# Mastering™
## MySQL™ 4

**Ian Gilfillan**

SYBEX®

San Francisco   London

Associate Publisher: Joel Fugazzotto

Acquisitions and Developmental Editor: Tom Cirtin

Freelance Editor: Kim Wimpsett

Production Editor: Donna Crossman

Technical Editor: Charlie Hornberger

Graphic Illustrator: Tony Jonick

Electronic Publishing Specialists: Rozi Harris, Bill Clark, Interactive Composition Corporation

Proofreaders: Amey Garber, Emily Hsuan, Dave Nash, Laurie O'Connell, Yariv Rabinovitch, Nancy Riddiough, and Monique van den Berg

Indexer: Nancy Guenther

Book Designer: Maureen Forys, Happenstance Type-O-Rama

Cover Designer: Design Site

Cover Illustrator: Tania Kac, Design Site

Library of Congress Card Number: 2002111957

ISBN: 0-7821-4162-5

Manufactured in the United States of America

10 9 8 7 6 5 4 3 2 1

For Superbabe and my parents!

# Acknowledgments

THIS IS MY FIRST book, but having written numerous articles, I thought a book would be like a big article. A few hundred pages and many gray hairs later, I know the truth. This book would never have been possible without the many people who helped me along the way. First, thanks to Anique van der Vlugt for installing software, testing code, proofreading many of the chapters, and keeping the bed warm on those long, lonely nights. Second, thanks to Bob Meredith for setting up a test server on short notice and constantly asking for more from the book. Thanks also to Rushdi Salie and Web Factory for introducing me to MySQL all those years ago and to Pieter Claassen for his passion with Linux, MySQL, Python, and Perl long before it was fashionable. Thanks to my employers IOL for not clock-watching too much while I wrote this book. Thanks to Technical Editor Charlie Hornberger for some superb comments, and thanks to all those at Sybex who helped make the book what it is: Developmental Editor Tom Cirtin, who was first to bite and who acquired the book, Production Editor Donna Crossman, Editor Kim Wimpsett, Associate Publisher Joel Fugazzotto, Illustrator Tony Jonick for making sense of my scrawlings, Composition Coordinator Rozi Harris, and Compositor Bill Clark, as well as Proofreaders Amey Garber, Emily Hsuan, Dave Nash, Laurie O'Connell, Yariv Rabinovitch, Nancy Riddiough, and Monique van den Berg, and Indexer Nancy Guenther.

And, of course, thanks to MySQL AB for a great product.

# Contents at a Glance

# Contents

# Introduction

MYSQL HAS GROWN UP. Once dismissed as a lightweight toy for websites, MySQL 4 is now a viable mission-critical data-management solution. Whereas before it was the ideal choice for websites, now it contains many of the features needed in other environments, all while maintaining its impressive speed. It has long been able to outperform many commercial solutions for raw speed and has an elegant and powerful permissions system, but now version 4 has the ACID-compliant InnoDB transactional storage engine.

MySQL 4 is faster, has online backup facilities, and has a multitude of new features. There is little reason not to consider MySQL for your database solution. MySQL AB, the company behind MySQL, offers efficient and low-cost support, and, like most open-source communities, you'll find lots of free support on the Web. Standard features not yet included in MySQL (such as views and stored procedures) are currently under development and may even be ready by the time you read this book.

There are many important reasons to choose MySQL as your mission-critical data-management solution:

**Cost**   MySQL is free for most purposes, and its support is inexpensive.

**Support**   MySQL AB offers inexpensive support contracts, and there's a large and active MySQL community.

**Speed**   MySQL outperforms most of its rivals.

**Functionality**   MySQL offers most of the features serious developers require, such as full ACID compliance, support for most of ANSI SQL, online backups, replication, Secure Sockets Layer (SSL) support, and integration with almost all programming environments. Also, it is being developed and updated faster than many of its rivals, so almost all of the "standard" features MySQL does not yet have are under development.

**Portability**   MySQL runs on the vast majority of operating systems, and in most cases data can be transferred from one system to another without difficulty.

**Ease of use**   MySQL is easy to use and administer. Many older databases suffer from legacy issues, making administration needlessly complex. MySQL's tools are powerful and flexible without sacrificing usability.

## Who Should Buy This Book?

This book is for developers, database administrators (DBAs), and MySQL users. It contains the following topics:

- Exploring Structured Query Language (SQL) as implemented by MySQL.
- Understanding and using the data and table types.
- Optimizing your queries and indexes.
- Backing up the database.

◆ Managing users and security.
◆ Administering and configuring MySQL (and optimizing the configuration for performance).
◆ Replicating MySQL onto multiple servers.
◆ Understanding database design and database normalization, and walking you through a complete case study. Knowledge of this topic is vital if you plan to use MySQL in serious applications.
◆ Programming with MySQL.
◆ Writing your own extensions to MySQL.
◆ Installing MySQL.

The book's appendixes contain the following:

◆ A thorough MySQL reference
◆ References containing PHP, Perl, C, Java, Python, and ODBC functions and methods for interacting with MySQL

## What Not to Expect from This Book

MySQL is a vast topic, and this book covers everything you need to become a skilled MySQL DBA and developer. However, it cannot explain everything, so it does not contain the following topics:

◆ How to program. This book assists you in programming with MySQL, but it will not teach you how to program from the beginning.
◆ Embedded MySQL.
◆ Thorough coverage of how to compile and install libraries. Writing your own extensions requires some knowledge of compiling and installing libraries on your platform. Although this topic is explained, the book cannot cover all possible configurations on all platforms, so if you plan to get to this advanced level, you'll need a good source of information about your platform.

## What Do You Need?

You'll need the following to work through the examples in this book:

◆ A copy of, or access to, a MySQL client and server. You can download the current version from the MySQL site: www.mysql.com.
◆ A system on which to install MySQL (if you don't have access to one already). MySQL can install on your desktop PC, but more often it runs on a dedicated server when it is used in serious applications.
◆ If you plan to develop applications with MySQL, you may need to download the latest drivers or application programming interfaces (APIs) for your development environment. MySQL integrates best with PHP, Perl, Java, C, C++, and Python, but you can use it in any programming environment, such as .NET via Open Database Connectivity (ODBC). Visit the MySQL website (www.mysql.com) to download current versions of the drivers.

## How to Use This Book

This book is divided into four parts. If you're new to databases, the best place to start is Part I, "Using MySQL," and specifically Chapter 1, "Quickstart to MySQL," which eases novice users into the world of SQL. Readers experienced in other database management systems may want to give Chapter 1 a quick read to familiarize themselves with the way MySQL does things, before exploring the MySQL data and table types in detail in Chapter 2, "Data Types and Table Types." Readers of an intermediate level can start with Chapter 3, "Advanced SQL," and Chapter 4, "Indexes and Query Optimization," which look at advanced SQL, indexes, and optimization. Readers wanting to use a programming language with MySQL should read Chapter 5, "Programming with MySQL," and also look at the appendix relevant to their language. Chapter 6, "Extending MySQL," is for those readers who understand MySQL and want to add their own functions to it.

Readers without formal database design knowledge will benefit from Part II, "Designing a Database," which covers the often-ignored database design issues required for developing large-scale databases.

Any readers wanting to administer MySQL will benefit from Part III, "MySQL Administration," which progresses from the basics for new users to the advanced issues for optimizing high-performance databases. It also explains backups, replication, security, and installation.

Finally, you should turn to the appendixes when you need MySQL SQL, function, and operator references, as well as references to the database functions and methods used by most popular programming languages.

All sample code is available for download at `www.sybex.com`.

## How to Contact the Author

For errata, please check the Sybex website (`www.sybex.com`) first. Feel free to contact the author with any queries at `mysql4@greenman.co.za`, and I'll do what I can to help out or point you in the right direction.

# Part I

# Using MySQL

## Chapter 1

# Quickstart to MySQL

So, YOU'VE OBTAINED A copy of this book. Some of you may be competent with MySQL already and want to dive into the murky waters of database replication or optimizing the server variables. If you're an advanced user, feel free to jump ahead. This chapter is not for you. But beginners need not worry. This book also contains everything you need to get started and eventually become an advanced user.

MySQL is the world's most popular open-source database. *Open source* means that the *source code*, the programming code that makes up MySQL, is freely available to anyone. People all over the world can add to MySQL, fix bugs, make improvements, or suggest optimizations. And they do. MySQL has developed from being a "toy" database a few years ago into a grown-up version 4, having overtaken many commercial databases along the way—and terrified most of the other database manufacturers. It's grown so quickly because of the countless dedicated people who have contributed to the project in some way, as well as the dedication of the MySQL team.

Unlike proprietary projects, where the source code is written by a few people and carefully guarded, open-source projects exclude no one who is interested in contributing if they are competent enough. In 2000 when MySQL was a young upstart of four years old, Michael "Monty" Widenius, the founder of MySQL, predicted big things for MySQL as he attended the first-ever open-source database convention. Many established database vendors scoffed at the time. Some of those vendors are no longer around.

With version 3, MySQL dominated the low end of the Internet market. And with MySQL's release of version 4, the product is now appealing to a much wider range of customers. With the open-source Apache dominating the web server market and various open-source operating systems (such as Linux and FreeBSD) performing strongly in the server market, MySQL's time has come in the database market.

Featured in this chapter:

◆ Essential database concepts and terminology

◆ Connecting to and disconnecting from MySQL server

◆ Creating and dropping databases

- Creating, updating, and dropping tables
- Adding data into a table
- Returning data and deleting data from a table
- Understanding basic statistical and date functions
- Joining more than one table

## Understanding MySQL Basics

MySQL is a *relational database management system* (RDBMS). It's a program capable of storing an enormous amount and a wide variety of data and serving it up to meet the needs of any type of organization, from mom-and-pop retail establishments to the largest commercial enterprises and governmental bodies. MySQL competes with well-known proprietary RDBMSs, such as Oracle, SQL Server, and DB2.

MySQL comes with everything needed to install the program, set up differing levels of user access, administer the system, and secure and back up the data. You can develop database applications in most programming languages used today and run them on most operating systems, including some of which you've probably never heard. MySQL utilizes Structured Query Language (SQL), the language used by all relational databases, which you'll meet later in this chapter (see the section titled "Creating and Using Your First Database"). SQL enables you to create databases, as well as add, manipulate, and retrieve data according to specific criteria.

But I'm getting ahead of myself. This chapter provides a brief introduction to relational database concepts. You'll learn exactly what a relational database is and how it works, as well as key terminology. Armed with this information, you'll be ready to jump into creating a simple database and manipulating its data.

### What Is a Database?

The easiest way to understand a database is as a collection of related files. Imagine a file (either paper or electronic) of sales orders in a shop. Then there's another file of products, containing stock records. To fulfill an order, you'd need to look up the product in the order file and then look up the stock levels for that particular product in the product file. A database and the software that controls the database, called a *database management system* (DBMS), helps with this kind of task. Most databases today are *relational* databases, named such because they deal with tables of data related by a common field. For example, Table 1.1 shows the Product table, and Table 1.2 shows the Invoice table. As you can see, the relation between the two tables is based on the common field stock_code. Any two tables can relate to each other simply by having a field in common.

**TABLE 1.1:** THE PRODUCT TABLE

| STOCK_CODE | DESCRIPTION | PRICE |
| --- | --- | --- |
| A416 | Nails, box | $0.14 |
| C923 | Drawing pins, box | $0.08 |

**TABLE 1.2:** THE INVOICE TABLE

| INVOICE_CODE | INVOICE_LINE | STOCK_CODE | QUANTITY |
|---|---|---|---|
| 3804 | 1 | A416 | 10 |
| 3804 | 2 | C923 | 15 |

## Database Terminology

Let's take a closer look at the previous two tables to see how they are organized:

◆ Each table consists of many *rows* and *columns*.

◆ Each row contains data about one single *entity* (such as one product or one order). This is called a *record*. For example, the first row in Table 1.1 is a record; it describes the A416 product, which is a box of nails that costs 14 cents. To reiterate, the terms *row* and *record* are interchangeable.

◆ Each column (also called a *tuple*) contains one piece of data that relates to the record, called an *attribute*. Examples of attributes are the quantity of an item sold or the price of a product. An attribute, when referring to a database table, is called a *field*. For example, the data in the Description column in Table 1.1 are fields. To reiterate, the terms *attribute* and *field* are interchangeable.

Given this kind of structure, the database gives you a way to manipulate this data: SQL. SQL is a powerful way to search for records or make changes. Almost all DBMSs use SQL, although many have added their own enhancements to it. This means that when you learn about SQL in this chapter and in more detail in later chapters, you aren't learning something specific to MySQL. Most of what you learn can be used on any other relational database, such as PostgreSQL, Oracle, Sybase, or SQL Server. But after tasting the benefits of MySQL, you probably won't want to change!

# Connecting to the MySQL Server

The machine where MySQL runs and stores the data is called the *MySQL server*. To connect to the server, you have several setup options. First, you can have the MySQL client and MySQL server on your desktop, as shown in Figure 1.1. Second, you can have the MySQL client set up on your desktop while the MySQL server is on another machine that you connect to, as shown in Figure 1.2. Finally, your desktop can be any machine connecting to another machine with a MySQL client, which in turn connects to a MySQL server, either on the same machine or another, as shown in Figure 1.3.

**FIGURE 1.1**

Your machine has both the MySQL client and the MySQL server on it.

MySQL client and server

**FIGURE 1.2**

Your machine has the MySQL client. The MySQL server exists on another machine to which you connect.

Desktop and MySQL client          MySQL server

**FIGURE 1.3**

In this case, your terminal can be any machine capable of connecting to another, as it doesn't even run the lightweight MySQL client on it.

Desktop                    MySQL client                MySQL server

If the MySQL client is not on your desktop and you need to connect to a second machine to use the MySQL client, you'll probably use something such as Telnet or a Secure Shell (SSH) client to do so. Using one of these is a matter of opening the Telnet program, entering the hostname, username, and password. If you're unsure about this, ask your system administrator for help.

Once you've logged into a machine on which the MySQL client program is installed, connecting to the server is easy:

- On a Unix machine (for example, Linux or FreeBSD), run the following command from the command line within your shell:

  ```
  % mysql -h hostname -u username -ppassword databasename
  ```

- On a Windows machine, run the same command from the command prompt:

  ```
  % mysql -h hostname -u username -ppassword databasename
  ```

The % refers to the shell prompt. It'll probably look different on your machine—for example, c:\> on some Windows setups or $ on some Unix shells. The -h and the -u can be followed by a space (you can also leave out the space), but the -p must be followed by the password immediately, with no intermediate spaces.

Once you've connected, you'll encounter the mysql> prompt, which appears in most distributions on the command line once you've connected. You don't need to type it in; it will appear automatically. Even if a slightly different prompt appears, don't worry, just enter the text in bold. This is the convention used throughout the book.

*TIP*    *There is a more secure way of entering the password, which I recommend in a multiuser environment. Just enter the -p and omit the password. You'll be prompted for it when MySQL starts; then you can enter the password without it appearing on the screen. This avoids anyone seeing your password entered in plain text.*

The hostname would be the machine hosting the server (perhaps something such as www.sybex.com or an IP such as 196.30.168.20). You don't need a hostname if you're already logged into the server (in other words, the MySQL client and server are on the same machine). The administrator assigns you the username and password (this is your MySQL password and username, which is not the same as your login to the client machine). Some insecure systems don't require any username or password.

*TIP*    *Sometimes the system administrator makes your life a little harder by not putting MySQL into the default path. So, when you type the* mysql *command, you may get a* command not found *error (Unix) or a* bad command or file name *error (Windows) even though you know you have MySQL installed. If this happens, you'll need to enter the full path to the MySQL client (for example,* /usr/local/build/mysql/bin/mysql, *or on Windows, something such as* C:\mysql\bin\mysql). *Ask your administrator for the correct path if this is a problem in your setup.*

To disconnect, simply type **QUIT** as shown:

```
mysql> QUIT
Bye
```

You can also type **EXIT** or press **Ctrl+D**.

*NOTE*    *MySQL does not distinguish between uppercase and lowercase here. You could have typed* **QUIT**, **quit**, *or even* **qUIt** *if you'd wanted.*

## Creating and Using Your First Database

The following sections describe how to create a database and perform queries on it. It assumes you have connected to the MySQL server and that you have permissions to use a database. If not, ask your administrator for permission. You will call your database *firstdb*, so ask your administrator to create and give you full permission to that database only. That way you won't run into permission problems later, but you also won't give your administrator a heart attack by causing havoc with existing databases. If your administrator looks flustered or if you have just installed MySQL yourself, then you or your administrator will need to perform one of the following two sets of commands to get started. Remember, just enter the text in bold.

### If You've Just Installed MySQL

First, connect to the MySQL database as *root*. Because you're just starting, you won't have a root password yet, and the first thing you should do is assign a password to the root user (See Chapter 14, "Database Security").

```
% mysql -u root mysql
Welcome to the MySQL monitor.  Commands end with ; or \g.
Your MySQL connection id is 15 to server version: 4.0.2-alpha-Max

Type 'help;' or '\h' for help. Type '\c' to clear the buffer.
mysql> SET PASSWORD=PASSWORD('g00r002b');
Query OK, 0 rows affected (0.00 sec)
```

For ease of use, you're going to use the same password for the root user, *g00r002b*, as you will for the user you're creating, *guru2b*.

Next, you will have to create the *firstdb* database that you're going to be working with throughout:

```
mysql> CREATE DATABASE firstdb;
Query OK, 1 row affected (0.01 sec)
```

Finally, the user you're going to be working as, *guru2b*, with a password of *g00r002b*, needs to be created and given full access to the *firstdb* database:

```
mysql> GRANT ALL ON firstdb.* to guru2b@localhost
  IDENTIFIED BY 'g00r002b';
Query OK, 0 rows affected (0.01 sec)
mysql> exit
Bye
```

### If an Administrator Needs to Give You Permission

First the administrator will have to connect to the MySQL database as *root* (or any other user that has permissions to grant a new user their own permissions):

```
% mysql -u root -p mysql
Enter password:
Welcome to the MySQL monitor.  Commands end with ; or \g.
Your MySQL connection id is 15 to server version: 4.0.2-alpha-Max
Type 'help;' or '\h' for help. Type '\c' to clear the buffer.
```

Next, your administrator will have to create the *firstdb* database that you're going to be working with throughout:

```
mysql> CREATE DATABASE firstdb;
Query OK, 1 row affected (0.01 sec)
```

Finally, the user you're going to be working as, *guru2b*, with a password of *g00r002b*, needs to be created and given full access to the *firstdb* database. Note that this assumes you will be connecting to the database from *localhost* (i.e., the database client and database server are on the same machine). If this is not the case, your administrator will have to replace *localhost* with the appropriate host name:

```
mysql> GRANT ALL ON firstdb.* to guru2b@localhost
  IDENTIFIED BY 'g00r002b';
Query OK, 0 rows affected (0.01 sec)
mysql> exit
Bye
```

*guru2b* is your MySQL username, and I'll use it throughout the book, and *g00r002b* is your password. You may choose, or be assigned, another username. You'll learn how to grant permissions in Chapter 14.

### Using Your Database

If you're new to SQL or MySQL, this is your chance to get your hands dirty. I suggest you do the examples in the next few sections in the order they're presented. But you only really learn when you go beyond the book and start to write your own queries. So, experiment as you go along. Try variations you think may work. Don't be afraid to make mistakes at this stage! Mistakes are the way you learn. None of the data is valuable. It'd be better to delete your sample database by accident now than the vital million records you're processing in a year's time.

You'll start by creating a table inside your sample database, and then populating this table with data. Once you've got some tables with data in them, you'll learn how to perform queries on these tables. First, connect to your newly created table with the following command:

```
% mysql -u guru2b -pg00r002b firstdb
Welcome to the MySQL monitor.  Commands end with ; or \g.
Your MySQL connection id is 15 to server version: 4.0.2-alpha-Max

Type 'help;' or '\h' for help. Type '\c' to clear the buffer.
```

If the permissions have not been set correctly, you'll get an error message, as follows:

```
ERROR 1044: Access denied for user: 'guru2be@localhost' to database 'firstdb'
```

You or your administrator will need to retrace the steps in the previous two sections if this is the case.

All these permission hassles may seem troublesome now, but they're a useful feature. At some stage you'll want to make sure that not just anybody can access your data, and permissions are the way you'll ensure this.

You can also connect without specifying a database, as follows:

```
% mysql -u guru2b -pg00r002b guru2b
Welcome to the MySQL monitor.  Commands end with ; or \g.
Your MySQL connection id is 15 to server version: 4.0.2-alpha-Max

Type 'help;' or '\h' for help. Type '\c' to clear the buffer.
```

Then to make sure you're using the right database, you'll need to let MySQL know which database to use. To make sure that any further work you do affects the right database, enter the following bold statement:

```
mysql> USE firstdb
Database changed
```

You can connect to your database either way for now, specifying the database when you connect or later once you are connected. In the future, when you have more than one database to use on the system, you'll find it much easier to change between databases with the USE statement.

## Creating a Table

Now that you've connected to your database, you'll want to put something in it. To get going, you're going to create a database that could track a sales team. As you learned, a database consists of many tables, and to start with, you'll create a table that can contains data about sales representatives. You will store their names, employee numbers, and commissions. To create a table, you're also going to use the CREATE command, but you need to specify TABLE rather than DATABASE, as well as a few extras. Enter the following CREATE statement:

```
mysql> CREATE TABLE sales_rep(
   employee_number INT,
   surname VARCHAR(40),
```

```
  first_name VARCHAR(30),
  commission TINYINT
);
Query OK, 0 rows affected (0.00 sec)
```

**WARNING** *Don't forget the semicolon at the end of the line. All MySQL commands must end with a semicolon. Forgetting it is one of the prime reasons for beginner frustration. Also be aware that if you've forgotten the semicolon and press Enter, you just need to add the semicolon before pressing Enter again. MySQL accepts commands over multiple lines.*

You don't need to enter the statement exactly as printed; I've used multiple lines to make it easier to follow, but entering it on one line will make it easier for you. Also, if you use a different case, it will still work. Throughout this book, I use uppercase to represent MySQL keywords and lowercase to represent names you can choose yourself. For example, you could have entered the following:

```
mysql> create table SALES_REPRESENTATIVE(
   EMPLOYEE_NO int,
   SURNAME varchar(40),
   FIRST_NAME varchar(30),
   COMMISSION tinyint
);
```

without any problems. However, entering the following:

```
mysql> CREATE TABLES sales_rep(
   employee_number INT,
   surname VARCHAR(40),
   first_name VARCHAR(30),
   commission TINYINT
);
```

would give you this error:

```
ERROR 1064: You have an error in your SQL syntax near
'TABLES sales_reps(employee_number INT,surname
VARCHAR(40),first_name VARCHAR(30)' at line 1
```

because you've misspelled TABLE. So take care to enter the capitalized text exactly; you can rename the text appearing in lowercase without any problems (as long as you are consistent and use the same names throughout).

You may be wondering about the INT, VARCHAR, and TINYINT terms that appear after the fieldnames. They're what are called *data types* or *column types.* INT stands for *integer,* or a whole number usually ranging from –2,147,483,648 to 2,147,483,647. That's about a third of the world's population, so it should cover the sales team no matter how large it grows. VARCHAR stands for *variable length character.* The number in brackets is the maximum length of the character string. An amount of 30 and 40 characters should suffice for the first name and surname, respectively. And TINYINT stands for *tiny integer,* usually a whole number from –128 to 127. The commission field refers to a percentage value, and because no one can earn more than 100 percent, a tiny integer is sufficient. Chapter 2, "Data Types and Table Types," goes into more detail about the various column types and when to use them.

### LISTING EXISTING TABLES IN A DATABASE WITH *SHOW TABLES*

Now that you have a table, you can confirm its existence with SHOW TABLES:

```
mysql> SHOW TABLES;
+-------------------+
| Tables_in_firstdb |
+-------------------+
| sales_rep         |
+-------------------+
1 row in set (0.00 sec)
```

SHOW TABLES lists all the existing tables in the current database. In the case of your newly created *firstdb* there's only one: *sales_rep*. So unless your short-term memory is really shot, this command probably wasn't much use. But in big databases with many tables, the name of that obscure table you created two months ago has slipped your mind. Or perhaps you're encountering a new database for the first time. That's when SHOW TABLES is invaluable.

### EXAMINING THE TABLE STRUCTURE WITH *DESCRIBE*

DESCRIBE is the command that shows you the structure of a table. To see that MySQL has created your table correctly, type the following:

```
mysql> DESCRIBE sales_rep;
+-----------------+-------------+------+-----+---------+-------+
| Field           | Type        | Null | Key | Default | Extra |
+-----------------+-------------+------+-----+---------+-------+
| employee_number | int(11)     | YES  |     | NULL    |       |
| surname         | varchar(40) | YES  |     | NULL    |       |
| first_name      | varchar(30) | YES  |     | NULL    |       |
| commission      | tinyint(4)  | YES  |     | NULL    |       |
+-----------------+-------------+------+-----+---------+-------+
4 rows in set (0.01 sec)
```

There are all kinds of extra columns in this table with which you're not yet familiar. For now, you should be interested in the field and the type. You'll learn about the other headings in Chapter 2. The fieldnames are exactly as you entered them, and the two VARCHAR fields have the size you allocated them. Notice that the INT and TINYINT fields have been allocated a size, too, even though you didn't specify one when you created them. Remember that a TINYINT by default ranges from −128 to 127 (four characters including the minus sign), and an INT ranges from −2,147,483,648 to 2,147,483,647 (11 characters including the minus sign), so the seemingly mysterious size allocation refers to the display width.

## Inserting New Records into a Table

Now that you have a table, you'll want to put some data into it. Let's assume there are three sales reps (as shown in Table 1.3).

**TABLE 1.3:** SALES REPS

| EMPLOYEE NUMBER | SURNAME | FIRST NAME | COMMISSION PERCENT |
|---|---|---|---|
| 1 | Rive | Sol | 10 |
| 2 | Gordimer | Charlene | 15 |
| 3 | Serote | Mike | 10 |

To enter this data into the table, you use the SQL statement INSERT to create a record, as follows:

```
mysql> INSERT INTO sales_rep(employee_number,surname,first_name,commission)
    VALUES(1,'Rive','Sol',10);
mysql> INSERT INTO sales_rep(employee_number,surname,first_name,commission)
    VALUES(2,'Gordimer','Charlene',15);
mysql> INSERT INTO sales_rep(employee_number,surname,first_name,commission)
    VALUES(3,'Serote','Mike',10);
```

*NOTE*  *The string field (a* VARCHAR *character field) needs a single quote around its value, but the numeric fields (*commission, employee_number*) don't. Make sure you have enclosed the right field values in quotes and that you have matched quotes correctly (whatever gets an open quote must get a close quote), as this often entraps newcomers to SQL.*

There is also a shortcut INSERT statement to enter the data. You could have used the following:

```
mysql> INSERT INTO sales_rep VALUES(1,'Rive','Sol',10);
mysql> INSERT INTO sales_rep VALUES(2,'Gordimer','Charlene',15);
mysql> INSERT INTO sales_rep VALUES(3,'Serote','Mike',10);
```

When entering commands in this way, you *must* enter the fields in the same order as they are defined in the database. You could not use the following:

```
mysql> INSERT INTO sales_rep VALUES(1,'Sol','Rive',10);
Query OK, 1 row affected (0.00 sec)
```

Although this seems to work, the data would have been entered in the wrong order, with *Sol* as the surname and *Rive* the first name.

*TIP*  *I suggest getting into the habit now of using the full* INSERT *statement, especially if you are planning to run queries through a programming language. First, it reduces the chances of error (you could not see just from the statement whether* first_name *and* surname *were in the wrong order), and second, it makes your programs more flexible. Chapter 5, "Programming with MySQL," discusses this topic in more detail.*

### INSERTING DATA WITHIN ONE *INSERT* STATEMENT

Another shortcut you could have used would have been to enter all the data within one INSERT statement, with each record separated with a comma, as follows:

```
mysql> INSERT INTO sales_rep (employee_number,surname,first_name,commission)
    VALUES
```

```
(1,'Rive','Sol',10),
(2,'Gordimer','Charlene',15),
(3,'Serote','Mike',10);
Query OK, 3 rows affected (0.05 sec)
Records: 3  Duplicates: 0  Warnings: 0
```

This method involves less typing of course, and the server also processes it more quickly.

### INSERTING HIGH VOLUMES OF DATA FROM A TEXT FILE WITH *LOAD DATA*

A final way for inserting data—and the best way if you're inserting high volumes of data all at once—is to use the LOAD DATA statement, as follows:

```
mysql> LOAD DATA LOCAL INFILE "sales_rep.sql" INTO TABLE sales_rep;
```

The format of the data file must be correct, with no exceptions. In this case, where you're using the defaults, the text file has each record on a new line, and each field separated by a tab. Assuming the \t character represents a tab, and each line ends with a newline character, the text file would have to look exactly as follows:

```
1\tRive\tSol\t10
2\tGordimer\tCharlene\t15
3\tSerote\tMike\t10
```

A variation of this is used for restoring backups, discussed in Chapter 11, "Database Backups." This is even more efficient than a multirecord INSERT statement. The LOCAL keyword tells the server that the file is found on the client machine (the machine from which you connect). Omitting it means MySQL looks for the file on the database server. By default, LOAD DATA assumes that the values are in the same order as in the table definition, that each field is separated by a tab, and that each record is separated with a newline.

## Retrieving Information from a Table

Getting information out of a table in MySQL is easy. You can use the powerful SELECT statement, for example:

```
mysql> SELECT commission FROM sales_rep WHERE surname='Gordimer';
+------------+
| commission |
+------------+
|         15 |
+------------+
1 row in set (0.01 sec)
```

The SELECT statement has several parts. The first part, immediately after the SELECT, is the list of fields. You could have returned a number of other fields, instead of just commission, as follows:

```
mysql> SELECT commission,employee_number FROM
  sales_rep WHERE surname='Gordimer';
```

```
+------------+-----------------+
| commission | employee_number |
+------------+-----------------+
|         15 |               2 |
+------------+-----------------+
1 row in set (0.00 sec)
```

You could also use a wildcard (*) to return all the fields, as follows:

```
mysql> SELECT * FROM sales_rep WHERE surname='Gordimer';
+-----------------+----------+------------+------------+
| employee_number | surname  | first_name | commission |
+-----------------+----------+------------+------------+
|               2 | Gordimer | Charlene   |         15 |
+-----------------+----------+------------+------------+
1 row in set (0.00 sec)
```

The * wildcard means all fields in the table. So in the previous example, all four fields are returned, in the same order they exist in the table structure.

The part of the SELECT statement after the WHERE is called the *WHERE clause*. The clause is highly flexible and can contain many conditions, of varying kinds. Take a look at the following example:

```
mysql> SELECT * FROM sales_rep WHERE commission>10
 OR surname='Rive' AND first_name='Sol';
+-----------------+----------+------------+------------+
| employee_number | surname  | first_name | commission |
+-----------------+----------+------------+------------+
|               1 | Rive     | Sol        |         10 |
|               2 | Gordimer | Charlene   |         15 |
+-----------------+----------+------------+------------+
2 rows in set (0.00 sec)
```

Understanding AND and OR is fundamental to using SQL properly. The conditions on both sides of an AND keyword must be true for the whole to be true. Only one of the conditions in an OR statement needs to be true. Table 1.4 shows the AND/OR truth table.

**TABLE 1.4:** AND/OR TRUTH TABLE

| KEYWORD | HOT | HUMID | OVERALL |
|---------|-----|-------|---------|
| AND | True | True | True, hot AND humid |
| AND | True | False | False, not hot AND humid as it's not humid |
| AND | False | True | False, not hot AND humid as it's not hot |
| AND | False | False | False, not hot AND humid as neither are true |
| OR | True | True | True, hot OR humid as both are true |

*Continued on next page*

**TABLE 1.4:** AND/OR TRUTH TABLE *(continued)*

| KEYWORD | HOT | HUMID | OVERALL |
|---------|-----|-------|---------|
| OR | True | False | True, hot OR humid as it's hot |
| OR | False | True | True, hot OR humid as it's humid |
| OR | False | False | False, not hot OR humid as neither are true |

### THE ORDER IN WHICH MYSQL PROCESSES CONDITIONS

The following example demonstrates a trap into which many have fallen. Let's assume a manager asks you for a list of all employees with the surname Rive and the first name Sol or a commission greater than 10 percent. You may well try the following query:

```
mysql> SELECT * FROM sales_rep WHERE surname='Rive'
 AND first_name='Sol' OR commission>10;
+-----------------+----------+------------+------------+
| employee_number | surname  | first_name | commission |
+-----------------+----------+------------+------------+
|               1 | Rive     | Sol        |         10 |
|               2 | Gordimer | Charlene   |         15 |
+-----------------+----------+------------+------------+
2 rows in set (0.00 sec)
```

This result may be exactly what you want. But what if the manager had meant something slightly different? The employee must have a surname of Rive and then can either have a first name of Sol or have a commission of greater than 10 percent. The second result would then not apply, as although her commission is greater than 10 percent, her first name is not Sol. The AND construct means that both clauses must be true. You would have to give the query as follows:

```
mysql> SELECT * FROM sales_rep WHERE surname='Rive'
 AND (first_name='Sol' OR commission>10);
+-----------------+---------+------------+------------+
| employee_number | surname | first_name | commission |
+-----------------+---------+------------+------------+
|               1 | Rive    | Sol        |         10 |
+-----------------+---------+------------+------------+
1 row in set (0.00 sec)
```

Note the parentheses in this query. When you have multiple conditions, it becomes critical to know the order in which the conditions must be processed. Does the OR part or the AND part come first? Often you will be given unclear verbal instructions, but this example shows you the importance of finding out getting clarity before you implement the query. Sometimes errors like these are never discovered! It's what's often meant by *computer error*, but it all comes down eventually to a person, usually someone who devised the wrong query.

Appendix B, "MySQL Function and Operator Reference," contains a list of operators and their precedence. I suggest that you use parentheses to determine precedence in your queries. Some books and people swear by learning the built-in precedence. For example, you may have learned at school that $1 + 1 * 3 = 4$, not 6, because you know that multiplication is performed before addition. The same applies to AND, which is performed before OR. But not everyone may know this, so use the parentheses to make it clear to everyone what you mean $1 + (1 * 3)$. Even after many years of programming, I still don't know the full list of operator precedence, and probably never will.

### PATTERN MATCHING: *LIKE* AND %

Let's look at some more additions to the SELECT statement. What if you want to return the details for Mike Serote? Simple, you say—you'd use the following query:

```
mysql> SELECT * FROM sales_rep WHERE surname='Serote' and first_name='Mike';
+-----------------+---------+------------+------------+
| employee_number | surname | first_name | commission |
+-----------------+---------+------------+------------+
|               3 | Serote  | Mike       |         10 |
+-----------------+---------+------------+------------+
1 row in set (0.00 sec)
```

But what if you've forgotten how to spell *Serote*? Was it *Serotte* or maybe *Serota*? You may have to try a number of queries before you succeed, and if you don't happen to remember the exact spelling you will never succeed. You may want to try just using *Mike*, but remember that many databases consist of hundreds of thousands of records. Luckily, there is a better way. MySQL allows the LIKE statement. If you remember the surname begins with Sero, you can use the following:

```
mysql> SELECT * FROM sales_rep WHERE surname LIKE 'Sero%';
+-----------------+---------+------------+------------+
| employee_number | surname | first_name | commission |
+-----------------+---------+------------+------------+
|               3 | Serote  | Mike       |         10 |
+-----------------+---------+------------+------------+
1 row in set (0.00 sec)
```

Take note of the %. It's a wildcard, similar to *, but specifically for use inside a SELECT condition. It means *0 or more characters*. So all of the earlier permutations on the spelling you were considering would have been returned. You can use the wildcard any number of times, which allows queries such as this:

```
mysql> SELECT * FROM sales_rep WHERE surname LIKE '%e%';
+-----------------+----------+------------+------------+
| employee_number | surname  | first_name | commission |
+-----------------+----------+------------+------------+
|               1 | Rive     | Sol        |         10 |
|               2 | Gordimer | Charlene   |         15 |
|               3 | Serote   | Mike       |         10 |
+-----------------+----------+------------+------------+
3 rows in set (0.00 sec)
```

This returns all the records, as it looks for any surname with an *e* in it. This is different from the following query, which only looks for surnames that start with an *e*:

```
mysql> SELECT * FROM sales_rep WHERE surname LIKE 'e%';
Empty set (0.00 sec)
```

You could also use a query such as the following, which searches for surnames that have an *e* anywhere in the name and then end with an *e*:

```
mysql> SELECT * FROM sales_rep WHERE surname LIKE '%e%e';
+-----------------+---------+------------+------------+
| employee_number | surname | first_name | commission |
+-----------------+---------+------------+------------+
|               3 | Serote  | Mike       |         10 |
+-----------------+---------+------------+------------+
1 row in set (0.00 sec)
```

Let's add a few more records to the table so that you can try some more complex queries. Add the following two records:

```
mysql> INSERT INTO sales_rep values(4,'Rive','Mongane',10);
mysql> INSERT INTO sales_rep values(5,'Smith','Mike',12);
```

### SORTING

Another useful and commonly used clause allows sorting of the results. An alphabetical list of employees would be useful, and you can use the ORDER BY clause to help you generate it:

```
mysql> SELECT * FROM sales_rep ORDER BY surname;
+-----------------+----------+------------+------------+
| employee_number | surname  | first_name | commission |
+-----------------+----------+------------+------------+
|               2 | Gordimer | Charlene   |         15 |
|               1 | Rive     | Sol        |         10 |
|               4 | Rive     | Mongane    |         10 |
|               3 | Serote   | Mike       |         10 |
|               5 | Smith    | Mike       |         12 |
+-----------------+----------+------------+------------+
5 rows in set (0.00 sec)
```

You may have noticed that this list is not quite correct if you want to sort by name because Sol Rive appears before Mongane Rive. To correct this, you need to sort on the first name as well when the surnames are the same. To achieve this, use the following:

```
mysql> SELECT * FROM sales_rep ORDER BY surname,first_name;
+-----------------+----------+------------+------------+
| employee_number | surname  | first_name | commission |
+-----------------+----------+------------+------------+
|               2 | Gordimer | Charlene   |         15 |
|               4 | Rive     | Mongane    |         10 |
|               1 | Rive     | Sol        |         10 |
|               3 | Serote   | Mike       |         10 |
|               5 | Smith    | Mike       |         12 |
+-----------------+----------+------------+------------+
5 rows in set (0.00 sec)
```

Now the order is correct. To sort in reverse order (descending order), you use the DESC keyword. The following query returns all records in order of commission earned, from high to low:

```
mysql> SELECT * FROM sales_rep ORDER BY commission DESC;
+-----------------+----------+------------+------------+
| employee_number | surname  | first_name | commission |
+-----------------+----------+------------+------------+
|               2 | Gordimer | Charlene   |         15 |
|               5 | Smith    | Mike       |         12 |
|               1 | Rive     | Sol        |         10 |
|               4 | Rive     | Mongane    |         10 |
|               3 | Serote   | Mike       |         10 |
+-----------------+----------+------------+------------+
5 rows in set (0.00 sec)
```

Again, you may want to further sort the three employees earning 10-percent commission. To do so, you can use the ASC keyword. Although not strictly necessary because it is the default sort order, the keyword helps add clarity:

```
mysql> SELECT * FROM sales_rep ORDER BY commission DESC,
    surname ASC,first_name ASC;
+-----------------+----------+------------+------------+
| employee_number | surname  | first_name | commission |
+-----------------+----------+------------+------------+
|               2 | Gordimer | Charlene   |         15 |
|               5 | Smith    | Mike       |         12 |
|               4 | Rive     | Mongane    |         10 |
|               1 | Rive     | Sol        |         10 |
|               3 | Serote   | Mike       |         10 |
+-----------------+----------+------------+------------+
5 rows in set (0.01 sec)
```

### LIMITING THE NUMBER OF RESULTS

So far you have always gotten the full number of results that satisfy the condition returned to you. In a real-world database, however, there may be many thousands of records, and you do not want to see them all at once. MySQL, therefore, allows you to use the LIMIT clause. LIMIT is non-standard SQL, which means you won't be able to use it in the same way with all other databases, but it is a powerful and useful MySQL enhancement. If you only wanted to find the employee with the highest commission (assuming there is only one, as with this dataset), you could run this query:

```
mysql> SELECT first_name,surname,commission FROM sales_rep
    ORDER BY commission DESC;
```

```
+------------+----------+------------+
| first_name | surname  | commission |
+------------+----------+------------+
| Charlene   | Gordimer |         15 |
| Mike       | Smith    |         12 |
| Sol        | Rive     |         10 |
| Mike       | Serote   |         10 |
| Mongane    | Rive     |         10 |
+------------+----------+------------+
5 rows in set (0.00 sec)
```

Clearly the employee you're after is Charlene Gordimer. But LIMIT allows you to return only that record, as follows:

```
mysql> SELECT first_name,surname,commission FROM sales_rep
 ORDER BY commission DESC LIMIT 1;
+------------+----------+------------+
| first_name | surname  | commission |
+------------+----------+------------+
| Charlene   | Gordimer |         15 |
+------------+----------+------------+
1 row in set (0.00 sec)
```

If there's only one number after the LIMIT clause, it determines the number of rows returned.

**NOTE**  LIMIT 0 *returns no records. This may seem useless, but it's a useful way to test your query on large databases without actually running it.*

The LIMIT clause does not only allow you to return a limited number of records starting from the beginning or end of the dataset. You can also tell MySQL what *offset* to use—in other words, from which result to start limiting. If there are two numbers after the LIMIT clause, the first is the offset and the second is the row limit. The next example returns the second record, in descending order:

```
mysql> SELECT first_name,surname,commission FROM
 sales_rep ORDER BY commission DESC LIMIT 1,1;
+------------+----------+------------+
| first_name | surname  | commission |
+------------+----------+------------+
| Mike       | Smith    |         12 |
+------------+----------+------------+
1 row in set (0.00 sec)
```

The default offset is 0 (computers always start counting at 0), so by specifying an offset of 1, you're taking the second record. You can check this by running this query:

```
mysql> SELECT first_name,surname,commission FROM sales_rep
 ORDER BY commission DESC LIMIT 0,1;
```

```
+------------+----------+------------+
| first_name | surname  | commission |
+------------+----------+------------+
| Charlene   | Gordimer |         15 |
+------------+----------+------------+
1 row in set (0.00 sec)
```

LIMIT 1 is the same as LIMIT 0,1 as the default 0 is assumed if it is not specified.

Now let's try another example. How would you return the third, fourth, and fifth records sorted in descending order on the commission field?

```
mysql> SELECT first_name,surname,commission FROM sales_rep
 ORDER BY commission DESC LIMIT 2,3;
+------------+----------+------------+
| first_name | surname  | commission |
+------------+----------+------------+
| Sol        | Rive     |         10 |
| Mike       | Serote   |         10 |
| Mongane    | Rive     |         10 |
+------------+----------+------------+
3 rows in set (0.00 sec)
```

The 2 is the offset (remember the offset starts at 0, so 2 is actually the third record), and the 3 is the number of records to return.

**NOTE** LIMIT *is often used in search engines running MySQL, for example, to display 10 results per page. The first page results would then use* LIMIT 0,10, *the second would use* LIMIT 10,10, *and so on.*

### RETURNING THE MAXIMUM VALUE WITH *MAX()*

MySQL has a vast number of functions that allow you to fine-tune your queries. If you happen to have glanced at Appendix B already, don't be put off by thinking you have to learn pages of terms. No one remembers them all, but once you know they exist, you can look up to see if there is one to do what you want it to do. And once you use them a lot, you'll find you've memorized the more common functions. This is much more effortless than memorizing them upfront! The first function you're going to look at is the MAX() function. To return the highest commission, you would use this query:

```
mysql> SELECT MAX(commission) from sales_rep;
+-----------------+
| MAX(commission) |
+-----------------+
|              15 |
+-----------------+
1 row in set (0.00 sec)
```

Notice the parentheses when you use functions. The function is applied to whatever is inside the parentheses. Throughout this book, I write functions with the parentheses whenever I refer to them to remind you that it is a function and how to use it—for example, MAX().

*WARNING*    *Be careful about spaces in your queries. In most cases they make no difference, but when you're dealing with functions (functions can usually be identified by the fact that they need to enclose something in parentheses), you need to be especially careful. If you'd put a space after the word COUNT, you'd have gotten a MySQL syntax error.*

### RETURNING DISTINCT RECORDS

Sometimes, you don't want to return duplicate results. Take a look at the following query:

```
mysql> SELECT surname FROM sales_rep ORDER BY surname;
+----------+
| surname  |
+----------+
| Gordimer |
| Rive     |
| Rive     |
| Serote   |
| Smith    |
+----------+
5 rows in set (0.00 sec)
```

This query is all well and good, but what if you just wanted to return a list of surnames, with each surname appearing only once? You don't want Rive to appear for both Mongane and Sol, but just once. The solution is to use DISTINCT, as follows:

```
mysql> SELECT DISTINCT surname FROM sales_rep ORDER BY surname;
+----------+
| surname  |
+----------+
| Gordimer |
| Rive     |
| Serote   |
| Smith    |
+----------+
4 rows in set (0.00 sec)
```

### COUNTING

As you can see beneath the results so far, MySQL displays the number of rows returned, such as 4 rows in set. Sometimes, all you really want to return is the number of results, not the contents of the records themselves. In this case, you'd use the COUNT() function:

```
mysql> SELECT COUNT(surname) FROM sales_rep;
+----------------+
| COUNT(surname) |
+----------------+
|              5 |
+----------------+
1 row in set (0.01 sec)
```

It doesn't really make much difference which field you counted in the previous example, as there are as many surnames as there are first names in the table. You would have gotten the same results if you used the following query:

```
mysql> SELECT COUNT(*) FROM sales_rep;
+----------+
| COUNT(*) |
+----------+
|        5 |
+----------+
1 row in set (0.00 sec)
```

To count the number of distinct surnames, you combine COUNT() with DISTINCT, as follows:

```
mysql> SELECT COUNT(DISTINCT surname) FROM sales_rep;
+------------------------+
| COUNT(DISTINCT surname) |
+------------------------+
|                      4 |
+------------------------+
1 row in set (0.00 sec)
```

### RETURNING THE AVERAGE, MINIMUM, AND TOTAL VALUES WITH *AVG()*, *MIN()*, AND *SUM()*

These functions work the same way as MAX(). You put whatever you want to work on inside the parentheses. So, to return the average commission, use the following:

```
mysql> SELECT AVG(commission) FROM sales_rep;
+-----------------+
| AVG(commission) |
+-----------------+
|         11.4000 |
+-----------------+
1 row in set (0.00 sec)
```

And to find the lowest commission that any of the sales staff is earning, use this:

```
mysql> SELECT MIN(commission) FROM sales_rep;
+-----------------+
| MIN(commission) |
+-----------------+
|              10 |
+-----------------+
1 row in set (0.00 sec)
```

SUM() works in the same way. It's unlikely you would find much use for totaling the commissions as shown here, but you can get an idea of how it works:

```
mysql> SELECT SUM(commission) from sales_rep;
```

```
+-----------------+
| SUM(commission) |
+-----------------+
|              57 |
+-----------------+
1 row in set (0.00 sec)
```

### PERFORMING CALCULATIONS IN A QUERY

SQL allows you to perform calculations in your query, as well. As a simple example, try the following:

```
mysql> SELECT 1+1;
+-----+
| 1+1 |
+-----+
|   2 |
+-----+
1 row in set (0.00 sec)
```

Obviously this is not the reason you use MySQL. There's no danger of schools embracing MySQL for students to use in mathematics examinations. But it's a useful feature inside a query. For example, if you want to see what commissions the sales reps would be earning if you increased everyone's commission by 1 percent, use this:

```
mysql> SELECT first_name,surname,commission + 1 FROM sales_rep;
+------------+----------+----------------+
| first_name | surname  | commission + 1 |
+------------+----------+----------------+
| Sol        | Rive     |             11 |
| Charlene   | Gordimer |             16 |
| Mike       | Serote   |             11 |
| Mongane    | Rive     |             11 |
| Mike       | Smith    |             12 |
+------------+----------+----------------+
5 rows in set (0.00 sec)
```

## Deleting Records

To delete a record, MySQL uses the DELETE statement. It's similar to SELECT, except that as the entire record is deleted, there is no need to specify any columns. You just need the table name and the condition. For example, Mike Smith resigns, so to remove him, you use this:

```
mysql> DELETE FROM sales_rep WHERE employee_number = 5;
Query OK, 1 row affected (0.00 sec)
```

You could also have used the first name and surname as a condition to delete, and in this case it would have worked as well. But for real-world databases, you'll want to use a unique field to identify the right person. Chapter 3 will introduce the topic of indexes, but for now keep in mind that *employee_number* is a unique field, and it is best to use it (Mike Smith is not that uncommon a name!). You will formalize the fact that *employee_number* is unique in your database structure in the section on indexes.

*WARNING*   *Be careful to use a condition with your* DELETE *statement. Simply entering* DELETE FROM sales_rep; *would have deleted all records in the table. There is no undo option, and as you haven't yet learned to back up your data, you'd be in trouble!*

## Changing Records in a Table

You've learned to add records using INSERT, remove them using DELETE, and return results using SELECT. All that's missing is learning how to change data in existing records. Let's assume that Sol Rive has just sold a huge shipment of sand to the desert dwellers in Namibia, and he is rewarded with an increase to a 12-percent commission. To correctly reflect this fact, you use the UPDATE statement, as follows:

```
mysql> UPDATE sales_rep SET commission = 12 WHERE
  employee_number=1;
Query OK, 1 row affected (0.00 sec)
Rows matched: 1  Changed: 1  Warnings: 0
```

*WARNING*   *Again, be careful to apply a condition. Without the* WHERE *clause, you would have changed everybody's commission to 12 percent!*

INSERT, SELECT, UPDATE, and DELETE make up the four standard statements for manipulating data. They are part of SQL's Data Manipulation Language (DML). With them, you have all the ammunition you need to make changes to the data in your records. You'll come across more advanced queries in Chapter 2.

## Dropping Tables and Databases

There are also statements to define the data structure, and these are said to be part of SQL's Data Definition Language (DDL). You've already seen one—the CREATE statement—which you used to create your database and then the tables and structures within that database. As with data manipulation, you may want to remove or change these tables. Let's create a table and then remove (or drop) it again:

```
mysql> CREATE TABLE commission (id INT);
Query OK, 0 rows affected (0.01 sec)
mysql> DROP TABLE commission;
Query OK, 0 rows affected (0.00 sec)d
```

*WARNING*   *No warnings, no notification—the table, and all data in it, has been dropped! Be careful with this statement.*

You can do the same with a database:

```
mysql> CREATE DATABASE shortlived;
Query OK, 1 row affected (0.01 sec)
mysql> DROP DATABASE shortlived;
Query OK, 0 rows affected (0.00 sec)
```

Now you get some idea why permissions become so important! Allowing anyone who can connect to MySQL such power would be disastrous. You'll learn how to prevent catastrophes like this with permissions in Chapter 14.

## Changing Table Structure

The final DDL statement, `ALTER`, allows you to change the structure of tables. You can add columns, change column definitions, rename tables, and drop columns.

### ADDING A COLUMN

Let's say that you realize you need to create a column in your *sales_reps* table to store the date the person joined. `UPDATE` won't do, as this only changes the data, not the structure. To make this change, you use the `ALTER` statement:

```
mysql> ALTER TABLE sales_rep ADD date_joined DATE;
Query OK, 4 rows affected (0.01 sec)
Records: 4  Duplicates: 0  Warnings: 0
```

*TIP* `DATE` *is a column type that stores data in the format year-month-day (YYYY-MM-DD). If you're used to entering dates in other ways, such as the U.S. format (MM/DD/YYYY), you'll need to make some adjustments.*

Your manager gives you another requirement for your database. (Although most changes are easy to perform, it's always better to get the design right from the beginning, as some changes will have unhappy consequences. Chapter 9, "Database Design," introduces the topic of database design.) You need to store the year that the sales rep was born, in order to perform analysis on the age distribution of the staff. MySQL has a `YEAR` column type, which you can use. Add the following column:

```
mysql> ALTER TABLE sales_rep ADD year_born YEAR;
Query OK, 4 rows affected (0.02 sec)
Records: 4  Duplicates: 0  Warnings: 0
```

### CHANGING A COLUMN DEFINITION

But seconds after adding the year, your manager comes up with a better idea. Why not store the sales rep's date of birth instead? That way the year is available as before, but the company can also surprise the reps with a birthday present. To change the column definition, use the following:

```
mysql> ALTER TABLE sales_rep CHANGE year_born birthday
  DATE;
Query OK, 4 rows affected (0.03 sec)
Records: 4  Duplicates: 0  Warnings: 0
```

After the `CHANGE` clause comes the old column name, then the new column name, followed by its definition. To change the definition, but not the name of the column, you would simply keep the name the same as before, as shown here:

```
mysql> ALTER TABLE tablename CHANGE oldname oldname new_column_definition;
```

Alternatively, use the MODIFY clause, which doesn't require the repetition of the name, as follows:

```
mysql> ALTER TABLE tablename MODIFY oldname new_column_definition;
```

### RENAMING A TABLE

One morning your manager barges in demanding that the term *sales rep* no longer be used. From henceforth, the employees are *cash-flow enhancers*, and records need to be kept of their *enhancement value*. Noting the wild look in your manager's eye, you decide to comply, first by adding the new field:

```
mysql> ALTER TABLE sales_rep ADD enhancement_value int;
Query OK, 4 rows affected (0.05 sec)
Records: 4  Duplicates: 0  Warnings: 0
```

and then renaming the table. To do so, use RENAME in the ALTER statement as follows:

```
mysql> ALTER TABLE sales_rep RENAME cash_flow_specialist;
Query OK, 4 rows affected (0.00 sec)
Records: 4  Duplicates: 0  Warnings: 0
```

The next day your manager is looking a little sheepish and red-eyed, and is mumbling something about doctored punch. You decide to change the table name back and drop the new column, before anyone notices.

```
mysql> ALTER TABLE cash_flow_specialist RENAME TO
  sales_rep;
Query OK, 4 rows affected (0.00 sec)
Records: 4  Duplicates: 0  Warnings: 0
```

**NOTE** *Note the difference between the two* ALTER RENAME *statements:* TO *has been included after the second* RENAME. *Both statements are identical in function, however. There are quite a few cases like this where MySQL has more than one way of doing something. In fact, there's even a third way to rename a table; you could use* RENAME old tablename TO new_tablename. *These sorts of things are often to provide compliance with other databases or to the ANSI SQL standard.*

### DROPPING A COLUMN

To remove the unwanted *enhancement_value* (what made us think INT was right for this mysterious field anyway?), use ALTER … DROP, as follows:

```
mysql> ALTER TABLE sales_rep DROP enhancement_value;
Query OK, 4 rows affected (0.06 sec)
Records: 4  Duplicates: 0  Warnings: 0
```

## Using Date Functions

Now that you've added a couple of date columns, let's look at some of MySQL's date functions. The table structure currently looks as follows:

```
mysql> DESCRIBE sales_rep;
```

```
+-----------------+-------------+------+-----+---------+-------+
| Field           | Type        | Null | Key | Default | Extra |
+-----------------+-------------+------+-----+---------+-------+
| employee_number | int(11)     | YES  |     | NULL    |       |
| surname         | varchar(40) | YES  |     | NULL    |       |
| first_name      | varchar(30) | YES  |     | NULL    |       |
| commission      | tinyint(4)  | YES  |     | NULL    |       |
| date_joined     | date        | YES  |     | NULL    |       |
| birthday        | date        | YES  |     | NULL    |       |
+-----------------+-------------+------+-----+---------+-------+
6 rows in set (0.00 sec)
```

If you do a query, returning *date_joined* and *birthday*, you get the following result:

```
mysql> SELECT date_joined,birthday FROM sales_rep;
+-------------+----------+
| date_joined | birthday |
+-------------+----------+
| NULL        | NULL     |
| NULL        | NULL     |
| NULL        | NULL     |
| NULL        | NULL     |
+-------------+----------+
4 rows in set (0.00 sec)
```

The NULL values indicate that you never entered anything into these fields. You'll have noticed the Null heading returned when you DESCRIBE a table. YES is the default for this; it means the field is allowed to have nothing in it. Sometimes you want to specify that a field can never contain a NULL value. You'll learn how to do this in Chapter 3. NULL values often affect the results of queries and have their own complexities, which are also examined in chapters 2 and 3. To make sure you have no NULL values, update the sales rep records as follows:

```
mysql> UPDATE sales_rep SET date_joined =
  '2000-02-15', birthday='1976-03-18'
  WHERE employee_number=1;
mysql> UPDATE sales_rep SET date_joined =
  '1998-07-09', birthday='1958-11-30'
  WHERE employee_number=2;
mysql> UPDATE sales_rep SET date_joined =
  '2001-05-14', birthday='1971-06-18'
  WHERE employee_number=3;
mysql> UPDATE sales_rep SET date_joined =
  '2002-11-23', birthday='1982-01-04'
  WHERE employee_number=4;
```

There are a host of useful date functions. These examples show just a few; see Appendix A, "MySQL Syntax Reference," and Appendix B for more information.

### SPECIFYING THE DATE FORMAT

All is not lost if you want to return dates in a format of your choice, rather than the standard YYYY-MM-DD format. To return the birthdays of all staff in the format MM/DD/YYYY, use the DATE_FORMAT() function, as follows:

```
mysql> SELECT DATE_FORMAT(date_joined,'%m/%d/%Y')
 FROM sales_rep WHERE employee_number=1;
+-----------------------------------+
| date_format(date_joined,'%m/%d/%Y') |
+-----------------------------------+
| 02/15/2000                        |
+-----------------------------------+
```

The part in single quotes after the *date_joined* column is called the *format string*. Inside the format string, you use a *specifier* to specify exactly what format to return. %m returns the month (01–12), %d returns the day (01–31), and %Y returns the year in four digits. There are a huge range of specifiers; see Appendix B for a full listing. In the meantime, some examples follow:

```
mysql> SELECT DATE_FORMAT(date_joined,'%W %M %e %y')
 FROM sales_rep WHERE employee_number=1;
+-----------------------------------+
| DATE_FORMAT(date_joined,'%W %M %e %y') |
+-----------------------------------+
| Tuesday February 15 00            |
+-----------------------------------+
```

%W returns the weekday name, %M returns the month name, %e returns the day (1–31), and %y returns the year in a two-digit format. Note that %d also returns the day (01-31), but is different to %e because the leading zeros are included.

In the following query, %a is the abbreviated weekday name, %D is the day of month with the suffix attached, %b is the abbreviated month name, and %Y is the four-digit year:

```
mysql> SELECT DATE_FORMAT(date_joined,'%a %D %b, %Y')
 FROM sales_rep WHERE employee_number=1;
+-----------------------------------------+
| DATE_FORMAT(date_joined,'%a %D %b, %Y') |
+-----------------------------------------+
| Tue 15th Feb, 2000                      |
+-----------------------------------------+
```

**NOTE**  *You can add any of your own characters in the format string. The previous examples have used a slash (/) and a comma (,). You can add any text you want to format the date as you want it.*

### RETURNING THE CURRENT DATE AND TIME

To find out what date it is, according to the server, you can use the CURRENT_DATE() function. There is another function, NOW(), which returns the time, as well:

```
mysql> SELECT NOW(),CURRENT_DATE();
```

```
+--------------------+----------------+
| NOW()              | CURRENT_DATE() |
+--------------------+----------------+
| 2002-04-07 18:32:31 | 2002-04-07    |
+--------------------+----------------+
1 row in set (0.00 sec)
```

**NOTE**  NOW() *returns the date and time. There is a column type called* DATETIME *that allows you to store data in the same format (YYYY-MM-DD HH:MM:SS) in your tables.*

You can do other conversions on the *birthday* field when you return it. Just in case you were worried about not being able to return the year, because you've replaced the year field with a date of birth, you can use the YEAR() function, as follows:

```
mysql> SELECT YEAR(birthday) FROM  sales_rep;
+----------------+
| YEAR(birthday) |
+----------------+
|           1976 |
|           1958 |
|           1982 |
|           1971 |
+----------------+
4 rows in set (0.00 sec)
```

MySQL has other functions for returning just a part of a date: MONTH() and DAYOFMONTH():

```
mysql> SELECT MONTH(birthday),DAYOFMONTH(birthday) FROM sales_rep;
+-----------------+----------------------+
| MONTH(birthday) | DAYOFMONTH(birthday) |
+-----------------+----------------------+
|               3 |                   18 |
|              11 |                   30 |
|               1 |                    4 |
|               6 |                   18 |
+-----------------+----------------------+
4 rows in set (0.00 sec)
```

## Creating More Advanced Queries

By now you should be comfortable with basic queries. The good news is that in the real world, most queries are fairly simple, like what you've done so far. And the better designed your databases (see Part II, "Designing a Database"), the more simple your queries. But there are situations where you'll need more—the most common being joining two or more tables together (this kind of query is called a *join*).

### GIVING COLUMNS A NEW HEADING WITH *AS*

The previous queries aren't too easy to read or understand. Let's tidy up the previous query, by sorting on the month and returning the sales rep names. You also introduce aliases with the AS keyword, where you give a column another name:

```
mysql> SELECT surname,first_name,MONTH(birthday)
 AS month,DAYOFMONTH(birthday) AS day FROM sales_rep
 ORDER BY month;
+----------+------------+-------+------+
| surname  | first_name | month | day  |
+----------+------------+-------+------+
| Rive     | Mongane    |     1 |    4 |
| Rive     | Sol        |     3 |   18 |
| Serote   | Mike       |     6 |   18 |
| Gordimer | Charlene   |    11 |   30 |
+----------+------------+-------+------+
4 rows in set (0.01 sec)
```

### JOINING COLUMNS WITH *CONCAT*

Sometimes you may prefer to display the person's name as one result field, rather than separate the first name and surname fields. You can join the results of columns together, using the CONCAT() function (which stands for *concatenate*), as follows:

```
mysql> SELECT CONCAT(first_name, ' ',surname)
 AS name,MONTH(birthday) AS month,DAYOFMONTH(birthday)
 AS day FROM sales_rep ORDER BY month;
+------------------+-------+------+
| name             | month | day  |
+------------------+-------+------+
| Mongane Rive     |     1 |    4 |
| Sol Rive         |     3 |   18 |
| Mike Serote      |     6 |   18 |
| Charlene Gordimer |   11 |   30 |
+------------------+-------+------+
4 rows in set (0.00 sec)
```

**NOTE** *Note the space used inside* CONCAT()*. Just as with date specifiers, you can use any characters to format your* CONCAT()*.*

### FINDING THE DAY IN A YEAR

To find out what day in the year (from 1–366) Sol Rive joined the company, use the following:

```
mysql> SELECT DAYOFYEAR(date_joined) FROM sales_rep
 WHERE employee_number=1;
+-----------------------+
| DAYOFYEAR(date_joined) |
+-----------------------+
|                    46 |
+-----------------------+
```

**WORKING WITH MULTIPLE TABLES**

The real power of relational databases comes from the fact that there are relations between tables. So far you've only been working on one table to get familiar with SQL syntax. But most real-world applications have more than one table, so you need to know how to work with these situations. First, let's add two new tables to the database. Table 1.5 will contain customer data (a customer ID, first name, and surname), and Table 1.6 will contain sales data (a customer ID, a sales rep ID, a sales value in dollars, and a unique code for the sale).

**TABLE 1.5:** THE CUSTOMER TABLE

| ID | FIRST_NAME | SURNAME |
|----|------------|---------|
| 1  | Yvonne     | Clegg   |
| 2  | Johnny     | Chaka-Chaka |
| 3  | Winston    | Powers  |
| 4  | Patricia   | Mankunku |

**TABLE 1.6:** THE SALES TABLE

| CODE | SALES_REP | CUSTOMER | VALUE |
|------|-----------|----------|-------|
| 1    | 1         | 1        | 2000  |
| 2    | 4         | 3        | 250   |
| 3    | 2         | 3        | 500   |
| 4    | 1         | 4        | 450   |
| 5    | 3         | 1        | 3800  |
| 6    | 1         | 2        | 500   |

Can you create these tables? Here are the statements I used:

```
mysql> CREATE TABLE customer(
   id int,
   first_name varchar(30),
   surname varchar(40)
);
Query OK, 0 rows affected (0.00 sec)
mysql> CREATE TABLE sales(
   code int,
   sales_rep int,
   customer int,
   value int
);
```

```
Query OK, 0 rows affected (0.00 sec)
mysql> INSERT INTO customer(id,first_name,surname) VALUES
(1,'Yvonne','Clegg'),
(2,'Johnny','Chaka-Chaka'),
(3,'Winston','Powers'),
(4,'Patricia','Mankunku');
Query OK, 4 rows affected (0.00 sec)
Records: 4  Duplicates: 0  Warnings: 0
mysql> INSERT INTO sales(code,sales_rep,customer,value) VALUES
(1,1,1,2000),
(2,4,3,250),
(3,2,3,500),
(4,1,4,450),
(5,3,1,3800),
(6,1,2,500);
Query OK, 6 rows affected (0.00 sec)
Records: 6  Duplicates: 0  Warnings: 0
```

### JOINING TWO OR MORE TABLES

As you can see, this uses the sales rep's employee number and the customer's ID in the sales table. If you examine the first sales record, you can see that it was made of sales_rep 1, which, looking up on the *sales_rep* table, is Sol Rive. The process you go through manually, of looking at the relation between the two tables, is the same one MySQL does, as long as you tell it what relation to use. Let's write a query that returns all the information from the first sales record, as well as the sales rep's name:

```
mysql> SELECT sales_rep,customer,value,first_name,surname
 FROM sales,sales_rep WHERE code=1 AND
 sales_rep.employee_number=sales.sales_rep;
+-----------+----------+-------+------------+---------+
| sales_rep | customer | value | first_name | surname |
+-----------+----------+-------+------------+---------+
|         1 |        1 |  2000 | Sol        | Rive    |
+-----------+----------+-------+------------+---------+
1 row in set (0.00 sec)
```

The first part of the query, after the SELECT, lists the fields you want to return. Easy enough—you just list the fields you want from both tables.

The second part, after the FROM, tells MySQL which tables to use. In this case it's two tables: the *sales* and *sales_rep* tables.

The third part, after the WHERE, contains the condition: code=1, which returns the first record from the sales table. The next part is what makes this query a join. This is where you tell MySQL which fields to join on or which fields the relation between the tables exists on. The relation between the *sales* table and the *sales_rep* table is between the *employee_number* field in *sales_rep*, and the *sales_rep* field in the *sales* table. So, because you find a 1 in the *sales_rep* field, you must look for employee_number 1 in the *sales_rep* table.

Let's try another one. This time you want to return all the sales that Sol Rive (employee_number 1) has made. Let's look at the thought process behind building this query:

◆ Which tables do you need? Clearly *sales_rep*, and *sales.* That's already part of the query: FROM sales_rep,sales.

◆ What fields do you want? You want all the sales information. So the field list becomes SELECT code,customer,value.

◆ And finally, what are your conditions? The first is that you only want Sol Rive's results, and the second is to specify the relation, which is between the *sales_rep* field in the *sales* table and the *employee_number* field in the *sales_rep* table. So, the conditions are as follows: WHERE first_name='Sol' and surname='Rive' AND sales.sales_rep = sales_rep.employee_number.

The final query is as follows:

```
mysql> SELECT code,customer,value FROM sales_rep,sales
  WHERE first_name='Sol' AND surname='Rive' AND
  sales.sales_rep = sales_rep.employee_number;
+------+----------+-------+
| code | customer | value |
+------+----------+-------+
|    1 |        1 |  2000 |
|    4 |        4 |   450 |
|    6 |        2 |   500 |
+------+----------+-------+
3 rows in set (0.00 sec)
```

Notice the notation in the relation's condition: sales.sales_rep or sales_rep.employee_number. Specifying the table name, then a dot, then the fieldname helps to make the queries clearer in the previous examples and is mandatory when different tables have fieldnames that are the same. You can also use this notation in the field list. For example, you could have written the previous query as follows:

```
mysql> SELECT code,customer,value FROM sales,
  sales_rep WHERE first_name='Sol' AND surname='Rive'
  AND sales_rep = employee_number;
+------+----------+-------+
| code | customer | value |
+------+----------+-------+
|    1 |        1 |  2000 |
|    4 |        4 |   450 |
|    6 |        2 |   500 |
+------+----------+-------+
3 rows in set (0.00 sec)
```

without table names before any fieldnames because there are no fields that have the same names in the different tables. Or you could have written it like this:

```
mysql> SELECT sales.code,sales.customer,sales.value
 FROM sales,sales_rep WHERE sales_rep.first_name='Sol'
 AND sales_rep.surname='Rive' AND sales.sales_rep =
 sales_rep.employee_number;
+------+----------+-------+
| code | customer | value |
+------+----------+-------+
|    1 |        1 |  2000 |
|    4 |        4 |   450 |
|    6 |        2 |   500 |
+------+----------+-------+
3 rows in set (0.00 sec)
```

Both queries give identical results.

To demonstrate what happens when you have fieldnames that are identical, let's change the *sales_rep* field in the sales table to *employee_number*. Don't worry; you'll change it back before anyone notices:

```
mysql> ALTER TABLE sales CHANGE sales_rep
 employee_number int;
Query OK, 6 rows affected (0.00 sec)
Records: 6  Duplicates: 0  Warnings: 0
```

Now let's try the join again, with the name corrected, but without using the dot notation to specify the table names:

```
mysql> SELECT code,customer,value FROM sales_rep,sales
 WHERE first_name='Sol' AND surname='Rive'AND employee_number = employee_number;
ERROR 1052: Column: 'employee_number' in where clause is ambiguous
```

Just from reading the query you can probably see it is not clear. So now you have to use the table names every time you reference one of the *employee_number* fields:

```
mysql> SELECT code,customer,value FROM sales_rep,sales
 WHERE sales_rep.employee_number=1 AND sales_rep.employee_number =
 sales.employee_number;
+------+----------+-------+
| code | customer | value |
+------+----------+-------+
|    1 |        1 |  2000 |
|    4 |        4 |   450 |
|    6 |        2 |   500 |
+------+----------+-------+
3 rows in set (0.00 sec)
```

*TIP* *You could have used* sales.employee_number *instead of* sales_rep.employee_number *in the* WHERE *clause, but it's best to use the smaller table because this gives MySQL less work to do to return the query. You will learn more about optimizing queries in Chapter 4.*

Let's change the fieldname back to what it was before going any further:

```
mysql> ALTER TABLE sales CHANGE employee_number sales_rep INT;
Query OK, 6 rows affected (0.00 sec)
Records: 6  Duplicates: 0  Warnings: 0
```

## Performing Date Calculations

Performing date calculations is relatively easy. We're going to work out someone's age based on their birthday in the next section, but first you'll try a more simple calculation. To find the number of years between the current date and the birthday, you use two functions, YEAR() and NOW():

```
mysql> SELECT YEAR(NOW()) - YEAR(birthday) FROM sales_rep;
+------------------------------+
| YEAR(NOW()) - YEAR(birthday) |
+------------------------------+
|                           26 |
|                           44 |
|                           31 |
|                           20 |
+------------------------------+
4 rows in set (0.00 sec)
```

**NOTE** *You can also use* CURRENT_DATE() *instead of* NOW(), *which will give you the same result.*

The previous query result does not return the age, only the difference in years. It does not take into account days and months. This section describes age calculation; it may be tricky for novice users. Don't be put off. Once you've practiced your basic queries, this type of query will be old hat!

You need to subtract the years as you've done previously but then subtract a further year if a full year has not passed. Someone born on the 10th of December in 2001 is not one year old in January 2002, but only after the 10th of December in 2002. A good way of doing this is to take the MM-DD components of the two date fields (the current date and the birthdate) and compare them. If the current one is larger, a full year has passed, and the year calculation can be left. If the current MM-DD part is less than the birth date one, less than a full year has passed, and you must subtract one from the calculation. This may sound tricky, and there are some quite complex ways of doing the calculation floating around, but MySQL makes it easier because it evaluates a true expression to 1 and a false expression to 0:

```
mysql> SELECT YEAR(NOW()) > YEAR(birthday) FROM
 sales_rep WHERE employee_number=1;
+------------------------------+
| YEAR(NOW()) > YEAR(birthday) |
+------------------------------+
|                            1 |
+------------------------------+
1 row in set (0.00 sec)
mysql> SELECT YEAR(NOW()) < YEAR(birthday) FROM
```

```
sales_rep WHERE employee_number=1;
+----------------------------+
| YEAR(NOW()) < YEAR(birthday) |
+----------------------------+
|                          0 |
+----------------------------+
1 row in set (0.00 sec)
```

The current year is greater than the birthday year of employee 1. That is true and evaluates to 1. The current year is not less than the birthday year. That is false and evaluates to 0.

Now you need a quick way to return just the MM-DD component of the date. And a shortcut way of doing this is to use the RIGHT() string function:

```
mysql> SELECT RIGHT(CURRENT_DATE,5),RIGHT(birthday,5) FROM sales_rep;
+----------------------+-------------------+
| RIGHT(CURRENT_DATE,5) | RIGHT(birthday,5) |
+----------------------+-------------------+
| 04-06                | 03-18             |
| 04-06                | 11-30             |
| 04-06                | 01-04             |
| 04-06                | 06-18             |
+----------------------+-------------------+
4 rows in set (0.00 sec)
```

The 5 inside the RIGHT() function refers to the number of characters from the right side of the string that the function returns. The full string is 2002-04-06, and the five rightmost characters are 04-06 (the dash is included). So, now you have all the components to do the date calculation:

```
mysql> SELECT surname, first_name, (YEAR(CURRENT_DATE) -
    YEAR(birthday)) -(RIGHT(CURRENT_DATE,5)<RIGHT(birthday,5))
    AS age FROM sales_rep;
+----------+------------+------+
| surname  | first_name | age  |
+----------+------------+------+
| Rive     | Sol        |   26 |
| Gordimer | Charlene   |   43 |
| Rive     | Mongane    |   20 |
| Serote   | Mike       |   30 |
+----------+------------+------+
4 rows in set (0.00 sec)
```

Your results may not match these results exactly because time marches on, and you'll be running the query at a later date than I did.

**WARNING**   *Be careful to match parentheses carefully when doing such a complex calculation. For every opening parenthesis, you need a closing parenthesis, and in the correct place!*

Can you spot a case when the previous age query will not work? When the current year is the same as the birth year, you'll end up with −1 as the answer. Once you've had a good look at the appendixes, try and work out your own way of calculating age. There are many possibilities and just as many plaintive cries to MySQL to develop an AGE() function.

## Grouping in a Query

Now that you have a sales table, let's put the SUM() function to better use than you did earlier, by returning the total value of sales:

```
mysql> SELECT SUM(value) FROM sales;
+------------+
| SUM(value) |
+------------+
|       7500 |
+------------+
1 row in set (0.00 sec)
```

Now you want to find out the total sales of each sales rep. To do this manually, you would need to group the sales table according to sales_rep. You would place all of the sales made by sales_rep 1 together, total the value, and then repeat with sales rep 2. SQL has the GROUP BY clause, which MySQL uses in the same way:

```
mysql> SELECT sales_rep,SUM(value) FROM sales GROUP BY
  sales_rep;
+-----------+------------+
| sales_rep | SUM(value) |
+-----------+------------+
|         1 |       2950 |
|         2 |        500 |
|         3 |       3800 |
|         4 |        250 |
+-----------+------------+
4 rows in set (0.00 sec)
```

If you had tried the same query without grouping, you'd have gotten an error:

```
mysql> SELECT sales_rep,SUM(value) FROM sales;
ERROR 1140: Mixing of GROUP columns
  (MIN(),MAX(),COUNT()...) with no GROUP columns
  is illegal if there is no GROUP BY clause
```

This query makes no sense, as it tries to mix a summary field, SUM(), with an ordinary field. What are you expecting? The sum of all values repeated next to each *sales_rep*?

You can sort the output of a grouped query as well. To return the total sales of each sales rep from highest to lowest, you just add an ORDER BY clause:

```
mysql> SELECT sales_rep,SUM(value) AS sum FROM sales
  GROUP BY sales_rep ORDER BY sum desc;
```

```
+-----------+------+
| sales_rep | sum  |
+-----------+------+
|         3 | 3800 |
|         1 | 2950 |
|         2 |  500 |
|         4 |  250 |
+-----------+------+
```

Now try a more complex query that uses a number of the concepts you have learned. Let's return the name of a sales rep with the fewest number of sales. First, you would have to return an employee number. You may get back a different number when you run the query, as there are three people who've made only one sale. It doesn't matter which one you return for now. You would do this as follows:

```
mysql> SELECT sales_rep,COUNT(*) as count from sales
  GROUP BY sales_rep ORDER BY count LIMIT 1;
+-----------+-------+
| sales_rep | count |
+-----------+-------+
|         4 |     1 |
+-----------+-------+
1 row in set (0.00 sec)
```

Can you take it even further? Can you perform a join as well to return the name of sales rep 4? If you can do this having started the book as a novice, you're well on the way to earning your username, "guru to be"! Here's the query to do so:

```
mysql> SELECT first_name,surname,sales_rep,COUNT(*) AS
  count from sales,sales_rep WHERE sales_rep=employee_number
  GROUP BY sales_rep,first_name,surname ORDER BY count
  LIMIT 1;
+------------+---------+-----------+-------+
| first_name | surname | sales_rep | count |
+------------+---------+-----------+-------+
| Mongane    | Rive    |         4 |     1 |
+------------+---------+-----------+-------+
1 row in set (0.00 sec)
```

## Summary

MySQL is a relational database management system. Logically, data is structured into tables, which are related to each other by means of a common field. Tables consist of rows (or records), and records consist of columns (or fields). Fields can be of differing types: a numeric type, a string type, or a date type. (This chapter merely introduces SQL. You will build your skills in the language throughout this book.)

The MySQL server is what stores the data and runs queries on it. To connect to the MySQL server, you need the MySQL client. This can be on the same machine as the server or a remote machine.

The power of a database management system comes from the capability to structure data and retrieve it for a wide variety of highly specific requirements. The industry standard for manipulating and defining data is SQL. Its most important commands are the following:

- The CREATE statement creates databases and the tables within the database.
- The INSERT statement places records into a table.
- The SELECT statement returns the results of a query.
- The DELETE statement removes records from a table.
- The UPDATE statement modifies the data in a table.
- The ALTER statement changes the structure of a table, utilizing clauses such as ADD to add a new column, CHANGE to change the name or definition of an existing column, RENAME to rename a table, or DROP to remove a table.

Functions add to the power of MySQL. You can recognize a function by the parentheses immediately following it. There are many MySQL functions—mathematical ones such as SUM() to calculate the total of a result set, date and time functions such as YEAR() to extract the year portion of a date, and string functions such as RIGHT() to extract part of a string starting on the right side of that string.

Armed with this basic information, you are now ready to learn the crucial intricacies of structuring data, move on to more advanced SQL, and encounter the various types of tables MySQL uses for different kinds of solutions.

# Chapter 2

# Data Types and Table Types

As YOU KNOW, MySQL uses a number of table types. By default, it uses the MyISAM table type, optimized for SELECT speed. Most websites use this table, as websites usually have infrequent INSERT or UPDATE statements and frequent SELECT statements. In this chapter you'll examine all the table types in detail. You've also looked briefly at the various data types in Chapter 1, "Quickstart to MySQL." Here, you'll explore all the data types available to you and learn when to use them.

Featured in this chapter:

◆ Numeric, string, and date column types

◆ MySQL command-line options

◆ Logical, arithmetic, comparison, and bit operators

◆ Exploring options for connecting to MySQL

◆ Understanding table types

## Exploring the Various Column Types

To use MySQL effectively it's important to understand the basic building blocks available to you. The MySQL mailing lists are full of cries for help where the solution is often as simple as using another column or table type or having a better understanding of its features. This chapter first discusses the various column types, and then goes on to look at the table types available to MySQL.

There are three main types of columns in MySQL: numeric, string, and date. Although there are many more specific types, which you'll learn about shortly, you can classify each of these into one of the three main types. Generally, you should choose the smallest possible column type, as this will save space and be faster to access and update. However, choosing too small a column can result in data being lost or cut off when you insert it, so be sure to choose a type that covers all eventualities. The following sections explore each type in detail.

**NOTE** *Column names are always case insensitive, so* SELECT field1 FROM tablename *is the same as* SELECT FieLD1 FROM tablename. *Note, however, that table and database names can be case sensitive! By default they are not case sensitive on Windows, but they are case sensitive on most versions of Unix, except MacOS X.*

## Numeric Column Types

Numeric types are designed for storing any kind of numeric data, such as prices, ages, or quantities. There are two main kinds of numeric types: integer types (whole numbers, without any decimal places or fractional parts) and floating-point types. All numeric types allow two options: UNSIGNED and ZEROFILL. UNSIGNED prohibits negative numbers (extending the positive range of the type for integer types), and ZEROFILL pads the value with zeroes instead of the usual spaces, as well as automatically making it UNSIGNED. For example:

```
mysql> CREATE TABLE test1(id TINYINT ZEROFILL);
Query OK, 0 rows affected (0.32 sec)

mysql> INSERT INTO test1 VALUES(3);
Query OK, 1 row affected (0.16 sec)

mysql> INSERT INTO test1 VALUES (-1)
Query OK, 1 row affected (0.16 sec)

mysql> INSERT INTO test1 VALUES (256)
Query OK, 1 row affected (0.16 sec)

mysql> SELECT * from test1;
+------+
| id   |
+------+
|  003 |
|  000 |
|  255 |
+------+
3 rows in set (0.00 sec)
```

Notice that because the field is UNSIGNED, the negative number is adjusted to fit into the bottom of the range, and because the 256 exceeds the maximum of the range, it is adjusted to 255, the maximum allowable positive value.

NOTE   *When performing a query on a numeric column type, you do not need to use quotes around the numeric value.*

Table 2.1 lists the numeric types available in MySQL.

**TABLE 2.1:** NUMERIC TYPES

| TYPE | DESCRIPTION |
|------|-------------|
| TINYINT[(M)] [UNSIGNED] [ZEROFILL] | A tiny integer, –128 to 127 (SIGNED), 0 to 255 (UNSIGNED), 1 byte of storage required. |
| BIT | A synonym for TINYINT(1). |
| BOOL | Another synonym for TINYINT(1). |

*Continued on next page*

**TABLE 2.1:** NUMERIC TYPES *(continued)*

| TYPE | DESCRIPTION |
|---|---|
| SMALLINT[(M)] [UNSIGNED] [ZEROFILL] | A small integer; −32,768 to 32,767 (SIGNED); 0 to 65,535 (UNSIGNED); 2 bytes of storage required. |
| MEDIUMINT[(M)] [UNSIGNED] [ZEROFILL] | A medium-size integer, −8,388,608 to 8,388,607 (SIGNED); 0 to 16,777,215 (UNSIGNED); 3 bytes of storage required. |
| INT[(M)] [UNSIGNED] [ZEROFILL] | An integer; −2,147,483,648 to 2,147,483,647 (SIGNED); 0 to 4,294,967,295 (UNSIGNED); 4 bytes of storage required. |
| INTEGER | A synonym for INT. |
| BIGINT[(M)] [UNSIGNED] [ZEROFILL] | A big integer, −9,223,372,036,854,775,808 to 9,223,372,036,854,775,807 (SIGNED); 0 to 18,446,744,073,709,551,615 (UNSIGNED); 8 bytes of storage required. See the rules after this table for some important considerations when using BIGINTs. |
| FLOAT(precision) [UNSIGNED] [ZEROFILL] | A floating-point number. precision <=24 is for a single-precision floating-point number. precision between 25 and 53 is for a double-precision floating-point number. FLOAT(X) has the same range as the corresponding FLOAT and DOUBLE types, but the display size and number of decimals are undefined. Prior to MySQL version 3.23, this was not a true floating-point value and always had two decimals. This may give some unexpected problems as all calculations in MySQL are done with double precision. |
| FLOAT[(M,D)] [UNSIGNED] [ZEROFILL] | A small or single-precision floating-point number. −3.402823466E+38 to −1.175494351E−38, 0, and 1.175494351E−38 to 3.402823466E+38. With UNSIGNED, the positive range stays the same, but negative numbers are disallowed. M refers to the total display width, and D refers to the number of decimals. FLOAT without arguments or FLOAT(X) where X <= 24 stands for a single-precision floating-point number. FLOAT(X) where X is between 25 and 53 stands for a double-precision floating-point number. 4 bytes of storage are required (single-precision). |
| DOUBLE[(M,D)] [UNSIGNED] [ZEROFILL] | A double-precision floating-point number. −1.7976931348623157E+308 to −2.2250738585072014E−308, 0, and 2.2250738585072014E−308 to 1.7976931348623157E+308. As with FLOAT, UNSIGNED will leave the positive range untouched, but disallow negative numbers. M refers to the total display width and D to the number of decimals. DOUBLE without arguments or FLOAT(X) where 25 <= X <= 53 stands for a double-precision floating-point number. 8 bytes of storage are required. |
| DOUBLE PRECISION[(M,D)] [UNSIGNED] [ZEROFILL] | A synonym for DOUBLE. |
| REAL[(M,D)] [UNSIGNED] [ZEROFILL] | Another synonym for DOUBLE. |

*Continued on next page*

**TABLE 2.1:** NUMERIC TYPES *(continued)*

| TYPE | DESCRIPTION |
|------|-------------|
| DECIMAL[(M[,D])] [UNSIGNED] [ZEROFILL] | A decimal number is stored like a string, one byte for each character (this is called *unpacked*—all other numeric types are packed). From −1.7976931348623157E+308 to −2.2250738585072014E−308, 0, and 2.2250738585072014E−308 to 1.7976931348623157E+308. M refers to the total number of digits (excluding the sign and decimal point, except for versions earlier than 3.23). D refers to the number of digits after the decimal point. It should always be less than M. D is by default 0 if omitted. Unlike other numeric types, M and D can constrain the range of allowed values. With UNSIGNED, negative values are disallowed. |
| DEC[(M[,D])] [UNSIGNED] [ZEROFILL] | A synonym for DECIMAL. |
| NUMERIC[(M[,D])] [UNSIGNED] [ZEROFILL] | Another synonym for DECIMAL. |

Use the following guidelines when deciding what numeric type to choose:

◆ Choose the smallest applicable type (TINYINT rather than INT if the value would never go beyond 127 signed).

◆ For whole numbers, choose an integer type. (Remember that money can also be stored as a whole number—for example, it can be stored in cents rather than dollars, which are integers.) It could also be reasonably stored as a DECIMAL.

◆ For high precision, use integer types rather than floating-point types (rounding errors afflict floating-point numbers).

The M value in Table 2.1 often causes confusion. Setting M to a higher value than the type allows *will not* allow you to extend its limit. For example:

```
mysql> CREATE TABLE test2(id TINYINT(10));
Query OK, 0 rows affected (0.32 sec)

mysql> INSERT INTO test2(id) VALUES(100000000);
Query OK, 1 row affected (0.00 sec)

mysql> SELECT id FROM test2;
+------+
| id   |
+------+
|  127 |
+------+
1 row in set (0.00 sec)
```

Even though the figure inserted was fewer than 10 digits, because it is a signed TINYINT, it is limited to a maximum positive value of 127.

This optional width specification left-pads the display of values whose width is less than the width specified for the column, but, with the exception of DECIMAL fields, it does not constrain the range of values that can be stored in the column or the number of digits that will be displayed for values whose width exceeds that specified for the column.

However, if you try to limit a type to less than its allowable limit, the value is not cut off. It neither constrains the range that can be stored nor the number of digits displayed. For example:

```
mysql> CREATE TABLE test3(id INT(1));
Query OK, 0 rows affected (0.32 sec)

mysql> INSERT INTO test3(id) VALUES(42432432);
Query OK, 1 row affected (0.00 sec)

mysql> SELECT id FROM test3;
+----------+
| id       |
+----------+
| 42432432 |
+----------+
1 row in set (0.16 sec)
```

The width specification is most often used with zerofill because you can easily see the results:

```
mysql> CREATE TABLE test4(id INT(3) ZEROFILL,id2 INT ZEROFILL);
Query OK, 0 rows affected (0.32 sec)

mysql> INSERT INTO test4(id,id2) VALUES (22,22);
Query OK, 1 row affected (0.00 sec)

mysql> SELECT * FROM test4;
+------+------------+
| id   | id2        |
+------+------------+
|  022 | 0000000022 |
+------+------------+
1 row in set (0.22 sec)
```

The effect of the width specification in id is to limit the display to three characters, while the id2 field uses the normal unsigned INT default (10).

## String Column Types

String columns are for storing any kind of character data, such as names, addresses, or newspaper articles. Table 2.2 describes the string types available to MySQL.

**TABLE 2.2:** STRING TYPES

| TYPE | DESCRIPTION |
|---|---|
| [NATIONAL] CHAR(M) [BINARY] | Character. A fixed-length string, right-padded with spaces to the specified length. From 0 to 255 characters (1 to 255 prior to MySQL version 3.23). Trailing spaces are removed when the value is retrieved. |
| CHAR | This is a synonym for CHAR(1). |
| [NATIONAL] VARCHAR(M) [BINARY] | Variable-length character. A variable-length string, where trailing spaces are removed when the value is stored (this is a bug, and can catch out those coming from another DBMS, where this is not the case). From 0 to 255 characters (1 to 255 prior to MySQL version 4.0.2). |
| TINYBLOB | Tiny binary large object. Maximum 255 characters ($2^8 - 1$). Requires length + 1 bytes storage. Same as TINYTEXT, except that searching is done case sensitively. In most situations, use rather use VARCHAR BINARY, as it should be faster. |
| TINYTEXT | Maximum 255 characters ($2^8 - 1$). Requires length + 1 bytes storage. Same as TINYBLOB, except that searching is done case insensitively. In most situations, rather use VARCHAR, as it should be faster. |
| BLOB | Binary large object. Maximum 65,535 characters ($2^{16} - 1$). Requires length + 2 bytes storage. Same as TEXT, except that searching is done case sensitively. |
| TEXT | Maximum 65,535 characters ($2^{16} - 1$). Requires length + 2 bytes storage. Same as BLOB, except that searching is done case insensitively. |
| MEDIUMBLOB | Medium-sized binary large object. Maximum 16,777,215 characters ($2^{24} - 1$). Requires length + 3 bytes storage. Same as MEDIUMTEXT, except that searching is done case sensitively. |
| MEDIUMTEXT | Maximum 16,777,215 characters ($2^{24} - 1$). Requires length + 3 bytes storage. Same as MEDIUMBLOB, except that searching is done case insensitively. |
| LONGBLOB | Large binary large object. Maximum of 4,294,967,295 characters ($2^{32} - 1$). Requires length + 4 bytes storage. Same as LONGTEXT, except that searching is done case sensitively. Note that because of external limitations, there is a limit of 16MB per communication packet/table row. |
| LONGTEXT | Maximum of 4,294,967,295 characters ($2^{32} - 1$). Requires length + 4 bytes storage. Same as LONGBLOB, except that searching is done case insensitively. Note that because of external limitations, there is a limit of 16MB per communication packet/table row. |
| ENUM('value1','value2',...) | Enumeration. Can only have one of the specified values, NULL or " ". Maximum of 65,535 values. |
| SET('value1','value2',...) | A set. Can contain zero to 64 values from the specified list. |

Use the following guidelines when deciding what string type to choose:

◆ Never store numbers in string columns. It is much more efficient to store them in numeric columns. Each digit in a string field takes up an entire byte, as opposed to a numeric field, which is stored in bits. Also, ordering numbers if they are stored as a string may yield inconsistent results.

◆ For speed, choose fixed columns, such as CHAR.

◆ To save space, use dynamic columns, such as VARCHAR.

◆ For limiting contents of a column to one choice, use ENUM.

◆ For allowing more than one entry in a column, choose SET.

◆ For text you want to search case insensitively, use TEXT.

◆ For text you want to search case sensitively, use BLOB.

◆ For images, and other binary objects, store them on the file system rather than directly in the database.

By default, CHAR and VARCHAR types are searched case insensitively, unless you use the BINARY keyword. For example:

```
mysql> CREATE TABLE test5(first_name CHAR(10));
Query OK, 0 rows affected (0.00 sec)

mysql> INSERT INTO test5(first_name) VALUES ('Nkosi');
Query OK, 1 row affected (0.06 sec)

mysql> SELECT first_name FROM test5 WHERE first_name='nkosi';
+------------+
| first_name |
+------------+
| Nkosi      |
+------------+
1 row in set (0.17 sec)
```

This search returned a result even though you specified *nkosi* rather than *Nkosi*. If you ALTER the table, specifying the first_name column as BINARY, you do not find the result, as follows:

```
mysql> ALTER TABLE test5 CHANGE first_name first_name CHAR(10) BINARY;
Query OK, 1 row affected (0.16 sec)
Records: 1  Duplicates: 0  Warnings: 0

mysql> SELECT first_name FROM test5 WHERE first_name='nkosi';
Empty set (0.17 sec)
```

**NOTE** *Searching CHAR and VARCHAR fields case insensitively is not common among most DBMSs, so be careful if you're moving to MySQL from another DBMS.*

The NATIONAL keyword is only there for ANSI SQL compliance. (ANSI stands for the American National Standards Institute, and they have developed a "standard" SQL. Most database management systems—DBMSs—adhere to this to some degree, but few do so entirely, and many have their own additions.) It tells the DBMS to use the MySQL default character set (which is the MySQL standard anyway).

NOTE   *Using* CHAR *as opposed to* VARCHAR *leads to larger tables, but usually faster processing, because MySQL knows exactly where each record starts. See a full discussion of this in the "MyISAM Tables" section.*

ENUM columns have some interesting features. If you add an invalid value, an empty string ("") is inserted instead, as follows:

```
mysql> CREATE TABLE test6(bool ENUM("true","false"));
Query OK, 0 rows affected (0.17 sec)

mysql> INSERT INTO test6(bool) VALUES ('true');
Query OK, 1 row affected (0.17 sec)

mysql> INSERT INTO test6(bool) VALUES ('troo');
Query OK, 1 row affected (0.06 sec)

mysql> SELECT bool from test6;
+------+
| bool |
+------+
| true |
|      |
+------+
2 rows in set (0.11 sec)
```

You can also perform queries on enumerated fields based on their indexes (the first value starts at 1). In the previous example, true would reflect as an index of 1, false as an index of 2, NULL as an index of NULL, and any other value ("") as an index of 0. For example:

```
mysql> SELECT * FROM test6 WHERE bool=0;
+------+
| bool |
+------+
|      |
+------+
1 row in set (0.17 sec)

mysql> SELECT * FROM test6 WHERE bool=1;
+------+
| bool |
+------+
| true |
+------+
1 row in set (0.16 sec)
```

The following example shows the query. If you insert an index directly, you'll see the full enumerated value when you return a result:

```
mysql> INSERT INTO test6(bool) VALUES(2);
Query OK, 1 row affected (0.00 sec)

mysql> SELECT * FROM test6;
+-------+
| bool  |
+-------+
| true  |
|       |
| false |
+-------+
3 rows in set (0.16 sec)
```

**WARNING**  LOAD DATA *does not allow you to add records to an enumerated field using the index because it treats all inputs as strings.*

Enumerated fields are sorted on their index values, not alphabetically. In other words, they are sorted in the order the values were defined:

```
mysql> SELECT * FROM test6 ORDER BY bool ASC;
+-------+
| bool  |
+-------+
|       |
| true  |
| false |
+-------+
3 rows in set (0.22 sec)
```

Sets work in a similar way to enumerated fields:

```
mysql> CREATE TABLE test7 (fruit SET('apple','mango','litchi','banana'));
Query OK, 0 rows affected (0.11 sec)

mysql> INSERT INTO test7 VALUES('banana');
Query OK, 1 row affected (0.17 sec)

mysql> INSERT INTO test7 VALUES('litchi');
Query OK, 1 row affected (0.05 sec)

mysql> INSERT INTO test7 VALUES('paw-paw');
Query OK, 1 row affected (0.00 sec)
```

The difference of a SET type is that you can add multiple instances:

```
mysql> INSERT INTO test7 VALUES('apple,mango');
Query OK, 1 row affected (0.06 sec)

mysql> SELECT * FROM test7;
+-------------+
| fruit       |
+-------------+
| banana      |
| litchi      |
|             |
| apple,mango |
+-------------+
4 rows in set (0.17 sec)
```

As with enumerations, sorting is by the index:

```
mysql> INSERT INTO test7 VALUES('mango,apple');
Query OK, 1 row affected (0.00 sec)

mysql> SELECT * FROM test7 ORDER BY fruit;
+-------------+
| fruit       |
+-------------+
|             |
| apple,mango |
| apple,mango |
| litchi      |
| banana      |
+-------------+
5 rows in set (0.11 sec)
```

Note that the order of the elements is always the same as they were specified by the CREATE TABLE statement, so *mango,apple* is stored as *apple,mango* and appears this way in the sorted results, too.

NOTE  *You can create a column of type* CHAR(0). *This may seem useless, but it can be useful when using old applications that depend on the existence of a field but don't actually store anything in it. You can also use it if you need a field that contains only two values,* NULL *and* " ".

## Date and Time Column Types

Date and time column types are designed for the special conditions required for working with temporal data, and can be used to store data such as time of day or date of birth. Table 2.3 describes the date column types available to MySQL.

**TABLE 2.3:** DATE TYPES

| TYPE | DESCRIPTION |
|------|-------------|
| DATETIME | YYYY-MM-DD HH:MM:SS from 1000-01-01 00:00:00 to 9999-12-31 23:59:59 |
| DATE | YYYY-MM-DD from 1000-01-01 to 9999-12-31 |
| TIMESTAMP | YYYYMMDDHHMMSS |
| TIME | HH:MM:SS |
| YEAR | YYYY |

The TIMESTAMP column type can be displayed in different ways, as shown in Table 2.4.

**TABLE 2.4:** TIMESTAMP TYPES

| TYPE | DESCRIPTION |
|------|-------------|
| TIMESTAMP(14) | YYYYMMDDHHMMSS |
| TIMESTAMP(12) | YYMMDDHHMMSS |
| TIMESTAMP(10) | YYMMDDHHMM |
| TIMESTAMP(8) | YYYYMMDD |
| TIMESTAMP(6) | YYMMDD |
| TIMESTAMP(4) | YYMM |
| TIMESTAMP(2) | YY |

This does not mean that data is lost, though. The number only affects the display; even in column defined as TIMESTAMP(2), the full 14 digits are stored, so if at a later stage you change the table definition, the full TIMESTAMP will be correctly displayed.

**WARNING** *Functions, except for* UNIX_TIMESTAMP(), *work on the display value. So the* DAYOFWEEK() *function will not work on a* TIMESTAMP(2) *or* TIMESTAMP(4).

MySQL is lenient in accepting date formats. You can replace the hyphen (–) and colon (:) characters with any other *punctuation* character without affecting validity. For example:

```
mysql> CREATE TABLE tt(ts DATETIME);

mysql> INSERT INTO tt(ts) VALUES('1999+11+11 23-24');
Query OK, 1 row affected (0.06 sec)
```

You can even replace the space with another character. The following example replaces it with an equals sign:

```
mysql> INSERT INTO tt(ts) VALUES('1999+12=12-12'12');
Query OK, 1 row affected (0.05 sec)
```

If the value entered is invalid, you will not get an error message; instead, the results are set to 0 (0000 for a YEAR type, 00:00:00 for a TIME type, and so on).

## MySQL Options

When you run the mysql command to connect to MySQL, you can use any of the options shown in Table 2.5.

**TABLE 2.5:** MySQL Options

| OPTION | DESCRIPTION |
| --- | --- |
| -?, --help | Displays the help and exits. |
| -A, --no-auto-rehash | Allows for quicker startup. Automatic rehashing is the feature that allows you to press Tab; MySQL will try to complete the table or field. MySQL hashes the field and table names on startup, but sometimes, when you have many tables and fields, startup can become too slow. Using this option switches this off. To use hashing when this option has been specified on startup, enter **rehash** on the command line. |
| -b, --no-beep | Turns off the beeping each time there's an error. |
| -B, --batch | Accepts SQL statements in batch mode. Displays results with tab separation. Doesn't use history file. |
| --character-sets-dir=... | Tells MySQL in which directory character sets are located. |
| -C, --compress | Uses compression in server/client protocol. |
| -#, --debug[=...] | Creates a debug log. The default is d:t:o:,/tmp/mysql.trace, which enables debugging, turns on function call entry and exit tracing, and outputs to /tmp/mysql.trace. You can override this by specifying another file. |
| -D, --database=... | Indicates which database to use. Ordinarily, you can select a database without specifying this option, but this is useful in the configuration file. |
| --default-character-set=... | Sets the default character set. |
| -e, --execute=... | Executes command and quits. The output is the same as with the -B option. |
| -E, --vertical | Prints the output of a query vertically, with each field on a different line. Without this option you can also force this output by ending your statements with \G. |
| -f, --force | Forces MySQL to continue processing even if you get a SQL error. Useful in batch mode when processing from files. |

*Continued on next page*

**TABLE 2.5:** MYSQL OPTIONS *(continued)*

| OPTION | DESCRIPTION |
| --- | --- |
| -g, --no-named-commands | Disables named commands. Uses \* form only, or uses named commands only in the beginning of a line ending with a semicolon ( ; ). Since version 10.9, the client starts with this option enabled by default! With the -g option, however, long format commands will still work from the first line. |
| -G, --enable-named-commands | Enables named commands. Long format commands are allowed as well as shortened \* commands. |
| -h, --host=... | Connects to the specified host machine. |
| -H, --html | Formats the results of a query in HTML. Most commonly you'll use a programming language to format this, but this option can be useful for a quick and dirty way to generate HTML. |
| -i, --ignore-space | Ignores spaces after function names. |
| -L, --skip-line-numbers | Causes MySQL not to write line number for errors. Can be useful when outputting to result files in which you later want to search for errors or compare. |
| --no-pager | Disables the pager and results in output going to standard output. See the -pager option. |
| --no-tee | Disables outfile. See interactive help (\h) also. |
| -n, --unbuffered | Flushes buffer after each query. |
| -N, --skip-column-names | Causes MySQL not to write column names in results. |
| -O, --set-variable var=option | Gives a variable a value. --help lists variables. |
| -o, --one-database | Only updates the default database. This can be useful for skipping updates to other databases in the update log. |
| --pager[=...] | Long results outputs will usually scroll off the screen. You can output the result to a pager. The default pager is your ENV variable PAGER. Valid pagers are less, more, cat [> filename], and so on. This option does not work in batch mode. Pager works only in Unix. |
| -p[password], --password[=...] | Password to use when connecting to server. If a password is not given on the command line, you will be prompted for it. If you enter the password on the command line, you can't have a space between the option and the password. |
| -P, --port=... | By default, you connect to a MySQL server through port 3306. You can change this by specifying the TCP/IP port number to use for connection. |

*Continued on next page*

**TABLE 2.5:** MYSQL OPTIONS (continued)

| OPTION | DESCRIPTION |
| --- | --- |
| -q, --quick | Causes the results to be displayed row by row. This speeds up output if the results are very large. This can slow down the server if the output is suspended. Doesn't use the history file. |
| -r, --raw | Write column values without escape conversion. Used with --batch. |
| -s, --silent | Does not display as much output. |
| -S, --socket=... | Socket file to use for connection. |
| -t, --table | Outputs in table format. This is default in nonbatch mode. |
| -T, --debug-info | Prints some debug information at exit. |
| --tee=... | Appends everything into outfile. See interactive help (\h) also. Does not work in batch mode. |
| -u, --user=# | Specifies a user for login. If a user is not specified, MySQL will assume it's the current user (if there is one). |
| -U, --safe-updates[=#], --i-am-a-dummy[=#] | Only allows UPDATE and DELETE that use keys. If this option is set by default, you can reset it by using --safe-updates=0. |
| -v, --verbose | Causes MySQL to give more verbose output (-v -v -v gives the table output format, -t). |
| -V, --version | Outputs the version information and exit. |
| -w, --wait | If the connection is down, this option will wait and try to connect later, rather than aborting. |

Automatic rehashing is the feature that allows you to press the Tab key and complete the table or field. MySQL creates this when you connect, but sometimes, when you have many tables and fields, startup can become too slow. Using the -A or -- no-auto-rehash option switches this off.

The -E option prints the results vertically. You can get this kind of output, even if you haven't connected to MySQL with this option active, by using \G at the end of a query:

```
mysql> SELECT * FROM customer\G;
*************************** 1. row ***************************
        id: 1
first_name: Yvonne
   surname: Clegg
*************************** 2. row ***************************
        id: 2
first_name: Johnny
   surname: Chaka-Chaka
```

```
*************************** 3. row ***************************
       id: 3
first_name: Winston
  surname: Powers
*************************** 4. row ***************************
       id: 4
first_name: Patricia
  surname: Mankunku
*************************** 5. row ***************************
       id: 5
first_name: Francois
  surname: Papo
*************************** 6. row ***************************
       id: 7
first_name: Winnie
  surname: Dlamini
*************************** 7. row ***************************
       id: 6
first_name: Neil
  surname: Beneke
7 rows in set (0.00 sec)
```

The ignore space option (-i) allows you to be more lax in using functions in your queries. For example, the following normally causes an error (note the space after MAX):

```
mysql> SELECT MAX (value) FROM sales;
ERROR 1064: You have an error in your SQL syntax near '(value) from
 sales' at line 1
```

But if you'd used the -i option to connect, there'd have been no problem:

```
mysql> SELECT MAX(value) FROM sales;
+-------------+
| MAX (value) |
+-------------+
|        3800 |
+-------------+
```

The -H (or --html) option places query results inside an HTML table. If you connect with this option, you'll see the following sort of output:

```
mysql> SELECT * FROM customer;
<TABLE BORDER=1><TR><TH>id</TH><TH>first_name</TH><TH>surname</TH></TR>
<TR><TD>1</TD><TD>Yvonne</TD><TD>Clegg</TD></TR>
<TR><TD>2</TD><TD>Johnny</TD><TD>Chaka-Chaka</TD></TR>
<TR><TD>3</TD><TD>Winston</TD><TD>Powers</TD></TR>
<TR><TD>4</TD><TD>Patricia</TD><TD>Mankunku</TD></TR>
<TR><TD>5</TD><TD>Francois</TD><TD>Papo</TD></TR>
<TR><TD>7</TD><TD>Winnie</TD><TD>Dlamini</TD></TR>
<TR><TD>6</TD><TD>Neil</TD><TD>Beneke</TD></TR></TABLE>
7 rows in set (0.00 sec)
```

The -o option only allows updates to the default database. If you connected with this option, you would not have been able to make an update to any tables in the *firstdb* database:

```
mysql> UPDATE customer SET first_name='John' WHERE first_name='Johnny';
Ignoring query to other database
```

The -U option (also called the "I am a dummy" option) helps avoid unpleasant surprises by not permitting an UPDATE or DELETE that does not use a key (you'll look at keys in detail in Chapter 4, "Indexes and Query Optimization"). If you connect with this option, the following command will not work:

```
mysql> DELETE FROM customer;
ERROR 1175: You are using safe update mode and you tried to update a
   table without a WHERE that uses a KEY column
```

## Exploring the Various Table Types

There are two transaction-safe table types (InnoDB and BDB), but the rest (ISAM, MyISAM, MERGE, and HEAP) are not transaction safe. Choosing the right table type can dramatically affect performance speed.

### ISAM Tables

The Indexed Sequential Access Method (ISAM) table type was the old MySQL standard. The MyISAM table type replaced it in version 3.23.0 (although ISAM types will still be available until MySQL 4.1). So, you'll probably only encounter the ISAM table type if you're dealing with old databases dating from that time. The main difference between the two is that the index on a MyISAM table is much smaller than on an ISAM table, so a SELECT using an index on a MyISAM table will use fewer system resources. The flipside is that MyISAM uses more processor power to insert a record into the more compressed index.

ISAM tables have the following features:

- ISAM stores the data files with an .ISD and the index file with an .ISM extension.
- It is not binary portable across different machines or operating systems. In other words, you cannot just copy the ISD and ISM files. You'll have to use one of the other backup methods, such as mysqldump (see Chapter 11, "Database Backups").

If you do run into the ISAM table type, you should change it to the more efficient MyISAM type. MyISAM tables also allow you to use more of MySQL's built-in functionality. To convert an ISAM table to a MyISAM table, use the following:

```
ALTER TABLE tablename TYPE = MYISAM;
```

### MyISAM Tables

The MyISAM table type replaced ISAM in version 3.23.0. MyISAM indexes are much smaller than ISAM indexes, so the system will use fewer resources when doing a SELECT using an index on a MyISAM table. However, MyISAM uses more processor power to insert a record into the more compressed index.

MyISAM data files are given the extension `.MYD`, and the indexes have the extension `.MYI`. MyISAM databases are stored in a directory, so if you've been doing the examples from Chapter 1 and have permission to look inside the directory `firstdb`, you'll see the following files:

◆ `sales_rep.MYI`

◆ `sales_rep.MYD`

◆ `sales.MYD`

◆ `sales.MYI`

◆ `customer.MYD`

◆ `customer.MYI`

The data files should always be larger than the index files. In Chapter 4 you'll see how to use indexes properly and what they actually contain.

There are three subtypes of MyISAM tables: static, dynamic, or compressed.

MySQL decides whether to use dynamic or static tables when the table is created. Static tables are the default format, which exist if there are no `VARCHAR`, `BLOB`, or `TEXT` columns. If any of these column types exist, the table type becomes dynamic.

### STATIC TABLES

Static tables (also more descriptively called *fixed-length tables*) are of a fixed length. Look at Figure 2.1, which shows the characters stored in one field of a mini-table. The field is a first name, set to `CHAR(10)`.

**FIGURE 2.1**

Data stored in static format

There are exactly 10 bytes stored for each record. If the actual name takes up fewer, the rest of the column is padded with spaces to fit the full 10 characters.

Characteristics of static tables include the following:

◆ Very quick (because MySQL knows the second name always starts at the 11th character)

◆ Easy to cache

◆ Easy to reconstruct after a crash (again, because the positions of records are fixed, MySQL knows where each record is, so only a record being written during the crash will be lost)

◆ Requires more disk space (30 characters needed for the 3 records, even though only 16 are used for the names)

◆ Not necessary to reorganize with myisamchk (see Chapter 10, "Basic Administration," for more on this)

### DYNAMIC TABLES

Columns in dynamic tables are of different lengths. If the same data used in the static table is placed into a dynamic table, it will be stored as shown in Figure 2.2.

**FIGURE 2.2**

Data stored in
dynamic format

Although this data format saves space, it is more complex. Each record has a header, which indicates how long it is.

Characteristics of dynamic table types include the following:

◆ All string columns are dynamic (unless they are less than 4 bytes. In this case, the space saved would be negligible, and the extra complexity would lead to a performance loss).

◆ Usually takes much less disk space than fixed tables.

◆ Tables require regular maintenance to avoid fragmentation. (For example, if you updated *Ian* to *Iane*, the *e* could not appear in the space immediately after the *n* because this space is occupied by the start of the next column or record.) See Chapter 10 for further details on maintenance.

◆ In the case of fragmented columns, each new link incurs a penalty of 6 bytes and will be at least 20 bytes in size (and may have links of its own as well if further updates increase the size beyond this).

◆ Not as easy to reconstruct after a crash, especially if heavily fragmented.

◆ Excluding links, the size of a dynamic record can be calculated with this formula:

3

+ (number of columns + 7) / 8

+ (number of char columns)

+ packed size of numeric columns

+ length of strings

+ (number of NULL columns + 7) / 8

◆ Each record has a header, which indicates which string columns are empty and which numeric columns contain a zero (not NULL records), in which case they are not stored to disk. Nonempty strings contain a length byte, plus the string contents.

### COMPRESSED TABLES

Compressed tables are read-only table types that use much less disk space. They are ideal for use with archival data which will not change (as they can only currently be read from, not written to), and where not much space is available, such as for a CD-ROM.

Characteristics of compressed tables include the following:

◆ Created using the myisampack utility (note that the ROW_FORMAT="compressed" option for CREATE TABLE will only work if the myisampack code has been added to the server).

◆ Tables are much smaller.

◆ Because each record is separately compressed, there is little access overhead.

◆ Each column could be compressed differently, using different compression algorithms.

◆ Can compress fixed or dynamic table formats.

◆ To create a compressed table with myisampack, simply run the following:

```
myisampack [options] filename
```

Table 2.6 shows the options for compressed tables.

**TABLE 2.6:** COMPRESSED TABLE OPTIONS

| OPTION | DESCRIPTION |
| --- | --- |
| -b, --backup | Creates a backup of the table, calling it `tablename.OLD`. |
| -#, --debug=debug_options | Outputs debug log. The `debug_options` string often is `d:t:o,filename`. |
| -f, --force | When compressing, MySQL creates a temporary file called `tablename.TMD`. If the compression process dies for some reason, this file may not have been deleted. This option forces MySQL to pack the table even if the temporary file exists, if the compression causes the table to become bigger, or if the table is too small to compress in the first place. |
| -?, --help | Displays a help message and exits. |
| -j big_tablename, --join=big_tablename | Joins all tables listed on the command line into one big table. All tables that you want to combine must be identical (in all aspects such as columns and indexes). |
| -p #, --packlength=# | Usually you'd only use this option when you're running myisampack a second time. myisampack stores all rows with a length pointer from 1–3. Occasionally, myisampack notices that it should have used a shorter-length pointer during the process (normally it gets it right!). Next time you pack the table, you can alert myisampack to use the optimal length storage size. |
| -s, --silent | Silent mode. Only outputs errors. |
| -t, --test | This option will not actually pack the table; it will just test the packing process. |
| -T dir_name, --tmp_dir=dir_name | Writes the temporary table into the directory you specify. |
| -v, --verbose | Verbose mode. Writes information about progress and result of the packing. |
| -V, --version | Displays version information and exits. |
| -w, --wait | If the table is in use, this option waits and retries. Using this option in conjunction with `--skip-external-locking` is not recommended if there is a possibility of the table being updated while you're packing. |

Let's compress one of the tables you've used so far. You have to use the -f option because the table is too small to compress normally:

```
C:\Program Files\MySQL\bin>myisampack -v -f   ..\data\firstdb\sales_~1
Compressing ..\data\firstdb\sales_~1.MYD: (5 records)
- Calculating statistics

normal:      3  empty-space:     0  empty-zero:       2  empty-fill:  1
pre-space:   0  end-space:       2  intervall-fields: 0  zero:        0
Original trees:  7  After join: 1
- Compressing file
Min record length:      10   Max length:      17   Mean total length:    40
-35.81%
```

To unpack a table, run myisamchk --unpack filename:

```
C:\Program Files\MySQL\bin>myisamchk --unpack ..\data\firstdb\sales_~1
- recovering (with keycache) MyISAM-table '..\data\firstdb\sales_~1'
Data records: 5
```

## MERGE Tables

MERGE tables are amalgamations of identical MyISAM tables. They were introduced in version 3.23.25. You'd normally use them only when your MyISAM tables are getting too big.

The advantages of MERGE tables include the following:

◆ More speed in some situations (you could split different tables onto different disks, and use a MERGE table to access them as one table).

◆ Smaller table size. Some operating systems have a file size limit, and splitting the tables and creating a MERGE table allows one to get around this. Also, files can more easily transferred, such as by copying them to CD.

◆ You can make most of the original tables read-only and allow INSERTs into the most recent table. This means you run the risk of only one small table getting corrupted during an UPDATE or INSERT, and the repairs on this table would be much quicker.

The disadvantages of MERGE tables include the following:

◆ They are much slower on eq_ref searches.

◆ You need to take care when changing one of the underlying tables, as this will corrupt the MERGE table (no actual harm is done, just the MERGE table may be unavailable).

◆ REPLACE doesn't work.

◆ Tables use slightly more file descriptors.

Let's create a MERGE table. First, you'll need to create two identical tables:

```
CREATE TABLE sales_repl (
  id INT AUTO_INCREMENT PRIMARY KEY,
  employee_number INT(11),
```

```
   surname VARCHAR(40),
   first_name VARCHAR(30),
   commission TINYINT(4),
   date_joined DATE,
   birthday DATE
   ) TYPE=MyISAM;

CREATE TABLE sales_rep2 (
   id INT AUTO_INCREMENT PRIMARY KEY,
   employee_number INT(11),
   surname VARCHAR(40),
   first_name VARCHAR(30),
   commission TINYINT(4),
   date_joined DATE,
   birthday DATE
   ) TYPE=MyISAM;

CREATE TABLE sales_rep1_2 (
   id INT AUTO_INCREMENT PRIMARY KEY,
   employee_number INT(11),
   surname VARCHAR(40),
   first_name VARCHAR(30),
   commission TINYINT(4),
   date_joined DATE,
   birthday DATE
   ) TYPE=MERGE
   UNION=(sales_rep1,sales_rep2);
```

Let's insert some data into the tables so you can test it later:

```
INSERT INTO sales_rep1 ('employee_number', 'surname',
 'first_name', 'commission', 'date_joined', 'birthday')
 VALUES (1,'Tshwete','Paul',15,'1999-01-03','1970-03-04');

INSERT INTO sales_rep2 ('employee_number', 'surname',
 'first_name', 'commission', 'date_joined', 'birthday')
 VALUES (2,'Grobler','Peggy-Sue',12,'2001-11-19','1956-08-25');
```

Now, if you do a query on the merged table, all the records in *sales_rep1* and *sales_rep2* are available:

```
mysql> SELECT first_name,surname FROM sales_rep1_2;
+------------+---------+
| first_name | surname |
+------------+---------+
| Paul       | Tshwete |
| Peggy-Sue  | Grobler |
+------------+---------+
2 rows in set (0.00 sec)
```

Based on the previous results, you don't know which underlying table any of the records are in. Fortunately, if you're updating a record, you don't need to know this. The following statement

```
mysql> UPDATE sales_rep1_2 set first_name = "Peggy"
  WHERE first_name="Peggy-Sue";
Query OK, 1 row affected (0.00 sec)
Rows matched: 1  Changed: 1  Warnings: 0
```

will update the record correctly. Because the record only physically exists on the underlying level, queries to both the MERGE table and the underlying MyISAM table will reflect the correct data, as the following demonstrates:

```
mysql> SELECT first_name,surname FROM sales_rep1_2;
+------------+---------+
| first_name | surname |
+------------+---------+
| Paul       | Tshwete |
| Peggy      | Grobler |
+------------+---------+
2 rows in set (0.00 sec

mysql> SELECT first_name,surname FROM sales_rep2;
+------------+---------+
| first_name | surname |
+------------+---------+
| Peggy      | Grobler |
+------------+---------+
1 row in set (0.00 sec)
```

The same applies to DELETE statements:

```
mysql> DELETE FROM sales_rep1_2 WHERE first_name='Peggy';
Query OK, 1 row affected (0.00 sec)
```

The record is removed at the underlying level, so it will disappear from queries to both the MERGE table and the underlying table:

```
mysql> SELECT first_name,surname FROM sales_rep1_2;
+------------+---------+
| first_name | surname |
+------------+---------+
| Paul       | Tshwete |
+------------+---------+
1 row in set (0.00 sec)

mysql> SELECT first_name,surname FROM sales_rep2;
Empty set (0.00 sec)
```

However, if you tried to perform an INSERT, MySQL would not know which underlying table to insert the record to, and so it will return an error:

```
mysql> INSERT INTO sales_rep1_2 ('surname', 'first_name',
 'commission', 'date_joined', 'birthday')
 VALUES ('Shephard','Earl',11,'2002-12-15','1961-05-31');
ERROR 1031: Table handler for 'sales_rep1_2' doesn't have this option
```

Luckily there is a solution, introduced in version 4 (before this, you could not insert into the MERGE table at all). When creating your MERGE table, you can specify which table to insert to. Look at the last clause of the following CREATE statement:

```
CREATE TABLE sales_rep1_2 (
    id INT AUTO_INCREMENT PRIMARY KEY,
    employee_number INT(11),
    surname VARCHAR(40),
    first_name VARCHAR(30),
    commission TINYINT(4),
    date_joined DATE,
    birthday DATE
    ) TYPE=MERGE
    UNION=(sales_rep1,sales_rep2)
    INSERT_METHOD = LAST
```

The INSERT_METHOD can be NO, FIRST, or LAST. Inserted records are then placed into the first table in the union list, the last table, or none at all. The default is NO.

**WARNING**    *If you perform any structural changes to the underlying tables, such as renaming them or rebuilding the indexes, you'll need to rebuild the MERGE table. Drop the MERGE table, then make your changes, and then rebuild the MERGE table. If you make the changes and forget to drop your MERGE table, you may find you are unable to access the MERGE table properly. Dropping and rebuilding will solve this.*

## HEAP Tables

HEAP tables are the fastest table types because they are stored in memory and use a hashed index. The downside is that, because they are stored in memory, all data will be lost in the case of a crash. They also can't hold quite so much data (unless you've got a big budget for RAM).

As with any table, you can create a table based on the contents of another table. HEAP tables are often used to give faster access to an already existing table—to leave the original table for inserting and updating and then have the new table for fast reading. Let's create one from the *sales_rep* table. If you haven't already created the *sales_rep* table, create and populate the *sales_rep* table with the following statements:

```
CREATE TABLE sales_rep (
    employee_number int(11) default NULL,
    surname varchar(40) default NULL,
    first_name varchar(30) default NULL,
    commission tinyint(4) default NULL,
    date_joined date default NULL,
```

```
     birthday date default NULL
) TYPE=MyISAM;

INSERT INTO sales_rep VALUES (1, 'Rive', 'Sol', 10,
  '2000-02-15', '1976-03-18');
INSERT INTO sales_rep VALUES (2, 'Gordimer', 'Charlene', 15,
  '1998-07-09', '1958-11-30');
INSERT INTO sales_rep VALUES (3, 'Serote', 'Mike', 10,
  '2001-05-14', '1971-06-18');
INSERT INTO sales_rep VALUES (4, 'Rive', 'Mongane', 10,
  '2002-11-23', '1982-01-04');
```

Now, you create a HEAP table that will take a subset of *sales_rep* and put it into memory for fast access:

```
mysql> CREATE TABLE heaptest TYPE=HEAP SELECT first_name,surname
  FROM sales_rep;
Query OK, 4 rows affected (0.02 sec)
Records: 4  Duplicates: 0  Warnings: 0

mysql> SELECT * FROM heaptest;
+------------+----------+
| first_name | surname  |
+------------+----------+
| Sol        | Rive     |
| Charlene   | Gordimer |
| Mike       | Serote   |
| Mongane    | Rive     |
+------------+----------+
4 rows in set (0.00 sec)
```

Characteristics of HEAP tables include the following:

◆ Because HEAP tables use memory, you don't want them hogging too much. The tables are always limited by the mysqld variable max_heap_table_size.

◆ Keys are not used in the same way as for MyISAM tables. They cannot be used for an ORDER BY.

◆ They only use the whole key to search for a row, not parts of a key.

◆ They only use = and <=> when searching indexes.

◆ MySQL's range optimizer cannot find out how many rows there are between two values.

◆ However, when keys are used properly in HEAP tables, they are fast!

◆ HEAP tables, unlike many other hashed tables, allow nonunique keys.

◆ They do not support an index on a NULL column.

◆ They do not support AUTO_INCREMENT columns.

◆ Do not support BLOB or TEXT columns.

As you can see, there are quite a few differences between MyISAM indexes and HEAP indexes. A HEAP table could actually be slower if you're relying on an index it does not use. See Chapter 4 for more on using keys.

**NOTE**   *Besides the* `max_heap_table_size` *limit and the memory limit on your machine, a limit of 4GB per table could be reached on some setups because this is the limit imposed by a 32-bit machine's address space.*

## InnoDB Tables

InnoDB tables are a transaction-safe table type (this means you have `COMMIT` and `ROLLBACK` capabilities. In a MyISAM table, the entire table is locked when inserting. Just for that fraction of a second, no other statements can be run on the table. InnoDB uses row-level locking so that only the row is locked, not the entire table, and statements can still be performed on other rows.

For performance purposes you should use InnoDB tables if your data performs large numbers of `INSERT`s or `UPDATE`s relative to `SELECT`s. MyISAM would be a better choice when your database performs large numbers of `SELECT`s relative to `UPDATE`s or `INSERT`s.

To use InnoDB tables, MySQL will need to have been compiled with InnoDB support (see Chapter 15, "Installing MySQL," for full details), such as the mysqld-max distribution. There are also a number of configuration parameters that you should set up before you can rely on this table type for good performance, so be sure to read Chapter 13, "Configuring and Optimizing MySQL," for more details.

When you start MySQL with InnoDB options compiled, and use only the defaults, you'll see something like the following:

```
C:\MySQL\bin>mysqld-max
InnoDB: The first specified data file .\ibdata1 did not exist:
InnoDB: a new database to be created!
InnoDB: Setting file .\ibdata1 size to 64 MB
InnoDB: Database physically writes the file full: wait...
InnoDB: Log file .\ib_logfile0 did not exist: new to be created
InnoDB: Setting log file .\ib_logfile0 size to 5 MB
InnoDB: Log file .\ib_logfile1 did not exist: new to be created
InnoDB: Setting log file .\ib_logfile1 size to 5 MB
InnoDB: Doublewrite buffer not found: creating new
InnoDB: Doublewrite buffer created
InnoDB: Creating foreign key constraint system tables
InnoDB: Foreign key constraint system tables created
020504 12:42:52  InnoDB: Started
C:\MYSQL\BIN\MYSQLD~2.EXE: ready for connections
```

**WARNING**   *Before version 4, you could not just start MySQL. You had to set at least the* `innodb_data_file_path` *in the configuration file. This config file is discussed more fully in Chapter 13.*

By default, MySQL creates a file `ibdata1` in the default data directory (usually `C:\MSQL\data` on `Windows`, or `/usr/local/mysql/data` or `/usr/local/var/` on Unix).

InnoDB tables are different from MyISAM tables in that the databases are not stored in a directory, with the tables as files. All tables and indexes are stored in an InnoDB *tablespace* (which can consist of one or more tables; in the previous example it's `ibdata1`).

The table data limit then is not limited to the operating system file size limit.

**NOTE** *In a MyISAM table, an operating system with a 2GB limit will allow a maximum table size of 2GB. InnoDB has no such limit, although the onus is then on the administrator to optimize the tablespace.*

The initial size of this table is set to 16MB. In early versions of MySQL 4, this was set to 64MB but was nonextending (meaning that once you ran out of space, that was it!). Later versions set this to auto-extending by default, meaning that as your data grows, so does the tablespace. You'll want to have some hands-on control over this to optimize performance. This is explained briefly in a bit and in more detail in Chapter 13.

To create an InnoDB table, use the following:

```
mysql> CREATE TABLE innotest (f1 INT,f2 CHAR(10),INDEX (f1)) TYPE=InnoDB;
Query OK, 0 rows affected (0.10 sec)
```

### BDB Tables

BDB stands for Berkeley Database (it was originally created at the University of California, Berkeley). It is also a transaction-capable table type. As with InnoDB tables, BDB support needs to be compiled into MySQL to make it work (the mysql-max distribution comes with BDB support).

To create a BDB table, simply use TYPE=BDB after your CREATE TABLE statement:

```
mysql> CREATE TABLE bdbtest(f1 INT,f2 CHAR(10)) TYPE=BDB;
Query OK, 0 rows affected (0.28 sec)
```

Currently, the interface between MySQL and BDB (which exists independently to MySQL) is still in beta. MySQL and BDB have both been around for ages, and are stable, but the interface between the two has not been. Check the latest documentation to see whether this is still the case.

## Summary

Choosing the types for your fields is important if you want to get the best performance out of MySQL. Numeric types allow you to do calculations and are usually smaller than string types. Date types allow you to easily store date and time data.

Similarly, to use MySQL properly, you need to have an understanding of the operators it employs. Logical operators such as AND and OR, and comparison operators such as = and LIKE, assist in narrowing the results from your queries down to just what you need. Bit operators are a useful feature for binary mathematical data.

MySQL has a number of table types, which are suited to different situations. The MyISAM table type (the default) is ideal for systems where there are large numbers of queries relative to updates (such as websites). MERGE tables are amalgamations of identical MyISAM tables, allowing you to split large tables into a number of smaller ones, for ease of updating, and giving extra speed in some situations.

HEAP tables are the fastest of the lot and are stored in memory. InnoDB and BDB tables are transaction safe, allowing statements to be grouped for integrity of data. InnoDB tables make use of consistent reads, which means results of tables are displayed as they appear after a completed transaction. This isn't always ideal, and you can override this behavior with read locks for updating or for sharing.

# Chapter 3

# Advanced SQL

YOU GOT A TASTE of SQL in Chapter 1, "Quickstart to MySQL," but there's much more to learn. To begin to appreciate the possibilities and approach MySQL mastery, you need to understand the various logical, arithmetic, comparison, and bit operators available to MySQL. These allow you to build much more complex queries than the simple kind that you learned in the first chapter. Similarly, you'll find the need to run queries that require data from more than one table, called *joins*. The vagaries of left joins, right joins, outer joins, inner joins, and natural joins can seem confusing. This chapter will introduce all these to you, showing you when and how to use them.

Featured in this chapter:

◆ Logical, arithmetic, comparison, and bit operators

◆ Advanced joins (inner, outer, left, right, and natural joins)

◆ Joining results with UNION

◆ Rewriting sub-selects as joins

◆ Removing records with DELETE and TRUNCATE

◆ User variables

◆ Running MySQL in batch mode

◆ Performing transactions with BEGIN and COMMIT

◆ Consistent reads

◆ Table locks

◆ Read locks for updating and for sharing

## Operators

Operators are the building blocks of complex queries. *Logical operators* (such as AND and OR) allow you to relate numbers of conditions in various ways. *Arithmetic operators* (such as are + or *) allow you to perform basic mathematical operations in your queries. *Comparison operators* (such as > or <) allow you to compare values, and narrow result sets in this way. Finally, *bit operators*, while not often used, allow you to work at a bit level in your queries.

## Logical Operators

Logical operators reduce to either true (1) or false (0). For example, if you are male, and I ask whether you're male OR female (assume I'm asking for a yes/no answer), the answer would be yes, or true. If I ask whether you're male AND female, the answer would be no, or false. The AND and OR in the questions are logical operators. Table 3.1 describes the operators in more detail.

**Table 3.1:** Logical Operators

| Operator | Syntax | Description |
|---|---|---|
| AND, && | c1 AND c2, c1 && c2 | Only true if both conditions c1 and c2 are true. |
| OR, \|\| | c1 OR c2, c1 \|\| c2 | True if either c1 or c2 is true. |
| !, NOT | ! c1, NOT c1 | True if c1 is false, false if c1 is true. |

Instead of populating a table and running queries against this, the following examples will produce either a 1 or a 0. Each row in the tables you query will also reduce to a 1 or a 0. 1s will be returned, and 0s will not be. If you understand this, you can apply the principles to any of your own tables. If you're going through these operators for the first time, see if you can predict the results based on Table 3.1.

```
mysql> SELECT 1 AND 0;
+---------+
| 1 AND 0 |
+---------+
|       0 |
+---------+

mysql> SELECT NOT(1 AND 0);
+--------------+
| NOT(1 AND 0) |
+--------------+
|            1 |
+--------------+

mysql> SELECT !((1 OR 0) AND (0 OR 1));
+-------------------------+
| !((1 OR 0) AND (0 OR 1)) |
+-------------------------+
|                       0 |
+-------------------------+
```

Remember that conditions inside the innermost parentheses are evaluated first. So, MySQL simplifies the complex statement in the previous example as follows:

```
!((1 OR 0) AND (0 OR 1))
!((1) AND (1))
!(1)
0
```

## Arithmetic Operators

Arithmetic operators are used to perform basic mathematical operations. For example, when I say that $2 + 3 = 5$, the plus sign $(+)$ is an arithmetic operator. Table 3.2 describes the arithmetic operators available in MySQL.

**TABLE 3.2:** ARITHMETIC OPERATORS

| OPERATOR | SYNTAX | DESCRIPTION |
|---|---|---|
| + | a + b | Adds a and b together, returning the sum of both |
| − | a - b | Subtracts b from a, returning the difference |
| * | a * b | Multiplies a and b, returning the product of both |
| / | a / b | Divides a by b, returning the quotient |
| % | a % b | a modulus b, returning the remainder after a / b |

For example, adding together two columns of type INT will produce an INT:

```
mysql> SELECT 2+1;
+-----+
| 2+1 |
+-----+
|   3 |
+-----+
```

```
mysql> SELECT 4-2/4;
+-------+
| 4-2/4 |
+-------+
|  3.50 |
+-------+
```

This returns 3.5, not 0.5, because the division is performed first (remember the rules of precedence you learned at school?). However, you should always use parentheses to make clear which operations are to be performed first to someone who doesn't know the rules. To make the previous query simpler, rewrite it as follows:

```
mysql> SELECT 4-(2/4);
+---------+
| 4-(2/4) |
+---------+
|    3.50 |
+---------+
```

*NOTE* *Even though all the values in this query are integers, because the result has a non-integer element, it is returned as a floating-point number.*

This next example demonstrates the modulus operator:

```
mysql> SELECT 5 % 3;
+-------+
| 5 % 3 |
+-------+
|     2 |
+-------+
```

Modulus returns the remainder of a division. In the previous example, 5 divided by 3 is 1, remainder 2.

## Comparison Operators

Comparison operators are used when making comparisons between values. For example, I can make the statement that 34 is greater than 2. The *is greater than* part is a comparison operator. Table 3.3 lists and describes the comparison operators used in MySQL.

**TABLE 3.3:** COMPARISON OPERATORS

| OPERATOR | SYNTAX | DESCRIPTION |
| --- | --- | --- |
| = | a = b | True if both a and b are equal (excluding NULL). |
| !=, <> | a != b, a <> b | True if a is not equal to b. |
| > | a > b | True if a is greater than b. |
| < | a < b | True if a is less than b. |
| >= | a >= b | True if a is greater than or equal to b. |
| <= | a <= b | True if a is less than or equal to b. |
| <=> | a <=> b | True if a and b are equal (including NULL). |
| IS NULL | a is NULL | True if a contains a NULL value. |
| IS NOT NULL | a IS NOT NULL | True if a does not contain a NULL value. |
| BETWEEN | a BETWEEN b and c | True if a is between the values of b and c, inclusive. |
| NOT BETWEEN | a NOT BETWEEN b and c | True if a is not between the values of b and c, inclusive. |
| LIKE | a LIKE b | True if a matches b on an SQL pattern match. |

*Continued on next page*

**TABLE 3.3:** COMPARISON OPERATORS *(continued)*

| OPERATOR | SYNTAX | DESCRIPTION |
| --- | --- | --- |
| NOT LIKE | a NOT LIKE b | True if a does not match b on an SQL pattern match. The two acceptable wildcard characters are % (which means any number of characters) and _ (which means one character). |
| IN | a IN (b1, b2, b3…) | True if a is equal to anything in the list. |
| NOT IN | a NOT IN (b1,b2,b3…) | True if a is not equal to anything in the list. |
| REGEXP, RLIKE | a REGEXP b, a RLIKE b | True if a matches b with a regular expression. |
| NOT REGEXP, NOT RLIKE | a NOT REGEXP b, a NOT RLIKE B | True if a does not match b with a regular expression. |

With comparison operators, you're also going to use 1 and 0 to represent true and false. Remember you'll be replacing these with constants of your own and fields from database tables. For example, take a table with two rows, as shown in Figure 3.1.

**FIGURE 3.1**

TABLE1

| FIELD1 |
| --- |
| 15 |
| 13 |

The following code represents the = comparison operator:

```
SELECT * FROM TABLE1 WHERE FIELD1 = 13.
```

Each row in the table is then compared to see whether the condition is true or false. For the first row, the expression reduces to this:

```
15 = 13
```

This is false, so the row is not returned. For the second row, the expression reduces to the following:

```
13 = 13
```

This is true, so this time the row is returned.
Once you understand this, you can apply it to your own tables.
Another example:

```
mysql> SELECT 13=11;
+-------+
| 13=11 |
+-------+
|   0   |
+-------+
```

If you come from a programming background, you'll probably know the complexities of comparing different types (such as strings with numbers). For example, what sort of answer do you expect when you ask if the string 'thirty' is less than the number 29? MySQL tries to be as helpful as possible when you want to compare values of different types (converting the types as well as it can, called *type conversions*). If you are comparing strings and numerics, or floating-point numbers and integers, MySQL will compare them as if they were the same type. For example:

```
mysql> SELECT '4200' = 4200.0;
+----------------+
| '4200' = 4200.0 |
+----------------+
|              1 |
+----------------+
```

The string '4200' converted to a number is equal to 4200.0. However, the two strings '4200' and '4200.0' are not the same:

```
mysql> SELECT '4200' = '4200.0';
+------------------+
| '4200' = '4200.0' |
+------------------+
|                0 |
+------------------+
```

The next example demonstrates the case-insensitive nature of string comparisons:

```
mysql> SELECT 'abc' = 'ABC';
+--------------+
| 'abc' = 'ABC' |
+--------------+
|            1 |
+--------------+
```

In the following example, a trailing space is ignored for purposes of equality in a case-insensitive search:

```
mysql> SELECT 'abc' = 'ABC ';
+--------------+
| 'abc' = 'ABC' |
+--------------+
|            1 |
+--------------+
1 row in set (0.00 sec)
```

The following example is an important one to note; the result is not 0 (false), it's NULL:

```
mysql> SELECT NULL=0;
+--------+
| NULL=0 |
+--------+
|   NULL |
+--------+
```

To evaluate `NULL` rows, you'd need to use the following:

```
mysql> SELECT NULL<=>0;
+----------+
| NULL<=>0 |
+----------+
|        0 |
+----------+
```

`NULL` is basically a third possible result of an evaluation: There's true, false, and then there's `NULL`. None of the following queries provides useful results when compared to a `NULL` value:

```
mysql> SELECT 200 = NULL, 200 <> NULL, 200 < NULL, 200 > NULL;
+------------+-------------+------------+------------+
| 200 = NULL | 200 <> NULL | 200 < NULL | 200 > NULL |
+------------+-------------+------------+------------+
|       NULL |        NULL |       NULL |       NULL |
+------------+-------------+------------+------------+
```

You need to use the `IS NULL` (or `IS NOT NULL`) comparison instead:

```
mysql> SELECT NULL IS NULL;
+--------------+
| NULL IS NULL |
+--------------+
|            1 |
+--------------+
```

```
mysql> SELECT 4.5 BETWEEN 4 and 5;
+---------------------+
| 4.5 BETWEEN 4 and 5 |
+---------------------+
|                   1 |
+---------------------+
```

The next example demonstrates a common mistake when using `BETWEEN`.

```
mysql> SELECT 5 BETWEEN 6 and 4;
+-------------------+
| 5 BETWEEN 6 and 4 |
+-------------------+
|                 0 |
+-------------------+
```

**WARNING** *MySQL does not sort the two values after a `BETWEEN`, so if you get the order wrong, the results for all rows will be false. Make sure that the first number is the lower number.*

Because *a* appears earlier in the alphabet than *b*, the result of the following is true. String comparisons are performed from left to right, one character at a time:

```
mysql> SELECT 'abc' < 'b';
```

```
+------------+
| 'abc' < 'b' |
+------------+
|          1 |
+------------+
```

In the following example, *b* is less than or equal to *b*; however, the next *b* is not less than or equal to nothing (the second character on the right string):

```
mysql> SELECT 'bbc' <= 'b';
+--------------+
| 'bbc' <= 'b' |
+--------------+
|            0 |
+--------------+
```

The `IN()` function can be used to test one value against a number of possible values. The field can match any of the comma-separated values listed inside the parentheses, as demonstrated in the next example:

```
mysql> SELECT 'a' IN ('b','c','a');
+----------------------+
| 'a' in ('b','c','a') |
+----------------------+
|                    1 |
+----------------------+
```

### USING *LIKE* WITH SQL PATTERN MATCHES

Often used together with the comparison operators are the wildcard characters, listed in Table 3.4. These allow you to compare against a character (or number of characters) you're not sure about instead of specific ones you know.

**TABLE 3.4:** WILDCARD CHARACTERS

| CHARACTER | DESCRIPTION |
| --- | --- |
| % | Any number of characters |
| _ | One character |

The following example demonstrates the usage of the % wildcard:

```
mysql> SELECT 'abcd' LIKE '%bc%';
+--------------------+
| 'abcd' LIKE '%bc%' |
+--------------------+
|                  1 |
+--------------------+
```

The % wildcard returns any number of characters, so the following would also match:

```
mysql> SELECT 'abcd' LIKE '%b%';
+-------------------+
| 'abcd' LIKE '%b%' |
+-------------------+
|                 1 |
+-------------------+
mysql> SELECT 'abcd' LIKE 'a_ _ _';
+---------------------+
| 'abcd' LIKE 'a_ _ _' |
+---------------------+
|                   1 |
+---------------------+
```

An underscore (_) matches only one character exactly, so if you'd only had two underscores, instead of the three as shown, it would not have matched. For example:

```
mysql> SELECT 'abcd' LIKE 'a_ _';
+-------------------+
| 'abcd' LIKE 'a_ _' |
+-------------------+
|                 0 |
+-------------------+
```

### REGULAR EXPRESSIONS

Regular expressions allow you to perform complex comparisons in MySQL. Hearing the term *regular expressions*, for many people, is like mentioning the plague to a medieval doctor. Immediately the face frowns, the excuses are prepared, and all hope is lost. And it can be complicated—entire books have been written on the topic. But using them in MySQL is not difficult, and they add a useful flexibility to comparisons in MySQL. Table 3.5 describes the regular expression operators available in MySQL.

**TABLE 3.5:** REGULAR EXPRESSIONS (REGEXP, RLIKE)

| CHARACTER | DESCRIPTION |
| --- | --- |
| * | Matches zero or more instances of the string preceding it |
| + | Matches one or more instances of the string preceding it |
| ? | Matches zero or one instances of the string preceding it |
| . | Matches any single character |
| [xyz] | Matches any of x, y, or z (the characters within the brackets) |
| [A-Z] | Matches any uppercase letter |

*Continued on next page*

**TABLE 3.5:** REGULAR EXPRESSIONS (REGEXP, RLIKE) *(continued)*

| CHARACTER | DESCRIPTION |
|---|---|
| [a-z] | Matches any lowercase letter |
| [0-9] | Matches any digit |
| ^ | Anchors the match from the beginning |
| $ | Anchors the match to the end |
| \| | Separates strings in the regular expression |
| {n,m} | String must occur at least n times, but no more than n |
| {n} | String must occur exactly n times |
| {n,\| | String must occur at least n times |

Regular expression matches (REGEXP) can produce similar results to SQL matches (LIKE), but there are some important differences, too. A regular expression, unless you specify otherwise, matches anywhere in the string. It is unnecessary to use wildcard characters on either side, as with LIKE. Note the difference between these two results:

```
mysql> SELECT 'abcdef' REGEXP 'abc';
+-----------------------+
| 'abcdef' REGEXP 'abc' |
+-----------------------+
|                     1 |
+-----------------------+

mysql> SELECT 'abcdef' LIKE 'abc';
+---------------------+
| 'abcdef' LIKE 'abc' |
+---------------------+
|                   0 |
+---------------------+
```

To get the equivalent with LIKE, you'd have had to use % wildcards at the end:

```
mysql> SELECT 'abcdef' LIKE 'abc%';
+----------------------+
| 'abcdef' LIKE 'abc%' |
+----------------------+
|                    1 |
+----------------------+
```

The following matches where *a* is the first character:

```
mysql> SELECT 'abc' REGEXP '^a';
```

```
+------------------+
| 'abc' REGEXP '^a' |
+------------------+
|                1 |
+------------------+
```

However, the following does not match, as the plus sign (+) indicates that *g* had to appear one or more times:

```
mysql> SELECT 'abcdef' REGEXP 'g+';
+---------------------+
| 'abcdef' REGEXP 'g+' |
+---------------------+
|                   0 |
+---------------------+
```

The next query does match because the asterisk (*) indicates zero or more. Effectively, this would match anything:

```
mysql> SELECT 'abcdef' REGEXP 'g*';
+---------------------+
| 'abcdef' REGEXP 'g*' |
+---------------------+
|                   1 |
+---------------------+
```

We could also try use the asterisk to try matching against the name *ian* or the alternative spelling, *iain*. Anything other letter after *a* should cause the match to fail. For example:

```
mysql> SELECT 'ian' REGEXP 'iai*n';
+---------------------+
| 'ian' REGEXP 'iai*n' |
+---------------------+
|                   1 |
+---------------------+
```

But the problem is that this also matches 'iaiiiin', as the asterisk matches any number of characters, as follows:

```
mysql> SELECT 'iaiiiiin' REGEXP 'iai*n';
+-------------------------+
| 'iaiiiiin' REGEXP 'iai*n' |
+-------------------------+
|                       1 |
+-------------------------+
```

To correct this, you'd have to limit the match on the 'i' to either zero or one. Changing the asterisk to a question mark character achieves this. It still matches 'ian' and 'iain,' but not 'iaiiin,' as follows:

```
mysql> SELECT 'iaiiiiin' REGEXP 'iai?n';
```

```
+-------------------------+
| 'iaiiiiin' REGEXP 'iai?n' |
+-------------------------+
|                       0 |
+-------------------------+
```

The following matches because {3,} means the *a* must occur at least three times:

```
mysql> SELECT 'aaaa' REGEXP 'a{3,}';
+---------------------+
| 'aaaa' REGEXP 'a{3,}' |
+---------------------+
|                   1 |
+---------------------+
```

At first glance, you may think the following should not match because the *a* matches four times, but {3} means it should match exactly three times. It does, however, match three times, as well as twice, once, and four times:

```
mysql> SELECT 'aaaa' REGEXP 'a{3}';
+--------------------+
| 'aaaa' REGEXP 'a{3}' |
+--------------------+
|                  1 |
+--------------------+
```

If you'd wanted only *aaa* to match, you'd need to do the following:

```
mysql> SELECT 'aaaa' REGEXP '^aaa$';
+---------------------+
| 'aaaa' REGEXP '^aaa$' |
+---------------------+
|                   0 |
+---------------------+
```

The caret (^) anchors the start, and the dollar sign ($) the end; omitting either would cause the match to succeed.

The following match fails because the {3} only refers to the *c*, not the entire *abc*:

```
mysql> SELECT 'abcabcabc' REGEXP 'abc{3}';
+---------------------------+
| 'abcabcabc' REGEXP 'abc{3}' |
+---------------------------+
|                         0 |
+---------------------------+
```

So, the following does match:

```
mysql> SELECT 'abccc' REGEXP 'abc{3}';
```

```
+------------------------+
| 'abccc' REGEXP 'abc{3}' |
+------------------------+
|                      1 |
+------------------------+
```

To match *abcabcabc*, you need to use parentheses, as follows:

```
mysql> SELECT 'abcabcabc' REGEXP '(abc){3}';
+------------------------------+
| 'abcabcabc' REGEXP '(abc){3}' |
+------------------------------+
|                            1 |
+------------------------------+
```

Note the difference between curly braces and square brackets in the next example. The curly braces group *abc* as a whole, and the square brackets would have allowed any of *a*, or *b*, or *c* to match, allowing a whole range of other possibilities, such as the following:

```
mysql> SELECT 'abcbbcccc' REGEXP '[abc]{3}';
+------------------------------+
| 'abcbbcccc' REGEXP '[abc]{3}' |
+------------------------------+
|                            1 |
+------------------------------+
```

The following uses parentheses to achieve the same effect, with the vertical bar character ( | ) being used to group alternate substrings:

```
mysql> SELECT 'abcbbcccc' REGEXP '(a|b|c){3}';
+--------------------------------+
| 'abcbbcccc' REGEXP '(a|b|c){3}' |
+--------------------------------+
|                              1 |
+--------------------------------+
```

## Bit Operators

To understand how bit operations work, you'll need to know a little bit about Boolean numbers and Boolean arithmetic. These kinds of queries aren't often used, but any self-respecting "guru2be" needs to have them as part of their repertoire. Table 3.6 describes the bit operators.

**TABLE 3.6:** BIT OPERATORS

| OPERATOR | SYNTAX | DESCRIPTION |
| --- | --- | --- |
| & | a & b | Bitwise AND |
| | | a | b | Bitwise OR |

*Continued on next page*

**TABLE 3.6:** BIT OPERATORS *(continued)*

| OPERATOR | SYNTAX | DESCRIPTION |
| --- | --- | --- |
| << | a << b | Left shift of a by b bit positions |
| >> | a >> b | Right shift of a by b bit positions |

The ordinary number system, called the *decimal number system*, works off a base 10. You have 10 fingers, after all, so it makes sense. You count from zero to nine, and then when you hit 10, you move to the "tens" column, and start at zero again:

00 01 02 03 04 05 06 07 08 09 10

The decimal number system has 10 digits, from zero to nine. But people working with computers have often found it useful to work with a number system based on two digits, zero and one. These represent the two states of an electrical connection, on and off:

00 01 10 11

Instead of moving to the "tens" column when you run out of digits (in decimal, after 9 comes 10), you move into the "twos" column (in binary, after 1 comes 10, which is pronounced "one-zero" to avoid confusion with the decimal number).

In decimal, the columns increase in size by powers of 10, as shown in Figure 3.2.

**FIGURE 3.2**

Powers of 10

| $10^6$ | $10^5$ | $10^4$ | $10^3$ | $10^2$ | $10^1$ | $10^0$ |
| --- | --- | --- | --- | --- | --- | --- |
| Millions | Hundred thousands | Ten thousands | Thousands | Hundreds | Tens | Ones |
| 4 | 3 | 9 | 2 | 4 | 2 | 1 |

So the number in this figure, which reads as four million, three hundred ninety-two thousand, four hundred and twenty-one could also be displayed as:

4 * 100 000 000 +

3 * 100 000 +

9 * 10 000 +

2 * 1000 +

4 * 100 +

2 * 10 +

1 * 1

If you can follow all that (imagining that you are a child learning to count in decimal helps), you'll see how to apply the same concepts to binary numbers.

In binary, columns increase in size by powers of 2, as shown in Figure 3.3.

**FIGURE 3.3**

Powers of 2

| $2^6$ | $2^5$ | $2^4$ | $2^3$ | $2^2$ | $2^1$ | $2^0$ |
|---|---|---|---|---|---|---|
| 64s | 32s | 16s | 8s | 4s | 2s | 1s |
| 1 | 1 | 1 | 1 | 1 | 1 | 1 |

The previous binary number—1111111—when converted to decimal, reads as the following:

1 * 64 +

1 * 32 +

1 * 16 +

1 * 8 +

1 * 4 +

1 * 2 +

1 * 1

which is equivalent to $64 + 32 + 16 + 8 + 4 + 2 + 1$, which in turn is 127.

Similarly, the binary number 101001 would be $1 * 1 + 1 * 8 + 1 * 32 = 41$.

So, converting binary numbers to decimal is easy enough, but how about the reverse, converting decimal numbers to binary? It's equally simple. To convert the number 18 to binary, start with Figure 3.4.

**FIGURE 3.4**

Step 1, Drawing up the columns

| $2^6$ | $2^5$ | $2^4$ | $2^3$ | $2^2$ | $2^1$ | $2^0$ |
|---|---|---|---|---|---|---|
| 64s | 32s | 16s | 8s | 4s | 2s | 1s |

Starting on the left, there are clearly no 64s in 18, and no 32s. There is, however, one 16 in 18. So you write a 1 in the 16 column, as shown in Figure 3.5.

**FIGURE 3.5**

Step 2, Filling in the values

| $2^6$ | $2^5$ | $2^4$ | $2^3$ | $2^2$ | $2^1$ | $2^0$ |
|---|---|---|---|---|---|---|
| 64s | 32s | 16s | 8s | 4s | 2s | 1s |
| 0 | 0 | 1 |  |  |  |  |

You've accounted for 16 of your 18, so you now subtract 16 from 18, leaving you with 2. Continuing to the right, there are no 8s, no 4s, and one 2, in 2. And since 2 minus 2 is 0, you stop once you've written the 1 in the two column, as shown in Figure 3.6.

**FIGURE 3.6**

Step 3, Converting decimal to binary

| $2^6$ | $2^5$ | $2^4$ | $2^3$ | $2^2$ | $2^1$ | $2^0$ |
|---|---|---|---|---|---|---|
| 64s | 32s | 16s | 8s | 4s | 2s | 1s |
| 0 | 0 | 1 | 0 | 0 | 1 | 0 |

In binary, 18 is then 10010. With larger numbers, you just use more columns to the left (representing 128s, 256s, and so on). Binary numbers can get very long very quickly, which is why you don't usually store numbers that way. Octal (base 8) and hexadecimal (base 16) are two other number systems that are more convenient.

Let's get back to the bit operators; take two numbers, 9 and 7. In binary they are 1001 and 111, respectively. The bit operators work on the individual bits of the binary number that make up the numbers 8 and 7.

For a bitwise AND operation, both bits need to be 1 for the result to be 1 (just like an ordinary AND). Figure 3.7 shows the two binary numbers.

**FIGURE 3.7**

Bitwise AND operation: 9&7

| 1 | 0 | 0 | 1 |
|---|---|---|---|
| 0 | 1 | 1 | 1 |
| **0** | **0** | **0** | **1** |

Starting on the left, 1 AND 0 is 0, so the leftmost column (the eights) is 0. Moving right, 0 AND 1 is 0, and again, 0 AND 1 is 0. Only in the rightmost column do you see 1 AND 1, which is 1.

So, the result of a bitwise AND between 7 and 9 is 1! For example:

```
mysql> SELECT 9&7;
+-----+
| 9&7 |
+-----+
|   1 |
+-----+
```

**NOTE** *A bitwise AND is the same no matter which way around you do it—in other words, 9&7 is the same as 7&9.*

For a bitwise OR, either digit should be 1 for the result to be 1. So, Figure 3.8 shows a bitwise OR performed on the same 9 and 7.

**FIGURE 3.8**

Bitwise OR operation: 9|7

| 1 | 0 | 0 | 1 |
|---|---|---|---|
| 0 | 1 | 1 | 1 |
| **1** | **1** | **1** | **1** |

All columns have at least one 1 present, so the result for each is a 1 overall. And 1111 is equivalent to 15 in binary:

```
mysql> SELECT 9|7;
+-----+
| 9|7 |
+-----+
|  15 |
+-----+
```

The << is the left shift operator, so << b means that the bits of a are shifted left by b columns. For example: 2 << 1. In binary, 2 is 10. If this is shifted left 1 bit, you get 100, which is 4. For example:

```
mysql> SELECT 2 << 1;
+--------+
| 2 << 1 |
+--------+
|      4 |
+--------+
```

```
mysql> SELECT 15 << 4;
+---------+
| 15 << 4 |
+---------+
|     240 |
+---------+
```

Now you have 15, which is 1111; when shifted 4 bits left, you get 11110000. Convert this to decimal in the usual way, as in Figure 3.9.

**FIGURE 3.9**

Converting the binary number 11110000 to decimal

| $2^7$ | $2^6$ | $2^5$ | $2^4$ | $2^3$ | $2^2$ | $2^1$ | $2^0$ |
|------|------|------|------|------|------|------|------|
| 128s | 64s | 32s | 16s | 8s | 4s | 2s | 1s |
| 1 | 1 | 1 | 1 | 0 | 0 | 0 | 0 |

Now total this:

$128 + 64 + 32 + 16 = 240$

Bitwise operations are performed as BIGINTs, meaning there's a limit of 64 bits. Shifting beyond 64 bits, or with a negative number, just returns 0. For example:

```
mysql> SELECT 3 << 64;
+---------+
| 3 << 64 |
+---------+
|       0 |
+---------+
```

The >> is the right shift operator, so a >> b shifts the bits of a right by b columns. Bits shifted beyond the "ones" column are lost. And, again, shifting by a negative number returns 0. For example:

```
mysql> SELECT 3 >> 1;
+--------+
| 3 >> 1 |
+--------+
|      1 |
+--------+
```

In binary, 3 is 11, shifted right by 1 with 1 floating past the ones column (or 1.1 if you'd like, although there is no decimal point in binary notation). Because you're dealing with integers, the numbers to the right of the "decimal point" are dropped (perhaps we should call it the *binary point*, but there's probably a Hollywood movie coming out by that name), and you're left with 1 (in both binary and decimal). For example:

```
mysql> SELECT 19 >> 3;
+---------+
| 19 >> 3 |
+---------+
|       2 |
+---------+
```

In the example above, 19 is 10011, shifted right by 3 is 10, with 011 dropping away. 10 is 2 in decimal.

```
mysql> SELECT 4 >> 3;
+--------+
| 4 >> 3 |
+--------+
|      0 |
+--------+
```

This one shifts too far to the right, losing all the bits.

## Advanced Joins

You've already looked at a basic two-table join in Chapter 1. But joins can get much more complicated than that, and badly written joins are the culprits in the majority of serious performance problems.

Let's return to the tables created in the previous chapter. If you skipped that chapter, you can re-create them by running the following statements:

```
CREATE TABLE customer (
  id int(11) default NULL,
  first_name varchar(30) default NULL,
  surname varchar(40) default NULL
) TYPE=MyISAM;

INSERT INTO customer VALUES (1, 'Yvonne', 'Clegg');
INSERT INTO customer VALUES (2, 'Johnny', 'Chaka-Chaka');
INSERT INTO customer VALUES (3, 'Winston', 'Powers');
INSERT INTO customer VALUES (4, 'Patricia', 'Mankunku');

CREATE TABLE sales (
  code int(11) default NULL,
  sales_rep int(11) default NULL,
```

```
    customer int(11) default NULL,
    value int(11) default NULL
) TYPE=MyISAM;

INSERT INTO sales VALUES (1, 1, 1, 2000);
INSERT INTO sales VALUES (2, 4, 3, 250);
INSERT INTO sales VALUES (3, 2, 3, 500);
INSERT INTO sales VALUES (4, 1, 4, 450);
INSERT INTO sales VALUES (5, 3, 1, 3800);
INSERT INTO sales VALUES (6, 1, 2, 500);

CREATE TABLE sales_rep (
    employee_number int(11) default NULL,
    surname varchar(40) default NULL,
    first_name varchar(30) default NULL,
    commission tinyint(4) default NULL,
    date_joined date default NULL,
    birthday date default NULL
) TYPE=MyISAM;

INSERT INTO sales_rep VALUES (1, 'Rive', 'Sol', 10,
 '2000-02-15', '1976-03-18');
INSERT INTO sales_rep VALUES (2, 'Gordimer', 'Charlene', 15,
 '1998-07-09', '1958-11-30');
INSERT INTO sales_rep VALUES (3, 'Serote', 'Mike', 10,
 '2001-05-14', '1971-06-18');
INSERT INTO sales_rep VALUES (4, 'Rive', 'Mongane', 10,
 '2002-11-23', '1982-01-04');
```

Let's start with a basic join:

```
mysql> SELECT sales_rep, customer,value, first_name,surname
 FROM sales, sales_rep WHERE code=1 AND
 sales_rep.employee_number=sales.sales_rep;
+-----------+----------+-------+------------+---------+
| sales_rep | customer | value | first_name | surname |
+-----------+----------+-------+------------+---------+
|         1 |        1 |  2000 | Sol        | Rive    |
+-----------+----------+-------+------------+---------+
```

Because the relationship between the *sales_rep* and *sales* tables is on the *employee_number*, or *sales_rep* field, those two fields form the join condition of the WHERE clause.

To do a more complex join over all three tables is not much more complicated. If you wanted to return the first names and surnames of both the sales rep and the customer, as well as the value of the sale, you'd use this query:

```
mysql> SELECT sales_rep.first_name,sales_rep.surname,
 value,customer.first_name, customer.surname FROM
```

```
sales,sales_rep,customer WHERE sales_rep.employee_number =
sales.sales_rep AND customer.id = sales.customer;
+------------+----------+-------+------------+-------------+
| first_name | surname  | value | first_name | surname     |
+------------+----------+-------+------------+-------------+
| Sol        | Rive     |  2000 | Yvonne     | Clegg       |
| Mike       | Serote   |  3800 | Yvonne     | Clegg       |
| Sol        | Rive     |   500 | Johnny     | Chaka-Chaka |
| Charlene   | Gordimer |   500 | Winston    | Powers      |
| Mongane    | Rive     |   250 | Winston    | Powers      |
| Sol        | Rive     |   450 | Patricia   | Mankunku    |
+------------+----------+-------+------------+-------------+
```

The *employee_number* field of the *sales_rep* table is related to the *sales_rep* field of the *sales* table. And the *id* field in the *customer* table is related to the *customer* field of the *sales* table. Hence, these make up the two join conditions of the WHERE clause. There are no other conditions, so this query lists all the sales for which there are corresponding rows in both the *sales_rep* and *customer* tables.

## Inner Joins

Inner joins are just another way of describing the first kind of join you learned. The following two queries are identical:

```
mysql> SELECT first_name,surname,value FROM customer,sales WHERE
    id=customer;
+------------+-------------+-------+
| first_name | surname     | value |
+------------+-------------+-------+
| Yvonne     | Clegg       |  2000 |
| Winston    | Powers      |   250 |
| Winston    | Powers      |   500 |
| Patricia   | Mankunku    |   450 |
| Yvonne     | Clegg       |  3800 |
| Johnny     | Chaka-Chaka |   500 |
+------------+-------------+-------+
6 rows in set (0.00 sec)

mysql> SELECT first_name,surname,value FROM customer INNER JOIN sales
    ON id=customer;
+------------+-------------+-------+
| first_name | surname     | value |
+------------+-------------+-------+
| Yvonne     | Clegg       |  2000 |
| Winston    | Powers      |   250 |
| Winston    | Powers      |   500 |
| Patricia   | Mankunku    |   450 |
| Yvonne     | Clegg       |  3800 |
| Johnny     | Chaka-Chaka |   500 |
+------------+-------------+-------+
```

## Left Joins (Left Outer Joins)

Let's say you make another sale. Except this time it's a cash sale, and the customer has left with the goods before you realize you forgot to capture their details. There's no problem because you can still add the data to the *sales* table using a NULL value for the customer:

```
mysql> INSERT INTO sales(code,sales_rep,customer,value) VALUES
  (7, 2,NULL,670);
```

Let's run the query that returns the value and the names of the sales reps and customers for each sale again:

```
mysql> SELECT sales_rep.first_name, sales_rep.surname, value,
  customer.first_name, customer.surname FROM sales,sales_rep,
  customer WHERE sales_rep.employee_number = sales.sales_rep
  AND customer.id = sales.customer;
```

| first_name | surname  | value | first_name | surname      |
|------------|----------|-------|------------|--------------|
| Sol        | Rive     | 2000  | Yvonne     | Clegg        |
| Mike       | Serote   | 3800  | Yvonne     | Clegg        |
| Sol        | Rive     | 500   | Johnny     | Chaka-Chaka  |
| Charlene   | Gordimer | 500   | Winston    | Powers       |
| Mongane    | Rive     | 250   | Winston    | Powers       |
| Sol        | Rive     | 450   | Patricia   | Mankunku     |

What's going on? Where is the new sale? The problem here is that, because the *customer* is NULL in the *sales* table, the join condition is not fulfilled. Remember, when you looked at the operators earlier in this chapter, you saw that the = operator excludes NULL values. The <=> operator won't help because there are no NULL records in the *customer* table, so even a null-friendly equality check won't help.

The solution here is to do an OUTER JOIN. These return a result for each matching result of the one table, whether or not there is an associated record in the other table. So even though the *customer* field is NULL in the *sales* table and has no relation with the *customer* table, a record will be returned. A LEFT OUTER JOIN is one which returns all matching rows from the left table, regardless of whether there is a corresponding row in the right table. The syntax for a LEFT JOIN (a shorter name for a LEFT OUTER JOIN) is as follows:

```
SELECT field1, field2 FROM table1 LEFT JOIN table2 ON field1=field2
```

Let's first try a simple example first, performing a LEFT JOIN on just the *customer* and *sales* tables.

```
mysql> SELECT first_name,surname,value FROM sales LEFT JOIN customer
  ON id=customer;
```

```
+------------+-------------+-------+
| first_name | surname     | value |
+------------+-------------+-------+
| Yvonne     | Clegg       |  2000 |
| Winston    | Powers      |   250 |
| Winston    | Powers      |   500 |
| Patricia   | Mankunku    |   450 |
| Yvonne     | Clegg       |  3800 |
| Johnny     | Chaka-Chaka |   500 |
| NULL       | NULL        |   670 |
+------------+-------------+-------+
```

All seven records are returned, as expected.

Table order in a LEFT JOIN is important. The table from which all matching rows are returned must be the left table (before the LEFT JOIN keywords). If you'd reversed the order and tried the following:

```
mysql> SELECT first_name,surname,value FROM customer LEFT JOIN sales
  ON id=customer;
+------------+-------------+-------+
| first_name | surname     | value |
+------------+-------------+-------+
| Yvonne     | Clegg       |  2000 |
| Yvonne     | Clegg       |  3800 |
| Johnny     | Chaka-Chaka |   500 |
| Winston    | Powers      |   250 |
| Winston    | Powers      |   500 |
| Patricia   | Mankunku    |   450 |
+------------+-------------+-------+
```

then you'd have seen only the six records. Because the left table is the *customer table in this query,* and the join matches only those records that exist in the left table, the *sales* record with the NULL customer (meaning there is no relation to the *customer* table) is not returned.

**NOTE**    *A LEFT JOIN was more frequently called a* LEFT OUTER JOIN *in the past. For the sake of familiarity, MySQL accepts this term, too.*

Of course, you can extend this across a third table to answer the original query (names of customers and sales reps, as well as sales values, for each sale). See if you can do it. This is my suggestion:

```
mysql> SELECT sales_rep.first_name, sales_rep.surname, value,
  customer.first_name, customer.surname FROM sales LEFT JOIN
  sales_rep ON sales_rep.employee_number = sales.sales_rep
  LEFT JOIN customer ON customer.id = sales.customer;
```

```
+------------+-----------+-------+------------+-------------+
| first_name | surname   | value | first_name | surname     |
+------------+-----------+-------+------------+-------------+
| Sol        | Rive      | 2000  | Yvonne     | Clegg       |
| Mongane    | Rive      | 250   | Winston    | Powers      |
| Charlene   | Gordimer  | 500   | Winston    | Powers      |
| Sol        | Rive      | 450   | Patricia   | Mankunku    |
| Mike       | Serote    | 3800  | Yvonne     | Clegg       |
| Sol        | Rive      | 500   | Johnny     | Chaka-Chaka |
| Charlene   | Gordimer  | 670   | NULL       | NULL        |
+------------+-----------+-------+------------+-------------+
```

## Right Joins (Right Outer Joins)

*Right joins* are exactly the same as left joins, except that the order of the join is reversed. To return for each sale the names of all customers, including those sales where there is no corresponding customer data, you have to put the *sales* table on the right in your join:

```
mysql> SELECT first_name,surname,value FROM customer RIGHT JOIN
  sales ON id=customer;
+------------+-------------+-------+
| first_name | surname     | value |
+------------+-------------+-------+
| Yvonne     | Clegg       | 2000  |
| Winston    | Powers      | 250   |
| Winston    | Powers      | 500   |
| Patricia   | Mankunku    | 450   |
| Yvonne     | Clegg       | 3800  |
| Johnny     | Chaka-Chaka | 500   |
| NULL       | NULL        | 670   |
+------------+-------------+-------+
```

*TIP  If you get confused by which table to put on which side for left and right joins, remember that a right join reads all records from the right table, including nulls, while a left join reads all records from the left table, including nulls.*

## Full Outer Joins

At the time of writing this, MySQL does not yet support *full outer joins*. These are joins where each record from the first table, including those with no match in the second table, is returned along with each record in the second table, including those with no match in the first. This is the equivalent of a left and a right join. MySQL will support this in the near future, so check the latest documentation. The syntax is the same as for the other joins:

```
SELECT field1,field2 FROM table1 FULL OUTER JOIN table2
```

## Natural Joins and the *USING* Keyword

The *id* field in the *customer* table and the *customer* field in the *sales* table are related. If you have given them the same name, SQL has a few shortcuts that make the JOIN statements less unwieldy. Let's rename *sales.customer* to *sales.id* for now, to demonstrate:

```
mysql> ALTER TABLE sales CHANGE customer id INT;
```

Now because the two tables have fields with identical names, you can perform a NATURAL JOIN, which looks for identically named fields on which to perform the JOIN:

```
mysql> SELECT first_name,surname,value FROM customer NATURAL JOIN
  sales;
+------------+-------------+-------+
| first_name | surname     | value |
+------------+-------------+-------+
| Yvonne     | Clegg       |  2000 |
| Winston    | Powers      |   250 |
| Winston    | Powers      |   500 |
| Patricia   | Mankunku    |   450 |
| Yvonne     | Clegg       |  3800 |
| Johnny     | Chaka-Chaka |   500 |
+------------+-------------+-------+
```

This is identical to the following:

```
mysql> SELECT first_name,surname,value FROM customer INNER JOIN
  sales ON customer.id=sales.id;
+------------+-------------+-------+
| first_name | surname     | value |
+------------+-------------+-------+
| Yvonne     | Clegg       |  2000 |
| Winston    | Powers      |   250 |
| Winston    | Powers      |   500 |
| Patricia   | Mankunku    |   450 |
| Yvonne     | Clegg       |  3800 |
| Johnny     | Chaka-Chaka |   500 |
+------------+-------------+-------+
```

There is only one field that is identical in both tables, but if there were more, each of these would become part of the join condition.

A NATURAL JOIN can also be a LEFT or RIGHT JOIN. The following two statements are identical:

```
mysql> SELECT first_name,surname,value FROM customer LEFT JOIN sales
  ON customer.id=sales.id;
```

```
+------------+-------------+-------+
| first_name | surname     | value |
+------------+-------------+-------+
| Yvonne     | Clegg       |  2000 |
| Yvonne     | Clegg       |  3800 |
| Johnny     | Chaka-Chaka |   500 |
| Winston    | Powers      |   250 |
| Winston    | Powers      |   500 |
| Patricia   | Mankunku    |   450 |
+------------+-------------+-------+
```

```
mysql> SELECT first_name,surname,value FROM customer NATURAL LEFT JOIN sales;
+------------+-------------+-------+
| first_name | surname     | value |
+------------+-------------+-------+
| Yvonne     | Clegg       |  2000 |
| Yvonne     | Clegg       |  3800 |
| Johnny     | Chaka-Chaka |   500 |
| Winston    | Powers      |   250 |
| Winston    | Powers      |   500 |
| Patricia   | Mankunku    |   450 |
+------------+-------------+-------+
```

The USING keyword allows a bit more control than a NATURAL JOIN. If there is more than one identical field in the two tables, this keyword allows you to specify which of these fields are used as join conditions. For example, taking two tables A and B with identical fields a,b,c,d, the following are equivalent:

```
SELECT * FROM A LEFT JOIN B USING (a,b,c,d)
SELECT * FROM A NATURAL LEFT JOIN B
```

The USING keyword allows more flexibility because it allows you to use only some of the four identical fields. For example:

```
SELECT * FROM A LEFT JOIN B USING (a,d)
```

*NOTE    For purposes of a NATURAL JOIN, identical means identical in name, not in type. The two id fields could be INT and DECIMAL, or even INT and VARCHAR, as long as they have the same name.*

## Returning Results Found in One Table, but Not the Other

So far you've returned rows that appear in both tables you're joining with an INNER JOIN. With the OUTER JOIN, you also returned records from one table where wasn't a corresponding match in the other table. Quite often it's useful to do the converse and return results that are found *only* in one table, but not the other. To demonstrate this, let's first add a new sales_rep:

```
mysql> INSERT INTO sales_rep VALUES(5, 'Jomo', 'Ignesund', 10,
  '2002-11-29', '1968-12-01');
```

Now, if you do an INNER JOIN, you can return all the sales reps who have made a sale:

```
mysql> SELECT DISTINCT first_name,surname FROM sales_rep
 INNER JOIN sales ON sales_rep=employee_number;
+------------+----------+
| first_name | surname  |
+------------+----------+
| Sol        | Rive     |
| Mongane    | Rive     |
| Charlene   | Gordimer |
| Mike       | Serote   |
+------------+----------+
```

You use the DISTINCT keyword to avoid duplicates because there are sales reps who have made more than one sale.

But the reverse is as useful. The boss is raging and heads must roll. Which sales reps have not made any sales? You can find this information by seeing which sales reps appear in the *sales_rep* table but do not have a corresponding entry in the *sales* table:

```
mysql> SELECT first_name,surname FROM sales_rep LEFT JOIN sales
 ON sales_rep=employee_number WHERE sales_rep IS NULL;
+------------+----------+
| first_name | surname  |
+------------+----------+
| Ignesund   | Jomo     |
+------------+----------+
```

You had to do a LEFT JOIN (an OUTER JOIN, as opposed to an INNER JOIN) because only an OUTER JOIN returns any records that don't correspond (or null values) in the first place.

## Joining Results with *UNION*

MySQL 4 introduced the long-awaited ANSI SQL UNION statement, which combines the results of different SELECT statements into one. Each statement must have the same number of columns.

To see the use of this statement, let's create another table, containing a list of customers handed over from the previous owner of your store:

```
mysql> CREATE TABLE old_customer(id int, first_name varchar(30),
 surname varchar(40));
mysql> INSERT INTO old_customer VALUES (5432, 'Thulani', 'Salie'),
 (2342, 'Shahiem', 'Papo');
```

Now, to get a list of all customers, both old and new, you can use the following:

```
mysql> SELECT id, first_name, surname FROM old_customer UNION SELECT
 id, first_name,surname FROM customer;
```

```
+------+------------+-------------+
| id   | first_name | surname     |
+------+------------+-------------+
| 5432 | Thulani    | Salie       |
| 2342 | Shahiem    | Papo        |
|    1 | Yvonne     | Clegg       |
|    2 | Johnny     | Chaka-Chaka |
|    3 | Winston    | Powers      |
|    4 | Patricia   | Mankunku    |
+------+------------+-------------+
```

You can also order the output as normal. You just need to be careful about whether the ORDER BY clause applies to the entire UNION or just to the one SELECT:

```
mysql> SELECT id, first_name, surname FROM old_customer UNION SELECT
    id, first_name, surname FROM customer ORDER BY surname,first_name;
+------+------------+-------------+
| id   | first_name | surname     |
+------+------------+-------------+
|    2 | Johnny     | Chaka-Chaka |
|    1 | Yvonne     | Clegg       |
|    4 | Patricia   | Mankunku    |
| 2342 | Shahiem    | Papo        |
|    3 | Winston    | Powers      |
| 5432 | Thulani    | Salie       |
+------+------------+-------------+
```

The sorting is performed on the entire UNION. If you just want to sort the second SELECT, you'd need to use parentheses:

```
mysql> SELECT id, first_name, surname FROM old_customer UNION
    (SELECT id, first_name, surname FROM customer ORDER BY surname,
    first_name);
+------+------------+-------------+
| id   | first_name | surname     |
+------+------------+-------------+
| 5432 | Thulani    | Salie       |
| 2342 | Shahiem    | Papo        |
|    2 | Johnny     | Chaka-Chaka |
|    1 | Yvonne     | Clegg       |
|    4 | Patricia   | Mankunku    |
|    3 | Winston    | Powers      |
+------+------------+-------------+
```

*TIP*   *Whenever there's possible ambiguity, such as where the sorting applies, use parentheses. It ensures the sort is applied to the correct part and also means that anyone else trying to interpret your statements will have an easier time. Don't assume everyone else knows as much as you!*

By default, UNION does not return duplicate results (similar to the DISTINCT keyword). You can override this by specifying that all results must be returned with the ALL keyword:

```
mysql> SELECT id FROM customer UNION ALL SELECT id FROM sales;
+------+
| id   |
+------+
|    1 |
|    2 |
|    3 |
|    4 |
|    1 |
|    3 |
|    3 |
|    4 |
|    1 |
|    2 |
| NULL |
+------+
```

UNION requires some thought. You can quite easily put together unrelated fields as long as the number of fields returned by each SELECT match, and the data types are the same. MySQL will happily return these results to you, even though they are meaningless:

```
mysql> SELECT id, surname FROM customer UNION ALL SELECT value,
    sales_rep FROM sales;
+------+-------------+
| id   | surname     |
+------+-------------+
|    1 | Clegg       |
|    2 | Chaka-Chaka |
|    3 | Powers      |
|    4 | Mankunku    |
| 2000 | 1           |
|  250 | 4           |
|  500 | 2           |
|  450 | 1           |
| 3800 | 3           |
|  500 | 1           |
|  670 | 2           |
+------+-------------+
```

## Sub-selects

Many queries make use of a SELECT within a SELECT. Sub-selects are scheduled for implementation in version 4.1. Until now, MySQL did not allow sub-selects, partly by design (they are often less efficient than alternatives, as you'll see later) and partly because it was low on a list of 1,001 other "vital" things to implement. With MySQL about to implement them, you'll need to see how they work.

## Rewriting Sub-selects as Joins

Let's take a query where you want to return all the sales reps who have made a sale with a value greater than $1,000. If you can run a sub-select, try the following:

```
mysql> SELECT first_name,surname FROM sales_rep WHERE
  sales_rep.employee_number IN (SELECT code FROM sales WHERE
  value>1000);
+------------+---------+
| first_name | surname |
+------------+---------+
| Sol        | Rive    |
+------------+---------+
```

Only Sol Rive has managed this feat.

The query resolves by first resolving the inner SELECT—that is, performing the following step first:

```
mysql> SELECT id FROM sales WHERE value>1000;
+------+
| id   |
+------+
|    1 |
|    1 |
+------+
```

and then the remainder:

```
mysql> SELECT first_name, surname FROM sales_rep WHERE
  sales_rep.employee_number IN (1);
+------------+---------+
| first_name | surname |
+------------+---------+
| Sol        | Rive    |
+------------+---------+
```

But you already know another, better way of doing this, which is the join:

```
mysql> SELECT DISTINCT first_name,surname FROM sales_rep INNER JOIN sales ON
  employee_number=id WHERE value>1000;
+------------+---------+
| first_name | surname |
+------------+---------+
| Sol        | Rive    |
| Sol        | Rive    |
+------------+---------+
```

or, alternatively:

```
mysql> SELECT DISTINCT first_name,surname FROM sales_rep,sales WHERE
  sales.id=sales_rep.employee_number AND value>1000;
+------------+---------+
| first_name | surname |
+------------+---------+
| Sol        | Rive    |
| Sol        | Rive    |
+------------+---------+
```

The reason I say *better* is that often the join is a more efficient way of doing the query and will return the results quicker. It may not make much difference on a tiny database, but in large, heavily used tables where performance is vital, you'll want every extra microsecond you can get out of MySQL.

To return all the sales reps who have not yet made a sale, you could again use a sub-select, if your DBMS allows it, as follows:

```
mysql> SELECT first_name,surname FROM sales_rep WHERE employee_number
  NOT IN (SELECT DISTINCT code from sales);
+------------+---------+
| first_name | surname |
+------------+---------+
| Ignesund   | Jomo    |
+------------+---------+
```

But you know another way, which is better:

```
mysql> SELECT DISTINCT first_name,surname FROM sales_rep LEFT JOIN sales ON
  sales_rep=employee_number WHERE sales_rep IS NULL;
+------------+---------+
| first_name | surname |
+------------+---------+
| Ignesund   | Jomo    |
+------------+---------+
```

## Adding Records to a Table from Other Tables with *INSERT SELECT*

The INSERT statement also allows you to add records, or parts of records, that exist in other tables. For example, let's say you want to create a new table containing the customer names and the values of all the purchases they have made. The query to return the results you want would be the following:

```
mysql> SELECT first_name,surname,SUM(value) FROM sales NATURAL JOIN
  customer GROUP BY first_name, surname;
```

```
+------------+-------------+------------+
| first_name | surname     | SUM(value) |
+------------+-------------+------------+
| Johnny     | Chaka-Chaka |        500 |
| Patricia   | Mankunku    |        450 |
| Winston    | Powers      |        750 |
| Yvonne     | Clegg       |       5800 |
+------------+-------------+------------+
```

First you'll need to create the table to receive the results:

```
mysql> CREATE TABLE customer_sales_values(first_name
  VARCHAR(30), surname VARCHAR(40), value INT);
```

Now, you insert the results into this table:

```
mysql> INSERT INTO customer_sales_values(first_name,surname,value)
  SELECT first_name,surname, SUM(value) FROM sales NATURAL JOIN
  customer GROUP BY first_name, surname;
```

The *customer_sales_values* table now contains the following:

```
mysql> SELECT * FROM customer_sales_values;
+------------+-------------+-------+
| first_name | surname     | value |
+------------+-------------+-------+
| Johnny     | Chaka-Chaka |   500 |
| Patricia   | Mankunku    |   450 |
| Winston    | Powers      |   750 |
| Yvonne     | Clegg       |  5800 |
+------------+-------------+-------+
```

## More about Adding Records

INSERT also allows a syntax similar to the one used by an UPDATE statement. Instead of saying the following:

```
mysql> INSERT INTO customer_sales_values(first_name, surname, value)
  VALUES('Charles', 'Dube', 0);
```

you could say this:

```
mysql> INSERT INTO customer_sales_values SET first_name =
  'Charles', surname='Dube', value=0;
```

You can also do a limited form of calculation when you add records. To demonstrate, add another field onto the *customer_sales_value* table:

```
mysql> ALTER TABLE customer_sales_values ADD value2 INT;
```

Now, you can insert into this table and populate `value2` with twice the *value*:

```
mysql> INSERT INTO customer_sales_values(first_name, surname, value,
  value2) VALUES('Gladys', 'Malherbe', 5, value*2);
```

This record now contains the following:

```
mysql> SELECT * FROM customer_sales_values WHERE first_name='Gladys';
+------------+----------+-------+--------+
| first_name | surname  | value | value2 |
+------------+----------+-------+--------+
| Gladys     | Malherbe |     5 |     10 |
+------------+----------+-------+--------+
```

## More about Removing Records (*DELETE* and *TRUNCATE*)

You already know how to remove a record with the DELETE statement. And you've probably taken note of the warning that if you don't use a WHERE clause, you'll remove all the records. A problem with removing all the records in that way is that it can be very slow in a large table! Luckily, there is a better way.

Let's first remove all the records in the *customer_sales_value* table with a DELETE statement:

```
mysql> DELETE FROM customer_sales_values;
Query OK, 7 rows affected (0.00 sec)
```

The quicker way to remove this is by using TRUNCATE. Let's add the records back, and then use a TRUNCATE statement:

```
mysql> INSERT INTO customer_sales_values(first_name, surname, value,
  value2) VALUES('Johnny', 'Chaka-Chaka', 500, NULL),('Patricia',
  'Mankunku', 450, NULL), ('Winston', 'Powers', 750, NULL),('Yvonne',
  'Clegg', 5800, NULL), ('Charles', 'Dube', 0, NULL), ('Charles',
  'Dube', 0, NULL), ('Gladys', 'Malherbe', 5, 10);

mysql> TRUNCATE customer_sales_values;
Query OK, 0 rows affected (0.00 sec)
```

Notice the difference between the outputs of the two statements. DELETE informs you how many rows have been removed, but TRUNCATE doesn't; TRUNCATE just removes the lot without counting them. It actually does this by dropping and re-creating the table.

## User Variables

MySQL has a feature that allows you to store values as temporary variables, which you can use again in a later statement. In the vast majority of cases you'd use a programming language to do this sort of thing (see Chapter 5, "Programming with MySQL"), but MySQL variables can be useful when working on the MySQL command line.

The value of a variable is set with the SET statement or in a SELECT statement with :=. To see all the sales reps with a commission higher than the average commission, you could do the following:

```
mysql> SELECT @avg := AVG(commission) FROM sales_rep;
+------------------------+
| @avg := AVG(commission) |
+------------------------+
|                11.0000 |
+------------------------+

mysql> SELECT surname,first_name FROM sales_rep WHERE commission>@avg;
+----------+------------+
| surname  | first_name |
+----------+------------+
| Gordimer | Charlene   |
+----------+------------+
```

The at (@) sign signifies a MySQL variable. The average commission is stored in the variable @avg, which can be accessed again at a later stage.

You can also set a variable specifically. For example, instead of repeating a complex calculation each time you require it, set the variable with the value once upfront:

```
mysql> SET @result = 22/7*33.23;

mysql> SELECT @result;
+-----------------+
| @result         |
+-----------------+
| 104.43714285714 |
+-----------------+
```

User variables can be strings, integers, or floating-point numbers. They can be set to an expression (excluding places where certain literal values are required, such as in the LIMIT clause). They cannot yet be used to replace part of the query, such as replacing the name of a table. For example:

```
mysql> SET @t = 'sales';
mysql> SELECT * FROM @t;
ERROR 1064: You have an error in your SQL syntax near '@t' at line 1


mysql> SET @v=2;
mysql> SELECT * FROM sales LIMIT 0,@v;
ERROR 1064: You have an error in your SQL syntax near '@v' at line 1
```

User variables are set in a particular thread (or connection to a server) and cannot be accessed by another thread. They are unset when the thread is closed or the connection lost.

Run the following from the first thread, Window1:

```
mysql> SET @a = 1;

mysql> SELECT @a;
+------+
| @a   |
+------+
|    1 |
+------+
```

You won't be able to access this variable from another thread. Run the following from Window2:

```
mysql> SELECT @a;
+------+
| @a   |
+------+
| NULL |
+------+
```

If you close the connection and reconnect from Window1, MySQL will have cleared the variable, as follows, from Window1:

```
mysql> exit

% mysql firstdb
Welcome to the MySQL monitor.  Commands end with ; or \g.
Your MySQL connection id is 14 to server version: 4.0.1-alpha-max

Type 'help;' or '\h' for help. Type '\c' to clear the buffer.

mysql> SELECT @a;
+------+
| @a   |
+------+
| NULL |
+------+
```

Note that in a SELECT statement, the WHERE clause is calculated first and then the field list. If no records are returned, the user variable will not be set for that statement. For example, because no records are returned from this statement, the user variable will not be set:

```
mysql> SELECT @a:=2 FROM sales WHERE value>10000;
Empty set (0.00 sec)

mysql> SELECT @a;
+------+
| @a   |
+------+
| NULL |
+------+
```

However, if you had returned at least one record, the user variable would have been set correctly:

```
mysql> SELECT @a:=2 FROM sales WHERE value>2000;
+-------+
| @a:=2 |
+-------+
|     2 |
+-------+

mysql> SELECT @a;
+------+
| @a   |
+------+
| 2    |
+------+
```

Similarly, a user variable set in the field list cannot be used as a condition. The following will not work because the user variable has not been set in time for the condition:

```
mysql> SELECT @d:=2000,value FROM sales WHERE value>@d;
Empty set (0.00 sec)
```

You would have had to set the variable specifically before the query, as follows:

```
mysql> SET @d=2000;
Query OK, 0 rows affected (0.00 sec)

mysql> SELECT @d,value FROM sales WHERE value>@d;
+------+-------+
| @d   | value |
+------+-------+
| 2000 | 3800  |
+------+-------+
```

You can also set a variable in the WHERE clause itself. Be aware then that it will not be correctly reflected in the field list unless you reset the variable again! For example:

```
mysql> SELECT @e,value FROM sales WHERE value>(@e:=2000);
+------+-------+
| @e   | value |
+------+-------+
| NULL | 3800  |
+------+-------+
```

To reflect this correctly, you'd have to set the variable again in the field list:

```
mysql> SELECT @f:=2000,value FROM sales WHERE value>(@f:=2000);
+----------+-------+
| @f:=2000 | value |
+----------+-------+
|     2000 | 3800  |
+----------+-------+
```

This is not an elegant way of implementing user variables; instead, set them separately beforehand.

*WARNING*    *Remember that user variables are set for the duration of the thread. You may not get the results you expect if you forget to initialize a user variable.*

## Running SQL Statements Stored in Files

Often groups of SQL statements are stored in a file for reuse. You can run these commands from your operating system's command line easily. Doing this is called running MySQL in *batch mode* (as opposed to interactively when you connect to the server and type in the commands yourself).

Create a text file test.sql containing the following two lines:

```
INSERT INTO customer(id,first_name,surname) VALUES(5,'Francois','Papo');
INSERT INTO customer(id,first_name,surname) VALUES(6,'Neil','Beneke');
```

You can run these two statements from within your operating system's command line as follows:

```
% mysql firstdb < test.sql
```

Remember to add a hostname, username, and password if required. (This example shows the shortened version for ease of reading.)

If you connect to the MySQL server now, you'll see that these two records have been added:

```
mysql> SELECT * FROM customer;
+------+------------+-------------+
| id   | first_name | surname     |
+------+------------+-------------+
|    1 | Yvonne     | Clegg       |
|    2 | Johnny     | Chaka-Chaka |
|    3 | Winston    | Powers      |
|    4 | Patricia   | Mankunku    |
|    5 | Francois   | Papo        |
|    6 | Neil       | Beneke      |
+------+------------+-------------+
```

If any of the lines in the file contains a SQL error, MySQL will immediately stop processing the rest of the file. Change test.sql to the following. You add the DELETE statement at the top so that if you rerun the set of statements a number of times, you won't be stuck with any duplicate records:

```
DELETE FROM customer WHERE id>=6;
INSERT INTO customer(id,first_name,surname) VALUES(6,'Neil','Beneke');
INSERT INTO customer(id,first_name,surname) VALUES(,'Sandile','Cohen');
INSERT INTO customer(id,first_name,surname) VALUES(7,'Winnie','Dlamini');
```

When you run this from the command line, you'll see MySQL returns an error:

```
% mysql firstdb < test.sql
ERROR 1064 at line 2: You have an error in your SQL syntax near
  ''Sandile','Cohen')' at line 1
```

If you look at what the *customer* table contains now, you'll see that the first record has been correctly inserted, but because the second line contains an error (the *id* field is not specified), MySQL stopped processing at that point:

```
mysql> SELECT * FROM customer;
+------+------------+-------------+
| id   | first_name | surname     |
+------+------------+-------------+
|    1 | Yvonne     | Clegg       |
|    2 | Johnny     | Chaka-Chaka |
|    3 | Winston    | Powers      |
|    4 | Patricia   | Mankunku    |
|    5 | Francois   | Papo        |
|    6 | Neil       | Beneke      |
+------+------------+-------------+
```

You can force MySQL to continue processing even if there are errors with the force option (see Chapter 2, "Data Types and Table Types," for a full list of MySQL options):

```
% mysql -f firstdb < test.sql
ERROR 1064 at line 2: You have an error in your SQL syntax near
  ''Sandile','Cohen')' at line 1
```

Even though the error is still reported, all the valid records have still been inserted, as you can see if you view the table again:

```
mysql> SELECT * FROM customer;
+------+------------+-------------+
| id   | first_name | surname     |
+------+------------+-------------+
|    1 | Yvonne     | Clegg       |
|    2 | Johnny     | Chaka-Chaka |
|    3 | Winston    | Powers      |
|    4 | Patricia   | Mankunku    |
|    5 | Francois   | Papo        |
|    7 | Winnie     | Dlamini     |
|    6 | Neil       | Beneke      |
+------+------------+-------------+
```

## Redirecting Output to a File

You can also capture the output in another file. For example, instead of running your SELECT statement from the MySQL command line, you can add it to the original file and output the results of the query to a third file. If you change the test.sql file to the following:

```
DELETE FROM customer WHERE id>=6;
INSERT INTO customer(id,first_name,surname) VALUES(6,'Neil','Beneke');
INSERT INTO customer(id,first_name,surname) VALUES(7,'Winnie','Dlamini');
SELECT * FROM customer;
```

then you can output the results to a file, `test_output.txt`, as follows:

```
% mysql firstdb < test.sql > test_output.txt
```

The file `test_output.txt` now contains the following:

```
id        first_name        surname
1         Yvonne            Clegg
2         Johnny            Chaka-Chaka
3         Winston           Powers
4         Patricia          Mankunku
5         Francois          Papo
7         Winnie            Dlamini
6         Neil              Beneke
```

Notice that the output is not exactly the same as it would be if you were running in interactive mode. The data is tab delimited, and there are no formatting lines around them. If you did want the interactive format in the output file, you could use the table option, `-t`, for example:

```
% mysql -t firstdb < test.sql > test_output.txt
```

### Using Files from within the MySQL Command Line

You can also run SQL statements stored in a file from the command line in MySQL, with the `SOURCE` command:

```
mysql> SOURCE test.sql
Query OK, 2 rows affected (0.00 sec)

Query OK, 1 row affected (0.00 sec)

Query OK, 1 row affected (0.00 sec)


+------+------------+-------------+
| id   | first_name | surname     |
+------+------------+-------------+
|    1 | Yvonne     | Clegg       |
|    2 | Johnny     | Chaka-Chaka |
|    3 | Winston    | Powers      |
|    4 | Patricia   | Mankunku    |
|    5 | Francois   | Papo        |
|    7 | Winnie     | Dlamini     |
|    6 | Neil       | Beneke      |
+------+------------+-------------+
7 rows in set (0.00 sec)
```

You can delete the records added through the text files, as you will not need them later:

```
mysql> DELETE FROM customer WHERE id > 4;
```

Reasons for using batch mode include the following:

◆ You can reuse SQL statements you need again.

◆ You can copy and send files to other people.

◆ It's easy to make changes to a file if there are any errors.

◆ Sometimes you have to run in batch mode, such as when you want to run certain SQL commands repeatedly at a certain time each day (for example, with Unix's `cron`).

# Transactions and Locking

Database queries run one after another. For a website serving pages, it doesn't matter which order the database performs the queries, as long as they all get served quickly. But some kinds of queries need to be performed in a specific order, such as those that are dependent on the results of a previous query, or groups of updates that need to be done as a whole. All table types can make use of locking, but only InnoDB and BDB tables have transactional capabilities built in. This section discusses the various transaction and locking mechanisms.

## Transactions in InnoDb Tables

The power of the InnoDB table type comes from using *transactions*, or SQL statements that are grouped as one. A typical example of this is in a bank transaction. For example, if money is transferred from one person's account to another, there will typically be at least two queries:

```
UPDATE person1 SET balance = balance-transfer_amount;
UPDATE person2 SET balance = balance+transfer_amount;
```

This is all fine and well, but what happens if something goes wrong, and the system crashes after the first query is completed, but before the second one is complete? Person1 will have the money removed from their account, and believe the payment has gone through, but person2 will be irate, believing the payment was never made. In this sort of case, it's vital that either both queries are processed together, or neither not at all. To do this, you wrap the queries together in what is called a *transaction*, with a `BEGIN` statement to indicate the start of the transaction, and a `COMMIT` statement to indicate the end. Only when the `COMMIT` is processed, will all queries be made permanent. If something goes wrong in between, you can use the `ROLLBACK` command to reverse the incomplete part of the transaction.

Let's run some queries to see how this works. You'll have to create the table only if you haven't already done so in Chapter 2:

```
mysql> CREATE TABLE innotest (f1 INT,f2 CHAR(10),INDEX (f1))TYPE=InnoDB;
Query OK,0 rows affected (0.10 sec)

mysql> INSERT INTO innotest(f1) VALUES(1);
Query OK, 1 row affected (0.00 sec)
```

```
mysql> SELECT f1 FROM innotest;
+------+
| f1   |
+------+
|    1 |
+------+
1 row in set (0.21 sec)
```

Nothing surprising so far! Now let's wrap a query in a BEGIN/COMMIT:

```
mysql> BEGIN;
Query OK, 0 rows affected (0.05 sec)

mysql> INSERT INTO innotest(f1) VALUES(2);
Query OK, 1 row affected (0.05 sec)

mysql> SELECT f1 FROM innotest;
+------+
| f1   |
+------+
|    1 |
|    2 |
+------+
2 rows in set (0.16 sec)
```

If you now do a ROLLBACK, you will undo this transaction, as it has not yet been committed:

```
mysql> ROLLBACK;
Query OK, 0 rows affected (0.00 sec)

mysql> SELECT f1 FROM innotest;
+------+
| f1   |
+------+
|    1 |
+------+
1 row in set (0.17 sec)
```

Now let's see what happens if you lost the connection before you completed the transaction:

```
mysql> BEGIN;
Query OK, 0 rows affected (0.00 sec)

mysql> INSERT INTO innotest(f1) VALUES(2);
Query OK, 1 row affected (0.00 sec)

mysql> EXIT
Bye
```

```
C:\MySQL\bin> mysql firstdb
Welcome to the MySQL monitor.  Commands end with ; or \g.
Your MySQL connection id is 8 to server version: 4.0.1-alpha-max

Type 'help;' or '\h' for help. Type '\c' to clear the buffer.

mysql> SELECT f1 FROM innotest;
+------+
| f1   |
+------+
|    1 |
+------+
1 row in set (0.11 sec)
```

You can repeat the previous statement, this time doing a COMMIT before you exit. Once the COMMIT is run, the transaction is complete, so when you reconnect, the new record will be present:

```
mysql> BEGIN;
Query OK, 0 rows affected (0.05 sec)

mysql> INSERT INTO innotest(f1) VALUES(2);
Query OK, 1 row affected (0.06 sec)

mysql> COMMIT;
Query OK, 0 rows affected (0.05 sec)

mysql> EXIT
Bye

C:\Program Files\MySQL\bin> mysql firstdb
Welcome to the MySQL monitor.  Commands end with ; or \g.
Your MySQL connection id is 9 to server version: 4.0.1-alpha-max

Type 'help;' or '\h' for help. Type '\c' to clear the buffer.

mysql> SELECT f1 FROM innotest;
+------+
| f1   |
+------+
|    1 |
|    2 |
+------+
2 rows in set (0.11 sec)
```

## Consistent Reads

By default, InnoDB tables perform a *consistent read*. What this means is that when a SELECT is performed, MySQL returns the values present in the database up until the most recently completed transaction. If any transactions are still in progress, any UPDATE or INSERT statements will not be reflected. Before you disagree, there is one exception: The open transaction itself can see the changes (you probably noticed that when you did the BEGIN-INSERT-SELECT, the inserted result was displayed). To demonstrate this, you need to have two windows open and be connected to the database.

First add a record from within a transaction in Window1:

```
mysql> BEGIN;
Query OK, 0 rows affected (0.11 sec)

mysql> INSERT INTO innotest(f1) VALUES(3);
Query OK, 1 row affected (0.05 sec)
```

Now switch to Window2:

```
mysql> SELECT f1 FROM innotest;
+------+
| f1   |
+------+
|    1 |
|    2 |
+------+
2 rows in set (0.16 sec)
```

The 3 you inserted, because it is part of an as yet incomplete transaction, is not returned. Returning results from an incomplete transaction would be an *inconsistent read*.

Now return to Window1:

```
mysql> SELECT f1 FROM innotest;
+------+
| f1   |
+------+
|    1 |
|    2 |
|    3 |
+------+
```

The 3 is visible here because you are inside the transaction.

Now commit the transaction, while still in Window1:

```
mysql> COMMIT;
```

And now the query in Window2 will reflect the completed transaction:

```
mysql> SELECT f1 FROM innotest;
+------+
| f1   |
+------+
|    1 |
|    2 |
|    3 |
+------+
```

## Read Locks for Updating

Consistent reads are not always what you need. What if more than one user is trying to add a new record to the *innotest* table? Each new record inserts a unique ascending number. As in this example, the *f1* field is not a PRIMARY KEY or an AUTO_INCREMENT field, so there is nothing in the table structure to prevent a duplicate occurring. But you want to ensure a duplicate could never occur. You would expect to read the existing value of *f1* and then insert a new value, incremented by 1. But this does not guarantee a unique value. Look at the following example, starting with Window1:

```
mysql> BEGIN;

mysql> SELECT MAX(f1) FROM innotest;
+---------+
| MAX(f1) |
+---------+
|       3 |
+---------+
```

At the same time, another user is doing the same in Window2:

```
mysql> BEGIN;

mysql> SELECT MAX(f1) FROM innotest;
+---------+
| MAX(f1) |
+---------+
|       3 |
+---------+
1 row in set (0.11 sec)
```

Now, both users (Window1 and Window2) add a new record and commit their transaction:

```
mysql> INSERT INTO innotest(f1) VALUES(4);
Query OK, 1 row affected (0.11 sec)

mysql> COMMIT;
Query OK, 0 rows affected (0.00 sec)
```

Now if either user does a SELECT, they'll see the following:

```
mysql> SELECT f1 FROM innotest;
+------+
| f1   |
+------+
|    1 |
|    2 |
|    3 |
|    4 |
|    4 |
+------+
```

The consistent read has not produced what you'd hoped for: records with values 4 and 5. The way to avoid this is with an update lock on the SELECT. By letting MySQL know you are reading in order to update, it will not let anyone else read that value until your transaction is finished.

First, let's remove the incorrect 4 from the table, so you can do it properly this time:

```
mysql> DELETE FROM innotest WHERE f1=4;
Query OK, 2 rows affected (0.00 sec)
```

Now, set the update lock as follows in Window1:

```
mysql> BEGIN;

mysql> SELECT MAX(f1) FROM innotest FOR UPDATE;
+---------+
| MAX(f1) |
+---------+
|       3 |
+---------+

mysql> INSERT INTO innotest(f1) VALUES(4);
Query OK, 1 row affected (0.05 sec)
```

Meantime, Window2 also tries to set an update lock:

```
mysql> BEGIN;

mysql> SELECT MAX(f1) FROM innotest FOR UPDATE;
```

Notice how no results are returned. MySQL is waiting for the transaction in Window1 to complete.

Complete the transaction in Window1:

```
mysql> COMMIT;
Query OK, 0 rows affected (0.00 sec)
```

Window2 will now return the results of its query, having waited for the INSERT to be completed.

```
mysql> SELECT MAX(f1) FROM innotest FOR UPDATE;
+---------+
| MAX(f1) |
+---------+
|       4 |
+---------+
1 row in set (4 min 32.65 sec)
```

Now, safe in the knowledge that 4 is the latest value, you can add 5 to the table in Window2:

```
mysql> INSERT INTO innotest(f1) VALUES(5);
Query OK, 1 row affected (0.06 sec)
```

```
mysql> COMMIT;
Query OK, 0 rows affected (0.00 sec)
```

## Read Locks for Sharing

There is another kind of read lock that does not return a value only if the value it is reading has been changed by another incomplete transaction. It only returns the latest data, but it is not part of a transaction that wants to change the value itself. For example, let's use the *f2* field created in the *innotest* table. Assume that the *f1* field is populated first, but then only at a later stage in the transaction is a value for *f2* added. When you SELECT, you never want to see a record that has a value for the *f1* field, but not a value for the *f2* field, but you always want the latest record. In this case, you need to wait for the transaction to be finished before you return the results. For example, a transaction begins in Window1:

```
mysql> BEGIN;
Query OK, 0 rows affected (0.00 sec)

mysql> INSERT INTO innotest(f1) VALUES(6);
Query OK, 1 row affected (0.00 sec)

mysql> UPDATE innotest set f2='Sebastian' WHERE f1=6;
Query OK, 1 row affected (0.05 sec)
Rows matched: 1  Changed: 1  Warnings: 0
```

If you do an ordinary SELECT now in Window2, you will not get the latest value (because the previous transaction is incomplete, and InnoDB defaults to a consistent read). However, if you do a SELECT with a LOCK IN SHARE MODE, you will not get a result until the transaction in Window1 is complete.

Running an ordinary query in Window2 returns the following:

```
mysql> SELECT MAX(f1) FROM innotest;
+---------+
| MAX(f1) |
+---------+
|       5 |
+---------+
1 row in set (0.17 sec)
```

Still in Window2, performing the same query with a LOCK IN SHARE MODE will not yet deliver any results:

```
mysql> SELECT MAX(f1) FROM innotest LOCK IN SHARE MODE;
```

Complete the transaction in Window1:

```
mysql> COMMIT;
Query OK, 0 rows affected (0.00 sec)
```

Now Window2 will return the correct result:

```
mysql> SELECT MAX(f1) FROM innotest LOCK IN SHARE MODE;
```

```
+---------+
| MAX(f1) |
+---------+
|       6 |
+---------+
1 row in set (4 min 32.98 sec)

mysql> COMMIT;
Query OK, 0 rows affected (0.00 sec)
```

## Automatic *COMMIT*s

By default, unless you specify a transaction with BEGIN, MySQL automatically commits statements. For example, a query in Window1 returns the following:

```
mysql> SELECT f1 FROM innotest;
+------+
| f1   |
+------+
|    1 |
|    2 |
|    3 |
|    4 |
|    5 |
|    6 |
+------+
6 rows in set (0.11 sec)
```

Now, the user in Window2 inserts a record:

```
mysql> INSERT INTO innotest(f1) VALUES (7);
Query OK, 1 row affected (0.00 sec)
```

It's immediately available in Window1 (remember to complete all your previous examples with a COMMIT statement):

```
mysql> SELECT f1 FROM innotest;
+------+
| f1   |
+------+
|    1 |
|    2 |
|    3 |
|    4 |
|    5 |
|    6 |
|    7 |
+------+
7 rows in set (0.11 sec)
```

The INSERT from Window2 is immediately available to other windows because the AUTOCOMMIT is set by default. However, with transaction-safe tables (InnoDB, BDB), you can change this behavior by setting AUTOCOMMIT to zero.

First, set AUTOCOMMIT to 0 in Window1:

```
mysql> SET AUTOCOMMIT=0;
Query OK, 0 rows affected (0.00 sec)
```

And run this query on Window2:

```
mysql> SELECT f1 FROM innotest;
+------+
| f1   |
+------+
|    1 |
|    2 |
|    3 |
|    4 |
|    5 |
|    6 |
|    7 |
+------+
7 rows in set (0.22 sec)
```

Now, Window1 inserts a record:

```
mysql> INSERT INTO innotest(f1) VALUES(8);
Query OK, 1 row affected (0.00 sec)
```

This time it's not immediately available to Window2:

```
mysql> SELECT f1 FROM innotest;
+------+
| f1   |
+------+
|    1 |
|    2 |
|    3 |
|    4 |
|    5 |
|    6 |
|    7 |
+------+
7 rows in set (0.16 sec)
```

Because you have AUTOCOMMIT off, the INSERT from Window1 will not be committed until a specific COMMIT is run.

Commit the transaction from Window1:

```
mysql> COMMIT;
Query OK, 0 rows affected (0.00 sec)
```

Now the new record is available to Window2:

```
mysql> SELECT f1 FROM innotest;
+------+
| f1   |
+------+
|    1 |
|    2 |
|    3 |
|    4 |
|    5 |
|    6 |
|    7 |
|    8 |
+------+
8 rows in set (0.11 sec)
```

However, AUTOCOMMIT=0 does not set this across the entire server, only for that particular session. If Window2 also sets AUTOCOMMIT to 0, you'll experience different behavior.

First, set AUTOCOMMIT in both Window1 and 2:

```
mysql> SET AUTOCOMMIT=0;
Query OK, 0 rows affected (0.00 sec)
```

Now, run the following in Window1 to see what's present:

```
mysql> SELECT f1 FROM innotest;
+------+
| f1   |
+------+
|    1 |
|    2 |
|    3 |
|    4 |
|    5 |
|    6 |
|    7 |
|    8 |
+------+
8 rows in set (0.17 sec)
```

Add a record in Window2, and commit the transaction:

```
mysql> INSERT INTO innotest(f1) VALUES(9);
Query OK, 1 row affected (0.00 sec)

mysql> COMMIT;
Query OK, 0 rows affected (0.00 sec)
```

And now see if it appears in Window1:

```
mysql> SELECT f1 FROM innotest;
```

```
+------+
| f1   |
+------+
|    1 |
|    2 |
|    3 |
|    4 |
|    5 |
|    6 |
|    7 |
|    8 |
+------+
8 rows in set (0.11 sec)
```

The 9 from the new record does not appear, even though you have committed the results! The reason is that the SELECT in Window1 is also part of a transaction. The consistent read has been assigned a *timepoint*, and this timepoint only moves forward when the transaction it was set in is completed.

Commit the transaction in Window1:

```
mysql> COMMIT;
Query OK, 0 rows affected (0.00 sec)
```

```
mysql> SELECT f1 FROM innotest;
+------+
| f1   |
+------+
|    1 |
|    2 |
|    3 |
|    4 |
|    5 |
|    6 |
|    7 |
|    8 |
|    9 |
+------+
9 rows in set (0.22 sec)
```

As you saw before, the only way to see the latest results is to SELECT with a LOCK IN SHARE MODE. This would have waited until the transaction doing the inserting had done a COMMIT.

## Transactions in BDB Tables

BDB tables handle transactions slightly differently than InnoDB tables. First create the table (only if you haven't already in Chapter 2) and then insert a record from Window1:

```
mysql> CREATE TABLE bdbtest(f1 INT,f2 CHAR(10))TYPE=BDB;
Query OK, 0 rows affected (0.28 sec)
```

```
mysql> BEGIN;
Query OK, 0 rows affected (0.06 sec)
```

```
mysql> INSERT INTO bdbtest(f1) VALUES(1);
Query OK, 1 row affected (0.00 sec)
```

Now try the following in Window2:

```
mysql> SELECT f1 FROM bdbtest;
```

Window2 waits for the transaction in Window1 to complete. (It does not return a set of results based on the situation before the Window1 transaction began, like InnoDB.)

Only after Window1 commits does Window2 receive the results. Complete the transaction in Window1:

```
mysql> COMMIT;
Query OK, 0 rows affected (0.00 sec)
```

And the query in Window2 completes (you don't need to type it again):

```
mysql> SELECT f1 FROM bdbtest;
+------+
| f1   |
+------+
|    1 |
+------+
1 row in set (3 min 13.99 sec)
```

Note the long period of time the query took. The fact that there is not a "quick" SELECT in BDB tables means that any transactions that are delayed could have serious performance problems.

As with InnoDB tables, the default mode is AUTOCOMMIT=1. That means that unless you place your changes within a transaction (starting with BEGIN), they are immediately finalized.

Run the following query from Window1:

```
mysql> SELECT f1 FROM bdbtest;
+------+
| f1   |
+------+
|    1 |
+------+
1 row in set (0.17 sec)
```

Now run an INSERT from Window2:

```
mysql> INSERT INTO bdbtest(f1) VALUES(2);
Query OK, 1 row affected (0.06 sec)
```

It is immediately retrievable from Window1:

```
mysql> SELECT f1 FROM bdbtest;
+------+
| f1   |
+------+
|    1 |
|    2 |
+------+
2 rows in set (0.16 sec)
```

By setting AUTOCOMMIT to 0, the effect is the same as having all statements wrapped in a BEGIN.

Set AUTOCOMMIT to 0 and insert a record in Window1:

```
mysql> SET OPTION AUTOCOMMIT=0;
Query OK, 0 rows affected (0.11 sec)
mysql> INSERT INTO bdbtest(f1) VALUES(3);
Query OK, 1 row affected (0.11 sec)
```

A query run from Window2 will wait while the transaction is active:

```
mysql> SELECT f1 FROM bdbtest;
```

Only when the transaction is committed will the result appear.
Commit the transaction in Window1:

```
mysql> COMMIT;
Query OK, 0 rows affected (0.05 sec)
```

And now the query retrieves its results in Window2 (you do not have to retype the query):

```
mysql> SELECT f1 FROM bdbtest;
+------+
| f1   |
+------+
|    1 |
|    2 |
|    3 |
+------+
```

3 rows in set (2 min 8.14 sec)

## Further Transactional Behavior

There are a number of other commands that automatically end a transaction (in other words, they behave as if you'd performed a COMMIT):

- ◆ BEGIN
- ◆ ALTER TABLE
- ◆ CREATE INDEX
- ◆ RENAME TABLE (this is a synonym for ALTER TABLE x RENAME)
- ◆ TRUNCATE
- ◆ DROP TABLE
- ◆ DROP DATABASE

Even if the command is unsuccessful, just attempting the command will effectively cause a COMMIT. For example, begin the following transaction inWindow1:

```
mysql> BEGIN;
```

```
mysql> SELECT MAX(f1) FROM innotest FOR UPDATE;
+---------+
| MAX(f1) |
+---------+
|       9 |
+---------+
```

And begin another transaction in Window2:

```
mysql> BEGIN;
```

```
mysql> SELECT MAX(f1) FROM innotest FOR UPDATE;
```

The results are not displayed, as Window1 has locked the row for updating. However, the user on Window1 changes their mind and decides to change the structure of the table first.

◆ Run the ALTER TABLE on Window1:

```
mysql> ALTER TABLE innotest add f1 INT;
ERROR 1060: Duplicate column name 'f1'
```

Even though the ALTER was a failure, the lock was released and the transaction committed, and the query waiting on Window2 completes (you do not need to retype).

```
mysql> SELECT MAX(f1) FROM innotest FOR UPDATE;
+---------+
| MAX(f1) |
+---------+
|       9 |
+---------+
1 row in set (2 min 23.52 sec)
```

## Locking Tables

In the discussions on InnoDB and BDB tables, you've come across the concept of row-level locking, where individual rows are locked for a period of time. Row-level locks are much more efficient when the table needs to perform high volumes of INSERTs or UPDATEs. Row-level locking, though, is available only to transaction-safe table types (BDB and InnoDB). MySQL also has table-level locking, which is available to all table types.

There are two kinds of table locks: *read locks* and *write locks*. Read locks mean that only reads may be performed on the table, and writes are locked. Write locks mean that no reads or writes may be performed on the table for the duration of the lock. The syntax to lock a table is as follows:

```
LOCK TABLE tablename {READ|WRITE}
```

To unlock a table simply use the UNLOCK TABLES statement, as follows:

```
UNLOCK TABLES
```

The following demonstrates a table-level lock in action, and will work with any table type. First, lock the table from Window1:

```
mysql> LOCK TABLE customer READ;
Query OK, 0 rows affected (0.01 sec)
```

Other threads can now read, but not write, as you can see by trying the following from Window2:

```
mysql> SELECT * FROM customer;
+------+------------+-------------+
| id   | first_name | surname     |
+------+------------+-------------+
|    1 | Yvonne     | Clegg       |
|    2 | Johnny     | Chaka-Chaka |
|    3 | Winston    | Powers      |
|    4 | Patricia   | Mankunku    |
+------+------------+-------------+

mysql> INSERT INTO customer(id,first_name,surname) VALUES(5,'Francois','Papo');
```

The INSERT statement is not processed until the lock is released by Window1:

```
mysql> UNLOCK TABLES;
```

The INSERT on Window2 now completes (no need to type it again):

```
mysql> INSERT INTO customer(id,first_name,surname) VALUES(5,'Francois','Papo');
Query OK, 1 row affected (7 min 0.74 sec)
```

You can also lock more than one table at a time. Place the following locks from Window1:

```
mysql> LOCK TABLE customer READ,sales WRITE;
```

Other threads can now read the customer table, but not the *sales* table. Try to run a SELECT from Window2:

```
mysql> SELECT * FROM sales;
```

If the thread that created the lock tries to add a record to the *customer* table, it will fail. It will not wait for the lock to be released (because it created the lock, if it hung it would never be able to release the lock); rather, the INSERT just fails. Try this from Window1:

```
mysql> INSERT INTO customer VALUES (1,'a','b');
ERROR 1099: Table 'customer' was locked with a READ lock and can't be updated
```

However, it can perform reads on the table it write locked, as follows, still on Window1:

```
mysql> SELECT * FROM sales;
```

```
+------+-----------+------+-------+
| code | sales_rep | id   | value |
+------+-----------+------+-------+
|   1  |        1  |   1  |  2000 |
|   2  |        4  |   3  |   250 |
|   3  |        2  |   3  |   500 |
|   4  |        1  |   4  |   450 |
|   5  |        3  |   1  |  3800 |
|   6  |        1  |   2  |   500 |
|   7  |        2  | NULL |   670 |
+------+-----------+------+-------+
```

```
mysql> UNLOCK TABLES;
```

And with the write lock released, Window2 now processes the SELECT (no need to retype):

```
mysql> SELECT * FROM sales;
+------+-----------+------+-------+
| code | sales_rep | id   | value |
+------+-----------+------+-------+
|   1  |        1  |   1  |  2000 |
|   2  |        4  |   3  |   250 |
|   3  |        2  |   3  |   500 |
|   4  |        1  |   4  |   450 |
|   5  |        3  |   1  |  3800 |
|   6  |        1  |   2  |   500 |
|   7  |        2  | NULL |   670 |
+------+-----------+------+-------+
7 rows in set (5 min 59.35 sec)
```

**NOTE** *You can use either the singular or the plural form. Both* [UN]LOCK TABLE *and* [UN]LOCK TABLES *are valid, no matter how many tables you're locking. MySQL doesn't care about grammar!*

Write locks have a higher priority than read locks, so if one thread is waiting for a read lock, and a request for a write lock comes along, the read lock has to wait until the write lock has been obtained, and released, before it obtains its read lock, as follows:

Place a write lock from Window1:

```
mysql> LOCK TABLE customer WRITE;
Query OK, 0 rows affected (0.00 sec)
```

And try to place a read lock from Window2:

```
mysql> LOCK TABLE customer READ;
```

The read lock cannot be obtained until the write lock is released. In the meantime, another request for a write lock comes along, which also has to wait until the first write lock is released.

Attempt to place another write lock from a third window, Window3:

```
mysql> LOCK TABLE customer WRITE;
```

Now release the lock from Window1:

```
mysql> UNLOCK TABLES;
Query OK, 0 rows affected (0.00 sec)
```

The write lock from Window 3 is now obtained, even though it was requested after the read lock, as follows (no need to retype the LOCK statement):

```
mysql> LOCK TABLE customer WRITE;
Query OK, 0 rows affected (33.93 sec)
mysql> UNLOCK TABLES;
Query OK, 0 rows affected (0.00 sec)
```

Only when the write lock on Window 3 is released can the read lock from Window2 be obtained (no need to retype):

```
mysql> LOCK TABLE customer READ;
Query OK, 0 rows affected (4 min 2.46 sec)
mysql> UNLOCK TABLES;
Query OK, 0 rows affected (0.00 sec)
```

You can override this behavior by specifying that the write lock should be a lower priority, with the LOW_PRIORITY keyword. If you run the previous example again with a low-priority request for a write lock, the earlier read lock will be obtained first.

First, place the write lock on Window1:

```
mysql> LOCK TABLE customer WRITE;
Query OK, 0 rows affected (0.00 sec)
```

Next attempt a read lock from Window2:

```
mysql> LOCK TABLE customer READ;
```

And a low priority write lock from Window3:

```
mysql> LOCK TABLE customer LOW_PRIORITY WRITE;
```

Now release the lock from Window1:

```
mysql> UNLOCK TABLES;
Query OK, 0 rows affected (0.00 sec)
```

This time Window2 is first to obtaining its lock (no need to retype the LOCK statement):

```
mysql> LOCK TABLE customer READ;
Query OK, 0 rows affected (20.88 sec)

mysql> UNLOCK TABLES;
Query OK, 0 rows affected (0.00 sec)
```

And finally the write lock from Window3 is obtained (no need to retype):

```
mysql> LOCK TABLE customer LOW_PRIORITY WRITE;
Query OK, 0 rows affected (1 min 25.94 sec)
```

Again, release the lock so that you can use the table later:

```
mysql> UNLOCK TABLES;
Query OK, 0 rows affected (0.00 sec)
```

**WARNING**    *The* LOCK TABLES *statement is not transaction safe. It will commit all active transactions before it attempts to lock the tables.*

Table locks are mostly used in this way on tables that do not support transactions. If you're using an InnoDB or a BDB table, use BEGIN and COMMIT instead to avoid anomalies in your data. The following is an example of where it could be used. If your *customer_sales_values* table is empty, populate it with some records:

```
mysql> INSERT INTO customer_sales_values(first_name, surname, value,
  value2) VALUES('Johnny', 'Chaka-Chaka', 500, NULL), ('Patricia',
  'Mankunku', 450, NULL), ('Winston', 'Powers', 750, NULL), ('Yvonne',
  'Clegg', 5800, NULL), ('Charles', 'Dube', 0, NULL), ('Charles',
  'Dube', 0, NULL), ('Gladys', 'Malherbe', 5, 10);
```

Now assume that Johnny Chaka-Chaka has made two sales, both of which are being processed by different clerks. The one sale is worth $100 and the other $300. Both clerks go through a process of reading the existing value, then adding either 100 or 300 to this, and then updating the record. The problem comes if both perform the SELECT before either is updated. Then the one update will overwrite the other, and the one value will be lost, as follows.

First, perform the query on Window1:

```
mysql> SELECT value from customer_sales_values WHERE
  first_name='Johnny' and surname='Chaka-Chaka';
+-------+
| value |
+-------+
|   500 |
+-------+
```

Then perform the query on Window2:

```
mysql> SELECT value from customer_sales_values WHERE
  first_name='Johnny' and surname='Chaka-Chaka';
+-------+
| value |
+-------+
|   500 |
+-------+
```

This is Window1:

```
mysql> UPDATE customer_sales_values SET value=500+100 WHERE
  first_name='Johnny' and surname='Chaka-Chaka';
Query OK, 1 row affected (0.01 sec)
```

This is Window2:

```
mysql> UPDATE customer_sales_values SET value=500+300 WHERE
  first_name='Johnny' and surname='Chaka-Chaka';
Query OK, 1 row affected (0.01 sec)
```

After both sales have been captured, the total value of Johnny's sales is $800, which is $100 short! If you'd taken the care to lock the table, you'd have avoided the problem.

After you reset the data and start again, run the following UPDATE:

```
mysql> UPDATE customer_sales_values SET value=500 WHERE
  first_name='Johnny' and surname='Chaka-Chaka';
Query OK, 1 row affected (0.00 sec)
```

Now, place a write lock with Window1:

```
mysql> LOCK TABLE customer_sales_values WRITE;
mysql> SELECT value from customer_sales_values WHERE
  first_name='Johnny' and surname='Chaka-Chaka';
+-------+
| value |
+-------+
|   500 |
+-------+
```

Window2 attempts to place a write lock as well:

```
mysql> LOCK TABLE customer_sales_values WRITE;
```

The lock is not obtained, as Window1 has obtained a write lock already. Now Window1 can update the record, before releasing the lock and allowing Window2 to continue.

Run the following UPDATE statement onWindow1, and release the lock:

```
mysql> UPDATE customer_sales_values SET value=500+100 WHERE
  first_name='Johnny' and surname='Chaka-Chaka';
Query OK, 1 row affected (0.00 sec)
mysql> UNLOCK TABLES;
```

Window2 obtains the lock (no need to retype), and can complete the rest of the transaction as follows:

```
mysql> LOCK TABLE customer_sales_values WRITE;
Query OK, 0 rows affected (1 min 35.87 sec)
mysql> SELECT value from customer_sales_values WHERE
  first_name='Johnny' and surname='Chaka-Chaka';
+-------+
| value |
+-------+
|   600 |
+-------+
1 row in set (0.00 sec)
```

```
mysql> UPDATE customer_sales_values SET value=600+300 WHERE
 first_name='Johnny' and surname='Chaka-Chaka';
Query OK, 1 row affected (0.01 sec)

mysql> UNLOCK TABLES;
Query OK, 0 rows affected (0.00 sec)
```

Johnny receives credit due to him; the table correctly reflects the $900 worth of sales he has made.

## Avoiding Table Locks

You should avoid table locks as much as possible in high-update volume tables, as, in the case of a write lock, no records from the table can be read or written for the duration of the lock. And because write locks have by default a higher priority than a read locks, no records can be read until all updates or inserts are complete, potentially causing MySQL to jam up horribly. There are ways to avoid table locks, though. One way is to perform the read and the update in the same statement (called an *incremental update*).

Run the following incremental update from Window1:

```
mysql> UPDATE customer_sales_values SET value=value+300 WHERE
 first_name='Johnny' and surname='Chaka-Chaka';
```

Window2 can perform its UPDATE as well:

```
mysql> UPDATE customer_sales_values SET value=value+100 WHERE
 first_name='Johnny' and surname='Chaka-Chaka';
```

Now, no matter which order the statements are placed, the update will always be performed on the most recent value.

## Transaction Levels

You can change the default behavior when dealing with transactions by setting the transaction level. There are a number of transaction levels in MySQL. MySQL supports the following transaction isolation levels:

**READ UNCOMMITTED**   This level allows transactions to read the uncommitted data from other transactions (called a *dirty read*).

**READ COMMITTED**   This level does not allow dirty reads.

**REPEATABLE READ**   This level does not allow nonrepeatable reads (which are when the data has been changed by another transaction, even if it has been committed).

**SERIALIZABLE**   This level does not allow phantom reads, which is when another transaction has committed a new row that matches the results of your query. The data will be the same each time. To change the transaction level, use the following syntax:

```
SET [scope] TRANSACTION ISOLATION LEVEL
{ isolation_level }
```

The *scope* option can be either GLOBAL or SESSION. This option overrides the usual scope of the statement, which is to set the transaction isolation level for the next transaction to be started. GLOBAL sets the level for all new transactions, and SESSION for all new transactions on that thread. The *isolation_level* option is one of the four transaction isolation levels listed above.

## Summary

Joins can be much more complicated than the simple two-table joins covered in Chapter 1, "Quick-start to MySQL." Inner joins ignore NULL values in a table being joined (or rows where there is no associated records), and outer joins include NULL data. Left outer joins return all data in the table specified first (on the left), including those without an associated record in the right table, while right outer joins return all data in the table specified on the right of the join. Full outer joins combine the features of a left and a right join, but MySQL does not yet support this.

Natural joins use the fact that common fields may be named the same, and simplify the syntax if this is the case.

The UNION command combines the results of more than one query into one.

Sub-selects are queries within queries. Often they perform more efficiently if they are rewritten as a join.

Deleting records one by one, as with the DELETE statement, is not efficient if you just want to remove all the records in a table. The TRUNCATE statement is a quicker way of doing this, though it doesn't return the number of records deleted, as DELETE does.

User variables allow you to store values for use in a later query. You need to take care when using them, however, that the user variable is set before it is required. In SELECT statements, the condition (the WHERE clause) is performed first, before the field list (immediately after the SELECT and where user variables are usually set).

MySQL can also be run in batch mode, with SQL statements stored in files for ease of editing and reuse. You can also redirect the output to a file, so for example, results of queries can be examined easily at a later stage.

All table types also allow table locking, where the entire table can be locked, as opposed to just the row as with transaction-safe tables.

In the next chapter, you'll sharpen your skills some more and look at how you can optimize the performance of our database. You'll explore creating indexes, writing queries more efficiently, and improving the server's performance.

# Chapter 4

# Indexes and Query Optimization

GETTING A QUERY TO work is one thing, but getting a query to work quickly when the clients are piling up is another. You can speed up your queries in some basic ways. Using indexes intelligently can make a huge difference, while carefully fine-tuning your system can also make a noticeable improvement.

Featured in this chapter:

◆ Creating and using indexes

◆ Primary keys, unique indexes, full-text indexes, and ordinary indexes

◆ Full-text searches

◆ Dropping or changing an index

◆ Auto increment fields

◆ Analyzing queries with EXPLAIN

◆ Optimizing SELECT statements

## Understanding Indexes

So far, none of the tables created in the previous chapters has an index. When you add each new record, it's usually just added onto the end of the table, but can be added to the middle of the table if another record has been deleted and if there is space. In other words, the records are not stored in any order. Consider, for instance, the customer table from Chapter 3, "Advanced SQL," which, assuming you followed the examples in that chapter, contains records in the following order:

```
+------+------------+-------------+
| id   | first_name | surname     |
+------+------------+-------------+
| 1    | Yvonne     | Clegg       |
| 2    | Johnny     | Chaka-Chaka |
| 3    | Winston    | Powers      |
| 4    | Patricia   | Mankunku    |
| 5    | Francois   | Papo        |
| 7    | Winnie     | Dlamini     |
| 6    | Neil       | Beneke      |
+------+------------+-------------+
```

Now, imagine you were doing the job of MySQL. If you wanted to return any records with the surname of Beneke, you'd probably start at the top and examine each record. Without any further information, there's no way for you, or MySQL itself, to know where to find records adhering to this criteria. Scanning the table in this way (from start to finish, examining all the records) is called a *full table scan*. When tables are large, this becomes inefficient; full table scans of tables consisting of many hundreds of thousands of records can run very slowly.

To overcome this problem, it would help if the records were sorted. Let's look for the same record as before, but on a table sorted by surname:

```
+------+------------+-------------+
| id   | first_name | surname     |
+------+------------+-------------+
| 6    | Neil       | Beneke      |
| 2    | Johnny     | Chaka-Chaka |
| 1    | Yvonne     | Clegg       |
| 7    | Winnie     | Dlamini     |
| 4    | Patricia   | Mankunku    |
| 5    | Francois   | Papo        |
| 3    | Winston    | Powers      |
+------+------------+-------------+
```

Now you can search this table much more quickly. Because you know the records are stored alphabetically by surname, you know once you reach the surname Chaka-Chaka, which begins with a *C*, that there can be no more Beneke records. You've only had to examine one record, as opposed to the seven you would have had to examine in the unordered table. That's quite a savings, and in a bigger table the benefits would be even greater.

Therefore, it may look like sorting the table is the solution. But, unfortunately, you may want to search the table in other ways, too. For example, perhaps you want to return the record with an id of 3. With the table still ordered by surname, you would have to examine all the records again, and once more you're stuck with slow, inefficient queries.

The solution is to create separate lists for each field that you need to order. These don't contain all the fields, just the fields that you need ordered and a pointer to the complete record in the full table. These lists are called *indexes*, and they are one of the most underused and misused aspects of relational databases (see Figure 4.1). Indexes are stored as separate files in some cases (MyISAM tables), or as part of the same tablespace in other cases (InnoDB tables).

**FIGURE 4.1**

The index records point to the associated customer table records.

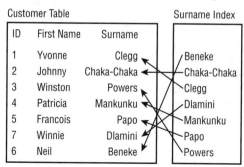

# Creating an Index

There are four kinds of indexes in MySQL: a primary key, a unique index, a full-text index, and an ordinary index.

## Creating a Primary Key

A *primary key* is an index on a field where each value is unique and none of the values are NULL.

**NOTE** *The term primary key is, strictly speaking, a logical term, but MySQL uses it to denote a physical index. When MySQL indicates that a primary key exists, there is always an associated index. Throughout this text, the term* key *indicates the presence of a physical index.*

To create a primary key when creating a table, use PRIMARY KEY at the end of the field definitions, with a list of the fields to be included:

```
CREATE TABLE tablename(fieldname columntype NOT NULL,
    [fieldname2...,] PRIMARY KEY(fieldname1 [,fieldname2...]));
```

Note that the keyword NOT NULL is mandatory when creating a primary key; primary keys cannot contain a null value. MySQL warns you if you forget to specify this:

```
mysql> CREATE TABLE pk_test(f1 INT, PRIMARY KEY(f1));
ERROR 1171: All parts of a PRIMARY KEY must be NOT NULL;
If you need NULL in a key, use UNIQUE instead
```

To create a primary key on an already existing table, you can use the ALTER keyword:

```
ALTER TABLE tablename ADD PRIMARY KEY(fieldname1 [,fieldname2...]);
```

Choosing a primary key for the customer table is fairly easy. The id field lends itself to this because each customer has a different id and there are no null fields. Either of the name fields would not be ideal, as there may be duplicates at some stage. To add a primary key to the id field of the customer table, you need to change the field to not allow nulls and then add the primary key. You can do this in one statement, as follows:

```
mysql> ALTER TABLE customer MODIFY id INT NOT NULL, ADD PRIMARY KEY(id);
Query OK, 7 rows affected (0.00 sec)
Records: 7  Duplicates: 0  Warnings: 0
```

You can see the changes you've made to the table with this statement by examining the columns:

```
mysql> DESCRIBE customer;
+------------+-------------+------+-----+---------+-------+
| Field      | Type        | Null | Key | Default | Extra |
+------------+-------------+------+-----+---------+-------+
| id         | int(11)     |      | PRI | 0       |       |
| first_name | varchar(30) | YES  |     | NULL    |       |
| surname    | varchar(40) | YES  |     | NULL    |       |
+------------+-------------+------+-----+---------+-------+
3 rows in set (0.00 sec)
```

The id field does not have a *YES* in the Null column, indicating that it no longer can accept null values. It also has *PRI* in the Key column, indicating the primary key.

Primary keys can also consist of more than one field. Sometimes there is no one field that can uniquely identify a record. To add a primary key in this instance, separate the fields with a comma:

```
mysql> CREATE TABLE pk2(id INT NOT NULL, id2 INT NOT NULL, PRIMARY KEY(id,id2));
Query OK, 0 rows affected (0.00 sec)
```

or as follows if the table already exists:

```
mysql> ALTER TABLE pk2 ADD PRIMARY KEY(id,id2);
Query OK, 0 rows affected (0.01 sec)
```

The sales table from earlier chapters does not yet have a key:

```
mysql> SHOW COLUMNS FROM sales;
+-----------+---------+------+-----+---------+-------+
| Field     | Type    | Null | Key | Default | Extra |
+-----------+---------+------+-----+---------+-------+
| code      | int(11) | YES  |     | NULL    |       |
| sales_rep | int(11) | YES  |     | NULL    |       |
| id        | int(11) | YES  |     | NULL    |       |
| value     | int(11) | YES  |     | NULL    |       |
+-----------+---------+------+-----+---------+-------+
4 rows in set (0.00 sec)
```

Let's assume you add a new record with the same code as an existing record:

```
mysql> SELECT * FROM sales;
+------+-----------+------+-------+
| code | sales_rep | id   | value |
+------+-----------+------+-------+
|    1 |         1 |    1 |  2000 |
|    2 |         4 |    3 |   250 |
|    3 |         2 |    3 |   500 |
|    4 |         1 |    4 |   450 |
|    5 |         3 |    1 |  3800 |
|    6 |         1 |    2 |   500 |
|    7 |         2 | NULL |   670 |
+------+-----------+------+-------+
7 rows in set (0.00 sec)
mysql> INSERT INTO sales VALUES(7,3,3,1000);
Query OK, 1 row affected (0.00 sec)
```

There is no problem so far. Even though there are now two records with a code of 7, there is nothing in the table structure that disallows this. But now, with your new knowledge of the reasons for using a primary key, you decide to make the code field a primary key:

```
mysql> ALTER TABLE sales MODIFY code INT NOT NULL,ADD PRIMARY KEY(code);
ERROR 1062: Duplicate entry '7' for key 1
```

You have a duplicate value for the code field, and by definition a primary key should always be unique. Here, you would have to either remove or update the duplicates or use an ordinary index that allows duplicates. Most tables work better with a primary key, though. In this situation, it's easy to update the responsible record:

```
mysql> UPDATE sales SET code=8 WHERE code=7 AND sales_rep=3;
Query OK, 1 row affected (0.00 sec)
Rows matched: 1  Changed: 1  Warnings: 0
mysql> ALTER TABLE sales MODIFY code INT NOT NULL,ADD PRIMARY KEY(code);
Query OK, 8 rows affected (0.01 sec)
Records: 8  Duplicates: 0  Warnings: 0
```

*TIP   I worked on one system where a "unique" field turned out to have thousands of duplicates because of a combination of having no primary key and nonexistent locking. It's always better to add keys, especially a primary key, when you create a table.*

## Creating an Ordinary Index

An index that is not primary allows duplicate values (unless the fields are specified as unique). As always, it's best to create the index at the same time as you create the table:

```
CREATE TABLE tablename(fieldname columntype, fieldname2
    columntype, INDEX [indexname] (fieldname1 [,fieldname2...]));
```

You can also create more than one index when the table is created, just separating them with commas:

```
CREATE TABLE tablename(fieldname columntype, fieldname2
    columntype, INDEX [indexname1] (fieldname1,fieldname2),INDEX
    [indexname2] (fieldname1 [,fieldname2...]));
```

You can always create an index at a later stage, though, with this code:

```
ALTER TABLE tablename ADD INDEX [indexname] (fieldname1 [,fieldname2...]);
```

or with the following code:

```
mysql> CREATE INDEX indexname on tablename(fieldname1 [,fieldname2...]);
```

Both of these statements ask for an index name, although with the CREATE INDEX statement the index name is mandatory. If, in the ALTER TABLE...ADD INDEX... statement, you do not name the index, MySQL will assign its own name based on the fieldname. MySQL takes the first field as the index name if there is more than one field in the index. If there is a second index starting with the same field, MySQL appends _2, then _3, and so on to the index name.

The following sales table has a primary key, but it could also do with an index on the value field. You may quite often be searching for records with a value greater or less than a certain amount, or ordering by the value:

```
mysql> SHOW COLUMNS FROM sales;
```

```
+-----------+---------+------+-----+---------+-------+
| Field     | Type    | Null | Key | Default | Extra |
+-----------+---------+------+-----+---------+-------+
| code      | int(11) |      | PRI | 0       |       |
| sales_rep | int(11) | YES  |     | NULL    |       |
| id        | int(11) | YES  |     | NULL    |       |
| value     | int(11) | YES  |     | NULL    |       |
+-----------+---------+------+-----+---------+-------+
4 rows in set (0.00 sec)
mysql> ALTER TABLE sales ADD INDEX(value);
Query OK, 8 rows affected (0.02 sec)
Records: 8  Duplicates: 0  Warnings: 0
```

*NOTE*  *You can use the keyword* KEY *instead of* INDEX *in MySQL statements if you want. I prefer* INDEX *because* KEY *usually refers to the logical structure, and* INDEX *usually refers to the actual physical index on the disk.*

## Creating a Full-Text Index

You can create full-text indexes in MyISAM tables, on any CHAR, VARCHAR, or TEXT fields. A full-text index is designed to allow easy searching for keywords in text fields in large tables.

To create a full-text index when the table is created, use this syntax:

```
CREATE TABLE tablename (fieldname columntype, fieldname2
    columntype, FULLTEXT(fieldname [,fieldname2...]));
```

The optional keyword INDEX can be added, as in this syntax:

```
CREATE TABLE tablename (fieldname columntype, fieldname2
    columntype, FULLTEXT INDEX(fieldname [,fieldname2...]));
```

To create a full-text index once the table is already in existence, use this syntax:

```
ALTER TABLE tablename ADD FULLTEXT [indexname] (fieldname [,fieldname2...]);
```

or the following code:

```
CREATE FULLTEXT INDEX indexname ON tablename(fieldname [,fieldname2...]);
```

Let's create a table and try to create full-text indexes on some of the fields, as follows:

```
mysql> CREATE TABLE ft(f1 VARCHAR(255),f2 TEXT,f3 BLOB,f4 INT);
Query OK, 0 rows affected (0.01 sec)
mysql> ALTER TABLE ft ADD FULLTEXT (f1,f2);
Query OK, 0 rows affected (0.01 sec)
Records: 0  Duplicates: 0  Warnings: 0
```

The fields f1 and f2 are VARCHAR and TEXT, respectively, so a full-text index is allowed:

```
mysql> ALTER TABLE ft ADD FULLTEXT (f1,f4);
```

```
ERROR 1005: Can't create table './firstdb/#sql-52eb_4f.frm' (errno: 140)
mysql> ALTER TABLE ft ADD FULLTEXT (f2,f3);
ERROR 1005: Can't create table './firstdb/#sql-52eb_4f.frm' (errno: 140)
```

In these examples, the field f4 is of type INT and f3 is of type BLOB, so a full-text index is not allowed in either case.

### USING A FULL-TEXT INDEX

Let's create a table with a full-text index and insert some book titles into it to test it:

```
mysql> CREATE TABLE ft2(f1 VARCHAR(255),FULLTEXT(f1));
Query OK, 0 rows affected (0.00 sec)
mysql> INSERT INTO ft2 VALUES('Waiting for the
    Barbarians'),
    ('In the Heart of the Country'),
    ('The Master of Petersburg'),
    ('Writing and Being'),
    ('Heart of the Beast'),
    ('Heart of the Beest'),
    ('The Beginning and the End'),
    ('Master Master'),
    ('A Barbarian at my Door');
Query OK, 9 rows affected (0.00 sec)
Records: 9  Duplicates: 0  Warnings: 0
```

To return the results of a full-text search, you use the MATCH() function, and MATCH() a field AGAINST() a value, as in this example, which looks for occurrences of the word *Master*:

```
mysql> SELECT * FROM ft2 WHERE MATCH(f1) AGAINST ('Master');
+-------------------------+
| f1                      |
+-------------------------+
| Master Master           |
| The Master of Petersburg |
+-------------------------+
2 rows in set (0.01 sec)
```

It's no coincidence that *Master Master* appeared first, even though it was added second. MySQL calculates a relevance result for each match and returns the results in this order.

**NOTE**   *Remember that searches on TEXT fields are not case sensitive, nor are they on VARCHAR or CHAR fields declared without the BINARY keyword.*

### NOISE WORDS

Now you run another search:

```
mysql> SELECT * FROM ft2 WHERE MATCH(f1) AGAINST ('The Master');
```

```
+---------------------------+
| f1                        |
+---------------------------+
| Master Master             |
| The Master of Petersburg  |
+---------------------------+
2 rows in set (0.00 sec)
```

These results are not as you may expect. Most of the titles contain the word *the*, and *The Beginning and the End* contains it twice, yet is not reflected. There are a number of reasons for this:

- MySQL has what is called a *50-percent threshold*. Any words that appear in more than 50 percent of the fields are treated as *noise words*, meaning that they are ignored.
- Any words of three or fewer letters are excluded from the index.
- There is a predefined list of noise words, with *the* included.

So, *The Beginning and the End* didn't have a chance!

**WARNING**   *If you have a table with only one record, all words will be noise words, so a full-text search would not return anything! Tables with very few records can also increase the likelihood of words being treated as noise words.*

The following query returns nothing, even though the word *for* does appear in the data because *for* is a word of three or fewer characters, and by default these are excluded from the index:

```
mysql> SELECT * FROM ft2 WHERE MATCH(f1) AGAINST ('for');
Empty set (0.00 sec)
```

### RELEVANCE

You are not limited to using the MATCH() function in the WHERE condition; you can return the results, too, as follows:

```
mysql> SELECT f1, (MATCH(f1) AGAINST ('Master')) FROM ft2;
+---------------------------+-------------------------------+
| f1                        | (MATCH(f1) AGAINST ('Master')) |
+---------------------------+-------------------------------+
| Waiting for the Barbarians |                             0 |
| In the Heart of the Country |                            0 |
| The Master of Petersburg  |                1.2245972156525 |
| Writing and Being         |                             0 |
| Heart of the Beast        |                             0 |
| Heart of the Beest        |                             0 |
| A Barbarian at my Door    |                             0 |
| Master Master             |                 1.238520026207 |
| The Beginning and the End |                             0 |
+---------------------------+-------------------------------+
9 rows in set (0.00 sec)
```

Your relevance scores may not match the examples, as MySQL occasionally makes changes to the weighting scheme.

The relevance calculation is quite intelligent. It is based on the number of words in the index field of the row, the number of unique words in that row, the total number of words in the result, the number of records that contain the particular word, and the weight of the word. Rare words are weighted more heavily, and the more records that contain the word, the less its weight.

MySQL can return the relevance as well as the required fields at no extra cost in time because the two calls to the MATCH() function are identical:

```
mysql> SELECT f1,(MATCH(f1) AGAINST ('Master')) FROM ft2
  WHERE MATCH(f1) AGAINST ('Master');
+------------------------+-------------------------------+
| f1                     | (MATCH(f1) AGAINST ('Master')) |
+------------------------+-------------------------------+
| Master Master          |                1.238520026207 |
| The Master of Petersburg |              1.2245972156525 |
+------------------------+-------------------------------+
```

## BOOLEAN FULL-TEXT SEARCHES

One of MySQL 4's most useful enhancements is the ability to perform a Boolean full-text search. This makes use of a full set of features to search for words, combinations of words, portions of words, and so on (see Table 4.1).

**TABLE 4.1:** BOOLEAN SEARCH OPERATORS

| OPERATOR | DESCRIPTION |
| --- | --- |
| + | The word following is mandatory and must be present in every row returned. |
| – | The word following is prohibited and must not be present in any row returned. |
| < | The word following has a lower relevance than other words. |
| > | The word following has a higher relevance than other words. |
| ( ) | Used to group words in subexpressions. |
| ~ | The word following makes a negative contribution to the row relevance (this is not the same as the – operator, which excludes the row altogether if the word is found, or as the < operator, which still assigns a positive, though lower, relevance to the word). |
| * | The wildcard, indicating zero or more characters. It can only appear on the end of a word. |
| " | Anything enclosed in double quotes is taken as a whole. |

Boolean full-text searches do not take the 50-percent threshold limit into account. To perform a Boolean full-text search, you use the IN BOOLEAN MODE clause:

```
mysql> SELECT * FROM ft2 WHERE MATCH(f1) AGAINST
  ('+Master -Petersburg' IN BOOLEAN MODE);
+---------------+
| f1            |
+---------------+
| Master Master |
+---------------+
1 row in set (0.00 sec)
```

In this example, the word *Petersburg* is excluded, so *The Master of Petersburg* is not returned even though *Master* appears in the title.

Note the difference between these two sets of results:

```
mysql> SELECT * FROM ft2 WHERE MATCH(f1) AGAINST
  ('Country Master' IN BOOLEAN MODE);
+----------------------------+
| f1                         |
+----------------------------+
| In the Heart of the Country |
| The Master of Petersburg   |
| Master Master              |
+----------------------------+
3 rows in set (0.00 sec)
mysql> SELECT * FROM ft2 WHERE MATCH(f1) AGAINST
  ('+Country Master' IN BOOLEAN MODE);
+----------------------------+
| f1                         |
+----------------------------+
| In the Heart of the Country |
+----------------------------+
1 row in set (0.00 sec)
```

The word *Country* is mandatory in the second search (by default a word is optional), so *The Master of Petersburg* and *Master Master* are not returned.

The next example demonstrates a common cause of confusion:

```
mysql> SELECT * FROM ft2 WHERE MATCH(f1) AGAINST
  ('+Dog Master' IN BOOLEAN MODE);
+-------------------------+
| f1                      |
+-------------------------+
| The Master of Petersburg |
| Master Master           |
+-------------------------+
2 rows in set (0.00 sec)
```

This result may seem surprising if you compare it to the previous example, but because the word *Dog* is three or fewer letters, it is excluded for purposes of the search.

The next two examples demonstrate the difference between searching for a whole word and a part of a word (making use of the * operator):

```
mysql> SELECT * FROM ft2 WHERE MATCH(f1) AGAINST
  ('Barbarian' IN BOOLEAN MODE);
+-----------------------+
| f1                    |
+-----------------------+
| A Barbarian at my Door |
+-----------------------+
1 row in set (0.00 sec)
mysql> SELECT * FROM ft2 WHERE MATCH(f1) AGAINST
  ('Barbarian*' IN BOOLEAN MODE);
+---------------------------+
| f1                        |
+---------------------------+
| A Barbarian at my Door    |
| Waiting for the Barbarians |
+---------------------------+
2 rows in set (0.01 sec)
```

By default only whole words are matched, unless the * operator is used.

The next three examples demonstrate the use of the > and < operators to increase and decrease the weightings respectively:

```
mysql> SELECT f1,MATCH(f1) AGAINST ('Heart Beest Beast'
  IN BOOLEAN MODE) AS m FROM ft2 WHERE MATCH(f1)
  AGAINST ('Heart Beest Beast' IN BOOLEAN MODE);
+--------------------------+------+
| f1                       | m    |
+--------------------------+------+
| In the Heart of the Country |   1 |
| Heart of the Beast       |    2 |
| Heart of the Beest       |    2 |
+--------------------------+------+
3 rows in set (0.00 sec)
mysql> SELECT f1,MATCH(f1) AGAINST ('Heart Beest >Beast'
  IN BOOLEAN MODE) AS m FROM ft2 WHERE MATCH(f1)
  AGAINST ('Heart Beest >Beast' IN BOOLEAN MODE);
+--------------------------+------+
| f1                       | m    |
+--------------------------+------+
| In the Heart of the Country |   1 |
| Heart of the Beast       |  2.5 |
| Heart of the Beest       |    2 |
+--------------------------+------+
3 rows in set (0.00 sec)
```

The > operator increases the relevance of *Heart of the Beast*.

```
mysql> SELECT f1,MATCH(f1) AGAINST ('Heart <Beest Beast'
 IN BOOLEAN MODE) As m FROM ft2 WHERE MATCH(f1)
 AGAINST ('Heart <Beest Beast' IN BOOLEAN MODE);
+-------------------------------+-----------------+
| f1                            | m               |
+-------------------------------+-----------------+
| In the Heart of the Country   |               1 |
| Heart of the Beast            |               2 |
| Heart of the Beest            | 1.6666667461395 |
+-------------------------------+-----------------+
3 rows in set (0.00 sec)
```

The < operator decreases the relevance of *Heart of the Beest*.

The next five examples demonstrate the difference between the < operator, which adds a decreased, yet positive, weight to the match; the ~ operator, which places a negative weight on the match; and the - operator, which prohibits the match. The first example is a basic Boolean search, with a weighting of 1 for a match:

```
mysql> SELECT *,MATCH(f1) AGAINST ('Door' IN BOOLEAN MODE)
    AS m FROM ft2 WHERE MATCH(f1) AGAINST ('Door' IN BOOLEAN MODE);
+-----------------------+------+
| f1                    | m    |
+-----------------------+------+
| A Barbarian at my Door |    1 |
+-----------------------+------+
1 row in set (0.00 sec)
```

Next, the < operator reduces this weighting to roughly 2/3, which is still a positive weight:

```
mysql> SELECT *,MATCH(f1) AGAINST ('<Door' IN BOOLEAN MODE)
    AS m FROM ft2 WHERE MATCH(f1) AGAINST ('<Door' IN BOOLEAN MODE);
+-----------------------+------------------+
| f1                    | m                |
+-----------------------+------------------+
| A Barbarian at my Door | 0.66666668653488 |
+-----------------------+------------------+
1 row in set (0.00 sec)
```

The ~ operator reduces this weight to a negative, and so, since the result is less than 0 when matched with *A Barbarian at my Door*, the row is not returned:

```
mysql> SELECT *,MATCH(f1) AGAINST ('~Door' IN BOOLEAN MODE)
    AS m FROM ft2 WHERE MATCH(f1) AGAINST ('~Door' IN BOOLEAN MODE);
Empty set (0.00 sec)
```

Using the ~ operator in conjunction with an ordinary match allows us to see how much the weighting is reduced by, which in this case is 0.5:

```
mysql> SELECT *,MATCH(f1) AGAINST ('~Door Barbarian*' IN BOOLEAN MODE)
    AS m FROM ft2 WHERE MATCH(f1) AGAINST ('~Door Barbarian*' IN BOOLEAN MODE);
```

```
+---------------------------+------+
| f1                        | m    |
+---------------------------+------+
| A Barbarian at my Door    | 0.5  |
| Waiting for the  Barbarians | 1  |
+---------------------------+------+
2 rows in set (0.01 sec)
```

Finally, this next example shows the difference between the ~ and - operators, where the - operator prohibits the match when *Door* is found:

```
mysql> SELECT *,MATCH(f1) AGAINST ('-Door Barbarian*' IN BOOLEAN MODE)
    AS m FROM ft2 WHERE MATCH(f1) AGAINST ('-Door Barbarian*' IN BOOLEAN MODE);
+---------------------------+------+
| f1                        | m    |
+---------------------------+------+
| Waiting for the  Barbarians | 1  |
+---------------------------+------+
1 row in set (0.00 sec)
```

The next example demonstrates grouping words into a sub-expression:

```
mysql> SELECT f1,MATCH(f1) AGAINST ('+Heart +(<Beest >Beast)'
 IN BOOLEAN MODE) As m FROM ft2 WHERE MATCH(f1)
 AGAINST ('+Heart +(<Beest >Beast)' IN BOOLEAN MODE);
+--------------------+------------------+
| f1                 | m                |
+--------------------+------------------+
| Heart of the Beast |             1.25 |
| Heart of the Beest | 0.83333337306976 |
+--------------------+------------------+
2 rows in set (0.00 sec)
```

The + operator applies to the entire substring in parentheses, which means that at least one of *Beest* and *Beast* must be present in the string. *In the Heart of the Country* does not appear then, because neither *Beest* nor *Beast* is present. Compare this to the following code:

The next example demonstrates a commonly used form of the search, where each of the supplied words is mandatory:

```
mysql> SELECT f1,MATCH(f1) AGAINST ('+Heart +<Beest +>Beast)' IN BOOLEAN MODE)
AS m FROM ft2 WHERE MATCH(f1) AGAINST ('+Heart +<Beest +>Beast)' IN BOOLEAN MODE);
Empty set (0.00 sec)
```

Nothing is returned because no rows contain all of Heart, Beest, and Beast at the same time.

The next two examples demonstrate the difference between a search using the " " operators and one without them. The " " operators allow you to search for an exact match on a phrase:

```
mysql> SELECT * FROM ft2 WHERE MATCH(f1)
  AGAINST ('the Heart of the' IN BOOLEAN MODE);
```

```
+----------------------------+
| f1                         |
+----------------------------+
| In the Heart of the Country |
| Heart of the Beast         |
| Heart of the Beest         |
+----------------------------+
3 rows in set (0.01 sec)

mysql> SELECT * FROM ft2 WHERE MATCH(f1)
  AGAINST ('"the Heart of the"' IN BOOLEAN MODE);
+----------------------------+
| f1                         |
+----------------------------+
| In the Heart of the Country |
+----------------------------+
1 row in set (0.00 sec)
```

Be careful not to leave out the initial single quotes when making use of the double quote operator. If you do, you'll effectively have no operators. For example:

```
mysql> SELECT * FROM ft2 WHERE MATCH(f1)
  AGAINST ("the Heart of the" IN BOOLEAN MODE);
+----------------------------+
| f1                         |
+----------------------------+
| In the Heart of the Country |
| Heart of the Beast         |
| Heart of the Beest         |
+----------------------------+
3 rows in set (0.00 sec)
```

**WARNING**   *Full-text indexes can take a long time to generate and cause* OPTIMIZE *statements to take a long time as well.*

## Creating a Unique Index

A *unique index* is the same as an ordinary index, except that no duplicates are allowed.

To create a unique index when the table is created, use the following syntax:

```
CREATE TABLE tablename (fieldname columntype, fieldname2
    columntype, UNIQUE(fieldname [,fieldname2...]));
```

Or, if the table already exists, you can use either this syntax:

```
ALTER TABLE tablename ADD UNIQUE [indexname ] (fieldname [,fieldname2...]);
```

or this syntax:

```
CREATE UNIQUE INDEX indexname ON tablename(fieldname [,fieldname2...]);
```

If the index contains a single field, that field cannot contain duplicate values:

```
mysql> CREATE TABLE ui_test(f1 INT,f2 INT,UNIQUE(f1));
Query OK, 0 rows affected (0.00 sec)
mysql> INSERT INTO ui_test VALUES(1,2);
Query OK, 1 row affected (0.01 sec)
mysql> INSERT INTO ui_test VALUES(1,3);
ERROR 1062: Duplicate entry '1' for key 1
```

Although the field f1 was not specified as UNIQUE when it was created, the existence of the unique index prevents any duplication. If the index contains more than one field, individual field values can be duplicated, but the combination of field values making up the entire index cannot be duplicated:

```
mysql> CREATE TABLE ui_test2(f1 INT,f2 INT,UNIQUE(f1,f2));
Query OK, 0 rows affected (0.00 sec)
mysql> INSERT INTO ui_test2 VALUES(1,2);
Query OK, 1 row affected (0.00 sec)
mysql> INSERT INTO ui_test2 VALUES(1,3);
Query OK, 1 row affected (0.00 sec)
mysql> INSERT INTO ui_test2 VALUES(1,3);
ERROR 1062: Duplicate entry '1-3' for key 1
```

## Creating Indexes from Part of a Field

For VARCHAR, CHAR, BLOB, and TEXT columns, MySQL allows you to create an index that does not use the entire field. For example, although the customer surname may be up to 40 characters, it's likely that the surname will differ in the first 10 characters. By only using the first 10 characters for the index, the index will be a lot smaller. This makes updates and inserts quicker (you're writing one quarter what you would have if you'd used the full column after all), and it won't affect SELECT speed as long as you don't cut the index too short. Making a one-character index for the surname would defeat the purpose of an index.

To create an index from part of a field, just put the size in parentheses after the column name. For example, to create a 10-character index on the surname field in the customer table, use the following code:

```
mysql> ALTER TABLE customer ADD INDEX (surname(10));
Query OK, 8 rows affected (0.00 sec)
Records: 8  Duplicates: 0  Warnings: 0
```

**NOTE**  *You cannot create an index (except for a full-text index) on an entire BLOB or TEXT field, so in this case you'd have to specify the index size.*

## Using an Auto Increment Field

An auto increment field is a useful feature that allows the value of a field to be automatically incremented each time a new record is inserted. Only one field in a record can be auto incremented, and this field must be a numeric primary key or a numeric unique index.

### Creating an Auto Increment Field

The syntax to create an auto increment field when creating a new table is:

```
CREATE TABLE tablename(fieldname INT AUTO_INCREMENT, [fieldname2...,]
    PRIMARY KEY(fieldname));
Query OK, 0 rows affected (0.00 sec)
```

To create an auto increment field in an already existing table, use this syntax:

```
ALTER TABLE tablename MODIFY fieldname columntype AUTO_INCREMENT;
Query OK, 0 rows affected (0.00 sec)
```

The customer table has an ideal candidate for an auto increment field, the id field:

```
mysql> SHOW COLUMNS FROM customer;
+------------+-------------+------+-----+---------+-------+
| Field      | Type        | Null | Key | Default | Extra |
+------------+-------------+------+-----+---------+-------+
| id         | int(11)     |      | PRI | 0       |       |
| first_name | varchar(30) | YES  |     | NULL    |       |
| surname    | varchar(40) | YES  | MUL | NULL    |       |
+------------+-------------+------+-----+---------+-------+
3 rows in set (0.00 sec)
```

The id field is a numeric field that is already a primary key, and because you've been assigning the id in sequence to date, turning the id into an auto increment field will allow MySQL to automate this process for you. The following code makes the id field auto increment:

```
mysql> ALTER TABLE customer MODIFY id INT AUTO_INCREMENT;
Query OK, 7 rows affected (0.01 sec)
Records: 7  Duplicates: 0  Warnings: 0
mysql> SHOW COLUMNS FROM customer;
+------------+-------------+------+-----+---------+----------------+
| Field      | Type        | Null | Key | Default | Extra          |
+------------+-------------+------+-----+---------+----------------+
| id         | int(11)     |      | PRI | NULL    | auto_increment |
| first_name | varchar(30) | YES  |     | NULL    |                |
| surname    | varchar(40) | YES  | MUL | NULL    |                |
+------------+-------------+------+-----+---------+----------------+
3 rows in set (0.00 sec)
```

## Inserting Records Containing an Auto Increment Field

Now, if you add a record, you don't need to specify the value of the id; MySQL will automatically add the next highest value:

```
mysql> SELECT * FROM customer;
+----+------------+-------------+
| id | first_name | surname     |
+----+------------+-------------+
|  1 | Yvonne     | Clegg       |
|  2 | Johnny     | Chaka-Chaka |
|  3 | Winston    | Powers      |
|  4 | Patricia   | Mankunku    |
|  5 | Francois   | Papo        |
|  7 | Winnie     | Dlamini     |
|  6 | Neil       | Beneke      |
+----+------------+-------------+
7 rows in set (0.00 sec)

mysql> INSERT INTO customer(first_name,surname) VALUES('Breyton','Tshbalala');
Query OK, 1 row affected (0.00 sec)
mysql> SELECT * FROM customer;
+----+------------+-------------+
| id | first_name | surname     |
+----+------------+-------------+
|  1 | Yvonne     | Clegg       |
|  2 | Johnny     | Chaka-Chaka |
|  3 | Winston    | Powers      |
|  4 | Patricia   | Mankunku    |
|  5 | Francois   | Papo        |
|  7 | Winnie     | Dlamini     |
|  6 | Neil       | Beneke      |
|  8 | Breyton    | Tshbalala   |
+----+------------+-------------+
8 rows in set (0.00 sec)
```

An important feature is that MySQL's auto increment counter remembers the most recently added number, even if this record is deleted. This ensures that the newly inserted record has a new id value and does not clash with any records related to the old entry:

```
mysql> DELETE FROM customer WHERE id=8;
Query OK, 1 row affected (0.00 sec)
mysql> INSERT INTO customer(first_name,surname)
    VALUES('Breyton','Tshbalala');
Query OK, 1 row affected (0.00 sec)
mysql> SELECT * FROM customer;
```

```
+----+------------+-------------+
| id | first_name | surname     |
+----+------------+-------------+
|  1 | Yvonne     | Clegg       |
|  2 | Johnny     | Chaka-Chaka |
|  3 | Winston    | Powers      |
|  4 | Patricia   | Mankunku    |
|  5 | Francois   | Papo        |
|  7 | Winnie     | Dlamini     |
|  6 | Neil       | Beneke      |
|  9 | Breyton    | Tshbalala   |
+----+------------+-------------+
8 rows in set (0.01 sec)
```

The id is now 9. Even though the next highest remaining record is 7, the most recently inserted value was 8.

## Returning and Resetting the Auto Increment Value

You can return the most recently inserted auto increment value with the LAST_INSERT_ID() function:

```
mysql> SELECT LAST_INSERT_ID() FROM customer LIMIT 1;
+------------------+
| last_insert_id() |
+------------------+
|                9 |
+------------------+
1 row in set (0.00 sec)
```

This can be useful for updates where you need to create a new auto increment value. For example, the following code finds the most recently inserted auto increment value, and adds 1 to it in order to set a new id value for Breyton Tshbalala:

```
mysql> UPDATE customer set id=LAST_INSERT_ID()+1 WHERE
  first_name='Breyton' AND surname='Tshbalala';
Query OK, 1 row affected (0.01 sec)
Rows matched: 1  Changed: 1  Warnings: 0
mysql> SELECT * FROM customer;
+----+------------+-------------+
| id | first_name | surname     |
+----+------------+-------------+
|  1 | Yvonne     | Clegg       |
|  2 | Johnny     | Chaka-Chaka |
|  3 | Winston    | Powers      |
|  4 | Patricia   | Mankunku    |
|  5 | Francois   | Papo        |
|  7 | Winnie     | Dlamini     |
|  6 | Neil       | Beneke      |
| 10 | Breyton    | Tshbalala   |
+----+------------+-------------+
8 rows in set (0.00 sec)
```

*WARNING*   LAST_INSERT_ID() *has problems when you reset the auto increment counter. See the "Problems with* LAST_INSERT_ID()*" section later in this chapter.*

If you want to reset the auto increment counter to start at a particular value, such as back to 1 after you've deleted all the records, you can use this:

```
ALTER TABLE tablename AUTO_INCREMENT=auto_inc_value;
```

Let's create a test to examine the behavior:

```
mysql> CREATE TABLE ai_test(id INT NOT NULL AUTO_INCREMENT,
 f1 VARCHAR(10),PRIMARY KEY (id));
Query OK, 0 rows affected (0.00 sec)
mysql> INSERT INTO ai_test(f1) VALUES('one'),('two');
Query OK, 2 rows affected (0.00 sec)
Records: 2  Duplicates: 0  Warnings: 0
mysql> SELECT * FROM ai_test;
+----+------+
| id | f1   |
+----+------+
|  1 | one  |
|  2 | two  |
+----+------+
2 rows in set (0.00 sec)
mysql> DELETE FROM ai_test;
Query OK, 2 rows affected (0.00 sec)
mysql> INSERT INTO ai_test(f1) VALUES('three');
Query OK, 1 row affected (0.01 sec)
mysql> SELECT * FROM ai_test;
+----+-------+
| id | f1    |
+----+-------+
|  3 | three |
+----+-------+
1 row in set (0.00 sec)
```

The auto increment counter has maintained its value, even though the table has been emptied. You can use TRUNCATE to clear the table, and this will reset the auto increment counter:

```
mysql> DELETE FROM ai_test;
Query OK, 1 row affected (0.00 sec)
mysql> ALTER TABLE ai_test AUTO_INCREMENT=1;
Query OK, 0 rows affected (0.01 sec)
Records: 0  Duplicates: 0  Warnings: 0
```

This statement has specifically reset the auto increment counter to 1:

```
mysql> INSERT INTO ai_test(f1) VALUES('four');
Query OK, 1 row affected (0.00 sec)
```

```
mysql> SELECT * FROM ai_test;
+----+------+
| id | f1   |
+----+------+
|  1 | four |
+----+------+
1 row in set (0.00 sec)
mysql> TRUNCATE ai_test;
Query OK, 0 rows affected (0.00 sec)
mysql> INSERT INTO ai_test(f1) VALUES('five');
Query OK, 1 row affected (0.01 sec)
mysql> SELECT * FROM ai_test;
+----+------+
| id | f1   |
+----+------+
|  1 | five |
+----+------+
1 row in set (0.00 sec)
```

By using TRUNCATE rather than DELETE, the auto increment counter is reset.

**WARNING**  *Currently, this only works with MyISAM tables. You'll need to manually set the auto increment counter with the other table types.*

Setting the auto increment value to something besides 1 is also easy. You can set it when the table is created, for example:

```
mysql> CREATE TABLE ai_test2(id INT NOT NULL AUTO_INCREMENT,
 f1 VARCHAR(5),PRIMARY KEY(id)) AUTO_INCREMENT=50;
Query OK, 0 rows affected (0.00 sec)
mysql> INSERT INTO ai_test2(f1) VALUES('one');
Query OK, 1 row affected (0.00 sec)
mysql> SELECT * FROM ai_test2;
+----+------+
| id | f1   |
+----+------+
| 50 | one  |
+----+------+
1 row in set (0.00 sec)
```

Or you can set the counter once the table is in existence:

```
mysql> DELETE FROM ai_test;
Query OK, 3 rows affected (0.00 sec)
mysql> ALTER TABLE ai_test AUTO_INCREMENT=1000;
Query OK, 0 rows affected (0.00 sec)
Records: 0  Duplicates: 0  Warnings: 0
```

```
mysql> INSERT INTO ai_test(f1) VALUES('one');
Query OK, 1 row affected (0.00 sec)
mysql> SELECT * FROM ai_test;
+------+------+
| id   | f1   |
+------+------+
| 1000 | one  |
+------+------+
1 row in set (0.01 sec)
```

In most cases you'd use this feature when the table is emptied, but this is not necessary; you can reset the counter even while there are records in the table:

```
mysql> ALTER TABLE ai_test2 AUTO_INCREMENT=500;
Query OK, 1 row affected (0.01 sec)
Records: 1  Duplicates: 0  Warnings: 0
mysql> INSERT INTO ai_test2(f1) VALUES('two');
Query OK, 1 row affected (0.01 sec)
mysql> SELECT * FROM ai_test2;
+-----+------+
| id  | f1   |
+-----+------+
|  50 | one  |
| 500 | two  |
+-----+------+
2 rows in set (0.00 sec)
```

**NOTE**  *Currently this too only works for MyISAM tables. You cannot set the auto increment counter to anything except 1 with an InnoDB table, for example.*

The previous examples have inserted records without specifying the id field. If you prefer to use an alternative syntax where the value for the auto increment field is specified, make the value of the auto incremented field either NULL or 0:

```
mysql> INSERT INTO ai_test VALUES(NULL,'two');
Query OK, 1 row affected (0.01 sec)
mysql> INSERT INTO ai_test VALUES(0,'three');
Query OK, 1 row affected (0.00 sec)
mysql> SELECT * FROM ai_test;
+------+-------+
| id   | f1    |
+------+-------+
| 1000 | one   |
| 1001 | two   |
| 1002 | three |
+------+-------+
3 rows in set (0.00 sec)
```

## Going Out of Bounds

Note that the auto increment counter can only be a positive number, even though the field it is attached to is a signed field. If you try to set it to a negative number, you'll run into strange problems:

```
mysql> ALTER TABLE ai_test2 AUTO_INCREMENT=-500;
Query OK, 2 rows affected (0.01 sec)
Records: 2  Duplicates: 0  Warnings: 0
mysql> INSERT INTO ai_test2(f1) VALUES('three');
Query OK, 1 row affected (0.00 sec)
mysql> SELECT * FROM ai_test2;
+------------+-------+
| id         | f1    |
+------------+-------+
|         50 | one   |
|        500 | two   |
| 2147483647 | three |
+------------+-------+
3 rows in set (0.00 sec)
```

Because the −500 was outside the positive range of values permissible for an auto increment, MySQL has set it to the maximum allowed for an INT: 2147483647. If you try to add another record, you'll get a duplicate key error because MySQL cannot make an INT value any higher:

```
mysql> INSERT INTO ai_test2(f1) VALUES('four');
ERROR 1062: Duplicate entry '2147483647' for key 1
```

**WARNING**    *Be careful to ensure that you always have enough space for your records. If you create an auto increment on a* SIGNED TINYINT *field, once you hit 127 you'll start getting duplicate key errors.*

## Problems with *LAST_INSERT_ID()*

The LAST_INSERT_ID() function has a number of features that could cause problems when using it:

◆ The value returned by LAST_INSERT_ID() is not reset to the same value to which you reset the auto increment counter. Instead, it returns to 1.

◆ The number is maintained on a per-connection basis, so if new inserts are added from another connection, the number returned by this function will not be updated.

The following are some examples:

```
mysql> SELECT * FROM ai_test2;
+------------+-------+
| id         | f1    |
+------------+-------+
|         50 | one   |
|        500 | two   |
| 2147483647 | three |
+------------+-------+
3 rows in set (0.00 sec)
```

```
mysql> ALTER TABLE ai_test2 AUTO_INCREMENT=501;
Query OK, 3 rows affected (0.00 sec)
Records: 3  Duplicates: 0  Warnings: 0
mysql> UPDATE ai_test2 SET id=LAST_INSERT_ID()+1 WHERE f1='three';
Query OK, 1 row affected (0.00 sec)
Rows matched: 1  Changed: 1  Warnings: 0
```

Here you would expect the id to have a value of 501. However, you'd receive a rude shock! Look at the following:

```
mysql> SELECT * FROM ai_test2;
+-----+-------+
| id  | f1    |
+-----+-------+
|  50 | one   |
| 500 | two   |
|   1 | three |
+-----+-------+
3 rows in set (0.00 sec)
```

The LAST_INSERT_ID has reset to 1 when you reset the auto increment counter. Even worse follows if you try it again:

```
mysql> ALTER TABLE ai_test2 AUTO_INCREMENT=501;
Query OK, 3 rows affected (0.01 sec)
Records: 3  Duplicates: 0  Warnings: 0
mysql> UPDATE ai_test2 SET id=LAST_INSERT_ID()+1 WHERE f1='two';
ERROR 1062: Duplicate entry '1' for key 1
```

Now you have a duplicate key, and the UPDATE fails. The other error occurs when multiple connections are made. Open two windows to get two connections to the database.

From Window1:

```
mysql> TRUNCATE ai_test2;
Query OK, 0 rows affected (0.01 sec)
mysql> INSERT INTO ai_test2(f1) VALUES('one');
Query OK, 1 row affected (0.00 sec)
mysql> SELECT * FROM ai_test2;
+----+------+
| id | f1   |
+----+------+
|  1 | one  |
+----+------+
1 row in set (0.01 sec)
mysql> SELECT LAST_INSERT_ID() FROM ai_test2;
+------------------+
| last_insert_id() |
+------------------+
|                1 |
+------------------+
1 row in set (0.00 sec)
```

So far, so good. Now go to the second window, and insert another record. From Window2:

```
mysql> INSERT INTO ai_test2(f1) VALUES('two');
Query OK, 1 row affected (0.00 sec)
Window1:
mysql> SELECT LAST_INSERT_ID() FROM ai_test2;
+------------------+
| last_insert_id() |
+------------------+
|                1 |
|                1 |
+------------------+
2 rows in set (0.00 sec)
```

The value returned is still 1, when it should be 2. So now if you try and use the value for an update, you'll get the familiar duplicate key error:

```
mysql> UPDATE ai_test2 SET id=LAST_INSERT_ID()+1 WHERE f1='one';
ERROR 1062: Duplicate entry '2' for key 1
```

## Multicolumn Indexes and Auto Increment Fields

With MyISAM and BDB tables, you can also make the second index field of a multicolumn index be an auto increment field. This is mainly useful when you're creating groupings of data. For this example, you're going to create a table for staff, where staff can be ranked according to whether they are a manager, an employee, or a contractor and then assigned a specific position on top of that:

```
mysql> CREATE TABLE staff(rank ENUM('Employee','Manager',
  'Contractor') NOT NULL,position VARCHAR(100),
  id INT NOT NULL AUTO_INCREMENT,PRIMARY KEY(rank,id));
Query OK, 0 rows affected (0.00 sec)
mysql> INSERT INTO staff(rank,position) VALUES
  ('Employee','Cleaner'),
  ('Contractor','Network maintenance'),
  ('Manager','Sales manager');
Query OK, 3 rows affected (0.01 sec)
mysql> SELECT * FROM staff;
+------------+---------------------+----+
| rank       | position            | id |
+------------+---------------------+----+
| Employee   | Cleaner             |  1 |
| Contractor | Network maintenance |  1 |
| Manager    | Sales manager       |  1 |
+------------+---------------------+----+
3 rows in set (0.00 sec)
```

All three records have the same id value, as the primary key consists of two fields: rank and id. Once you start adding other records to each rank, you'll see the familiar incremental behavior:

```
mysql> INSERT INTO staff(rank,position) VALUES
  ('Employee','Security guard'),
```

```
 ('Employee', 'Receptionist'),
 ('Manager','Head of security');
Query OK, 3 rows affected (0.00 sec)
Records: 3  Duplicates: 0  Warnings: 0
mysql> SELECT * FROM staff;
+------------+---------------------+----+
| rank       | position            | id |
+------------+---------------------+----+
| Employee   | Cleaner             |  1 |
| Contractor | Network maintenance |  1 |
| Manager    | Sales manager       |  1 |
| Employee   | Security guard      |  2 |
| Employee   | Receptionist        |  3 |
| Manager    | Head of security    |  2 |
+------------+---------------------+----+
6 rows in set (0.01 sec)
```

In this example, you have an employee 1, 2, and 3; a manager 1 and 2; and a contractor 1. The auto increment counter is maintained correctly for each group.

In this situation you cannot, however, reset the auto increment counter:

```
mysql> ALTER TABLE staff AUTO_INCREMENT=500;
Query OK, 6 rows affected (0.01 sec)
Records: 6  Duplicates: 0  Warnings: 0

mysql> INSERT INTO staff(rank,position) VALUES
  ('Employee','Stationary administrator'),
  ('Manager','Personnel manager'),
  ('Contractor','Programmer');
Query OK, 3 rows affected (0.01 sec)
Records: 3  Duplicates: 0  Warnings: 0
mysql> SELECT * FROM staff;
+------------+--------------------------+----+
| rank       | position                 | id |
+------------+--------------------------+----+
| Employee   | Cleaner                  |  1 |
| Contractor | Network maintenance      |  1 |
| Manager    | Sales manager            |  1 |
| Employee   | Security guard           |  2 |
| Employee   | Receptionist             |  3 |
| Manager    | Head of security         |  2 |
| Employee   | Stationary administrator |  4 |
| Manager    | Personnel manager        |  3 |
| Contractor | Programmer               |  2 |
+------------+--------------------------+----+
9 rows in set (0.00 sec)
```

The auto increments continue from where they left off, regardless of the ALTER statement.

## Dropping or Changing an Index

Sometimes, indexes outlive their usefulness, and they need to be changed or dropped (removed). When making any change to an index, you'll need to drop the index first and then rebuild it with the new definition.

To drop a primary key, use this syntax:

```
ALTER TABLE tablename DROP PRIMARY KEY;
```

To drop an ordinary, unique, or full-text index, you need to specify the index name, like this:

```
ALTER TABLE tablename DROP INDEX indexname;
```

or like this:

```
DROP INDEX indexname ON tablename;
```

If you're not sure what the index name is, SHOW KEYS will reveal all:

```
SHOW KEYS FROM tablename;
```

## Understanding Table Types and Indexes

Each table type has its own behavior when it comes to indexes, and each will handle them differently. Not all index types are available to each table type. It's important to understand how you're going to be using a table, and therefore what indexes you may require, before you commit to a table type. Sometimes what looks like an ideal table type turns out to be no good because a certain type of index is not available. The following lists highlight features and differences of indexes for each table type.

MyISAM tables have the following attributes:

◆ Indexes are stored in files with the extension .MYI.

◆ Number indexes are stored with the high byte first to allow better compression of the index.

◆ BLOB and TEXT indexes can exist.

◆ Null values are permissible in indexes (not primary keys).

◆ The data and the index can be in different directories (which allows greater speed).

MERGE tables have the following attributes:

◆ A MERGE table contains no indexes of its own.

◆ The .MRG file contains a list of the .MYI index files from the component MyISAM tables.

◆ You still need to specify indexes when you create a MERGE table.

HEAP tables have the following attributes:

◆ Use a hash index stored in memory, which is very fast.

◆ Can only use indexes with the = and <=> operators.

◆ Cannot use an index on a column that allows NULL values.

◆ Indexes are not used with an ORDER BY clause.

◆ MySQL cannot find out approximately how many rows there are between two values (this result is used by the query optimizer to decide which index is most efficient to use). See the "Helping MySQL's Query Optimizer with ANALYZE" section later in this chapter for more on this.

ISAM tables use a B-Tree index stored in files with an extension of .ism.
InnoDB tables cannot use full-text indexes.

## Using Indexes Effectively

Tables with too few indexes will return results very slowly. But adding too many indexes, although less common, is still problematic. They take up disk space. And, because an index is sorted, each time an insert or an update is performed, the index has to be re-sorted to include the changes, resulting in a significant extra load. The following sections explain when you should and shouldn't use indexes. Also note that index efficiency is dependent on the configuration; see Chapter 13, "Configuring and Optimizing MySQL," for more on this.

### Where Are Indexes Used?

The most common use of an index is to retrieve rows that match a condition in a WHERE clause:

```
mysql> SELECT first_name FROM customer WHERE surname>'C';
+------------+
| first_name |
+------------+
| Yvonne     |
| Johnny     |
| Winston    |
| Patricia   |
| Francois   |
| Winnie     |
| Breyton    |
+------------+
7 rows in set (0.00 sec)
```

An index on the surname field would be useful in this example. An index on the first_name field would not be used in this query, as it is not part of the condition. Any fields appearing only in the field list (immediately after the SELECT) do not make use of an index.

When searching for the MAX() or MIN() values, MySQL only needs to look at the first or last value in the sorted index table, which is extremely quick. If there are frequent requests for MAX() or MIN() values, an index on the appropriate field would be extremely useful.

```
mysql> SELECT MAX(id) FROM customer;
+---------+
| MAX(id) |
+---------+
|      10 |
+---------+
```

An index on the id field would assist this query tremendously.

There's another case where MySQL never needs to look at the full table and can just look at the index: when all the fields to be returned are part of an index. Take this example:

```
mysql> SELECT id FROM customer;
+----+
| id |
+----+
|  1 |
|  2 |
|  3 |
|  4 |
|  5 |
|  6 |
|  7 |
| 10 |
+----+
8 rows in set (0.01 sec)
```

If the id field were indexed here, MySQL would never even need to look at the data file. This would not apply if the index consisted only of a portion of the full column data (for example, the field is a VARCHAR of 20 characters, but the index was created on the first 10 characters only).

Another case where an index is useful is where you ORDER BY a field, as with this example:

```
mysql> SELECT * FROM customer ORDER BY surname;
+----+------------+-------------+
| id | first_name | surname     |
+----+------------+-------------+
|  6 | Neil       | Beneke      |
|  2 | Johnny     | Chaka-Chaka |
|  1 | Yvonne     | Clegg       |
|  7 | Winnie     | Dlamini     |
|  4 | Patricia   | Mankunku    |
|  5 | Francois   | Papo        |
|  3 | Winston    | Powers      |
| 10 | Breyton    | Tshbalala   |
+----+------------+-------------+
8 rows in set (0.01 sec)
```

Because the records are returned in sorted order, which is exactly what an index is, an index on the surname field would be useful for this query. If the ORDER BY is DESC, the index is simply read in reverse order.

**WARNING**    *Currently, indexes cannot be used in ORDER BY clauses with HEAP tables.*

Indexes are employed to speed up joins as well, as in this example:

```
mysql> SELECT first_name,surname,commission FROM sales,sales_rep
    WHERE code=8 AND sales.sales_rep=sales_rep.employee_number;
```

```
+------------+---------+------------+
| first_name | surname | commission |
+------------+---------+------------+
| Mike       | Serote  |         10 |
+------------+---------+------------+
1 row in set (0.00 sec)
```

An index would be used to perform the join condition—in other words, to look up both the sales.sales_rep and sales_rep.employee_number fields. This of course applies even if you use the alternative syntax:

```
mysql> SELECT first_name,surname,commission FROM sales INNER
    JOIN sales_rep ON sales.sales_rep=sales_rep.employee_number
    WHERE code=8;
+------------+---------+------------+
| first_name | surname | commission |
+------------+---------+------------+
| Mike       | Serote  |         10 |
+------------+---------+------------+
1 row in set (0.00 sec)
```

An index can be used when your query condition contains a wildcard, such as:

```
mysql> SELECT * FROM sales_rep WHERE surname LIKE 'Ser%';
+------------+---------+------------+
| first_name | surname | commission |
+------------+---------+------------+
| Mike       | Serote  |         10 |
+------------+---------+------------+
1 row in set (0.00 sec)
```

But an index cannot be used in the following case:

```
mysql> SELECT * FROM sales_rep WHERE surname LIKE '%Ser%';
+------------+---------+------------+
| first_name | surname | commission |
+------------+---------+------------+
| Mike       | Serote  |         10 |
+------------+---------+------------+
1 row in set (0.00 sec)
```

The difference is that the latter has a wildcard as the first character. Because the index is sorted alphabetically from the first character, the presence of the wildcard renders the index useless.

## Choosing Indexes

Now that you know where MySQL uses indexes, here are a few tips to help you with choosing indexes.

◆ It should go without saying that you should only create indexes where you have queries that will make use of them (on fields in your WHERE condition, for example), and not on fields where they will not be used (such as where the first character of the condition is a wildcard).

- Create indexes that return as few rows as possible. A primary key is the best here, as each primary key is uniquely associated with one record. Similarly, indexes on enumerated fields will not be particularly useful (for example, an index on a field containing the values *yes* or *no* would only serve to reduce the selection to half, with all the overhead of maintaining an index).

- Use short indexes (index only the first 10 characters of a name, for example, rather than the entire field).

- Don't create too many indexes. An index adds to the time to update or add a record, so if the index is for a rarely used query that can afford to run slightly more slowly, consider not creating the index.

- Make use of leftmost prefixing (see the next section).

## Using Leftmost Prefixes

You already know you can create an index on more than one field. Surnames and first names are good examples of this, so that, although there may be many duplicate surnames, the first name would make the index close to unique. In effect, there are two indexes available to MySQL here. The first is surname and first_name, and the second is just surname. Starting from the left of the list of fields in the index, MySQL can use each of these in turn, as long as they keep to the sequence starting from the left. Some examples will make this clearer. Let's add an initial field to the customer table and add some values, as well as an index:

```
mysql> ALTER TABLE customer ADD initial VARCHAR(5);
Query OK, 8 rows affected (0.01 sec)
Records: 8  Duplicates: 0  Warnings: 0
mysql> ALTER TABLE customer ADD INDEX (surname,initial, first_name);
Query OK, 8 rows affected (0.01 sec)
Records: 8  Duplicates: 0  Warnings: 0
mysql> UPDATE customer SET initial='X' WHERE id=1;
Query OK, 1 row affected (0.00 sec)
Rows matched: 1  Changed: 1  Warnings: 0
mysql> UPDATE customer SET initial='B' WHERE id=2;
Query OK, 1 row affected (0.00 sec)
Rows matched: 1  Changed: 1  Warnings: 0
mysql> UPDATE customer SET initial='M' WHERE id=3;
Query OK, 1 row affected (0.00 sec)
Rows matched: 1  Changed: 1  Warnings: 0
mysql> UPDATE customer SET initial='C' WHERE id=4;
Query OK, 1 row affected (0.00 sec)
Rows matched: 1  Changed: 1  Warnings: 0
mysql> UPDATE customer SET initial='P' WHERE id=5;
Query OK, 1 row affected (0.00 sec)
Rows matched: 1  Changed: 1  Warnings: 0
mysql> UPDATE customer SET initial='B' WHERE id=10;
Query OK, 1 row affected (0.01 sec)
Rows matched: 1  Changed: 1  Warnings: 0
```

If you performed a query with all three of these fields in the condition, you'd be making the most use of this index:

```
mysql> SELECT * FROM customer WHERE surname='Clegg' AND
 initial='X' AND first_name='Yvonne';
```

You would also make the most of the index if you searched for surname and initial:

```
mysql> SELECT * FROM customer WHERE surname='Clegg' AND initial='X';
```

or just surname:

```
mysql> SELECT * FROM customer WHERE surname='Clegg';
```

However, if you broke the leftmost sequence and searched for either first name or initial, or both first name and initial, MySQL would not use the index. For example, none of the following makes use of an index:

```
mysql> SELECT * FROM customer WHERE initial='X' AND first_name='Yvonne';
mysql> SELECT * FROM customer WHERE first_name='Yvonne';
mysql> SELECT * FROM customer WHERE initial='X';
```

If you searched on the first and third fields of the index (surname and first_name), you'd be breaking the sequence, so the index would not be fully used. However, because surname is the first part of the index, this portion of the index would still be used:

```
mysql> SELECT * FROM customer WHERE surname='Clegg' AND first_name='Yvonne';
+----+------------+---------+---------+
| id | first_name | surname | initial |
+----+------------+---------+---------+
|  1 | Yvonne     | Clegg   | X       |
+----+------------+---------+---------+
1 row in set (0.00 sec)
```

You can use leftmost prefixing whenever an index is used, such as with an ORDER BY clause.

## Analyzing How MySQL Uses Indexes with *EXPLAIN*

One of the best-kept secrets in MySQL is the EXPLAIN statement. Even people who've been using MySQL for years seem to have missed this statement, and it makes your life a lot easier!

EXPLAIN shows (explains!) how MySQL processes SELECT statements, uses indexes, and joins the tables. It can help you select better indexes and write your queries more optimally.

To use it, place it before a SELECT statement:

```
mysql> EXPLAIN SELECT surname,first_name FROM customer WHERE id=1;
+----------+-------+---------------+---------+---------+-------+------+-------+
| table    | type  | possible_keys | key     | key_len | ref   | rows | Extra |
+----------+-------+---------------+---------+---------+-------+------+-------+
| customer | const | PRIMARY       | PRIMARY |       4 | const |    1 |       |
+----------+-------+---------------+---------+---------+-------+------+-------+
1 row in set (0.00 sec)
```

So what do all these columns mean? See Table 4.2 for an explanation.

**TABLE 4.2:** WHAT THE EXPLAIN COLUMNS MEAN

| COLUMN | DESCRIPTION |
|---|---|
| table | Shows you which table the rest of the row is about (it's trivial in this example, but it's useful when you join more than one table in a query). |
| type | This is an important column, as it tells you which type of join is being used. From best to worst, the join types are system, const, eq_ref, ref, range, index, and ALL. |
| possible_keys | Shows which indexes could possibly apply to this table. If it's empty, there are no possible indexes. You could make one available by looking for a relevant field from the WHERE clause. |
| key | The index that was actually used. If this is NULL, then no index was used. Rarely, MySQL chooses a less optimal index. In this case, you could force the use of an index by employing **USE INDEX(indexname)** with your SELECT statement or force MySQL to ignore an index with **IGNORE INDEX(indexname)**. |
| key_len | The length of the index used. The shorter you can make this without losing accuracy, the better. |
| ref | Tells you which column of the index is used, or a constant if this is possible. |
| rows | Number of rows MySQL believes it must examine to be able to return the required data. |
| extra | Extra information about how MySQL will resolve the query. This is discussed more fully in Table 4.3, but the bad ones to see here are Using temporary and Using filesort, which mean that MySQL is unable to make much use of an index at all, and the results will be slow to retrieve. |

Table 4.3 looks at what the descriptions returned by the extra column mean.

**TABLE 4.3:** WHAT THE DESCRIPTIONS IN THE extra EXPLAIN COLUMN MEAN

| EXTRA COLUMN DESCRIPTION | DESCRIPTION |
|---|---|
| Distinct | Once MySQL has found one row that matches the row combination, it will not search for more. |
| Not exists | MySQL optimized the LEFT JOIN and once it has found one row that matches the LEFT JOIN criteria, it will not search for more. |
| range checked for each record (index map: #) | No ideal index was found, so for each row combination from the earlier tables, MySQL checks which index to use and uses this to return rows from the table. This is one of the slowest joins with an index. |

*Continued on next page*

**TABLE 4.3:** WHAT THE DESCRIPTIONS IN THE extra EXPLAIN COLUMN MEAN *(continued)*

| EXTRA COLUMN DESCRIPTION | DESCRIPTION |
|---|---|
| Using filesort | When you see this, the query needs to be optimized. MySQL will need to do an extra step to find out how to sort the rows it returns. It sorts by going through all rows according to the join type and storing the sort key and a pointer to the row for all rows that match the condition. The keys are then sorted and finally the rows returned in the sorted order. |
| Using index | The column data is returned from the table using only information in the index, without having to read the actual row. This occurs when all the required columns for the table are part of the same index. |
| Using temporary | When you see this, the query needs to be optimized. Here, MySQL needs to create a temporary table to hold the result, which usually occurs when you perform an ORDER BY on a different column set than what you did a GROUP BY on. |
| Where used | A WHERE clause is used restrict which rows will be matched against the next table or returned to the client. If you don't want to return all rows from the table, and the join type is either ALL or index, this should appear, or else there may be a problem with your query. |

The type column returned by EXPLAIN tells you the type of join being used. Table 4.4 explains the join type, listing them in order of most to least efficient.

**TABLE 4.4:** THE DIFFERENT JOIN TYPES

| JOIN | DESCRIPTION |
|---|---|
| system | The table has only one row: a system table. This is a special case of the const join type. |
| const | A maximum of one record from the table can match this query (the index would be either a primary key or a unique index). With only one row, the value is effectively a constant, as MySQL reads this value first and then treats it identically to a constant. |
| eq_ref | In a join, MySQL reads one record from this table for each combination of records from the earlier tables in the query. It is used when the query uses all parts of an index that is either a primary key or a unique key. |
| ref | This join type occurs if the query uses a key that is not a unique or primary key or is only part of one of these types (for instance, makes use of leftmost prefixing). All records that match will be read from this table for each combination of rows from earlier tables. This join type is heavily dependent on how many records are matched by the index—the fewer the better. |
| range | This join type uses the index to return rows from within a range, such as what occurs if you search for something using > or <. |

*Continued on next page*

**TABLE 4.4:** THE DIFFERENT JOIN TYPES *(continued)*

| JOIN | DESCRIPTION |
|------|-------------|
| index | This join type scans the entire index for each combination of records from the earlier tables (which is better than ALL, as the indexes are usually smaller than the table data). |
| ALL | This join scans the entire table for each combination of records from earlier tables. This is usually very bad and should be avoided as much as possible. |

Let's return to the example:

```
mysql> EXPLAIN SELECT surname,first_name FROM customer WHERE id=1;
+----------+-------+---------------+---------+---------+-------+------+-------+
| table    | type  | possible_keys | key     | key_len | ref   | rows | Extra |
+----------+-------+---------------+---------+---------+-------+------+-------+
| customer | const | PRIMARY       | PRIMARY |       4 | const |    1 |       |
+----------+-------+---------------+---------+---------+-------+------+-------+
1 row in set (0.00 sec)
```

You already have a primary key in the customer table on the id field, and, because there is only one condition in our query, the id field is equivalent to a constant, and the query is as optimal as it can be. The *rows* column tells you that MySQL only needed to look at one row to return the results. You can't get better than that! Also, the *type* of the join (in this case, it's not really a join) is const, standing for constant, which is the best type. Let's look at what happens if you perform a similar query on a table with no indexes:

```
mysql> EXPLAIN SELECT * FROM sales_rep WHERE employee_number=2;
+-----------+------+---------------+------+---------+------+------+------------+
| table     | type | possible_keys | key  | key_len | ref  | rows | Extra      |
+-----------+------+---------------+------+---------+------+------+------------+
| sales_rep | ALL  | NULL          | NULL |    NULL | NULL |    5 | where used |
+-----------+------+---------------+------+---------+------+------+------------+
1 row in set (0.00 sec)
```

This query is as bad as you can get. The join type is ALL, the worst of the lot, there were no possible keys, and five rows were examined to return the results (there are currently only five records in the sales_rep table). Let's see how you can improve the situation:

```
mysql> SHOW COLUMNS FROM sales_rep;
+-----------------+-------------+------+-----+---------+-------+
| Field           | Type        | Null | Key | Default | Extra |
+-----------------+-------------+------+-----+---------+-------+
| employee_number | int(11)     | YES  |     | NULL    |       |
| surname         | varchar(40) | YES  |     | NULL    |       |
| first_name      | varchar(30) | YES  |     | NULL    |       |
| commission      | tinyint(4)  | YES  |     | NULL    |       |
| date_joined     | date        | YES  |     | NULL    |       |
| birthday        | date        | YES  |     | NULL    |       |
+-----------------+-------------+------+-----+---------+-------+
6 rows in set (0.00 sec)
```

```
mysql> SELECT * FROM sales_rep;
+-----------------+-----------+------------+------------+-------------+------------+
| employee_number | surname   | first_name | commission | date_joined | birthday   |
+-----------------+-----------+------------+------------+-------------+------------+
|               1 | Rive      | Sol        |         10 | 2000-02-15  | 1976-03-18 |
|               2 | Gordimer  | Charlene   |         15 | 1998-07-09  | 1958-11-30 |
|               3 | Serote    | Mike       |         10 | 2001-05-14  | 1971-06-18 |
|               4 | Rive      | Mongane    |         10 | 2002-11-23  | 1982-01-04 |
|               5 | Jomo      | Ignesund   |         10 | 2002-11-29  | 1968-12-01 |
+-----------------+-----------+------------+------------+-------------+------------+
5 rows in set (0.01 sec)
```

An obvious choice for a primary key here is the employee_number field. There are no duplicate values, and you would not want any, so you can make it a primary key without any complications:

```
mysql> ALTER TABLE sales_rep MODIFY employee_number INT NOT NULL
    PRIMARY KEY;
Query OK, 5 rows affected (0.00 sec)
Records: 5  Duplicates: 0  Warnings: 0
```

The result is immediately noticeable if you rerun the EXPLAIN on the query:

```
mysql> EXPLAIN SELECT * FROM sales_rep WHERE employee_number=2;
+-----------+-------+---------------+---------+---------+-------+------+-------+
| table     | type  | possible_keys | key     | key_len | ref   | rows | Extra |
+-----------+-------+---------------+---------+---------+-------+------+-------+
| sales_rep | const | PRIMARY       | PRIMARY |       4 | const |    1 |       |
+-----------+-------+---------------+---------+---------+-------+------+-------+
1 row in set (0.00 sec)
```

This is a vast improvement!

EXPLAIN is also a synonym for DESCRIBE tablename or SHOW COLUMNS FROM tablename if used before a table name.

## Calculating during a Query

Let's examine some more complex situations. For example, you want to return all the sales representatives who would have a commission of less than 20 percent if you were to give them all a 5-percent increase in commission earned. The following is one possible query with EXPLAIN:

```
mysql> EXPLAIN SELECT * FROM sales_rep WHERE (commission+5)<20;
+-----------+------+---------------+------+---------+------+------+------------+
| table     | type | possible_keys | key  | key_len | ref  | rows | Extra      |
+-----------+------+---------------+------+---------+------+------+------------+
| sales_rep | ALL  | NULL          | NULL |    NULL | NULL |    5 | where used |
+-----------+------+---------------+------+---------+------+------+------------+
```

Not so good! This query doesn't make use of any indexes. This isn't surprising because there's only one index so far, a primary key on employee_number. It looks like adding an index on the commission field will improve matters. Because the commission field has duplicate values, it cannot be a primary key (of which you are only allowed one per table anyhow) or a unique key. And it's not a character field, so the only key available to you is an ordinary index:

```
mysql> ALTER TABLE sales_rep ADD INDEX(commission);
Query OK, 5 rows affected (0.01 sec)
Records: 5  Duplicates: 0  Warnings: 0
```

Now, if you rerun the check on the query, you get the following result:

```
mysql> EXPLAIN SELECT * FROM sales_rep WHERE (commission+5)<20;
+-----------+------+---------------+------+---------+------+------+------------+
| table     | type | possible_keys | key  | key_len | ref  | rows | Extra      |
+-----------+------+---------------+------+---------+------+------+------------+
| sales_rep | ALL  | NULL          | NULL | NULL    | NULL |    5 | where used |
+-----------+------+---------------+------+---------+------+------+------------+
1 row in set (0.00 sec)
```

There's no improvement! MySQL is still examining every record. The reason is that commission+5 has to be calculated for each record. The commission field is read from each record in order to add 5 to it, and then compared to the constant 20. You should try not to perform any calculations on the index field. The solution is to perform the calculation on the constant, not the indexed field. In algebraic terms, $(x + 5 < y)$ is the same as $(x < y - 5)$, so you can rewrite the query as follows:

```
mysql> EXPLAIN SELECT * FROM sales_rep WHERE commission<20-5;
+-----------+-------+---------------+------------+---------+------+------+------------+
| table     | type  | possible_keys | key        | key_len | ref  | rows | Extra      |
+-----------+-------+---------------+------------+---------+------+------+------------+
| sales_rep | range | commission    | commission |       2 | NULL |    3 | where used |
+-----------+-------+---------------+------------+---------+------+------+------------+
1 row in set (0.00 sec)
```

This is much better. MySQL performs the calculation once, coming up with a constant of 15, and can search the index for values less than this. You could also have entered the query as this:

```
mysql> EXPLAIN SELECT * FROM sales_rep WHERE commission<15;
+-----------+-------+---------------+------------+---------+------+------+------------+
| table     | type  | possible_keys | key        | key_len | ref  | rows | Extra      |
+-----------+-------+---------------+------------+---------+------+------+------------+
| sales_rep | range | commission    | commission |       2 | NULL |    3 | where used |
+-----------+-------+---------------+------------+---------+------+------+------------+
1 row in set (0.00 sec)
```

where you worked out the constant yourself, but this would not be noticeably faster. Subtracting 5 from 20 costs MySQL almost an immeasurably small amount of time (or at least you'd be challenged to take a measurement!). Notice what happens if you wanted to return all the sales representatives who would earn a commission of exactly 20 percent after the 5-percent increase:

```
mysql> EXPLAIN SELECT * FROM sales_rep WHERE commission=15;
```

```
+-----------+------+---------------+------------+---------+-------+------+------------+
| table     | type | possible_keys | key        | key_len | ref   | rows | Extra      |
+-----------+------+---------------+------------+---------+-------+------+------------+
| sales_rep | ref  | commission    | commission |       2 | const |    1 | where used |
+-----------+------+---------------+------------+---------+-------+------+------------+
1 row in set (0.00 sec)
```

The query type changes from range to ref, which is a better one to use if possible. This can be easily understood because returning an exact value is less work than returning a range of values (or many exact values).

## Using *EXPLAIN* with Leftmost Prefixing

Let's revisit the topic of leftmost prefixing and see how EXPLAIN can help you understand it better. Consider the following query:

```
mysql> EXPLAIN SELECT * FROM customer WHERE first_name='Yvonne';
+----------+------+---------------+------+---------+------+------+------------+
| table    | type | possible_keys | key  | key_len | ref  | rows | Extra      |
+----------+------+---------------+------+---------+------+------+------------+
| customer | ALL  | NULL          | NULL |    NULL | NULL |    8 | where used |
+----------+------+---------------+------+---------+------+------+------------+
1 row in set (0.01 sec)
```

Because the first_name field is not the leftmost part of the index, it is useless to you for indexing purposes, and the join type ALL tells you this fact clearly. The next example shows what EXPLAIN makes of leftmost prefixing:

```
mysql> EXPLAIN SELECT * FROM customer WHERE surname='Clegg'
 AND initial='X' AND first_name='Yvonne';
+----------+------+---------------+---------+---------+-------------------+------+------------+
| table    | type | possible_keys | key     | key_len | ref               | rows | Extra      |
+----------+------+---------------+---------+---------+-------------------+------+------------+
| customer | ref  | surname       | surname |      78 | const,const,const |    1 | where used |
+----------+------+---------------+---------+---------+-------------------+------+------------+
1 row in set (0.01 sec)
```

In this example, the full three fields of the index are used, and the join type is ref because the index in question allows duplicates. If the table structure excluded the possibility of a duplicate combination of surname, initial, and first_name, the join type would have been eq_ref. Note the ref column, const,const,const, indicating that all three parts of the index are compared against a constant value. The next example shows a similar situation:

```
mysql> EXPLAIN SELECT * FROM customer WHERE
   surname='Clegg' AND initial='X';
+----------+------+---------------+---------+---------+-------------+------+------------+
| table    | type | possible_keys | key     | key_len | ref         | rows | Extra      |
+----------+------+---------------+---------+---------+-------------+------+------------+
| customer | ref  | surname       | surname |      47 | const,const |    1 | where used |
+----------+------+---------------+---------+---------+-------------+------+------------+
1 row in set (0.00 sec)
```

Again, the index is used correctly, but only the first two fields are used. The key length here is shorter (meaning MySQL has less to scan and is thus a little quicker). The next case makes no use of leftmost prefixing:

```
mysql> EXPLAIN SELECT * FROM customer WHERE initial='X';
+----------+------+---------------+------+---------+------+------+------------+
| table    | type | possible_keys | key  | key_len | ref  | rows | Extra      |
+----------+------+---------------+------+---------+------+------+------------+
| customer | ALL  | NULL          | NULL |    NULL | NULL |    8 | where used |
+----------+------+---------------+------+---------+------+------+------------+
1 row in set (0.00 sec)
```

This query does not adhere to the principles of leftmost prefixing and makes no use of an index. The next example also makes no use of leftmost prefixing, but does still make use of an index:

```
mysql> EXPLAIN SELECT * FROM customer WHERE surname='Clegg'
  AND first_name='Yvonne';
+----------+------+---------------+---------+---------+-------+------+------------+
| table    | type | possible_keys | key     | key_len | ref   | rows | Extra      |
+----------+------+---------------+---------+---------+-------+------+------------+
| customer | ref  | surname       | surname |      41 | const |    1 | where used |
+----------+------+---------------+---------+---------+-------+------+------------+
1 row in set (0.00 sec)
```

Although leftmost prefixing is not used here, because the first_name field is out of sequence, the surname is still enough to make good use of the index. In this case, it narrows the number of rows that MySQL needs to scan to only one, because the surname Clegg is unique, irrespective of any first names or initials.

## Optimizing Selects

In a join, you can calculate the number of rows MySQL needs to search by multiplying all the rows together. In the following example, MySQL would need to examine 5*8*1 rows, giving a total of 40:

```
mysql> EXPLAIN SELECT * FROM customer,sales_rep,sales
WHERE sales.sales_rep=sales_rep.employee_number
AND customer.id=sales.id;
+-----------+--------+---------------+---------+---------+----------+------+------------+
| table     | type   | possible_keys | key     | key_len | ref      | rows | Extra      |
+-----------+--------+---------------+---------+---------+----------+------+------------+
| sales_rep | ALL    | PRIMARY       | NULL    |    NULL | NULL     |    5 |            |
| sales     | ALL    | NULL          | NULL    |    NULL | NULL     |    8 | where used |
| customer  | eq_ref | PRIMARY       | PRIMARY |       4 | sales.id |    1 |            |
+-----------+--------+---------------+---------+---------+----------+------+------------+
3 rows in set (0.00 sec)
```

You can see that the more tables that are joined, the greater the rows searched. Part of good database design is balancing the choice between smaller database tables that require more joins with larger tables that are harder to maintain. Chapter 8, "Database Normalization," will introduce some useful techniques to help you achieve this.

For purposes of optimizing, I'm going to concentrate on the join between sales_rep and sales from the previous query. I've re-created just that join below (using the alternative LEFT JOIN syntax):

```
mysql> EXPLAIN SELECT * FROM sales_rep LEFT JOIN sales
    ON sales.sales_rep = sales_rep.employee_number;
+-----------+------+---------------+------+---------+------+------+-------+
| table     | type | possible_keys | key  | key_len | ref  | rows | Extra |
+-----------+------+---------------+------+---------+------+------+-------+
| sales_rep | ALL  | NULL          | NULL | NULL    | NULL | 5    |       |
| sales     | ALL  | NULL          | NULL | NULL    | NULL | 8    |       |
+-----------+------+---------------+------+---------+------+------+-------+
2 rows in set (0.00 sec)
```

The number of rows to examine in this query is five times eight (from the rows column), which gives you 40. No indexes are used here. If you examine the structure of the first two tables, you can see why:

```
mysql> DESCRIBE sales;
+-----------+---------+------+-----+---------+-------+
| Field     | Type    | Null | Key | Default | Extra |
+-----------+---------+------+-----+---------+-------+
| code      | int(11) |      | PRI | 0       |       |
| sales_rep | int(11) | YES  |     | NULL    |       |
| id        | int(11) | YES  |     | NULL    |       |
| value     | int(11) | YES  |     | NULL    |       |
+-----------+---------+------+-----+---------+-------+
4 rows in set (0.00 sec)
mysql> DESCRIBE sales_rep;
+-----------------+-------------+------+-----+---------+-------+
| Field           | Type        | Null | Key | Default | Extra |
+-----------------+-------------+------+-----+---------+-------+
| employee_number | int(11)     |      | PRI | 0       |       |
| surname         | varchar(40) | YES  |     | NULL    |       |
| first_name      | varchar(30) | YES  |     | NULL    |       |
| commission      | tinyint(4)  | YES  | MUL | NULL    |       |
| date_joined     | date        | YES  |     | NULL    |       |
| birthday        | date        | YES  |     | NULL    |       |
+-----------------+-------------+------+-----+---------+-------+
6 rows in set (0.00 sec)
```

Because you have no WHERE condition, the query will return all records from the first table—sales_rep. The join is then performed between the employee_number field from the sales_rep table (which you cannot use an index for because you are returning all records) and the sales_rep field from the sales table (which is not indexed). The problem is that the join condition does not make use of an index. If you added an index to the sales_rep field, you'd improve performance:

```
mysql> CREATE INDEX sales_rep ON sales(sales_rep);
Query OK, 8 rows affected (0.01 sec)
Records: 8  Duplicates: 0  Warnings: 0
mysql> EXPLAIN SELECT * FROM sales_rep LEFT JOIN sales
 ON sales.sales_rep = sales_rep.employee_number;
```

| table | type | possible_keys | key | key_len | ref | rows | Extra |
|-------|------|---------------|-----|---------|-----|------|-------|
| sales_rep | ALL | NULL | NULL | NULL | NULL | 5 | |
| sales | ref | sales_rep | sales_rep | 5 | sales_rep.employee_number | 2 | |

```
2 rows in set (0.00 sec)
```

You've reduced the number of rows that MySQL needs to read from 40 to 10 (5*2), a fourfold improvement.

If you performed the LEFT JOIN the other way around (with the sales table containing the possible nulls, not the sales_rep table), you'd get a different result with EXPLAIN:

```
mysql> EXPLAIN SELECT * FROM sales LEFT JOIN sales_rep ON
 sales.sales_rep = sales_rep.employee_number;
```

| table | type | possible_keys | key | key_len | ref | rows | Extra |
|-------|------|---------------|-----|---------|-----|------|-------|
| sales | ALL | NULL | NULL | NULL | NULL | 8 | |
| sales_rep | eq_ref | PRIMARY | PRIMARY | 4 | sales.sales_rep | 1 | |

```
2 rows in set (0.00 sec)
```

Only eight rows are examined because while all rows from the sales table are being returned, the primary key on the sales_rep table (employee_number) is being used to perform the join.

As a further example, examine the following:

```
mysql> EXPLAIN SELECT * FROM sales_rep LEFT JOIN sales
 ON sales.sales_rep = sales_rep.employee_number
 WHERE sales.sales_rep IS NULL;
```

| table | type | possible_keys | key | key_len | ref | rows | Extra |
|-------|------|---------------|-----|---------|-----|------|-------|
| sales_rep | ALL | NULL | NULL | NULL | NULL | 5 | |
| sales | ref | sales_rep | sales_rep | 5 | sales_rep.employee_number | 2 | where used |

```
2 rows in set (0.00 sec)
```

Now, if you change the sales_rep field to not allow nulls, you'll see some changes:

```
mysql> ALTER TABLE sales CHANGE sales_rep sales_rep INT NOT NULL;
Query OK, 8 rows affected (0.00 sec)
Records: 8  Duplicates: 0  Warnings: 0
mysql> EXPLAIN SELECT * FROM sales_rep LEFT JOIN sales ON
 sales.sales_rep = sales_rep.employee_number WHERE
 sales.sales_rep IS NULL;
```

| table | type | possible_keys | key | key_len | ref | rows | Extra |
|-------|------|---------------|-----|---------|-----|------|-------|
| sales_rep | ALL | NULL | NULL | NULL | NULL | 5 | |
| sales | ref | sales_rep | sales_rep | 4 | sales_rep.employee_number | 2 | where used; Not exists |

```
2 rows in set (0.00 sec)
```

Notice that the index length (shown in key_len) is now 4, not 5. Because nulls are no longer permissible, each record does not have to store whether the field is null or not, so overall it is one byte shorter. Also, notice the *Not exists* comment in the extra column. Because the sales_rep field can no longer contain nulls, once MySQL finds a record that matches the LEFT JOIN criteria, it no longer needs to search for any more.

The order in which the tables are presented to MySQL can, in some cases, also make a difference in the speed of the query. MySQL tries its best to choose the best options, but it doesn't always know in advance which the quickest route will be. The next section explains how to help MySQL garner in advance as much information as possible about the index composition, but, as the following example demonstrates, sometimes even this isn't enough.

First, create four identical tables:

```
mysql> CREATE TABLE t1 (f1 int unique not null, primary key(f1));
Query OK, 0 rows affected (0.15 sec)
mysql> CREATE TABLE t2 (f2 int unique not null, primary key(f2));
Query OK, 0 rows affected (0.15 sec)
mysql> CREATE TABLE t3 (f3 int unique not null, primary key(f3));
Query OK, 0 rows affected (0.15 sec)
mysql> CREATE TABLE t4 (f4 int unique not null, primary key(f4));
Query OK, 0 rows affected (0.15 sec)
```

Next, add two records to each:

```
mysql> INSERT INTO t1 VALUES(1),(2);
Query OK, 2 rows affected (0.12 sec)
Records: 2  Duplicates: 0  Warnings: 0
mysql> INSERT INTO t2 VALUES(1),(2);
Query OK, 2 rows affected (0.12 sec)
Records: 2  Duplicates: 0  Warnings: 0
mysql> INSERT INTO t3 VALUES(1),(2);
Query OK, 2 rows affected (0.12 sec)
Records: 2  Duplicates: 0  Warnings: 0
mysql> INSERT INTO t4 VALUES(1),(2);
Query OK, 2 rows affected (0.12 sec)
Records: 2  Duplicates: 0  Warnings: 0
```

Now, imagine you need to perform a join on these tables. The following query will give you the required results:

```
mysql> SELECT * FROM t1,t2 LEFT JOIN t3 ON (t3.f3=t1.f1)
    LEFT JOIN t4 ON (t4.f4=t1.f1) WHERE t2.f2=t4.f4;
```

```
+----+----+------+------+
| f1 | f2 | f3   | f4   |
+----+----+------+------+
|  1 |  1 |   1  |   1  |
|  2 |  2 |   2  |   2  |
+----+----+------+------+
2 rows in set (0.02 sec)
```

If you use EXPLAIN to examine the record, you'll notice the following:

```
mysql> EXPLAIN SELECT * FROM t1,t2 LEFT JOIN t3 ON
(t3.f3=t1.f1) LEFT JOIN t4 ON (t4.f4=t1.f1)
WHERE t2.f2=t4.f4;
```

| table | type  | possible_keys | key     | key_len | ref   | rows | Extra                  |
|-------|-------|---------------|---------|---------|-------|------|------------------------|
| t1    | index | NULL          | PRIMARY | 4       | NULL  | 2    | Using index            |
| t2    | index | PRIMARY,b,f2  | PRIMARY | 4       | NULL  | 2    | Using index            |
| t3    | eq_ref| PRIMARY,c,f3  | PRIMARY | 4       | t1.f1 | 1    | Using index            |
| t4    | eq_ref| PRIMARY,d,f4  | PRIMARY | 4       | t1.f1 | 1    | where used; Using index|

```
4 rows in set (0.00 sec)
```

There are two index scans, one on t1 and another on t2, meaning that MySQL needs to scan the entire index. Looking carefully at the query, you'll see that the LEFT JOIN is what requires t2 to be read before t4. You can get around this by changing the order of the tables and separating t2 from the LEFT JOIN:

```
mysql> EXPLAIN SELECT * FROM t2,t1 LEFT JOIN t3
ON (t3.f3=t1.f1) LEFT JOIN t4 ON (t4.f4=t1.f1)
WHERE t2.f2=t4.f4;
```

| table | type   | possible_keys | key     | key_len | ref   | rows | Extra       |
|-------|--------|---------------|---------|---------|-------|------|-------------|
| t1    | index  | NULL          | PRIMARY | 4       | NULL  | 2    | Using index |
| t3    | eq_ref | PRIMARY,c,f3  | PRIMARY | 4       | t1.f1 | 1    | Using index |
| t4    | eq_ref | PRIMARY,d,f4  | PRIMARY | 4       | t1.f1 | 1    | Using index |
| t2    | eq_ref | PRIMARY,b,f2  | PRIMARY | 4       | t4.f4 | 1    | Using index |

```
4 rows in set (0.01 sec)
```

Notice the difference! According to the rows column, only 2*1*1*1 rows need to be read (2 in total), as opposed to 2*2*1*1 (4 in total) with the earlier query. Of course, the results are the same:

```
mysql> SELECT * FROM t2,t1 LEFT JOIN t3 ON (t3.f3=t1.f1)
LEFT JOIN t4 ON (t4.f4=t1.f1) WHERE t2.f2=t4.f4;
```

```
+----+----+------+------+
| f2 | f1 | f3   | f4   |
+----+----+------+------+
|  1 |  1 |    1 |    1 |
|  2 |  2 |    2 |    2 |
+----+----+------+------+
2 rows in set (0.00 sec)
```

Once again, this demonstrates the importance of testing your queries with EXPLAIN. Without a good understanding of the inner workings of MySQL, you may never have known which of the above queries was quicker, even if you had an inkling there would be a difference. EXPLAIN quantifies your hunches, which develop with experience.

## Helping MySQL's Query Optimizer with *ANALYZE*

The brain inside MySQL that decides which key, if any, to use is called the *query optimizer*. It takes a quick look at the index to see which indexes are the best to use. A human does something similar when looking for a book. For example, say that you were searching for a book by the author Zakes Mda entitled *Ways of Dying*, and you knew only that there were two indexes. If one is alphabetical by author name and consists of 4,000 entries, and the other is alphabetical by book title and consists of 12,000 entries, you'd probably decide to use the author index. But if you knew that Zakes Mda had written 200 books but that there was only one book entitled *Ways of Dying*, you'd probably use the other index. MySQL too performs better if it has an idea of what each index contains. You can provide this kind of information (called the *cardinality*, or number of unique values) by running the following command: ANALYZE TABLE tablename. There's not much point in running this on the sample tables, but on large tables with many inserts, updates, and deletes, regularly analyzing the table can help the performance.

ANALYZE TABLE updates the key distribution for the table if it is not up-to-date. (Running ANALYZE is equivalent to running myisamchk -a or myismachk --analyze. See Chapter 12, "Database Replication," for more information.)

**WARNING**    *This only works with MyISAM and BDB tables, and the table is locked with a read lock for the duration of this process. Therefore, you don't want to do this when your database is busy.*

You can see the information available to MySQL by running the command SHOW INDEX:

```
mysql> SHOW INDEX FROM customer;
+----------+------------+----------+--------------+-------------+-----------+-------------+----------+--------+---------+
| Table    | Non_unique | Key_name | Seq_in_index | Column_name | Collation | Cardinality | Sub_part | Packed | Comment |
+----------+------------+----------+--------------+-------------+-----------+-------------+----------+--------+---------+
| customer |          0 | PRIMARY  |            1 | id          | A         |           8 | NULL     | NULL   |         |
| customer |          1 | surname  |            1 | surname     | A         |           8 | NULL     | NULL   |         |
| customer |          1 | surname  |            2 | initial     | A         |           8 | NULL     | NULL   |         |
| customer |          1 | surname  |            3 | first_name  | A         |           8 | NULL     | NULL   |         |
+----------+------------+----------+--------------+-------------+-----------+-------------+----------+--------+---------+
4 rows in set (0.01 sec)
```

Table 4.5 explains the meanings of the columns returned by a SHOW INDEX statement.

**TABLE 4.5:** MEANINGS OF THE COLUMNS RETURNED BY SHOW INDEX

| COLUMN | DESCRIPTION |
| --- | --- |
| Table | Name of the table you're looking at. |
| Non_unique | 0 or 1. 0 means the index can't contain duplicates (a primary key or unique index), and 1 means it can. |
| Key_name | Name of the index. |
| Seq_in_index | Order of columns in the index, starting with 1. |
| Column_name | Column name. |
| Collation | A or NULL. A means the index is sorted in ascending order, and NULL means it's not sorted. |
| Cardinality | Number of unique values in the index. This specifically is updated by running ANALYZE TABLE or myisamchk -a. |
| Sub_part | NULL if the entire column is indexed, otherwise the size of the index, in characters. |
| Packed | Whether the index is packed or not. |
| Null | YES if the column can contain NULL values. |
| Comment | Various remarks. |

Deletes and updates can leave gaps in the table (especially when your tables contain TEXT, BLOB, or VARCHAR fields. This means the drive is doing too much work because the head needs to skip over these gaps when reading.

OPTIMIZE TABLE solves this problem, removing the gaps in the data by rejoining fragmented records, doing the equivalent of a defrag on the table data.

*TIP   See Chapter 10, "Basic Administration," for more on the* OPTIMIZE *statement. Note that the table is locked for the duration of the process, so you don't want to run it during peak hours!*

## Optimizing *SELECT* Statements and Security

The more complex your permissions (see Chapter 14, "Database Security"), the more overhead you'll experience on your queries. This is hardly a reason to skimp on security, but if you have some high-volume queries, and another set of low-volume queries with complex permissions, it may be useful to keep the low-volume set as separate as possible.

## Benchmarking Functions

The BENCHMARK() function tells you how long it takes MySQL to perform a function a certain number of times. It can help to give a basic idea of the difference in capabilities between machines. The syntax is as follows:

```
SELECT BENCHMARK(number_of_repetitions,expression)
```

Compare the difference between the following benchmarks, where MySQL calculates the square root of 999 10 million times. The first one was run on a fairly inactive 1GB Duron running Windows 98, and the second was run on a slightly busier Pentium III 850MhZ running Linux Red Hat 7. Just for good measure, I ran it a third time, on an ancient Cyrix 200MMX running FreeBSD 4.6, doing nothing else:

```
mysql> SELECT BENCHMARK(10000000,SQRT(999));
+------------------------------+
| BENCHMARK(10000000,SQRT(999)) |
+------------------------------+
|                            0 |
+------------------------------+
1 row in set (0.66 sec)
mysql> SELECT BENCHMARK(10000000,SQRT(999));
+------------------------------+
| BENCHMARK(10000000,SQRT(999)) |
+------------------------------+
|                            0 |
+------------------------------+
1 row in set (2.73 sec)
mysql> SELECT BENCHMARK(10000000,SQRT(999));
+------------------------------+
| BENCHMARK(10000000,SQRT(999)) |
+------------------------------+
|                            0 |
+------------------------------+
1 row in set (13.24 sec)
```

**WARNING**   *You should use* BENCHMARK() *with caution to compare machines. For a live database, there are many other factors, such as disk speed, which are not taken into account with this test. Its main aim is to help in the optimization of functions.*

## Optimizing Updates, Deletes, and Inserts

An UPDATE is basically the same as a SELECT, but with a write operation afterward. For example, for the purposes of optimizing, the following code:

```
UPDATE fieldname FROM tablename WHERE condition
```

is the same as this code:

```
SELECT fieldname FROM tablename WHERE condition
```

You can optimize an UPDATE statement in the same way as you would the equivalent SELECT statement. Also note that the fewer indexes you use and the smaller the data, the quicker the operation will be. Take care not to use superfluous indexes or make the fields or indexes larger than they need to be.

The speed of a DELETE statement depends on the number of indexes. When deleting, each record needs to be deleted from any associated indexes as well as the main data file. This is the reason that TRUNCATE tablename is much faster than DELETE tablename, as the entire table is dropped at once, without the need to delete each individual index and data record.

The best method to insert data is to use LOAD DATA rather than INSERT, as this is up to 20 times faster.

You can speed up the process by disabling keys for the duration of the period you're adding data. MySQL will then only have to concentrate on adding the data and not worry about adding to the index files at the same time. The data itself is then added much quicker, and when the indexes are built separately, the process will be more optimal as well. You can use the following procedure:

```
ALTER TABLE tbl_name DISABLE KEYS;
LOAD DATA INFILE filename INTO TABLE tablename
ALTER TABLE tbl_name ENABLE KEYS;
```

You're not always going to be able to insert from a text file, though. But if you can group your inserts, multiple value lists are added much quicker than the separate statements. For instance, the following query:

```
INSERT INTO tablename VALUES(record1),(record2)…(recordn);
```

is much faster than this alternative:

```
INSERT INTO tablename VALUES(record1);
INSERT INTO tablename VALUES(record1);
…
INSERT INTO tablename VALUES(recordn);
```

The reason for this is that the indexes are only flushed once per INSERT statement. If you require multiple INSERT statements, you can use locking to achieve the same result. For nontransactional tables, use statements like this:

```
LOCK TABLES tablename WRITE;
INSERT INTO tablename VALUES (record1),(record2),(record3);
INSERT INTO tablename VALUES (record4),(record5),(record6);
UNLOCK TABLES;
```

Be aware that no one will be able to read your tables while the previous statements are in progress. To achieve the same with transactional tables, use these statements instead:

```
BEGIN;
INSERT INTO tablename VALUES (record1),(record2),(record3);
INSERT INTO tablename VALUES (record4),(record5),(record6);
COMMIT;
```

Matters become slightly more complex when you're adding records from many threads. Consider a scenario where the first thread adds 10,000 records, and the second thread adds one record. Using locking, the overall speed will be a lot faster, but the second thread will only complete after the first thread. Without locking, the second thread will complete much more quickly, but the overall speed will be slower. The importance of the second thread relative to the first will determine which method you choose.

However, your application may need to do many unrelated inserts continually. If you're not using row-level locking (such as is possible with InnoDB tables), you may find that the vast hordes of people querying your tables are waiting an inordinately long time for the few to carry out their inserts. But don't despair—there are ways to minimize this effect.

The first is to use INSERT LOW PRIORITY. This causes the insert to lose its usual pushy behavior and to wait until there are no more read queries waiting in the queue. The problem, though, is that if your database is very busy, the client performing the INSERT LOW PRIORITY may take a long time to find a gap, if ever!

An alternative here is INSERT DELAYED. The client is immediately freed, and the insert put into a queue (with all the other INSERT DELAYED statements still waiting for the queue to end). A downside of this is that no meaningful information is passed back to the client (such as the auto_increment value), as the INSERT has not been processed when the client is freed. But some things aren't worth waiting for! Also, be aware that there is the possibility of all inserts in the queue being lost if there is a catastrophe, such as a power failure.

*WARNING*   *For neither* INSERT LOW PRIORITY *nor* INSERT DELAYED *do you have any idea when the data will be inserted, if at all, so use them with caution.*

## Summary

Poor use of indexes is probably the single most important cause of performance problems. An index is a small, sorted file that points to the main data file. Finding a particular record is then quicker because only the small index file has to be searched.

An index can be a primary key (a unique index that cannot contain nulls), a unique index, an ordinary index (that can contain duplicates), or a full-text index. Full-text indexes allow a high level of sophistication in searching text fields for certain combinations of keywords.

Auto increment fields are associated with the primary key and allow MySQL to automatically take care of the sequencing of the field. If a record is inserted, MySQL will add 1 to the previous auto incremented value and use this for the value of the inserted auto increment field.

EXPLAIN returns useful information about how MySQL uses indexes in a particular query. You can use it to see whether MySQL is using the indexes you've created, and if the query is not optimal, get information about what fields to create indexes on or how to change the query to make it more optimal.

# Chapter 5

# Programming with MySQL

THIS CHAPTER IS NOT going to teach you how to program. Too many books try to teach both MySQL and a programming language and instead end up doing incomplete jobs of both. This book assumes you're already a competent programmer, you're going to learn, or you're going to focus only on the database administrator (DBA) role, and are not interested in programming.

You can begin to tap into the real power of a database when it becomes part of a larger *information system*, with fully functional applications adding their own value to the system. A news website, for example, needs tools to add and sort the news articles, to display them on a website, and to track the most popular stories. Most journalists have no interest in learning Structured Query Language (SQL), however, so they need a well-designed interface to link them to the database. This interface could be a web page with a Hypertext Markup Language (HTML) form, with a submit button that calls a script to run an INSERT statement. Or the interface could be a news feed that takes articles from the newspaper's QuarkXPress system and automatically adds them to the database.

Another information system could involve an application for financial advisors, where the backend is fed with the latest stock and currency prices, so the advisors can access and analyze the information to monitor trends for their clients.

The possibilities for information systems are endless. What these scenarios have in common is that they include a developed application to add extra levels of logic that MySQL cannot supply. In theory, you can use any programming language to develop applications. Languages commonly used are Java, C, PHP, Perl, C++, Visual Basic, Python, and Tcl, which mostly have well-developed Application Programming Interfaces (APIs) for interfacing with MySQL. The appendixes in this book contain APIs for most of these programming languages.

Throughout this chapter, all examples are in PHP—not because you should all be using PHP, but simply because so many of you already do, because its syntax is familiar to anyone with a C-like background (C, Perl, or C++), and because it's simple enough for other programmers to follow. It's the programming principles that are important, however—not the syntax. All code is extensively commented in this chapter so that you can follow it no matter what language you are familiar with or your level of competency.

Featured in this chapter:

◆  Using persistent connections
◆  Making your code portable and easier to maintain
◆  Assessing the database's vs. the application's workload
◆  Exploring the application development process

# Using Good Database Programming Techniques

The following sections will introduce some of the most common techniques used by database programmers to ensure that their applications are robust (do not break down easily), portable (easy to move to new environments and platforms), and easy to maintain. Persistent connections are a useful technique when the application makes high numbers of connection requests that mostly come from the same source in a short period of time. It's also all too easy for inexperienced, hurried, or lazy programmers to create code that makes the tasks of subsequent programmers (and often themselves, too) more difficult than need be by not considering portability and maintainability or placing too much burden on the application instead of the database. By doing some simple planning at the beginning, you can avoid needless problems later.

## Using Persistent Connections

MySQL has always been fairly quick to connect to, compared to other databases. However, connecting to the database is still a fairly heavy task, and, if you are doing a large number of connections in a short space of time (such as when connecting from a web server), you want to make this as easy on your resources as possible. Using *persistent connections* will keep the connection open after the script has completed. When the next connection request comes along, it will reuse the existing connection, saving the overhead. In PHP, you can use the `mysql_pconnect()` function to create a persistent connection:

```
mysql_pconnect($host,$user,$pass);
    // the mysql_pconnect function creates a persistent connection to a
    // mysql database, taking host, user and password parameters
```

You don't always want the connections to hang around too long, though. In most cases, the web server will clean up after itself. However, I have encountered a web server that was having problems, resulting in it restarting itself but not cleaning up the connections. The web server was set to allow 400 instances, and MySQL could take 750 connections. With the web server misbehaving and not cleaning up, it effectively doubled the number of connections it was making to the database server, allowing a potential 800. Suddenly the database server was running out of available connections. You can minimize the risk of persistent connections hanging around for too long by reducing the `wait_timeout` mysqld variable (or `interactive_timeout`, depending how you connect), which determines the amount of time MySQL allows a connection to remain inactive before closing it. (Chapter 10, "Basic Administration," and Chapter 13, "Configuring and Optimizing MySQL," explain how to set these variables.) The default is 28,800 seconds (8 hours). By reducing this to 600 seconds, I prevented the problem from recurring. Then there was just the web server to worry about!

## Making Code Portable and Easy to Maintain

Some simple steps can vastly improve the flexibility of the code. These include keeping connection details separate and in a single location, as well as building database queries flexibly so that future changes in database structure do not needlessly affect the application.

### CONNECTING

Most programming languages make it easy to connect to a database through native functions. For example, PHP has a host of functions for use with MySQL, such as `mysql_connect()`, `mysql_query()`, and so on.

When programming a tiny application with one connection to the database, using the native classes, it's easy to use something simple to connect to MySQL (see Listing 5.1).

---

**LISTING 5.1:** TOTALLY_IMPORTABLE.PHP

```
$db = mysql_pconnect("dbhostname.co.za", "db_app", "g00r002b");
   // the mysql_pconnect function creates a persistent connection to a
   // mysql database, taking host, user and password parameters
   // where 'dbhostname' is the host, 'db_app' the user and
   // 'g00r002b' the password
if (!$db) {
    echo "There was a problem connecting to the database.";
    exit;
}
   // basic error checking - if the connection is not successful, print
   // an error message and exit the script
```

---

Many examples you'll come across connect in this way because it's simple to understand and fine for small situations. But to use a database in a more serious application, you'll want to make it as portable, as easy to maintain, and as secure as possible.

Imagine you have 10 scripts that connect to the database. If all 10 scripts connected in the same way, and then one day you had to move the database to a new server or wanted to change your password, you'd have to change all 10 scripts.

Now imagine you had 100 scripts.

I inherited a situation like this once before, and, facing the possibility of the password having been compromised (with the password in hundreds of locations, it's more likely to be found as well), I had to do lots of grunt work! The best solution is to build the application correctly from the beginning. Place your database connection details in a separate location, which is then included in scripts that connect to the database. Then, when you need to change the details, you only need to change them in one place (and you *know* that nothing has been forgotten). Changing the password in hundreds of locations involves the risk of missing a location and only finding out when functionality fails.

The solutions shown in Listings 5.2 and 5.3 are better.

---

**LISTING 5.2:** DB.INC

```
$host = "dbhostname.co.za";
$user = "db_app";
$pass = "g00r002b";
```

---

**LISTING 5.3:** NOT_TOO_PORTABLE.PHP

```
require_once "$include_path/db.inc";
// includes the file containing the connection details, db.inc
// located in the path: $include_path, which should be a safe location
$db = mysql_pconnect($host, $user, $pass);
  // the mysql_pconnect function creates a persistent connection to a
  // mysql database, taking host, user and password parameters
if (!$db) {
    echo "There was a problem connecting to the database.";
    exit;
}
  // basic error checking - if the connection is not successful, print
  // an error message and exit the script
```

---

In this example, the password, hostname, and username are stored in a single file, so you only need to change the details in one place (db.inc).

**WARNING**  *If you're creating a web application, make sure that* db.inc *is not inside the web tree. (Your web server should usually not be able to serve* .inc *files, but in any case, you'll want to keep sensitive information as far removed as possible.)*

A further improvement comes from a slightly higher level of abstraction. Imagine, with Listings 5.2 and 5.3, that management decides to move to another DBMS. It happens; MySQL is not ideal for every kind of situation, and, besides, management often makes strange decisions—such as another situation I walked into, where management had spent thousands on another database when all that was needed was to configure MySQL properly. (Luckily I managed to talk them out of it because, once again, the code was not very portable!)

To make your code as portable as possible, you only want to change the DBMS details in one place. This involves creating a second function that handles the connection details, as shown in Listings 5.4 and 5.5. The db_pconnect() function is placed in the file db.inc, and in portable.php this function is used to connect to the database instead of mysql_pconnect().

---

**LISTING 5.4:** DB.INC

```
// this function connects to the database, and returns the connection
function db_pconnect() {
  $host = "dbhostname.co.za";
```

```
    $user = "db_app";
    $pass = "g00r002b";
    return mysql_pconnect($host, $user, $pass);
}
```

---

**LISTING 5.5:** PORTABLE.PHP

```
require_once "$include_path/db.inc";
 // includes the file containing the connection details, db.inc
 // located in the path: $include_path, which should be a safe location
$db = db_pconnect($host, $user, $pass);
if (!$db) {
  echo "There was a problem connecting to the database.";
  exit;
}
 // basic error checking - if the connection is not successful, print
 // an error message and exit the script
```

---

Now, if you want to change from MySQL to another database, simply replace `mysql_pconnect()` with the appropriate function, such as **odbc_pconnect()**.

*NOTE   This book is not trying to impose a programming style upon you. Each language has its own strengths and weaknesses. Java is a much more object-oriented language than PHP, for example, so the previous examples will not work well if just directly translated into Java. What's important is the principle of making your applications as easy to maintain (by storing connection information in one location) and as portable (by avoiding database-specific code) as possible.*

### DATABASE QUERIES

It's acceptable to use shortcuts such as SELECT * when querying MySQL directly. But you should avoid this in your applications, as they make them less portable. Take a situation where there are three fields in the entrants database table; in order, they are id, first_name, and surname. Your programming code may look something like Listing 5.6.

---

**LISTING 5.6:** TOTALLY_INFLEXIBLE_SELECT.PHP

```
  // assuming the connection $db has already been made
$result = mysql_query("SELECT * FROM entrants",$db);
  // run the query on the active connection
while ($row = mysql_fetch_array($result,MYSQL_NUM)) {
    // mysql_fetch_array when called with MYSQL_NUM
    // as a parameter, returns a numerically indexed
    // array, each element corresponding to a
    // field returned from a returned row
  $id = $row[0];
    // Because the id is the first field in the database,
```

```
    // it is returned as the first element of the array,
    // which of course starts at 0
  $first_name = $row[1];
  $surname = $row[2];
  // .. do some processing with the details
}
```

This works at first. But now, somebody (it's always somebody else) makes a change to the database structure, adding a new field between first_name and surname, called initial. Your code does not need the initial. Suddenly your code does not work, as the initial is the third element of the array (or $row[2]), and it is stored as $surname. The actual surname, now in $row[3], is never accessed.

There are a number of problems with the totally_inflexible_select.php script that need to be addressed. Besides the fact that it will not work if the database structure is changed, the function used to return fields returns a numeric array, rather than an associative array. Your code is then less readable, as someone with no knowledge of the database structure cannot know what is being returned from the database. In PHP, you can correct this by using a function that returns an associative array, as shown in Listing 5.7.

**LISTING 5.7: INFLEXIBLE_SELECT.PHP**

```
  // assuming the connection $db has already been made
$result = mysql_query("SELECT * FROM entrants",$db);
while ($row = mysql_fetch_array($result,MYSQL_ASSOC)) {
    // mysql_fetch_array when called with MYSQL_ASSOC
    // as a parameter, returns an associative array,
    // with each key of the array being the name of a
    // field returned from the row
  $id = $row["id"];
  $first_name = $row["first_name"];
  $surname = $row["surname"];
  // .. do some processing with the details
}
```

This is better, because now, even after the initial field has been added to the database table, your code will work. It can handle some changes in database structure, and it is more readable. A programmer with no knowledge of the database structure will know what fields are being returned. But you can still make an improvement. By running a SELECT * query, you're asking MySQL to return all the fields from the table. Your code only needs to use three fields, so why waste the resources in returning all of them, with the extra disk input/output and greater pressure on your network this involves? Rather, just specify the fields you want to return. Not only does this waste fewer resources, but it also makes your code even more readable. In fact, in some instances returning the associative array is more resource hungry than returning a numeric array. In this case, you can still keep your code readable, even when returning a numeric array, by specifying the fields as shown in Listing 5.8.

**LISTING 5.8:** FLEXIBLE_SELECT.PHP

```
    // assuming the connection $db has already been made
$result = mysql_query("SELECT id,first_name,surname FROM entrants",$db);
while ($row = mysql_fetch_array($result,MYSQL_NUM)) {
    // mysql_fetch_array when called with MYSQL_NUM
    // as a parameter, returns a numerically indexed
    // array, each element corresponding to a
    // field returned from a returned row
  $id = $row[0];
  $first_name = $row[1];
  $surname = $row[2];
  // .. do some processing with the details
}
```

The same principle applies to INSERT queries. Never use an INSERT query without a list of fields inside an application. For example, taking the original entrants table with three fields—id, first_name, and surname—you could use code as shown in Listing 5.9.

**LISTING 5.9:** INFLEXIBLE_INSERT.PHP

```
    // assuming the connection $db has already been made
$result = mysql_query("INSERT INTO entrants↵
 VALUES('$id','$first_name','$surname')",$db);
```

If the table structure changes, once again the code will break. By adding a field, initial, the number of fields being inserted will not match the number of fields in the table, and the query will fail.

The way to solve this is to specify the database fields you are inserting into, as shown in Listing 5.10.

**LISTING 5.10:** FLEXIBLE_INSERT.PHP

```
    // assuming the connection $db has already been made
$result = mysql_query("INSERT INTO entrants(id, first_name,↵
 surname) VALUES('$id','$first_name','$surname')",$db);
```

This also has the advantage of being more readable, especially considering that the field values will not always match the field names as in this example.

## How Much Work Should the Database Server Do?

One of the perennial debates raging among architects is that of how much work the database server must do and how much the application should do.

MySQL developers initially came out heavily in favor of passing the burden to the application, partly as justification for not supporting features such as stored procedures and triggers and partly as a matter of principle. They were criticized for this, and the lack of these features led people to dismiss MySQL as a serious database—a tag MySQL is only now, with version 4, starting to shake off.

In general, the database should do as much work as it can. Take the following two examples, which produce the same output but are done in different ways. Listing 5.11 returns all the data, unsorted, and then uses the PHP `sort()` function to sort the data. Listing 5.12, on the other hand, uses MySQL's `ORDER BY` clause to sort the data.

---

**LISTING 5.11:** `WORK_THE_SCRIPT.PHP`

```
    // assuming the connection $db has already been made
$result = mysql_query("SELECT surname FROM entrants",$db);
while ($row = mysql_fetch_array($result,MYSQL_ASSOC)) {
    // mysql_fetch_array when called with MYSQL_ASSOC
    // as a parameter, returns an associative array,
    // with each key of the array being the name of a
    // field returned from the row
  $surname[] = $row["surname"];
    // add the surname as the next element of the
    // surname array (and creates the array if not yet done)
}
  sort($surname)
  // the sort() function sorts the array
  // … continue processing the sorted data
```

---

**LISTING 5.12:** `WORK_THE_DB.PHP`

```
    // assuming the connection $db has already been made
$result = mysql_query("SELECT surname FROM entrants ORDER BY surname",$db);
while ($row = mysql_fetch_array($result,MYSQL_ASSOC)) {
    // mysql_fetch_array when called with MYSQL_ASSOC
    // as a parameter, returns an associative array,
    // with each key of the array being the name of a
    // field returned from the row
  $surname[] = $row["surname"];
    // add the surname as the next element of the
    // surname array (and creates the array if not yet done)
}
  // … continue processing the sorted data
```

---

Listing 5.12 makes a lot more sense. MySQL could (or should) have an index on the surname field if this is a commonly performed operation, and reading the data in order, from an index, is much quicker than reading the data in the unordered format and then using the application to perform the sort.

In fact, it's possible that reading the sorted data from the database will be quicker than reading the unsorted data (even before taking the `sort()` function into account) because the sorted data may only need to be read from the index, not the data file.

There are possible exceptions (perhaps situations where an index is not possible and the database server is the main bottleneck), but in the vast majority of cases, the technique shown in Listing 5.12 will be far superior.

A similar, more extreme (but still all too common) example is one where the application is performing the work of the `WHERE` clause, as Listing 5.13 demonstrates.

**LISTING 5.13:** `WORK_THE_SCRIPT2.PHP`

```php
   // assuming the connection $db has already been made
 $result = mysql_query("SELECT surname FROM entrants",$db);
 while ($row = mysql_fetch_array($result,MYSQL_ASSOC)) {
    // mysql_fetch_array when called with MYSQL_ASSOC
    // as a parameter, returns an associative array,
    // with each key of the array being the name of a
    // field returned from the row
  if ($row["surname"] == 'Johnson') {
    $johnson[] = $row["surname"];
      // add the surname as the next element of the
      // johnson array (and creates the array if not yet done)
  }
  elseif ($row["surname"] == 'Makeba') {
    $makeba[] = $row["surname"];
    // add the surname as the next element of the
    // makeba array (and creates the array if not yet done)


  }
 }
   // ... process the makeba and johnson arrays
```

A far better solution is to use the `WHERE` clause, as shown in Listing 5.14, and not waste time retrieving all the unwanted extra records.

**LISTING 5.14:** `WORK_THE_DB2.PHP`

```php
   // assuming the connection $db has already been made
 $result = mysql_query("SELECT surname FROM↵
  entrants WHERE surname = 'Makeba' OR surname='Johnson'",$db);
 while ($row = mysql_fetch_array($result,MYSQL_ASSOC)) {
    // mysql_fetch_array when called with MYSQL_ASSOC
    // as a parameter, returns an associative array,
    // with each key of the array being the name of a
    // field returned from the row
  if ($row["surname"] == 'Johnson') {
    $johnson[] = $row["surname"];
```

```
        // add the surname as the next element of the
        // johnson array (and creates the array if not yet done)
    }
    elseif ($row["surname"] == 'Makeba') {
      $makeba[] = $row["surname"];
        // add the surname as the next element of the
        // makeba array (and creates the array if not yet done)
    }
}
    // … continue processing the sorted data
```

You can write these code snippets more elegantly if you're processing many names, but the point is that Listing 5.14 is much more efficient because MySQL is doing the work, limiting the results returned and reducing the resources used.

Listing 5.15 demonstrates a solution often implemented by people from other database backgrounds. Because MySQL version 4.0 does not fully implement sub-selects (although this will be rectified in version 4.1), people often assume there is no alternative but using the application. For example, in a situation where you have two customer tables and want to see which customers from one table do not appear in the other table, the following standard ANSI query does not work in MySQL:

```
SELECT first_name,surname FROM entrants WHERE code NOT IN
    (SELECT code FROM referred_entrants);
```

For this reason, the sort of code shown in Listing 5.15 is all too frequently implemented.

**LISTING 5.15: WORK_THE_SCRIPT3.PHP**

```
    // assuming the connection $db has already been made
$result = mysql_query("SELECT code FROM entrants",$db);
$codelist = "";
    // initialise the list of codes
while ($row = mysql_fetch_array($result,MYSQL_ASSOC)) {
    // mysql_fetch_array when called with MYSQL_ASSOC
    // as a parameter, returns an associative array,
    // with each key of the array being the name of a
    // field returned from the row
  $codelist .= $row["code"].",";
    // add the code, followed by a comma to the $codelist variable
}
$codelist = substr($codelist, 0, -1);
    // removes the last comma, resulting in a list
    // such as "1,3,4,8,12";
$result = mysql_query("SELECT first_name,surname FROM⏎
 referred_entrants WHERE code NOT IN($codelist)",$db);
while ($row = mysql_fetch_array($result,MYSQL_ASSOC)) {
    // … process the entrant details
}
```

Listing 5.15 would function, but again it is placing far too much of a load on the application. Instead, with some thought, MySQL could perform a query to return the results, as Listing 5.16 demonstrates.

---

**LISTING 5.16:** WORK_THE_DB3.PHP

```php
    // assuming the connection $db has already been made
$result = mysql_query("SELECT entrants.first_name,↵
   entrants.surname FROM entrants LEFT JOIN referred_entrants↵
   ON entrants.code = referred_entrants.code WHERE↵
   referred_entrants.code IS NULL",$db);
while ($row = mysql_fetch_array($result,MYSQL_ASSOC)) {
    // … process the entrant details
}
```

---

When sub-selects are implemented (version 4.1 according the current schedule), the resulting code, shown in Listing 5.17, is even simpler.

---

**LISTING 5.17:** WORK_THE_DB3_2.PHP

```php
    // assuming the connection $db has already been made
$result = mysql_query("SELECT first_name,surname FROM↵
   entrants WHERE code NOT IN (SELECT code FROM↵
   referred_entrants", $db);
while ($row = mysql_fetch_array($result,MYSQL_ASSOC)) {
    // … process the entrant details
}
```

---

# The Stages of Application Development

This chapter assumes you can already program or you can get another book to help you to learn. But what many new programmers forget about, especially those who have not been formally trained, is to take a step back and look at their application development project in context and to plan for future situations. Too many programmers are continually putting out fires, reinventing the wheel, and generally making poor use of their time, all while blaming project managers, users, and everyone else around them. Of course, others may not be blameless, but because this book is targeted at MySQL developers, I'll make a number of suggestions aimed at improving the way developers run the projects in which they are involved. Web developers in particular, who've often progressed through learning HTML and JavaScript up to MySQL and a programming language, are not aware of the complexities of larger projects and often get caught when projects get big.

The following sections briefly discuss the stages of application development. It is not a rigid prescription of steps; rather, it's one of many possible frameworks. Any good application development will allow a level of flexibility depending on the resources available and the specific conditions of the project. There are many good development methodologies, and you should use one appropriate to your needs, although the general principles usually remain the same. Reading this chapter in conjunction with Chapter 9, "Database Design," will help you grasp the bigger picture.

## Phase 1: Analyzing the Requirements

Analyzing the requirements of a project is an obvious step in developing an application. This rule is repeated time and time again by experts bemoaning the poor state of software development. Yet all too often, "We didn't know you wanted that" or "You never told us that at the beginning" is offered as an excuse for the poor outcome of a project. The first and possibly most important phase of a project is determining its requirements.

### DETERMINING USER REQUIREMENTS

Most requests that users make are trivial, often much to their surprise. I've encountered users who, after dealing with incompetent or lazy developers, are terrified to make a request that turns out to be no more complex than an extra field in a table. In most cases, anything is possible as long as it's requested upfront. The main difficulty is not in fulfilling the user requirements, but in fulfilling different requirements after the original framework has been built. Users do not always know what they want. They need to be helped to formalize their requirements. But, seeing as this book is aimed at developers, not business decision makers, I'll place the burden on the developer. Make sure, upfront, that the user requirements are clear, understood by the development team, and understood by the users themselves.

The project team needs to undertake the following when determining user requirements:

◆ Engage the users to determine their requirements. Guide the users, explaining why certain suggestions are not practical or suggesting better alternatives. The team needs to use their experience. Bring unsaid requirements into the open so that they can be documented. What's obvious to the user may not be obvious to the developers, and important requirements may go missing. Requirements need to be as complete as possible. For example, a user may request that a reservation system "take the booking." However, this is no good. Each field is required for a booking, and the processes behind it needs to be spelled out.

◆ Once you understand the user requirements, write them down and return them to both the users and to the project owners (the people paying for the project) for confirmation. Users need to be sure what they are going to be getting; there should be no surprises later.

◆ Get the owners to sign off on the requirements. That way, there is less likelihood of either party being unhappy. *Scope creep*—when a project's requirements continue to grow during development—is an insidious problem that occurs frequently, usually when the requirements have not been formally agreed upon beforehand. Either the project owners demand more and more or someone from either party discovers critical new issues that no one thought of until then.

### DETERMINING TECHNOLOGY REQUIREMENTS

Determining the technology requirements is as important as determining the user requirements. It may not be impossible to run a database-intensive website that gets more than 20 million page requests a month on one server, but at the least it's going to require a fine machine and specific conditions. The team should not impose any requirements on the project, for example, "It should run Linux and MySQL." The reason the technology requirements are listed afterward is so that the technology can best match the project—within any constraints. Questions to answer include the following:

- How many machines? What kind of architecture is needed to link them?
- What kind of machines do these need to be?
- What operating systems, DBMSs, or other software is required (such as web servers, mail clients, and so on)?
- What languages will be used to develop the application? Will they be object oriented?

## Phase 2: Designing the Application

Once the requirements are crystallized, it's time to begin designing the application.

### MODELING

A model simplifies the program structure and transforms the user requirements into a form that the programmer can easily understand. These can be formal models, such as required by Unified Modeling Language (UML), a data flow diagram, or simply a drawing on a piece of paper. The basics to include are what data each process needs and what data the process produces.

### USING PSEUDOCODE

Pseudocode is another step that can help the programmer develop an application more quickly and more easily. Instead of worrying about the exact syntax requirements of the programming language, pseudocode tackles the logical requirements, creating the algorithms needed to solve the problems.

## Phase 3: Coding

This is the step that is often the only step. But coding becomes much easier when the documentation produced in the previous stages exists. Use the following tips during the coding phase:

- Always document your code. Include comments inside the code, and create separate documents noting how the application is put together and how it works. If not for yourself, do this for anyone else to follow you. (You'll be surprised how easy it is to forget some "trivial" detail after a few months.) A coder is selfish if they have not left ample documents for someone else to follow. Make sure you build in time for this, though; don't let the pressure of a deadline make you skimp on this aspect.
- Use clear filenames, function names, and variable names. For example, the function f3() is not very intuitive, but calculate_interest() is clearer.
- Don't reinvent the wheel. There are ample classes and sample code available. Rarely will coders need to do something unique. Mostly the job is repetitive, and coders play the job of librarian, tracking down the right code for the job.
- Initialize all your variables and document them in one place, even when coding in languages that allow variables to be used before they are initialized. This is not only more readable, but it is more secure.

◆ Break your code up into small parts. This makes it easier to understand, easier to debug, and easier to maintain. In web development, for example, some sources have espoused the virtues of one script to handle everything, and the result is usually a jumbled mess.

◆ Use directories intelligently. All parts of the application do not, and usually should not, appear in the same directory. Group them logically and for security purposes.

◆ Reuse your own code. Know what functions and classes have been created, and use these again and again. Write them so that they can be used for slightly different tasks. This makes changing code at a later stage much easier. This applies especially to things such as database connections.

◆ Separate logic from presentation (in a web environment, HTML and scripting languages are intermingled too frequently).

◆ When debugging a query, it can help to run the query directly in MySQL and not through the application (I often display the query and then paste this into the MySQL client). This allows you to narrow down the error, so you know whether it's in the query you're running or something in the application.

◆ Get into the habit of closing connections (running `mysql_close()` in PHP) and cleaning up resources, even if you're working in an environment where this is not necessary. Web developers often struggle when making the move to other kinds of applications, as they're used to a tolerant web environment, where everything is cleaned up after the web server process is complete. Similarly, languages such as PHP are much less strict than languages such as C++.

◆ Simple code is good code. Writing a chunk of code on one unreadable line, just because you can, may make you look clever, but it just frustrates those who have to read your code later. Coders who overly complicate their code are failing to do what coders are supposed to do: simplifying complexities. Simple code is usually as fast, too. It can even be faster, such as when you use simple string functions instead of regular expressions.

◆ In projects with more than one coder, use coding standards. That way when members of the coding team work on each other's code, they will be more productive because it will take them less time to adjust to the new standard (or lack of it). Coding standards include such things as the number of spaces (or tabs) to use when indenting and variable name conventions (such as whether to use capitalization, for example, `$totalConnects`; underscores, for example, `$total_connects`; or no spaces, for example, `$totalconnects`). The standards could go so far as to prescribe the editor to use, because different editors could align code differently, making it less readable.

◆ Larger projects too need some sort of version control. This ensures that when more than one person works on a piece of code, their work does not conflict. Even one-person projects can easily get out of hand if, like me, you have a tendency to work on different machines and save versions all over the place. Larger projects can use something such as CVS or Visual SourceSafe (these can be found at `http://www.cvshome.org/` and `http://msdn.microsoft.com/ssafe/`, respectively), and small projects can simply use a numbering scheme.

◆ Use prototyping if the project warrants it (especially if there are doubts about all the project requirements being set). Prototyping is where a model of the final system is developed, without all the functionality, and this is worked and reworked until the final system is ready. Prototyping demands more of a role from the users and can be used to make them feel more included.

## Phase 4: Testing and Implementation

Never skimp on the testing phase! Deadline pressure may tempt you to cut down the scheduled three weeks of testing to one, for example, but this is bound to backfire. You should not look at testing as an unnecessary burden; rather, it's a vital part of fine-tuning the application and ensuring that it runs smoothly.

There are a number of kinds of testing:

**Unit testing**    These tests ensure that each class, method, and function works properly in its own right. You need to test whether the returned results are correct no matter what the input; in other words, account for every possible scenario.

**Integration testing**    These tests ensure that each unit works as it should when integrated with other units.

**System testing**    The entire system is tested as a whole. This would include testing the performance of the system under load (stress testing), multiple users, and so on.

**Regression testing**    These are the tests that take place to see if the fixes have broken any other functionality. It's extremely common for "quick fixes" to have unforeseen circumstances.

After you've finished analyzing the requirements, designing the application, coding it, and then testing it, you're ready to implement the application. You may want to roll out the application for a small group of users or a single office first, allowing you to deal with any unforeseen problems, or take the big bang approach and move everyone to the new system at a single point in time. Then, be ready to start this process all over again when users request new features.

# Summary

There are a number of techniques to make your database applications more portable and easier to maintain, especially regarding database queries. Separate your connection details from the scripts that make the connections, and make sure they are stored in only one place so that you can easily change the details. Make sure future changes in the database table structure do not affect your scripts if the change is unrelated. Specify field names in your SELECT and INSERT queries.

Certain environments (particularly web applications) may benefit from persistent connections. Use these to reduce the connection overhead when using frequent connections from the same place.

MySQL is usually more efficient at performing a task than a programming language. MySQL is optimized for speed, and makes use of indexes, caches, and memory to access information quickly. For example, using an application language instead of MySQL to sort data, though possible, is not efficient. In general, use MySQL whenever possible.

When developing applications, careful planning is important. Gather and formalize all the requirements from the users before determining the technology requirements, designing a model, and coding the application.

When coding, be sure to avoid the common pitfalls so that your code is flexible, portable, and easily maintainable. Then, before you implement the application, be prepared to test it extensively, which should be just as important as coding the application.

# Chapter 6

# Extending MySQL

ONE OF THE GREAT advantages of MySQL is that it's always been relatively easy to extend MySQL. When early versions of MySQL were accused of being lacking in features, the comeback was always, "Write your own." MySQL has made it easy to do that for anyone competent in C or C++.

You can add functions to MySQL in two ways. Create a *user-defined function* (UDF) or add a native (built-in) function. You can add UDFs to source and binary distributions, adding or dropping them at any time, but you can add built-in functions only to a source distribution (you modify the source code and compile your additions). This chapter only discusses UDFs. (This chapter uses the term *UDF* to describe the related set of C/C++ functions that correspond to a single MySQL function. The term *function* describes a single C/C++ function.)

Featured in this chapter:

◆ Standard user-defined functions
◆ Aggregate user-defined functions
◆ UDF functions and parameters

## User-Defined Functions

You would mostly write UDFs in C or C++. You can use them with binary or source distributions that have been configured with `--with-mysqld-ldflags=-rdynamic`. Once added, UDFs are always available when the server restarts, unless the `--skip-grant-tables` option is used.

There are two kinds of UDFs: *standard* and *aggregate*. Standard UDFs are like ordinary built-in functions such as `POW()` and `SIN()` and work on a single row of data, and aggregate functions are similar to the built-in `SUM()` and `AVG()` functions that work with groups.

To implement a UDF you need to do the following:

1. Write the C or C++ functions (you can use other languages as long as you can compile them into a native code shared library).

2. Compile and install the library.

3. Load the UDF into MySQL.

Once a UDF is added, details are stored in the *func* table in the *mysql* database. The *func* table looks as follows:

```
mysql> SHOW COLUMNS FROM func;
+-------+----------------------------+------+-----+---------+-------+
| Field | Type                       | Null | Key | Default | Extra |
+-------+----------------------------+------+-----+---------+-------+
| name  | char(64) binary            |      | PRI |         |       |
| ret   | tinyint(1)                 |      |     | 0       |       |
| dl    | char(128)                  |      |     |         |       |
| type  | enum('function','aggregate') |    |     | function |      |
+-------+----------------------------+------+-----+---------+-------+
4 rows in set (0.00 sec)
```

The *name* field contains the name of the UDF (and the name of the main C/C++ function). The *ret* field indicates whether the UDF can return nulls, the *dl* field indicates the name of the library containing the UDF (many UDFs can be bundled into one library), and the *type* field indicates whether the UDF is a standard or aggregate UDF.

**NOTE** *If you've upgraded from an older version of MySQL, you may not have all the columns. Run the* `mysql_fix_privilege_tables` *script (in the* `bin` *directory) to add the missing columns to your table.*

In this section, you'll first look at compiling and installing the sample UDFs that come with a MySQL distribution and then go on to writing your own. Before you get started, create and add records to a small table, which you'll use to test the UDFs once you've added them:

```
mysql> USE firstdb;
Database changed
mysql> CREATE TABLE words (id tinyint(4), word varchar(50));
Query OK, 0 rows affected (0.00 sec)
mysql> INSERT INTO words VALUES (1,'aeiou');
Query OK, 1 row affected (0.00 sec)
mysql> INSERT INTO words VALUES (2,'bro');
Query OK, 1 row affected (0.00 sec)
mysql> INSERT INTO words VALUES (3,'so');
Query OK, 1 row affected (0.00 sec)
mysql> INSERT INTO words VALUES (4,'kisso');
Query OK, 1 row affected (0.00 sec)
mysql> INSERT INTO words VALUES (5,'lassoo');
Query OK, 1 row affected (0.00 sec)
mysql> INSERT INTO words VALUES (2,'bro');
Query OK, 1 row affected (0.00 sec)
mysql> INSERT INTO words VALUES (3,'so');
Query OK, 1 row affected (0.00 sec)
mysql> INSERT INTO words VALUES (4,'kisso');
Query OK, 1 row affected (0.00 sec)
mysql> INSERT INTO words VALUES (4,'kisso');
Query OK, 1 row affected (0.00 sec)
```

```
mysql> INSERT INTO words VALUES (5,'lassoo');
Query OK, 1 row affected (0.00 sec)
```

MySQL comes with five sample UDFs, bundled in the file udf_example.cc, usually stored in the mysql/sql directory of a source distribution. You'll need to compile this file as a sharable object file. On Unix systems, these files usually have a .so extension, and on Windows the extension is usually .dll. The command (on Unix) you'll use will be something like this:

```
% gcc -shared -o udf_example.so udf_example.cc
```

This book is not a guide to programming and compiling, so although the topics are explained reasonably thoroughly, it cannot cover all possible combinations. You may need to be experienced or get some assistance in those areas to get the most out of this chapter.

To find the correct compiler options for your system, you can use the make utility, which checks for dependencies. Each system will differ, but after running make you may get output something like this:

```
% make udf_example.o
g++ -DMYSQL_SERVER -DDEFAULT_MYSQL_HOME="\"/usr/local\""
-DDATADIR="\"/usr/local/var\"" -DSHAREDIR="\"/usr/local/share/mysql\""
-DHAVE_CONFIG_H -I../innobase/include -I./../include -I./../regex
-I. -I../include -I. -O3 -DDBUG_OFF    -fno-implicit-templates
-fno-exceptions -fno-rtti -c udf_example.cc
```

Take the options supplied, and use them to compile the UDF. Again, your system may differ—some will require the -c option to be left out, others will need it. You should know your system well enough, know someone who does, or have enough patience to try again if your first (and second and third…) attempts result in a dead end. Your final command may look something like this:

```
% gcc -shared -o udf_example.so udf_example.cc -I../innobase/include↩
 -I./../include -I./../regex -I. -I../include -I.
```

**NOTE**  *On some systems you'll have to do this in two steps: first compile* udf_example.cc *as* udf_example.o, *then create the shared library from* udf_example.o *(using* gcc -shared -o udf_example.so udf_example.o*).*

Once you've compiled the UDF, move it to the place your shared libraries usually go. With Unix systems, it's any directory searched by ld (mostly /usr/lib or /lib), or you can set an environment variable to point to the directory you're storing your library. Typing **man dlopen** will give you the name of the environment variable (usually LD_LIBRARY or LD_LIBRARY_PATH). You would set this in your startup script (mysql.server or mysqld_safe). With Windows systems, you'll usually place the UDF in the WINDOWS\System32 or WINNT\System32 directory. Copy your compiled file to the appropriate location, for example:

```
% cp udf_example.so /usr/lib
```

Once you have placed the file, some systems may require you to create the necessary links (such as by running ldconfig) or restarting MySQL before you can load the function.

To load the UDF from the MySQL command line, use the CREATE FUNCTION statement. The syntax is as follows:

```
CREATE [AGGREGATE] FUNCTION function_name RETURNS {STRING|REAL|INTEGER}
        SONAME shared_library_name
```

The example comes with a number of UDFs (you can bundle more than one in a single library). For now, you'll load just three of the functions, as follows:

```
mysql> CREATE FUNCTION metaphon RETURNS STRING SONAME "udf_example.so";
Query OK, 0 rows affected (0.03 sec)
mysql> CREATE FUNCTION myfunc_double RETURNS REAL SONAME "udf_example.so";
Query OK, 0 rows affected (0.00 sec)
mysql> CREATE AGGREGATE FUNCTION avgcost RETURNS REAL SONAME "udf_example.so";
Query OK, 0 rows affected (0.00 sec)
```

Now you can test the new UDF. To see what all the UDFs do, you should look at the udf_example.cc file. The metaphon UDF (the correct name for the algorithm is actually *metaphone*) takes a string and returns a result based on the way the string sounds. It is similar to the more well-known soundex algorithm, but tuned more for English.

```
mysql> SELECT METAPHON(word) FROM words;
+----------------+
| METAPHON(word) |
+----------------+
| E              |
| BR             |
| S              |
| KS             |
| LS             |
| BR             |
| S              |
| KS             |
| KS             |
| LS             |
+----------------+
10 rows in set (0.00 sec)
```

This is not particularly useful, but at least now you know how to add functions. Test that the aggregate function is working by using this code:

```
mysql> SELECT AVGCOST(id,1.5) FROM words;
+-----------------+
| AVGCOST(id,1.5) |
+-----------------+
|          1.5000 |
+-----------------+
1 row in set (0.00 sec)
```

There is only one result, as the function works with a group. You didn't use a GROUP BY clause, so the entire result set is taken as a single group. If you grouped by the contents of id, you'd get five results, as there are five unique id values:

```
mysql> SELECT id,AVGCOST(id,1.5) FROM words GROUP BY id;
+------+-----------------+
| id   | AVGCOST(id,1.5) |
+------+-----------------+
|    1 |          1.5000 |
|    2 |          1.5000 |
|    3 |          1.5000 |
|    4 |          1.5000 |
|    5 |          1.5000 |
+------+-----------------+
```

You can drop a UDF with the DROP FUNCTION statement, for example:

```
mysql> DROP FUNCTION myfunc_double;
Query OK, 0 rows affected (0.01 sec)
```

You can view the list of available UDFs by looking at the contents of the *func* table in the *mysql* database, as follows:

```
mysql> SELECT * FROM mysql.func;
+----------+-----+----------------+-----------+
| name     | ret | dl             | type      |
+----------+-----+----------------+-----------+
| metaphon |   0 | udf_example.so | function  |
| avgcost  |   1 | udf_example.so | aggregate |
+----------+-----+----------------+-----------+
2 rows in set (0.01 sec)
```

This implies that the user adding or removing the function needs to have INSERT or DELETE permission for the *func* table, or *mysql* database. You would usually only give this to an administrator, as besides the security risk of access to the *mysql* database, a UDF can potentially cause a lot of harm.

Now let's create a UDF from scratch. You're first going to create a standard (not aggregate) UDF, called count_vowels.

## Standard UDFs

A standard UDF has one main function, which is named the same as the UDF and is required, and two optional functions, which are named similarly but with _init and _deinit appended to the end. All these functions must be in the same library.

### THE INIT FUNCTION

The init function is the initialization function, called once at the beginning of processing the UDF. It checks the arguments passed to the UDF (for example, whether they're the right type or number) and specifies details about the result (whether it can be NULL, how many decimal places it has, and so on).

It is declared as follows:

```
my_bool function_name_init(UDF_INIT *initid, UDF_ARGS *args, char *message);
```

The function returns a Boolean type, which you set to `false` if the function did not pick up any errors or `true` if an error was spotted.

### The initd Parameter

The `initd` parameter is the UDF's main data structure. It is passed to all three functions. Any changes to the default settings are made in this function. The structure contains the following members:

**my_bool maybe_null**   This is a Boolean that specifies whether the UDF can return a `NULL` value (if set to `true`) or not (if set to `false`). It's set to `false` by default, unless any of the function's arguments can be `NULL`.

**unsigned int decimals**   Specifies the maximum number of decimals that can be returned. By default it takes the most number of decimals passed into the main function by any of the arguments. So, if 203.2, 219.12, and 341.456 are passed, `decimals` would default to 3 (based on the .456 of the last argument). You can set a maximum limit in the init function, though.

**unsigned int max_length**   Specifies the maximum length of the returned result. For string UDFs, the default is the length of the longest string argument. For integers, the default is 21 characters (including the sign). For reals, the default is 13 (including the sign and decimal point) plus the number of `decimals`.

**char *ptr**   This is a pointer that the UDF can use—for example, to pass data across all three functions. Allocate the memory in the init function if the pointer is used for new data.

### The args Parameter

The second parameter, `args`, is a structure containing the arguments passed in from the query. It contains the following members:

**unsigned int arg_count**   Contains the number of arguments passed in from the query. If your UDF takes a set number of arguments, check this value for error handling.

**enum Item_result *arg_type**   Contains an array of types. Each element corresponds to one of the arguments, so the total number of elements is the same as the value of `arg_count`. The possible types are `STRING_RESULT`, `INT_RESULT`, and `REAL_RESULT`. Use this for error checking, or cast the argument into the specific type you require.

**char **args**   Contains an array of the actual arguments passed from the query. If the argument is constant, it can be accessed as `args->args[i]`, where `i` is the element number of the argument. For a nonconstant `args->args[i]` is 0, as the actual value from the row is passed to the main function. This is discussed further in "The Main Function."

**unsigned long *lengths**   An array containing the maximum possible string length for each argument passed by the query. It differs in the main function, so see the discussion in "The Main Function."

### *The* message *Parameter*

The message parameter contains a character pointer, which is used for any error messages that arise during the initialization. It should always be given a value when the init function returns true, indicating an error. The default character buffer is 200 bytes, but you'd usually want a much shorter error message than this (80 characters is the width of a standard terminal). You must also terminate it with a null byte.

## THE MAIN FUNCTION

The main function is the only one required for a standard UDF, and it is called once for each row returned from the query. The return value from this function is the same as the return value for the whole UDF and can be a string, a real, or an integer. The function should be declared as one of the following corresponding to its return value.

If the UDF returns a string:

```
char *function_name(UDF_INIT *initid, UDF_ARGS *args, char *result,
  unsigned long *length, char *is_null, char *error);
```

If the UDF returns a real:

```
double function_name(UDF_INIT *initid, UDF_ARGS *args,
  char *is_null, char *error);
```

If the UDF returns an integer:

```
long long function_name(UDF_INIT *initid, UDF_ARGS *args,
  char *is_null, char *error);
```

For numeric types, the return value of the main function is simply the value. If it's a string type, the return value is a pointer to the result, with the length stored in the length argument. The result buffer is defaulted to 255 bytes, so if the result is less than this, the pointer should be the result pointer passed into the main function. If it's more, it should be the pointer allocated in the init function (you'll need to allocate space with malloc() and then later deallocate the space in the deinit function).

### *The* initd *Parameter*

All of the attributes of this structure (discussed previously) are available to the main function. There should be no need to modify any of these values in the main function.

### *The* args *Parameter*

The attributes from this structure were discussed previously. In the main function, however, the args array contains the actual arguments passed from each row to the function. Because these can differ in type, you must case them to the appropriate type. For an argument of type INT_RESULT, cast args->args[i] to a long long, as follows:

```
long long int_val;
int_val = *((long long*) args->args[i]);
```

For an argument of type REAL_RESULT, cast to a double, as follows:

```
double    real_val;
real_val = *((double*) args->args[i]);
```

For an argument of type STRING_RESULT, the string is available as args->args[i], and the length of the string as args->length[i], excluding any trailing nulls (for numeric types, args->length[i] still contains the maximum length it was given in the init function).

### The length *Parameter*

This is a pointer to an integer that you set to the length of the returned value (excluding trailing nulls).

### The is null *Parameter*

Set this to 1 if the UDF returns a null value; otherwise, leave it at the default, 0.

### The result *Parameter*

This is a pointer to a character array and is where you place the return value of the UDF; 255 bytes are allocated, so if the result is longer, you'll need to use the ptr parameter from the init function. You'll need to allocate and deallocate this memory.

### THE DEINIT FUNCTION

This function frees memory allocated by the init function and takes care of any other required cleanup, specifically the pointer that may have been allocated in the init function. You declare the function as follows:

```
void function_name_deinit(UDF_INIT *initid)
```

## Creating a Sample Standard UDF

After all the introductions, let's create a small UDF called count_vowels. It takes one argument only (which must be a string) and returns the number of vowels in the string. Listing 6.1 contains the UDF.

---

**LISTING 6.1: COUNT_VOWELS.CC**

```
#ifdef STANDARD
#include <stdio.h>
#include <string.h>
#else
#include <my_global.h>
#include <my_sys.h>
#endif
#include <mysql.h>
#include <m_ctype.h>
#include <m_string.h>

/* These must be right or mysqld will not find the symbol! */
```

```
extern "C" {
my_bool count_vowels_init(UDF_INIT *initid, UDF_ARGS *args, char *message);
void count_vowels_deinit(UDF_INIT *initid);
long long count_vowels(UDF_INIT *initid, UDF_ARGS *args,
 char *is_null, char *error);
}

/* Makes sure there is one argument passed, and that it's a string. */
my_bool count_vowels_init(UDF_INIT *initid, UDF_ARGS *args, char *message) {
  if (args->arg_count != 1 || args->arg_type[0] != STRING_RESULT) {
    strcpy(message,"You can only pass one argument, and it must be a string");
    return 1;
  }
  return 0;
}

/* no need for a deinit function, as we don't allocate extra memory */
void count_vowels_deinit(UDF_INIT *initid){
}

/* count the number of vowels in the string */
long long count_vowels(UDF_INIT *initid, UDF_ARGS *args,char *is_null,↵
 char *error) {
 long long num_vowels = 0; /* the same type as the result of the function */
 char *word = args->args[0];  /* pointer to string */
 int i = 0; /* to loop through the word */
 char c;    /* to contain the letter  */
 while ( ( c = word[ i++ ] ) != '\0' ) {
  switch ( c ) {
   case 'a':
   case 'e':
   case 'i':
   case 'o':
   case 'u':
   num_vowels++; /* if the letter in c is a vowel, increment the counter */
  }
 }
 return num_vowels;
}
```

Once you've saved the file, make and compile it, and then copy it to the directory where you place your libraries, as discussed earlier:

```
% make count_vowels.o
g++ -DMYSQL_SERVER -DDEFAULT_MYSQL_HOME="\"/usr/local/mysql\""
  -DDATADIR="\"/usr/local/mysql/var\""
  -DSHAREDIR="\"/usr/local/mysql/share/mysql\""
```

```
    -DHAVE_CONFIG_H -I../innobase/include -I./../include
    -I./../regex -I. -I../include -I. -O3 -DDBUG_OFF
    -fno-implicit-templates -fno-exceptions -fno-rtti -c repeat_str.cc
% gcc -shared -o count_vowels.so count_vowels.cc -I../innobase/include↵
    -I./../include -I./../regex -I. -I../include -I.
```

Now connect to MySQL, load the function, and run a test:

```
mysql> CREATE FUNCTION count_vowels RETURNS INTEGER SONAME "count_vowels.so";
Query OK, 0 rows affected (0.02 sec)
mysql> SELECT id,word,count_vowels(word) FROM words;
+------+--------+--------------------+
| id   | word   | count_vowels(word) |
+------+--------+--------------------+
|    1 | aeiou  |                  5 |
|    2 | bro    |                  1 |
|    3 | so     |                  1 |
|    4 | kisso  |                  2 |
|    5 | lassoo |                  3 |
|    2 | bro    |                  1 |
|    3 | so     |                  1 |
|    4 | kisso  |                  2 |
|    4 | kisso  |                  2 |
|    5 | lassoo |                  3 |
+------+--------+--------------------+
10 rows in set (0.00 sec)
```

If you passed a nonstring argument such as from the *id* field, or more than one argument, you'd get the error message you specified:

```
mysql> SELECT id,word,count_vowels(id) FROM words;
ERROR:
You can only pass one argument, and it must be a string
```

***WARNING*** *If you make a change to the UDF, be sure to* **DROP** *the function first from MySQL before you upload it again. You're quite likely to crash MySQL and have to restart if you don't!*

## Understanding Aggregate Functions

Aggregate functions are those that can be used with a GROUP BY clause, such as SUM() and AVG(). To create an aggregate UDF, you use the same functions as with a standard UDF, except that there are two more required: the reset and add functions. The behavior of the other functions is different as well:

**The Reset Function**   This function is called at the beginning of each new group. Data used for group calculations are reset here. You declare the function as follows:

```
char *xxx_reset(UDF_INIT *initid, UDF_ARGS *args,
                char *is_null, char *error);
```

**The Add Function**  This is called for each row of the group except the first row. You'll probably want it to be called for every row, in which case you'll need to call it from within the reset function.

**The Main Function**  The main function is only called once per group of data (at the end), so it performs any necessary calculations on the entire group of data (usually accessed by `initd->ptr`).

**The Init Function**  Behaves the same as with a standard UDF, except the `ptr` attribute becomes much more important in an aggregate function. It stores data about each group, which is added within the add function. The main function can then access it to get data about the entire group.

**The Deinit Function**  Plays the same role as with a standard UDF, except that it will almost always exist, as you need to clean up `ptr`.

## Creating a Sample Aggregate UDF

For the aggregate UDF, you're going to make some changes to the `count_vowels` UDF so that it counts groups of vowels. You're going to create a structure called `data` with an element count. You'll increment `data->count` each time you encounter a vowel in the add function (which is called every row), and reset the value in the reset function (called once per group). Because the add function is not explicitly called for the first row, you'll call it from the reset function to make sure the first row of the group is also counted. Listing 6.2 contains the aggregate UDF.

---

**LISTING 6.2:** `COUNT_AGG_VOWELS.CC`

```
#ifdef STANDARD
#include <stdio.h>
#include <string.h>
#else
#include <my_global.h>
#include <my_sys.h>
#endif
#include <mysql.h>
#include <m_ctype.h>
#include <m_string.h>          // To get strmov()

#ifdef HAVE_DLOPEN

/* These must be right or mysqld will not find the symbol! */

extern "C" {
my_bool count_agg_vowels_init( UDF_INIT* initid, UDF_ARGS* args, char* message );
void count_agg_vowels_deinit( UDF_INIT* initid );
void count_agg_vowels_reset( UDF_INIT* initid, UDF_ARGS* args,↵
char* is_null, char *error );
```

```
void count_agg_vowels_add( UDF_INIT* initid, UDF_ARGS* args,↵
char* is_null, char *error );
long long count_agg_vowels( UDF_INIT* initid, UDF_ARGS* args,↵
char* is_null, char *error );
}

struct count_agg_vowels_data {
  unsigned long long count;
};


/* Count the number of vowels */
my_bool
count_agg_vowels_init( UDF_INIT* initid, UDF_ARGS* args, char* message ) {
  struct count_agg_vowels_data* data;

  if (args->arg_count != 1 || args->arg_type[0] != STRING_RESULT) {
    strcpy(message,"You can only pass one argument, and it must be a string");
    return 1;
  }

  initid->max_length = 20;
  data = new struct count_agg_vowels_data;
  data->count = 0;
  initid->ptr = (char*)data;

  return 0;
}

/* free the memory allocated to from ptr */
void
count_agg_vowels_deinit( UDF_INIT* initid ) {
  delete initid->ptr;
}

/* called once at the beginning of each group. Needs to call the add
function as well resets data->count to 0 for the new group */
 void
count_agg_vowels_reset( UDF_INIT* initid, UDF_ARGS* args,↵
char* is_null, char* message ) {
  struct count_agg_vowels_data* data = (struct count_agg_vowels_data*)initid->ptr;
  data->count          = 0;

  *is_null = 0;
  count_agg_vowels_add( initid, args, is_null, message );
}
```

```
/* called for every row, add the number of vowels to data->count */
void
count_agg_vowels_add( UDF_INIT* initid, UDF_ARGS* args, char* is_null,↵
char* message ) {
  struct count_agg_vowels_data* data    =↵
(struct count_agg_vowels_data*)initid->ptr;
  char *word = args->args[0];  /* pointer to string */
  int I = 0;
  char c;

  while ( ( c = word[ I++ ] ) != '\0' ) {
   switch ( c ) {
    case 'a':
    case 'e':
    case 'i':
    case 'o':
    case 'u':
    data->count++;
   }
 }
}
/* returns data->count, or a null if it cannot find anything */
long long
count_agg_vowels( UDF_INIT* initid, UDF_ARGS* args, char* is_null, char* error )
{
  struct count_agg_vowels_data* data = (struct count_agg_vowels_data*)initid->ptr;
  if (!data->count)
  {
    *is_null = 1;
    return 0;
  }

  *is_null = 0;
  return data->count;
}

#endif /* HAVE_DLOPEN */
% make count_agg_vowels.o
g++ -DMYSQL_SERVER -DDEFAULT_MYSQL_HOME="\"/usr/local/mysql\""
 -DDATADIR="\"/usr/local/mysql/var\""
 -DSHAREDIR="\"/usr/local/mysql/share/mysql\""
 -DHAVE_CONFIG_H -I../innobase/include -I../include
 -I./../regex -I. -I../include -I. -O3 -DDBUG_OFF
 -fno-implicit-templates -fno-exceptions -fno-rtti -c repeat_str.cc
% gcc -shared -o count_agg_vowels.so count_agg_vowels.cc -I../innobase/include↵
 -I./../include -I./../regex -I. -I../include -I.
```

Now connect to MySQL, load the function, and run a test:

```
mysql> CREATE AGGREGATE FUNCTION count_agg_vowels RETURNS INTEGER
  SONAME "count_vowels.so";
Query OK, 0 rows affected (0.02 sec)

mysql> SELECT count_agg_vowels(word) FROM words;
+-----------------------+
| count_agg_vowels(word) |
+-----------------------+
|                    21 |
+-----------------------+
1 row in set (0.01 sec)
mysql> SELECT id,count_agg_vowels(word) FROM words GROUP BY id;
+------+-----------------------+
| id   | count_agg_vowels(word) |
+------+-----------------------+
|    1 |                     5 |
|    2 |                     2 |
|    3 |                     2 |
|    4 |                     6 |
|    5 |                     6 |
+------+-----------------------+
5 rows in set (0.00 sec)
```

## Troubleshooting the UDF

There are quite a few reasons that your UDF may not have worked. It's common for MySQL to crash if the UDF is not properly implemented, so be careful about implementing an untried UDF on a running, live system. Each system will have its own intricacies, but the following are some of the more common problems:

- Make sure you've dropped any pre-existing functions of the same name (if you're updating a function) before you upload them or reload them. You may have to manually delete the function from the *func* table if you've previously added broken UDF that you can't DROP in the normal way.

- You can also try stopping and restarting MySQL before reloading the function though this is not usually necessary.

- Make sure the return type when you CREATE FUNCTION matches the type you return from the main function in your code (string, real or integer).

- You may have to configure MySQL with --with-mysqld-ldflags=-rdynamic in order to implement the UDF.

# Summary

MySQL allows you to add user-defined functions (UDFs). You use these as you would a normal function inside a query. There are two kinds of UDFs: aggregate and standard. Aggregate UDFs work on groups of data and can be used with the `GROUP BY` clause. Standard UDFs work on single rows of data.

Standard UDFs consist of three functions: the main function, which is required and called for every row, and the initialization and deinitialization functions, called once at the beginning and end, respectively. Aggregate functions also utilize the add function (called every row, in place of the main function, which is called only once at the end of every group) and the reset function (called at the start of every group).

# Part II

# Designing a Database

**In this section:**
- Chapter 7: Understanding Relational Databases
- Chapter 8: Database Normalization
- Chapter 9: Database Design

# Chapter 7

# Understanding Relational Databases

JUST AS PERHAPS WE take movie special effects for granted until we see what the state of the art was in previous eras, so we can't fully appreciate the power of relational databases without seeing what preceded them.

Relational databases allow any table to relate to any other table through means of common fields. It is a highly flexible system, and most modern databases are relational.

Featured in this chapter:

◆ The hierarchical database model
◆ The network database model
◆ The relational database model
◆ Learning basic terms
◆ Table keys and foreign keys
◆ Views

## Exploring Early Database Models

Before the advent of databases, the only way to store data was from unrelated files. Programmers had to go to great lengths to extract the data, and their programs had to perform complex parsing and relating.

Languages such as Perl, with its powerful regular expressions ideal for processing text, have made the job a lot easier than before; however, accessing data from files is still a challenging task. Without a standard way to access data, systems are more prone to errors, are slower to develop, and are more difficult to maintain. Data redundancy (where data is duplicated unnecessarily) and poor data integrity (where data is not changed in all the necessary locations, leading to wrong or outdated data being supplied) are frequent consequences of the file access method of data storage. For these reasons, database management systems (DBMSs) were developed to provide a standard and reliable way to access and update data. They provide an intermediary layer between the application and the data, and the programmer is able to concentrate on developing the application, rather than worrying about data access issues.

A *database model* is a logical model concerned with how the data is represented. Instead of database designers worrying about the physical storage of the data, the database model allows them to look at a higher, or more conceptual, level, reducing the gap between the real-world problem for which the application is being developed and the technical implementation.

There are a number of database models. First you'll learn about two common models, the hierarchical database model and the network database model. Then you'll investigate the one that MySQL (along with most modern DBMSs) uses, the relational model.

## Understanding the Hierarchical Database Model

The earliest model was the hierarchical database model, resembling an upside-down tree. Files are related in a parent-child manner, with each parent capable of relating to more than one child, but each child only being related to one parent. Most of you will be familiar with this kind of structure—it's the way most filesystems work. There is usually a root, or top-level, directory that contains various other directories and files. Each subdirectory can then contain more files and directories, and so on. Each file or directory can only exist in one directory itself—it only has one parent. As you can see in Figure 7.1, A1 is the root directory, and its children are B1 and B2. B1 is a parent to C1, C2, and C3, which in turn has children of its own.

**FIGURE 7.1**

The hierarchical database model

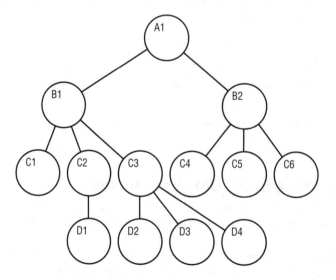

This model, although being a vast improvement on dealing with unrelated files, has some serious disadvantages. It represents one-to-many relationships well (one parent has many children; for example, one company branch has many employees), but it has problems with many-to-many relationships. Relationships such as that between a product file and an orders file are difficult to implement in a hierarchical model. Specifically, an order can contain many products, and a product can appear in many orders. Also, the hierarchical model is not flexible because adding new relationships can result in wholesale changes to the existing structure, which in turn means all existing applications need to change as well. This is not fun when someone has forgotten a file type and wants to add it to the structure shortly before the project is due to launch!

Developing the applications is complex also because the programmer needs to know the data structure well in order to traverse the model to access the needed data. As you've seen in the earlier chapters, when accessing data from two related tables, you only need to know the fields you require from those two tables. In the hierarchical model, you'd need to know the entire chain between the two. For example, to relate data from A1 and D4, you'd need to take the route: A1, B1, C3, and D4.

### Understanding the Network Database Model

The network database model was a progression from the hierarchical database model and was designed to solve some of that model's problems, specifically the lack of flexibility. Instead of only allowing each child to have one parent, this model allows each child to have multiple parents (it calls the children *members* and the parents *owners*). It addresses the need to model more complex relationships, such as the orders/parts many-to-many relationship mentioned earlier. As you can see in Figure 7.2, A1 has two members, B1 and B2. B1 is the owner of C1, C2, C3, and C4. However, in this model, C4 has two owners, B1 and B2.

**FIGURE 7.2**

The network database model

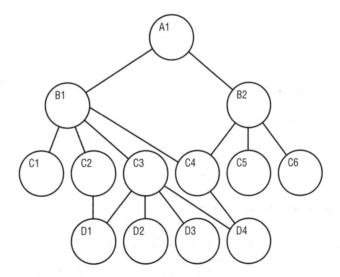

Of course, this model has its problems, or everyone would still be using it. It is more difficult to implement and maintain, and, although more flexible than the hierarchical model, it still has flexibility problems. Not all relations can be satisfied by assigning another owner, and the programmer still has to understand the data structures well in order to make the model efficient.

## Understanding the Relational Database Model

The relational database model was a huge leap forward from the network database model. Instead of relying on a parent-child or owner-member relationship, the relational model allows any file to be related to any other by means of a common field. Suddenly, the complexity of the design was greatly reduced because changes could be made to the database schema without affecting the system's ability to access data. And because access was not by means of paths to and from files, but from a direct relationship between files, new relations between these files could be easily added.

In 1970, when E. F. Codd developed the model, it was thought to be impractical. The increased ease of use comes at a large performance penalty, and the hardware in those days was not able to implement the model. Since then, of course, hardware has taken huge strides to where today even the simplest computers can run sophisticated relational database management systems.

Relational databases go hand in hand with the development of SQL, which is covered in Part I, "Using MySQL." The simplicity of SQL—where even a novice can learn to perform basic queries in a short period of time—is a large part of the reason for the popularity of the relational model.

Tables 7.1 and 7.2 relate to each other through the stock_code field. Any two tables can relate to each other simply by creating a field they have in common.

**TABLE 7.1:** THE PRODUCT TABLE

| STOCK_CODE | DESCRIPTION | PRICE |
|---|---|---|
| A416 | Nails, box | $0.14 |
| C923 | Drawing pins, box | $0.08 |

**TABLE 7.2:** THE INVOICE TABLE

| INVOICE_CODE | INVOICE_LINE | STOCK_CODE | QUANTITY |
|---|---|---|---|
| 3804 | 1 | A416 | 10 |
| 3804 | 2 | C923 | 15 |

## Introducing Basic Terms

The relational model uses certain terms to describe its components. If you've gone through Part I, "Using MySQL," you'll be familiar with many of them:

- *Data* are the values kept in the database. On their own, the data mean very little. CA 684-213 is an example of data in a DMV (Division of Motor Vehicles) database.

- *Information* is processed data. For example, CA 684-213 is the car registration number of Lyndon Manson in a DMV database.

- A *database* is a collection of *tables*.

- Each table is made up of *records* (the horizontal rows in the table, also called *tuples*). Each record should be unique, and can be stored in any order in the table.

- Each record is made up of *fields* (which are the vertical columns of the table, also called *attributes*). Basically, a record is one fact (for example, one customer or one sale).

- These fields can be of various *types*. MySQL has many types, as you saw in Chapter 2 ("Data Types and Table Types"), but generally the types fall into three kinds: character, numeric, and date. For example, a customer name is a character field, a customer's birthday is a date field, and a customer's number of children is a numeric field.

- The range of allowed values for a field is called the *domain* (also called a *field specification*). For example, a credit_card field may be limited to only the values Mastercard, Visa, and Amex.

- A field is said to contain a null value when it contains nothing at all. Null fields can create complexities in calculations and have consequences for data accuracy. For this reason, many fields are specifically set not to contain null values.

- A *key* accesses specific records in a table.

- An *index* is a mechanism to improve the performance of a database. Indexes are often confused with keys. They are, strictly speaking, part of the physical structure, and keys are part of the logical structure. You'll often see the terms used interchangeably, however.

- A *view* is a virtual table made up of a subset of the actual tables.

- A *one-to-one* (1:1) relationship is where for each instance of the first table in a relationship, only one instance of the second table exists. An example of this would be a case where a chain of stores carries a vending machine. Each vending machine can only be in one store, and each store carries only one vending machine (see Figure 7.3).

**FIGURE 7.3**

A one-to-one relationship

- A *one-to-many* (1:M) relationship is where for each instance of the first table in the relationship, many instances of the second table exist. This is a common kind of relationship. An example is the relationship between a sculptor and their sculptures. Each sculptor may have created many sculptures, but each sculpture has been created by only one sculptor (see Figure 7.4).

**FIGURE 7.4**

A one-to-many relationship

- A *many-to-many* (M:N) relationship occurs where, for each instance of the first table, there are many instances of the second table, and for each instance of the second table, there are many instances of the first. For example, a student can have many lecturers, and a lecturer many students (see Figure 7.5).

**FIGURE 7.5**

A many-to-many relationship

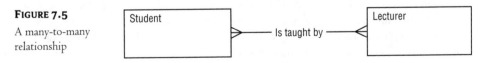

◆ A *mandatory* relationship exists where for each instance of the first table in a relationship, one or more instances of the second *must* exist. For example, for a music group to exist, there must exist at least one musician in that group.

◆ An *optional* relationship is where for each instance of the first table in a relationship, there *may* exist instances of the second. For example, if an author can be listed in the database without having written a book (in other words, a prospective author), that relationship is optional. The reverse isn't necessarily true, though; for example, for a book to be listed, it must have an author.

◆ *Data integrity* refers to the condition where data is accurate, valid, and consistent. An example of poor integrity would be if a customer telephone number is stored differently in two different locations. Another is where a course record contains a reference to a lecturer who is no longer present at the school. In Chapter 8, "Database Normalization," you'll learn a technique that assists you to minimize the risk of these sorts of problems: database normalization.

Now that you've been introduced to some of the basic terms, the next section will cover table keys, a fundamental aspect of relational databases, in more detail.

## Introducing Table Keys

A *key*, as the term itself indicates, unlocks access to the tables. If you know the key, you know how to identify specific records and the relationships between tables.

A *candidate key* is a field, or combination of fields, that uniquely identifies a record. It cannot contain a null value, and its value must be unique. (With duplicates, you would no longer be identifying a unique record.)

A *primary key* is a candidate key that has been designated to identify unique records in the table throughout the database structure. As an example, Table 7.3 shows the customer table.

**TABLE 7.3:** THE CUSTOMER TABLE

| CUSTOMER_CODE | FIRST_NAME | SURNAME | TELEPHONE_NUMBER |
| --- | --- | --- | --- |
| 1 | John | Smith | 448-2143 |
| 2 | Charlotte | Smith | 448-2143 |
| 3 | John | Smith | 9231-5312 |

At first glance, there are two possible candidate keys for this table. Either customer_code or a combination of first_name, surname, and telephone_number would suffice. It is always better to choose the candidate key with the least number of fields for the primary key, so you would choose customer_code in this example. Upon reflection, there is also the possibility of the second combination not being unique. The combination of first_name, surname, and telephone_number could in theory be duplicated, such as where a father has a son of the same name who is contactable at the same telephone number. This system would have to expressly exclude this possibility for these three fields to be considered for the status of primary key.

There may be many John Smiths in the average English-speaking country, but you avoid confusion by assigning each a unique number. Once a primary key has been created, the remaining candidate keys are labeled as alternate keys.

## Introducing Foreign Keys

You already know that a relation between two tables is created by assigning a common field to the two tables. This common field must be a primary key to the one table. Consider a relation between a customer table and a sale table. The relation is not much good if instead of using the primary key, customer_code, in the sale table, you use another field that is not unique, such as the customer's first name. You could never know for sure which customer made the sale in that case. So, in Figure 7.6, customer_ code is called the *foreign key* in the sale table; in other words, it is the primary key in a foreign table.

**FIGURE 7.6**

Setting foreign keys

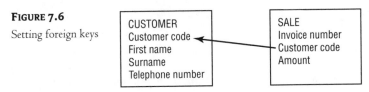

Foreign keys allow for something called *referential integrity*. What this means is that if a foreign key contains a value, this value refers to an existing record in the related table. For example, take a look at Table 7.4 and Table 7.5.

**TABLE 7.4:** THE LECTURER TABLE

| CODE | FIRSTNAME | SURNAME |
|------|-----------|---------|
| 1 | Anne | Cohen |
| 2 | Leonard | Clark |
| 3 | Vusi | Cave |

**TABLE 7.5:** THE COURSE TABLE

| COURSE TITLE | LECTURER |
|--------------|----------|
| Introduction to Programming | 1 |
| Information Systems | 2 |
| Systems Software | 3 |

Referential integrity exists here, as all the lecturers in the course table exist in the lecturer table. However, let's assume Anne Cohen leaves the institution, and you remove her from the lecturer table. In a situation where referential integrity is not enforced, she would be removed from the lecturer table, but not from the course table, shown in Table 7.6 and Table 7.7.

**TABLE 7.6:** THE LECTURER TABLE

| CODE | FIRSTNAME | SURNAME |
|------|-----------|---------|
| 2 | Leonard | Clark |
| 3 | Vusi | Cave |

**TABLE 7.7:** THE COURSE TABLE

| COURSE TITLE | LECTURER |
|--------------|----------|
| Introduction to Programming | 1 |
| Information Systems | 2 |
| Systems Software | 3 |

Now, when you look up who lectures Introduction to Programming, you are sent to a nonexistent record. This is called poor data integrity.

Foreign keys also allow cascading deletes and updates. For example, if Anne Cohen leaves, taking the Introduction to Programming course with her, all trace of her can be removed from both the lecturer and course table by using one statement. The delete "cascades" through the relevant tables, removing all relevant records. Since version 3.23.44, MySQL has supported checking of foreign key with the InnoDB table type, and cascading deletes have been supported since version 4.0.0. Remember, though, that enforcing referential integrity does have a performance cost. Though without it, it becomes the responsibility of the application to maintain data integrity.

Foreign keys can contain null values, indicating that no relationship exists.

## Introducing Views

Views are virtual tables. They are only a structure and contain no data. Their purpose is to allow a user to see a subset of the actual data. Views are one of the most frequent MySQL feature requests, and are due to be implemented in version 5.

A view can consist of a subset of one table. For example, Table 7.8 is a subset of the full table, shown in Table 7.9.

**TABLE 7.8:** THE STUDENT VIEW

| STUDENT VIEW |
|--------------|
| First_name |
| Surname |
| Grade |

**TABLE 7.9:** THE STUDENT TABLE

| **STUDENT** |
| --- |
| Student_id |
| First_name |
| Surname |
| Grade |
| Address |
| Telephone |

This view could be used to allow other students to see their fellow students' marks but not allow them access to personal information.

Or a view could be a combination of a number of tables, such as the view shown in Table 7.10. It's a combination of Table 7.11, Table 7.12, and Table 7.13.

**TABLE 7.10:** THE STUDENT GRADE VIEW

| **STUDENT GRADE VIEW** |
| --- |
| First_name |
| Surname |
| Course description |
| Grade |

**TABLE 7.11:** THE STUDENT TABLE

| **STUDENT** |
| --- |
| Student_id |
| First_name |
| Surname |
| Address |
| Telephone |

**TABLE 7.12:** THE COURSE TABLE

**COURSE**

Course_id

Course description

**TABLE 7.13:** THE GRADE TABLE

**GRADE**

Student_id

Course_id

Grade

Views are also useful for security. In larger organizations, where many developers may be working on a project, views allow developers access to only the data they need. What they don't need, even if it is in the same table, is hidden from them, safe from being seen or manipulated. It also allows queries to be simplified for developers. For example, without the view, a developer would have to retrieve the fields in the view with the following sort of query:

```
SELECT first_name,surname,course_description,grade FROM student,
  grade, course WHERE grade.student_id = student.student_id AND
  grade.course_id = course.course_id;
```

With the view, a developer could do the same with the following:

```
SELECT first_name,surname,course_description,grade FROM student_grade_view;
```

This is much more simple for a junior developer who hasn't yet learned how to do joins, and it's just less hassle for a senior developer, too!

## Summary

Before databases, programmers stored data in files. However, accessing data from files is inefficient for the programmer, so databases were created.

Hierarchical databases store data in a top-down, one-to-many structure. They are inflexible and also create a lot of work for the programmers.

Network databases allow easier representation of many-to-many relationships, but they are difficult to develop and maintain.

Relational databases allow any table to relate to any other table through means of common fields. It is a highly flexible system, and most modern databases are relational.

Table keys allow access to the records in a database. A primary key is an attribute, or a number of attributes, that uniquely identifies a row. A foreign key is an attribute, or a number of attributes, that is a primary key in another table.

Table views are logical subsets of existing tables. They contain no data but make it easier for developers, ensure security, and so on.

# Chapter 8

# Database Normalization

THIS CHAPTER INTRODUCES YOU to a powerful tool for optimizing your database design: normalization. Developed in the 1970s by E.F. Codd, normalization is now a standard requirement of most database designs. By following the steps outlined in this chapter, you'll be able to reduce data anomalies and ease maintenance.

Featured in this chapter:

- ◆ 1st normal form
- ◆ 2nd normal form
- ◆ 3rd normal form
- ◆ Boyce-Codd normal form
- ◆ 4th normal form
- ◆ 5th normal form
- ◆ Denormalization

## Understanding Normalization

In Part I, "Using MySQL," you created some tables in MySQL. Perhaps you've been using MySQL for a while with small projects where the databases contain one or two tables. But as you become more experienced and begin to tackle bigger projects, you may find that the queries you need become more complex and unwieldy, you begin to experience performance problems, or data anomalies start to creep in. Without some knowledge of database design and normalization, these problems may become overwhelming, and you will be unable to take the next step in your mastery of MySQL. Database *normalization* is a technique that can help you avoid data anomalies and other problems with managing your data. It consists of transforming a table through various stages: 1st normal form, 2nd normal form, 3rd normal form, and beyond. It aims to:

- ◆ Eliminate data redundancies (and therefore use less space)
- ◆ Make it easier to make changes to data, and avoid anomalies when doing so

◆ Make referential integrity constraints easier to enforce
◆ Produce an easily comprehensible structure that closely resembles the situation the data represents, and allows for growth

Let's begin by creating a sample set of data. You'll walk through the process of normalization first, without worrying about the theory, to get an understanding of the reasons you'd want to normalize. Once you've done that, I'll introduce the theory and steps of the various stages of normalization, which will make the whole process you're about to carefully go through now much simpler the next time you do it.

Imagine you are working on a system that records plants placed in certain locations and the soil descriptions associated with them.

The location:

Location code: 11

Location name: Kirstenbosch Gardens

contains the following three plants:

Plant code: 431
Plant name: Leucadendron
Soil category: A
Soil description: Sandstone

Plant code: 446
Plant name: Protea
Soil category: B
Soil description: Sandstone/Limestone

Plant code: 482
Plant name: Erica
Soil category: C
Soil description: Limestone

The location:

Location code: 12

Location name: Karbonkelberg Mountains

contains the following two plants:

Plant code: 431
Plant name: Leucadendron

Soil category: A

Soil description: Sandstone

Plant code: 449

Plant name: Restio

Soil category: B

Soil description: Sandstone/Limestone

There is a problem with the previous data. Tables in relational databases are in a grid, or table, format (MySQL, like most modern databases, is a relational database), with each row being one unique record. Let's try and rearrange this data is the form of a tabular report (as shown in Table 8.1).

**TABLE 8.1:** PLANT DATA DISPLAYED AS A TABULAR REPORT

| LOCATION CODE | LOCATION NAME | PLANT CODE | PLANT NAME | SOIL CATEGORY | SOIL DESCRIPTION |
| --- | --- | --- | --- | --- | --- |
| 11 | Kirstenbosch Gardens | 431 | Leucadendron | A | Sandstone |
| | | 446 | Protea | B | Sandstone/ Limestone |
| | | 482 | Erica | C | Limestone |
| 12 | Karbonkelberg Mountains | 431 | Leucadendron | A | Sandstone |
| | | 449 | Restio | B | Sandstone/ Limestone |

How are you to enter this data into a table in the database? You could try to copy the layout you see in the report above, resulting in a table something like Table 8.2. The null fields reflect the fields where no data was entered.

**TABLE 8.2:** TRYING TO CREATE A TABLE WITH THE PLANT DATA

| LOCATION CODE | LOCATION NAME | PLANT CODE | PLANT NAME | SOIL CATEGORY | SOIL DESCRIPTION |
| --- | --- | --- | --- | --- | --- |
| 11 | Kirstenbosch Gardens | 431 | Leucadendron | A | Sandstone |
| NULL | NULL | 446 | Protea | B | Sandstone/ Limestone |

*Continued on next page*

**TABLE 8.2:** TRYING TO CREATE A TABLE WITH THE PLANT DATA *(continued)*

| LOCATION CODE | LOCATION NAME | PLANT CODE | PLANT NAME | SOIL CATEGORY | SOIL DESCRIPTION |
|---|---|---|---|---|---|
| NULL | NULL | 482 | Erica | C | Limestone |
| 12 | Karbonkelberg Mountains | 431 | Leucadendron | A | Sandstone |
| NULL | NULL | 449 | Restio | B | Sandstone/ Limestone |

This table is not much use, though. The first three rows are actually a group, all belonging to the same location. If you take the third row by itself, the data is incomplete, as you cannot tell the location the Erica is to be found. Also, with the table as it stands, you cannot use the location code, or any other field, as a primary key (remember, a primary key is a field, or list of fields, that uniquely identify one record). There is not much use in having a table if you can't uniquely identify each record in it.

So, the solution is to make sure that each table row can stand alone, and is not part of a group, or set. To achieve this, remove the groups, or sets of data, and make each row a complete record in its own right, which results in Table 8.3.

**TABLE 8.3:** EACH RECORD STANDS ALONE

| *LOCATION CODE* | LOCATION NAME | *PLANT CODE* | PLANT NAME | SOIL CATEGORY | SOIL DESCRIPTION |
|---|---|---|---|---|---|
| 11 | Kirstenbosch Gardens | 431 | Leucadendron | A | Sandstone |
| 11 | Kirstenbosch Gardens | 446 | Protea | B | Sandstone/ Limestone |
| 11 | Kirstenbosch Gardens | 482 | Erica | C | Limestone |
| 12 | Karbonkelberg Mountains | 431 | Leucadendron | A | Sandstone |
| 12 | Karbonkelberg Mountains | 449 | Restio | B | Sandstone/ Limestone |

NOTE   *The primary keys are shown in italics in Table 8.3 and the following tables.*

Notice that the location code cannot be a primary key on its own. It does not uniquely identify a row of data. So, the primary key must be a combination of location code and plant code. Together these two fields uniquely identify one row of data. Think about it: You would never add the same plant type more than once to a particular location. Once you have the fact that it occurs in that location, that's enough. If you want to record quantities of plants at a location—for this example you're just interested in the spread of plants—you don't need to add an entire new record for each plant; rather, just add a quantity field. If for some reason you would be adding more than one instance of a plant/location combination, you'd need to add something else to the key to make it unique.

So, now the data can go in table format, but there are still some problems with it. The table stores the information that code 11 refers to the Kirstenbosch Gardens three times! Besides the waste of space, there is another serious problem. Look carefully at the data in Table 8.4.

**TABLE 8.4:** A DATA ANOMALY

| LOCATION CODE | LOCATION NAME | PLANT CODE | PLANT NAME | SOIL CATEGORY | SOIL DESCRIPTION |
| --- | --- | --- | --- | --- | --- |
| 11 | Kirstenbosch Gardens | 431 | Leucadendron | A | Sandstone |
| 11 | Kirstenbosh Gardens | 446 | Protea | B | Sandstone/ Limestone |
| 11 | Kirstenbosch Gardens | 482 | Erica | C | Limestone |
| 12 | Karbonkelberg Mountains | 431 | Leucadendron | A | Sandstone |
| 12 | Karbonkelberg Mountains | 449 | Restio | B | Sandstone/ Limestone |

Did you notice anything strange in the data in Table 8.4? Congratulations if you did! *Kirstenbosch* is misspelled in the second record. Now imagine trying to spot this error in a table with thousands of records! By using the structure in Table 8.4, the chances of data anomalies increase dramatically.

The solution is simple. You remove the duplication. What you are doing is looking for partial dependencies—in other words, fields that are dependent on a part of a key and not the entire key. Because both the location code and the plant code make up the key, you look for fields that are dependent only on location code or on plant name.

There are quite a few fields where this is the case. Location name is dependent on location code (plant code is irrelevant in determining project name), and plant name, soil code, and soil name are all dependent on plant number. So, take out all these fields, as shown in Table 8.5.

**TABLE 8.5:** REMOVING THE FIELDS NOT DEPENDENT ON THE ENTIRE KEY

| LOCATION CODE | PLANT CODE |
|---|---|
| 11 | 431 |
| 11 | 446 |
| 11 | 482 |
| 12 | 431 |
| 12 | 449 |

Clearly you can't remove the data and leave it out of the database completely. You take it out and put it into a new table, consisting of the fields that have the partial dependency and the fields on which they are dependent. For each of the *key* fields in the partial dependency, you create a new table (in this case, both are already part of the primary key, but this doesn't always have to be the case). So, you identified plant name, soil description, and soil category as being dependent on plant code. The new table will consist of plant code as a key, as well as plant name, soil category, and soil description, as shown in Table 8.6.

**TABLE 8.6:** CREATING A NEW TABLE WITH PLANT DATA

| PLANT CODE | PLANT NAME | SOIL CATEGORY | SOIL DESCRIPTION |
|---|---|---|---|
| 431 | Leucadendron | A | Sandstone |
| 446 | Protea | B | Sandstone/Limestone |
| 482 | Erica | C | Limestone |
| 449 | Restio | B | Sandstone/Limestone |

You do the same process with the location data, as shown in Table 8.7.

**TABLE 8.7:** CREATING A NEW TABLE WITH LOCATION DATA

| LOCATION CODE | LOCATION NAME |
|---|---|
| 11 | Kirstenbosch Gardens |
| 12 | Karbonkelberg Mountains |

See how these tables remove the earlier duplication problem? There is only one record that contains *Kirstenbosch Gardens*, so the chances of noticing a misspelling are much higher. And you aren't wasting space storing the name in many different records. Notice that the location code and plant code fields are repeated in two tables. These are the fields that create the relation, allowing you to associate the various plants with the various locations. Obviously there is no way to remove the duplication of these fields without losing the relation altogether, but it is far more efficient storing a small code repeatedly than a large piece of text.

But the table is still not perfect. There is still a chance for anomalies to slip in. Examine Table 8.8 carefully.

**TABLE 8.8:** ANOTHER ANOMALY

| PLANT CODE | PLANT NAME | SOIL CATEGORY | SOIL DESCRIPTION |
|---|---|---|---|
| 431 | Leucadendron | A | Sandstone |
| 446 | Protea | B | Sandstone/Limestone |
| 482 | Erica | C | Limestone |
| 449 | Restio | B | Sandstone |

The problem in Table 8.8 is that the Restio has been associated with sandstone, when in fact, having a soil category of B, it should be a mix of sandstone and limestone. (The soil category determines the soil description in this example). Once again you are storing data redundantly: The soil category to soil description relationship is being stored in its entirety for each plant. As before, the solution is to take out this excess data and place it in its own table. What you are in fact doing at this stage is looking for *transitive* relationships, or relationships where a nonkey field is dependent on another nonkey field. Soil description, although in one sense dependent on plant code (it did seem to be a partial dependency when we looked at it in the previous step), is actually dependent on soil category. So, soil description must be removed: Once again, take it out and place it in a new table, along with its actual key (soil category), as shown in Table 8.9 and Table 8.10.

**TABLE 8.9:** PLANT DATA AFTER REMOVING THE SOIL DESCRIPTION

| PLANT CODE | PLANT NAME | SOIL CATEGORY |
|---|---|---|
| 431 | Leucadendron | A |
| 446 | Protea | B |
| 482 | Erica | C |
| 449 | Restio | B |

**TABLE 8.10:** CREATING A NEW TABLE WITH THE SOIL DESCRIPTION

| SOIL CATEGORY | SOIL DESCRIPTION |
|---|---|
| A | Sandstone |
| B | Sandstone/Limestone |
| C | Limestone |

You've cut down the chance of anomalies once again. It is now impossible to mistakenly assume soil category B is associated with anything but a mix of sandstone and limestone. The soil description to soil category relationships is stored in only one place: the new soil table, where you can be sure they are accurate.

Let's look at this example without the data tables to guide you. Often when you're designing a system you don't yet have a complete set of test data available, and it's not necessary if you understand how the data relates. I've used the tables to demonstrate the consequences of storing data in tables that were not normalized, but without them you have to rely on dependencies between fields, which is the key to database normalization.

At first, the data structure was as follows:

Location code

Location name

1–n Plant numbers (1–n is a shorthand for saying there are many occurrences of this field—in other words, it is a repeating group)

1–n Plant names

1–n Soil categories

1–n Soil descriptions

This is a completely unnormalized structure—in other words, it is in *zero normal form*. So, to begin the normalization process, you start by moving from zero normal form to 1st normal form.

## 1st Normal Form

Tables in 1st normal form follow these rules:

- There are no repeating groups.
- All the key attributes are defined.
- All attributes are dependent on the primary key.

What this means is that data must be able to fit into a tabular format, where each field contains one value. This is also the stage where the primary key is defined. Some sources claim that defining the primary key is not necessary for a table to be in 1st normal form, but it's usually done at this stage, and is necessary before we can progress to the next stage. Theoretical debates aside, you'll have to define your primary keys at this point.

**TIP** *Although not always seen as part of the definition of 1st normal form, the principle of atomicity is usually applied at this stage as well. This means that all columns must contain their smallest parts, or be indivisible. A common example of this is where someone creates a name field, rather than first name and surname fields. They usually regret it later.*

So far, the plant example has no keys, and there are repeating groups. To get it into 1st normal form, you'll need to define a primary key and change the structure so that there are no repeating groups; in other words, each row/column intersection contains one, and only one, value. Without this, you cannot put the data into the ordinary two-dimensional table that most databases require. You define location code and plant code as the primary key together (neither on its own can uniquely identify a record), and replace the repeating groups with a single-value attribute. After doing this, you are left with the data shown in Table 8.11.

**TABLE 8.11:** 1ST NORMAL FORM

**PLANT LOCATION TABLE**

*Location code*

Location name

*Plant code*

Plant name

Soil category

Soil description

This table is in now in 1st normal form. Is it in 2nd normal form?

## 2nd Normal Form

A table is in 2nd normal form if it follows these rules:

◆ Is in 1st normal form

◆ Includes no partial dependencies (where an attribute is only dependent on part of a primary key)

*TIP    For an attribute to be only dependent on part of a primary key, the primary key must consist of more than one field. If the primary key contains only one field, the table is automatically in 2nd normal form if it is in 1st normal form.*

Let's examine all the fields. Location name is only dependent on location code. Plant name, soil category, and soil description are only dependent on plant code. (This assumes that each plant only occurs in one soil type, which is the case in this example). So you remove each of these fields, and place them in a separate table, with the key being that part of the original key on which they are dependent. For example, with plant name, the key is plant code. This leaves you with Table 8.12, Table 8.13, and Table 8.14.

**TABLE 8.12:** THE PLANT LOCATION TABLE WITH PARTIAL DEPENDENCIES REMOVED

**PLANT LOCATION TABLE**

*Plant code*

*Location code*

**TABLE 8.13:** TABLE RESULTING FROM FIELDS DEPENDENT ON PLANT CODE

**PLANT TABLE**

*Plant code*

Plant name

Soil category

Soil description

**TABLE 8.14:** TABLE RESULTING FROM FIELDS DEPENDENT ON LOCATION CODE

**LOCATION TABLE**

*Location code*

Location name

The resulting tables are now in 2nd normal form. Are they in 3rd normal form?

## 3rd Normal Form

A table is in 3rd normal form if it follows these rules:

- ◆ Is in 2nd normal form
- ◆ Contains no transitive dependencies (where a nonkey attribute is dependent on the primary key through another nonkey attribute)

*TIP   If a table only contains one nonkey attribute, it is obviously impossible for a nonkey attribute to be dependent on another nonkey attribute. Any tables like these that are in 2nd normal form are then automatically in 3rd normal form.*

As only the plant table has more than one nonkey attribute, you can ignore the others because they are in 3rd normal form already. All fields are dependent on the primary key in some way, since the tables are in 2nd normal form. But is this dependency through another nonkey field? Plant name is not dependent on either soil category or soil description. Nor is soil category dependent on either soil description or plant name. However, soil description is dependent on soil category. You use the same procedure as before, removing it, and placing it in its own table with the attribute that it was dependent on as the key. You are left with Table 8.15, Table 8.16, Table 8.17, and Table 8.18.

**TABLE 8.15:** THE PLANT LOCATION TABLE REMAINS UNCHANGED

**PLANT LOCATION TABLE**

*Plant code*

*Location code*

**TABLE 8.16:** THE PLANT TABLE WITH SOIL DESCRIPTION REMOVED

**PLANT TABLE**

*Plant code*

Plant name

Soil category

**TABLE 8.17:** THE NEW SOIL TABLE

**SOIL TABLE**

*Soil category*

Soil description

**TABLE 8.18:** THE LOCATION TABLE IS UNCHANGED

**LOCATION TABLE**

*Location code*

Location name

All of these tables are now in 3rd normal form. 3rd normal form is usually sufficient for most tables, because it avoids the most common kind of data anomalies. I suggest getting most tables you work with to 3rd normal form before you implement them, as this will achieve the aims of normalization listed at the beginning of the chapter in the vast majority of cases. The normal forms beyond this, such as Boyce-Codd normal form and 4th normal form, are rarely useful for business applications. In most cases, tables in 3rd normal form are already in these normal forms anyway. But any skillful database practitioner should know the exceptions, and be able to normalize to the higher levels when required.

## Boyce-Codd Normal Form

E.F. Codd and R.F. Boyce, two of the people instrumental in the development of the database model, have been honored by the name of this normal form. E.F. Codd developed and expanded the relational model, and also developed normalization for relational models in 1970, while R.F. Boyce was one of the creators of Structured Query Language (then called SEQUEL).

In spite of some resources stating the contrary, Boyce-Codd normal form is not the same as 4th normal form. Let's look at an example of data anomalies, which are presented in 3rd normal form and solved by transforming into Boyce-Codd normal form, before defining it (see Table 8.19).

**TABLE 8.19:** A TABLE CONTAINING DATA ABOUT THE STUDENT, COURSE, AND INSTRUCTOR RELATIONSHIP

**STUDENT COURSE INSTRUCTOR TABLE**

Student

Course

Instructor

Assume that the following is true for Table 8.19:

◆ Each instructor takes only one course.

◆ Each course can have one or more instructors.

◆ Each student has only one instructor per course.

◆ Each student can take one or more courses.

What would the key be? None of the fields on their own would be sufficient to uniquely identify a record, so you have to use two fields. Which two should you use?

Perhaps student and instructor seem like the best choice, as that would allow you to determine the course. Or you could use student and course, which would determine the instructor. For now, let's use student and course as the key (see Table 8.20).

**TABLE 8.20:** USING STUDENT AND COURSE AS THE KEY

**STUDENT COURSE INSTRUCTOR TABLE**

*Student*

*Course*

Instructor

What normal form is this table in? It's in first normal form, as it has a key and no repeating groups. It's also in 2nd normal form, as the instructor is dependent on both other fields (students have many courses and therefore instructors, and courses have many instructors). Finally, it's also in 3rd normal form, as there is only one nonkey attribute.

But there are still some data anomalies. Look at the data sample in Table 8.21.

**TABLE 8.21:** MORE DATA ANOMALIES

| STUDENT | COURSE | INSTRUCTOR |
| --- | --- | --- |
| Conrad Pienaar | Biology | Nkosizana Asmal |
| Dingaan Fortune | Mathematics | Kader Dlamini |

*Continued on next page*

**TABLE 8.21:** MORE DATA ANOMALIES *(continued)*

| STUDENT | COURSE | INSTRUCTOR |
|---------|--------|------------|
| Gerrie Jantjies | Science | Helen Ginwala |
| Mark Thobela | Biology | Nkosizana Asmal |
| Conrad Pienaar | Science | Peter Leon |
| Alicia Ncita | Science | Peter Leon |
| Quinton Andrews | Mathematics | Kader Dlamini |

The fact that Peter Leon teaches science is stored redundantly, as are Kader Dlamini with mathematics and Nkosizana Asmal with biology. The problem is that the instructor determines the course. Or put another way, course is determined by instructor. The table conforms to 3rd normal form rules because no nonkey attribute is dependent upon another nonkey attribute. However, a key attribute is dependent upon a nonkey attribute! Again, you can use the familiar method of removing this field and placing it into another table, along with its key (see Table 8.22 and Table 8.23).

**TABLE 8.22:** STUDENT INSTRUCTOR TABLE AFTER REMOVING COURSE

**STUDENT INSTRUCTOR TABLE**

*Student*

*Instructor*

After removing the course field, the primary key needs to include both remaining fields to uniquely identify a record.

**TABLE 8.23:** RESULTING INSTRUCTOR COURSE TABLE

**INSTRUCTOR COURSE TABLE**

*Instructor*

Course

Although we had chosen course as part of the primary key in the original table, the instructor determines the course, which is why we make it the primary key in this table. As you can see, the redundancy problem has been solved.

Thus, a table is in Boyce-Codd normal form if it meets the following conditions:

◆ It is in 3rd normal form.

◆ Each determinant is a candidate key.

That sounds scary! For most people new to database design, these are new terms. If you followed along with this example, however, the terms will soon become clear:

◆ A *determinant* is an attribute that determines the value of another attribute.

◆ A *candidate key* is either the key or an alternate key (in other words, the attribute could be a key for that table).

Instructor is not a candidate key (alone it cannot uniquely identify the record), yet it determines the course, so the table is not in Boyce-Codd normal form.

Let's look at the example again, and see what happens if you chose student and instructor as the key, as shown in Table 8.24. What normal form is the table in this time?

**TABLE 8.24:** USING STUDENT AND INSTRUCTOR AS THE KEY

**STUDENT COURSE INSTRUCTOR TABLE**

Student

Instructor

Course

Once again it's in 1st normal form because there is a primary key and there are no repeating groups. This time, though, it's not in 2nd normal form because course is determined by only part of the key: the instructor. By removing course and its key, instructor, you get the data shown in Table 8.25 and Table 8.26.

**TABLE 8.25:** REMOVING COURSE

**STUDENT INSTRUCTOR TABLE**

Student

Instructor

**TABLE 8.26:** CREATING A NEW TABLE WITH COURSE

**INSTRUCTOR COURSE TABLE**

Instructor

Course

Either way you do it, by making sure the tables are normalized into Boyce-Codd normal form, you get the same two resulting tables. It's usually the case that when there are alternate fields to choose as a key, it doesn't matter which ones you choose initially because after normalizing the results you get the same results either way.

## 4th Normal Form

Let's look at situation where redundancies can creep in even though a table is in Boyce-Codd normal form. Let's take the previous student/instructor/course example but change one of the initial assumptions. This time, a student can have several instructors for a single course (see Table 8.27).

**TABLE 8.27:** STUDENT COURSE INSTRUCTOR DATA, WITH SEVERAL INSTRUCTORS PER COURSE

| STUDENT | COURSE | INSTRUCTOR |
| --- | --- | --- |
| Conrad Pienaar | Biology | Nkosizana Asmal |
| Dingaan Fortune | Mathematics | Kader Dlamini |
| Gerrie Jantjies | Science | Helen Ginwala |
| Mark Thobela | Biology | Nkosizana Asmal |
| Conrad Pienaar | Science | Peter Leon |
| Alicia Ncita | Science | Peter Leon |
| Quinton Andrews | Mathematics | Kader Dlamini |
| Dingaan Fortune | Mathematics | Helen Ginwala |

The data is the same as before, except that Helen Ginwala is teaching science to Gerrie Jantjies as well as mathematics to Dingaan Fortune, and Dingaan Fortune is being taught by both Helen Ginwala and Kader Dlamini for mathematics.

The only possible key is a combination of all three attributes, as shown in Table 8.28. No other combination will uniquely identify a particular record.

**TABLE 8.28:** THREE ATTRIBUTES AS KEY

**STUDENT COURSE INSTRUCTOR TABLE**

*Student*

*Instructor*

*Course*

But this still has some potentially anomalous behavior. The fact that Kader Dlamini teaches mathematics is still stored more than once, as is the fact that Dingaan Fortune takes mathematics. The real problem is that the table stores more than one kind of fact: that of a student-to-course relationship, as well as that of a student-to-instructor relationship. You can avoid this, as always, by separating the data into two tables, as shown in Table 8.29 and Table 8.30.

**TABLE 8.29:** CREATING A TABLE FOR THE STUDENT TO INSTRUCTOR RELATIONSHIP

**STUDENT INSTRUCTOR TABLE**

Student

Instructor

**TABLE 8.30:** CREATING A TABLE FOR THE STUDENT TO COURSE RELATIONSHIP

**STUDENT COURSE TABLE**

Student

Course

This situation exists when you have multiple multivalued dependencies. A multivalued dependency exists between two attributes when, for each value of the first attribute, there is one or more associated values of the second attribute. For each value of student, there were many values of course. This is the first multivalued dependency. Then for each value of student, there are one or more associated values of instructor. This is the second multivalued dependency.

Thus, a table is in 4th normal form if it meets the following criteria:

◆ Is in Boyce-Codd normal form

◆ Does not contain more than one multivalued dependency

## 5th Normal Form and Beyond

There are further normal forms that are mainly of academic interest, as the problems they exist to solve rarely appear in practice. I won't go into them in much detail, but for those who are interested, the following example provides a taste (see Table 8.31):

**TABLE 8.31:** THE SALES REP EXAMPLE

| SALES REP | COMPANY | PRODUCT |
|---|---|---|
| Felicia Powers | Exclusive | Books |
| Afzal Ignesund | Wordsworth | Magazines |
| Felicia Powers | Exclusive | Magazines |

Usually you would store this data in one table, as you need all three records to see which combinations are valid. Afzal Ignesund sells magazines for Wordsworth, but not necessarily books. Felicia Powers happens to sell both books and magazines for Exclusive. However, let's add another condition: If a sales rep sells a certain product, and they sell it for a particular company, then they must sell that product for that company.

Let's look at a larger data set adhering to this condition (see Table 8.32).

**TABLE 8.32:** LOOKING AT A LARGER SET OF DATA

| SALES REP | COMPANY | PRODUCT |
| --- | --- | --- |
| Felicia Powers | Exclusive | Books |
| Felicia Powers | Exclusive | Magazines |
| Afzal Ignesund | Wordsworth | Books |
| Felicia Powers | Wordsworth | Books |
| Felicia Powers | Wordsworth | Magazines |

Now, with this extra dependency, you could normalize Table 8.32 further into three separate tables without losing any facts, as shown in Table 8.33, Table 8.34, and Table 8.35.

**TABLE 8.33:** CREATING A TABLE WITH SALES REP AND PRODUCT

| SALES REP | PRODUCT |
| --- | --- |
| Felicia Powers | Books |
| Felicia Powers | Magazines |
| Afzal Ignesund | Books |

**TABLE 8.34:** CREATING A TABLE WITH SALES REP AND COMPANY

| SALES REP | COMPANY |
| --- | --- |
| Felicia Powers | Exclusive |
| Felicia Powers | Wordsworth |
| Afzal Ignesund | Wordsworth |

**TABLE 8.35:** CREATING A TABLE WITH COMPANY AND PRODUCT

| COMPANY | PRODUCT |
| --- | --- |
| Exclusive | Books |
| Exclusive | Magazines |

*Continued on next page*

| **TABLE 8.35:** CREATING A TABLE WITH COMPANY AND PRODUCT *(continued)* | |
|---|---|
| **COMPANY** | **PRODUCT** |
| Wordsworth | Books |
| Wordsworth | Magazines |

Basically, a table is in 5th normal form if it cannot be made into any smaller tables with different keys (most tables can obviously be made into smaller tables with the same key!).

Beyond 5th normal form, you enter the heady realms of domain key normal form, a kind of theoretical ideal. Its practical use to a database designer is similar to that of the concept of infinity to a bookkeeper—i.e., it exists in theory, but is not going to be used in practice. Even the most corrupt executive is not going to expect that of the bookkeeper!

For those interested in pursuing this academic and highly theoretical topic further, I suggest obtaining a copy of *An Introduction to Database Systems* by C.J. Date (Addison-Wesley, 1999).

# Understanding Denormalization

*Denormalization* is the process of reversing the transformations made during normalization for performance reasons. It's a topic that stirs controversy among database experts; there are those who claim the costs are too high and never denormalize, and there are those who tout its benefits and routinely denormalize.

For proponents of normalization, the thinking is as follows: Normalization creates more tables as you proceed toward the higher normal forms, but more tables mean there are more joins to be made when data is retrieved, which in turn slows down your queries. For that reason, to improve the speed of certain queries, you can override the advantages to data integrity and return the data structure to a lower normal form.

I suggest a practical approach, taking into account the limitations of SQL, and MySQL in particular, but being cautious not to needlessly denormalize. The following tips will help you in your decision:

- If your performance with a normalized structure is acceptable, you should not denormalize.
- If your performance is unacceptable, make sure denormalizing will cause it to become acceptable. Also investigate alternatives, such as better hardware, which may avoid the need to denormalize. It's hard to undo structural changes later.
- Be sure you are willing to trade the decreased data integrity for the increase in performance.
- Consider possible future scenarios, where applications may place different requirements on the data. Denormalizing to enhance performance of a specific application makes your data structure dependent on that application, when in an ideal situation it will be application independent.

Table 8.36 introduces a common structure where it may not be in your best interests to denormalize. Can you tell which normal form the table is in?

**TABLE 8.36:** CUSTOMER TABLE

**CUSTOMER TABLE**

*ID*

First name

Surname

Address line 1

Address line 2

Town

ZIP code

Table 8.36 must be in 1st normal form because it has a primary key and there are no repeating groups. It must be in 2nd normal form because there's only one key, so there cannot be any partial dependencies. And 3rd normal form? Are there any transitive dependencies? It looks like it. ZIP code is probably determined by the town attribute. To make it into 3rd normal form, you should take out ZIP code, putting it in a separate table with town as the key. In most cases, I would suggest not doing this though. Although this table is not really in 3rd normal form, separating this table is not worth the trouble. The more tables you have, the more joins you need to do, which slows the system down. The reason you normalize at all is to reduce the size of tables by removing redundant data (which can often speed up the system). But you also need to look at how your tables are used. Town and ZIP code would almost always be returned together, as part of the address. In most cases, the small amount of space you save by removing the duplicate town/ZIP code combinations would not offset the slowing down of the system because of the extra joins. In some situations, this may be useful, perhaps where you need to sort addresses according to ZIP codes or towns for thousands of customers, and the distribution of the data means that a query to the new, smaller table can return the results substantially quicker. In the end, experienced database designers can go beyond rigidly following the steps, as they understand how the data will be used. And that is something only experience can teach you. Normalization is just a helpful set of steps that most often produces an efficient table structure and not a rule for database design.

*TIP*   *I've seen some scary database designs out there, almost always because of not normalizing rather than too much normalization. So if you're unsure, normalize!*

## Summary

Database normalization is a process performed on your tables to make them less likely to fall prey to various common kinds of data anomaly:

- 1st normal form contains no repeating groups and guarantees that all attributes are dependent on a primary key.
- 2nd normal form contains no partial dependencies.
- 3rd normal form contains no transitive dependencies.
- For practical purposes, 3rd normal form is usually sufficient; indeed, overnormalizing can lead to performance issues, with the database having to perform too many joins.
- Boyce-Codd normal form ensures each determinant is a candidate key.
- 4th normal form contains no more than one multivalued dependency.
- 5th normal form ensures tables cannot be reduced to smaller tables with different keys.
- Domain key normal form is a theoretical ideal beyond the scope of this book.

# Chapter 9

# Database Design

DATABASES EXIST BECAUSE OF the need to change data into information. Data are the raw and unprocessed facts. Information is obtained by processing the data into something useful. For example, the millions of names and telephone numbers in a phone book are data. Information is the telephone number of the fire department when your house is burning down.

A database is a large repository of facts, designed in such a way that processing the facts into information is easy. If the phone book was structured in a less convenient way, such as with the names and numbers placed in chronological order according to when the numbers were issued, converting the data into information would be much more difficult. Not knowing when the fire department was issued their latest phone number, you could search for hours. By the time you find the number, your house would be a charred pile of ash. So, it's a good thing your phone book is designed as it is.

A database is much more flexible; a similar set of data to what's in your phone book could be ordered by MySQL according to name, telephone number, address, or chronologically. But databases are of course more complex, containing many different kinds of information. People, job titles, and a company's products can all mingle to provide complex information. But this complexity makes the design of databases more complex as well. Poor design could make for slow queries, or it could even make certain kinds of information impossible to reach. This chapter introduces good database design.

Featured in this chapter:

- The database lifecycle
- Entity-relationship modeling
- Common mistakes in database design
- Real-world example: creating a publishing tracking system
- Concurrency control with transactions

## The Database Lifecycle

Like everything else, databases have a finite lifespan. They are born in a flush of optimism and make their way through life achieving fame, fortune, and peaceful anonymity, or notoriety as the case may be, before fading out once more. Even the most successful database at some time is replaced by another, more flexible, and up-to-date structure, and so begins its life anew. Although exact definitions may differ, there are generally six stages of the database lifecycle:

**Analysis**   The Analysis phase is where the stakeholders are interviewed and any existing system is examined to identify problems, possibilities, and constraints. The objectives and scope of the new system are determined.

**Design**   The Design phase is where a conceptual design is created from the previously determined requirements, and a logical and physical design are created that will ready the database for implementation.

**Implementation**   The Implementation phase is where the database management system (DBMS) is installed, the databases are created, and the data are loaded or imported.

**Testing**   The Testing phase is where the database is tested and fine-tuned, usually in conjunction with the associated applications.

**Operation**   The Operation phase is where the database is working normally, producing information for its users.

**Maintenance**   The Maintenance phase is where changes are made to the database in response to new requirements or changed operating conditions (such as heavier load).

Database development is not independent of systems development, often being one component of the greater systems development process. The stages of systems development basically mirror the stages of a database lifecycle but are a superset. Whereas database design deals with designing the system to store the data, systems design is also concerned with the processes that will impact on the data.

## Phase 1: Analysis

Your existing system can no longer cope. It's time to move on. Perhaps the existing paper system is generating too many errors, or the old Perl script based on flat files can no longer handle the load. Or perhaps an existing news database for a website is struggling under its own popularity and needs an upgrade. This is the stage where the existing system is reviewed.

Depending on the size of the project, the designer may be an individual, responsible for the database implementation and coding, or may be a whole team of analysts. For now, the term *designer* will represent all these possibilities.

The following are the steps in the Analysis phase:

1. Analyze the organization.
2. Define any problems, possibilities, and constraints.
3. Define the objectives.
4. Agree on the scope.

When reviewing a system, the designer needs to look at the bigger picture—not just the hardware or existing table structures, but the whole situation of the organization calling for the redesign. For example, a large bank with centralized management would have a different structure and a different way of operating from a decentralized media organization, where anyone can post news onto a website. This may seem trivial, but understanding the organization you're building the database for is vital to designing a good database for it. The same demands in the bank and media organizations should lead to different designs because the organizations are different. In other words, a solution that was constructed for the bank cannot be unthinkingly implemented for the media organization, even when the situation seems similar. A culture of central control at the bank may mean that news posted on the bank website has to be moderated and authorized by central management, or may require the designer to keep detailed audit trails of who modified what and when. On the flip side, the media organization may be more *laissez-faire* and will be happy with news being modified by any authorized editor. Understanding an organization's culture helps the designer to ask the right questions. The bank may not ask for the audit trail, it may simply expect it; and when the time comes to roll out the implementation, the audit trail would need to be patched on, requiring more time and resources.

Once you understand the organization structure, you can question the users of any existing system as to what their problems and needs are, what constraints exist currently, and what the objectives of the new database system are, as well as what constraints will exist then. You need to question different role players, as each can add a new understanding as to what the database may need. For example, the media organization's marketing department may want to track movements from one news article to another on its website, but the editorial department may want detailed statistics about the times of day certain articles are read. You may also be alerted to possible future requirements. Perhaps the editorial department is planning to expand the website, which will give them the staff to cross-link web articles. Keeping this future requirement in mind could make it easier to add the cross-linking feature when the time comes.

Constraints can include hardware ("We have to use our existing database server, an AMD Duron 900MHz") or people ("We only have one data capturer on shift at any one time"). Constraints also refer to the limitations on values. For example, a student's grade in a university database may not be able to go beyond 100 percent, or the three categories of seats in a theatre database are small, medium, and large.

It is rarely sufficient to rely on one level of management, or an individual, to supply objectives and current problems, except in the smallest of organizations. Top management may be paying for the database design, but lower levels will need to use it, and their input is probably even more important for a successful design.

Of course, although anything is possible given infinite time and money, this is almost never forthcoming. Determining scope, and formalizing it, is an important part of the project. If the budget is for one month's work but the ideal solution requires three, the designer must make clear these constraints and agree with the project owners on which facets are not going to be implemented.

## Phase 2: Design

The Design phase is where the requirements identified in the previous phase are used as the basis to develop the new system. Another way of putting it is that the business understanding of the data structures is converted into a technical understanding. The *what* questions ("What data are required? What are the problems to be solved?") are replaced by *how* questions ("How will the data be structured? How is the data to be accessed?").

This phase consists of three parts: the conceptual design, the logical design, and the physical design. Some methodologies merge the logical design phase into the other two phases. Note that this chapter is not aimed at being a definitive discussion of database design methodologies (there are whole books written on that!); rather it aims to introduce you to the topic.

## CONCEPTUAL DESIGN

The purpose of the conceptual design phase is to build a conceptual model based upon the previously identified requirements but closer to the final physical model. The most useful and common conceptual model is called an *entity-relationship model.*

### Entities and Attributes

*Entities* are basically people, places, or things you want to keep information about. For example, a library system may have `book`, `library`, and `customer` entities. Learning to identify what should be an entity, what should be a number of entities, and what should be an *attribute* of an entity takes practice, but there are some good rules of thumb. The following questions can help to identify whether something is an entity:

◆ Can it vary in number independently of other entities? For example, `person height` is probably not an entity, as it cannot vary in number independently of `person`. It is not fundamental, so it cannot be an entity in this case.

◆ Is it important enough to warrant the effort of maintaining? For example, `customer` may not be important for a grocery store and will not be an entity in that case, but it will be important for a video store and will be an entity in that case.

◆ Is it its own thing that cannot be separated into subcategories? For example, a car-rental agency may have different criteria and storage requirements for different kinds of vehicles. `Vehicle` may not be an entity as it can be broken up into `car` and `boat`, which are the entities.

◆ Does it list a type of thing, not an instance? The video game `blow-em-up 6` is not an entity, rather an instance of the `game` entity.

◆ Does it have many associated facts? If it only contains one attribute, it is unlikely to be an entity. For example, `city` may be an entity in some cases, but if it contains only one attribute, `city name`, it is more likely to be an attribute of another entity, such as `customer`.

The following are examples of entities involving a university with the possible attributes in parentheses:

◆ Course (`name, code, course prerequisites`)

◆ Student (`first name, surname, address, age`)

◆ Book (`title, ISBN, price, quantity in stock`)

An *instance* of an entity is one particular occurrence of that entity. For example, the student Rudolf Sono is one instance of the `student` entity. There will probably be many instances. If there is only one instance, consider whether the entity is warranted. The top level usually does not warrant an entity. For example, if the system is being developed for a particular university, `university` will not be an entity because the whole system is for that one university. However, if the system was developed to track registration at all universities in the country, then `university` would be a valid entity.

### Relationships

Entities are related in certain ways. For example, a customer can belong to a library and can take out books. A book can be found in a particular library. Understanding what you are storing data about, and how the data relate, leads you a large part of the way to a physical implementation in the database.

There are a number of possible relationships:

**Mandatory**    For each instance of entity A, there must exist one or more instances of entity B. This does not necessarily mean that for each instance of entity B, there must exist one or more instances of entity A. Relationships are optional or mandatory in one direction only, so the A-to-B relationship can be optional while B-to-A is mandatory.

**Optional**    For each instance of entity A, there may or may not exist instances of entity B.

**One-to-one relationship (1:1)**    This is where for each instance of entity A, there exists one instance of entity B, and vice versa. If the relationship is optional, there can exist zero or one instances, and if the relationship is mandatory, there exists one and only one instance of the associated entity.

**One-to-many relationship (1:M)**    For each instance of entity A, many instances of entity B exist, while for each instance of entity B, only one instance of entity A exists. Again, these can be either optional or mandatory relationships.

**Many-to-many relationship (M:N)**    For each instance of entity A, many instances of entity B exist, and vice versa. These can be either optional or mandatory relationships.

There are numerous ways of showing these relationships. Figure 9.1 shows `student` and `course` entities. In this case, each student must have registered for at least one course, but a course does not necessarily have to have any students registered. The student-to-course relationship is mandatory, and the course-to-student relationship is optional.

**FIGURE 9.1**

A many-to-many relationship

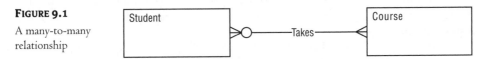

Figure 9.2 shows `invoice line` and `product` entities. Each invoice line must have at least one product (but no more than one); however, each product can appear on many invoice lines or none at all. The invoice line-to-product relationship is mandatory, while the product to-invoice-line relationship is optional.

**FIGURE 9.2**

A one-to-many relationship

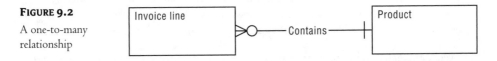

Figure 9.3 shows husband and wife entities. Each husband must have one and only one wife, and each wife must have one, and only one, husband. Both relationships are mandatory.

**FIGURE 9.3**

A one-to-one relationship

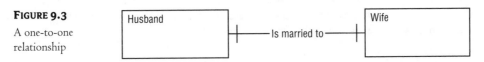

An entity can also have a relationship with itself. Such an entity is called a *recursive entity*. Take a `person` entity: If you're interested in storing data about which people are brothers, you will have an "is a brother to" relationship. In this case, the relationship is an M:N relationship.

Conversely, a *weak entity* is an entity that cannot exist without another entity. For example, in a school, the `scholar` entity is related to the weak entity "parent/guardian." Without the scholar, the parent or guardian cannot exist in the system. Weak entities usually derive their primary key, in part or in totality, from the associated entity. `Parent/guardian` could take the primary key from the scholar table as part of its primary key (or the entire key if the system only stored one `parent/guardian` per `scholar`).

The term *connectivity* refers to the relationship classification (1:1, 1:M, or M:N).

The term *cardinality* refers to the specific number of instances possible for a relationship. *Cardinality limits* list the minimum and maximum possible occurrences of the associated entity. In the husband and wife example, the cardinality limit is (1,1), and in the case of a student who can take between one and eight courses, the cardinality limits would be represented as (1,8).

### Developing an Entity-Relationship Diagram

An entity-relationship diagram models how the entities relate to each other. It's made up of multiple relationships, the kind that you've seen in Figures 9.1, 9.2, and 9.3. In general, these entities go on to become to the database tables.

The first step in developing the diagram is to identify all the entities in the system. In the initial stage, it is not necessary to identify the attributes, but this may help to clarify matters if the designer is unsure about some of the entities. Once the entities are listed, relationships between these entities are identified and modeled according to their type: one-to-many, optional, and so on. There are many software packages that can assist in drawing an entity-relationship diagram, but any graphical package should suffice.

Once the initial entity-relationship diagram has been drawn, it is often shown to the stakeholders. Entity-relationship diagrams are easy for nontechnical people to understand, especially if they are guided through the process. This can help identify any errors that have crept in. Part of the reason for modeling is that models are much easier to understand than pages of text, and they are much more likely to be viewed by stakeholders, which reduces the chances of errors slipping through to the next stages, when they may be more difficult to fix.

*TIP   It's important to remember that there is no one right or wrong answer. The more complex the situation, the more possible designs that will work. Database design is an acquired skill, though, and more experienced designers will have a good idea of what works and of possible problems at a later stage, having gone through the process before.*

Once the diagram has been approved, the next stage is to replace many-to-many relationships with two one-to-many relationships. A DBMS cannot directly implement many-to-many relationships, so they are decomposed into two smaller relationships. To achieve this, you have to create an *intersection*, or *composite* entity type. Because intersection entities are less "real-world" than ordinary entities, they are sometimes difficult to name. In this case, you can name them according to the two entities being intersected. For example, you can intersect the many-to-many relationship between `student` and `course` by a `student-course` entity (see Figure 9.4).

**FIGURE 9.4**

Creating the student-course intersection entity

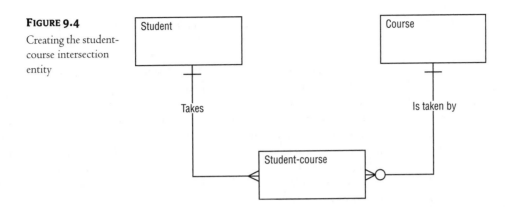

The same applies even if the entity is recursive. The person entity that has an M:N relationship "is brother to" also needs an intersection entity. You can come up with a good name for the intersection entity in this case: brother. This entity would contain two fields, one for each person of the brother relationship—in other words, the primary key of the first brother and the primary key of the other brother (see Figure 9.5).

**FIGURE 9.5**

Creating the brother intersection entity

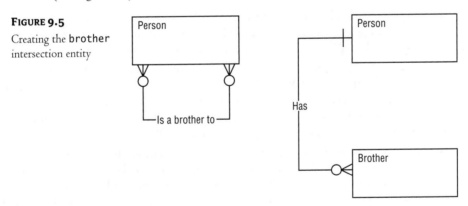

### LOGICAL AND PHYSICAL DESIGN

Once the conceptual design is finalized, it's time to convert this to the logical and physical design. Usually, the DBMS is chosen at this stage, depending on the requirements and complexity of the data structures. Strictly speaking, the logical design and the physical design are two separate stages, but are often merged into one. They overlap because most current DBMSs (including MySQL) match logical records to physical records on disk on a 1:1 basis.

Each entity will become a database table, and each attribute will become a field of this table. Foreign keys can be created if the DBMS supports them and the designer decides to implement them. If the relationship is mandatory, the foreign key must be defined as NOT NULL, and if it is optional, the foreign key can allow nulls. For example, because of the invoice line-to-product relationship in the previous example, the product code field is a foreign key in the invoice line table. Because the invoice line must contain a product, the field must be defined as NOT NULL. Currently, InnoDB tables do support foreign key constraints, and MyISAM tables do not support foreign keys in version 4, but they probably will in version 4.1. A DBMS that does support foreign keys uses ON DELETE CASCADE and ON DELETE RESTRICT clauses in their definitions. ON DELETE RESTRICT means that records cannot be deleted unless all records associated with that foreign key are deleted. In the invoice line-to-product case, ON DELETE RESTRICT in the invoice line table means that if a product is deleted, the deletion will not take place unless all associated invoice lines with that product are deleted as well. This avoids the possibility of an invoice line existing that points to a nonexistent product. ON DELETE CASCADE achieves a similar effect but more automatically (and more dangerously!). If the foreign key was declared with ON DELETE CASCADE, associated invoice lines would automatically be deleted if a product was deleted. ON UPDATE CASCADE is similar to ON DELETE CASCADE, in that all foreign key references to a primary key are updated when the primary key is updated.

Normalizing your tables is an important step when designing the database (see Chapter 8, "Database Normalization"). This process helps avoid data redundancy and improves your data integrity.

Novice database designers usually make a number of common errors. If you've carefully identified entities and attributes and you've normalized your data, you'll probably avoid these errors. However, designers who rush through the design process often end up with large tables of unrelated data. Implementing the following tips will help you to avoid some of the more frequently made errors:

- Keep unrelated data in different tables. People who are used to using spreadsheets often make this mistake because they are used to seeing all their data in one two-dimensional table. A relational database is much more powerful; don't "hamstring" it in this way.

- Don't store values you can calculate. Let's say you're interested in three numbers: A, B, and the product of A and B (A * B). Don't store the product. It wastes space and can easily be calculated if you need it. And it makes your database more difficult to maintain: If you change A, you also have to change all of the products as well. Why waste your database's efforts on something you can calculate when you need it?

- Does your design cater to all the conditions you've analyzed? In the heady rush of creating an entity-relationship diagram, you can easily overlook a condition. Entity-relationship diagrams are usually better at getting stakeholders to spot an incorrect rule than spot a missing one. The business logic is as important as the database logic and is more likely to be overlooked. For example, it's easy to spot that you cannot have a sale without an associated customer, but have you built in that a customer cannot be approved for a sale of less than $500 if another approved customer has not recommended them?

- Are your attributes, which are about to become your field names, well chosen? Fields should be clearly named. For example, if you use f1 and f2 instead of surname and first_name, the time saved in less typing will be lost in looking up the correct spelling of the field or in mistakes where a developer thought f1 was the first name, and f2 the surname. Similarly, try to avoid the same names for different fields. If six tables have a primary key of code, you're making life unnecessarily difficult. Rather, use more descriptive terms, such as sales_code or customer_code.

- Don't create too many relationships. Almost every table in a system can be related by some stretch of the imagination, but there's no need to do this. For example, a tennis player belongs to a sports club. A sports club belongs to a region. The tennis players then also belong to a region, but this relationship can be derived through the sports club, so there's no need to add another foreign key (except to achieve performance benefits for certain kinds of queries). Normalizing can help you avoid this sort of problem (and even when you're trying to optimize for speed, it's usually better to normalize and then consciously denormalize rather than not normalize at all).

♦ Conversely, have you catered to all relations? Do all relations from your entity-relationship diagram appear as common fields in your table structures? Have you covered all relations? Are all many-to-many relationships broken up into two one-to-many relationships, with an intersection entity?

♦ Have you listed all the constraints? Constraints include a gender that can only be m or f, ages of schoolchildren that cannot exceed 20, or e-mail addresses that need to have an at sign (@) and at least one period (.); don't take these limits for granted. At some stage the system will need to implement them, and you're going to either forget to do so, or have to go back to gather more data if you don't list these up front.

♦ Are you planning to store too much data? Should a customer be asked to supply their eye color, favorite kind of fish, and names of their grandparents if they are simply trying to register for an online newsletter? Sometimes stakeholders want too much information from their customers. If the user is outside the organization, they may not have a voice in the design process, but they should always be thought of foremost. Consider also the difficulty and time taken to capture all the data. If a telephone operator needs to take all this information down before making a sale, imagine how much slower they will be. Also consider the impact data has on database speed. Larger tables are generally slower to access, and unnecessary BLOB, TEXT, and VARCHAR fields lead to record and table fragmentation.

♦ Have you combined fields that should be separate? Combining first name and surname into one name field is a common mistake. Later you'll realize that sorting names alphabetically is tricky if you've stored them as John Ellis and Alfred Ntombela. Keep distinct data discrete.

♦ Has every table got at least a primary key? There had better be a good reason for leaving out a primary key. How else are you going to identify a unique record quickly? Consider that an index speeds up access time tremendously, and when kept small it adds very little overhead. Also, it's usually better to create a new field for the primary key rather than take existing fields. First name and surname may be unique in your current dataset, but they may not always be. Creating a system-defined primary key ensures that it will always be unique.

♦ Give some thought to your other indexes. What fields are likely to be used in the condition to access the table? You can always create more fields later when you test the system, but add any you think you need at this stage.

♦ Are your foreign keys correctly placed? In a one-to-many relationship, the foreign key appears in the "many" table, and the associated primary key in the "one" table. Mixing these up can cause errors.

♦ Do you ensure referential integrity? Foreign keys should not relate to a primary key in another table that no longer exists.

◆ Have you covered all character sets you may need? German letters, for example, have an expanded character set, and if the database is to cater to German users it will have to take this into account. Similarly, dates and currency formats should be carefully considered if the system is to be international.

◆ Is your security sufficient? Remember to assign the minimum permissions you can. Do not allow anyone to view a table if they do not need to do so. Allowing malicious users to view data, even if they cannot change it, is often the first step in for an attacker.

## Phase 3: Implementation

The Implementation phase is where you install the DBMS on the required hardware, optimize the database to run best on that hardware and software platform, and create the database and load the data. The initial data could be either new data captured directly or existing data imported from a MySQL database or other DBMS. You also establish database security in this phase and give the various users that you've identified access applicable to their requirements. Finally, you also initiate backup plans in this phase.

The following are steps in the Implementation phase:

1. Install the DBMS.
2. Tune the setup variables according to the hardware, software, and usage conditions.
3. Create the databases and tables.
4. Load the data.
5. Set up the users and security.
6. Implement the backup regime.

## Phase 4: Testing

The Testing phase is where the performance, security, and integrity of the data are tested. Usually this will occur in conjunction with the applications that have been developed. You test the performance under various load conditions to see how the database handles multiple concurrent connections or high volumes of updating and reading. Are the reports generated quickly enough? For example, an application designed with MyISAM tables may prove too slow because the impact of the updates was underestimated. The table type may have to be changed to InnoDB in response.

Data integrity also needs to be tested, as the application may have logical flaws that result in transactions being lost or other inaccuracies. Further, security needs to be tested to ensure that users can access and change only the data they should.

The logical or physical designs may have to be modified. Perhaps new indexes are required (which the tester may discover after careful use of MySQL's EXPLAIN statement, explained in Chapter 4, "Indexes and Query Optimization"), or certain tables may need to be denormalized for performance reasons (see Chapter 8).

The testing and fine-tuning process is an iterative one, with multiple tests performed and changes implemented.

The following are the steps in the Testing phase:

1. Test the performance.
2. Test the security.
3. Test the data integrity.
4. Fine-tune the parameters or modify the logical or physical designs in response to the tests.

## Phase 5: Operation

The Operation phase takes place when the testing is complete and the database is ready to be rolled out for everyday use. The users of the system begin to operate the system, load data, read reports, and so on. Inevitably, problems come to light. The designer needs to manage the database's scope carefully at this stage, as users may expect all their desires to be pandered to. Poor database designers may find themselves extending the project well beyond their initial time estimate, and the situation may also become unpleasant if the scope has not been clearly defined and agreed upon. Project owners will feel wronged if their needs are not met, and the database designers will feel overworked and underpaid. Even when scope has been well managed, there will always be new requirements. These then lead into the next stage.

There are numerous strategies for implementing a rollout. The low-key approach often works well, where the relatively low number of users in the early stage make bug fixing easy. Hugely publicized rollouts often end with egg on the stakeholders' faces, as the best testers of all, the users, invariably find an unforeseen bug, which is best done away from the spotlight. Alternatively, rollouts can occur in a distributed manner, where a pilot branch or office is selected, and when the system has proven its stability, it's rolled out to the remaining branches.

The following are the steps in the Operation phase:

1. Hand over operation of the database to the users.
2. Make any final changes based on problems discovered by users.

## Phase 6: Maintenance

The database Maintenance phase incorporates general maintenance, such as maintaining the indexes, optimizing the tables, adding and removing users, and changing passwords, as well as backups and restoration of backups in case of a failure. (See Chapter 10, "Basic Administration," for more information about maintenance.) New requirements also start to be requested, and this may result in new fields, or new tables, being created.

As the system and organization changes, the existing database becomes less and less sufficient to meet the organization's needs. For example, the media organization may be amalgamated with media bodies from other countries, requiring integration of many data sources, or the volumes and staff may expand (or reduce) dramatically. Eventually, there comes a time, whether it's 10 months after completion or 10 years, when the database system needs to be replaced. The maintenance of the existing database begins to drain more and more resources, and the effort to create a new design is matched by the current maintenance effort. At this point, the database is coming to the end of its life, and a new project begins its life in the Analysis phase.

The following are the steps in the Maintenance phase:

1. Maintain the indexes (for example, with MySQL's `ANALYZE`).
2. Maintain the tables (MySQL's `OPTIMIZE`).
3. Maintain the users (MySQL's `GRANT` and `REVOKE`).
4. Change passwords.
5. Back up.
6. Restore backups.
7. Change the design based upon new requirements.

# Real-World Example: Creating a Publishing Tracking System

You'll now walk through the database design process with a step-by-step example. The Poet's Circle is a publisher that publishes poetry and poetry anthologies. It is keen to develop a new system that tracks poets, poems, anthologies, and sales. The following sections show the steps taken from the initial analysis to the final, working database.

## Poet's Circle Database Phase 1: Analysis

The following information is gleaned from speaking to the various stakeholders at Poet's Circle: They want to develop a database system to track the poets they have recorded, the poems they write, and the publications they appear in, as well as the sales to customers that these publications make.

The designer asks various questions to get more detailed information, such as "What is a poet, as far as the system goes? Does Poet's Circle keep track of poets even if they haven't written or published poems? Are publications recorded even before there are any associated poems? Does a publication consist of one poem or many? Are potential customer details recorded?" The following summarizes the responses:

◆ Poet's Circle is a publisher that bases its choices of publications on an active poetry community on its website. If enough of the community wants a poem published, Poet's Circle will do so.

◆ A poet can be anybody who wants to be a poet, not necessarily someone who has a poem captured in the system or someone who has even written a poem.

◆ Poems can be submitted through a web interface, by e-mail, or on paper.

◆ All captured poems are written by an associated poet, whose details are already in the system. There can be no poems submitted and stored without a full set of details of the poet.

◆ A publication can be a single poem, a poetry anthology, or a work of literary criticism.

◆ Customers can sign up through a web interface and may order publications at that point in time or express interest in receiving updates for possible later purchases.

◆ Sales of publications are made to customers whose details are stored in the system. There are no anonymous sales.

◆ A single sale can be for one publication, but many publications can also be purchased at the same time. If more than one customer is involved in this sale, Poet's Circle treats it as more than one sale. Each customer has their own sale.

◆ Not all publications make sales—some may be special editions, others never sell any copies!

## Poet's Circle Database Phase 2: Design

Based on this information, you can begin your logical design and should be able to identify the initial entities:

◆ Poet

◆ Poem

◆ Publication

◆ Sale

◆ Customer

The Poet's Circle is not an entity or even an instance of the `publisher` entity. Only if the system were developed for many publishers would `publisher` be a valid entity.

Neither `website` nor `poetry community` is an entity. There is only one website, and anyway, a website is merely a means of processing the data to populate the database. There is also only one poetry community as far as this system is concerned, and there is not much you'd want to store about it.

Next, you need to determine the relationships between these entities. You can identify the following:

◆ A poet can write many poems. The analysis identified the fact that a poet can be stored in the system even if there are no associated poems. Poems may be captured at a later point in time, or the poet may still be a potential poet. Conversely, many poets could conceivably write a poem, though the poem must have been written by at least one poet.

◆ A publication may contain many poems (an anthology) or just one. It can also contain no poems (poetry criticism, for example). A poem may or may not appear in a publication.

◆ A sale must be for at least one publication but may be for many. A publication may or may not have made any sales.

◆ A customer may be made many sales or none at all. A sale is made for one and only one customer.

You can identify the following attributes:

◆ Poet: `first name, surname, address, telephone number`

◆ Poem: `poem title, poem contents`

◆ Publication: `title, price`

◆ Sales: `date, amount`

◆ Customer: `first name, surname, address, telephone number`

Based on these entities and relationships, you can construct the entity-relationship diagram shown in Figure 9.6.

**FIGURE 9.6**

Poet's Circle entity-
relationship diagram

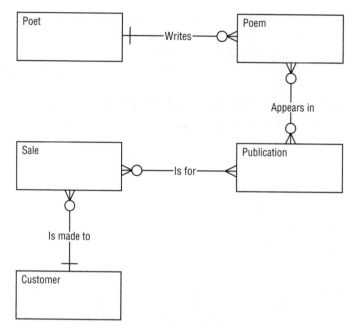

As shown in Figure 9.6, there are two many-to-many relationships. These need to be converted into one-to-many relationships before you can implement them in a DBMS. The result is Figure 9.7, with the intersection entities `poem-publication` and `sale-publication`.

**FIGURE 9.7**

Poet's Circle entity-
relationship diagram,
with the many-to-
many relationships
removed

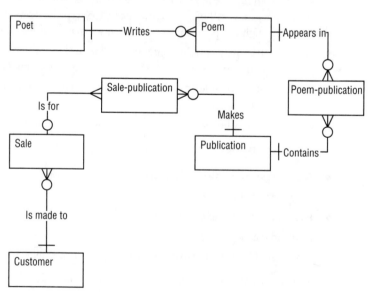

Now, to begin the logical and physical design, you need to add attributes that can create the relationship between the entities, and specify primary keys. You do what's usually best and create new, unique primary keys. Tables 9.1 through 9.7 show the structures for the tables created from each of the entities.

**TABLE 9.1:** POET TABLE

| FIELD | DEFINITION |
| --- | --- |
| poet code | primary key, integer |
| first name | character (30) |
| surname | character (40) |
| address | character (100) |
| postcode | character (20) |
| telephone number | character (30) |

**TABLE 9.2:** POEM TABLE

| FIELD | DEFINITION |
| --- | --- |
| poem code | primary key, integer |
| poem title | character (50) |
| poem contents | text |
| poet code | foreign key, integer |

**TABLE 9.3:** POEM-PUBLICATION TABLE

| FIELD | DEFINITION |
| --- | --- |
| poem code | joint primary key, foreign key, integer |
| publication code | joint primary key, foreign key, integer |

**TABLE 9.4:** PUBLICATION TABLE

| FIELD | DEFINITION |
| --- | --- |
| publication code | primary key, integer |
| title | character (100) |
| price | numeric (5.2) |

**TABLE 9.5:** SALE-PUBLICATION TABLE

| FIELD | DEFINITION |
| --- | --- |
| sale code | joint primary key, foreign key, integer |
| publication code | joint primary key, foreign key, integer |

**TABLE 9.6:** SALE TABLE

| FIELD | DEFINITION |
| --- | --- |
| sale code | primary key, integer |
| date | date |
| amount | numeric (10.2) |
| customer code | foreign key, integer |

**TABLE 9.7:** CUSTOMER TABLE

| FIELD | DEFINITION |
| --- | --- |
| customer code | primary key, integer |
| first name | character (30) |
| surname | character (40) |
| address | character (100) |
| postcode | character (20) |
| telephone number | character (30) |

MySQL will have no problem with this design and is selected as the DBMS. Existing hardware and operating system platforms are also selected.

## Poet's Circle Database Phase 3: Implementation

With the design complete, it is time to install MySQL and run the CREATE statements, as follows:

```
mysql> CREATE TABLE poet (poet_code INT NOT NULL, first_name VARCHAR(30),
  surname VARCHAR(40), address VARCHAR(100), postcode VARCHAR(20),
  telephone_number VARCHAR(30), PRIMARY KEY(poet_code));
Query OK, 0 rows affected (0.02 sec)
mysql> CREATE TABLE poem(poem_code INT NOT NULL, title VARCHAR(50),
  contents TEXT, poet_code INT NOT NULL, PRIMARY KEY(poem_code),
```

```
    INDEX(poet_code), FOREIGN KEY(poet_code) REFERENCES poem(poet_code))
    type=InnoDB;
Query OK, 0 rows affected (0.00 sec)
mysql> CREATE TABLE publication(publication_code INT NOT NULL,
 title VARCHAR(100),price MEDIUMINT UNSIGNED,
 PRIMARY KEY(publication_code)) type=InnoDB;
Query OK, 0 rows affected (0.05 sec)
mysql> CREATE TABLE poem_publication(poem_code INT NOT NULL,
 publication_code INT NOT NULL, PRIMARY KEY(poem_code,
 publication_code), INDEX(poem_code), INDEX(publication_code),
 FOREIGN KEY(poem_code) REFERENCES poem(poem_code),
 FOREIGN KEY(publication_code) REFERENCES
 publication(publication_code)) TYPE=InnoDB;
Query OK, 0 rows affected (0.09 sec)
mysql> CREATE TABLE sales_publication(sales_code INT NOT NULL,
 publication_code INT NOT NULL,PRIMARY KEY(sales_code,
 publication_code)) TYPE =InnoDB;
Query OK, 0 rows affected (0.07 sec)
mysql> CREATE TABLE customer(customer_code INT NOT NULL, first_name
 VARCHAR(30), surname VARCHAR(40), address VARCHAR(100), postcode
 VARCHAR(20), telephone_number VARCHAR(30), PRIMARY KEY(customer_code))
 TYPE=InnoDB;
Query OK, 0 rows affected (0.06 sec)
mysql> CREATE TABLE sale(sale_code INT NOT NULL, sale_date DATE,
 amount INT UNSIGNED, customer_code INT NOT NULL, PRIMARY
 KEY(sale_code), INDEX(customer_code), FOREIGN KEY(customer_code)
 REFERENCES customer(customer_code)) TYPE = InnoDB;
Query OK, 0 rows affected (0.08 sec)
```

## Poet's Circle Database Phases 4–6: Testing, Operation, and Maintenance

Once the database is ready and the application programs have been rolled out, it's time for the testing to begin. While the other phases of the database lifecycle can occur reasonably independently of the systems development process, part of the testing phase is testing how all components of the system run together.

Load testing may indicate that MySQL has not been set up to handle the expected 600 concurrent connections, and the configuration file needs to be changed. Other tests may indicate that in certain circumstances, duplicate key errors are received, as the locking mechanism is not uniformly implemented, and the application does not handle locking correctly. The application needs to be fixed. Backups also need to be tested, as well as the ability to smoothly restore from backup with a minimum of downtime.

*WARNING*  *Testing is one of the most neglected and critical phases. A designer or manager who does not properly account for testing is simply incompetent. No matter how tiny your system, make sure you allocate time for thorough testing and time for fixing the inevitable bugs.*

Once testing is complete, the system can be rolled out. You decide on a low-key rollout and give a few selected poets access to the website to upload their poems. You discover other problems: Obscure browsers have incompatibilities that lead to garbled poems being submitted. Strictly speaking, this doesn't fall into the database programmer's domain, but it's the kind of situation testing will reveal once all the elements of the system are working together. You decide to insist that users make use of browsers that can render the developed pages correctly, and browsers that don't adhere to these standards are barred from uploading.

And soon enough, the system is rolled out completely. Maintenance, though, is a never-ending task, and with large numbers of updates and deletes being performed, the database has a tendency to become fragmented. The administrator must run regular OPTIMIZE statements, and of course, the inevitable disk failure leads to an all-night restore session and much thankfulness for the ease of use of mysqldump.

# Concurrency Control with Transactions

Database requests happen in a linear fashion, one after another. When many users are accessing a database, or one user has a related set of requests to run, it becomes important to ensure that the results remain consistent. To achieve this, you use *transactions*, which are groups of database requests that are processed as a whole. Put another way, they are logical units of work.

To ensure data integrity, transactions need to adhere to four conditions: atomicity, consistency, isolation, and durability (also known as ACID).

## Atomicity

*Atomicity* means the entire transaction must complete. If this is not the case, the entire transaction is aborted. This ensures that the database can never be left with partially completed transactions, which lead to poor data integrity. If you remove money out of one bank account, for example, but the second request fails and the system cannot place the money in another bank account, both requests must fail. The money cannot simply be lost or taken from one account without going into the other.

## Consistency

*Consistency* refers to the state the data is in when certain conditions are met. For example, one rule may be that each invoice must relate to a customer in the customer table. These rules may be broken during the course of a transaction if, for example, the invoice is inserted without a related customer, which is added at a later stage in the transaction. These temporary violations are not visible outside of the transaction, and will always be resolved by the time the transaction is complete.

## Isolation

*Isolation* means that any data being used during the processing of one transaction cannot be used by another transaction until the first transaction is complete. For example, if two people deposit $100 into an account with a balance of $900, the first transaction must add $100 to $900, and the second must add $100 to $1,000. If the second transaction reads the $900 before the first transaction has completed, both transactions will seem to succeed, but $100 has gone missing. The second transaction must wait until it alone is accessing the data.

## Durability

*Durability* refers to the fact that once data from a transaction has been committed, its effects will remain, even after a system failure. While a transaction is under way, the effects are not persistent. If the database crashes, backups will always restore it to a consistent state prior to the transaction commencing. Nothing a transaction does should be able to change this fact.

# Summary

Good database design ensures a longer-living and more efficient database system. By spending the time to design it carefully, designers can avoid most of the commonly repeated errors that plague many existing databases.

The database lifecycle (DBLC) can be defined in many ways, but it comes down to the same main steps. First, the Analysis phase is where information is gathered and the existing system is examined to identify current problems, possible solutions, and so on. Then, the Design phase is where the new system is carefully designed, first conceptually for the stakeholders and then logically and physically for implementation. Next, the Implementation phase physically rolls out the database, before the Testing phase brings any problems to light. Then, when the Testing phase has succeeded, the system is put into operation for day-to-day use. Almost immediately, the Maintenance phase starts. As change requests come in, routine optimizations and backups need to be performed. Finally, once maintenance becomes too intensive, a new database cycle begins to replace the aging system.

Transactions ensure that the database remains in a consistent state throughout its existence. There are four principles that keep this so. Atomicity states that all requests within a transaction succeed or fail as one. Consistency ensures that the database will always return to a coherent state between transactions. Isolation ensures that all requests from one transaction are completed before the next transaction that affects the same data is allowed to begin processing. And durability keeps the database consistent even in the case of failures.

# Part III

# MySQL Administration

# Chapter 10

# Basic Administration

ALTHOUGH MySQL IS EASY to maintain and administer, it does not look after itself. This chapter covers the basic administrative tasks, some of which are covered in more detail in the following chapters. Specifically, you'll learn how to start and stop the server, both manually and automatically. You'll also get to know some of the indispensable tools for a MySQL administrator, learn how to use logs, and how to configure MySQL.

Featured in this chapter:

◆  The MySQL utilities
◆  Starting and shutting down MySQL
◆  Starting mysqld automatically upon booting up
◆  Configuring MySQL
◆  Logging
◆  Rotating logs
◆  Optimizing, checking, analyzing, and repairing tables

## Meeting MySQL as an Administrator

As an administrator, you'll need to know a lot more about how MySQL works than if you were just running queries. You'll need to be familiar with the utilities supplied with the MySQL distribution, as well as how your MySQL is set up. The main utilities you will use as an administrator are the following:

**mysqladmin**   This is probably the most useful administration utility; it allows you to create and drop databases, stop the server, view the server variables, view and kill MySQL processes, set passwords, and flush log files…among other things!

**mysqldump**   Creates SQL backups of the database.

**mysqld**   This is not really a utility, as it's the MySQL server. You'll come across terms such as *the mysqld variables*, and you should know this is nothing more esoteric than the server variables.

**mysqlimport**   Imports text files into database tables.

**mysqlcheck**   Checks, analyzes, and repairs database tables.

**mysqlhotcopy**   A Perl script that backs up database tables quickly.

**myisampack**   Compresses MyISAM tables.

The first question you should ask about a new system is fairly fundamental: Where is the data stored?

The default location is usually `/usr/local/var` on a source Unix distribution, `/usr/local/mysql/data` on a binary Unix distribution, and `C:\mysql\data` on Windows. When MySQL is compiled, a data directory is selected, but this can be set to another location by specifying the new data directory in the configuration file. You'll learn about the configuration file in more detail later in this chapter in the section "Configuring MySQL," but for now, it's sufficient to know it's usually called `my.cnf` in Unix, or `my.ini` in Windows only, and it contains the MySQL configuration data. If you wanted to force MySQL to use a new location, the line would be something like this:

```
datadir = C:/mysqldata
```

To discover what the data directory is on an existing installation, you can use the variables option of mysqladmin. The sample output is a little intimidating for novices; there are many, many variables (and each new MySQL update seems to add more), but they're listed alphabetically:

```
% mysqladmin -uroot -pg00r002b variables;
+----------------------+------------------------------------------+
| Variable_name        | Value                                    |
+----------------------+------------------------------------------+
| back_log             | 50                                       |
| basedir              | /usr/local/mysql-max-4.0.1-alpha-pc-     |
|                      |   linux-gnu-i686/                        |
| bdb_cache_size       | 8388600                                  |
| bdb_log_buffer_size  | 32768                                    |
| bdb_home             | /usr/local/mysql/data/                   |
| bdb_max_lock         | 10000                                    |
| bdb_logdir           |                                          |
| bdb_shared_data      | OFF                                      |
| bdb_tmpdir           | /tmp/                                    |
| bdb_version          | Sleepycat Software: Berkeley DB 3.2.9a:  |
|                      |   (December 23, 2001)                    |
| binlog_cache_size    | 32768                                    |
| character_set        | latin1                                   |
| character_sets       | latin1 big5 czech euc_kr gb2312 gbk      |
|                      |   latin1_de sjis tis620 ujis dec8 dos    |
|                      |   german1 hp8 koi8_ru latin2 swe7 usa7   |
|                      |   cp1251 danish hebrew win1251 estonia   |
|                      |   hungarian koi8_ukr win1251ukr greek    |
|                      |   win1250 croat cp1257 latin5            |
| concurrent_insert    | ON                                       |
| connect_timeout      | 5                                        |
| datadir              | /usr/local/mysql/data/                   |
```

You can also just get the variable you're interested in by using grep (Unix) or find (Windows), as follows, first on Unix, then on Windows:

```
% mysqladmin -uroot -pg00r002b variables | grep 'datadir'
| datadir                   | /usr/local/mysql/data/                      |
```

or

```
C:\mysql\bin>mysqladmin variables | find "datadir"
| datadir                   | C:\mysql\data\                              |
```

The data directory in this case is /usr/local/mysql/data, the default for most binary installations on Unix, and c:\mysql\data with the Windows example.

The data directory usually contains the log files (they are placed there by default, though you can change this) as well as the actual data. In the case of MyISAM tables (the default), each database has its own directory, and within this directory each table has three corresponding files: an .MYD file for the data, an .MYI for the indexes, and an .frm file for the definition. BDB tables are also stored in the same directory, but they consist of a .db file and an .frm definition file. InnoDB tables have their .frm definition file in the database directory, but the actual data is stored one level up, on the same level as the database directories.

MySQL clients can access the server in three ways:

**Unix sockets**   These are used on Unix machines when connecting to a server on the same machine. The socket file is placed in the default location (usually /tmp/mysql.sock or /var/lib/mysql.sock), unless otherwise specified.

**Named pipes**   These are used on Windows NT/2000/XP machines where the --enable-named-pipe option is used with an executable that allows named pipes (mysqld-max-nt or mysqld-nt).

**TCP/IP through a port**   This is the slowest method but is the only way to connect to a server running on Windows 95/98/Me or to connect remotely to a Unix machine.

# Starting and Shutting Down MySQL

MySQL runs on most flavors of operating system, but the procedures differ with each. The following sections are divided into Windows and Unix discussions.

## Starting and Shutting Down in Unix

The most basic way to start MySQL is to run mysqld directly. However, most distributions come with a starter script called mysqld_safe (older versions of MySQL called it safe_mysqld), which you should use instead when starting MySQL manually. This script has some extra safety features, such as logging errors and automatically restarting the server when an error occurs. To start MySQL, log in as root and run the following command from the directory in which MySQL was installed (usually /usr/local/mysql):

```
% bin/mysqld_safe  --user=mysql &
```

Note that the user is set as mysql. It's important to run MySQL as the mysql user to avoid permission and security problems.

*WARNING    If you are unfamiliar with the system—especially if you didn't install it—speak to your systems admin-istrator before trying to start the server in this way. There are multiple ways to start a server, and trying the wrong one could cause problems! Most production systems use a script to automatically start MySQL upon booting up, and you should use this if one is in place.*

Some distributions come with a script called mysql.server, which may even be automatically installed for you (sometimes renamed just to mysql). This would usually be placed in a directory where processes are automatically activated upon booting. If this is the case, you'd use this script to start. mysql.server takes start and stop options. The following is a common startup used on Red Hat Linux:

```
% /etc/rc.d/init.d/mysql start
% Starting mysqld daemon with databases from /usr/local/mysql/data
```

On FreeBSD, the file may be placed in /usr/local/etc/rc.d, in which case you'd use the following:

```
% /usr/local/etc/rc.d/mysql.sh start
```

To shut down, you can use mysqladmin:

```
% mysqladmin shutdown -uroot -p
Enter password:
020706 16:56:02  mysqld ended
```

or the equivalent option from the startup script, such as this:

```
% /etc/rc.d/init.d/mysql stop
Killing mysqld with pid 2985
Wait for mysqld to exit\c
.\c
.\c
.\c
.\c
.\c
.\c
020706 17:07:49  mysqld ended
```

### STARTING MYSQL AUTOMATICALLY UPON BOOTING UP

In production systems, all but the greatest of control freaks will want MySQL to be running as soon as the system boots up. To achieve this, if it isn't already done for you, you'll need to know how your version of Unix starts and stops processes upon booting or shutting down. It can differ quite mark-edly from system to system. If you're unsure of this, especially if you didn't install the version of MySQL yourself, the best person to speak to is your system administrator. They should know your system's ins and outs better than I can explain in a book.

This example is from Red Hat Linux:

```
% cp /usr/share/mysql/mysql.server /etc/rc.d/init.d
```

This line copies the mysql.server script to the initialization directory.

The next two lines ensure that MySQL is started when the system boots up and reaches multiuser mode (run level 3) and shuts down with the system (run level 0). They create a link from the appropriate level to the mysql.server script:

```
% ln -s /etc/rc.d/init.d/mysql.server /etc/rc.d/rc3.d/S99mysql
% ln -s /etc/rc.d/init.d/mysql.server /etc/rc.d/rc0.d/S01mysql
```

The next example is from a recent version of FreeBSD, where the startup scripts just need to be copied to the rc.d directory and given an .sh extension:

```
% cp /usr/local/mysql/support-files/mysql.server /usr/local/etc/rc.d/mysql.sh
```

Make sure your script is executable, and not accessible to any unauthorized eyes, with the following:

```
% chmod 700 /usr/local/etc/rc.d/mysql.sh
```

Some older systems may use /etc/rc.local to start scripts, in which case you should add something like the following to the file:

```
/bin/sh -c 'cd /usr/local/mysql ; ./bin/safe_mysqld --user=mysql &'
```

### AVOIDING COMMON PROBLEMS WITH STARTING MYSQL IN UNIX

The most common cause for problems is permissions. If you're not logged in as root and you try to start MySQL, you'll get an error such as the following:

```
% /usr/local/mysql/bin/mysqld_safe --user=mysql &
% The file /usr/local/mysql/libexec/mysqld doesn't exist or is not executable
Please do a cd to the mysql installation directory and restart
this script from there as follows:
./bin/mysqld_safe.
```

To solve it, log in as root:

```
% su
Password:
% /usr/local/mysql/bin/mysqld_safe --user=mysql &
[1] 24756
% Starting mysqld daemon with databases from
 /usr/local/mysql-max-4.0.2-alpha-unknown-freebsdelf4.6-i386/data
```

For other problems, the MySQL error log may give you some assistance. See the section titled "The Error Log" later in this chapter.

## Starting and Shutting Down in Windows

There are a number of executable files that come with a Windows distribution (see Table 10.1). You'll need to choose which one you'd like to run depending on how you're going to be using MySQL.

**TABLE 10.1:** THE MYSQL EXECUTABLES

| EXECUTABLE | DESCRIPTION |
| --- | --- |
| mysqld | A binary that supports debugging, automatic memory allocation checking, transactional tables (InnoDB and BDB), and symbolic links. |
| mysqld-opt | An optimized binary that comes with no support for transactional tables (InnoDB or BDB). |
| mysqld-nt | An optimized binary that supports named pipes (for use with NT/2000/XP). It can run on 95/98/Me, but no named pipes will be created, as these operating systems do not support it. |
| mysqld-max | An optimized binary that supports transactional tables (InnoDB and BDB) and symbolic links. |
| mysqld-max-nt | An optimized binary that supports transactional tables (InnoDB and BDB) as well as named pipes when run on NT/2000/XP and symbolic links. |

To start MySQL, simply run the executable you'd like to use, for example:

```
C:\> c:\mysql\bin\mysqld-max
020706 18:53:45  InnoDB: Started
```

Replace \mysql\bin\ with the directory where you've installed MySQL, if it is different. Many Windows users prefer to use the following:

```
C:\> c:\progra~1\mysql\bin\mysqld-max
```

You can also use the winmysqladmin utility that comes with Windows distributions to start MySQL.

**NOTE** *If you're still using Windows 95, make sure Winsock 2 is installed. Older versions of Windows 95 do not come with Winsock 2, and MySQL will not run. You can download it from* `www.microsoft.com`.

### STARTING MYSQL AUTOMATICALLY

With Windows 95/98/Me, create a shortcut to the executable file winmysqladmin in the `StartUp` folder. This file is stored in the same place as the other executables—in other words, in `c:\mysql\bin` by default.

Make sure your `my.ini` file contains the executable you want to use. You may run mysqld-max manually and then want to start it automatically with winmysqladmin. However, if your file contains the following, for example:

```
[WinMySQLAdmin]
Server=C:/PROGRAM FILES/MYSQL/bin/mysqld-opt.exe
```

you won't be able to use the transactional capability you may have been expecting. You can edit the `my.ini` file manually, or you can use winmysladmin to modify it, selecting `my.ini` `Setup` and changing the mysqld file (see Figure 10.1).

**FIGURE 10.1**

Using winmysqladmin to update the my.ini configuration file

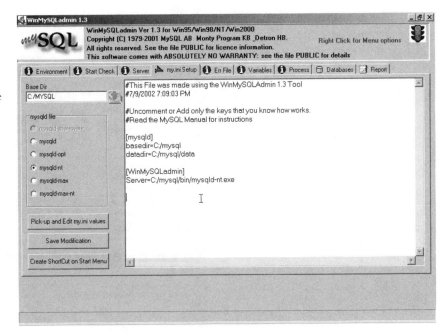

With NT/2000/XP, install MySQL as a service as follows:

```
C:\> c:\mysql\bin\mysqld-max-nt -install
```

If you don't want MySQL to start automatically, but you still want it as a service, run the same command with the `manual` option:

```
C:\mysql\bin> mysqld-max-nt --install-manual
```

You can then start the service with the following:

```
C:\> net start mysql
The MySql service is starting.
The MySql service was started successfully.
```

And stop it with the usual `mysqladmin shutdown` or the following:

```
C:\> net stop mysql
The MySql service is stopping...........
The MySql service was stopped successfully.
```

To remove it as a service, run mysqld with the remove option, as follows:

```
C:\> c:\mysql\bin\mysqld-max-nt -remove
```

You can also use the Services Control Panel, and click Start or Stop (see Figure 10.2).

**FIGURE 10.2**

Starting MySQL
as a service in
Windows 2000

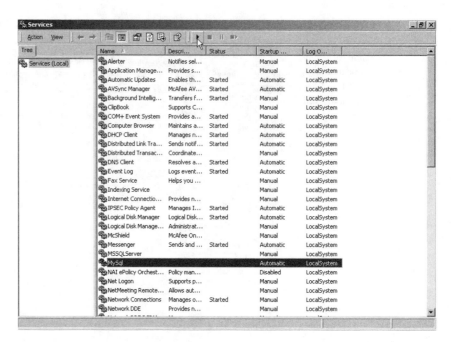

### AVOIDING COMMON PROBLEMS WITH STARTING MySQL IN WINDOWS

A common problem with starting MySQL on Windows occurs when MySQL is installed in a non-default directory (such as `c:\Program Files\MySQL\bin`). Sometimes the locations are not correctly reflected in the `my.ini` configuration file. For example, if you've installed MySQL in `c:\Program Files\MySQL`, then `my.ini` should contain something like the following:

```
[mysqld]
basedir=C:/Program Files/mysql
datadir=C:/Program Files/data

[WinMySQLAdmin]
Server=C:/Program Files/mysql/bin/mysqld-max-nt.exe
```

*NOTE*   *Windows pathnames are specified with forward slashes, not the usual Windows backslash, in option files. If you want to use backslashes, you'll need to escape them (with another backslash), as the backslash is a special MySQL character, for example:* `Server=C:\\Program Files\\mysql\\bin\\mysqld-opt.exe`.

You may have wanted to use spaces in your filename and tried something like this:

```
C:/program files/mysql
```

instead of this:

```
C:/progra~1/mysql
```

Starting winmysqladmin may create a `my.ini` file that interferes with an existing configuration. Try removing the newly created `my.ini` file (restoring the original if necessary).

If the problem still eludes you, try examining the error log to see if there is an obvious reason. The error log is in `C:\MySQL\data\mysql.err` by default.

You can also start MySQL in stand-alone mode (`mysqld --standalone`), which may give more useful output, or, as a final roll of the dice, in debug mode, which will write a trace file (usually to `C:\mysqld.trace`) that may be of some use.

## Configuring MySQL

To get MySQL to run smoothly in the way you want, you'll need to configure it in certain ways, such as to set the default table type to InnoDB or to display error messages in a certain language. You can set most options in three ways: from the command line, from a configuration file, or from a preset environment variable. Setting options from the command line is useful for testing, but it's not useful if you want to keep those options over a long period of time. Environment variables are almost never used. The most common, and the most useful method, is through a configuration file.

On Unix, the startup configuration file is usually called `my.cnf` and can be placed in the following locations. MySQL reads this from top to bottom, so the lower positions have a higher precedence (see Table 10.2).

**TABLE 10.2:** PRECEDENCE OF THE CONFIGURATION FILES ON UNIX

| FILE | DESCRIPTION |
| --- | --- |
| `/etc/my.cnf` | Global options that apply to all servers and users. If you're unsure where to put a configuration file, place it here. |
| `DATA_DIRECTORY/my.cnf` | Options specific to the server that stores its data in the specified DATA_DIRECTORY. This is usually `/usr/local/mysql/data` for binary or `/usr/local/var` for source installations. Be warned that this is not necessarily the same as the `--datadir` option specified for mysqld. Rather, it's the one specified when the system was set up. |
| `defaults-extra-file` | Options specific to server or client utilities started with the `--defaults-extra-file=filename` command-line option. |
| `~/.my.cnf` | Options specific to the user. |

On Windows, the startup configuration file is usually called `my.ini` or `my.cnf` depending on its location (see Table 10.3).

**TABLE 10.3:** PRECEDENCE OF THE CONFIGURATION FILES IN WINDOWS

| FILE | DESCRIPTION |
| --- | --- |
| `C:WINDOWS_SYSTEM_FOLDER\my.ini` | Global options that apply to all servers and users. The Windows system folder is usually `C:WINNT\System32`, `C:\WINNT`, or `C:\WINDOWS`. If you're unsure which configuration file to use, I suggest this one. |
| `C:\my.cnf` | Global options that apply to all servers and users (could just use the previous `my.ini` file instead). |

*Continued on next page*

**TABLE 10.3:** PRECEDENCE OF THE CONFIGURATION FILES IN WINDOWS *(continued)*

| FILE | DESCRIPTION |
|---|---|
| C:\DATA_DIRECTORY\ my.cnf | Options specific to the server that stores its data in the specified DATA_DIRECTORY (which is usually C:\mysql\data). |
| defaults-extra-file=filename | Options specific to server or client utilities started with the --defaults-extra-file=filename command-line option. |

In Windows, if the C drive is not the boot drive, or you use the winmysqladmin utility, you have to use a my.ini configuration file (in the Windows system folder).

*NOTE* *Windows has no configuration file for options specific to the user.*

A sample configuration file follows:

```
# The following options will be passed to all MySQL clients
[client]
#password       = your_password
port            = 3306
socket          = /tmp/mysql.sock

# The MySQL server
[mysqld]
port            = 3306
socket          = /tmp/mysql.sock
skip-locking
set-variable    = key_buffer=16M
set-variable    = max_allowed_packet=1M
set-variable    = table_cache=64
set-variable    = sort_buffer=512K
set-variable    = net_buffer_length=8K
set-variable    = myisam_sort_buffer_size=8M
#set-variable   = ft_min_word_length=3
log-bin
server-id       = 1

[mysqldump]
quick
set-variable    = max_allowed_packet=16M

[mysql]
no-auto-rehash
# Remove the next comment character if you are not familiar with SQL
#safe-updates
```

```
[myisamchk]
set-variable      = key_buffer=20M
set-variable      = sort_buffer=20M
set-variable      = read_buffer=2M
set-variable      = write_buffer=2M

[mysqlhotcopy]
interactive-timeout
```

The hash (#) denotes a comment, and the square brackets ([]) are section markers. Terms inside square brackets denote which program the settings that follow will affect. In this example, the setting `interactive-timeout` will apply when running the program mysqlhotcopy only. The options set beneath a section marker setting apply for the previously set section, until the next section marker.

In the previous example, the first port applies to clients, and the second port applies to the MySQL server. They're usually the same, but they don't have to be (such as when you run multiple MySQL servers on the same machine).

Options come in three types:

♦ `option=value` (such as `port=3306`).

♦ `option` (such as `log-bin`). These are Boolean options that are not set if the option is absent (the default is used) and are set if the option is present.

♦ `set-variable = variable=value` (such as `set-variable = write_buffer=2M`). This allows you to set the MySQL server variables.

**WARNING**  *The sample configurations come with a password option for clients that's commented out. It may be convenient to connect this way, but I don't suggest doing it in most cases for security reasons. Anyone who could possibly read this file could then access MySQL.*

The following programs support option files: myisamchk, myisampack, mysql, mysql.server, mysqladmin, mysqlcheck, mysqld, mysqld_safe, mysqldump, mysqlimport, and mysqlshow.

Basically, almost any option that can be used with a MySQL program from the command line can be set in a configuration file as well.

A large part of mastering MySQL is in getting the configuration just right for your situation. Later in this chapter, you'll see what the various server options mean and how you can configure them to get the most performance from MySQL. Most MySQL distributions come with four sample configurations:

**my-huge.cnf**  For systems with more than 1GB memory mostly dedicated to MySQL.

**my-large.cnf**  For systems with at least 512MB memory mostly dedicated to MySQL.

**my-medium.cnf**  For systems with at least 32MB memory dedicated entirely to MySQL, or at least 128MB on a machine that serves multiple purposes (such as a dual web/database server.

**my-small.cnf**  For systems with less than 64MB memory where MySQL cannot take up too much of the resources.

Some distributions come with just the one sample: `my-example.cnf`.

View the files to check the latest documentation, though; 512MB is not going to remain a "large" system forever. I suggest copying the one that comes closest to your needs to the directory you're storing it in and then making any further modifications.

*TIP    Keep a backup of your configuration file as well. If your system fails, you may lose quite a lot of time reconfiguring the server.*

# Logging

Examining log files may not sound like your idea of fun on a Friday evening, but it can be an invaluable aid in not only identifying problems that have already occurred, but spotting situations that, if left untouched, may soon cause you to lose more than a Friday night. MySQL has a number of different log files:

**The error log**    This is the place to look for problems with starting, running, or stopping MySQL.

**The query log**    All connections and executed queries are logged here.

**The binary update log**    All SQL statements that change data are stored.

**The slow query log**    All queries that took more than `long_query_time` to execute, or that didn't make use of any indexes, are logged here.

**The update log**    This has been deprecated and should be replaced by the binary update log in all instances. It stores SQL statements that change data.

**The ISAM log**    Logs all changes to the ISAM tables. Used only for debugging the ISAM code.

## The Error Log

On Windows, the MySQL error log is called `mysql.err`, and on Unix it is called `hostname.err` (for example, `test.mysqlhost.co.za.err`). It is located in the data directory (usually `C:\MySQL\data` on Windows, `/usr/local/mysql/data` for binary Unix installations, `/usr/local/var` for source Unix installations, or `/var/lib/mysql` on Red Hat Linux flavors).

It contains startup and shutdown information and any critical errors that occur while running. It will log if the server died and was automatically restarted or if MySQL notices that a table needs to be automatically checked or repaired. The log may also contain a stack trace when MySQL dies. A sample error log follows:

```
010710 19:52:43  mysqld started
010710 19:52:43  Can't start server: Bind on TCP/IP port: Address already in use
010710 19:52:43  Do you already have another mysqld server running on port: 3306 ?
010710 19:52:43  Aborting

010710 19:52:43  /usr/local/mysql-3.23.39-pc-linux-gnu-i686/bin/mysqld:
 Shutdown Complete

010710 19:52:43  mysqld ended
```

```
010710 19:55:23  mysqld started
/usr/local/mysql-3.23.39-pc-linux-gnu-i686/bin/mysqld: ready for connections
010907 17:50:38  /usr/local/mysql-3.23.39-pc-linux-gnu-i686/bin/mysqld:
 Normal shutdown

010907 17:50:38  /usr/local/mysql-3.23.39-pc-linux-gnu-i686/bin/mysqld:
 Shutdown Complete

010907 17:50:38  mysqld ended
```

This logs a situation you were warned about at the beginning of the chapter, where MySQL has been improperly started. Then, when you attempted to start MySQL properly, you could not because another process had already started. To solve the problem, you had to end the rogue process (such as by running kill s 9 PID or kill -9 PID on Unix, or using the Task Manager on Windows).

### The Query Log

You can start the query log with the following option:

```
log =[query_log_filename]
```

in my.cnf. If you don't specify query_log_filename, the query log will be given the hostname.

It will log all connections and executed queries. It can be useful to see who is connecting (and when) for security purposes, as well as for debugging to see if the server is receiving queries correctly.

This kind of log has performance implications, so you should deactivate it if performance is a concern. The binary update log (which logs only update queries) can be useful in its place.

A sample query log follows:

```
/usr/local/mysql-max-4.0.1-alpha-pc-linux-gnu-i686/bin/mysqld, Version:
 4.0.1-alpha-max-log, started with:
Tcp port: 3306  Unix socket: /tmp/mysql.sock
Time                    Id Command      Argument
020707  1:01:29          1 Connect      root@localhost on
020707  1:01:35          1 Init DB      firstdb
020707  1:01:38          1 Query        show tables
020707  1:01:51          1 Query        select * from innotest
020707  1:01:54          1 Quit
```

### The Binary Update Log

Binary logging is activated when the log-bin option is used in the my.cnf or my.ini configuration file, as follows:

```
--log-bin[=binlog_filename]
```

Any extension will be dropped, as MySQL adds its own extension to the binary log. If no filename is specified, the binary log is named as the host machine, with -bin appended. MySQL also creates a binary index file, with the same name and an extension of .index. The index can be given a different name (and location) with the following option:

```
--log-bin-index=binlog_index_filename
```

The binary update logs contain all the SQL statements that update the database, as well as how long the query took to execute and a timestamp of when the query was processed. Statements are logged in the same order as they are executed (after the query is complete but before transactions are completed or locks removed). Updates that have not yet been committed are placed in a cache first.

The binary update log is also useful for restoring backups (see Chapter 11, "Database Backups") and for when you are replicating a slave database from a master (see Chapter 12, "Database Replication").

Binary update logs start with an extension 001. A new one is created, with the number incremented by one, each time the server is restarted or one of mysqladmin refresh, mysqladmin flush-logs, or FLUSH LOGS is run. A new binary log is also created (and incremented) when the binary log reaches max_bin_log_size.

The max_bin_log_size value is set in the my.cnf or my.ini file as follows:

```
set-variable    = max_binlog_size = 1000M
```

You can see what size it has defaulted to, in bytes, by examining the variables:

```
% mysqladmin -u root -pg00r002b variables | grep 'max_binlog_size'
max_binlog_size                | 1073741824
```

The binary update index file contains a list of all the binary logs used to date. A sample could be as follows:

```
./test-bin.001
./test-bin.002
./test-bin.003
./test-bin.004
```

If you now flushed the logs, the binary update index would be appended with the new binary log:

```
% mysqladmin -u root -pg00r002b flush-logs
```

The sample now contains the following:

```
./test-bin.001
./test-bin.002
./test-bin.003
./test-bin.004
./test-bin.005
```

You can delete all the unused binary update logs with RESET MASTER:

```
mysql> RESET MASTER;
Query OK, 0 rows affected (0.00 sec)
```

The binary update index now reflects that there is only one binary update log:

```
./test-bin.006
```

**WARNING**  *Do not remove binary update logs until you are sure they are not going to be needed. If you use replication, be especially careful (see Chapter 12 for more on this). If you use the binary logs to restore backups, make sure you don't remove any that are more recent than your most recent backup.*

Not all updates to all databases need to be logged; in many cases, you may only want to store updates to certain databases. The `binlog-do-db` and `binlog-ignore-db` options in the `my.cnf` and `my.ini` configuration files allow you to control this. The first specifically sets which database updates are to be logged. For example, the following:

```
binlog-do-db = firstdb
```

will log updates only to the firstdb database, but the following:

```
binlog-ignore-db = test
```

will log updates to all databases except test. You can add multiple lines if you want to log multiple databases:

```
binlog-do-db = test
binlog-do-db = firstdb
```

When updates that are part of a transaction are to be logged, MySQL creates a buffer of the size specified by `binlog-cache-size` in your configuration file (the default is 32KB, or 32,768 bytes). Each thread can create one of these buffers. To avoid too many buffers being used at the same time, the variable `max-binlog-cache-size` is also set. The default maximum for this is 4GB, or 4,294,967,295 bytes.

Because the binary update log is a binary file, the data is stored more efficiently than in the old text update log. It also means that you cannot view the data with a text editor. The mysqlbinlog utility allows you to view the data:

```
C:\Program Files\MySQL\data>..\bin\mysqlbinlog test-bin.002
# at 4
#020602 18:40:02 server id  1    Start: binlog v 2, server v 4.0.1-alpha-max-log
created 020602 18:40:02
# at 79
#020602 18:41:27 server id  1    Query    thread_id=3      exec_time=0
 error_code=0
use firstdb;
SET TIMESTAMP=1023036087;
CREATE TABLE customer(id INT);
# at 146
#020602 18:41:40 server id  1    Query    thread_id=3      exec_time=0
 error_code=0
SET TIMESTAMP=1023036100;
INSERT INTO customer(id) VALUES(1);
# at 218
#020602 18:43:12 server id  1    Query    thread_id=5      exec_time=0
 error_code=0
SET TIMESTAMP=1023036192;
INSERT INTO customer VALUES(12);
# at 287
#020602 18:45:00 server id  1    Stop
```

To use a binary update log to update the contents of a MySQL server, simply pipe the results to the required server, for example:

```
% mysqlbinlog ..\data\test-bin.022 | mysql
```

*NOTE*   *One of the consequences of using the binary update log is that concurrent inserts will not work with* CREATE...INSERT *or* INSERT...SELECT. *Concurrent inserts are where MySQL allows reads and writes to happen at the same time in MyISAM tables, but enabling them with these two kinds of statement would mean that the binary update log could not be reliably used for restoring backups or for replication.*

## The Slow Query Log

You start the slow query log with the following option:

```
log-slow-queries[=slow_query_log_filename]
```

in the configuration file. If slow_query_log_filename is not supplied, the slow query log will be given the name of the host machine, with -slow.log appended (for example, test.mysqlhost.co.za-slow.log).

All SQL statements that take longer to execute than long_query_time are logged.

This is set in the my.cnf or my.ini config file as follows:

```
set-variable    = long_query_time = 20
```

It is measured in seconds (though MySQL is planning to change soon to measure in microseconds, so check the latest documentation).

If the option log-long-format is set, then all queries that do not make use of an index are also logged. Place the following line:

```
log-long-format
```

in your my.cnf or my.ini file to do this.

This is a useful log to have in place; the performance impact is not high (assuming most of your queries are not slow!), and it highlights the queries that most need attention (where indexes are missing or not optimally used).

A sample slow query log follows:

```
/usr/local/mysql-max-4.0.1-alpha-pc-linux-gnu-i686/bin/mysqld, Version:
 4.0.1-alpha-max-log, started with:
Tcp port: 3306  Unix socket: /tmp/mysql.sock
Time                Id Command    Argument
# Time: 020707 13:57:57
# User@Host: root[root] @ localhost []
# Query_time: 0  Lock_time: 0  Rows_sent: 8  Rows_examined: 8
use firstdb;
select id from sales;
# Time: 020707 13:58:47
# User@Host: root[root] @ localhost []
# Query_time: 0  Lock_time: 0  Rows_sent: 6  Rows_examined: 8
```

In this log, the `select id from sales` query is there because it did not make use of an index. The query could have made use of an index on the *id* field. See Chapter 4, "Indexes and Query Optimization," for a discussion on where to use indexes.

You can also use the mysqldumpslow utility to display the results of the slow query log:

```
% mysqldumpslow test-slow.log
```

```
Reading mysql slow query log from test-slow.log
Count: 1  Time=0.00s (0s)  Lock=0.00s (0s)  Rows=0.0 (0), root[root]@localhost
  # Query_time: N  Lock_time: N  Rows_sent: N  Rows_examined: N
  use firstdb;
  select id from sales

Count: 1  Time=0.00s (0s)  Lock=0.00s (0s)  Rows=0.0 (0), root[root]@localhost
  # Query_time: N  Lock_time: N  Rows_sent: N  Rows_examined: N
  DELETE FROM sales WHERE id>N

Count: 1  Time=0.00s (0s)  Lock=0.00s (0s)  Rows=0.0 (0), root[root]@localhost
  # Query_time: N  Lock_time: N  Rows_sent: N  Rows_examined: N
  select id from sales where id<N
```

## Rotating Logs

Log files, although extremely useful, have a cancerous nature in that they continue to grow until there is no space left for anything else. Eventually you'll need to remove the excess logs, and there is no better way of doing this than having some scripts that automatically perform this task for you.

For the noncritical logs, doing the following will suffice (assuming you start in the directory containing the log files). The following is on a Unix system:

```
mv logfile backup_directory/logfile.old
mysqladmin flush-logs
```

And the following is on a Windows system:

```
move logfile backup_directory\logfile.old
mysqladmin flush-logs
```

Flushing the logs (which you can also do while connected the server with the SQL statement FLUSH LOGS) closes and reopens log files that do not increment in sequence (such as the slow query log). Or, in the case of logs that are incremented (the binary update log), flushing the logs creates a new log file with an extension incremented by one from the previous one and forces MySQL to use this new file.

The old log file can be either removed to backup or just deleted if it will be of no further use. Any queries that are processed between the two statements are not logged, as the query log for that moment in time does not exist. Logging is only re-created when the logs are flushed. For example, assuming that the query log is called `querylog`, the following set of commands shows one way to rotate logs. You need to have two windows open, Window1 connected to your shell or command line, and Window2 connected to MySQL.

First, from Window1:

```
% mv querylog querylog.old
```

Now run a query fromWindow2 (connected to MySQL):

```
mysql> SELECT * FROM sales;
```

See if the query has been logged, from Window1:

```
% tail querylog
tail: querylog: No such file or directory
```

Until you flush the logs, no log file exists and no queries will be logged:

```
% mysqladmin -uroot -pg00r002b flush-logs
```

Run another query from Window2:

```
mysql> SELECT * FROM customer;
```

This time it's been added to the query log, as you can see from Window1:

```
% tail querylog
/usr/local/mysql-max-4.0.1-alpha-pc-linux-gnu-i686/bin/mysqld, Version:
 4.0.1-alpha-max-log, started with:
Tcp port: 3306  Unix socket: /tmp/mysql.sock
Time                 Id Command    Argument
020707 20:45:23       5 Quit
020707 20:45:26       4 Query         select * from customer
```

This technique cannot be used with the critical log files (such as the binary update log) because if they are to be useful for replication or for restoration of backups, there cannot be the possibility of any queries being missed. For this reason, a new binary update log, with an extension that increments by one each time, is created whenever the logs are flushed. Records will only be added to the latest log, meaning you can move older ones without worrying about queries going missing. Assuming the binary update log is called gmbinlog and starting with one binary update log, try the following:

```
C:\Program Files\MySQL\data>dir *-bin*

 Volume in drive C has no label
 Volume Serial Number is 2D20-1303
 Directory of C:\Program Files\MySQL\data

GMBINLOG 001          272  07-07-02  8:50p gmbinlog.001
GMBINL~1 IND            0  07-07-02  8:48p gmbinlog.index
        2 file(s)          398 bytes
        0 dir(s)    33,868.09 MB free
C:\Program Files\MySQL\data>..\bin\mysqladmin flush-logs
C:\Program Files\MySQL\data>dir *-bin*
```

```
 Volume in drive C has no label
 Volume Serial Number is 2D20-1303
 Directory of C:\Program Files\MySQL\data

GMBINLOG 001          272  07-07-02   8:50p gmbinlog.001
GMBINL~1 IND            0  07-07-02   8:48p gmbinlog.index
GMBINLOG 002            0  07-07-02   8:50p gmbinlog.001
        3 file(s)            398 bytes
        0 dir(s)      33,868.09 MB free
C:\Program Files\MySQL\data> move gmbinlog.001 D:\backup_directory\gmbinlog001.old
```

**WARNING**   *If you're using replication, do not remove old binary log files until you are sure no slave servers will still need them. See Chapter 12 for more details.*

MySQL for Red Hat Linux comes with a log rotation script. If the distribution you're using does not, you can use this one as the basis to create your own:

```
# This logname is set in mysql.server.sh that ends up in /etc/rc.d/init.d/mysql
#
# If the root user has a password you have to create a
# /root/.my.cnf configuration file with the following
# content:
#
# [mysqladmin]
# password = <secret>
# user= root
#
# where "<secret>" is the password.
#
# ATTENTION: This /root/.my.cnf should be readable ONLY
# for root !

/usr/local/var/mysqld.log {
        # create 600 mysql mysql
        notifempty
        daily
        rotate 3
        missingok
        compress
    postrotate
        # just if mysqld is really running
        if test -n "`ps acx|grep mysqld`"; then
                /usr/local/bin/mysqladmin flush-logs
        fi
    endscript
}
```

## Optimizing, Analyzing, Checking, and Repairing Tables

A regular part of a database administrator's job is to do preventative maintenance, as well as to repair things when they go wrong. In spite of the best efforts, data errors can occur, such as in the case of a power failure that interrupts a write. Usually you can correct these fairly painlessly.

There are four main tasks involved in checking and repairing:

- Optimizing tables
- Analyzing tables (analyzes and stores the key distribution for MyISAM and BDB tables)
- Checking tables (checks the tables for errors, and, for MyISAM tables, updates the key statistics)
- Repairing tables (repairs corrupted MyISAM tables)

### Optimizing Tables

Tables that contain BLOB and VARCHAR fields will, over time, become less optimized. Because these field types are variable in length, when records are updated, inserted, or deleted, they will not always take the same amount of space, the records will start to become fragmented, and empty spaces will remain. Just like with a fragmented disk, this situation will slow performance, so to keep MySQL in tiptop shape, you should regularly defragment it. The way to do this is to optimize the table, which can be done in a number of ways. There's the OPTIMIZE TABLE statement, the mysqlcheck utility (if the server is running), or the myisamchk utility (if the server is not running or there is no interaction with the table).

Optimizing currently works only with MyISAM and partially with BDB tables. With MyISAM tables, optimizing does the following:

- Defragments tables where rows are split or have been deleted
- Sorts the indexes if they have not been already
- Updates the index statistics if they have not been already

With BDB tables, optimizing analyzes the key distribution (the same as ANALYZE TABLE; see the "Analyzing Tables with ANALYZE TABLE" section later in this chapter).

#### OPTIMIZING TABLES WITH THE *OPTIMIZE* STATEMENT

The OPTIMIZE statement is a SQL statement used when connected to a MySQL database. The syntax is as follows:

```
OPTIMIZE TABLE tablename
```

You can also optimize many tables at once, separating each with a comma:

```
mysql> OPTIMIZE TABLE customer,sales;
+------------------+----------+----------+-----------------------------+
| Table            | Op       | Msg_type | Msg_text                    |
+------------------+----------+----------+-----------------------------+
| firstdb.customer | optimize | status   | Table is already up to date |
| firstdb.sales    | optimize | status   | OK                          |
+------------------+----------+----------+-----------------------------+
2 rows in set (0.02 sec)
```

The customer table in this instance has already been optimized.

### OPTIMIZING TABLES WITH MYSQLCHECK

mysqlcheck is a command-line utility that can perform numerous checking and repairing tasks besides optimization. A full description of all the mysqlcheck features follows later in the chapter in the section titled "Using mysqlcheck." The server must be running for you to use mysqlcheck. To optimize the customer table from the firstdb database, use the -o mysqlcheck option, as follows:

```
% mysqlcheck -o firstdb customer  -uroot -pg00r002b
firstdb.customer                 Table is already up to date
```

mysqlcheck allows you to optimize more than one table at a time by listing all the tables after the database name:

```
% mysqlcheck -o firstdb customer sales  -uroot -pg00r002b
firstdb.customer                 Table is already up to date
firstdb.sales                    Table is already up to date
```

You could also optimize the entire database by leaving out any table references, with the following:

```
% mysqlcheck -o firstdb -uroot -pg00r002b
```

### OPTIMIZING TABLES WITH MYISAMCHK

Finally, you can use the myisamchk command-line utility when the server is down or not interacting with the server. (Flush the tables before running this statement if the server is up with `mysqladmin flush-tables`. You still need to make sure the server is not interacting with the table, though, or else corruption may result.) This is the oldest way of checking tables. You have to run myisamchk from the exact location of the table or specify the path leading to the table. A full description of all the myisamchk features follows later in this chapter in the section titled "Using myisamchk."

The equivalent of an optimize statement is as follows:

```
myisamchk --quick --check-only-changed --sort-index --analyze tablename
```

or as follows:

```
myisamchk -q -C -S -a tablename
```

For example:

```
% myisamchk --quick --check-only-changed --sort-index --analyze customer
- check key delete-chain
- check record delete-chain
- Sorting index for MyISAM-table 'customer'
```

The -r option repairs the table, but also eliminates wasted space:

```
% myisamchk -r sales
- recovering (with sort) MyISAM-table 'sales'
Data records: 8
- Fixing index 1
- Fixing index 2
```

If you do not specify the path to the table index file, and you're not in the right directory, you'll get the following error:

```
% myisamchk -r customer
myisamchk: error: File 'customer' doesn't exist
```

Specifying the full path to the .MYI file corrects this:

```
% myisamchk -r /usr/local/mysql/data/firstdb/customer
- recovering (with keycache) MyISAM-table '/usr/local/mysql/data/firstdb/customer'
Data records: 0
```

*WARNING*    *Tables are locked during the optimization, so don't run this during peak hours! Also, make sure you have a reasonable amount of free space on the system when running* OPTIMIZE TABLE. *If you try to run it when your system has almost or already run out of disk space, MySQL may not be able to complete the optimization, leaving your table unusable.*

Optimizing is an important part of any administrative routine for databases that contain MyISAM tables and should be performed regularly.

## Analyzing Tables

Analyzing tables improves performance by updating the index information for a table so that MySQL can make a better decision on how to join tables. The distribution of the various index elements is stored for later usage. (Analyzing currently only works with MyISAM and BDB tables.)

There are three ways to analyze a table:

♦ When connected to MySQL, with the ANALYZE TABLE statement
♦ With the mysqlcheck command-line utility
♦ With the myisamcheck command-line utility

Regular analysis of tables can help performance and should be a regular part of any maintenance routine.

### ANALYZING TABLES WITH *ANALYZE TABLE*

ANALYZE TABLE is a statement used when connected to a database on the server. The syntax is as follows:

```
ANALYZE TABLE tablename
```

For example:

```
mysql> ANALYZE TABLE sales;
+---------------+---------+----------+----------+
| Table         | Op      | Msg_type | Msg_text |
+---------------+---------+----------+----------+
| firstdb.sales | analyze | status   | OK       |
+---------------+---------+----------+----------+
1 row in set (0.00 sec)
```

The Msg_type (message type) is one of status, error, info, or warning. Here's what would happen if the index file was missing altogether and you tried to analyze the table:

```
mysql> ANALYZE TABLE zz;
+------------+---------+----------+--------------------------------+
| Table      | Op      | Msg_type | Msg_text                       |
+------------+---------+----------+--------------------------------+
| firstdb.zz | analyze | error    | Table 'firstdb.zz' doesn't exist |
+------------+---------+----------+--------------------------------+
1 row in set (0.00 sec)
```

The table will only be analyzed again if it has changed since the last time it was analyzed:

```
mysql> ANALYZE TABLE sales;
+---------------+---------+----------+---------------------------+
| Table         | Op      | Msg_type | Msg_text                  |
+---------------+---------+----------+---------------------------+
| firstdb.sales | analyze | status   | Table is already up to date |
+---------------+---------+----------+---------------------------+
1 row in set (0.00 sec)
```

### ANALYZING TABLES WITH MYSQLCHECK

The mysqlcheck command-line utility is discussed fully later in this chapter in the section titled "Using mysqlcheck." The server needs to be running for you to use mysqlcheck, and it works only with MyISAM tables. To use it to analyze tables, you use the -a option:

```
% mysqlcheck -a firstdb sales -uroot -pg00r002b
firstdb.sales                                    OK
```

You can also analyze more than one table from a database by listing the tables after the database name:

```
% mysqlcheck -a firstdb sales customer -uroot -pg00r002b
firstdb.sales            Table is already up to date
firstdb.customer         Table is already up to date
```

If you tried to analyze a table that does not support analysis (such as an InnoDB table), no harm would be done and the operation would just fail. For example:

```
% mysqlcheck -a firstdb innotest -uroot -pg00r002b
firstdb.innotest
error    : The handler for the table doesn't support check/repair
```

You could also analyze all tables in the database with by leaving out any table names:

```
% mysqlcheck -a firstdb innotest -uroot -pg00r002b
```

### ANALYZING TABLES WITH MYISAMCHK

The myisamchk command-line utility is discussed fully later in this chapter in the section titled "Using myisamchk." The server should either not be running, or you must be sure that there is no interaction with the tables with which you're working. If the `--skip-external-locking` option is not on, you can safely use myisamchk to analyze tables, even if the server is running. The tables will be locked, affecting access, but there will be no erroneous reports. If `--skip-external-locking` is used, you'll need to flush the tables before starting the analysis (with `mysqladmin flush-tables`) and ensure that there is no access. You may get invalid results if mysqld or anything else accesses the table while myisamchk is running. To analyze tables, use the -a option:

```
% myisamchk -a /usr/local/mysql/data/firstdb/sales
Checking MyISAM file: /usr/local/mysql/data/firstdb/sales
Data records:       9  Deleted blocks:        0
- check file-size
- check key delete-chain
- check record delete-chain
- check index reference
- check data record references index: 1
- check data record references index: 2
```

## Checking Tables

Errors can occur when the indexes are not synchronized with the data. System crashes or power failures can all cause situations where the tables have become corrupted. Corruption of the data is fairly rare; in most cases, the corruption is of the index files. These can be hard to spot, though you may notice information being returned slowly or data not being found that should be there. Checking tables should be the first thing you do when you suspect an error. Some of the symptoms of corrupted tables include errors such as the following:

◆ Unexpected end of file.

◆ Record file is crashed.

◆ `tablename.frm` is locked against change.

◆ Can't find file `tablename.MYI` (Errcode: ###).

◆ Got error ### from table handler. The perror utility gives more information about the error number. Just run perror (which is stored in the same directory as the other binaries such as mysqladmin) and the error number. For example:

```
% perror 126
126 = Index file is crashed / Wrong file format
```

Some of the other more common errors include:

```
126 = Index file is crashed / Wrong file format
127 = Record-file is crashed
132 = Old database file
134 = Record was already deleted (or record file crashed)
135 = No more room in record file
136 = No more room in index file
141 = Duplicate unique key or constraint on write or update
144 = Table is crashed and last repair failed
145 = Table was marked as crashed and should be repaired
```

Once connected to the MySQL server, you can issue a CHECK TABLE command, make use of the mysqlcheck utility (when the server is running), or use the myisamchk utility when the server has been stopped. Checking updates the index statistics and checks for errors.

If any errors are found, the table will need to be repaired (see the "Repairing Tables" section later in this chapter). Serious errors mark the table as corrupt, in which case it can no longer be used until it is repaired.

*TIP* *Always check tables after a power failure or a system crash. You can usually fix any corruption that has occurred before users notice any problems.*

### CHECKING TABLES WITH *CHECK TABLES*

The syntax for CHECK TABLE is as follows:

```
CHECK TABLE tablename [option]
```

For example:

```
mysql> CHECK TABLE customer;
+------------------+-------+----------+----------+
| Table            | Op    | Msg_type | Msg_text |
+------------------+-------+----------+----------+
| firstdb.customer | check | status   | OK       |
+------------------+-------+----------+----------+
1 row in set (0.01 sec)
```

CHECK can check only MyISAM and InnoDB tables.

There are five options depending on the level of checking you want to do, as shown in Table 10.4.

**TABLE 10.4:** CHECK TABLE Options

| OPTION | DESCRIPTION |
|---|---|
| QUICK | This is the quickest check and does not scan the rows to check for wrong links. |
| FAST | Only checks tables that haven't been closed properly. |
| CHANGED | Only checks tables that haven't been closed properly or have been changed since last check. |
| MEDIUM | The default option. It scans rows to check that deleted links are correct. It also calculates a key checksum for the rows and verifies this with a calculated checksum for the keys. |
| EXTENDED | This is the slowest method, but it checks the table for complete consistency by doing a full key lookup for every index associated with each row. |

The QUICK option is useful for checking tables where you don't suspect any errors.

If an error or warning is returned, you should try and repair the table.

You can check more than one table at a time by listing the tables one after another, for example:

```
mysql> CHECK TABLE sales,customer;
+-------------------+-------+----------+----------+
| Table             | Op    | Msg_type | Msg_text |
+-------------------+-------+----------+----------+
| firstdb.sales     | check | status   | OK       |
| firstdb.customer  | check | status   | OK       |
+-------------------+-------+----------+----------+
2 rows in set (0.01 sec)
```

### CHECKING TABLES WITH MYSQLCHECK

The mysqlcheck command-line utility can be used when the server is running and works only with MyISAM tables. It is described fully later in this chapter in the section titled "Using mysqlcheck." Table 10.5 lists the options.

The syntax is as follows:

```
mysqlcheck [options] databasename tablename[s]
```

For example:

```
% mysqlcheck -c firstdb customer -uroot -pg00r002b
firstdb.customer                                 OK
```

**TABLE 10.5:** THE MYSQLCHECK OPTIONS THAT APPLY TO TABLE CHECKING

| OPTION | DESCRIPTION |
| --- | --- |
| --auto-repair | Used in conjunction with one of the check options, it will automatically begin to repair corrupted tables after the checks have completed. |
| -c, --check | Checks tables. |
| -C, --check-only-changed | Checks tables that have changed since the last check or were not closed properly. |
| -F, --fast | Checks tables that haven't been closed properly. |
| -e, --extended | This is the slowest form for checking, but it will make sure the table is completely consistent. You can also use this option to repair, though it is usually not necessary. |
| -m, --medium-check | This is much faster than the extended check, and it finds the vast majority of errors. |
| -q, --quick | The fastest check, this does not check table rows when checking. When repairing, it only repairs the index tree. |

You can check more than one table by listing a number of tables after the database name:

```
% mysqlcheck -c firstdb sales customer -uroot -pg00r002b
firstdb.sales                                    OK
firstdb.customer                                 OK
```

You can check all tables in the database by just specifying the name of the database.

```
% mysqlcheck -c firstdb -uroot -pg00r002b
```

### CHECKING TABLES WITH MYISAMCHK

When the server is shut down or there is no interaction with the tables you're checking, you can use the myisamchk command-line option (described fully in the "Using myisamchk" section later in this chapter). If the `--skip-external-locking` option is not on, you can safely use myisamchk to check tables, even if the server is running. The tables will be locked, affecting access, but there will be no erroneous reports. If `--skip-external-locking` is used, you'll need to flush the tables before starting the check (with `mysqladmin flush-tables`) and ensure that there is no access. You may get wrong results (with tables being marked as corrupted even when they are not) if mysqld or anything else accesses the table while myisamchk is running.

The syntax is as follows:

```
mysiamchk [options] tablename
```

The equivalent to the `CHECK TABLE` statement is the medium option:

```
myisamchk -m table_name
```

The default for myisamchk is the ordinary check option (`-c`). There is also the fast check (`-F`), which only checks tables that haven't been closed properly. This is not the same as the lowercase `-f` option, which is the force option, meaning the check continues even if errors occur. There is also the medium check (`-m`), slightly slower and more complete. The most extreme option is the `-e` option (that performs an extended check), which is the most thorough and slowest option. It's also usually a sign of desperation; use this only when all other options have failed. Increasing the `key_buffer_size` variable can speed up the extended check (if you have enough memory). See Table 10.6 for the checking options.

**TABLE 10.6:** MYISAMCHK CHECKING OPTIONS

| OPTION | DESCRIPTION |
| --- | --- |
| `-c, --check` | Ordinary check and the default option. |
| `-e, --extend-check` | Slowest and most thorough form of check. If you are using `--extended-check` and have much memory, you should increase the value of `key_buffer_size` a lot! |
| `-F, --fast` | Fast check, which only checks tables that haven't been closed properly. |
| `-C, --check-only-changed` | Checks only the tables that have been changed since the last check. |
| `-f, --force` | This runs the repair option if any errors are found in the table. |

*Continued on next page*

**TABLE 10.6:** MYISAMCHK CHECKING OPTIONS *(continued)*

| OPTION | DESCRIPTION |
| --- | --- |
| -i, --information | Displays statistics about the table that is checked. |
| -m, --medium-check | Medium check, faster than an extended check, and good enough for most cases. |
| -U, --update-state | Keeps information about when the table was checked and whether the table has crashed, which is useful for the -C option. Should not be used when the table is being used and the --skip-external-locking option is active. |
| -T, --read-only | Does not mark the table as checked (useful for running myisamchk when the server is active and the --skip-external-locking option is in use). |

The following is a sample myisamchk output when errors are found:

```
% myisamchk largetable.MYI
Checking MyISAM file: Hits.MYI
Data records: 2960032    Deleted blocks:        0
myisamchk: warning: 1 clients is using or hasn't closed the table
properly
- check file-size
myisamchk: warning: Size of datafile is: 469968400 Should be: 469909252
- check key delete-chain
- check record delete-chain
- check index reference
- check data record references index: 1
- check data record references index: 2
- check data record references index: 3
myisamchk: error: Found 2959989 keys of 2960032
- check record links
myisamchk: error: Record-count is not ok; is 2960394 Should be: 2960032
myisamchk: warning: Found    2960394 parts    Should be: 2960032 parts
```

## Repairing Tables

If you have checked the tables and errors have been found, you'll need to repair them. There are various repair options available, depending on which method you use, but you may not have success. If the disk has failed, or if none of them work, the only option is to restore from your backup. Repairing a table can take up significant resources, both disk and memory:

♦ Generally, repairing a table takes up twice as much disk space as the original data file (on the same disk). A quick repair (see the options in the following sections) is an exception because the data file is not modified.

♦ Some space for the new index file (on the same disk as the original). The old index is deleted at the start, so this is usually not significant, but it will be if the disk is close to full.

◆ With the standard and --sort-recover options, a sort buffer is created. This takes up the following amount of space (largest_key + row_pointer_length) * number_of_rows * 2. You can move some or all of this to memory (and increase the speed of the process) by increasing the size of the mysqld variable sort_buffer_size if you have the available memory. Otherwise, it is created as specified by the TMPDIR environment variable or the -t myisamchk option.

◆ Memory usage is determined by the mysqld variables or the options set in the myisamchk command line (see the section titled "Using myisamchk").

If the error is caused by the table running out of space and the table type is InnoDB, you will have to enlarge the InnoDB tablespace. MyISAM tables have a huge theoretical size limit (eight million terabytes), but by default pointers are only allocated for 4GB. If the table reaches this limit, you can extend it by using the MAX_ROWS and AVG_ROW_LENGTH ALTER TABLE parameters. To prepare the table called *limited* for great things (currently it only has three records), you use the following:

```
mysql> ALTER TABLE limited MAX_ROWS=999999999999 AVG_ROW_LENGTH=100;
Query OK, 3 rows affected (0.28 sec)
Records: 3  Duplicates: 0  Warnings: 0
```

This allocates pointers for a much greater number of records. The AVG_ROW_LENGTH is used when BLOB and TEXT fields are present, and it gives MySQL an idea of the average size of a record, which it can then use for optimization purposes.

### REPAIRING NON-MyISAM TABLE TYPES

The three methods of repairing discussed in the following sections work only with MyISAM tables. Some of the options have been reported to work occasionally with BDB tables, but they were not designed for this. Currently, the only way to repair corrupted BDB and InnoDB tables is to restore from backup.

### REPAIRING TABLES WITH *REPAIR TABLE*

You can run the REPAIR TABLE statement when connected to the MySQL server. It currently only works with MyISAM tables. See Table 10.7 for the options.

The syntax is as follows:

```
REPAIR TABLE tablename[s] option[s]
```

**TABLE 10.7:** AVAILABLE REPAIR TABLE OPTIONS

| OPTION | DESCRIPTION |
| --- | --- |
| QUICK | Fastest repair because the data file is not modified. It uses much less disk space as well because the data file is not modified. |
| EXTENDED | Attempts to recover every possible row from the data file. This option should not be used unless as a last resort because it may produce garbage rows. |
| USE_FRM | This is the option to use if the .MYI file is missing or has a corrupted header. It will rebuild the indexes from the definitions found in the .frm table definition file. |

The following is an example of using REPAIR in the case of a missing .MYI file. Let's delete the .MYI file of an existing table, t4.

```
% ls -l t4.*
-rw-rw----  1 mysql  mysql    10 Jun 14 02:00 t4.MYD
-rw-rw----  1 mysql  mysql  4096 Jun 14 02:00 t4.MYI
-rw-rw----  1 mysql  mysql  8550 Jun  8 10:46 t4.frm
% rm t4.MYI
% mysql -uguru2b -pg00r002b firstdb
```

A normal REPAIR does not work:

```
mysql> REPAIR TABLE t4;
+------------+--------+----------+------------------------------------+
| Table      | Op     | Msg_type | Msg_text                           |
+------------+--------+----------+------------------------------------+
| firstdb.t4 | repair | error    | Can't find file: 't4.MYD' (errno: 2) |
+------------+--------+----------+------------------------------------+
1 row in set (0.47 sec)
```

The current error message (4.0.3) indicates that the .MYD file cannot be found, when it's actually the .MYI file that's missing. The error message is likely to have been clarified by the time you read this. To repair the table in this instance, you need to use the USE_FRM option, which, as the name suggests, uses the .frm definition file to re-create the .MYI index file:

```
mysql> REPAIR TABLE t4 USE_FRM;
+------------+--------+----------+------------------------------------+
| Table      | Op     | Msg_type | Msg_text                           |
+------------+--------+----------+------------------------------------+
| firstdb.t4 | repair | warning  | Number of rows changed from 0 to 2 |
| firstdb.t4 | repair | status   | OK                                 |
+------------+--------+----------+------------------------------------+
2 rows in set (0.46 sec)
```

### REPAIRING TABLES WITH MYSQLCHECK

The mysqlcheck command-line utility is used while the server is still running and works only with MyISAM tables. It is described fully later in this chapter in the "Using mysqlcheck" section. To repair tables, you use the -r option:

```
% mysqlcheck -r firstdb customer -uroot -pg00r002b
firstdb.customer                                    OK
```

You can repair multiple tables at the same time by listing the table names after the database name:

```
% mysqlcheck -r firstdb customer sales -uroot -pg00r002b
firstdb.customer                                    OK
firstdb.sales                                       OK
```

If for some reason all tables in a database are corrupt, you can repair them all by just supplying the database name:

```
% mysqlcheck -r firstdb -uroot -pg00r002b
```

### REPAIRING TABLES WITH MYISAMCHK

You can use the myisamchk command-line utility (described fully later in this chapter in the "Using myisamchk" section) repair tables (see Table 10.8).

The server should either not be running, or you must be sure there is no interaction with the tables with which you're working, such as when you start MySQL with the `--skip-external-locking` option. If the `--skip-external-locking` option is not on, you can only safely use myisamchk to repair tables if you are sure there will be no simultaneous access. Whether `--skip-external-locking` is used or not, you'll need to flush the tables before starting the repair (with `mysqladmin flush-tables`) and ensure that there is no access. You may get wrong results (with tables being marked as corrupted even when they are not) if mysqld or anything else accesses the table while myisamchk is running.

The syntax is as follows:

```
myisamchk [options] [tablenames]
```

**TABLE 10.8:** REPAIRING TABLES WITH MYISAMCHK

| OPTION | DESCRIPTION |
| --- | --- |
| `-D #,--data-file-length=#` | Specifies the maximum length of the data file when re-creating it. |
| `-e,--extend-check` | Attempts to recover every possible row from the data file. This option should not be used unless as a last resort because it may produce garbage rows. |
| `-f,--force` | Overwrites old temporary files (that have an extension of .TMD) instead of aborting if it encounters a preexisting one. |
| `-k #,keys-used=#` | Specifies which keys to use, which can make the process faster. Each binary bit stands for one key starting at 0 for the first key. |
| `-r,--recover` | Repairs most corruption and should be the first option attempted. You can increase the `sort_buffer_size` to make the recovery go more quickly if you have the memory. This option will not recover from the rare form of corruption where a unique key is not unique. |
| `-o,--safe-recover` | A more thorough, yet slower repair option than `-r` that should be used only if `-r` fails. This reads through all rows and rebuilds the indexes based on the rows. It also uses less disk space than `-r` because a sort buffer is not created. You can increase the size of `key_buffer_size` to improve repair speed. |
| `-n,--sort-recover` | Forces MySQL to use sorting to resolve the indexes, even if the resulting temporary files are large. |

*Continued on next page*

**TABLE 10.8:** REPAIRING TABLES WITH MYISAMCHK (*continued*)

| OPTION | DESCRIPTION |
|---|---|
| `--character-sets-dir=...` | The directory containing the character sets. |
| `--set-character-set=name` | Specifies a new character set for the index. |
| `-t, --tmpdir=path` | Specifies a new path for storing temporary files if you don't want to use whatever the TMPDIR environment variable specifies. |
| `-q, --quick` | Fastest repair because the data file is not modified. Specifying the *q* twice (-q -q) will modify the data file if there are duplicate keys. Uses much less disk space as well because the data file is not modified. |
| `-u, --unpack` | Unpacks a file that has been packed with the myisampack utility. |

You must run myisamchk from the directory containing the .MYI files or supply the path. The following examples show a repair in action, with MySQL deciding whether to use sorting or a keycache:

```
% myisamchk -r customer
- recovering (with keycache) MyISAM-table 'customer.MYI'
Data records: 0
% myisamchk -r sales
- recovering (with sort) MyISAM-table 'sales.MYI'
Data records: 9
- Fixing index 1
- Fixing index 2
```

If you have lots of memory, besides increasing the size of sort_buffer_size and key_buffer_size as described previously, you can also set some other variables to make myisamchk perform more snappily. See the full myisamchk description later in this chapter in the "Using myisamchk" section.

### USING MYSQLCHECK

The mysqlcheck utility is a boon to more recent users of MySQL because, beforehand, much of the repairing and checking functionality could only be used when the server was shut down. Luckily this limitation is a thing of the past with the mysqlcheck utility.

mysqlcheck uses the CHECK, REPAIR, ANALYZE, and OPTIMIZE statements to perform these tasks from the command line, which is useful for automated maintenance of your databases (see Table 10.9).

The syntax is as follows:

```
mysqlcheck [options] databasename [tablenames]
```

or as follows:

```
mysqlcheck [options] --databases databasename1 [databasename2 databasename 3 ...]
```

or as follows:

```
mysqlcheck [options] --all-databases
```

**TABLE 10.9:** MYSQLCHECK OPTIONS

| OPTION | DESCRIPTION |
| --- | --- |
| -A, --all-databases | Checks all available databases. |
| -1, --all-in-1 | Combines queries for tables into one query per database (instead of one per table). Tables are in a comma-separated list. |
| -a, --analyze | Analyzes the listed tables. |
| --auto-repair | Automatically repairs tables if they are corrupted (after all tables in the query have been checked). |
| -#, --debug=... | Outputs a debug log. |
| --character-sets-dir=... | This specifies the directory where the character sets are. |
| -c, --check | Checks tables. |
| -C, --check-only-changed | Checks tables that have changed since the last check or were not closed properly. |
| --compress | Uses compression in the client/server protocol. |
| -?, --help | Displays the help message and exits. |
| -B, --databases | Lists a number of databases to check (all tables in the databases are checked). |
| --default-character-set=... | Sets the default character set. |
| -F, --fast | Checks tables that haven't been closed properly. |
| -f, --force | Forces the process to continue even if it encounters an error. |
| -e, --extended | This is the slowest form for checking but will make sure the table is completely consistent. You can also use this option to repair, though it is usually not necessary. |
| -h, --host=... | Hostname to which to connect. |
| -m, --medium-check | Much faster than the extended check and finds the vast majority of errors. |
| -o, --optimize | Optimizes the tables. |
| -p, --password[=...] | The password with which to connect. |
| -P, --port=... | The port to use for connecting. |

*Continued on next page*

**TABLE 10.9:** MYSQLCHECK OPTIONS *(continued)*

| OPTION | DESCRIPTION |
|--------|-------------|
| -q, --quick | The fastest check, this does not check table rows when checking. When repairing, it only repairs the index tree. |
| -r, --repair | Repairs most errors, except unique keys that somehow contain duplicates. |
| -s, --silent | Displays no output except for error messages. |
| -S, --socket=... | Specifies the socket file to use when connecting. |
| --tables | List of tables to check. With the -B option, this will take precedence. |
| -u, --user=# | Specifies the user to connect as. |
| -v, --verbose | Prints lots of output about the process. |
| -V, --version | Displays the version information and exits. |

The mysqlcheck utility also has a feature that allows it to be run in different ways without specifying the options. By simply creating a copy of mysqlcheck with one of the following names, it will take that default behavior:

♦ mysqlrepair: The default option is -r.

♦ mysqlanalyze: The default option is -a.

♦ mysqloptimize: The default option is -o.

The default option when it is named mysqlcheck is -c. All of these renamed files can have the full mysqlcheck functionality—it's just that their default behavior is changed.

### USING MYISAMCHK

The myisamchk utility is the older utility, available since the early days of MySQL. It is also used to analyze, check, and repair tables, but care needs to be taken if you want to use it when the server is running. Table 10.10 describes the general myisamchk options, Table 10.11 describes the check options, Table 10.12 describes the repair options, and Table 10.13 describes other options.

The server should either not be running, or you must be sure there is no interaction with the tables with which you're working, such as when you start MySQL with the --skip-external-locking option. If the --skip-external-locking option is not on, you can only safely use myisamchk to repair tables if you are sure there will be no simultaneous access. Whether or not --skip-external-locking is used, you'll need to flush the tables before starting the repair (with mysqladmin flush-tables) and ensure that there is no access.

I suggest you rather use one of the other options if the server is running.

The syntax is as follows:

```
myisamchk [options] tablename[s]
```

You must run myisamchk from the directory where the .MYI index files are located unless you specify the path to them; otherwise you'll get the following error:

```
% myisamchk -r sales.MYI
myisamchk: error: File 'sales.MYI' doesn't exist
```

Specifying the path solves the problem:

```
% myisamchk -r /usr/local/mysql/data/firstdb/sales.MYI
- recovering (with sort) MyISAM-table '/usr/local/mysql/data/firstdb/sales.MYI'
Data records: 9
- Fixing index 1
- Fixing index 2
```

The table name can be specified with or without the .MYI extension.

```
% myisamchk -r sales
- recovering (with sort) MyISAM-table 'sales'
Data records: 9
- Fixing index 1
- Fixing index 2
% myisamchk -r sales.MYI
- recovering (with sort) MyISAM-table 'sales.MYI'
Data records: 9
- Fixing index 1
- Fixing index 2
```

**WARNING** *A common mistake is to try run myisamchk on an* .MYD *data file. Always use the* .MYI *index file!*

You can use wildcard character to search all tables in a database directory (*.MYI) or even all tables in all databases:

```
% myisamchk -r /usr/local/mysql/data/*/*.MYI
```

**TABLE 10.10:** GENERAL MYISAMCHK OPTIONS

| OPTION | DESCRIPTION |
| --- | --- |
| -#, --debug=debug_options | Outputs a debug log. A common debug_option string is d:t:o,filename. |
| -?, --help | Displays a help message and exits. |
| -O var=option, --set-variable var=option | Sets the value of a variable. The possible variables and their default values for myisamchk can be examined with myisamchk --help. |
| -s, --silent | Only outputs error messages. A second s can be used to completely silence myisamchk. |
| -v, --verbose | Displays more information than usual. As with silent, multiple v's can be used to output more information (-vv or -vvv). |

*Continued on next page*

**TABLE 10.10:** GENERAL MYISAMCHK OPTIONS *(continued)*

| OPTION | DESCRIPTION |
|---|---|
| -V, --version | Displays the myisamchk version details and exits. |
| -w, --wait | If the table is locked, -w will wait for the table to be unlocked rather than exiting with an error. If mysqld was running with the --skip-external-locking option, the table can only be locked by another myisamchk command. |

By running myisamchk --help, besides the general options, you can see what variables you can change with the -O option and what the current settings are:

```
% myisamchk --help
..
Possible variables for option --set-variable (-O) are:
key_buffer_size         current value: 520192
myisam_block_size       current value: 1024
read_buffer_size        current value: 262136
write_buffer_size       current value: 262136
sort_buffer_size        current value: 2097144
sort_key_blocks         current value: 16
decode_bits             current value: 9
ft_min_word_len         current value: 4
ft_max_word_len         current value: 254
ft_max_word_len_for_sort  current value: 20
```

The space allocated by the key_buffer_size is used when doing an extended check or when indexes are inserted one row at a time (using the safe-recover option). sort_buffer_size is used in the default repair, when indexes are sorted in the repair.

To achieve a faster repair, set the sort_buffer_size to about one-quarter of the total available memory. Only one of the two variables is used at a time, so you don't need to worry about running out of memory by making both values large.

*NOTE   Inside the my.cnf (or my.ini) file, there are separate sections for mysqld and myisamchk. You can quite easily set the sort_buffer_size to a high value for repairing, and keep it lower if your system has other requirements for day-to-day running.*

**TABLE 10.11:** MYISAMCHK CHECK OPTIONS

| OPTION | DESCRIPTION |
|---|---|
| -c, --check | Ordinary check and the default option. |
| -e, --extend-check | Slowest and most thorough form of check. If you are using --extended-check and don't have much memory, you should increase the value of key_buffer_size a lot! |
| -F, --fast | Fast check that only checks tables that haven't been closed properly. |

*Continued on next page*

**TABLE 10.11:** MYISAMCHK CHECK OPTIONS *(continued)*

| OPTION | DESCRIPTION |
|---|---|
| -C, --check-only-changed | Checks only the tables that have been changed since the last check. |
| -f, --force | This runs the repair option if any errors are found in the table. |
| -i, --information | Displays statistics about the table that is checked. |
| -m, --medium-check | Medium check, faster than an extended check and good enough for most cases. |
| -U, --update-state | Keeps information about when the table was checked and whether the table has crashed, which is useful for the -C option. Should not be used when the table is being used and the --skip-external-locking option is active. |
| -T, --read-only | Does not mark the table as checked (useful for running myisamchk when the server is active and the --skip-external-locking option is in use). |

**TABLE 10.12:** MYISAMCHK REPAIR OPTIONS

| OPTION | DESCRIPTION |
|---|---|
| -D #, --data-file-length=# | Specifies the maximum length of the data file when re-creating it. |
| -e, --extend-check | Attempts to recover every possible row from the data file. This option should not be used unless as a last resort because it may produce garbage rows. |
| -f, --force | Overwrites old temporary files (that have an extension of .TMD) instead of aborting if it encounters a preexisting one. |
| -k #, keys-used=# | Specifies the keys to use, which can make the process faster. Each binary bit stands for one key starting at 0 for the first key (for example, 1 is the first index, 10 is the second index). |
| -r, --recover | Repairs most corruption and should be the first option attempted. You can increase the sort_buffer_size to make the recover go more quickly if you have the memory. This option will not recover from the rare form of corruption where a unique key is not unique. |
| -o, --safe-recover | A more thorough, slower repair option than -r, which should be used only if -r fails. This reads through all rows and rebuilds the indexes based on the rows. It also uses less disk space than -r because a sort buffer is not created. You can increase the size of key_buffer_size to improve repair speed. |
| -n, --sort-recover | Forces MySQL to uses sorting to resolve the indexes, even if the resulting temporary files are large. |
| --character-sets-dir=... | The directory containing the character sets. |

*Continued on next page*

**TABLE 10.12:** MYISAMCHK REPAIR OPTIONS *(continued)*

| OPTION | DESCRIPTION |
| --- | --- |
| `--set-character-set=name` | Specifies a new character set for the index. |
| `-t, --tmpdir=path` | Specifies a new path for storing temporary files if you don't want to use the contents of the TMPDIR environment variable. |
| `-q, --quick` | Fastest repair as the data file is not modified. Running this option a second time will modify the data file if there are duplicate keys. Uses much less disk space as well because the data file is not modified. |
| `-u, --unpack` | Unpacks a file that has been packed with the myisampack utility. |

**TABLE 10.13:** OTHER MYISAMCHK OPTIONS

| OPTION | DESCRIPTION |
| --- | --- |
| `-a, --analyze` | Analyzing tables improves performance by updating the index information for a table so that MySQL can make a better decision on how to join tables. The distribution of the various index elements is stored for later usage. This option is the same as ANALYZE TABLE. |
| `-d, --description` | Displays a description of the table. |
| `-A, --set-auto-increment[=value]` | Sets the AUTO_INCREMENT counter to the specified value (or increments it by one if no value is supplied). |
| `-S, --sort-index` | Sorts the index tree blocks in descending order, which improves the performance of seeks and table scanning by key. |
| `-R, --sort-records=#` | Sorts records according to the index specified (index numbers begin from 1; you can use SHOW INDEX to see an ordered list). This can speed up queries that are ordered on this index, as well as ranged selects. It will probably be very slow if you sort a large table for the first time. |

Running myisamchk with the -d option produces the following kind of output:

```
% myisamchk -d customer
MyISAM file:        customer
Record format:      Packed
Character set:      latin1 (8)
Data records:       3  Deleted blocks:          0
Recordlength:       75
table description:
Key Start Len Index   Type
1    2     4       unique   long
```

# Summary

MySQL has a host of tools to make administering the database server as painless a task as possible. But the more critical your data, and the larger your tables, the more important it is that you can competently and quickly handle problems when they occur. You can stop and start the MySQL server in a number of ways, such as using mysqld directly, but it is highly recommended that you use a wrapper script, such as the mysqld_safe script supplied with distributions.

Windows and Unix have quite different methods of automating startups, but both are fairly easy to implement once you know what you are doing.

The configuration files are a flexible way of controlling the server's behavior, and you'll learn more about them for optimization purposes in Chapter 13, "Configuring and Optimizing MySQL."

When disaster strikes, the log files can be invaluable in helping to identify the problem, whether it was a query or some other unforeseen error. They are also helpful in restoring from backups. They can also help with more mundane tasks, such as identifying slow queries for optimization purposes. Of course, they can grow out of control quite quickly, and rotating them so as to avoid the problem of them infinitely growing is also an important task.

Regular maintenance of the tables is the best way to avoid problems. Optimizing tables defragments them, and it is also useful to update the key information to assist MySQL in making query join decisions based upon up-to-date information about the data. But in spite of the best efforts, unforeseen power spikes, hardware failures, or human error can lead to data corruption (especially in indexes), in which case the various repair options are invaluable. The older myisamchk utility is more useful when the server is down, and the mysqlcheck utility can perform maintenance tasks while the server is still running (as can the related SQL statements).

The next chapters will investigate these topics in more detail: database security, replication, and configuration.

# Chapter 11

# Database Backups

BACKING UP IS ONE of the most important tasks for your database and one of the most neglected. Unpredictable events can be disastrous simply because of their unpredictability. Many have learned that the hard way by putting off a backup for some future date, which never seemed to come around, and then paying the price with a complete loss of data. The more important the data and the more frequent the changes, the more frequent the backup needs to be. For a news database, where changes are happening continually, a daily backup is prudent, with logging enabled to allow recovery of the day's work. For a small website where the data is changed weekly, a weekly backup makes more sense. However large or small your database, there's no avoiding it. A backup is a critical component of any data storage system.

I suggest also keeping a backup of your configuration file (`my.cnf` or `my.ini`), as the work you did tuning the server is also worth saving. I've been in the unpleasant situation of breezing through a restore from a disk failure, only to find that my lovingly crafted config file was lost.

This chapter shows various ways you can back up and restore with MySQL. Once you know the complexities and the possibilities involved in backing up, you'll be in a better position to implement the best strategy for your situation.

Featured in this chapter:

◆ The `BACKUP` and `RESTORE` commands
◆ Backing up by directly copying files
◆ mysqldump
◆ mysqlhotcopy
◆ Using `SELECT INTO` to back up
◆ Using `LOAD DATA INFILE` to restore
◆ Security issues with `LOAD DATA LOCAL`
◆ Using the binary update log
◆ Backing up InnoDB tables
◆ Replication as a means of backup

## Backing Up MyISAM Tables with *BACKUP*

One of the easiest ways to back up is with the `BACKUP` command. This currently works only with MyISAM tables. The syntax is as follows:

```
BACKUP TABLE tablename TO '/db_backup_path';
```

The backup path needs to be the full path to the directory you want to save to, and should not be a filename. This makes a copy of the `.frm` (definition) and `.MYD` (data) files, but not the `.MYI` (index) file. You can rebuild the index once the database has been restored.

When dealing with files, you'll need to watch out for file permissions. MySQL does not give the most friendly error message to warn you if, when backing up, you do not have the correct permissions to all the files and directories.

### Using *BACKUP* with Unix

The following example is run on a Unix machine, where the user performing the operations is the root user (see the next section for a Windows example):

```
% cd /
% mkdir db_backups
```

This creates the directory off the root directory, where you want to place the backups in this case. Connect to the *firstdb* database, and run the `BACKUP` command, as follows:

```
% mysql firstdb
Welcome to the MySQL monitor.  Commands end with ; or \g.
Your MySQL connection id is 13 to server version: 4.0.1-alpha-max-log
mysql> BACKUP TABLE sales TO '/db_backups';
+---------------+--------+----------+-------------------------------------+
| Table         | Op     | Msg_type | Msg_text                            |
+---------------+--------+----------+-------------------------------------+
| firstdb.sales | backup | error    | Failed copying .frm file: errno = 13 |
| firstdb.sales | backup | status   | Operation failed                    |
+---------------+--------+----------+-------------------------------------+
```

The problem in this example is that MySQL does not have permission to write files to the `/db_backups` directory. You need to exit MySQL, and from the command line make the mysql user the owner of the directory:

```
mysql> exit
Bye
% chown mysql db_backups/
```

**WARNING** *You need to have the correct permissions to do this. Ensure that the user you're working as has the correct permissions. In this example it's root, so there is no problem, but you may not be working as root. If you have problems, you may need help from your systems administrator.*

Now the `BACKUP` statement will run correctly:

```
% mysql firstdb;
```

```
Welcome to the MySQL monitor.  Commands end with ; or \g.
Your MySQL connection id is 15 to server version: 4.0.1-alpha-max-log

Type 'help;' or '\h' for help. Type '\c' to clear the buffer.

mysql> BACKUP TABLE sales TO '/db_backups';
+---------------+--------+----------+----------+
| Table         | Op     | Msg_type | Msg_text |
+---------------+--------+----------+----------+
| firstdb.sales | backup | status   | OK       |
+---------------+--------+----------+----------+
1 row in set (0.00 sec)
mysql> exit
Bye
```

This time the backup has been successful, and you can view the newly created files by exiting to the command line once again:

```
% ls -l db_backups/
total 10
-rw-rw----   1 mysql     mysql          136 May 26 14:07 sales.MYD
-rw-rw----   1 mysql     mysql         8634 May 26 14:07 sales.frm
```

There are the two files, newly created.

*TIP*   *If you have any problems making a backup in this way, it's likely to be because of file permissions. Ask your systems administrator for help if you don't have access to create the files or if you're not sure. Also, remember that **BACKUP** currently only works for MyISAM tables (check your latest documentation though, as this may no longer be the case by the time you read this).*

BACKUP places a read lock on the table before backing it up to ensure that the backed-up table is consistent.

You can also back up more than one table at a time, by listing more than one table name:

```
mysql> BACKUP TABLE sales,sales_rep,customer TO '/db_backups';
+-------------------+--------+----------+----------+
| Table             | Op     | Msg_type | Msg_text |
+-------------------+--------+----------+----------+
| firstdb.sales     | backup | status   | OK       |
| firstdb.sales_rep | backup | status   | OK       |
| firstdb.customer  | backup | status   | OK       |
+-------------------+--------+----------+----------+
3 rows in set (0.05 sec)
```

The lock is placed on one table at a time, first sales, then after sales is backed up, on sales_rep, and so on. This allows for consistent individual tables, but if you want to achieve a consistent snapshot of all the tables at the same time, you'll have to place your own locks on the tables:

```
mysql> LOCK TABLES customer READ,sales READ,sales_rep READ;
Query OK, 0 rows affected (0.00 sec)
```

```
mysql> BACKUP TABLE sales,sales_rep,customer TO '/db_backups';
+------------------+--------+----------+----------+
| Table            | Op     | Msg_type | Msg_text |
+------------------+--------+----------+----------+
| firstdb.sales    | backup | status   | OK       |
| firstdb.sales_rep| backup | status   | OK       |
| firstdb.customer | backup | status   | OK       |
+------------------+--------+----------+----------+
3 rows in set (0.00 sec)
```

Note that you cannot lock tables individually:

```
mysql> LOCK TABLE sales READ;
Query OK, 0 rows affected (0.00 sec)

mysql> LOCK TABLE sales_rep READ;
Query OK, 0 rows affected (0.00 sec)

mysql> LOCK TABLE customer READ;
Query OK, 0 rows affected (0.00 sec)

mysql> BACKUP TABLE sales,sales_rep,customer TO '/db_backups';
+------------------+--------+----------
+--------------------------------------------------+
| Table            | Op     | Msg_type | Msg_t   |
+------------------+--------+----------
+--------------------------------------------------+
  firstdb.sales    | backup | error
| Table 'sales' was not locked with LOCK TABLES     |
| firstdb.sales_rep| backup | error
| Table 'sales_rep' was not locked with LOCK TABLES |
| firstdb.customer | backup | status
| OK                                                |
+------------------+--------+----------
+--------------------------------------------------+
3 rows in set (0.00 sec)
```

LOCK TABLE automatically releases all locks held by the same thread, so the only lock still held by the time of the backup was on the customer table.

**NOTE**  *To be able to lock a table, you need the* LOCK TABLES *privilege and the* SELECT *privilege for the table you're trying to lock.*

```
mysql> UNLOCK TABLES;
Query OK, 0 rows affected (0.00 sec)
```

## Using *BACKUP* with Windows

You should read through the preceding example, even if you are not using Unix, as it explains some of the concepts of the BACKUP statement. The following example deals with a problem specific to

Windows. Windows may not have the same complexity with file permissions, but it does have its own problems. Take a look at this example, and see if you can spot what's causing the error:

```
C:\MySQL\bin>cd \
C:\>mkdir db_backups
C:\>mysql firstdb
Welcome to the MySQL monitor.  Commands end with ; or \g.
Your MySQL connection id is 3 to server version: 4.0.1-alpha-max

Type 'help;' or '\h' for help. Type '\c' to clear the buffer.

mysql> BACKUP TABLE sales TO 'c:\db_backups';
+---------------+--------+----------+------------------------------------+
| Table         | Op     | Msg_type | Msg_text                           |
+---------------+--------+----------+------------------------------------+
| firstdb.sales | backup | error    | Failed copying .frm file: errno = 2 |
| firstdb.sales | backup | status   | Operation failed                   |
+---------------+--------+----------+------------------------------------+
2 rows in set (0.33 sec)
```

Unfortunately, the error message is not too clear. The problem is that the backslash (\) is the MySQL escape character, used to escape other special characters such as single or double quotes. To use the backslash for a path in Windows, you need to escape it with another escape character:

```
mysql> BACKUP TABLE sales TO 'c:\\db_backups';
+---------------+--------+----------+----------+
| Table         | Op     | Msg_type | Msg_text |
+---------------+--------+----------+----------+
| firstdb.sales | backup | status   | OK       |
+---------------+--------+----------+----------+
1 row in set (0.55 sec)
```

## Restoring MyISAM Tables with *RESTORE*

The converse of BACKUP is RESTORE, which restores MyISAM tables previously created with BACKUP. It also re-creates the indexes, which can take some time for larger tables. The syntax is as follows:

```
RESTORE TABLE tablename FROM '/db_backup_path'
```

You cannot restore over an existing table. If you tried to restore the *sales* table you'd backed up earlier, you'd get the following result:

```
mysql> RESTORE TABLE sales FROM '/db_backups';
+-------+---------+----------+-------------------------------------------+
| Table | Op      | Msg_type | Msg_text                                  |
+-------+---------+----------+-------------------------------------------+
| sales | restore | error    | table exists, will not overwrite on restore |
+-------+---------+----------+-------------------------------------------+
1 row in set (0.01 sec)
```

At least this message is clearer than the failure to successfully complete a backup.

To test this backup, you're going to have to take a leap of faith and drop the sales table.

**WARNING**    *It may be obvious, but please don't test a backup of a live table by dropping the original table. Try and restore to a different database or server. If I'm too late, and the restoration fails, don't say you heard it from this book!*

Now DROP and attempt to RESTORE the table:

```
mysql> DROP TABLE sales;
Query OK, 0 rows affected (0.01 sec)

mysql> RESTORE TABLE sales FROM 'db_backups';
+-------+---------+----------+-------------------------+
| Table | Op      | Msg_type | Msg_text                |
+-------+---------+----------+-------------------------+
| sales | restore | error    | Failed copying .frm file |
+-------+---------+----------+-------------------------+
1 row in set (0.01 sec)
```

Don't panic. Can you see the error in the previous code? The path is not correct. One of your worst enemies when something does go wrong will be panic. After seeing the previous result in a crisis situation, you could easily run screaming from the building cursing MySQL's dodgy software. But there's usually a simple reason that something does not work, such as the previous typo. The correct path will correctly restore the table, as this Unix example shows:

```
mysql> RESTORE TABLE sales FROM '/db_backups';
+---------------+---------+----------+----------+
| Table         | Op      | Msg_type | Msg_text |
+---------------+---------+----------+----------+
| firstdb.sales | restore | status   | OK       |
+---------------+---------+----------+----------+
1 row in set (0.00 sec)
```

And this is the correct statement on Windows:

```
mysql> RESTORE TABLE sales FROM 'c:\\db_backups';
+---------------+---------+----------+----------+
| Table         | Op      | Msg_type | Msg_text |
+---------------+---------+----------+----------+
| firstdb.sales | restore | status   | OK       |
+---------------+---------+----------+----------+
1 row in set (0.66 sec)
```

And, just to placate the most paranoid, let's see if the *sales* table did in fact restore correctly:

```
mysql> SELECT * FROM sales;
```

```
+------+-----------+------+-------+
| code | sales_rep |   id | value |
+------+-----------+------+-------+
|    1 |         1 |    1 |  2000 |
|    2 |         4 |    3 |   250 |
|    3 |         2 |    3 |   500 |
|    4 |         1 |    4 |   450 |
|    5 |         3 |    1 |  3800 |
|    6 |         1 |    2 |   500 |
|    7 |         2 | NULL |   670 |
|    8 |         3 |    3 |  1000 |
+------+-----------+------+-------+
8 rows in set (0.00 sec)
```

## Backing Up MyISAM Tables by Directly Copying the Files

MyISAM tables are stored as files (.frm for the definition, .MYD for the data, and .MYI for the indexes) inside a directory named after the database, so an easy way to back up the data is to copy the files. Unlike BACKUP, directly copying the files does not automatically lock the tables, so you need to lock the tables yourself to get a consistent picture. Alternatively, you can do a direct copy while the server is down. Once the tables have been locked, you should flush the tables to make sure any unwritten indexes are written to disk. For this example, you'll need to have two windows open.

LOCK and FLUSH the tables from Window1:

```
mysql> LOCK TABLES sales READ,sales_rep READ,customer READ;
Query OK, 0 rows affected (0.00 sec)
mysql> FLUSH TABLES sales,sales_rep,customer;
Query OK, 0 rows affected (0.02 sec)
```

And now copy the tables from Window2 (on Unix):

```
% cd /usr/local/mysql/data/firstdb
% cp sales.* /db_backups
% cp sales_rep.* /db_backups
% cp customer.* /db_backups
%
```

Or on Windows (from Window2):

```
C:\MySQL\data\firstdb>copy customer.* c:\db_backup
customer.frm
customer.MYI
customer.MYD
        3 file(s) copied
C:\MySQL\data\firstdb>copy sales.* c:\db_backup
sales.frm
sales.MYI
sales.MYD
        3 file(s) copied
```

```
C:\MySQL\data\firstdb>copy sales_rep.* c:\db_backup
sales_rep.frm
sales_rep.MYI
sales_rep.MYD
        3 file(s) copied
```

Once you've copied the files, you can release the locks from Window1, as follows:

```
mysql> UNLOCK TABLES;
Query OK, 0 rows affected (0.00 sec)
```

**WARNING**   *For the duration of the backup, while the locks are in place, you will not be able to add new records to the tables and will also experience a performance penalty for reads. If at all possible, do not perform backups during peak hours!*

Again, to test the backup, you're going to drop a table.
From Window1, drop the table:

```
mysql> DROP TABLE sales;
Query OK, 0 rows affected (0.00 sec)
```

Copy the tables from Window2 (this example is from Unix):

```
% cp /db_backups/sales.* .
```

And our table is restored. You can verify this with the following, from Window2:

```
mysql> SELECT * FROM sales;
+------+-----------+------+-------+
| code | sales_rep |   id | value |
+------+-----------+------+-------+
|    1 |         1 |    1 |  2000 |
|    2 |         4 |    3 |   250 |
|    3 |         2 |    3 |   500 |
|    4 |         1 |    4 |   450 |
|    5 |         3 |    1 |  3800 |
|    6 |         1 |    2 |   500 |
|    7 |         2 | NULL |   670 |
|    8 |         3 |    3 |  1000 |
+------+-----------+------+-------+
8 rows in set (0.00 sec)
```

There's also a possibility that the Unix permissions could come back to haunt you. If you did not back the files up as the mysql user (you would usually have done this as the root user), you're likely to see the following:

```
mysql> SELECT * FROM sales;
ERROR 1017: Can't find file: './firstdb/sales.frm' (errno: 13)
```

The problem is that you've copied the file back, but the mysql user cannot access this file. The following snippet, from Window1, shows that I've backed up the files as the root user.

```
[root@test firstdb]# ls -l
total 183
...
-rw-r-----   1 root     root         153 May 27 22:27 sales.MYD
-rw-r-----   1 root     root        3072 May 27 22:27 sales.MYI
-rw-r-----   1 root     root        8634 May 27 22:27 sales.frm
-rw-rw----   1 mysql    mysql        156 May 22 21:50 sales_rep.MYD
-rw-rw----   1 mysql    mysql       3072 May 22 21:50 sales_rep.MYI
-rw-rw----   1 mysql    mysql       8748 May 22 21:50 sales_rep.frm
...
```

To restore permission to mysql, from Window1 change the owner of the sales table to mysql:

```
% chown mysql sales.*
%
```

And now everything should work correctly, as you can see from running a query in Window2:

```
mysql> SELECT * FROM sales;
+------+-----------+------+-------+
| code | sales_rep |   id | value |
+------+-----------+------+-------+
|    1 |         1 |    1 |  2000 |
|    2 |         4 |    3 |   250 |
|    3 |         2 |    3 |   500 |
|    4 |         1 |    4 |   450 |
|    5 |         3 |    1 |  3800 |
|    6 |         1 |    2 |   500 |
|    7 |         2 | NULL |   670 |
|    8 |         3 |    3 |  1000 |
+------+-----------+------+-------+
8 rows in set (0.00 sec)
```

MyISAM tables are platform independent, so they can be transferred to MySQL on a machine with different hardware or a different operating system. MyISAM tables created on an old MySQL version 3 system can be used in version 4, but not the other way round. To move data from MySQL version 4 to MySQL version 3, you need to use an option such as mysqldump, discussed in the next section.

## Backing Up with mysqldump

The previous two methods directly copy the files—and only work with MyISAM tables. (InnoDB tables are not stored as files, so they cannot make use of the earlier methods.)

Another method, mysqldump, makes a dump of the SQL statements needed to create the tables being backed up. This also potentially allows the database to be ported to other database systems (bearing in mind that not all MySQL features are standard to other databases). If you do have to do a move to another DBMS, expect a long, laborious task ahead.

To back up the customer table, run the following from the Unix shell:

```
% mysqldump firstdb customer > /db_backups/customer_2002_11_12.sql
```

Or run the following from the command line on Windows:

```
C:\MySQL\bin>mysqldump firstdb customer > c:\db_backups\customer_2002_11_12.sql

C:\MySQL\bin>
```

Remember to specify the path, username, and password if you need to. This creates a file in the db_backups directory containing the SQL statements needed to re-create the customer table. You can view this file in any text editor, such as Notepad or vi. The first part of the file contains the following:

```
# MySQL dump 8.14
#
# Host: localhost        Database: firstdb
#--------------------------------------------------------
# Server version        4.0.1-alpha-max-log
```

The hashes (#) are just comments, inefficacious information about versions and so on. Later in the file are the important SQL statements needed to re-create the various tables. This snippet is what can re-create the customer table:

```
#
# Table structure for table 'customer'
#

CREATE TABLE customer (
  id int(11) NOT NULL auto_increment,
  first_name varchar(30) default NULL,
  surname varchar(40) default NULL,
  initial varchar(5) default NULL,
  PRIMARY KEY  (id),
  KEY surname (surname,initial,first_name)
) TYPE=MyISAM;


#
# Dumping data for table 'customer'
#

INSERT INTO customer VALUES (1,'Yvonne','Clegg','X');
INSERT INTO customer VALUES (2,'Johnny','Chaka-Chaka','B');
INSERT INTO customer VALUES (3,'Winston','Powers','M');
INSERT INTO customer VALUES (4,'Patricia','Mankunku','C');
INSERT INTO customer VALUES (5,'Francois','Papo','P');
INSERT INTO customer VALUES (7,'Winnie','Dlamini',NULL);
INSERT INTO customer VALUES (6,'Neil','Beneke',NULL);
INSERT INTO customer VALUES (10,'Breyton','Tshabalala','B');
```

**WARNING**    *Using the results of a default mysqldump to restore a database can be time consuming. Because the index buffer is flushed after each INSERT statement, large tables can take a long time to restore. See the mysqldump options later in the next section to see how to speed this up.*

## Restoring a Database Backed Up with mysqldump

You can test your backup by dropping and re-creating the data:

```
mysql> DROP TABLE customer;
Query OK, 0 rows affected (0.31 sec)
mysql> exit
Bye
```

**WARNING**    *Once again, don't do this to test the backup of a live database. This is just a way to simulate the loss of your database.*

To restore the table on a Unix machine, run:

```
% mysql firstdb < /db_backups/customer_2002_11_12.sql
```

Or to restore from Windows:

```
C:\MySQL\bin>mysql firstdb < c:\db_backups\customer_2002_11_12.sql
```

The table has now been restored.

Table 11.1 describes the various options available to mysqldump.

**TABLE 11.1:** MYSQLDUMP OPTIONS

| OPTION | DESCRIPTION |
|---|---|
| --add-locks | Places a LOCK TABLES statement before, and an UNLOCK TABLE statement after, each table dump. This causes the INSERT statements to be processed much more quickly (as the key buffer is only flushed after the UNLOCK TABLE statement). |
| --add-drop-table | Adds a DROP TABLE before each CREATE TABLE statement. If the table already exists, it may interfere with the restoration, so this ensures a clean slate for the restored table. |
| -A, --all-databases | Dumps all existing databases. It is equivalent to the -B or --databases option with all the databases listed. |
| -a, --all | Includes all MySQL-specific CREATE options. |
| --allow-keywords | Usually column names cannot be the same as a keyword. This allows the creation of column names that are keywords by beginning each column name with the table name. |

*Continued on next page*

**Table 11.1:** Mysqldump Options *(continued)*

| Option | Description |
| --- | --- |
| -c, --complete-insert | Uses complete insert statements—in other words, INSERT INTO tablename(x,y,z) VALUES (a,b,c) rather than INSERT INTO tablename VALUES (a,b,c). |
| -C, --compress | Compresses the data transferred between the client and server if both support compression. |
| -B, --databases | Dumps several databases. No table names can be specified if this option is chosen—all tables in a database are dumped. The output places a USE databasename statement before each new database. |
| --delayed | Rows are inserted with the INSERT DELAYED command rather than just INSERT. |
| -e, --extended-insert | Uses the multiline INSERT syntax. The output is more compact and also runs faster because the index buffer is flushed only after each INSERT statement. |
| -#, --debug[=option_string] | Traces program usage for debugging purposes. |
| --help | Displays a help message and exits. |
| --fields-terminated-by=... | Same as the LOAD DATA INFILE options. See the sections on SELECT INTO and LOAD DATA INFILE. |
| --fields-enclosed-by=... | Same as the LOAD DATA INFILE options. See the sections on SELECT INTO and LOAD DATA INFILE. |
| --fields-optionally-enclosed-by=... | Same as the LOAD DATA INFILE options. See the sections on SELECT INTO and LOAD DATA INFILE. |
| --fields-escaped-by=... | Same as the LOAD DATA INFILE options. See the sections on SELECT INTO and LOAD DATA INFILE. |
| --lines-terminated-by=... | Same as the LOAD DATA INFILE options. See the sections on SELECT INTO and LOAD DATA INFILE. |
| -F, --flush-logs | Flushes the log file before starting the dump. |
| -f, --force | Continues even if there are MySQL errors during the dump. |
| -h, --host=... | Dumps data from the MySQL server found on the named host. The default host is localhost. |
| -l, --lock-tables | Locks all tables before starting the dump. The tables are locked with READ LOCAL, which allows concurrent inserts for MyISAM tables. |
| -K, --disable-keys | Indexes are disabled before the INSERT statements, and enabled afterward, which makes the insertions much quicker. |

*Continued on next page*

**TABLE 11.1:** MYSQLDUMP OPTIONS *(continued)*

| OPTION | DESCRIPTION |
| --- | --- |
| -n, --no-create-db | A CREATE DATABASE statement will not be placed in the output. It usually is if the --databases or --all-databases option is used. |
| -t, --no-create-info | Does not include the CREATE TABLE statement, so the tables are assumed to exist already. |
| -d, --no-data | Only dumps the table structure and does not include any INSERT statements for the table. |
| --opt | Equivalent to --quick --add-drop-table --add-locks --extended-insert --lock-tables. This results in the fastest restore. |
| -ppassphrase, --password[=passphrase] | Specifies the password to use when connecting to the server. As usual, if you don't specify the password, you will be prompted for it, which is a safer option. |
| -P portnumber, --port=portnumber | Specifies the TCP/IP port number to use when connecting to the host. This does not apply in the case of connections to localhost. See the -S option. |
| -q, --quick | Does not buffer the query, but dumps directly to stdout. Uses mysql_use_result() to do this. You may have to do this with large tables. |
| -Q, --quote-names | Places table and column names within single quotes. |
| -r, --result-file=... | Outputs directly to a given file. This is useful in DOS because it prevents Unix newline \n characters from being converted to a newline and carriage return \n\r. |
| -S /path/to/socket, --socket=/path/to/socket | Specifies the socket file to use when connecting to localhost (the default). |
| --tables | Overrides the -B or --databases option. |
| -T, --tab=path-to-some-directory | Creates two files for each table: tablename.sql, containing the CREATE statements, and tablename.txt, containing the data. This option only works when mysqldump is run on the server. |
| -u username, --user=username | Specifies the MySQL username to use when connecting to the server. The default value is your Unix login name. |
| -O var=option, --set-variable var=option | Sets the value of a variable. |
| -v, --verbose | Makes MySQL more talkative by forcing it to display more information on the mysqldump process. |
| -V, --version | Displays version information and exits. |

*Continued on next page*

**TABLE 11.1:** MYSQLDUMP OPTIONS *(continued)*

| OPTION | DESCRIPTION |
|---|---|
| -w, --where='where-condition' | Dumps only the records that satisfy the `where` condition. The condition must appear in quotes. |
| -X, --xml | Dumps the database as well-formed XML. |
| -x, --first-slave | Locks all tables across all databases. |
| -O net_buffer_length=n | Creates rows of up to *n* size when it creates multirow-insert statements (the -e or --opt options. *n* must be less than 16MB, and the `mysqld` variable `max_allowed_packet` must be larger than n. |

You can use mysqldump in three main ways.

```
% mysqldump [OPTIONS] database [tables]
```

or:

```
% mysqldump [OPTIONS] --databases [OPTIONS] DB1 [DB2 DB3...]
```

or:

```
% mysqldump [OPTIONS] --all-databases [OPTIONS]
```

The following examples demonstrate some of the available options. Specifically, the next example dumps all tables in the *firstdb* database:

```
% mysqldump firstdb > /db_backups/firstdb_2002_11-12.sql
```

The -v (verbose) option gives more information as it goes through the process, which could be useful for debugging if there are problems:

```
% mysqldump -v firstdb customer > /db_backups/customer_2002_11-12.sql
# Connecting to localhost...
# Retrieving table structure for table customer...
# Sending SELECT query...
# Retrieving rows...
# Disconnecting from localhost...
%
```

The following example uses where to limit the backup to only those records where the id>5:

```
% mysqldump --where='id>5' firstdb customer > /db_backups/customer_2002_11-12.sql
```

This leaves the output looking like this:

```
#
# Dumping data for table 'customer'
# WHERE:  id>5
#
```

```
INSERT INTO customer VALUES (7,'Winnie','Dlamini',NULL);
INSERT INTO customer VALUES (6,'Neil','Beneke',NULL);
INSERT INTO customer VALUES (10,'Breyton','Tshabalala','B');
```

The -e (extended) option allows for faster inserts:

```
% mysqldump -e firstdb customer > /db_backups/customer_2002_11-12.sql
```

This makes use of the multi-line INSERT statement, as you can see from viewing the text file:

```
#
# Dumping data for table 'customer'
#

INSERT INTO customer VALUES
(1,'Yvonne','Clegg','X'),
(2,'Johnny','Chaka-Chaka','B'),
(3,'Winston','Powers','M'),
(4,'Patricia','Mankunku','C'),
(5,'Francois','Papo','P'),
(7,'Winnie','Dlamini',NULL),
(6,'Neil','Beneke',NULL),(10,'Breyton','Tshabalala','B');
```

As there is only one INSERT statement, the index buffer is only flushed once, which is faster than doing it after every insert.

## Backing Up with *SELECT INTO*

Another way to perform a backup is to use SELECT INTO. This is similar to mysqldump in that it creates a file that is used to re-create the backed-up table. It is also the opposite of the LOAD DATA INTO statement. The resulting file can only be created on the MySQL server, not any other host. The syntax is as follows:

```
SELECT … INTO OUTFILE 'path_and_filename'
```

Any valid SELECT can be used to create a file.
To create a backup of the *customer* table, you would do the following, firstly on Unix:

```
mysql> SELECT * FROM customer INTO OUTFILE '/db_backups/customer.dat';
Query OK, 8 rows affected (0.00 sec)
```

And then on Windows:

```
mysql> SELECT * FROM customer INTO OUTFILE 'c:\\db_backups\\bdb.dat';
Query OK, 8 rows affected (0.33 sec)
```

Once again, you need to be careful when doing this. The following error is common:

```
mysql> SELECT * FROM customer INTO OUTFILE '/db_backups/customer.dat';
ERROR 1086: File '/db_backups/customer.dat' already exists
```

You cannot overwrite an existing file (which provides some sort of security, as a badly set up system may allow critical files to be overwritten).

Another common error is the following, from Windows:

```
mysql> SELECT * FROM customer INTO OUTFILE 'c:\db_backups\customer.dat';
ERROR 1: Can't create/write to file 'c:db_backupscustomer.dat' (Errcode: 2)
```

The error message here is quite clear: MySQL cannot write to this directory because you've forgotten to escape \ characters. \ in Windows is the escape character, and because it's also part of the Windows path, it needs to be escaped when used in that context. On Unix, a similar error is common:

```
mysql> SELECT * FROM customer INTO OUTFILE '\db_backups\customer.dat';
Query OK, 8 rows affected (0.18 sec)
```

In this case, though, MySQL does not even warn you of an error. Somebody from a Windows environment could easily put the slashes the wrong way and not get their backup. Always check that your backup has been created.

Looking at the file in any text editor (such as vi or Notepad), you'll see the following:

```
1       Yvonne  Clegg   X
2       Johnny  Chaka-Chaka     B
3       Winston Powers  M
4       Patricia        Mankunku        C
5       Francois        Papo    P
7       Winnie  Dlamini \N
6       Neil    Beneke  \N
10      Breyton Tshabalala      B
```

Tabs separate the fields, and newlines separate the records, which is the same default used by LOAD DATA INTO. You can also change these defaults by adding options at the end of the statement. The full set of options for SELECT INTO (and LOAD DATA INTO) is as follows:

```
[FIELDS
        [TERMINATED BY '\t']
        [[OPTIONALLY] ENCLOSED BY '']
        [ESCAPED BY '\\' ]
    ]
    [LINES TERMINATED BY '\n']
```

Here are some examples of using non-default options when using SELECT INTO, and the resulting text files:

```
mysql> SELECT * FROM customer INTO OUTFILE '/db_backups/customer2.dat'
 FIELDS TERMINATED BY 'zz';
Query OK, 8 rows affected (0.00 sec)
```

The data looks like the following:

```
1zzYvonnezzCleggzzX
2zzJohnnyzzChaka-ChakazzB
3zzWinstonzzPowerszzM
4zzPatriciazzMankunkuzzC
```

```
5zzFrancoiszzPapozzP
7zzWinniezzDlaminizz\N
6zzNeilzzBenekezz\N
10zzBreytonzzTshabalalazzB
```

The default tab character is replaced by the characters *zz* between each field.

***WARNING*** *The characters zz are used here just to make a point. It is dangerous to use ordinary characters like this as terminators. If the text contained the phrase zzz, the fields would all be out of alignment, as MySQL would think the first two characters were a terminator. Use conventional characters such as tabs, newlines, or piping (|) for your terminators.*

This next statement creates one long line:

```
mysql> SELECT * FROM customer INTO OUTFILE '/db_backups/customer3.dat'
  FIELDS TERMINATED BY '|' LINES TERMINATED BY '[end]';
Query OK, 8 rows affected (0.00 sec)
```

The data appears as shown:

```
1|Yvonne|Clegg|X[end]2|Johnny|Chaka-Chaka|B[end]⏎
3|Winston|Powers|M[end]4|Patricia|Mankunku|C[end]⏎
5|Francois|Papo|P[end]7|Winnie|Dlamini|\N[end]⏎
6|Neil|Beneke|\N[end]10|Breyton|Tshabalala|B[end]
```

The line breaks are replaced by the characters *[end]*.
In the following example, the ENCLOSED keyword surrounds all fields by the specified characters:

```
mysql> SELECT * FROM customer INTO OUTFILE '/db_backups/customer4.dat'
  FIELDS TERMINATED BY '|' ENCLOSED BY '"' LINES TERMINATED BY \n';
Query OK, 8 rows affected (0.00 sec)
```

The data appears as the following:

```
"1"|"Yvonne"|"Clegg"|"X"
"2"|"Johnny"|"Chaka-Chaka"|"B"
"3"|"Winston"|"Powers"|"M"
"4"|"Patricia"|"Mankunku"|"C"
"5"|"Francois"|"Papo"|"P"
"7"|"Winnie"|"Dlamini"|\N
"6"|"Neil"|"Beneke"|\N
"10"|"Breyton"|"Tshabalala"|"B"
```

The OPTIONALLY keyword results in only character fields being enclosed (just as you enclose character fields in single quotes when adding records, but not numeric fields). For example:

```
mysql> SELECT * FROM customer INTO OUTFILE '/db_backups/customer5.dat'
  FIELDS TERMINATED BY '|' OPTIONALLY ENCLOSED BY '"' LINES TERMINATED
  BY '\n';
Query OK, 8 rows affected (0.00 sec)
```

The first field of the data (it's type INT) is not enclosed with quotes:

```
1|"Yvonne"|"Clegg"|"X"
2|"Johnny"|"Chaka-Chaka"|"B"
3|"Winston"|"Powers"|"M"
4|"Patricia"|"Mankunku"|"C"
5|"Francois"|"Papo"|"P"
7|"Winnie"|"Dlamini"|\N
6|"Neil"|"Beneke"|\N
10|"Breyton"|"Tshabalala"|"B"
```

You can also back up a subset of the data, using a condition in your SELECT statement:

```
mysql> SELECT * FROM customer WHERE id<10 INTO OUTFILE
 '/db_backups/customer6.dat' FIELDS TERMINATED BY '|' LINES TERMINATED
 BY '\n';
Query OK, 7 rows affected (0.01 sec)
```

Only the seven applicable records appear in the file:

```
1|Yvonne|Clegg|X
2|Johnny|Chaka-Chaka|B
3|Winston|Powers|M
4|Patricia|Mankunku|C
5|Francois|Papo|P
7|Winnie|Dlamini|\N
6|Neil|Beneke|\N
```

## Restoring a Table with *LOAD DATA*

To restore a table created with SELECT INTO, use the LOAD DATA statement. You can also use LOAD DATA to add data that has been created in some other way, perhaps an application or a spreadsheet. It is the fastest way to add data, especially large quantities of data. The syntax is as follows:

```
LOAD DATA [LOW_PRIORITY | CONCURRENT] [LOCAL] INFILE 'filename'
    [REPLACE | IGNORE]
    INTO TABLE tbl_name
    [FIELDS
        [TERMINATED BY '\t']
        [[OPTIONALLY] ENCLOSED BY '']
        [ESCAPED BY '\\' ]
    ]
    [LINES TERMINATED BY '\n']
    [IGNORE number LINES]
    [(col_name,...)]
```

Let's remove the data from the customer table and restore it using LOAD DATA:

```
mysql> TRUNCATE customer;
Query OK, 0 rows affected (0.02 sec)
```

To restore the table on Unix, use:

```
mysql> LOAD DATA INFILE '/db_backups/customer.dat' INTO TABLE customer;
Query OK, 8 rows affected (0.01 sec)
Records: 8  Deleted: 0  Skipped: 0  Warnings: 0
```

And to restore it on Windows, use:

```
mysql> LOAD DATA INFILE 'c:\\db_backups\\customer.dat' INTO TABLE customer;
Query OK, 8 rows affected (0.01 sec)
Records: 8  Deleted: 0  Skipped: 0  Warnings: 0
```

As you can see, the data has been successfully restored:

```
mysql> SELECT * FROM customer;
+----+------------+-------------+---------+
| id | first_name | surname     | initial |
+----+------------+-------------+---------+
|  1 | Yvonne     | Clegg       | X       |
|  2 | Johnny     | Chaka-Chaka | B       |
|  3 | Winston    | Powers      | M       |
|  4 | Patricia   | Mankunku    | C       |
|  5 | Francois   | Papo        | P       |
|  7 | Winnie     | Dlamini     | NULL    |
|  6 | Neil       | Beneke      | NULL    |
| 10 | Breyton    | Tshabalala  | B       |
+----+------------+-------------+---------+
8 rows in set (0.00 sec)
```

### WHAT IF SOMETHING GOES WRONG?

Something can go wrong for a number of reasons:

- If you're trying unsuccessfully to use LOAD DATA, perhaps you don't have permission to read a file on the server. The user doing the LOAD DATA needs to have the FILE privilege (see Chapter 14, "Database Security"), and the file needs to either exist in the database directory or be readable by all.

- A common mistake is not to match the terminators and enclosure characters. They must be exactly the same as they are in the data file (or were specified in the SELECT INTO statement). If not, the result is that everything seems to work, but the table remains blank or full of NULL values. See the next section for more information.

- If you're using the LOCAL keyword, it will not work if MySQL has been started with the --local-infile=0 option (see Chapter 13, "Configuring and Optimizing MySQL").

- The pathname or filename was not specified correctly (remember to use the escape character for Windows pathnames).

### USING *LOAD DATA* WITH OPTIONS

Let's restore from some of the other backups, using some of the other options:

```
mysql> LOAD DATA INFILE '/db_backups/customer2.dat' INTO TABLE customer;
```

```
Query OK, 8 rows affected (0.01 sec)
Records: 8  Deleted: 0  Skipped: 0  Warnings: 32
```

Although this seemed to work, it didn't restore the data correctly:

```
mysql> SELECT * FROM customer;
+----+------------+---------+---------+
| id | first_name | surname | initial |
+----+------------+---------+---------+
|  1 | NULL       | NULL    | NULL    |
|  2 | NULL       | NULL    | NULL    |
|  3 | NULL       | NULL    | NULL    |
|  4 | NULL       | NULL    | NULL    |
|  5 | NULL       | NULL    | NULL    |
|  7 | NULL       | NULL    | NULL    |
|  6 | NULL       | NULL    | NULL    |
| 10 | NULL       | NULL    | NULL    |
+----+------------+---------+---------+
8 rows in set (0.00 sec)
```

The problem was that you did not match the terminators correctly. Remember that customer2.dat was created with the FIELDS TERMINATED BY 'zz' option. So, you need to restore it in the same way:

```
mysql> TRUNCATE customer;
Query OK, 0 rows affected (0.00 sec)
mysql> LOAD DATA INFILE '/db_backups/customer2.dat' INTO TABLE customer
  FIELDS TERMINATED BY 'zz';
Query OK, 8 rows affected (0.01 sec)
Records: 8  Deleted: 0  Skipped: 0  Warnings: 0
mysql> SELECT * FROM customer;
+----+------------+-------------+---------+
| id | first_name | surname     | initial |
+----+------------+-------------+---------+
|  1 | Yvonne     | Clegg       | X       |
|  2 | Johnny     | Chaka-Chaka | B       |
|  3 | Winston    | Powers      | M       |
|  4 | Patricia   | Mankunku    | C       |
|  5 | Francois   | Papo        | P       |
|  7 | Winnie     | Dlamini     | NULL    |
|  6 | Neil       | Beneke      | NULL    |
| 10 | Breyton    | Tshabalala  | B       |
+----+------------+-------------+---------+
8 rows in set (0.00 sec)
```

The same applies to the LINES TERMINATED BY clause used to create customer3.dat:

```
mysql> TRUNCATE customer;
```

```
Query OK, 0 rows affected (0.00 sec)
mysql> LOAD DATA INFILE '/db_backups/customer3.dat' INTO TABLE customer
 FIELDS TERMINATED BY '|' LINES TERMINATED BY '[end]';
Query OK, 8 rows affected (0.00 sec)
Records: 8  Deleted: 0  Skipped: 0  Warnings: 0
mysql> SELECT * FROM customer;
+----+------------+-------------+---------+
| id | first_name | surname     | initial |
+----+------------+-------------+---------+
|  1 | Yvonne     | Clegg       | X       |
|  2 | Johnny     | Chaka-Chaka | B       |
|  3 | Winston    | Powers      | M       |
|  4 | Patricia   | Mankunku    | C       |
|  5 | Francois   | Papo        | P       |
|  7 | Winnie     | Dlamini     | NULL    |
|  6 | Neil       | Beneke      | NULL    |
| 10 | Breyton    | Tshabalala  | B       |
+----+------------+-------------+---------+
8 rows in set (0.00 sec)
```

The ENCLOSED BY clause also needs to be added if it has been used, as with customer4.dat:

```
mysql> TRUNCATE customer;
Query OK, 0 rows affected (0.00 sec)
mysql> LOAD DATA INFILE '/db_backups/customer4.dat' INTO TABLE customer
 FIELDS TERMINATED BY '|' ENCLOSED BY '"' LINES TERMINATED BY '\n';
Query OK, 8 rows affected (0.01 sec)
Records: 8  Deleted: 0  Skipped: 0  Warnings: 0
mysql> SELECT * FROM customer;
+----+------------+-------------+---------+
| id | first_name | surname     | initial |
+----+------------+-------------+---------+
|  1 | Yvonne     | Clegg       | X       |
|  2 | Johnny     | Chaka-Chaka | B       |
|  3 | Winston    | Powers      | M       |
|  4 | Patricia   | Mankunku    | C       |
|  5 | Francois   | Papo        | P       |
|  7 | Winnie     | Dlamini     | NULL    |
|  6 | Neil       | Beneke      | NULL    |
| 10 | Breyton    | Tshabalala  | B       |
+----+------------+-------------+---------+
8 rows in set (0.00 sec)
```

And of course the same applies to the OPTIONALLY ENCLOSED clause as well, used to create customer5.dat:

```
mysql> TRUNCATE customer;
Query OK, 0 rows affected (0.00 sec)
```

```
mysql> LOAD DATA INFILE '/db_backups/customer5.dat' INTO TABLE customer
 FIELDS TERMINATED BY '|' OPTIONALLY ENCLOSED BY '"' LINES TERMINATED BY '\n';
Query OK, 8 rows affected (0.01 sec)
Records: 8  Deleted: 0  Skipped: 0  Warnings: 0
mysql> SELECT * FROM customer;
+----+------------+-------------+---------+
| id | first_name | surname     | initial |
+----+------------+-------------+---------+
|  1 | Yvonne     | Clegg       | X       |
|  2 | Johnny     | Chaka-Chaka | B       |
|  3 | Winston    | Powers      | M       |
|  4 | Patricia   | Mankunku    | C       |
|  5 | Francois   | Papo        | P       |
|  7 | Winnie     | Dlamini     | NULL    |
|  6 | Neil       | Beneke      | NULL    |
| 10 | Breyton    | Tshabalala  | B       |
+----+------------+-------------+---------+
8 rows in set (0.00 sec)
```

You can also update from the partially backed-up file, `customer6.dat`:

```
mysql> TRUNCATE customer;
Query OK, 0 rows affected (0.00 sec)
mysql> LOAD DATA INFILE '/db_backups/customer6.dat' INTO TABLE customer
 FIELDS TERMINATED BY '|' LINES TERMINATED BY '\n';
Query OK, 7 rows affected (0.01 sec)
Records: 7  Deleted: 0  Skipped: 0  Warnings: 0
mysql> SELECT * FROM customer;
+----+------------+-------------+---------+
| id | first_name | surname     | initial |
+----+------------+-------------+---------+
|  1 | Yvonne     | Clegg       | X       |
|  2 | Johnny     | Chaka-Chaka | B       |
|  3 | Winston    | Powers      | M       |
|  4 | Patricia   | Mankunku    | C       |
|  5 | Francois   | Papo        | P       |
|  7 | Winnie     | Dlamini     | NULL    |
|  6 | Neil       | Beneke      | NULL    |
+----+------------+-------------+---------+
7 rows in set (0.00 sec)
```

What if you now realize you made a mistake and want to restore the entire table? If you immediately LOAD DATA from a file containing a full backup, you'd come across the following problem:

```
mysql> LOAD DATA INFILE '/db_backups/customer.dat' INTO
    TABLE customer;           ERROR 1062: Duplicate entry '1'
    for key 1                                    mysql> SELECT * FROM customer;
```

```
+----+------------+-------------+---------+
| id | first_name | surname     | initial |
+----+------------+-------------+---------+
|  1 | Yvonne     | Clegg       | X       |
|  2 | Johnny     | Chaka-Chaka | B       |
|  3 | Winston    | Powers      | M       |
|  4 | Patricia   | Mankunku    | C       |
|  5 | Francois   | Papo        | P       |
|  7 | Winnie     | Dlamini     | NULL    |
|  6 | Neil       | Beneke      | NULL    |
+----+------------+-------------+---------+
7 rows in set (0.00 sec)
```

You've got a duplicate key error, and the file stopped processing at that point. You could of course simply clear the table beforehand, as you've been doing before all the restores to date, but if you were trying to restore a table that already contains records, you may not want to remove everything and start again. The two keywords that become useful here are REPLACE and IGNORE. The latter ignores any rows that duplicate an existing row on a unique index or primary key. So, as in this situation, IGNORE is useful where you know the records have not changed and you don't want to drop and restore all the records again:

```
mysql> LOAD DATA INFILE '/db_backups/customer.dat' IGNORE INTO TABLE customer;
Query OK, 1 row affected (0.00 sec)
Records: 8  Deleted: 0  Skipped: 7  Warnings: 0
```

You can see that of the eight rows, seven were skipped and only the missing record was inserted. On a large file this would save a lot of time and prevent the inconvenience of temporarily having no data available. All records are now present again:

```
mysql> SELECT * FROM customer;
+----+------------+-------------+---------+
| id | first_name | surname     | initial |
+----+------------+-------------+---------+
|  1 | Yvonne     | Clegg       | X       |
|  2 | Johnny     | Chaka-Chaka | B       |
|  3 | Winston    | Powers      | M       |
|  4 | Patricia   | Mankunku    | C       |
|  5 | Francois   | Papo        | P       |
|  7 | Winnie     | Dlamini     | NULL    |
|  6 | Neil       | Beneke      | NULL    |
| 10 | Breyton    | Tshabalala  | B       |
+----+------------+-------------+---------+
8 rows in set (0.00 sec)
```

The REPLACE keyword comes in useful where the values of the records have changed, and you want to restore the records existing on disk. To demonstrate, you'll make the far-too-common mistake of updating all records when you only mean to update one, accidentally changing all surnames to *Fortune*:

```
mysql> UPDATE customer SET surname='Fortune';
Query OK, 8 rows affected (0.00 sec)
Rows matched: 8  Changed: 8  Warnings: 0
```

You realize your error after you check the table!

```
mysql> SELECT * FROM customer;
+----+------------+---------+---------+
| id | first_name | surname | initial |
+----+------------+---------+---------+
|  1 | Yvonne     | Fortune | X       |
|  2 | Johnny     | Fortune | B       |
|  3 | Winston    | Fortune | M       |
|  4 | Patricia   | Fortune | C       |
|  5 | Francois   | Fortune | P       |
|  7 | Winnie     | Fortune | NULL    |
|  6 | Neil       | Fortune | NULL    |
| 10 | Breyton    | Fortune | B       |
+----+------------+---------+---------+
8 rows in set (0.00 sec)
```

Now, restore using the REPLACE keyword:

```
mysql> LOAD DATA INFILE '/db_backups/customer.dat' REPLACE INTO TABLE customer;
Query OK, 16 rows affected (0.00 sec)
Records: 8  Deleted: 8  Skipped: 0  Warnings: 0
mysql> SELECT * FROM customer;
+----+------------+-------------+---------+
| id | first_name | surname     | initial |
+----+------------+-------------+---------+
|  1 | Yvonne     | Clegg       | X       |
|  2 | Johnny     | Chaka-Chaka | B       |
|  3 | Winston    | Powers      | M       |
|  4 | Patricia   | Mankunku    | C       |
|  5 | Francois   | Papo        | P       |
|  7 | Winnie     | Dlamini     | NULL    |
|  6 | Neil       | Beneke      | NULL    |
| 10 | Breyton    | Tshabalala  | B       |
+----+------------+-------------+---------+
8 rows in set (0.00 sec)
```

LOAD DATA LOCAL is an option that allows the contents of a file that exists on the MySQL client machine to be uploaded to the database server.

LOW PRIORITY causes the addition of the new records to wait until there are no other clients reading from a table (as it does with an ordinary INSERT).

The CONCURRENT keyword is a useful one if you still want the table to be read. It allows other threads to read from a MyISAM table (but slows the LOAD DATA process down).

### SECURITY ISSUES WITH *LOAD DATA LOCAL*

Restoring from a client machine may be convenient, but it does come with a security risk. Someone could use LOAD DATA LOCAL to read any files to which the user they are connecting as has access. They could do this by creating a table and reading from the table after they have loaded the data. If they were connecting as the same user as the web server and have the right access to run queries, this becomes dangerous. By default, MySQL allows LOAD DATA LOCAL. To prevent this and disallow all LOAD DATA LOCAL, start the MySQL server with the --local-infile=0 option. You could also compile MySQL without the --enable-local-infile option.

## Using mysqlimport Instead of *LOAD DATA*

Instead of LOAD DATA, which is run from inside MySQL, you can use the command-line equivalent, mysqlimport. The syntax is as follows:

```
% mysqlimport [options] databasename filename1 [filename2 ...]
```

Many of the options are the same as the LOAD DATA equivalents. The table to import the data into is determined from the filename. To do this, mysqlimport drops the extension of the filename, so customer.dat is imported into the customer table.

Use mysqlimport to restore the customer data, as follows:

```
mysql> SELECT * FROM customer;
+----+------------+-------------+---------+
| id | first_name | surname     | initial |
+----+------------+-------------+---------+
|  1 | Yvonne     | Clegg       | X       |
|  2 | Johnny     | Chaka-Chaka | B       |
|  3 | Winston    | Powers      | M       |
|  4 | Patricia   | Mankunku    | C       |
|  5 | Francois   | Papo        | P       |
|  7 | Winnie     | Dlamini     | NULL    |
|  6 | Neil       | Beneke      | NULL    |
| 10 | Breyton    | Tshabalala  | B       |
+----+------------+-------------+---------+
8 rows in set (0.00 sec)
mysql> TRUNCATE customer;
Query OK, 0 rows affected (0.01 sec)
mysql> exit
Bye
% mysqlimport firstdb /db_backups/customer.dat
firstdb.customer: Records: 8  Deleted: 0  Skipped: 0  Warnings: 0
[root@test data]# mysql firstdb;
Welcome to the MySQL monitor.  Commands end with ; or \g.
Your MySQL connection id is 7 to server version: 4.0.1-alpha-max-log

Type 'help;' or '\h' for help. Type '\c' to clear the buffer.
```

```
mysql> SELECT * FROM customer;
+----+------------+-------------+---------+
| id | first_name | surname     | initial |
+----+------------+-------------+---------+
|  1 | Yvonne     | Clegg       | X       |
|  2 | Johnny     | Chaka-Chaka | B       |
|  3 | Winston    | Powers      | M       |
|  4 | Patricia   | Mankunku    | C       |
|  5 | Francois   | Papo        | P       |
|  7 | Winnie     | Dlamini     | NULL    |
|  6 | Neil       | Beneke      | NULL    |
| 10 | Breyton    | Tshabalala  | B       |
+----+------------+-------------+---------+
8 rows in set (0.00 sec)
```

And the data is restored.

Table 11.2 describes the options available to mysqlimport.

**TABLE 11.2:** MYSQLIMPORT OPTIONS

| OPTION | DESCRIPTION |
| --- | --- |
| -c, --columns=... | Takes a comma-separated list of field names as an argument. These are used to create a LOAD DATA INFILE command. |
| --character-sets-dir=name | Tells MySQL the directory where the character sets are. |
| -C, --compress | Compresses the data transferred between the client and server if both support compression. |
| -#, --debug[=option_string] | Traces program usage for debugging purposes. |
| -d, --delete | Empties the table before importing the text file. |
| --fields-terminated-by=... | Same as the LOAD DATA INFILE option. |
| --fields-enclosed-by=... | Same as the LOAD DATA INFILE option. |
| --fields-optionally-enclosed-by=... | Same as the LOAD DATA INFILE option. |
| --fields-escaped-by=... | Same as the LOAD DATA INFILE option. |
| --lines-terminated-by=... | Same as the LOAD DATA INFILE option. |
| -f, --force | Continues even if there are MySQL errors during the dump. |
| --help | Displays a help message and exits. |

*Continued on next page*

**TABLE 11.2:** MYSQLIMPORT OPTIONS *(continued)*

| OPTION | DESCRIPTION |
|---|---|
| -h host_name, --host= host_name | Imports data to the MySQL server found on the named host. The default host is localhost. |
| -i, --ignore | Added records that would cause a duplicate key error are ignored. Usually they result in an error and cause the process to stop at that point. |
| -l, --lock-tables | Locks all tables for writing before processing any text files, which keeps the tables synchronized on the server. |
| -L, --local | Reads input files from the client machine. If you connect to localhost (the default), text files are assumed to be on the server. |
| -ppassphrase, --password[=passphrase] | Specifies the password to use when connecting to the server. As usual, if you don't specify the password, you will be prompted for it, which is a safer option. |
| -P portnumber, --port=portnumber | Specifies the TCP/IP port number to use when connecting to the host. This does not apply in the case of connections to localhost. See the -S option. |
| -r, --replace | A record to be added that would result in a duplicate key replaces the original record of that same key. Usually this results in an error and causes the process to stop at that point. |
| -s, --silent | Displays output only when errors occur. |
| -S /path/to/socket, --socket=/path/to/socket | Specifies the socket file to use when connecting to localhost (the default). |
| -u username, --user=username | Specifies the MySQL username to use when connecting to the server. The default value is your Unix login name. |
| -v, --verbose | Displays more information during the run. |
| -V, --version | Displays version information and exits. |

# Using mysqlhotcopy to Back Up

The mysqlhotcopy utility is a Perl script to ease backups. It's still in beta (check the latest documentation to see if this is still the case by the time you read this), so it may not work properly in all situations. It's fast and convenient to use, and it works by locking and flushing the tables and then copying the files to the directory you specify (see Table 11.3). It can only copy files to elsewhere on the server. The syntax is as follows:

```
% mysqlhotcopy databasename backup_directory_path
```

Table 11.3 describes the options available to mysqlhotcopy.

**TABLE 11.3:** MYSQLHOTCOPY OPTIONS

| OPTION | DESCRIPTION |
|---|---|
| -?, --help | Displays a help screen and exits. |
| -u, --user=# | Username for connecting to the server. |
| -p, --password=# | Password for connecting to the server. |
| -P, --port=# | Port to use when connecting to local server. |
| -S, --socket=# | Socket to use when connecting to local server. |
| --allowold | If the files already exist, mysqlhotcopy usually aborts. This option appends _old to the filenames and continues operating. |
| --keepold | The renamed files from --allowold are usually deleted after the operation. This option leaves them there. |
| --noindices | This option does not include the index files in the backup, which speeds the process. After restoring the files, the indexes can be rebuilt with myisamchk -rq. |
| --method=# | Allows you to specify whether to use cp or scp to copy the files. |
| -q, --quiet | Only errors are outputted. |
| --debug | Enables debugging. |
| -n, --dryrun | Outputs messages, but does not do the actions. |
| --regexp=# | Copies all databases with names that match the regular expression. |
| --suffix=# | Gives a suffix for the names of copied databases. |
| --checkpoint=# | Inserts checkpoint entries into specified database table. |
| --flushlog | Flushes the logs once all the tables are locked. |
| --tmpdir=# | Allows you to specify a temporary directory. |

mysqlhotcopy gets its options from the client and mysqlhotcopy groups in the option files.

To restore a backup made with mysqlhotcopy, replace the files in the data directory, as if you'd made the direct copies yourself.

There are a number of prerequisites to meet in order to run mysqlhotcopy:

◆ You need to be able to run Perl scripts on your database server.

◆ mysqlhotcopy depends on the following Perl classes in order to run: Getopt::Long, Data::Dumper, File::Basename, File::Path, DBI, and Sys::Hostname.

◆ You need write access to the directory to which you're trying to back up.

◆ You need select privileges on the databases you are backing up.

◆ In order to flush the table, you need reload privileges.

## Using the Binary Update Log to Restore a Database to the Most Recent Position

The binary update log is an ideal way to restore your database to a point as close as possible to when a crash happened (see Chapter 10, "Basic Administration"). The binary update log logs all changes made to your database. The binary update log is enabled when MySQL is started with the `--log-bin` option. You can specify a name with `--log-bin = filename`; otherwise the default name will be the name of the server machine, with `-bin` appended. A new log file is created every time the server is restarted, the logs flushed, the server refreshed, or the maximum size (set in `max_bin_log_size`) is reached.

After you've made a backup with mysqldump, restart MySQL with the `--log-bin` option. When the time comes to restore, restore the mysqldump file, and then use the binary log files to return the database to its most recent status.

For example, let's assume that the last backup was from `customer.dat`, which restores it to the 10 records shown here:

```
mysql> SELECT * FROM customer;
+----+------------+-------------+---------+
| id | first_name | surname     | initial |
+----+------------+-------------+---------+
|  1 | Yvonne     | Clegg       | X       |
|  2 | Johnny     | Chaka-Chaka | B       |
|  3 | Winston    | Powers      | M       |
|  4 | Patricia   | Mankunku    | C       |
|  5 | Francois   | Papo        | P       |
|  7 | Winnie     | Dlamini     | NULL    |
|  6 | Neil       | Beneke      | NULL    |
| 10 | Breyton    | Tshabalala  | B       |
+----+------------+-------------+---------+
8 rows in set (0.00 sec)
```

Once you're at this stage (having just made the backup), start the server with binary logging enabled if you haven't already:

```
C:\MySQL\bin> mysqladmin shutdown
020601 23:59:01  mysqld ended
```

If it's not there already, place the following option inside your `my.cnf` or `my.ini` file to enable binary logging:

```
log-bin
```

Now restart the server:

```
C:\MySQL\bin> mysqld-max
020602 18:58:21  InnoDB: Started
C:\MySQL\bin> mysql firstdb;
```

```
Welcome to the MySQL monitor.  Commands end with ; or \g.
Your MySQL connection id is 3 to server version: 4.0.1-alpha-max-log

Type 'help;' or '\h' for help. Type '\c' to clear the buffer.
mysql> INSERT INTO customer VALUES(11,'Robin','McKenzie',NULL);
Query OK, 1 row affected (0.00 sec)
```

Now let's simulate a crash by stopping the server and deleting the customer data and index files:

```
mysql> exit
Bye
C:\MySQL\bin> del c:\MySQL\data\firstdb\customer.*
```

Depending on your setup, you may not have permission to remove the files until you shut the server down or change to root.

If you delete the files, and still have a connection active, and then try to perform a query on the customer table, you may still get results, as the results may be cached. But when you shut the server down and restart, you will not be able to find any customer data:

```
C:\MySQL\bin> mysqladmin shutdown
020601 23:59:01  mysqld ended
C:\MySQL\bin> mysqld-max
020602 18:58:21  InnoDB: Started
C:\MySQL\bin> mysql firstdb;
Welcome to the MySQL monitor.  Commands end with ; or \g.
Your MySQL connection id is 3 to server version: 4.0.1-alpha-max-log

Type 'help;' or '\h' for help. Type '\c' to clear the buffer.
mysql> SELECT * FROM customer;
ERROR 1146: Table 'firstdb.customer' doesn't exist
mysql> exit
Bye
```

Now restore the backup made earlier:

```
C:\MySQL\bin> copy c:\db_backups\customer.* c:\MySQL\data\firstdb
```

Doing a query, you see you have lost the most recent record, which was added after the backup:

```
C:\MySQL\bin> mysql firstdb;
Welcome to the MySQL monitor.  Commands end with ; or \g.
Your MySQL connection id is 3 to server version: 4.0.1-alpha-max-log

Type 'help;' or '\h' for help. Type '\c' to clear the buffer.
mysql> SELECT * FROM customer;
```

```
+----+------------+-------------+---------+
| id | first_name | surname     | initial |
+----+------------+-------------+---------+
|  1 | Yvonne     | Clegg       | X       |
|  2 | Johnny     | Chaka-Chaka | B       |
|  3 | Winston    | Powers      | M       |
|  4 | Patricia   | Mankunku    | C       |
|  5 | Francois   | Papo        | P       |
|  7 | Winnie     | Dlamini     | NULL    |
|  6 | Neil       | Beneke      | NULL    |
| 10 | Breyton    | Tshabalala  | B       |
+----+------------+-------------+---------+
8 rows in set (0.00 sec)
```

In order to restore it, you need to use the binary update log. First, let's look at what's in the binary update log. It's not a text file, so you can't use an ordinary text editor, but MySQL comes with a utility, mysqlbinlog. Running this utility on one of the binary update log files will output the contents of the log. The syntax is as follows:

```
mysqlbinlog path_to_binary_update_log
```

Let's see what's in the log:

```
C:\MySQL\bin>mysqlbinlog ..\data\speed_demon-bin.001
# at 4
#020602 18:58:21 server id 1    Start: binlog v 2, server v 4.0.1-alpha-max-log
created 020602 18:58:21
# at 79
#020602 19:01:11 server id 1    Query    thread_id=2 exec_time=0  error_code=0
use firstdb;
SET TIMESTAMP=1023037271;
INSERT INTO customer VALUES(11,'Robin','McKenzie');
# at 167
#020602 19:01:48 server id 1    Stop
```

If you'd already been running binary update logging, you may have many log files. Choose the second most recent one that would have captured the latest INSERT statement.

Of course, this output is not much good on the screen. You can pipe it to the actual database as follows:

```
C:\MySQL\bin>mysqlbinlog ..\data\speed_demon-bin.001 | mysql firstdb
```

Now, you can view your table and see that the record has been restored:

```
C:\MySQL\bin> mysql firstdb;
Welcome to the MySQL monitor.  Commands end with ; or \g.
Your MySQL connection id is 3 to server version: 4.0.1-alpha-max-log

Type 'help;' or '\h' for help. Type '\c' to clear the buffer.
mysql> SELECT * FROM customer;
```

```
+----+-----------+-------------+---------+
| id | first_name | surname    | initial |
+----+-----------+-------------+---------+
|  1 | Yvonne    | Clegg       | X       |
|  2 | Johnny    | Chaka-Chaka | B       |
|  3 | Winston   | Powers      | M       |
|  4 | Patricia  | Mankunku    | C       |
|  5 | Francois  | Papo        | P       |
|  7 | Winnie    | Dlamini     | NULL    |
|  6 | Neil      | Beneke      | NULL    |
| 10 | Breyton   | Tshabalala  | B       |
| 11 | Robin     | McKenzie    | NULL    |
+----+-----------+-------------+---------+
9 rows in set (0.00 sec)
```

The record has been successfully restored.

Table 11.4 describes the options available to mysqlbinlog.

**TABLE 11.4:** MYSQLBINLOG OPTIONS

| OPTION | DESCRIPTION |
| --- | --- |
| -?, --help | Displays help and exits |
| -d, --database=dbname | Only lists entries for the specified database |
| -s, --short-form | Shows only the queries, not any extra info |
| -o, --offset=N | Skips a number of entries starting from the beginning, specified by N |
| -h, --host=server | Gets the binary log from the specified server |
| -P, --port=port | Uses the specified port to connect to the remote server |
| -u, --user=username | Username to connect to the server |
| -p, --password=password | Password to connect to the server |
| -r, --result-file=file | Places the output in the specified file |
| -j, --position=N | Starts reading the binary log at position N |
| -t, --table=name | Gets the raw table dump using COM_TABLE_DUMB |
| -V, --version | Displays the version and exits |

## Backing Up and Restoring InnoDB Tables

It is currently impossible to do a standard online backup of an InnoDB table while the server is running with the standard distribution. This will be changing soon, though, so keep an eye on the MySQL documentation.

There is a paid-for tool that allows online backup of InnoDB tables, called InnoDB HotBackup. Go to www.innodb.com/hotbackup.html for details.

Ordinarily, to make a backup, you need to either take the database server down or shut out access from clients. There are two main ways to back up, and for critical data you should use both methods. One is to use mysqldump (the same as for MyISAM tables), with no write access permitted for the duration of the backup. This creates a text file with the SQL statements needed to restore the tables. The second is to make copies of the binary database files. To do this, you need to shut down the database without any errors and then copy the data files, InnoDB log files, configuration file (my.cnf or my.ini file), and the definition files (.frm) to a safe place:

```
% mysqladmin shutdown
% ls -l
total 76145
drwx------  2 mysql     mysql         2048 Jun  1 21:01 firstdb
-rw-rw----  1 mysql     mysql        25088 May  4 20:08 ib_arch_log_0000000000
-rw-rw----  1 mysql     mysql      5242880 Jun  1 21:04 ib_logfile0
-rw-rw----  1 mysql     mysql      5242880 May  4 20:08 ib_logfile1
-rw-rw----  1 mysql     mysql     67108864 Jun  1 21:04 ibdata1
drwxrwx---  2 mysql     mysql         1024 May  4 20:07 mysql
drwxrwx---  2 mysql     mysql         1024 Dec 23 17:44 test
-rw-rw----  1 mysql     mysql           98 May 19 15:03 test-bin.001
-rw-rw----  1 mysql     mysql        30310 Jun  1 21:04 test-bin.002
-rw-rw----  1 mysql     mysql           30 May 19 15:09 test-bin.index
-rw-r--r--  1 mysql     mysql         7292 Jun  1 21:04 test.dummymysql.co.za.err
```

You should copy all the files from the data directory starting with ib, as these are the InnoDB logs and data. For instance:

```
% cd /usr/local/mysql/data/
% cp ib*/db_backups/
```

Now copy the configuration files (remember to copy them all if you have more than one):

```
% cp /etc/my.cnf /db_backups/
```

Then copy the definition files, in this case innotest inside the firstdb directory (all definition files, as well as MySQL data and index files, exist inside a directory with the same name as the database):

```
% cp firstdb/innotest.frm /db_backups/
```

Now, let's restart the server in order so that a malicious user can destroy the data:

```
% mysqld-max
% Starting mysqld daemon with databases from /usr/local/mysql/data
% mysql firstdb
mysql> TRUNCATE innotest;
Query OK, 11 rows affected (0.00 sec)
```

All the data has been deleted. Your phone will soon start ringing, and it's time to restore the backup. Once again you need to bring down the server to prevent interference:

```
% mysqladmin shutdown
020601 21:20:34  mysqld ended
```

```
% cp /db_backups/ib* /usr/local/mysql/data/
cp: overwrite '/usr/local/mysql/data/ib_arch_log_0000000000'? y
cp: overwrite '/usr/local/mysql/data/ib_logfile0'? y
cp: overwrite '/usr/local/mysql/data/ib_logfile1'? y
cp: overwrite '/usr/local/mysql/data/ibdata1'? y
```

There's no need in this case to restore the configuration or definition files, as these have remained unscathed. In the case of hardware failure, you would have to restore these as well:

```
% mysqld-max
% Starting mysqld daemon with databases from /usr/local/mysql/data
% mysql firstdb
mysql> SELECT * FROM innotest;
+------+------+
|  f1  |  f2  |
+------+------+
|    1 | NULL |
|    2 | NULL |
|    3 | NULL |
|    4 | NULL |
|    5 | NULL |
|    6 | NULL |
|    7 | NULL |
|    8 | NULL |
|    9 | NULL |
|   10 | NULL |
+------+------+
10 rows in set (0.12 sec)
```

The data has been successfully restored.

In the case of a server crash to restore InnoDB data you simply need to restart the server. If general logging and log archiving are on (which is recommended), the InnoDB tables will automatically restore themselves from the MySQL logs (the MySQL logs are the "ordinary" logs, not the InnoDB logs). Any uncommitted transactions present at the time of the crash will be rolled back. The output will look similar to this:

```
InnoDB: Database was not shut down normally.
InnoDB: Starting recovery from log files...
InnoDB: Starting log scan based on checkpoint at
InnoDB: log sequence number 0 24785115
InnoDB: Doing recovery: scanned up to log sequence number 0 24850631
InnoDB: Doing recovery: scanned up to log sequence number 0 24916167
InnoDB: 1 uncommitted transaction(s) which must be rolled back
InnoDB: Starting rollback of uncommitted transactions
InnoDB: Rolling back trx no 982
InnoDB: Rolling back of trx no 98 completed
InnoDB: Rollback of uncommitted transactions completed
```

```
InnoDB: Starting an apply batch of log records to the database...
InnoDB: Apply batch completed
InnoDB: Started
mysqld: ready for connections
```

*TIP   InnoDB files are not as portable as MyISAM files. They can only be used on other platforms if that machine has the same floating-point number format as the machine on which they were generated. This means, for example, you can move the files between Intel x86 machines, no matter what operating systems you're using.*

## Replication as a Means of Backup

Replication is another means of keeping a backup (see Chapter 12, "Database Replication"). It protects against hardware failures on one of the replicated databases, but not against user stupidity or maliciousness! If a user deletes a number of records, this process will then be replicated onto the other replicated servers, making replication useless as a reliable form of backup. If you do replicate, you may be able to worry less about hardware failure, but you still need to make use of another form of backup.

## Summary

Backups are a vital part of any MySQL administrator's toolbox. There are a number of methods to use:

◆ The BACKUP statement creates a copy of the definition and data files of a MyISAM table. The RESTORE statement restores the data.

◆ Directly copying the files. You need to do your own locking. Returning the data files to the data directory restores the data.

◆ mysqldump, which creates a text file containing the SQL statements needed to regenerate the tables. Using the file as input to the MySQL daemon restores the data.

◆ Using SELECT INTO statements create a text file that can be used to restore the data with the LOAD DATA command or the mysqlimport utility.

◆ Using the mysqlhotcopy utility. This is a Perl script that copies the data files to another directory. Returning the data files to the data directory restores the data.

◆ Replication, which backs up onto another machine, but also replicates data loss across machines if it's caused by SQL statements.

The binary update log, if enabled, keeps a record of all changes to the database tables. The mysqlbinlog utility can be used to view the contents of the log or be used to restore updates to the database made because of a backup. InnoDB tables are not in stored in files, like MyISAM tables, and so they require extra care. They also have their own logging mechanism.

# Chapter 12

# Database Replication

MySQL HAS A USEFUL feature called *replication*, which is where one or more databases from a server (called the *master*) are automatically mirrored onto one or more other servers (called *slaves*). Replication is useful as a backup strategy and a performance-tuning technique. This chapter explains how replication works and shows you how to set up and configure it.

Featured in this chapter:

- ◆ Setting up replication
- ◆ Configuring slave and master files
- ◆ Understanding slave and master SQL statements

## Understanding Replication

Replication works as follows: The slave starts with an exact copy of the data on the master. Binary logging is then enabled on the master, and the slave connects to the master periodically and views the binary log to see what changes have been made since the last time it connected. The slave will then automatically repeat these statements on its server. The `master.info` file on the slave allows it to keep track of which point it is at on the master binary log. The relation between the master binary log and the slave `master.info` file is important; if these two fall out of sync, the data may no longer be identical on both servers. Replication can be useful as a form of backup (against disk error, not human error) and also to speed up performance. It is a practical way of running multiple databases, particularly in an environment where `SELECT` statements far outnumber `INSERT` or `UPDATE` statements. (The slaves can then be optimized entirely for `SELECT` statements, and the master can handle the `INSERT` and `UPDATE` statements.)

Replication is not a solution to all performance problems, though. Updates still need to be repeated on the slave, and although they are done more optimally, if your MyISAM tables are performing too many updates and becoming locked too frequently, then converting them to InnoDB may be a better solution than hoping replication will solve the problem. Also, there will be a lag between the updates being replicated on the slaves, the length of which is dependent upon your network capacity and the database servers themselves. So, it is not possible for your application to simply assume it can use the master or a slave as a database server. A record on the master may not immediately appear on the slave, which could cause problems for an application.

Replication is normally performed in a hierarchical manner (as shown in Figures 12.1 and 12.2), but you can set up circular structures (as shown in Figures 12.3 and 12.4). Your client code needs to make sure there are no conflicts, though; otherwise, replication can easily fail because of data irregularities, so Figures 12.3 and 12.4 are much less common structures.

**FIGURE 12.1**

One master, one slave

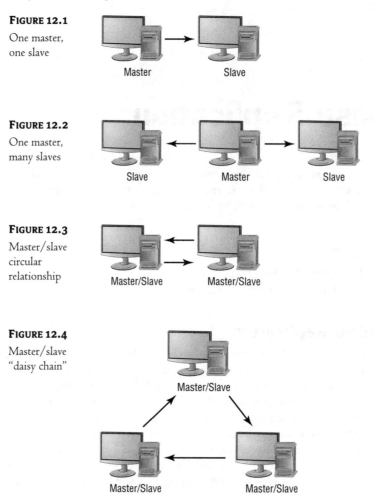

**FIGURE 12.2**

One master, many slaves

**FIGURE 12.3**

Master/slave circular relationship

**FIGURE 12.4**

Master/slave "daisy chain"

There is no need for the connection to be continuous. If the link is broken for whatever reason, the slave will keep trying to reconnect and will start updating from where it left off as soon as the link is restored.

## Setting Up Replication

A number of scenarios exist for setting up a master and slave relationship. You'll see some of these in the examples later in this chapter. The steps that follow are the basic ones to get replication started.

Perform the following steps on the master:

**1.** Set up a replication user, with the REPLICATION SLAVE permission:

```
GRANT REPLICATION_SLAVE ON *.* TO replication_user IDENTIFIED BY
  'replication_password';
```

**2.** Make a copy of the tables and data. If the database has been used a while and binary logging is already in place (see Chapter 10, "Basic Administration," for details on binary logging), take note of the offset immediately after the backup. (See the "Replication Commands" section later in the chapter for more information.) The LOAD DATA FROM MASTER operation on the slave can take the place of this step. LOAD DATA FROM MASTER currently only works with MyISAM tables, and is best used with small datasets or with situations where data on the master can be locked for the duration of the operation. Version 4.1 should solve some of these deficiencies.

**3.** Add the code below to the configuration file (my.cnf or my.ini). log-bin indicates that the master will use binary update logging, and server-id is a unique number to differentiate each of the master and slave machines. By convention, the master is usually set to 1, and the slaves from 2 upward:

```
[mysqld]
log-bin
server-id=1
```

Perform the following steps on the slave/s:

**1.** Add the following to the configuration file (my.cnf or my.ini). The master_hostname is the hostname of the master, the master_user and master_password values are the username and password, respectively, set up on the master for replication (with the replication slave privilege). The master_TCP/IP_port is the port number the master listens on (which is only needed if the port is nonstandard), and the unique number is a number starting from 2 up to 2^32-1:

```
[mysqld]
master-host=master_hostname
master-user=replication_user
master-password=replication_password
master-port=master_TCP/IP_port
server-id=unique_number
```

**2.** Copy the data taken from the master onto the slave (if you're not running LOAD DATA FROM MASTER).

**3.** Start the slave server.

**4.** If you haven't yet got the data, use LOAD DATA FROM MASTER to access it.

Now, with both servers running, you should start to see replication occurring.

## Replication Options

Table 12.1 describes the various replication options available to the master, and Table 12.2 describes the various replication options available to the slave.

**TABLE 12.1:** MASTER CONFIGURATION FILE OPTIONS

| OPTION | DESCRIPTION |
| --- | --- |
| log-bin=filename | Activates binary logging. This option must be present on the master for replication to occur. The filename is optional. To clear the log, run RESET MASTER, and do not forget to run RESET SLAVE on all slaves. By default the binary log will be called hostname.xxx, with xxx being a number starting at 001 and incrementing by one each time the log is rotated. |
| log-bin-index=filename | Specifies the name of the binary log index file (which lists the binary log files in order, so the slave will always know the active one). The default is hostname.index. |
| sql-bin-update-same | If set, setting SQL_LOG_BIN to either 1 or 0 will automatically set SQL_LOG_UPDATE to the same value, and vice versa. SQL_LOG_UPDATE should not be needed any more, so this option is unlikely to be used. |
| binlog-do-db=database_name | Only logs updates to the binary log from the database_name database. All other databases are ignored. You can restrict databases from the slave as well. |
| binlog-ignore-db=database_name | Logs all updates to the binary log except from the database_name database. You can also set the database to ignore on the slave. |

**TABLE 12.2:** SLAVE CONFIGURATION FILE OPTIONS

| OPTION | DESCRIPTION |
| --- | --- |
| master-host=host | Specifies the hostname or IP address of the master to which to connect. Has to be set for replication to begin. Once replication has begun, the master.info data will determine this, and you'll need to use a CHANGE MASTER TO statement to change it. |
| master-user=username | Specifies the username the slave will connect to the master with. The user should have REPLICATION SLAVE permission on the master. Defaults to test. Once replication has begun, the master.info data will determine this, and you'll need to use a CHANGE MASTER TO statement to change it. |
| master-password=password | Specifies the password with which the slave will connect to the master. Defaults to an empty string. Once replication has begun, the master.info data will determine this, and you'll need to use a CHANGE MASTER TO statement to change it. |
| master-port=portnumber | Specifies the port the master listens on (defaults to the value of MYSQL_PORT, usually 3306). Once replication has begun, the master.info data will determine this, and you'll need to use a CHANGE MASTER TO statement to change it. |

*Continued on next page*

**TABLE 12.2:** SLAVE CONFIGURATION FILE OPTIONS *(continued)*

| OPTION | DESCRIPTION |
|---|---|
| `master-connect-retry= seconds` | If the connection between the master and slave goes down, MySQL will wait this many seconds before trying to reconnect (default 60). |
| `master-ssl` | Specifies that replication take place using Secure Sockets Layer (SSL). |
| `master-ssl-key=key_name` | If SSL is set to be used (the `master-ssl` option), this specifies the master SSL key filename. |
| `master-ssl-cert= certificate_name` | If SSL is set to be used (the `master-ssl` option), this specifies the master SSL certificate name. |
| `master-info-file=filename` | Specifies the master information file (default `master.info` in the data directory), which keeps track of the point in the binary logs that the slave is at in the replication process. |
| `report-host` | Specifies the hostname or IP address that the slave will announce itself as to the master (for use during a SHOW SLAVE HOSTS statement). Not set by default. Other methods of determining the host are not reliable; hence the need for this option. |
| `report-port` | Specifies the port for connecting to the slave reported to the master. You should only need this if the slave is on a nondefault port, or connection takes place in a nonstandard way. |
| `replicate-do-table= db_name.table_name` | Ensures that the slave only replicates the specified table name, from the specified database. You can use this option multiple times to replicate multiple tables. |
| `replicate-ignore-table= db_name.table_name` | Tells the slave not to replicate a statement that updates the specified table (even if other tables are also updated by the same statement). You can specify multiple instances of this option. |
| `replicate-wild-do-table= db_name.table_name` | Tells the slave to replicate statements only where they match the specified table (similar to the `replicate_do_table` option), but where the match takes into account wildcards. For example, where the table name is db%.tb%, the match will apply to any database beginning with the letters *db*, and any table beginning with the letters *tb*. |
| `replicate-wild-ignore- table=db_name.table_name` | Tells the slave not to replicate a statement that updates the specified table, even if other tables are also updated by the same statement, similar to the `replicate-ignore-table` option, except that wildcards are taken into account. For example, where the table name is db%.tb% replication will not be performed where the database begins with the letters *db*, and the table begins with the letters *tb*). You can specify multiple instances of this option. |
| `replicate-ignore-db= database_name` | Tells the slave not to replicate any statement when the current database is database_name. You can use this option multiple times to specify multiple databases to ignore. |

*Continued on next page*

**TABLE 12.2:** SLAVE CONFIGURATION FILE OPTIONS *(continued)*

| OPTION | DESCRIPTION |
| --- | --- |
| `replicate-do-db=database_name` | Tells the slave thread to replicate a statement only when the database is database_name. You can use this option multiple times to replicate multiple databases. |
| `log-slave-updates` | Tells the slave to log replicated updates to the binary log. Not set by default. If you plan to use the slave as a master to another slave, you'll need to set this option. |
| `replicate-rewrite-db=master_database->slave_database` | If the database on your slave has a different name to that on the master, you'll need to map the relationship with this option. |
| `slave-skip-errors= [err_code1,err_code2,... | all]` | When replication encounters an error, it will stop (since an error usually means the data is inconsistent, and manual steps are needed). This option tells MySQL to continue replicating if the error is one of the listed errors. Error codes are supplied as a number (the same number given in the error log) and separated by a comma. You can also use the `all` option to cater for any possible errors. You should not normally use this option, as mistaken use of it can lead to your data getting out of sync with the master, with no realistic way of getting it back in sync besides recopying the master data. |
| `skip-slave-start` | With this option set, replication will not begin when the server starts. You can manually begin it with the SLAVE START command. |
| `slave_compressed_protocol=#` | If set to 1, then MySQL uses compression to transfer the data between slave and master if both servers support this. |
| `slave_net_timeout=#` | Determines the number of seconds to wait for more data from the master before a read is aborted. |

## Replication Commands

You should be familiar with both the slave and the master replication commands. The following are the slave replication commands:

♦ SLAVE START and SLAVE STOP start and stop the replication process, respectively.

♦ SHOW SLAVE STATUS returns information about the slave, including the important fact whether the slave is connected to the master (Slave_IO_Running), replication is running (Slave_SQL_Running), what binary log is being used (Master_Log_File and Relay_Master_Log_File), and what position is current in the binary log (Read_Master_Log_Pos and Exec_master_log_pos).

♦ The CHANGE MASTER TO statement is an important one for keeping the replication in sync or starting it off at the right place. The MASTER_LOG_FILE refers to the binary log on the master from which the slave must start replicating, and the MASTER_LOG_POS is the position in that file. (You'll see examples of this later in the chapter.) This statement is also used when the master fails, and you need to change the master to which the slave connects. The full set of CHANGE MASTER TO options is:

```
CHANGE MASTER TO MASTER_HOST = 'master_hostname',
    MASTER_USER='replication_username',
    MASTER_PASSWORD=''replication_user_password',
    MASTER_PORT='master_port',
    MASTER_LOG_FILE='master_binary_logfile',
    MASTER_LOG_POS='master_binary_log_position'
```

◆ The RESET SLAVE statement causes the slave to forget its position in the master logs.

◆ LOAD DATA FROM MASTER takes a copy of the data on the master and brings it onto the slave. Currently, this is not useful for large datasets or for situations where the master cannot be unavailable for long, as it acquires a global read lock when copying the data. It also updates the value of MASTER_LOG_FILE and MASTER_LOG_POS. Currently it only works with MyISAM tables. This statement is likely to become the standard way of preparing the slave in future, so be sure to read your latest documentation.

◆ The SET GLOBAL SQL_SLAVE_SKIP_COUNTER=n statement causes the slave to skip the next n statements from the master's binary log.

The following are the master replication commands:

◆ The SET SQL_LOG_BIN = n statement either deactivates binary update logging (if set to 0) or reactivates it (if set to 1). You need the SUPER privilege to run this statement.

◆ RESET MASTER removes all binary logs and starts numbering again at 001.

◆ SHOW MASTER STATUS shows the current binary log, the position in the binary log, and whether any databases are being ignored for binary logging.

◆ PURGE MASTER LOGS TO binary_log_filename removes all logs prior to the specified binary log. Be sure that no slaves still need the binary logs you're about to remove. See the example later in the "Removing Old Binary Logs from the Master and Starting" section.

◆ SHOW MASTER LOGS shows the list of binary log files available. You'd usually use this before purging the logs.

◆ SHOW SLAVE HOSTS returns a list of slaves registered with the master (note that by default a slave does not register itself but requires the report-host configuration option to be set).

◆ The SHOW BINLOG EVENTS [ IN 'logname' ] [ FROM pos ] [ LIMIT [offset,] rows ] statement reads statements from the binary logs.

## Replication Complexities

The following are a few crucial issues you need to keep in mind when setting up and configuring replication:

◆ FLUSH statements are not replicated, which will affect you if you update the permission tables directly on the master and then use FLUSH to activate the changes. The changes will not take effect on the slaves until you run a FLUSH statement there as well.

- Make sure your masters and slaves have the same character set.

- The RAND() function does not work properly when passed a random expression as an argument. You can safely use something like UNIX_TIMESTAMP().

- Queries that update data and use user variables are not replicated safely (although this is set to change. Check your latest documentation).

- Replication usually works with different MySQL versions, even between version 3.23.*x* and version 4.0.*x*, but there have been exceptions (none of 4.0.0, 4.0.1, or 4.0.2 worked with each other), so check the latest documentation to be sure. Instead, use the latest stable versions throughout if possible.

## Replicating One Database

For this example, you're going to create a new database, with a table, and replicate this onto another server. You need to have two servers running MySQL (ideally the same version), and the two servers need to be able to see each other to test this example.

First, on the master create a database called *replication_db*, a table called *replication_table*, and add some data to this table, as follows:

```
mysql> CREATE DATABASE replication_db;
Query OK, 1 row affected (0.01 sec)
mysql> USE replication_db;
Database changed
mysql> CREATE TABLE replication_table(f1 INT,f2 VARCHAR(20));
Query OK, 0 rows affected (0.03 sec)
mysql> INSERT INTO replication_table (f1,f2) VALUES(1,'first');
Query OK, 1 row affected (0.03 sec)
```

Now grant permission to a slave to replicate. The slave user will be *replication_user*, with a password of *replication_pwd*:

```
mysql> GRANT REPLICATION SLAVE ON *.* TO replication_user IDENTIFIED BY
  'replication_pwd';
```

On the slave, shut the server down, and add the code below to the configuration file (my.cfg or my.ini). Replace the master-host setting with the IP of your slave server. The server_id can be any number, as long as it's not the same as the server_id on the master:

```
master-host      = 192.168.4.100
master-user      = replication_user
master_password = replication_pwd
server-id        = 3
replicate-do-db = replication_db
```

On the slave create the replication_db database, and copy the replication_table data from the master to the slave (being MyISAM tables, the data will be in the replication_db directory). See Chapter 11, "Database Backups," if you are not sure how to do this. Make sure when you copy the files to the slave that the permissions are correct (in Unix, **chown mysql.mysql \***, **chmod 700 \***). Also, be aware that if your master server has already been using binary logging, you'll need to reset the binary log with **RESET MASTER** so that the slave can start updating from the beginning of the first binary log. Now start the slave server and connect. Once you've connected, check the slave status to see if replication has begun properly:

```
mysql> SHOW SLAVE STATUS;
+---------------+------------------+-------------+---------------+------
---------------+------------------+-------------+-----------------------+------
----------+------------------+-----------------+------------------
--+-----------------+-------------------+------------+------------+---
-----------+--------------------+----------------+
| Master_Host   | Master_User      | Master_Port | Connect_retry |
Master_Log_File    | Read_Master_Log_Pos | Relay_Log_File          |
Relay_Log_Pos | Relay_Master_Log_File | Slave_IO_Running |
Slave_SQL_Running | Replicate_do_db | Replicate_ignore_db | Last_errno
| Last_error | Skip_counter | Exec_master_log_pos | Relay_log_space |
+---------------+------------------+-------------+---------------+------
---------------+------------------+-------------+-----------------------+------
----------+------------------+-----------------+------------------
--+-----------------+-------------------+------------+------------+---
-----------+--------------------+----------------+
| 192.168.4.100 | replication_user | 3306        | 60            |
g-bin.001 | 79                      | s-bin.002 |
124            | g-bin.001    | Yes                  | Yes
| replication_db |                    | 0           |              | 0
| 79                       | 132          |
+---------------+------------------+-------------+---------------+------
---------------+------------------+-------------+-----------------------+------
----------+------------------+-----------------+------------------
--+-----------------+-------------------+------------+------------+---
-----------+--------------------+----------------+
1 row in set (0.00 sec)
mysql> INSERT INTO replication_table (f1,f2) VALUES(2,'second');
Query OK, 1 row affected (0.06 sec)
mysql> SELECT * FROM replication_table;
+------+--------+
| f1   | f2     |
+------+--------+
|    1 | first  |
|    2 | second |
+------+--------+
2 rows in set (0.00 sec)

mysql> SHOW SLAVE STATUS;
+---------------+------------------+-------------+---------------+------
---------------+------------------+-------------+-----------------------+------
----------+------------------+-----------------+------------------
--+-----------------+-------------------+------------+------------+---
-----------+--------------------+----------------+
```

```
| Master_Host    | Master_User     | Master_Port | Connect_retry |
Master_Log_File    | Read_Master_Log_Pos | Relay_Log_File         |
Relay_Log_Pos | Relay_Master_Log_File | Slave_IO_Running |
Slave_SQL_Running | Replicate_do_db | Replicate_ignore_db | Last_errno
| Last_error | Skip_counter | Exec_master_log_pos | Relay_log_space |
+---------------+-------------------+-------------+---------------+-----
--------------+--------------------+-------------------------+------
---------+----------------------+-----------------+------------------
-+----------------+-------------------+-------------+------------+---
-----------+---------------------+-----------------+
| 192.168.4.100 | replication_user | 3306        | 60            |
g-bin.001 | 180                   | s-bin.002 |
 225           | g-bin.001   | Yes                 | Yes
| replication_db |                   | 0         |           | 0
| 180           | 233                 |
+---------------+-------------------+-------------+---------------+-----
--------------+--------------------+-------------------------+------
---------+----------------------+-----------------+------------------
-+----------------+-------------------+-------------+------------+---
-----------+---------------------+-----------------+
1 row in set (0.00 sec)
```

Back on the master you can run DELETE and UPDATE statements, and these will be mirrored on the slave. For example:

```
mysql> DELETE FROM replication_table WHERE f1=1;
Query OK, 1 row affected (0.34 sec)
mysql> UPDATE replication_table SET f1=1;
Query OK, 1 row affected (0.05 sec)
```

Checking on the slave, you'll see the following:

```
mysql> SELECT * FROM replication_table;
+------+--------+
| f1   | f2     |
+------+--------+
|    1 | second |
+------+--------+
1 row in set (0.01 sec)
```

The slave does not have to stay connected to the master at all times to remain in sync as long as the binary logs are correct, as the next example demonstrates. First, shut down the slave:

```
% /usr/local/mysql/bin/mysqladmin -uroot -pg00r002b shutdown
020821 17:25:37  mysqld ended
```

Then add another record to the master:

```
mysql> INSERT INTO replication_table (f1,f2) VALUES(3,'third');
Query OK, 1 row affected (0.03 sec)
```

Back on the slave, restart the server, connect to the replication_db database, and you'll see the new record has been added:

```
% bin/mysqld_safe &
[1] 1989
% /usr/local/mysql/bin/mysql -uroot -pg00r002b mysql
Welcome to the MySQL monitor.  Commands end with ; or \g.
Your MySQL connection id is 3 to server version: 4.0.2-alpha-max-log

Type 'help;' or '\h' for help. Type '\c' to clear the buffer.
mysql> SELECT * FROM replication_table;
+------+--------+
| f1   | f2     |
+------+--------+
|    3 | third  |
|    1 | second |
+------+--------+
2 rows in set (0.02 sec)
```

The master could go down as well, and the slave would keep trying to reconnect (every master-connect-retry seconds, which has a default of 60) until the master was up again.

Be careful when making changes to the binary logs, though, because this is the only thing the slave has to go on. The next example shows an example where data can get lost. First, shut down the slave:

```
% /usr/local/mysql/bin/mysqladmin -uroot -pg00r002b shutdown
020821 17:25:37  mysqld ended
```

As before, add another record to the master, but this time run the RESET MASTER statement afterward (this removes all old binary logs and starts again with binary log 1):

```
mysql> INSERT INTO replication_table (f1,f2) VALUES(4,'fourth');
Query OK, 1 row affected (0.01 sec)
mysql> RESET MASTER;
Query OK, 0 rows affected (0.03 sec)
```

Now, when you restart the slave, it will not pick up the change:

```
% bin/mysqld_safe &
[1] 1989
% /usr/local/mysql/bin/mysql -uroot -pg00r002b mysql
Welcome to the MySQL monitor.  Commands end with ; or \g.
Your MySQL connection id is 3 to server version: 4.0.2-alpha-max-log

Type 'help;' or '\h' for help. Type '\c' to clear the buffer.
```

```
mysql> SELECT * FROM replication_table;
+------+--------+
| f1   | f2     |
+------+--------+
|    3 | third  |
|    1 | second |
+------+--------+
2 rows in set (0.00 sec)
```

You can see why by looking at the slave status:

```
mysql> SHOW SLAVE STATUS;
+--------------+-------------------+-------------+----------------+-----
--------------+--------------------+-------------+----------------------+------
---------+---------------------+-------------------+-------------------
-+-------------------+--------------------+-------------+-------------+---
-----------+-------------------+------------------+
| Master_Host  | Master_User       | Master_Port | Connect_retry |
Master_Log_File    | Read_Master_Log_Pos | Relay_Log_File           |
Relay_Log_Pos | Relay_Master_Log_File | Slave_IO_Running |
Slave_SQL_Running | Replicate_do_db | Replicate_ignore_db | Last_errno
| Last_error | Skip_counter | Exec_master_log_pos | Relay_log_space |
+--------------+-------------------+-------------+----------------+-----
--------------+--------------------+-------------+----------------------+------
---------+---------------------+-------------------+-------------------
-+-------------------+--------------------+-------------+-------------+---
-----------+---------------------+------------------+
| 192.168.4.100 | replication_user | 3306         | 60             |
g-bin.001 | 443                     | s-bin.004 | 4
| g-bin.001 | Yes                   | Yes                      |
replication_db |                      | 0                |          | 0
| 443                    | 500                     |
+--------------+-------------------+-------------+----------------+-----
--------------+--------------------+-------------+----------------------+------
---------+---------------------+-------------------+-------------------
-+-------------------+--------------------+-------------+-------------+---
-----------+---------------------+------------------+
1 row in set (0.00 sec)
```

The master log is supposed to be at position 443—compare this to what the master binary log is actually at, on the master:

```
mysql> SHOW MASTER STATUS;
+-----------+----------+---------------+------------------+
| File      | Position | Binlog_do_db  | Binlog_ignore_db |
+-----------+----------+---------------+------------------+
| g-bin.001 | 79       |               |                  |
+-----------+----------+---------------+------------------+
1 row in set (0.00 sec)
```

You can bring them back into sync by resetting the slave, as follows:

```
mysql> RESET SLAVE;
Query OK, 0 rows affected (0.01 sec)
```

The slave status has now changed and will again be looking at the beginning of binary log 1, or position 79:

```
mysql> SHOW SLAVE STATUS;
```

| Master_Host | Master_User | Master_Port | Connect_retry | Master_Log_File | Read_Master_Log_Pos | Relay_Log_File | Relay_Log_Pos | Relay_Master_Log_File | Slave_IO_Running | Slave_SQL_Running | Replicate_do_db | Replicate_ignore_db | Last_errno | Last_error | Skip_counter | Exec_master_log_pos | Relay_log_space |
|---|---|---|---|---|---|---|---|---|---|---|---|---|---|---|---|---|---|
| 192.168.4.100 | replication_user | 3306 | 60 | g-bin.001 | 79 | s-bin.002 | 124 | g-bin.001 | Yes | Yes | replication_db | | 0 | | 0 | 79 | 132 |

```
1 row in set (0.00 sec)
```

Now back on the master, add the record again, and take a look at the master status, where the binary log has moved to position 180:

```
mysql> INSERT INTO replication_table (f1,f2) VALUES(4,'fourth');
Query OK, 1 row affected (0.00 sec)
mysql> SHOW MASTER STATUS;
```

| File | Position | Binlog_do_db | Binlog_ignore_db |
|---|---|---|---|
| g-bin.001 | 180 | | |

```
1 row in set (0.00 sec)
```

And the slave has once again picked up the INSERT:

```
mysql> SELECT * FROM replication_table;
+------+--------+
| f1   | f2     |
+------+--------+
|    3 | third  |
|    1 | second |
|    4 | fourth |
+------+--------+
3 rows in set (0.00 sec)
```

If you're having an astute day, you may have noticed that the record has been added twice on the master:

```
mysql> SELECT * FROM replication_table;
+------+--------+
| f1   | f2     |
+------+--------+
|    3 | third  |
|    1 | second |
|    4 | fourth |
|    4 | fourth |
+------+--------+
4 rows in set (0.00 sec)
```

This example serves as a warning that just because replication is working, there is no guarantee that the data on both servers is identical. With good design (such as adding a primary key to the table), you could have avoided this problem; but it pays to carefully monitor your slave and master statuses and be careful when working with the binary logs.

## Replicating with an Active Binary Log on the Master

This example demonstrates how to handle the situation where the master has been running for a while with binary logging activated, and you want to set up a replication. First, shut down the slave to avoid any conflicts from the previous example:

```
% /usr/local/mysql/bin/mysqladmin -uroot -pg00r002b shutdown
020821 23:40:49  mysqld ended.
```

You'll use the same table as in the previous example. On the master, delete it and reset the binary logs to start afresh before inserting some records, as follows:

```
mysql> DELETE FROM replication_table;
Query OK, 4 rows affected (0.09 sec)
mysql> RESET MASTER;
Query OK, 0 rows affected (0.02 sec)
mysql> INSERT INTO replication_table (f1,f2) VALUES(1,'first');
Query OK, 1 row affected (0.01 sec)
```

```
mysql> INSERT INTO replication_table (f1,f2) VALUES(2,'second');
Query OK, 1 row affected (0.01 sec)
```

Now copy this data to the slave, and check the offset on the master's binary log. Make sure no new data was written to the master after you copied the data but before you could check the status:

```
mysql> SHOW MASTER STATUS;
+-----------+----------+---------------+------------------+
| File      | Position | Binlog_do_db  | Binlog_ignore_db |
+-----------+----------+---------------+------------------+
| g-bin.001 | 280      |               |                  |
+-----------+----------+---------------+------------------+
1 row in set (0.00 sec)
```

Now, on the slave, perform the same options as in the previous example—that is, copy the data, set the configuration options (with the following change), delete the master.info file if it exists (it would have been created in the previous example in the data directory, as C:\mysql\data or /usr/local/mysql/data), and restart the server. The only difference is that the configuration file should contain the option:

**skip-slave-start**

You don't want to start the slave replicating until you have set it to begin at the right point. Now add some more records to the master:

```
mysql> INSERT INTO replication_table (f1,f2) VALUES(3,'third');
Query OK, 1 row affected (0.01 sec)
mysql> INSERT INTO replication_table (f1,f2) VALUES(4,'fourth');
Query OK, 1 row affected (0.01 sec)
```

Now, on the slave, you'll need to tell it to start with the correct binary log file and the correct offset. To do this, set the MASTER_LOG_FILE to g-bin.001 (or whatever was shown when you ran SHOW MASTER STATUS), and set the MASTER_LOG_POS to 280 (or whatever is applicable in your case). Once this is done, start the slave replicating and test the results.

```
mysql> CHANGE MASTER TO MASTER_LOG_FILE='g-bin.001',
  MASTER_LOG_POS=280;
Query OK, 0 rows affected (0.00 sec)
mysql> SLAVE START;
Query OK, 0 rows affected (0.00 sec)
mysql> SELECT * FROM replication_table;
+------+--------+
| f1   | f2     |
+------+--------+
|    1 | first  |
|    2 | second |
|    3 | third  |
|    4 | fourth |
+------+--------+
4 rows in set (0.01 sec)
```

## Removing Old Binary Logs from the Master and Then Starting

When using replication, removing binary logs is risky because a slave may not yet have finished with one of the logs you plan to remove.

For this example you'll need to delete the data and reset the master, to start from a clean slate, and then add some data:

```
mysql> DELETE FROM replication_table;
mysql> RESET MASTER;
mysql> INSERT INTO replication_table (f1,f2) VALUES(1,'first');
mysql> INSERT INTO replication_table (f1,f2) VALUES(2,'second');
mysql> INSERT INTO replication_table (f1,f2) VALUES(3,'third');
```

Copy this data onto a clean slave (if you've run previous examples on the slave server, make sure you delete the master.info file, and start the slave with the skip-slave-start option).

Now flush the logs on the master, simulating a server that's been running a while:

```
mysql> FLUSH LOGS;
mysql> FLUSH LOGS;
```

Now, when you look at the master status, you'll see that the server is already onto its third binary log:

```
mysql> SHOW MASTER STATUS;
+-----------+----------+---------------+------------------+
| File      | Position | Binlog_do_db  | Binlog_ignore_db |
+-----------+----------+---------------+------------------+
| g-bin.003 | 4        |               |                  |
+-----------+----------+---------------+------------------+
1 row in set (0.00 sec)
```

Now start the slave, and start it replicating from the correct point:

```
mysql> CHANGE MASTER TO MASTER_LOG_FILE='g-bin.003',MASTER_LOG_POS=4;
Query OK, 0 rows affected (0.01 sec)
mysql> SLAVE START;
Query OK, 0 rows affected (0.00 sec)
```

The slave will now start from the correct log on the master. You still have two other binary logs on the master server, taking up space, and you'll need to start maintaining the log files to ensure they don't get out of hand. You may feel tempted to delete logs one and two, but you cannot safely do this if there is still the possibility that slaves may need to make use of them.

To check this, you'll need to check the slave status for each slave. In this case, there's only one:

```
mysql> SHOW SLAVE STATUS;
+--------------+-------------------+-------------+---------------+-----
--------------+-------------------+-------------+---------------+------
---------+---------------------+----------------+----------------
-+------------------+---------------------+------------+------------+---
----------+---------------------+----------------+
```

```
| Master_Host    | Master_User      | Master_Port | Connect_retry |
Master_Log_File    | Read_Master_Log_Pos | Relay_Log_File            |
Relay_Log_Pos | Relay_Master_Log_File | Slave_IO_Running |
Slave_SQL_Running | Replicate_do_db | Replicate_ignore_db | Last_errno
| Last_error | Skip_counter | Exec_master_log_pos | Relay_log_space |
+---------------+------------------+-------------+--------------+-----
--------------+--------------------+------------------------+------
---------+--------------------+------------------+-----------------
-+----------------+--------------------+-----------+-----------+---
-----------+--------------------+----------------+
| 192.168.4.100 | replication_user | 3306        | 60            |
g-bin.003 | 4                   | s-bin.003 |
830            | g-bin.003     | Yes              | Yes
| replication_db |                  | 0          |           | 0
| 4                   | 1885            |
```

You can see that the slave is using g-bin.003 and is up-to-date (position 4). If all slaves are up-to-date, you can safely remove binary logs 1 and 2 from the master, with the PURGE MASTER LOGS statement, as follows:

```
mysql> PURGE MASTER LOGS TO "g-bin.003";
Query OK, 0 rows affected (0.00 sec)
```

If you did a listing in the data directory (or wherever you've specified the binary logs to be), you'll see that the two earlier ones have been removed. This statement will fail if an active slave is attempting to read a log you're trying to delete, giving the following error:

```
mysql> PURGE MASTER LOGS TO "g-bin.003";
ERROR:
A purgeable log is in use, will not purge
```

If slave is not connected, and you purge a binary log that has not yet been used, that slave will be unable to continue replicating. At some stage this process may be automated, but for now you'll have to check each slave manually to see its position. Let's see what would happen if you didn't check. First, stop the slave:

```
mysql> SLAVE STOP;
Query OK, 0 rows affected (0.00 sec)
```

Now, on the master, flush the logs once more, add a new record, and then purge the binary logs:

```
mysql> FLUSH LOGS;
Query OK, 0 rows affected (0.00 sec)
mysql> INSERT INTO replication_table (f1,f2) VALUES(4,'fourth');
Query OK, 1 row affected (0.00 sec)
mysql> FLUSH LOGS;
Query OK, 0 rows affected (0.00 sec)
```

```
mysql> SHOW MASTER STATUS;
+-----------+----------+--------------+------------------+
| File      | Position | Binlog_do_db | Binlog_ignore_db |
+-----------+----------+--------------+------------------+
| g-bin.005 | 4        |              |                  |
+-----------+----------+--------------+------------------+
1 row in set (0.00 sec)
mysql> PURGE MASTER LOGS TO "g-bin.005";
Query OK, 0 rows affected (0.02 sec)
```

Now, if you restart the slave, it will not replicate, as it's looking for a nonexistent binary log:

```
mysql> SLAVE START;
Query OK, 0 rows affected (0.00 sec)
```

The problem now is that the most recent INSERT statement on the master does not appear in a log anywhere because all "old" logs have been purged. If you've made a backup of the binary logs, you can easily restore it, but if not, you can manually rerun the statement and then make the slave look at the most recent log, as follows:

```
mysql> INSERT INTO replication_table (f1,f2) VALUES(4,'fourth');
Query OK, 1 row affected (0.00 sec)
mysql> CHANGE MASTER TO MASTER_LOG_FILE='g-bin.005',MASTER_LOG_POS=4;
Query OK, 0 rows affected (0.01 sec)
```

Now, if you add another record to the master:

```
mysql> INSERT INTO replication_table (f1,f2) VALUES(5,'fifth');
Query OK, 1 row affected (0.00 sec)
```

it will be smoothly replicated onto the slave:

```
mysql> SELECT * FROM replication_table;
+------+--------+
| f1   | f2     |
+------+--------+
|    1 | first  |
|    2 | second |
|    3 | third  |
|    4 | fourth |
|    5 | fifth  |
+------+--------+
5 rows in set (0.00 sec)
```

This example demonstrates that replication is not about an exact copy of the data. Rather, it's about replicating the statements from one server onto the other. This will result in an exact copy of the data, but if the master.info file or the binary logs are tampered with, MySQL will not be able to follow the commands in sequence, which may result in the data getting out of sync.

## Avoiding Too Many Updates

This example shows what can happen if you do not start the slave at the correct point in the master binary log.

Starting with a clean master, add a few records, and take note of the binary log details immediately after making the copy:

```
mysql> DELETE FROM replication_table;
mysql> RESET MASTER;
mysql> INSERT INTO replication_table (f1,f2) VALUES(1,'first');
mysql> INSERT INTO replication_table (f1,f2) VALUES(2,'second');
mysql> SHOW MASTER STATUS;
+-----------+----------+--------------+------------------+
| File      | Position | Binlog_do_db | Binlog_ignore_db |
+-----------+----------+--------------+------------------+
| g-bin.001 | 280      |              |                  |
+-----------+----------+--------------+------------------+
1 row in set (0.00 sec)
```

Copy the data to the slave, and start the slave. The slave should be clean (no `master.info` file and no data in the replication_db database) and contain what looks like an ordinary set of options in its configuration file, as follows:

```
master-host      = 192.168.4.100
master-user      = replication_user
master_password  = replication_pwd
server-id        = 3
replicate-do-db  = replication_db
```

Start the slave server and take a look at the slave status to see that replication has started correctly:

```
mysql> SHOW SLAVE STATUS;
+---------------+------------------+-------------+---------------+-----
--------------+------------------+-------------+---------------+------
---------+---------------------+------------------+-----------------
-+---------------+---------------------+-----------+-----------+---
-----------+---------------------+----------------+
| Master_Host   | Master_User      | Master_Port | Connect_retry |
Master_Log_File    | Read_Master_Log_Pos | Relay_Log_File          |
Relay_Log_Pos | Relay_Master_Log_File | Slave_IO_Running |
Slave_SQL_Running | Replicate_do_db | Replicate_ignore_db | Last_errno
| Last_error | Skip_counter | Exec_master_log_pos | Relay_log_space |
+---------------+------------------+-------------+---------------+-----
--------------+------------------+-------------+---------------+------
---------+---------------------+------------------+-----------------
-+---------------+---------------------+-----------+-----------+---
-----------+---------------------+----------------+
```

```
| 192.168.4.100 | replication_user | 3306         | 60               |
g-bin.001 | 280                    | s-bin.003 |
325             | g-bin.001    | Yes                | Yes
| replication_db |                             | 0        |           | 0
| 280                     | 329              |
  +--------------+------------------+-------------+--------------+-----
  --------------+--------------------+------------------------+------
  ---------+--------------------+------------------+------------------
  -+---------------+--------------------+------------+-----------+---
  -----------+--------------------+-----------------+
1 row in set (0.00 sec)
```

Everything seems to be working smoothly. Replication has begun, and the slave is at the same point as the master, that is binary log `g-bin.001` and position 280. However, when you examine the data on the slave, you're in for a nasty surprise:

```
mysql> SELECT * FROM replication_table;
+------+--------+
| f1   | f2     |
+------+--------+
|    1 | first  |
|    2 | second |
|    1 | first  |
|    2 | second |
+------+--------+
4 rows in set (0.00 sec)
```

The problem is that the slave started replicating from the beginning of the first binary log, which means it repeated the two INSERT statements even though the copy of the data was made after that. There are two solutions. You can either run RESET MASTER on the master immediately after making the copy, or run a CHANGE MASTER TO... statement on the slave before starting to replicate to set it to begin at the right point, as you did in the "Replicating with an Active Binary Log on the Master" section (which entails starting the server with the `skip-slave-start` option).

## Avoiding Key Errors

This example shows what happens when data is updated onto the slave, which causes a key error. This error is commonly caused when you have the master and slave replicating in a circular manner or you make updates directly to a slave.

For this, you're going to add a primary key to the *replication_table* table. You can modify the existing table, as follows:

```
mysql> ALTER TABLE replication_table MODIFY f1 INT NOT NULL,ADD PRIMARY KEY(f1);
Query OK, 0 rows affected (0.36 sec)
```

Or you can create the table anew, as follows:

```
mysql> CREATE TABLE replication_table(f1 INT NOT NULL,f2 VARCHAR(20),
  PRIMARY KEY(f1));
Query OK, 0 rows affected (0.03 sec)
```

Add a few records onto the master and reset the master, so you do not repeat the error of the previous example:

```
mysql> INSERT INTO replication_table (f1,f2) VALUES(1,'first');
mysql> INSERT INTO replication_table (f1,f2) VALUES(2,'second');
mysql> RESET MASTER;
```

Copy the data to the slave and start the server replicating. Add a new record on the master:

```
mysql> INSERT INTO replication_table (f1,f2) VALUES(3,'third');
Query OK, 1 row affected (0.01 sec)
```

The data on the slave should now appear as follows:

```
mysql> SELECT * FROM replication_table;
+----+--------+
| f1 | f2     |
+----+--------+
|  1 | first  |
|  2 | second |
|  3 | third  |
+----+--------+
3 rows in set (0.00 sec)
```

So far everything is running smoothly. The problem comes if you add a record on the slave and then add the same record on the master. In this example, you purposely set the key to be the same, but it's most likely to happen when using AUTO_INCREMENT fields. Insert the following record first on the slave, then the master:

```
mysql> INSERT INTO replication_table (f1,f2) VALUES(4,'fourth');
Query OK, 1 row affected (0.01 sec)
```

Although if you checked the data on both servers they'd be identical, there's actually an error on the slave, as it has attempted to INSERT the record twice. Unless you used the risky slave-skip-errors option in the configuration file, replication would now stop, and the slave will report the erroneous query, as follows:

```
mysql> SHOW SLAVE STATUS;
+---------------+-----------------+------------+--------------+-----
---------------+--------------------+------------------------+------
---------+----------------------------+-----------------+------------------
-+---------------+--------------------+------------+----------------
--------------------------------------------------------------------
------------------+--------------+--------------------+--------------
---+
```

```
| Master_Host   | Master_User     | Master_Port | Connect_retry |
Master_Log_File    | Read_Master_Log_Pos | Relay_Log_File       |
Relay_Log_Pos | Relay_Master_Log_File | Slave_IO_Running |
Slave_SQL_Running | Replicate_do_db | Replicate_ignore_db | Last_errno
| Last_error
| Skip_counter | Exec_master_log_pos | Relay_log_space |
+---------------+------------------+-------------+---------------+-----
---------------+--------------------+-------------------------+------
---------+--------------------+-----------------+-------------------
-+---------------+--------------------+-------------+-----------------
-------------------------------------------------------------------
--------------------+-------------+--------------------+-------------
---+
| 192.168.4.100 | replication_user | 3306        | 60            |
g-bin.001 | 279                   | s-bin.002 |
224          | g-bin.001   | Yes         | No
| replication_db |                   | 1062        | error 'Duplicate
entry '4' for key 1' on query 'INSERT INTO replication_table(f1,f2)
values(4,'fourth')' | 0           | 179               | 332
|
+---------------+------------------+-------------+---------------+-----
---------------+--------------------+-------------------------+------
---------+--------------------+-------------------+-------------
-------+---------------+--------------------+-------------+----------
-------------------------------------------------------------------
--------------------+-------------+--------------------+--------
---------+
1 row in set (0.00 sec)
```

The error is clearly reported so that you can investigate the cause of the error and take action. In this case, the error was that the statement was repeated on the slave when it shouldn't have been. You can get the slave replicating correctly once more by telling it to skip the next command in the master binary log and continue from there. You use the SET SQL_SLAVE_SKIP_COUNTER command for this. Once this is run, you can start the slave (you can only tell a slave to skip when replication is stopped), and it will continue as before, as follows:

```
mysql> SET GLOBAL SQL_SLAVE_SKIP_COUNTER=1;
Query OK, 0 rows affected (0.00 sec)
mysql> SLAVE START;
Query OK, 0 rows affected (0.00 sec)
mysql> SHOW SLAVE STATUS;
+---------------+------------------+-------------+---------------+-----
---------------+--------------------+-------------------------+------
---------+--------------------+-------------------+-------------------
-+---------------+--------------------+-------------+-----------+---
-----------+--------------------+---------------+
```

```
| Master_Host   | Master_User       | Master_Port | Connect_retry |
Master_Log_File    | Read_Master_Log_Pos | Relay_Log_File         |
Relay_Log_Pos | Relay_Master_Log_File | Slave_IO_Running       |
Slave_SQL_Running | Replicate_do_db | Replicate_ignore_db | Last_errno
| Last_error | Skip_counter | Exec_master_log_pos | Relay_log_space |
+--------------+------------------+-------------+--------------+-----
--------------+--------------------+-------------------------+------
---------+--------------------+-----------------+--------------------
-+----------------+--------------------+------------+------------+---
-----------+--------------------+-----------------+
| 192.168.4.100 | replication_user | 3306        | 60            |
g-bin.001 | 378                   | s-bin.002 |
423            | g-bin.001   | Yes               | Yes
| replication_db |                  | 0           |            | 0
| 378            | 431              |
+--------------+------------------+-------------+--------------+-----
--------------+--------------------+-------------------------+------
---------+--------------------+-----------------+--------------------
-+----------------+--------------------+------------+------------+---
-----------+--------------------+-----------------+
1 row in set (0.00 sec)
```

Insert a record on the master:

```
mysql> INSERT INTO replication_table(f1,f2) values(5,'fifth');
Query OK, 1 row affected (0.00 sec)
```

Once again it will be replicated on the slave:

```
mysql> SELECT * FROM replication_table;
+----+--------+
| f1 | f2     |
+----+--------+
|  1 | first  |
|  2 | second |
|  3 | third  |
|  4 | fourth |
|  5 | fifth  |
+----+--------+
5 rows in set (0.00 sec)
```

# Summary

Replication is a useful feature that allows you to keep an exact copy of data from one server on another server. The master database writes to the binary log, and any number of slave servers connect to the master, read the binary update log, and replicate these statements on their servers.

Replication is useful as a form of backup and also to improve performance.

The relationship between the binary log on the master and the master.info file on the slave is the key to keeping replication in sync. If the master binary logs are removed before the slaves have used them, replication will fail.

# Chapter 13

# Configuring and Optimizing MySQL

YOU CAN ONLY REALLY claim to understand MySQL if you grasp the intricacies of the mysqld variables and how they impact MySQL's performance. This chapter shows you how to configure and optimize MySQL by explaining how to set the variables and what to look for if you need a boost in performance.

Featured in this chapter:

- ◆ The mysqld options and variables
- ◆ A detailed look optimizing the `table_cache`, `key_buffer_size`, `delayed_queue`, `back_log`, and `sort_buffer` variables.
- ◆ Handling more connections
- ◆ Changing the variables without restarting the server.
- ◆ Configuring InnoDB tables
- ◆ Making hardware improvements
- ◆ Running benchmarks
- ◆ Running MySQL in ANSI mode
- ◆ Using different languages and character sets

## Optimizing the mysqld Variables

To look at what the existing values for the mysqld variables are, you can use mysqladmin from the command line:

```
% mysqladmin -uroot -pg00r002b variables;
```

or when connected to MySQL:

```
mysql> SHOW VARIABLES
```

```
+---------------------+------------------------------+
| Variable_name       | Value                        +
+---------------------+------------------------------+
| back_log            | 50                           |
| basedir             | /usr/local/mysql-max-4.0.1-  |
|                     |  alpha-pc-linux-gnu-i686     |
| bdb_cache_size      | 8388600                      |
| bdb_log_buffer_size | 32768                        |
| bdb_home            | /usr/local/mysql/data/       |
| bdb_max_lock        | 10000                        |
| bdb_logdir          |                              |
| bdb_shared_data     | OFF                          |
| bdb_tmpdir          | /tmp/                        |
| bdb_version         | Sleepycat Software: Berkeley DB |
|                     | 3.2.9a: (December 23, 2001)  |
| binlog_cache_size   | 32768                        |
| character_set       | latin1                       |
| character_sets      | latin1 big5 czech euc_kr gb2312 |
|                     |  gbk latin1_de sjis tis620 ujis |
|                     |  dec8 dos german1 hp8 koi8_ru   |
|                     |  latin2 swe7 usa7 cp1251 danish |
|                     |  hebrew win1251 estonia      |
|                     |  hungarian koi8_ukr win1251ukr |
|                     |  greek win1250 croat cp1257  |
|                     |  latin5                      |
| concurrent_insert   | ON                           |
| connect_timeout     | 5                            |
| datadir             | /usr/local/mysql/data/       |
| delay_key_write     | ON                           |
| delayed_insert_limit | 100                         |
| delayed_insert_     |                              |
|  timeout            | 300                          |
| delayed_queue_size  | 1000                         |
| flush               | OFF                          |
| flush_time          | 0                            |
| ft_min_word_len     | 4                            |
| ft_max_word_len     | 254                          |
| ft_max_word_len_for_ |                             |
|  sort               | 20                           |
| ft_boolean_syntax   | + -><()~*:""&|               |
| have_bdb            | YES                          |
| have_innodb         | YES                          |
| have_isam           | YES                          |
| have_raid           | NO                           |
| have_symlink        | YES                          |
| have_openssl        | NO                           |
| init_file           |                              |
| innodb_additional_  |                              |
|  mem_pool_size      | 1048576                      |
```

| | | |
|---|---|---|
| innodb_buffer_pool size | 8388608 | |
| innodb_data_file_path | ibdata1:64M | |
| innodb_data_home_dir | | |
| innodb_file_io_ threads | 9 | |
| innodb_force_recovery | 0 | |
| innodb_thread_ concurrency | 8 | |
| innodb_flush_log_at_ trx_commit | OFF | |
| innodb_fast_shutdown | OFF | |
| innodb_flush_method | | |
| innodb_lock_wait_ timeout | 1073741824 | |
| innodb_log_arch_dir | | |
| innodb_log_archive | OFF | |
| innodb_log_buffer_ size | 1048576 | |
| innodb_log_file_size | 5242880 | |
| innodb_log_files_in_ group | 2 | |
| innodb_log_group_ home_dir | ./ | |
| innodb_mirrored_log_ groups | 1 | |
| interactive_timeout | 28800 | |
| join_buffer_size | 131072 | |
| key_buffer_size | 16773120 | |
| language | /usr/local/mysql-max-4.0.1-alpha -pc-linux-gnu-i686/share/mysql/ english/ | |
| large_files_support | ON | |
| locked_in_memory | OFF | |
| log | ON | |
| log_update | OFF | |
| log_bin | ON | |
| log_slave_updates | OFF | |
| log_long_queries | ON | |
| long_query_time | 20 | |
| low_priority_updates | OFF | |
| lower_case_table_ names | 0 | |
| max_allowed_packet | 1047552 | |
| max_binlog_cache_size | 4294963200 | |
| max_binlog_size | 1073741824 | |
| max_connections | 100 | |
| max_connect_errors | 10 | |

```
| max_delayed_threads  | 20                            |
| max_heap_table_size  | 16777216                      |
| max_join_size        | 4294967295                    |
| max_sort_length      | 1024                          |
| max_user_connections | 0                             |
| max_tmp_tables       | 32                            |
| max_write_lock_count | 4294967295                    |
| myisam_bulk_insert_  |                               |
|   tree_size          | 8388608                       |
| myisam_max_extra_    |                               |
|   sort_file_size     | 256                           |
| myisam_max_sort_     |                               |
|   file_size          | 2047                          |
| myisam_recover_      |                               |
|   options            | OFF                           |
| myisam_sort_buffer_  |                               |
|   size               | 8388608                       |
| net_buffer_length    | 7168                          |
| net_read_timeout     | 30                            |
| net_retry_count      | 10                            |
| net_write_timeout    | 60                            |
| open_files_limit     | 0                             |
| pid_file             | /usr/local/mysql/data/host.pid |
| port                 | 3306                          |
| protocol_version     | 10                            |
| record_buffer        | 131072                        |
| record_rnd_buffer    | 131072                        |
| rpl_recovery_rank    | 0                             |
| query_buffer_size    | 0                             |
| query_cache_limit    | 1048576                       |
| query_cache_size     | 0                             |
| query_cache_startup_ |                               |
|   type               | 1                             |
| safe_show_database   | OFF                           |
| server_id            | 1                             |
| slave_net_timeout    | 3600                          |
| skip_external_locking| ON                            |
| skip_networking      | OFF                           |
| skip_show_database   | OFF                           |
| slow_launch_time     | 2                             |
| socket               | /tmp/mysql.sock               |
| sort_buffer          | 524280                        |
| sql_mode             | 0                             |
| table_cache          | 64                            |
| table_type           | MYISAM                        |
| thread_cache_size    | 0                             |
| thread_stack         | 65536                         |
| transaction_isolation| READ-COMMITTED                |
```

```
| timezone         | SAST                 |
| tmp_table_size   | 33554432             |
| tmpdir           | /tmp/                |
| version          | 4.0.1-alpha-max-log  |
| wait_timeout     | 28800                |
```

Also important when tuning is the information supplied by the server itself. You can view this from the command line with the following:

```
% mysqladmin extended-status
```

or when connected to the server:

```
mysql> SHOW STATUS
+-------------------------+----------+
| Aborted_clients         | 142      |
| Aborted_connects        | 5        |
| Bytes_received          | 9005619  |
| Bytes_sent              | 15444786 |
| Connections             | 794      |
| Created_tmp_disk_tables | 1        |
| Created_tmp_tables      | 716      |
| Created_tmp_files       | 0        |
| Delayed_insert_threads  | 0        |
| Delayed_writes          | 0        |
| Delayed_errors          | 0        |
| Flush_commands          | 1        |
| Handler_delete          | 27       |
| Handler_read_first      | 1534     |
| Handler_read_key        | 608840   |
| Handler_read_next       | 652228   |
| Handler_read_prev       | 164      |
| Handler_read_rnd        | 14143    |
| Handler_read_rnd_next   | 1133372  |
| Handler_update          | 90       |
| Handler_write           | 131624   |
| Key_blocks_used         | 6682     |
| Key_read_requests       | 2745899  |
| Key_reads               | 6026     |
| Key_write_requests      | 63925    |
| Key_writes              | 63790    |
| Max_used_connections    | 20       |
| Not_flushed_key_blocks  | 0        |
| Not_flushed_delayed_rows| 0        |
| Open_tables             | 64       |
| Open_files              | 128      |
| Open_streams            | 0        |
| Opened_tables           | 517      |
| Questions               | 118245   |
```

```
| Select_full_join        | 0       |
| Select_full_range_join  | 0       |
| Select_range            | 2300    |
| Select_range_check      | 0       |
| Select_scan             | 642     |
| Slave_running           | OFF     |
| Slave_open_temp_tables  | 0       |
| Slow_launch_threads     | 0       |
| Slow_queries            | 8       |
| Sort_merge_passes       | 0       |
| Sort_range              | 3582    |
| Sort_rows               | 16287   |
| Sort_scan               | 806     |
| Table_locks_immediate   | 82957   |
| Table_locks_waited      | 2       |
| Threads_cached          | 0       |
| Threads_created         | 793     |
| Threads_connected       | 1       |
| Threads_running         | 1       |
| Uptime                  | 1662790 |
+-------------------------+---------+
```

The list of variables and status information grows longer with each new release. Your version will probably have more than this, and you should read the latest documentation to see exactly what these extras do. A full explanation of those currently in use is given later in this chapter, in Table 13.2.

Most MySQL distributions come with four sample configuration files:

**my-huge.cnf**   For systems with more than 1GB memory that are mostly dedicated to MySQL.

**my-large.cnf**   For systems with at least 512MB memory that are mostly dedicated to MySQL.

**my-medium.cnf**   For systems with at least 32MB memory dedicated entirely to MySQL or with at least 128MB on a machine that serves multiple purposes (such as a dual web/database server).

**my-small.cnf**   For systems with less than 64MB memory where MySQL cannot take up too much of the resources.

These files can usually be found in /usr/share/doc/packages/MySQL/ (an RPM installation), /usr/local/mysql-max-4.x.x-platform-operating-system-extra/support-files/ (Unix binary installation), or C:\mysql\ (Windows).

**WARNING**   *On Windows, the* .cnf *extension can conflict with FrontPage and NetMeeting.*

As a starting point, I suggest replacing your my.cnf file (or my.ini) with one of these configurations, choosing the configuration closest to the your needs.

Choosing the right configuration for your system will get you a large step of the way toward optimality, but to achieve optimal usage requires fine-tuning the configuration for your system and usage specifics. You'll see some of the variables in the following sections.

## Optimizing *table_cache*

The `table_cache` variable is one of the most useful variables to adjust. Every time MySQL accesses a table, if there is space in the cache, that table is placed there. It's faster to access the table in memory than the table on disk. You can see whether you need to increase the value of your `table_cache` by examining the value of `open_tables` at peak times (one of the extended status values you saw with SHOW STATUS or `mysqladmin variables`). If you find that `open_tables` is at the same value as your `table_cache`, and the value of `opened_tables` (another extended status value) is increasing, you should increase the `table_cache` if you have enough memory.

NOTE *The number of open tables can be higher than the number of tables in your databases. MySQL is multithreaded, and there may be many queries running at a time, each of which may open a table.*

Look at the following three scenarios, all during peak hours.

**Scenario 1** This scenario is taken from a live server that's not particularly busy:

```
table_cache - 512
open_tables - 103
opened_tables - 1723
uptime - 4021421 (measured in seconds)
```

It looks like the `table_cache` is set too high in this case. The server has been up for a long time (if the server had just come up you wouldn't know if the `table_cache` would be reached soon or if the `opened_tables` would soon begin to increase). The number of opened tables is reasonably low, and the number of open tables is well below what it could be, considering that this is a peak time.

**Scenario 2** This scenario is taken from a development server:

```
table_cache - 64
open_tables - 64
opened_tables - 431
uptime - 1662790 (measured in seconds)
```

Here, although the `open_tables` is at its maximum, the number of `open_tables` is reasonably low, considering that the server has been up a while. There is probably not much benefit to be gained from upping the `table_cache`.

**Scenario 3** This scenario is taken from an underperforming live server:

```
table_cache - 64
open_tables - 64
opened_tables - 22423
uptime - 19538
```

The `table_cache` in this instance is set too low. The `open_tables` is at its maximum, and the number of `opened_tables` is high, even though the `uptime` is less than six hours. If your system has spare memory available, you should increase the `table_cache`.

*WARNING* *Don't blindly set the* `table_cache` *to a high value. If you do not need a high value, keep the value of the* `table_cache` *to something reasonable. If it is set too high, you may run out of file descriptors, and consequently see unreliable performance or connections being refused.*

## Optimizing *key_buffer_size*

The `key_buffer_size` affects the size of the index buffers, which in turn affects the speed of index handling, in particular index reads. The higher the value, the more of the indexes MySQL can hold in memory, which is much faster to access than from disk. A suggested rule of thumb is to set it from between a quarter to half of the available memory on your server (if your server is dedicated to MySQL). You can get a good idea how to adjust the `key_buffer_size` by comparing the `key_read_requests` and `key_reads` status values. The ratio of `key_reads` to `key_read_requests` should be as low as possible, with 1:100 being about the highest acceptable limit (1:1000 is better, 1:10 is terrible). The `key_reads` value indicates how many times the key needs to be read from disk, which is what you want to avoid by setting the key buffer to as high a value as possible.

The following scenarios examine two possibilities.

**Scenario 1**  A healthy situation:

```
key_buffer_size - 402649088 (384M)
key_read_requests - 597579931
key_reads - 56188
```

**Scenario 2**  Alarm bells ringing:

```
key_buffer_size - 16777216 (16M)
key_read_requests - 597579931
key_reads - 53832731
```

Scenario 1 reflects a healthy situation. The ratio is over 1:10000, but alarm bells should be ringing in scenario 2, where the ratio is about a worrying 1:11. As a solution, you should increase the `key_buffer_size` to as much as the memory allows. A hardware upgrade is necessary if you don't have enough memory to cater for this.

The ratio of `key_writes` to `key_write_requests` can also be a useful one to look at. It's usually close to 1 if you do mainly inserts and updates of one record at a time, but if you often insert or update large volumes of data at a time, you would want this lower. Using INSERT DELAYED statements will also reduce this ratio.

## Dealing with Too Many Connections

A common, and sometimes easily fixable, error that can occur when systems get too busy is the Too many connections error. When the number of `threads_connected` goes beyond the number of `max_connections` often, it's time to make a change. If the queries are being handled smoothly, the solution can be as simple as increasing the value of `max_connections`.

Most applications should make use of persistent connections rather than ordinary connections (for example, in PHP, using the `pconnect()` function rather than the `connect()` function). Persistent connections remain open even after the query has finished running, which, on busy servers, means that the next query does not have to take any resources to connect again. Maintaining a large number of persistent, but unused, connections is less resource intensive than rapidly connecting, disconnecting, and reconnecting in quick succession.

**NOTE** *Persistent connections cannot be used in CGI mode, and are affected by the KeepAlive settings in the Apache web server.*

This scenario examines a web server under heavy load that uses persistent connections:

```
max_connections - 250
max_used_connections - 210
threads_connected - 202
threads_running - 1
```

It may look like MySQL is wasting resources in this scenario, but in this case it's simply that the 202 `threads_connected` are persistent, based upon the number of instances of the web server, and are hardly taking up any resources. Only one thread is actually running, so the database is probably not taking much strain. If the `threads_connected` gets ever closer to the `max_connections` without any problems, you may even want to increase the `max_connections` to avoid exceeding the connections limit. You can see how close the connections have ever gotten to maximum by looking at the `max_used_connections` value. If this is close, or equal to the `max_connections`, it's certainly time to make allowances for an increase.

Personally, I've always found persistent connections to be better, though there are some reports that, because the MySQL connection overhead is much lighter than other databases (such as Oracle, where you *have* to use persistent connections in most cases), it makes little difference or even penalizes performance. The best suggestion is to test performance on your own systems.

**WARNING** *When testing, make sure to test properly under load. There are some documents on the Web with all kinds of erroneous comparisons between persistent and nonpersistent connections.*

In a system such as the previous scenario, a climbing `threads_running` value is often an indicator that the database server is not handling the load. Examining the process list can help identify the queries causing the blockage. What follows is a portion of the output from a database server just before it crashed. The number of `threads_connected` continued increasing until the server could handle it no longer and fell over. The `processlist` output helped to identify the problematic queries:

```
% mysqladmin processlist;
Id      User    Host        Db      Command Time State  Info
6464    mysql   websrv2…     news    Sleep   590
6482    mysql   websrv2…     news    Sleep   158
6486    mysql   websrv2…     news    Sleep   842
7549    mysql   websrv2…     news    Sleep   185
8126    mysql   websrv2...news      Sleep   349
9938    mysql   websrv2...news      Sleep   320
1696    mysql   websrv2...news      Sleep   100
4143    mysql   websrv2...news      Sleep   98
```

```
5071   mysql  websrv2...news    Sleep    843
5135   mysql  websrv2...news    Sleep    155
92707  mysql  zubat...  news    Sleep    530
93014  mysql  zubat...  news    Query    13  Locked  select s_id from arts
                                                     where a_id =
                                                     'E232625'

93060  mysql  zubat...  news    Sleep    190
93096  mysql  zubat...  news    Query   171  Copying
                                             to tmp
                                             table   select distinct
                                                     arts.a_id,
                                                     arts.headline1,
                                                     nartsect.se_id,
                                                     arts.mdate,
                                                     arts.set_

93153  mysql  zubat...  news    Sleep    207
93161  mysql  zubat...  news    Query    30  Locked  SELECT DISTINCT
                                                     arts.a_id FROM
                                                     arts,keywordmap
                                                     WHERE arts.s_id in
                                                     (1) AND arts.
93165  mysql  zubat...  news    Query    36  Locked  select arts.name,
                                                     arts.headline1,
                                                     arts.se_id,
                                                     n_blurb.blurb,
                                                     slook.name as
                                                     sectna
93204  mysql  zubat...  news    Query    31  Locked  select arts.name,
                                                     arts.headline1,
                                                     arts.se_id,
                                                     n_blurb.blurb,
                                                     slook.name as
                                                     sectna
93205  mysql  zubat...  news    Query   156  Copying
                                             to tmp
                                             table   select distinct
                                                     arts.a_id,
                                                     arts.headline1,
                                                     nartsect.se_id,
                                                     arts.mdate,
                                                     arts.set_
93210  mysql  zubat...  news    Query    50  Locked  select arts.a_id,
                                                     arts.headline1,
                                                     nartfpg.se_id,
                                                     nartfpg.se_id,
                                                     arts.mdate,
                                                     nartfpg.p
```

```
93217  mysql  zubat...  news  Query   38  Locked         select arts.name,
                                                          arts.headline1,
                                                          arts.se_id,
                                                          n_blurb.blurb,
                                                          slook.name as
                                                          sectna
93222  mysql  zubat...  news  Query    8  Locked         select arts.name,
                                                          arts.headline1,
                                                          arts.se_id,
                                                          n_blurb.blurb,
                                                          slook2.name as
                                                          sectn
93226  mysql  zubat...  news  Query   39  Locked         select arts.name,
                                                          arts.headline1,
                                                          arts.se_id,
                                                          n_blurb.blurb,
                                                          slook.name as
                                                          sectna
93237  mysql  zubat...  news  Query   33  Locked         select arts.a_id,
                                                          arts.headline1,
                                                          nartfpg.se_id,
                                                          nartfpg.se_id,
                                                          arts.mdate,
                                                          nartfpg.p
93244  mysql  zubat...  news  Query   99  Copying
                                          to tmp
                                          table          select distinct
                                                          arts.a_id,
                                                          arts.headline1,
                                                          nartsect.se_id,
                                                          arts.mdate,
                                                          arts.set_
93247  mysql  zubat...  news  Query   64  Locked         select s_id from
                                                          arts where
                                                          a_id='32C436'
93252  mysql  zubat...  news  Query  120  Copying
                                          to tmp
                                          table          select distinct
                                                          arts.a_id,
                                                          arts.headline1,
                                                          nartsect.se_id,
                                                          arts.mdate,
                                                          arts.set_
93254  mysql  zubat...  news  Sleep   47
93256  mysql  zubat...  news  Sleep  171
```

| 93257 | mysql | zubat... | news | Query | 176 | Copying to tmp table | select distinct arts.a_id, arts.headline1, nartsect.se_id, arts.mdate, arts.set_ |
|-------|-------|----------|------|-------|-----|----------------------|----------------------------------------------------------------------------------|
| 93261 | mysql | zubat... | news | Sleep | 349 | | |
| 93262 | mysql | zubat... | news | Sleep | 1 | | |
| 93263 | mysql | zubat... | news | Query | 153 | Copying to tmp table | select distinct arts.a_id, arts.headline1, nartsect.se_id, arts.mdate, arts.set_ |
| 93267 | mysql | zubat... | news | Query | 27 | Locked | select arts.name, arts.headline1, arts.se_id, n_blurb.blurb, slook.name as sectna |
| 93276 | mysql | zubat... | news | Query | 29 | Locked | select arts.name, arts.headline1, arts.se_id, n_blurb.blurb, slook.name as sectna |
| 93278 | mysql | zubat... | news | Query | 183 | Copying to tmp table | select distinct arts.a_id, arts.headline1, nartsect.se_id, arts.mdate, arts.set |
| 93280 | mysql | zubat... | news | Sleep | 36 | | |
| 93285 | mysql | zubat... | news | Sleep | 10 | | |
| 93284 | mysql | zubat... | news | Query | 49 | Locked | select arts.name, arts.headline1, arts.se_id, n_blurb.blurb, slook.name as sectna |

Of the two web servers indicated in the list, websrv2 is behaving normally (all its threads are completed, and the connections are sleeping), but zubat has problem queries piling up.

There are many queries, and this is only a small portion of the whole list, but the query you should examine in this case is the one beginning like this:

```
select distinct arts.a_id, arts.headline1, nartsect.se_id, arts.mdate, arts.set ...
```

Notice how the status for all of these queries is `Copying to tmp table`, and the others were `Locked`. In this case, the problem was that a developer had made a change to the query so that it no longer used an index. Chapter 4, "Indexes and Query Optimization," discusses this topic in more detail.

Routinely examining the `processlist` output can help identify queries that are slow even before they cause something as drastic as the server to fail.

The `slow_queries` value is another good one you should examine. If it creeping up all the time, it probably indicates a problem. A well-tuned system should have as few slow queries as possible. Some complex joins may be unavoidably slow, but it's more likely that slow queries are just badly optimized.

## Optimizing the *delayed_queue_size* and *back_log* Variables

As discussed in Chapter 4, `INSERT DELAYED` frees the client but does not process the query immediately if there is anything else in the queue. Instead, MySQL waits for a gap so the inserts can be processed. The `delayed_queue_size` plays a role here. If the variable is set to its default value, 1,000, this means that after 1,000 delayed statements are in the queue, the client will no longer be freed and will have to wait. Having so many queued queries is not usually healthy, but if your system is one where a large number of inserts are made at a similar time, and you find clients having to wait even though you're using `INSERT DELAYED`, you should increase the `delayed_queue_size`.

Another variable that helps manage short bursts of activity is the `back_log` variable. If a system receives a large number of connection requests in a short space of time, MySQL will count those it has not yet processed as part of the backlog. As soon as the `back_log` limit is reached, any more requests that would be queued are instead refused. If your system is one that gets large numbers of connection requests in short bursts, and you find that some are getting refused for this reason, you should increase the `back_log` value. If your system is just busy, and the requests are a constant stream, increasing the `back_log` on its own will not do much. It gives your server breathing space to handles short bursts, but it does not help with an overloaded system.

## Optimizing the *sort_buffer* Variable

The `sort_buffer` variable has already been discussed as far as it pertains to speeding up the operations of myisamchk (in Chapter 10, "Basic Administration") but it can also be a useful variable to fine-tune for everyday operations. If you do lots of sorting normally (frequently using `ORDER BY` on large tables, for example), the `sort_buffer` is a useful one to change. Each thread that performs a sort allocates a buffer of `sort_buffer` size. The `my-huge.cnf` configuration file (for systems with at least 1 GB memory) defaults the `sort_buffer` to 256M for myisamchk, and 2M for mysqld. Although you want the mysqld figure to be able to handle large sorts, if you have many simultaneous connections performing `ORDER BY` clauses, because each is assigned a `sort_buffer`, you can run into memory problems.

## Configuring InnoDB Tables

To get InnoDB tables running smoothly, it is even more critical to configure the variables correctly than with MyISAM tables. The most important is the `innodb_data_file_path`, which specifies the space available to the tables (data and indexes). It specifies one or more data files, as well as allocating a size to them. You should make the last data file auto extend (only the last data file can do this). So, instead of simply running out of space when all the space is taken, the auto extended data file will grow (in chunks of 8MB) to accommodate the extra data. For example:

```
innodb_data_file_path=/disk1/ibdata1:900M;/disk2/ibdata2:50M:autoextend
```

Here the two data files are placed on different disks (called `disk1` and `disk2`). The data will first be placed in `ibdata1`, until the 900MB limit is reached, and then will be placed into `ibdata2`. Once the 50MB limit is reached, `ibdata2` will automatically extend in 8MB chunks.

If a disk becomes physically full, you'll need to add another data file on another disk, which requires some manual work for configuration. To do this, look at the physical size of the final data file and round it down to the nearest megabyte. Set this data file size specifically, and add the new data file definition. For example, if the `disk2` specified previously fills up with `ibdata2` at 109MB, you'll use something like the following definition:

```
innodb_data_file_path=/disk1/ibdata1:900M;/disk2/ibdata2:109M;/disk3/
ibdata3:500M:autoextend
```

You'll need to restart the server for the changes to take effect.

## Introducing the mysqld Options

Table 13.1 describes the mysqld options.

**TABLE 13.1:** THE MYSQLD OPTIONS

| OPTION | DESCRIPTION |
| --- | --- |
| `--ansi` | MySQL not only has a number of extensions but also a number of differences to standard ANSI (standard SQL, as defined by the American National Standards Institute) behavior. If this is set, MySQL will run in ANSI mode (the changes this causes are discussed later in this chapter in the section "Running MySQL in ANSI Mode"). |
| `-b, --basedir=path` | The path to the base directory or the MySQL installation directory. Other paths are usually taken relative to this. |
| `--big-tables` | Allows large result sets by saving all temporary sets on file when memory is not sufficient. |
| `--bind-address=IP` | The Internet Protocol (IP) address or hostname to which to bind MySQL. |
| `--character-sets-dir=path` | The directory where the character sets are located. |

*Continued on next page*

**TABLE 13.1:** THE MYSQLD OPTIONS *(continued)*

| OPTION | DESCRIPTION |
| --- | --- |
| `--chroot=path` | For security purposes, you can start MySQL in a chroot environment with this option. This causes MySQL to run in a subset of the directories, hiding the full directory structure. This does, however, limit the usage of LOAD DATA INFILE and SELECT . . . INTO OUTFILE. |
| `--core-file` | This option causes a core file to be written if mysqld dies unexpectedly. Some systems may require you to specify a `--core-file-size`. Some systems may also not write a core file if the `--user` option is used. |
| `-h, --datadir=path` | Path to the data directory. |
| `--debug[...]=` | If MySQL is configured with `--with-debug`, this option can be used to generate a trace file of what mysqld does. |
| `--default-character-set=charset` | Sets the default character set (the default is latin1). |
| `--default-table-type=type` | Sets the default table type (tables of this type are created if no table type is specified in the CREATE statement). By default, this will be MyISAM. |
| `--delay-key-write-for-all-tables` | With this option, MySQL does not flush the key buffers between writes for any MyISAM table. |
| `--des-key-file=filename` | The default keys are read from this file. This is used by the DES_ENCRYPT() and DES_DECRYPT() functions. |
| `--enable-external-locking` | This option enables system locking. It should not be used on systems where the locked daemon does not work fully. (This applied to Linux, although this may no longer be the case with newer versions.) |
| `--enable-named-pipe` | On Windows NT/2000/XP, this option enables support for named pipes. |
| `-T, --exit-info` | A bit mask of different flags used in debugging. Not suggested you use this unless you know what you're doing! |
| `--flush` | This option ensures MySQL flushes all changes to disk after each SQL statement. Usually the operating system handles this. You should not need to use this unless you're having problems. |
| `-?, --help` | Displays a help list and exits. |
| `--init-file=file` | Tells MySQL to execute SQL statements contained in this file when it starts up. |
| `-L, --language=...` | This option sets the language to be used for client error messages. Can be the language or the full path to the language file. |
| `-l, --log[=file]` | Connections and queries will be logged to the specified file. |

*Continued on next page*

**TABLE 13.1:** THE MYSQLD OPTIONS *(continued)*

| OPTION | DESCRIPTION |
| --- | --- |
| `--log-isam[=file]` | This option logs all changes to MyISAM or ISAM files to the specified file (only used when debugging these table types). |
| `--log-slow-queries[=file]` | Logs all queries that take longer than the value of the variable `long_query_time` (in seconds) to execute to the slow query log. |
| `--log-update[=file]` | Logs all updates to the specified update log. Instead use `--log-bin`. |
| `--log-bin[=file]` | Logs all updates to the specified binary update log. |
| `--log-long-format` | Logs more information. If the slow query log is being used (`--log-slow-queries`), any queries that do not use an index are logged there as well. |
| `--low-priority-updates` | If this option is used, all inserts, updates, and deletes will have a lower priority than selects. Where you don't want this to apply to all queries, you can use SET OPTION SQL_LOW_PRIORITY_UPDATES=1 to apply it to a specific thread or LOW_PRIORITY . . . to apply it to a specific INSERT, UPDATE, or DELETE query. |
| `--memlock` | Locks mysqld into memory. This option is only available if your system supports the `mlockall()` function (as Solaris does). You'd normally only use this if the operating system is having problems and mysqld is swapping to disk. You can see if `--memlock` has been used by looking at the value of the `locked_in_memory` variable. |
| `--myisam-recover [=option[,option...]]]` | The available options are DEFAULT, BACKUP, FORCE, QUICK, or "". If this is set to anything but "", when MySQL starts it will check tables to see if they are marked as crashed or not closed properly. If so, it will run a check on the table and attempt to repair corrupted tables. If the BACKUP option is used, MySQL will create a backup copy of the `.MYD` data file if any changes are made during the course of the repair (giving it the extension `.BAK`). The FORCE option forces the repair even if data is to be lost, and the QUICK option does not check the rows if there are no delete blocks in the data. All errors will be noted in the error log, so you can see what happened. Setting the BACKUP and FORCE options together allow MySQL to recover automatically from many problems (with the backup in case things go wrong). DEFAULT is the same as not giving any options. |
| `--pid-file=path` | Specifies the path to the pid (process id) file. |
| `-P, --port=...` | The port number that MySQL uses to listen for TCP/IP connections. |
| `-o, --old-protocol` | Specifies that MySQL use the ancient 3.20 protocol for compatibility with some equally ancient clients. |
| `--one-thread` | Specifies that MySQL only use one thread. You only want to use this for debugging! |

*Continued on next page*

**TABLE 13.1:** THE MYSQLD OPTIONS *(continued)*

| OPTION | DESCRIPTION |
| --- | --- |
| -O, --set-variable var=option | Sets a variable to allow you to optimize it. The full list of variables follows this table, in Table 13.2. |
| --safe-mode | Skips some optimizing stages. This option implies the --skip-delay-key-write option. |
| --safe-show-database | Not used in any but the earliest versions of MySQL 4. If set, users who do not have any privileges having anything to do with a database will not see that database listed when they perform a SHOW DATABASES statement (the SHOW DATABASES privilege removes the need for this). |
| --safe-user-create | This option adds to security by not allowing users to create new users (with the GRANT statement) unless they have INSERT privilege on the mysql.user table or one of the columns in that table. |
| --skip-concurrent-insert | Nullifies concurrent inserts (where selects and inserts can be performed at the same time on optimized tables). You should not need to do this unless debugging. |
| --skip-delay-key-write | Causes MySQL to ignore the delay_key_write option for all tables. |
| --skip-grant-tables | This option starts MySQL without the privilege tables (giving everyone full access). Never use this unless you have to (such as when you, as root, have forgotten the password). Once you've finished, run mysqladmin flush-privileges or mysqladmin reload to start using the privilege tables again. |
| --skip-host-cache | Hostnames are usually cached, but you can force MySQL to query the DNS server for every connect instead. This will slow down connection speeds. |
| --skip-external-locking | Disables system locking. This has important consequences for myisamchk; see "Analyzing Tables with myisamchk" in Chapter 10. |
| --skip-name-resolve | MySQL does not resolve hostnames, so all Host column values in the privilege tables must be a specific IP (or localhost). Hostnames are not resolved. This option can improve connection speeds if you have many hosts or slow DNS. |
| --skip-networking | This option causes MySQL to allow only local connections. It will not listen for TCP/IP (Transmission Control Protocol/Internet Protocol) connections at all. This is a good security measure if possible. |
| --skip-new | MySQL uses ISAM as a default table type and does not use some of the options that were new in version 3.23. It also implies --skip-delay-key-write. This option should not be needed anymore, unless its behavior changes. |

*Continued on next page*

**TABLE 13.1:** THE MYSQLD OPTIONS *(continued)*

| OPTION | DESCRIPTION |
| --- | --- |
| `--skip-symlink` | This option ensures that one cannot delete or rename files to which a symlinked file in the data directory points. You should use it if you are not using symlinks as a security measure to ensure no one can drop or rename a file outside of the mysqld data directory. |
| `--skip-safemalloc` | This options speeds up performance as it avoids checking for overruns for each memory allocation and memory freeing (these checks are done when MySQL is configured with `--with-debug=full`). |
| `--skip-show-database` | If set, the SHOW DATABASES statement does not return results unless the client has the PROCESS privilege. (The SHOW DATABASES privilege, introduced in early versions of MySQL 4, removes the need for this.) |
| `--skip-stack-trace` | Does not use stack traces (which is useful if running mysqld under a debugger). Some systems require this option to get a core file. |
| `--skip-thread-priority` | Disables the use of thread priorities for a faster response time. |
| `--socket=path` | The path to the socket file for use for local connections (instead of the default, usually `/tmp/mysql.sock`). |
| `--sql-mode=option[,option[, option...]]` | The various differences between ANSI standard and MySQL can be set using these options. They are REAL_AS_FLOAT, PIPES_AS_CONCAT, ANSI_QUOTES, IGNORE_SPACE, SERIALIZE, ONLY_FULL_GROUP_BY, or " " (to reset). Using them all is the same as the `--ansi` option. See the discussion later in this chapter, "Running MySQL in ANSI Mode," for what each difference is. |
| `--temp-pool` | This option should only be needed when an operating system leaks memory when creating large numbers of new files with different names (as happened with some versions of Linux). Instead, MySQL will use a small set of names for temporary files. |
| `--transaction-isolation= { READ-UNCOMMITTED \| READ-COMMITTED \| REPEATABLE-READ \| SERIALIZABLE }` | Sets the default transaction isolation level. See the discussion in Chapter 4. |
| `-t, --tmpdir=path` | The directory used to store temporary files and tables. It's useful to make it different to your usual temporary space if that is too small to hold temporary tables. |
| `-u, --user= [user_name \| userid]` | Supplies a username to run MySQL as. When starting mysqld as root, this option must be used. |
| `-V, --version` | Displays version information and exits. |
| `-W, --warnings` | Warnings will be displayed in the error file. |

## Exploring the mysqld Variables

When running `mysqladmin variables` from the command line, or `SHOW VARIABLES` from the `mysql` prompt, a long list of variables will be displayed. Most often, they relate to an option that you can set in the configuration file. Table 13.2 explains the variables displayed. Depending on your system setup and version, you may not have all these options—or, more likely, as MySQL keeps adding to them, you may have more.

**TABLE 13.2:** THE MYSQLD VARIABLES

| VARIABLE | DESCRIPTION |
| --- | --- |
| ansi_mode | MySQL not only has a number of extensions but also a number of differences to standard ANSI behavior. If this is set, MySQL will run in ANSI mode (the changes this causes are discussed later in this chapter, in the section "Running MySQL in ANSI Mode"). |
| back_log | The number of queued connection requests MySQL can have waiting before it starts refusing connections. This is the same as the size of the listen queue for incoming TCP/IP connections, which is also limited by the operating system. The lower of back_log and the operating system limit will apply. See the operating system documentation (for example, man listen on Unix) for more information. |
| basedir | The path to the base directory or the MySQL installation directory. |
| bdb_cache_size | The size of the buffer allocated cache data and indexes for BDB tables. If your system does not use BDB tables, use the --skip-bdb option to avoid wasting memory. |
| bdb_lock_detect | The Berkeley lock detect, which can be one of DEFAULT, OLDEST, RANDOM, or YOUNGEST. |
| bdb_log_buffer_size | The size of the buffer for BDB logs. If your system does not use BDB tables, use the --skip-bdb to avoid wasting memory. |
| bdb_home | The base directory for BDB tables, which should be the same as --datadir. |
| bdb_max_lock | The maximum number of locks that can be applied to a BDB table. Increase this if your transactions are likely to be long or your queries require many rows to be examined. Errors such as bdb: Lock table is out of available locks or Got error 12 from ... indicate a need to increase the value. The default value is 10000. |
| bdb-no-recover | If set, MySQL does not start BDB in recover mode. Usually you should only set this if there is corruption in the BDB logs that prevents a successful startup. |
| bdb-no-sync | If set, MySQL will not synchronously flush the logs. |
| bdb_logdir | The directory containing the BDB logs. |

*Continued on next page*

**TABLE 13.2:** THE MYSQLD VARIABLES *(continued)*

| VARIABLE | DESCRIPTION |
| --- | --- |
| bdb_shared_data | If set, MySQL starts BDB in multiprocess mode, meaning that DB_PRIVATE is not used. |
| bdb_tmpdir | The directory location for BDB temporary files. |
| binlog_cache_size | The cache size for transactions to be written to the binary log. If the transactions are large and take more than the default 32KB cache, you should increase this. |
| character_set | The character set to use when no other is specified (usually latin1). |
| character_sets | The full list of supported character sets. If you are compiling MySQL from source and know you are never going to use them, you can compile MySQL not to support the extra character sets. |
| concurrent_inserts | If active (by default it is), you can insert into MyISAM tables at the same time as querying, giving a performance gain (as long as the table contains no gaps from previously deleted records. You can ensure this by regularly optimizing the tables). The --safe or --skip-new options nullify this. |
| connect_timeout | The time in seconds MySQL waits for packets before it times out with a Bad handshake. The default is 5 seconds. This helps to prevent denial of service attacks where many bad connection attempts are made in order to prevent legitimate users from connecting. |
| datadir | The directory where the data is stored. |
| delay_key_write | If active (the default), MySQL will not flush the key buffer for a table on every index update for tables with the DELAY_KEY_WRITE option. Rather, it will only be flushed when the table is closed. This increases the speed of key writes, but it also increases the chance of corruption, so you should regularly check the tables. You can specify that the DELAY_KEY_WRITE option is default for all tables by using the --delay-key-write-for-all-tables option. The --safe or --skip-new options nullifies this option. |
| delayed_insert_limit | After inserting delayed_insert_limit rows, MySQL checks to see if there are any SELECT statements pending, and processes these, before continuing with the remaining INSERT DELAYED statements. The default is 100 rows. |
| delayed_insert_timeout | This determines how long an INSERT DELAYED thread should wait for INSERT statements before terminating. |
| delayed_queue_size | The number of rows allocated for the INSERT DELAYED queue. If this limit is reached, clients performing INSERT DELAYED will wait until there is space. |
| flush | If set, MySQL flushes all changes to disk after each SQL statement. Usually the operating system handles this. Defaults to OFF as you should not need to use this unless you're having problems. |

*Continued on next page*

**TABLE 13.2:** THE MYSQLD VARIABLES *(continued)*

| VARIABLE | DESCRIPTION |
|---|---|
| flush_time | The time in seconds between automatic flushes (where the tables are closed and synchronized to disk). This is usually set to 0 unless you're running a system with very little resources or Windows 95/98/Me. |
| ft_min_word_len | The minimum length of words to be included in a FULLTEXT index. After changing this value, any FULLTEXT indexes will need to be rebuilt. The default is 4. |
| ft_max_word_len | The maximum length of words to be included in a FULLTEXT index. After changing this value, any FULLTEXT indexes will need to be rebuilt. The default is 254. |
| ft_max_word_len_sort | Words of this length or less are inserted into the FULLTEXT index with the fast index re-creation when the index is rebuilt. Words longer than this length are inserted into the index the slow way. You are unlikely to want to change the default (20) unless the words in your index are of unusual average lengths. If the value is set too high, the process will be slower as the temporary files will be bigger, and fewer keys will be in one sort block. If the value is too low, too many words will be inserted the slow way. |
| ft_boolean_syntax | The list of operators supported by the MATCH . . . AGAINST( . . . IN BOOLEAN MODE) statement (+ -><()~*:" "&\|). |
| have_innodb | Set to YES if MySQL supports InnoDB tables or DISABLED if the --skip-innodb option is used. |
| have_bdb | Set to YES if MySQL supports BDB tables or DISABLED if the --skip-bdb option is used. |
| have_raid | Set to YES if MySQL supports the RAID (Redundant Array of Inexpensive Disks) option. |
| have_openssl | Set to YES if MySQL supports SSL (Secure Sockets Layer) encryption between client and server. |
| init_file | The name of a file containing SQL statements to be executed when the server starts (by default none is specified). |
| innodb_data_home_dir | The home directory for InnoDB data files and used as the common part of the path. If this is not mentioned, it will be the same as datadir. By setting this to an empty string, you can use absolute file paths in innodb_data_file_path. |
| innodb_data_file_path | The paths to individual data files and their sizes. The innodb_data_home_dir part of the path is added to this to give the full path. File sizes are specified in megabytes (M) or gigabytes (G). Can be larger than 4GB on operating systems that support big files, and the sum of the sizes should be at least 10MB. |

*Continued on next page*

**TABLE 13.2:** THE MYSQLD VARIABLES *(continued)*

| VARIABLE | DESCRIPTION |
| --- | --- |
| innodb_mirrored_ log_groups | Specifies the number of identical copies of log groups to keep for the database. Currently this should be 1. |
| innodb_log_group_ home_dir | Specifies the directory path to InnoDB log files. |
| innodb_log_files_in_ group | Specifies the number of log files in the log group. 3 is the suggested value (logs are written in rotation). |
| innodb_log_file_size | Specifies the size in megabytes of each log file in a log group. Suggested values are from 1MB to 1/innodb_log_files_in_group of the innodb_buffer_ pool_size. A high value saves disk input/output (I/O) because less flush activity is needed, but slows recovery after a crash. The total size of the log files should not be more than 4GB on 32-bit computers. |
| innodb_log_buffer_size | Specifies the size of the buffer used to write logs. A suggested value is 8MB. The larger the buffer, the less disk I/O because then transactions do not need to be written to disk until they are committed. |
| innodb_flush_log_at_ trx_commit | If set, logs are flushed to disk as soon as the transaction is committed (and are therefore permanent and able to survive a crash). This should not normally be set to anything but ON if your transactions are important. You can set this to OFF if performance is more critical and you want to reduce disk I/O at the cost of safety. |
| innodb_log_arch_dir | Specifies the directory where the logs are to be archived. Currently this should be the same as innodb_log_group_home_dir because log archiving is not currently used. |
| innodb_log_archive | If set, InnoDB log files will be archived. Currently, MySQL recovers using its own log files, so this should be set to OFF. |
| innodb_buffer_pool_size | Specifies the size in bytes of the memory buffer used to cache table indexes and data. The larger this is, the better the performance because less disk I/O is then required. Up to 80 percent of memory is suggested on a dedicated database server because any larger may cause operating system paging. |
| innodb_additional_mem_ pool_size | Specifies the size in bytes of a memory pool used to store information about the internal data structures. 2MB is a possibility, but if you have many tables, make sure there is enough memory allocated; otherwise MySQL will use operating system memory (you can see the warnings in the error log if this occurs and increase the value). |
| innodb_file_io_threads | The number of file I/O threads in InnoDB. The suggested value is 4, but it is suspected Windows may benefit from a higher setting. |

*Continued on next page*

**TABLE 13.2:** THE MYSQLD VARIABLES *(continued)*

| VARIABLE | DESCRIPTION |
|---|---|
| innodb_lock_wait_timeout | The time in seconds an InnoDB transaction waits for a lock before rolling back. InnoDB detects deadlocks automatically in its own lock tables, but if they come from outside (such as a LOCK TABLES statement), deadlock may arise, in which case this value is used. |
| innodb_flush_method | Flushing method. The default is fdatasync, and the alternative is O_DSYNC. Usually fdatasync is faster, though on some versions of Linux and Unix it has proven to be slower. |
| interactive_timeout | The time in seconds that the server waits for any activity on an interactive connection (one using the CLIENT_INTERACTIVE option when connecting) before closing it. The wait-timeout option applies to ordinary connections. The default is 28800. |
| join_buffer_size | The size in bytes of the buffer used for full joins (joins where no index is used). The buffer is allocated to each full join. Increasing this will make full joins faster, although the best way to speed up a join is by adding appropriate indexes. |
| key_buffer_size | The size in bytes of the buffer used for index blocks. This is discussed fully in the section "Optimizing Key Buffer Size." |
| language | The location of the language file used for error messages. |
| large_file_support | ON if MySQL was compiled with support for large files. The default is ON. |
| locked_in_memory | ON if MySQL was locked in memory (in other words, if mysqld was started with the --memlock option). The default is OFF. You normally only want this ON if the operating system is having problems and mysqld is swapping to disk. |
| log | ON if logging of all queries is enabled. |
| log_update | ON if update logging is enabled (you should rather use the binary log for this). |
| log_bin | ON if binary update logging is enabled. |
| log_slave_updates | ON if updates from a slave are logged. |
| long_query_time | The time in seconds that defines a slow query. Queries that take longer than this will cause the slow queries counter to be incremented and will be logged in the slow query log file if slow query logging is enabled. |
| lower_case_table_names | Set to 1 if table names are stored in lowercase and are case insensitive. The default is 0. |
| max_allowed_packet | The maximum allowable size in bytes of one packet of data. The message buffer is initialized to the size specified by net_buffer_length, but it can grow up to this size. If you use large BLOB or TEXT columns, set this to the size of the largest column. |

*Continued on next page*

**TABLE 13.2:** THE MYSQLD VARIABLES *(continued)*

| VARIABLE | DESCRIPTION |
| --- | --- |
| max_binlog_cache_size | The largest amount of memory in bytes a multistatement transaction can use without throwing the error: "Multistatement transaction required more than max_binlog_cache_size bytes of storage. |
| max_binlog_size | As soon as the current binary log exceeds this size, the logs will be rotated and a new one created. |
| max_connections | The maximum number of connections allowed. See the earlier discussion, "Dealing with Too Many Connections." |
| max_connect_errors | The maximum number of times a host can attempt a connection that becomes interrupted before the host is blocked from any further connections. This limit is imposed to reduce the possibility of denial of service attacks. Hosts can be unblocked by running FLUSH HOSTS. |
| max_delayed_threads | The maximum number of threads that can handle INSERT DELAYED statements. Once this is reached, further INSERT statements will be ordinary inserts and not make use of the DELAYED attribute. |
| max_heap_table_size | Maximum size in bytes that HEAP tables can become. |
| max_join_size | Joins that MySQL determines will return more rows than this limit will return an error. This prevents users from accidentally (or maliciously) running huge queries that could take return many millions of rows and take up too many resources. |
| max_sort_length | When sorting BLOB or TEXT fields, only up to this number of bytes will be used. For example, if this is set to 1024, only the first 1024 characters will be used in sorting. |
| max_user_connections | Determines the maximum number of connections a single user can have active. The default, 0, indicates there is no limit (except for max_connections). |
| max_tmp_tables | The maximum number of temporary tables a client can keep open at the same time. (At the time of this writing, this is not used; check the latest documentation.) |
| max_write_lock_count | If this many consecutive write locks occur, MySQL will allow a number of read locks to run. |
| myisam_bulk_insert_ tree_size | When MySQL inserts in bulk (for example, LOAD DATA INFILE...), it uses a tree-like cache to speed up the process. This is the maximum size in bytes of the cache for each thread. The default is 8MB, and setting it to 0 disables this feature. The cache is only used when adding to a table that is not empty. |

*Continued on next page*

**TABLE 13.2:** THE MYSQLD VARIABLES *(continued)*

| VARIABLE | DESCRIPTION |
|---|---|
| myisam_recover_options | The available options are DEFAULT, BACKUP, FORCE, QUICK, or OFF. If this is set to anything but OFF, when MySQL starts it will check tables to see if they are marked as crashed or not closed properly. If so, it will run a check on the table and attempt to repair corrupted tables. If the BACKUP option is used, MySQL will create a backup copy of the .MYD data file if any changes are made during the course of the repair (giving it the extension .BAK). The FORCE option forces the repair even if data is to be lost, and the QUICK option does not check the rows if there are no delete blocks in the data. All errors will be noted in the error log, so you can see what happened. Setting the BACKUP and FORCE options together allow MySQL to recover automatically from many problems (with the backup in case things go wrong). |
| myisam_sort_buffer_size | The size in bytes of the buffer allocated when sorting or repairing an index. |
| myisam_max_extra_sort_file_size | When MySQL creates an index, it subtracts the key cache size from the size of the temporary table it would use with fast index creation. If the difference is larger than this amount (specified in megabytes), MySQL uses the key cache method. |
| myisam_max_sort_file_size | The maximum size (in megabytes) of the temporary file MySQL creates when creating or repairing indexes. If this size would be exceeded, MySQL uses the slower key cache method to create or repair the index. |
| net_buffer_length | The size in bytes that the communication buffer is set to between queries. To save memory is systems with low memory, set this to the expected length of SQL statements sent by clients. It is automatically enlarged to the size of max_allowed_packet if the statement exceeds this length. |
| net_read_timeout | Time in seconds that MySQL waits for data from a connection before aborting the read. If no data is expected, the net_write_timeout is used, and slave_net_timeout is used for the master/slave connection. |
| net_retry_count | The number of times to retry a read on a communication port before aborting. |
| net_write_timeout | The number of seconds to wait for a block to be written to a connection before aborting. |
| open_files_limit | MySQL uses this value to reserve file descriptors. Increase this if you get the error Too many open files. Usually this is set to 0, in which case MySQL uses the larger of max_connections*5 or max_connections + table_cache*2. |
| pid_file | The path to the pid file. |
| port | The port number that MySQL uses to listen for TCP/IP connections. |
| protocol_version | The protocol version that MySQL uses. |
| record_buffer | MySQL allocates a buffer of this size in bytes for each thread that performs a *sequential scan* (where records are read in order, one after another). If you do many sequential scans, you may want to increase this value. |

*Continued on next page*

**Table 13.2:** The mysqld Variables *(continued)*

| Variable | Description |
| --- | --- |
| record_rnd_buffer | A buffer of this size in bytes is allocated when reading rows in nonsequential order (for example, after a sort), and rows read through this avoid disk seeks. If not set, it will be the same as the record_buffer. |
| query_buffer_size | The initial size in bytes allocated to the query buffer. It should be sufficient for most queries; otherwise it should be increased. |
| query_cache_limit | The limit in bytes for the query cache. Results larger than this will not be cached. The default is 1MB. |
| query_cache_size | The size in bytes allocated to the query cache (where results are stored from old queries). 0 indicates the cache is disabled. |
| query_cache_startup_type | This can be one of 0, 1, or 2. 0 (off) means MySQL does not cache or retrieve results. 1 (on) means MySQL caches all results unless they come with SQL_NO_CACHE. 2 (demand) means that only queries with SQL_CACHE are cached. |
| safe_show_database | Not used in any but the earliest versions of MySQL 4. If set, users who do not have any privileges having anything to do with a database will not see that database listed when they perform a SHOW DATABASES statement (the SHOW DATABASES privilege removes the need for this). |
| server_id | The ID of the server. Important for replication purposes to identify servers. |
| skip_external_locking | Disables system locking if ON. Has important consequences for myisamchk (see Chapter 10 for information on analyzing tables with myisamchk). |
| skip_networking | Is ON if MySQL allows only local connections. |
| skip_show_database | If set, the SHOW DATABASES statement does not return results unless the client has the PROCESS privilege. (The SHOW DATABASES privilege, introduced in early versions of MySQL 4, removes the need for this.) |
| slave_net_timeout | Time in seconds MySQL waits for more data from a master/slave connection before the read aborts. |
| slow_launch_time | Time in seconds before the launch of a thread increments the slow_launch_threads counter. |
| socket | The path to the Unix socket used by the server. |
| sort_buffer | The size in bytes allocated to the buffer used by sorts. See the discussion earlier in this chapter titled "Optimizing the *sort_buffer* variable." |
| table_cache | The number of open tables for all threads. See the discussion earlier in this chapter titled "Optimizing *table_cache*." |
| table_type | The default table type (usually MyISAM). |

*Continued on next page*

**TABLE 13.2:** THE MYSQLD VARIABLES *(continued)*

| VARIABLE | DESCRIPTION |
| --- | --- |
| thread_cache_size | The number of threads kept in a cache for reuse. New threads are taken from the cache if any are available, while a client's threads are placed in the cache when disconnecting if space is available. If you have lots of new connections, you can increase this value to improve performance. Systems with good thread implementation normally don't benefit much from this. You can see its efficiency by comparing the Connections and Threads_created status variables. |
| thread_concurrency | On Solaris systems, MySQL uses this value to determine whether to call the thr_setconcurrency() function, which assists the threads system in knowing the number of threads that should be running at the same time. |
| thread_stack | The size in bytes of the stack for each thread. The behavior of the crash-me benchmark depends on this value. |
| timezone | The server time zone. |
| tmp_table_size | The maximum size for a temporary table in memory. If it becomes larger, it will automatically become a MyISAM table on disk. If you perform lots of queries that result in large temporary tables (such as with complex GROUP BY clauses) and have enough memory, increase this value. |
| tmpdir | The directory used to store temporary files and tables. |
| version | The server version number. |
| wait_timeout | The time in seconds MySQL waits for activity on a connection before closing it. The interactive_timeout applies to interactive connections. |

## Exploring All the Status Variables

Status variables are reset every time the server restarts. They allow you to monitor the behavior of your server and to identify potential bottlenecks, problems, and improvements you can make. Table 13.3 contains a comprehensive list.

**TABLE 13.3:** THE MYSQL STATUS VALUES

| VALUE | DESCRIPTION |
| --- | --- |
| Aborted_clients | Indicates the number of connections that were aborted because for some reason the client did not close the connection properly. This could happen if the client does not call the mysql_close() function before exiting, the wait_timeout or interactive_timeout limits have been exceeded, or the client closed in the middle of a transfer. |

*Continued on next page*

**TABLE 13.3:** THE MYSQL STATUS VALUES *(continued)*

| VALUE | DESCRIPTION |
| --- | --- |
| Aborted_connects | Indicates the number of failed attempts to connect to MySQL server that failed. This could occur because the client tried to connect with the wrong password, does not have permission to connect, takes longer than `connect_timeout` seconds to obtain a connect packet, or the packet doesn't contain the correct information. |
| Bytes_received | The number of bytes that has been received from all clients. |
| Bytes_sent | The number of bytes that has been sent to all clients. |
| Com_[statement] | One of these variables exists for each kind of statement. The value indicates the number of times this statement has been executed. |
| Connections | The number of attempts to connect to the MySQL server. |
| Created_tmp_disk_tables | The number of implicit temporary tables on disk that were created while executing statements. |
| Created_tmp_tables | The number of implicit temporary tables in memory that were created while executing statements. |
| Created_tmp_files | The number of temporary files created by mysqld. |
| Delayed_insert_threads | The number of delayed insert handler threads currently in use. |
| Delayed_writes | The number of records written by an INSERT DELAYED statement. |
| Delayed_errors | The number of records written by an INSERT DELAYED where an error occurred. The most usual error is a duplicate key. |
| Flush_commands | The number of FLUSH statements executed. |
| Handler_commit | The number of internal COMMIT commands. |
| Handler_delete | The number of times a row was deleted from a table. |
| Handler_read_first | The number of times the first entry of an index was read, usually indicating a full index scan (for example, assuming `indexed_col` is indexed, the statement SELECT `indexed_col` from `tablename` results in a full index scan). |
| Handler_read_key | The number of requests where an index is used when reading a row. You'll want this to increase quickly, as it indicates your queries are using indexes. |
| Handler_read_next | The number of requests to read the next row in order of an index. This would get increased if you are doing a full-index scan or querying an index based on a range constant. |
| Handler_read_prev | The number of requests to read the previous row in index order. This would be used by an SELECT `fieldlist` ORDER BY `fields` DESC type of statement. |

*Continued on next page*

**TABLE 13.3:** THE MYSQL STATUS VALUES *(continued)*

| VALUE | DESCRIPTION |
|---|---|
| Handler_read_rnd | The number of requests to read a row based on a fixed position. Queries that require the results to be sorted would increment this counter. |
| Handler_read_rnd_next | The number of requests to read the next row in the data file. You would usually not want this to be high because it means that queries are not making use of indexes and have to read from the data file. |
| Handler_rollback | The number of internal ROLLBACK commands. |
| Handler_update | The number of requests to update a record in a table. |
| Handler_write | The number of requests to insert a record into a table. |
| Key_blocks_used | The number of blocks used in the key cache. |
| Key_read_requests | The number of requests causing a key block to be read from the key cache. The Key_reads:Key_read_requests ratio should be no higher than 1:100 (i.e., 1:10 is bad). |
| Key_reads | The number of physical reads causing a key block to be read from disk. The Key_reads:Key_read_requests ratio should be no higher than 1:100 (again, 1:10 is bad). |
| Key_write_requests | The number of requests causing a key block to be written to the cache. |
| Key_writes | The number of times there has been a physical write of a key block to disk. |
| Max_used_connections | The maximum number of connections in use at any one time. See the connections discussion earlier in this chapter ("Dealing with Too Many Connections"). |
| Not_flushed_key_blocks | The number of key blocks in the key cache that have changed but have not yet been flushed to disk. |
| Not_flushed_delayed_rows | The number of records currently in INSERT DELAY queues waiting to be written. |
| Open_tables | The number of tables that are currently open. See the table cache discussion earlier in this chapter ("Optimizing *table_cache*"). |
| Open_files | The number of files that are currently open. |
| Open_streams | The number of streams that are open. These are mostly used for logging. |
| Opened_tables | The number of tables that have been opened. See the table cache discussion earlier in this chapter ("Optimizing *table_cache*"). |
| Qcache_queries_in_cache | The number of queries in the cache. |
| Qcache_inserts | The number of queries added to the cache. |

*Continued on next page*

**TABLE 13.3:** THE MYSQL STATUS VALUES *(continued)*

| VALUE | DESCRIPTION |
|---|---|
| Qcache_hits | The number of times the query cache has been accessed. |
| Qcache_not_cached | The number of queries that were not cached (due to being too large, or because of the QUERY_CACHE_TYPE). |
| Qcache_free_memory | The amount memory still available for the query cache. |
| Qcache_total_blocks | The total number of blocks in the query cache. |
| Qcache_free_blocks | The number of free memory blocks in the query cache. |
| Questions | Total number of queries initiated. |
| Rpl_status | The status of failsafe replication. (This is only used by later versions of MySQL 4.) |
| Select_full_join | The number of joins that have been performed without using indexes. You do not want this to be high. |
| Select_full_range_join | The number of joins performed using a range search on the reference table. |
| Select_range | The number of joins performed using ranges on the first table (a large number here is normally fine). |
| Select_range_check | The number of joins performed without indexes that checked for indexes after each row. |
| Select_scan | The number of joins performed that did a full scan of the first table. |
| Slave_open_temp_tables | The number of currently open temporary tables held by a slave. |
| Slave_running | ON or OFF. Is ON if the server is a slave connected to a master. |
| Slow_launch_threads | The number of threads that took more than slow_launch_time to create. |
| Slow_queries | The number of queries that took more than long_query_time. |
| Sort_merge_passes | The number of merge passes performed during a sort. If this becomes too large, you should increase the sort_buffer. |
| Sort_range | The number of sorts performed with ranges. |
| Sort_rows | The number of sorted rows. |
| Sort_scan | The number of sorts performed by scanning the table. |
| ssl_[variables] | Contents of various variables used by SSL. This is not implemented in early versions of MySQL 4. |
| Table_locks_immediate | The number of times a table lock was immediately acquired. |

*Continued on next page*

**TABLE 13.3:** THE MYSQL STATUS VALUES *(continued)*

| VALUE | DESCRIPTION |
|---|---|
| Table_locks_waited | The number of times a table lock was not immediately acquired. A high value is usually a symptom of performance problems. You'll need to optimize by improving your queries and indexes, using another table type, splitting your tables, or using replication. |
| Threads_cached | The number of threads currently in the thread cache. |
| Threads_connected | The number of currently open connections. |
| Threads_created | The number of threads created to handle connections. |
| Threads_running | The number of active (not sleeping) threads. |
| Uptime | The time in seconds the server has been running. |

# Changing Variable Values with the Server Running

Until MySQL version 4.0.3, you always had to restart the server to change the variable values. Now, you can use the much more convenient SET statement to make a change without shutting down the server.

You can use the SET statement in two ways. The default is for the change you make to affect the SESSION only, meaning that when you connect next time (and for all other connections) the variable will still be at the setting specified in the configuration file. If you specify the GLOBAL keyword, all new connections will use the new value. When the server restarts, however, it will always use the values set in the configuration file, so you always need to make the changes there as well. To set a variable with the GLOBAL option, you need to have the SUPER permission.

The syntax is as follows:

```
SET [GLOBAL | SESSION] sql_variable=expression, [[GLOBAL | SESSION]↵
    sql_variable=expression...]
```

For example, the following:

```
mysql> SET SESSION max_sort_length=2048;
```

is the same as this:

```
mysql> SET max_sort_length=2048;
```

There is an alternate syntax too, used for compatibility with other database management systems (DBMSs), using the @@ syntax, as follows:

```
SET @@{global | local}.sql_variable=expression, [@@{global |↵
    local}.sql_variable=expression]
```

To repeat the previous example in this syntax, you use the following:

```
mysql> SET @@local.max_sort_length=2048;
```

SESSION and LOCAL are synonyms.

If, after experimenting with the new variable, you decide to return to the old value, there's no need to trust your memory or to look it up in the configuration file. You can use the DEFAULT keyword to restore a GLOBAL value to the value in configuration file, or a SESSION value to the GLOBAL value. For example:

```
mysql> SET SESSION max_sort_length=DEFAULT;
```

and

```
mysql> SET GLOBAL max_sort_length=DEFAULT;
```

Table 13.4 shows variables that you set in a nonstandard way.

**TABLE 13.4:** Nonstandard Variables

| SYNTAX | DESCRIPTION |
| --- | --- |
| AUTOCOMMIT= 0 \| 1 | When set (1), MySQL automatically COMMITs statements unless you wrap them in BEGIN and COMMIT statements. MySQL also automatically COMMITs all open transactions when you set AUTOCOMMIT. |
| BIG_TABLES = 0 \| 1 | When set (1), all temporary tables are stored on disk instead of in memory. This makes temporary tables slower, but it prevents the problem of running out of memory. The default is 0. |
| INSERT_ID = # | Sets the AUTO_INCREMENT value (so the next INSERT statement that uses an AUTO_INCREMENT field will use this value). |
| LAST_INSERT_ID = # | Sets the value returned from the next LAST_INSERT_ID( ) function. |
| LOW_PRIORITY_UPDATES = 0 \| 1 | When set (1), all update statements (INSERT, UPDATE, DELETE, LOCK TABLE WRITE) wait for there to be no pending reads (SELECT, LOCK TABLE READ) on the table they're accessing. |
| MAX_JOIN_SIZE = value \| DEFAULT | By setting a maximum size in rows, you can prevent MySQL from running queries that may not make use indexes properly or may have the potential to slow the server down when run in bulk or at peak times. Setting this to anything but DEFAULT resets SQL_BIG_SELECTS. If SQL_BIG_SELECTS is set, then MAX_JOIN_SIZE is ignored. If the query is already cached, MySQL will ignore this limit and return the results. |
| QUERY_CACHE_TYPE = OFF \| ON \| DEMAND | Sets the query cache setting for the thread. |
| QUERY_CACHE_TYPE = 0 \| 1 \| 2 | Sets the query cache setting for the thread. |
| SQL_AUTO_IS_NULL = 0 \| 1 | If set (1, the default), then the last inserted row for an AUTO_INCREMENT can be found with WHERE auto_increment_column IS NULL. MS Access and other ODBC programs make use of this. |

*Continued on next page*

**TABLE 13.4:** NONSTANDARD VARIABLES *(continued)*

| SYNTAX | DESCRIPTION |
|---|---|
| `SQL_BIG_SELECTS = 0 \| 1` | If set (1, the default), MySQL allows large queries. If not set (0), MySQL will not allow queries where it will have to examine more than `max_join_size` rows. This is useful to avoid running accidental or malicious queries that could bring the server down. |
| `SQL_BUFFER_RESULT = 0 \| 1` | If set (1), MySQL places query results into a temporary table (in some cases, speeding up performance by releasing table locks earlier). |
| `SQL_LOG_OFF = 0 \| 1` | If set (1), MySQL will not log for the client (this is not the update log). The SUPER permission is required. |
| `SQL_LOG_UPDATE = 0 \| 1` | If not set (0), MySQL will not use the update log for the client. Requires the SUPER permission. |
| `SQL_QUOTE_SHOW_CREATE = 0 \| 1` | If set (1, the default), MySQL will quote table and column names. |
| `SQL_SAFE_UPDATES = 0 \| 1` | If set (1), MySQL will not perform UPDATE or DELETE statements that don't use an index or a LIMIT clause, which helps prevent unpleasant accidents. |
| `SQL_SELECT_LIMIT = value \| DEFAULT` | Sets the maximum number of records (default unlimited) that can be returned with a SELECT statement. LIMIT takes precedence over this. |
| `TIMESTAMP = timestamp_value \| DEFAULT` | Sets the time for the client. You can use this to get the original timestamp when using the update log to restore rows. The `timestamp_value` is a Unix epoch timestamp. |

# Improving Hardware to Speed Up the Server

Hardware is one of the easiest improvements (if you have the cash) you can make to a poorly performing database server. As a general rule of thumb, pack in as much memory as you can first, then use the fastest disks you can get, and finally get the fastest CPU (Central Processing Unit). The best is to benchmark your system, using the various tools available to your operating system to see whether it's the CPU, memory, disk speed, or a combination that is the bottleneck. This will give you the best idea of the vagaries of your usage and assist you in upgrading. Running the benchmark suite (see "Using Benchmarks" later in this chapter) will also help show the performance of different kinds of tasks.

## Memory

Memory is the most important element because it allows you to tweak the mysqld variables. Large amounts of memory mean you can create large key and table caches. Memory that is as large as possible allows MySQL to use quicker memory rather than disk as much as possible, and the quicker the memory is, the faster MySQL can access the data stored there. Large amounts of memory on its own is not as useful as if you actively tweaked the mysqld variables to make use of the extra memory, so you can't be too lazy and just stick in the memory and wait for fireworks.

## Disks

Ultimately, MySQL has to fetch the data from disk, and this is where fast disk access plays a role. The disk seek time is important because it determines how fast the physical disk can move to get to the data it needs, so you should choose the disk with the best disk seek time. Also, SCSI (small computer system interface) disks are usually faster than IDE (Intelligent [or Integrated] Drive Electronics) disks, so you'll probably want these.

An important improvement you can make is to stripe data across multiple disks (where the OS breaks data in parts, spreading it evenly over multiple disks), as well as symlinking (where you create a link from the data directory to another disk). InnoDB tables have a mechanism to split data across multiple disks quite easily, but MyISAM tables do not (being made up of single files), so striping or other forms of RAID can be quite useful. Chapter 16, "Multiple Drives," looks at these topics in more detail.

## CPU

The faster the processor, the quicker any calculations can be done and the quicker the results sent back to the client. Besides processor speed, the bus speed and the size of the cache are important. An analysis of available processors is beyond the scope of this book and will probably be outdated before this book is even published, but be sure to investigate your processor possibilities carefully to see how it performs in various benchmarks.

# Using Benchmarks

MySQL distributions come with a benchmark suite called `run-all-tests`. You can use it to test various DBMSs to see how well they perform. To use it, you need to have Perl, the Perl DBI module, and the DBD module for the DBMS you want to test. Table 13.5 explains the options for `run-all-tests`.

**TABLE 13.5:** OPTIONS FOR *RUN-ALL-TESTS*

| OPTION | DESCRIPTION |
| --- | --- |
| `--comments` | Adds a comment to the benchmark output. |
| `--cmp=server[,server...]` | Runs the test with limits from the specified servers. By running all servers with the same `--cmp`, the test results will be comparable between the different SQL servers. |
| `--create-options=#` | Specifies an extra argument to all create statements. For example, to create all tables as BDB tables, you would use `--create-options=TYPE=BDB`. |
| `--database` | Specifies the database in which the test tables are created. The default is the test database. |
| `--debug` | Displays debugging information. You normally only use this when debugging a test. |

*Continued on next page*

**TABLE 13.5:** OPTIONS FOR *RUN-ALL-TESTS* *(continued)*

| OPTION | DESCRIPTION |
| --- | --- |
| `--dir` | Indicates where the test results should be stored. The default is the default output. |
| `--fast` | Allows the use of nonstandard ANSI SQL commands to make the test go faster. |
| `--fast-insert` | Uses fast inserts where possible, which include multiple value lists, such as INSERT INTO tablename VALUES (values),(values) or simply INSERT INTO tablename VALUES (values) rather than INSERT INTO tablename(fields) VALUES (values). |
| `--field-count` | Specifies how many fields there are to be in the test table. Usually only used when debugging a test. |
| `--force` | Continues the test even when encountering an error. Deletes tables before creating new ones. Usually only used when debugging a test. |
| `--groups` | Indicates how many different groups there are to be in the test. Usually only used when debugging a test. |
| `--lock-tables` | Allows the use of table locking to get more speed. |
| `--log` | Saves the results to the `--dir` directory. |
| `--loop-count (Default)` | Indicates how many times each test loop is to be executed. Usually only used when debugging a test. |
| `--help` | Displays a list of options. |
| `--host='host name'` | Specifies the host where the database server is located. The default is localhost. |
| `--machine="machine or os_name"` | The machine/operating system name that is added to the benchmark output filename. The default is the operating system name + version. |
| `--odbc` | Uses the DBI ODBC driver to connect to the database. |
| `--password='password'` | Specifies the password for the user the test connects as. |
| `--socket='socket'` | Specifies the socket to connect with (if sockets are supported). |
| `--regions` | Specifies how AND levels should be tested. Usually only used when debugging a test. |
| `--old-headers` | Gets the old benchmark headers from the old RUN- file. |
| `--server='server name'` | Specifies which DBMS on which to run the test. These can include Access, Adabas, AdabasD, Empress, Oracle, Informix, DB2, mSQL, MS-SQL, MySQL, Pg, Solid, and Sybase. The default is MySQL. |

*Continued on next page*

**TABLE 13.5:** OPTIONS FOR *RUN-ALL-TESTS* (continued)

| OPTION | DESCRIPTION |
| --- | --- |
| --silent | Does not output information about the server when the test starts. |
| --skip-delete | Specifies that the test tables created are not deleted. Usually only used when debugging a test. |
| --skip-test=test1[,test2,...] | Excludes the specified tests when running the benchmark. |
| --small-test | Speeds up the tests by using smaller limits. |
| --small-tables | Uses fewer rows to run the tests. This would be used if the database cannot handle large tables for some reason (they could have small partitions, for example). |
| --suffix | Adds a suffix to the database name in the benchmark output filename. Used when you want to run multiple tests without overwriting the results. When using the --fast option, the suffix is automatically _fast. |
| --random | Generates random initial values for the sequence of test executions, which could be used to imitate real conditions. |
| --threads=# | Specifies the number of threads to use for multiuser benchmarks. The default is 5. |
| --tcpip | Use TCP/IP to connect to the server. This allows the test to do many new connections in a row as the TCP/IP stack can be filled. |
| --time-limit | Specifies a time limit in seconds for a test loop before the test ends, and the result estimated. The default is 600 seconds. |
| --use-old-results | Uses the old results from the --dir directory instead of actually running the tests. |
| --user='user_name' | Specifies the user to connect as. |
| --verbose | Displays more info. Usually only used when debugging a test. |
| --optimization='some comments' | Adds comments about optimizations done before the test. |
| --hw='some comments' | Adds comments about hardware used for this test. |

To run run-all-tests, change to the sql-bench directory from the base directory. The following is a sample output of the benchmark:

```
% cd sql-bench
% perl run-all-tests --small-test --password='g00r002b'
Benchmark DBD suite: 2.14
Date of test:        2002-07-21 21:35:42
```

```
Running tests on:    Linux 2.2.5-15 i686
Arguments:           --small-test
Comments:
Limits from:
Server version:      MySQL 4.0.1 alpha max log
Optimization:        None
Hardware:
```

ATIS: Total time: 19 wallclock secs ( 5.23 usr  0.96 sys +  0.00 cusr
  0.00 csys =  0.00 CPU)
alter-table: Total time:  2 wallclock secs ( 0.12 usr  0.03 sys +  0.00
 cusr  0.00 csys =  0.00 CPU)
big-tables: Total time:  1 wallclock secs ( 0.43 usr  0.10 sys +  0.00
 cusr  0.00 csys =  0.00 CPU)
connect: Total time:  8 wallclock secs ( 2.90 usr  0.66 sys +  0.00
 cusr  0.00 csys =  0.00 CPU)
create: Total time:  0 wallclock secs ( 0.15 usr  0.01 sys +  0.00
 cusr  0.00 csys =  0.00 CPU)
insert: Total time: 31 wallclock secs ( 8.47 usr  1.43 sys +  0.00
 cusr  0.00 csys =  0.00 CPU)
select: Total time: 55 wallclock secs (17.76 usr  1.71 sys +  0.00
 cusr  0.00 csys =  0.00 CPU)
transactions: Test skipped because the database doesn't support
 transactions
wisconsin: Total time: 42 wallclock secs ( 9.55 usr  1.84 sys +  0.00
 cusr  0.00 csys =  0.00 CPU)

All 9 test executed successfully

Totals per operation:

| Operation | seconds | usr | sys | cpu | tests |
|---|---|---|---|---|---|
| alter_table_add | 1.00 | 0.07 | 0.00 | 0.00 | 92 |
| alter_table_drop | 0.00 | 0.03 | 0.00 | 0.00 | 46 |
| connect | 0.00 | 0.22 | 0.02 | 0.00 | 100 |
| connect+select_1_row | 1.00 | 0.27 | 0.04 | 0.00 | 100 |
| connect+select_simple | 1.00 | 0.27 | 0.04 | 0.00 | 100 |
| count | 1.00 | 0.13 | 0.00 | 0.00 | 100 |
| count_distinct | 1.00 | 0.13 | 0.02 | 0.00 | 100 |
| count_distinct_2 | 1.00 | 0.16 | 0.02 | 0.00 | 100 |
| count_distinct_big | 1.00 | 0.12 | 0.04 | 0.00 | 30 |
| count_distinct_group | 1.00 | 0.17 | 0.00 | 0.00 | 100 |
| count_distinct_group_on_key | 1.00 | 0.13 | 0.01 | 0.00 | 100 |
| count_distinct_group_on_key_parts | 1.00 | 0.16 | 0.01 | 0.00 | 100 |
| count_distinct_key_prefix | 1.00 | 0.12 | 0.01 | 0.00 | 100 |
| count_group_on_key_parts | 1.00 | 0.09 | 0.00 | 0.00 | 100 |
| count_on_key | 20.00 | 6.11 | 0.60 | 0.00 | 5100 |
| create+drop | 0.00 | 0.01 | 0.00 | 0.00 | 10 |
| create_MANY_tables | 0.00 | 0.01 | 0.00 | 0.00 | 10 |

| | | | | | |
|---|---|---|---|---|---|
| create_index | 1.00 | 0.00 | 0.00 | 0.00 | 8 |
| create_key+drop | 0.00 | 0.12 | 0.01 | 0.00 | 100 |
| create_table | 1.00 | 0.03 | 0.00 | 0.00 | 31 |
| delete_all_many_keys | 1.00 | 0.08 | 0.00 | 0.00 | 1 |
| delete_big | 0.00 | 0.01 | 0.00 | 0.00 | 1 |
| delete_big_many_keys | 1.00 | 0.07 | 0.00 | 0.00 | 128 |
| delete_key | 0.00 | 0.06 | 0.01 | 0.00 | 100 |
| delete_range | 1.00 | 0.01 | 0.00 | 0.00 | 12 |
| drop_index | 0.00 | 0.00 | 0.00 | 0.00 | 8 |
| drop_table | 0.00 | 0.01 | 0.00 | 0.00 | 28 |
| drop_table_when_MANY_tables | 0.00 | 0.00 | 0.00 | 0.00 | 10 |
| insert | 57.00 | 13.90 | 2.51 | 0.00 | 44768 |
| insert_duplicates | 1.00 | 0.29 | 0.04 | 0.00 | 1000 |
| insert_key | 0.00 | 0.04 | 0.01 | 0.00 | 100 |
| insert_many_fields | 0.00 | 0.12 | 0.00 | 0.00 | 200 |
| insert_select_1_key | 0.00 | 0.00 | 0.00 | 0.00 | 1 |
| insert_select_2_keys | 0.00 | 0.00 | 0.00 | 0.00 | 1 |
| min_max | 1.00 | 0.06 | 0.01 | 0.00 | 60 |
| min_max_on_key | 17.00 | 8.12 | 0.64 | 0.00 | 7300 |
| multiple_value_insert | 0.00 | 0.03 | 0.00 | 0.00 | 1000 |
| order_by_big | 1.00 | 0.30 | 0.10 | 0.00 | 10 |
| order_by_big_key | 1.00 | 0.29 | 0.14 | 0.00 | 10 |
| order_by_big_key2 | 1.00 | 0.28 | 0.12 | 0.00 | 10 |
| order_by_big_key_desc | 0.00 | 0.35 | 0.08 | 0.00 | 10 |
| order_by_big_key_diff | 0.00 | 0.35 | 0.05 | 0.00 | 10 |
| order_by_big_key_prefix | 1.00 | 0.31 | 0.09 | 0.00 | 10 |
| order_by_key2_diff | 0.00 | 0.01 | 0.00 | 0.00 | 10 |
| order_by_key_prefix | 0.00 | 0.02 | 0.00 | 0.00 | 10 |
| order_by_range | 0.00 | 0.03 | 0.00 | 0.00 | 10 |
| outer_join | 1.00 | 0.01 | 0.00 | 0.00 | 10 |
| outer_join_found | 1.00 | 0.01 | 0.01 | 0.00 | 10 |
| outer_join_not_found | 1.00 | 0.03 | 0.01 | 0.00 | 10 |
| outer_join_on_key | 0.00 | 0.01 | 0.00 | 0.00 | 10 |
| select_1_row | 1.00 | 0.27 | 0.06 | 0.00 | 1000 |
| select_1_row_cache | 1.00 | 0.18 | 0.07 | 0.00 | 1000 |
| select_2_rows | 1.00 | 0.43 | 0.05 | 0.00 | 1000 |
| select_big | 0.00 | 0.31 | 0.10 | 0.00 | 17 |
| select_big_str | 1.00 | 0.55 | 0.22 | 0.00 | 100 |
| select_cache | 4.00 | 0.95 | 0.18 | 0.00 | 1000 |
| select_cache2 | 4.00 | 1.28 | 0.11 | 0.00 | 1000 |
| select_column+column | 1.00 | 0.35 | 0.06 | 0.00 | 1000 |
| select_diff_key | 0.00 | 0.02 | 0.00 | 0.00 | 10 |
| select_distinct | 1.00 | 0.30 | 0.06 | 0.00 | 80 |
| select_group | 4.00 | 0.61 | 0.09 | 0.00 | 391 |
| select_group_when_MANY_tables | 0.00 | 0.00 | 0.00 | 0.00 | 10 |
| select_join | 1.00 | 0.06 | 0.03 | 0.00 | 10 |
| select_key | 0.00 | 0.02 | 0.01 | 0.00 | 20 |
| select_key2 | 0.00 | 0.02 | 0.00 | 0.00 | 20 |

| | | | | | |
|---|---|---|---|---|---|
| select_key2_return_key | 1.00 | 0.12 | 0.00 | 0.00 | 20 |
| select_key2_return_prim | 0.00 | 0.00 | 0.00 | 0.00 | 20 |
| select_key_prefix | 0.00 | 0.05 | 0.00 | 0.00 | 20 |
| select_key_prefix_join | 2.00 | 0.62 | 0.16 | 0.00 | 10 |
| select_key_return_key | 0.00 | 0.02 | 0.00 | 0.00 | 20 |
| select_many_fields | 1.00 | 0.31 | 0.10 | 0.00 | 200 |
| select_range | 2.00 | 0.23 | 0.05 | 0.00 | 41 |
| select_range_key2 | 1.00 | 0.43 | 0.02 | 0.00 | 505 |
| select_range_prefix | 1.00 | 0.42 | 0.05 | 0.00 | 505 |
| select_simple | 0.00 | 0.21 | 0.04 | 0.00 | 1000 |
| select_simple_cache | 0.00 | 0.14 | 0.05 | 0.00 | 1000 |
| select_simple_join | 0.00 | 0.13 | 0.05 | 0.00 | 50 |
| update_big | 1.00 | 0.01 | 0.00 | 0.00 | 10 |
| update_of_key | 1.00 | 0.20 | 0.03 | 0.00 | 500 |
| update_of_key_big | 0.00 | 0.02 | 0.01 | 0.00 | 13 |
| update_of_primary_key_many_keys | 0.00 | 0.12 | 0.02 | 0.00 | 256 |
| update_with_key | 4.00 | 1.03 | 0.12 | 0.00 | 3000 |
| update_with_key_prefix | 1.00 | 0.58 | 0.01 | 0.00 | 1000 |
| wisc_benchmark | 2.00 | 0.70 | 0.16 | 0.00 | 34 |
| TOTALS | 156.00 | 43.84 | 6.55 | 0.00 | 76237 |

The benchmark suite is useful for comparing various platforms. MySQL comes with a set of results, but these are dated and not particularly useful. I suggest repeating the test yourself to make them meaningful in your situation.

It's also important to benchmark your own applications (under the highest possible load) before you roll them out. An application that can help you impose load on your server is super-smack, downloadable from the MySQL site.

Another useful script distributed with MySQL is `crash-me`, which verifies the functionality on a specific installation and tests the reliability of the server under stress (see Table 13.6). It gets its name from the results when an installation fails the test. It's also portable and can test multiple database platforms for comparison purposes. As a result of its behavior, it should never be run in a live environment. It can crash not only the database server, but it also takes significant amounts of memory, meaning it can impact on other programs running on the server. Be aware, though, that MySQL has developed it, so it naturally highlights MySQL strengths and downplays MySQL weaknesses for comparison purposes. For example, triggers and procedures, which MySQL does not currently implement, may seem from viewing the `crash-me` output to be as important as nonstandard MySQL features, such as using || for OR instead of string concatenation.

**TABLE 13.6:** THE *CRASH-ME* OPTIONS

| OPTION | DESCRIPTION |
|---|---|
| --help, --Information | Displays a help list of options. |
| --batch-mode | Runs the test without asking for input and exits if it encounters errors. |
| --comment='some comment' | Adds the specified comment to the crash-me limit file. |

*Continued on next page*

**TABLE 13.6:** THE *CRASH-ME* OPTIONS *(continued)*

| OPTION | DESCRIPTION |
|---|---|
| --check-server | Does a new connection to the server every time it checks if the server is still running. This can be useful if a previous query causes wrong data to start being returned. |
| --database='database' | Creates the test tables in this database. The default is test. |
| --dir='directory_name' | Saves the output to this directory |
| --debug | Displays lots of output to assist in debugging if there is a problem. |
| --fix-limit-file | Reformats the crash-me limit file. This does not rerun the crash-me. |
| --force | Begins the test immediately, without warning and without waiting for input. Use this option to automate the test. |
| --log-all-queries | Displays all executed queries. Mostly used for debugging crash-me. |
| --log-queries-to-file='filename' | Logs full queries to the specified file. |
| --host='hostname' | Runs the test on the specified host. The default is localhost. |
| --password='password' | Specifies the password for the current user. |
| --restart | Saves states during each test, making it possible, in the case of a crash, to continue from where it left off by restarting with the same options. |
| --server='server name' | Specifies the server on which to run the test. These include Access, Adabas, AdabasD, Empress, Oracle, Informix, DB2, Mimer, mSQL, MS-SQL, MySQL, Pg, Solid, or Sybase. The default is MySQL. Other servers will not have their names reported. |
| --user='user_name' | Specifies the username to connect as. |
| --start-cmd='command to restart server' | Will use the specified command to restart the database server in the case of it dying. (The availability of this option says everything!) |
| --sleep='time in seconds' | Specifies the time in seconds to wait before restarting the server. The default is 10 seconds. |

A sample display of crash-me follows:

```
% perl crash-me --password='g00r002b'
Running crash-me 1.57 on 'MySQL 4.0.1 alpha max log'

I hope you didn't have anything important running on this server....
Reading old values from cache: /usr/local/mysql-max-4.0.1-alpha-pc-
linux-gnu-i686/sql-bench/limits/mysql.cfg

NOTE: You should be familiar with 'crash-me --help' before continuing!
```

This test should not crash MySQL if it was distributed together with
 the running MySQL version.
If this is the case you can probably continue without having to worry
 about destroying something.

Some of the tests you are about to execute may require a lot of
memory.  Your tests WILL adversely affect system performance. It's
not uncommon that either this crash-me test program, or the actual
database back-end, will DIE with an out-of-memory error. So might
any other program on your system if it requests more memory at the
wrong time.

Note also that while crash-me tries to find limits for the database server
it will make a lot of queries that can't be categorized as 'normal'.
It's not unlikely that crash-me finds some limit bug in your server so
if you run this test you have to be prepared that your server may die
during it!

We, the creators of this utility, are not responsible in any way if
your database server unexpectedly crashes while this program tries to
find the limitations of your server. By accepting the following
question with 'yes', you agree to the above!

You have been warned!

Start test (yes/no) ?
Tables without primary key: yes
SELECT without FROM: yes
Select constants: yes
Select table_name.*: yes
Allows ' and " as string markers: yes
Double '' as ' in strings: yes
Multiple line strings: yes
" as identifier quote (ANSI SQL): error
` as identifier quote: yes
[] as identifier quote: no
Column alias: yes
Table alias: yes
Functions: yes
Group functions: yes
Group functions with distinct: yes
Group by: yes
Group by position: yes
Group by alias: yes
Group on unused column: yes
Order by: yes
Order by position: yes
Order by function: yes

```
Order by on unused column: yes
Order by DESC is remembered: no
Compute: no
INSERT with Value lists: yes
INSERT with set syntax: yes
allows end ';': yes
LIMIT number of rows: with LIMIT
SELECT with LIMIT #,#: yes
Alter table add column: yes
Alter table add many columns: yes
Alter table change column: yes
Alter table modify column: yes
Alter table alter column default: yes
Alter table drop column: yes
Alter table rename table: yes
rename table: yes
truncate: yes
Alter table add constraint: yes
Alter table drop constraint: no
Alter table add unique: yes
Alter table drop unique: with drop key
Alter table add primary key: with constraint
Alter table add foreign key: yes
Alter table drop foreign key: with drop foreign key
Alter table drop primary key: drop primary key
Case insensitive compare: yes
Ignore end space in compare: yes
Group on column with null values: yes
Having: yes
Having with group function: yes
Order by alias: yes
Having on alias: yes
binary numbers (0b1001): no
hex numbers (0x41): yes
binary strings (b'0110'): no
hex strings (x'1ace'): no
Value of logical operation (1=1): 1
Simultaneous connections (installation default): 101
query size: 1048574

Supported sql types
Type character(1 arg): yes
Type char(1 arg): yes
Type char varying(1 arg): yes
Type character varying(1 arg): yes
Type boolean: no
Type varchar(1 arg): yes
Type integer: yes
```

```
Type int: yes
Type smallint: yes
Type numeric(2 arg): yes
Type decimal(2 arg): yes
Type dec(2 arg): yes
Type bit: yes
Type bit(1 arg): yes
Type bit varying(1 arg): no
Type float: yes
Type float(1 arg): yes
Type real: yes
Type double precision: yes
Type date: yes
Type time: yes
Type timestamp: yes
Type interval year: no
Type interval year to month: no
Type interval month: no
Type interval day: no
Type interval day to hour: no
Type interval day to minute: no
Type interval day to second: no
Type interval hour: no
Type interval hour to minute: no
Type interval hour to second: no
Type interval minute: no
Type interval minute to second: no
Type interval second: no
Type national character varying(1 arg): yes
Type national character(1 arg): yes
Type nchar(1 arg): yes
Type national char varying(1 arg): yes
Type nchar varying(1 arg): yes
Type national character varying(1 arg): yes
Type timestamp with time zone: no

Supported odbc types
Type binary(1 arg): yes
Type varbinary(1 arg): yes
Type tinyint: yes
Type bigint: yes
Type datetime: yes

Supported extra types
Type blob: yes
Type byte: no
Type long varbinary: yes
Type image: no
```

```
Type text: yes
Type text(1 arg): no
Type mediumtext: yes
Type long varchar(1 arg): no
Type varchar2(1 arg): no
Type mediumint: yes
Type middleint: yes
Type int unsigned: yes
Type int1: yes
Type int2: yes
Type int3: yes
Type int4: yes
Type int8: yes
Type uint: no
Type money: no
Type smallmoney: no
Type float4: yes
Type float8: yes
Type smallfloat: no
Type float(2 arg): yes
Type double: yes
Type enum(1 arg): yes
Type set(1 arg): yes
Type int(1 arg) zerofill: yes
Type serial: no
Type char(1 arg) binary: yes
Type int not null auto_increment: yes
Type abstime: no
Type year: yes
Type datetime: yes
Type smalldatetime: no
Type timespan: no
Type reltime: no
Type int not null identity: no
Type box: no
Type bool: yes
Type circle: no
Type polygon: no
Type point: no
Type line: no
Type lseg: no
Type path: no
Type interval: no
Type serial: no
Type inet: no
Type cidr: no
Type macaddr: no
```

```
Type varchar2(1 arg): no
Type nvarchar2(1 arg): no
Type number(2 arg): no
Type number(1 arg): no
Type number: no
Type long: no
Type raw(1 arg): no
Type long raw: no
Type rowid: no
Type mlslabel: no
Type clob: no
Type nclob: no
Type bfile: no
Remembers end space in char(): no
Remembers end space in varchar(): no
Supports 0000-00-00 dates: yes
Supports 0001-01-01 dates: yes
Supports 9999-12-31 dates: yes
Supports 'infinity dates: error
Type for row id: auto_increment
Automatic row id: _rowid


Supported sql functions


Supported odbc functions


Supported extra functions


Supported where functions


Supported sql group functions
Group function AVG: yes
Group function COUNT (*): yes
Group function COUNT column name: yes
Group function COUNT(DISTINCT expr): yes
Group function MAX on numbers: yes
Group function MAX on strings: yes
Group function MIN on numbers: yes
Group function MIN on strings: yes
Group function SUM: yes
Group function ANY: no
Group function EVERY: no
Group function SOME: no


Supported extra group functions
Group function BIT_AND: yes
Group function BIT_OR: yes
```

```
Group function COUNT(DISTINCT expr,expr,...): yes
Group function STD: yes
Group function STDDEV: yes
Group function VARIANCE: no

mixing of integer and float in expression: yes
No need to cast from integer to float: yes
Is 1+NULL = NULL: yes
Is concat('a',NULL) = NULL: yes
LIKE on numbers: yes
column LIKE column: yes
update of column= -column: yes
String functions on date columns: yes
char are space filled: no
DELETE FROM table1,table2...: no
Update with sub select: no
Calculate 1--1: yes
ANSI SQL simple joins: yes
max text or blob size: 1048543 (cache)
constant string size in where: 1048539 (cache)
constant string size in SELECT: 1048565 (cache)
return string size from function: 1047552 (cache)
simple expressions: 1837 (cache)
big expressions: 10 (cache)
stacked expressions: 1837 (cache)
tables in join: 63 (cache)
primary key in create table: yes
unique in create table: yes
unique null in create: yes
default value for column: yes
default value function for column: no
temporary tables: yes
create table from select: yes
index in create table: yes
null in index: yes
null in unique index: yes
null combination in unique index: yes
null in unique index: yes
index on column part (extension): yes
different namespace for index: yes
case independent table names: no
drop table if exists: yes
create table if not exists: yes
inner join: yes
left outer join: yes
natural left outer join: yes
left outer join using: yes
left outer join odbc style: yes
```

```
right outer join: yes
full outer join: no
cross join (same as from a,b): yes
natural join: yes
union: no
union all: no
intersect: no
intersect all: no
except: no
except all: no
except: no
except all: no
minus: no
natural join (incompatible lists): yes
union (incompatible lists): no
union all (incompatible lists): no
intersect (incompatible lists): no
intersect all (incompatible lists): no
except (incompatible lists): no
except all (incompatible lists): no
except (incompatible lists): no
except all (incompatible lists): no
minus (incompatible lists): no
subqueries: no
insert INTO ... SELECT ...: yes
atomic updates: no
views: no
foreign key syntax: yes
foreign keys: no
Create SCHEMA: no
Column constraints: no
Table constraints: no
Named constraints: no
NULL constraint (SyBase style): yes
Triggers (ANSI SQL): no
PSM procedures (ANSI SQL): no
PSM modules (ANSI SQL): no
PSM functions (ANSI SQL): no
Domains (ANSI SQL): no
many tables to drop table: yes
drop table with cascade/restrict: yes
-- as comment (ANSI): yes
// as comment: no
# as comment: yes
/* */ as comment: yes
insert empty string: yes
Having with alias: yes
table name length: 64 (cache)
```

```
column name length: 64 (cache)
select alias name length: +512 (cache)
table alias name length: +512 (cache)
index name length: 64 (cache)
max char() size: 255 (cache)
max varchar() size: 255 (cache)
max text or blob size: 1048543 (cache)
Columns in table: 3398 (cache)
unique indexes: 32 (cache)
index parts: 16 (cache)
max index part length: 255 (cache)
index varchar part length: 255 (cache)
indexes: 32
index length: 500 (cache)
max table row length (without blobs): 65534 (cache)
table row length with nulls (without blobs): 65502 (cache)
number of columns in order by: +64 (cache)
number of columns in group by: +64 (cache)
crash-me safe: yes
reconnected 0 times
```

## Running MySQL in ANSI Mode

Running MySQL in ANSI mode causes it to behave in a more standard way than usual, making it easier to move to another database at a later stage. If you start MySQL with the `--ansi` option, the following differences apply to MySQL's behavior:

- The || symbol does not mean OR; instead, it applies to string concatenation. This is the `PIPES_AS_CONCAT` mysqld `sql-mode` option.

- Having spaces before function names no longer results in an error. This has the consequence that all function names become reserved words. This is the `IGNORE_SPACE` mysqld `sql-mode` option.

- `REAL` is a synonym for `FLOAT`, not for `DOUBLE`. This is the `REAL_AS_FLOAT` mysqld `sql-mode` option.

- The default transaction isolation level is set to `SERIALIZABLE`. This is the `SERIALIZE` mysqld `sql-mode` option.

- The double quote (") character will be an identifier quote character, not a string quote character. This is the `ANSI_QUOTES` mysqld `sql-mode` option.

## Using Different Languages in MySQL

Of course, the data you put into MySQL can be any language you want, but many people around the world who do not speak English as a first language use MySQL. MySQL AB, the company now responsible for MySQL, is based in Sweden, and most of the primary developers are Scandinavian. So, it comes as no surprise that MySQL distributions come with support for other languages. The following languages are currently supported, and more are likely to be added: Czech, Danish, Dutch, English (the default), Estonian, French, German, Greek, Hungarian, Italian, Korean, Norwegian, Norwegian-ny, Polish, Portuguese, Romanian, Russian, Slovak, Spanish, and Swedish.

## Displaying Error Messages in Another Language

Starting MySQL so that it displays error messages in one of these languages is as easy as using the `--language` or `-L` options at startup. To do so in the config file, simply add a line such as the following:

```
language=french
```

You can also edit the error messages yourself (perhaps you want your database to have that personal touch) or contribute your own set in another language, and give something back to the MySQL community. To change the error messages, simply edit the `errmsg.txt` file in the appropriate language directory (usually `/share/language_name` from the MySQL base directory), run the `cmp_error` utility, and restart the server. For example:

```
% cp errmsg.txt errmsg.bak
% vi errmsg.txt
```

Here I edited the error message that read as follows:

```
"No Database Selected",
```

to read as follows instead:

```
"Haven't you forgotten something - No Database Selected",
```

and then saved it:

```
"errmsg.txt" 229 lines, 12060 characters written
% comp_err errmsg.txt errmsg.sys
Found 226 messages in language file errmsg.sys
```

Then restart the server, and the new error messages will take effect:

```
% mysqladmin shutdown
% /etc/rc.d/init.d/mysql start
% mysql -uroot -pg00r002b
mysql> SELECT * FROM a;
ERROR 1046: Haven't you forgotten something - No Database Selected
```

You'll have to repeat the changes if you upgrade to a newer version of MySQL.

## Using a Different Character Set

By default, MySQL uses the Latin1 (ISO-8859-1) character set. The character set determines what characters can be used, as well as the sorting order for queries. You can change the character set by changing the value of the `--default-character-set` option when you start the server. The available character sets currently include the following:

| | | |
|---|---|---|
| latin1 | dos | estonia |
| big5 | german1 | hungarian |
| czech | hp8 | koi8_ukr |
| euc_kr | koi8_ru | win1251ukr |
| gb2312 | latin2 | greek |
| gbk | swe7 | win1250 |
| latin1_de | usa7 | croat |
| sjis | cp1251 | cp1257 |
| tis620 | danish | latin5 |
| ujis | hebrew | |
| dec8 | win1251 | |

You can see what character sets are available in your distribution by looking at the value of the `character_sets` variable.

When you change a character set, you'll need to rebuild your indexes to ensure they sort according to the rules of the new character set.

By default, MySQL is compiled with `--with-extra-charsets=complex`, which makes the other character sets available if necessary. If you are compiling MySQL yourself, and you know you are never going to need other character sets, you can use the `--with-extra-charsets=none` option.

## Adding Your Own Character Set

You can add your own character set as well. If it is a simple character set and does not need multibyte character support or string collating routines for sorting, adding it is easy. It becomes more complex if these extras are required. To add a character set, perform the following steps:

1. Add the new character set to the `sql/share/charsets/Index` file, and give it a unique ID. The path may differ on some distributions, but it'll always be the `Index` file. Here, you can call the new character set `martian`, with an ID of 31:

```
# sql/share/charsets/Index
#
# This file lists all of the available character sets.

big5        1
czech       2
dec8        3
dos         4
german1     5
```

```
hp8                6
koi8_ru            7
latin1             8
latin2             9
swe7              10
usa7              11
ujis              12
sjis              13
cp1251            14
danish            15
hebrew            16
# The win1251 character set is deprecated.  Please use cp1251 instead.
win1251           17
tis620            18
euc_kr            19
estonia           20
hungarian         21
koi8_ukr          22
win1251ukr        23
gb2312            24
greek             25
win1250           26
croat             27
gbk               28
cp1257            29
latin5            30
martian           31
```

2. Create the .conf and place it in the directory, for example, sql/share/charsets/martian.conf. Use one of the existing .conf files as a starting point for this.

In the .conf file, lines beginning with a # are comments, words are separated by any amount of whitespace, and every word must be in hexadecimal format. There are four arrays. In order, they are ctype (containing 257 elements), to_lower and to_upper (each containing 256 elements), and sort_order (also containing 256 elements). The following is a sample .conf file (this is the standard latin1.conf):

```
# Configuration file for the latin1 character set

# ctype array (must have 257 elements)
  00
  20 20 20 20 20 20 20 20 20 28 28 28 28 28 20 20
  20 20 20 20 20 20 20 20 20 20 20 20 20 20 20 20
  48 10 10 10 10 10 10 10 10 10 10 10 10 10 10 10
  84 84 84 84 84 84 84 84 84 84 10 10 10 10 10 10
  10 81 81 81 81 81 81 01 01 01 01 01 01 01 01 01
  01 01 01 01 01 01 01 01 01 01 01 10 10 10 10 10
```

```
10  82  82  82  82  82  82  02  02  02  02  02  02  02  02  02
02  02  02  02  02  02  02  02  02  02  02  10  10  10  10  20
00  00  00  00  00  00  00  00  00  00  00  00  00  00  00  00
00  00  00  00  00  00  00  00  00  00  00  00  00  00  00  00
48  10  10  10  10  10  10  10  10  10  10  10  10  10  10  10
10  10  10  10  10  10  10  10  10  10  10  10  10  10  10  10
01  01  01  01  01  01  01  01  01  01  01  01  01  01  01  01
01  01  01  01  01  01  01  10  01  01  01  01  01  01  01  02
02  02  02  02  02  02  02  02  02  02  02  02  02  02  02  02
02  02  02  02  02  02  02  10  02  02  02  02  02  02  02  02
```

```
# to_lower array (must have 256 elements)
00  01  02  03  04  05  06  07  08  09  0A  0B  0C  0D  0E  0F
10  11  12  13  14  15  16  17  18  19  1A  1B  1C  1D  1E  1F
20  21  22  23  24  25  26  27  28  29  2A  2B  2C  2D  2E  2F
30  31  32  33  34  35  36  37  38  39  3A  3B  3C  3D  3E  3F
40  61  62  63  64  65  66  67  68  69  6A  6B  6C  6D  6E  6F
70  71  72  73  74  75  76  77  78  79  7A  5B  5C  5D  5E  5F
60  61  62  63  64  65  66  67  68  69  6A  6B  6C  6D  6E  6F
70  71  72  73  74  75  76  77  78  79  7A  7B  7C  7D  7E  7F
80  81  82  83  84  85  86  87  88  89  8A  8B  8C  8D  8E  8F
90  91  92  93  94  95  96  97  98  99  9A  9B  9C  9D  9E  9F
A0  A1  A2  A3  A4  A5  A6  A7  A8  A9  AA  AB  AC  AD  AE  AF
B0  B1  B2  B3  B4  B5  B6  B7  B8  B9  BA  BB  BC  BD  BE  BF
E0  E1  E2  E3  E4  E5  E6  E7  E8  E9  EA  EB  EC  ED  EE  EF
F0  F1  F2  F3  F4  F5  F6  D7  F8  F9  FA  FB  FC  FD  FE  DF
E0  E1  E2  E3  E4  E5  E6  E7  E8  E9  EA  EB  EC  ED  EE  EF
F0  F1  F2  F3  F4  F5  F6  F7  F8  F9  FA  FB  FC  FD  FE  FF
```

```
# to_upper array (must have 256 elements)
00  01  02  03  04  05  06  07  08  09  0A  0B  0C  0D  0E  0F
10  11  12  13  14  15  16  17  18  19  1A  1B  1C  1D  1E  1F
20  21  22  23  24  25  26  27  28  29  2A  2B  2C  2D  2E  2F
30  31  32  33  34  35  36  37  38  39  3A  3B  3C  3D  3E  3F
40  41  42  43  44  45  46  47  48  49  4A  4B  4C  4D  4E  4F
50  51  52  53  54  55  56  57  58  59  5A  5B  5C  5D  5E  5F
60  41  42  43  44  45  46  47  48  49  4A  4B  4C  4D  4E  4F
50  51  52  53  54  55  56  57  58  59  5A  7B  7C  7D  7E  7F
80  81  82  83  84  85  86  87  88  89  8A  8B  8C  8D  8E  8F
90  91  92  93  94  95  96  97  98  99  9A  9B  9C  9D  9E  9F
A0  A1  A2  A3  A4  A5  A6  A7  A8  A9  AA  AB  AC  AD  AE  AF
B0  B1  B2  B3  B4  B5  B6  B7  B8  B9  BA  BB  BC  BD  BE  BF
C0  C1  C2  C3  C4  C5  C6  C7  C8  C9  CA  CB  CC  CD  CE  CF
D0  D1  D2  D3  D4  D5  D6  D7  D8  D9  DA  DB  DC  DD  DE  DF
C0  C1  C2  C3  C4  C5  C6  C7  C8  C9  CA  CB  CC  CD  CE  CF
D0  D1  D2  D3  D4  D5  D6  F7  D8  D9  DA  DB  DC  DD  DE  FF
```

```
# sort_order array (must have 256 elements)
  00  01  02  03  04  05  06  07  08  09  0A  0B  0C  0D  0E  0F
  10  11  12  13  14  15  16  17  18  19  1A  1B  1C  1D  1E  1F
  20  21  22  23  24  25  26  27  28  29  2A  2B  2C  2D  2E  2F
  30  31  32  33  34  35  36  37  38  39  3A  3B  3C  3D  3E  3F
  40  41  42  43  44  45  46  47  48  49  4A  4B  4C  4D  4E  4F
  50  51  52  53  54  55  56  57  58  59  5A  5B  5C  5D  5E  5F
  60  41  42  43  44  45  46  47  48  49  4A  4B  4C  4D  4E  4F
  50  51  52  53  54  55  56  57  58  59  5A  7B  7C  7D  7E  7F
  80  81  82  83  84  85  86  87  88  89  8A  8B  8C  8D  8E  8F
  90  91  92  93  94  95  96  97  98  99  9A  9B  9C  9D  9E  9F
  A0  A1  A2  A3  A4  A5  A6  A7  A8  A9  AA  AB  AC  AD  AE  AF
  B0  B1  B2  B3  B4  B5  B6  B7  B8  B9  BA  BB  BC  BD  BE  BF
  41  41  41  41  5C  5B  5C  43  45  45  45  45  49  49  49  49
  44  4E  4F  4F  4F  4F  5D  D7  D8  55  55  55  59  59  DE  DF
  41  41  41  41  5C  5B  5C  43  45  45  45  45  49  49  49  49
  44  4E  4F  4F  4F  4F  5D  F7  D8  55  55  55  59  59  DE  FF
```

The ctype array contains bit values, with one element for one character. The to_lower and to_upper arrays simply hold the uppercase and lowercase characters that correspond to each member of the character set. For example, to_lower['A'] contains a, while to_upper['z'] contains Z.

The sort_order array indicates the order that characters are to be sorted (it usually corresponds to to_upper, in which case the sorting will be case insensitive. All of the arrays are indexed by character value, except ctype, which is indexed by character value + 1 (an old legacy).

**3.** Add the new character set (martian.conf) to the CHARSETS_AVAILABLE and COMPILED_CHARSETS lists in the file configure.in.

**4.** Reconfigure and recompile MySQL, and test the new character set.

If you're brave enough to tackle adding a new complex character set, there are a few more steps to this process. See the MySQL documentation for what is required (as well as the documentation in the existing complex character sets: czech, gbk, sjis, and tis160).

# Summary

To understand how to get the most out of your database server, it's important to understand the number of options you have when fine-tuning the server. To see how an existing server has been set up, use the SHOW VARIABLES statement, as well as SHOW STATUS to see how it's been handling. The output of these two statements can reveal many hidden problems, including queries that are not optimized, poor use of available memory, or simply that it's time for an upgrade.

MySQL supplies four configuration files that can help to get better performance from the server. Just choose the closest of my-huge.cnf, my-large.cnf, my-medium.cnf or my-small.cnf for your server situation.

Two of the easiest and most important variables to tweak are `table_cache` (the number of tables MySQL can keep open) and the `key_buffer_size` (how much of the indexes MySQL can keep in memory, minimizing disk access).

InnoDB databases have their own vagaries and work in a fundamentally different way than MyISAM tables, where each table is related to specific files. InnoDB configuration requires careful planning because disk space is allocated in advance.

Hardware too can be an easy way of improving the performance of a server, with memory, CPU, and disks being of primary importance.

MySQL comes with a benchmark suite, which can be used to compare the performance of various platforms, including other databases.

MySQL was developed in Scandinavia and has had good support for other languages besides English. It is easy to display error messages in other languages or add a character set.

# Chapter 14

# Database Security

SECURITY IS NOT AN optional extra. Plugging leaks in your data security once everything is established is much harder than securing the data properly in the first place. And, as a database administrator (DBA), you may trust your users, but when they accidentally delete a table they didn't even know was there, it's you who'll be blamed. Most of this chapter deals with managing users and ensuring they can do only what they need to do.

Featured in this chapter:

- Security when connecting
- Changing and assigning passwords
- Managing users and permissions
- The MySQL permission tables
- GRANT and REVOKE
- Dangerous privileges
- Application and system security
- Security issues with LOAD DATA LOCAL

## Security When Connecting

When connecting, it is insecure to connect in the following manner:

```
% mysql -uusername -ppassword
```

I use this throughout this chapter for convenience, to make the password visible for purposes of the examples, but a security-conscious user should not connect in this way for the following reasons:

- Anyone looking over your shoulder can see the password in plain text.
- The password could be visible in the history (for example, in Unix, someone getting access to someone else's terminal could scroll through the most recent commands and be able to see the password).
- Programs that view the system status (such as the Unix ps) could see the password in plain text.

Instead, connect by entering the password when prompted for it:

```
% mysql -uroot -p
Enter password:
```

If you need to store the password in a file, make sure it is properly secured. For example, if the password is stored in the my.cnf file in the user's home directory on a server, this file should not be readable by anyone else. The root user of the system can of course read this file. Be aware that the root user of the system is not necessarily the same as the MySQL root user. Similarly, applications often make use of a configuration file to store the database password. Make sure this is secure too.

**WARNING**   *Never store a configuration file that contains a database password for a web application, or any password for that matter, in the web tree.*

Finally, don't use the MYSQL_PWD environment variable to store your password if you desire any form of security, for similar reasons of not specifying the password on the command line. Environment variables are not secure.

## Managing Users and Permissions

MySQL has a well-designed, flexible, and easy-to-manage permissions system. Permissions are what allow or disallow certain users or host machines from connecting to the database server and from performing certain operations on the databases, tables, or even certain columns in the tables.

For example, take some possible scenarios:

◆ A news website includes a database server, a web server, and an intranet where staff update the news. Connections from the web server should only have permission to perform SELECT queries on the database, and connections from the intranet would allow UPDATE and INSERT queries for the staff.

◆ A financial transactions system has one database containing a log of records and one database containing customer balances. UPDATEs are permitted on the customer balance database, but not on the log database.

◆ A booking system has ordinary users who can only insert records to a particular table and an administrator who can update this table.

### The *mysql* Database

When MySQL is installed, the mysql database is one of those automatically created. A thorough knowledge of the tables in this database is vital to be able to effectively administer security on the system (see Table 14.1). Six tables in the mysql database affect system access:

```
mysql> USE mysql;
Database changed
mysql> SHOW TABLES;
```

```
+-----------------+
| Tables_in_mysql |
+-----------------+
| columns_priv    |
| db              |
| func            |
| host            |
| tables_priv     |
| user            |
+-----------------+
6 rows in set (0.00 sec)
```

**TABLE 14.1:** THE MySQL TABLES

| TABLE | DESCRIPTION |
|---|---|
| user | Lists users and the associated hosts and passwords that may access the server, as well as the global permissions they have. It's best to disallow any global permissions and instead specifically allow them access in one of the other tables. |
| db | Lists databases that users may access. Permissions granted here apply to all tables in the database. |
| host | Together with the db table allows a more controlled form of access based on the particular host. |
| tables_priv | Lists access to specific tables. Permissions granted here apply to all columns in the table. |
| columns_priv | Lists access to specific columns. |
| func | Not yet used. |

## WHAT FIELDS THE TABLES CONTAIN

Let's take a look at the tables in the mysql database. Your distribution may contain some slight differences.

```
mysql> SHOW COLUMNS FROM user;
+----------------------+--------------+------+-----+---------+-------+
| Field                | Type         | Null | Key | Default | Extra |
+----------------------+--------------+------+-----+---------+-------+
| Host                 | varchar(60)
                         binary       |      | PRI |         |       |
| User                 | varchar(16)
                         binary       |      | PRI |         |       |
| Password             | varchar(16)
                         binary       |      |     |         |       |
| Select_priv          | enum('N','Y')|      |     | N       |       |
| Insert_priv          | enum('N','Y')|      |     | N       |       |
| Update_priv          | enum('N','Y')|      |     | N       |       |
| Delete_priv          | enum('N','Y')|      |     | N       |       |
```

| | | | | | |
|---|---|---|---|---|---|
| Create_priv | enum('N','Y')| | | N | | |
| Drop_priv | enum('N','Y')| | | N | | |
| Reload_priv | enum('N','Y')| | | N | | |
| Shutdown_priv | enum('N','Y')| | | N | | |
| Process_priv | enum('N','Y')| | | N | | |
| File_priv | enum('N','Y')| | | N | | |
| Grant_priv | enum('N','Y')| | | N | | |
| References_priv | enum('N','Y')| | | N | | |
| Index_priv | enum('N','Y')| | | N | | |
| Alter_priv | enum('N','Y')| | | N | | |
| Show_db_priv | enum('N','Y')| | | N | | |
| Super_priv | enum('N','Y')| | | N | | |
| Create_tmp_table_priv | enum('N','Y')| | | N | | |
| Lock_tables_priv | enum('N','Y')| | | N | | |
| Execute_priv | enum('N','Y')| | | N | | |
| Repl_slave_priv | enum('N','Y')| | | N | | |
| Repl_client_priv | enum('N','Y')| | | N | | |
| ssl_type | enum('','ANY','X509','SPECIFIED') | | | | | |
| ssl_cipher | blob | | | | | |
| x509_issuer | blob | | | | | |
| x509_subject | blob | | | | | |
| max_questions | int(11) unsigned | | | 0 | | |
| max_updates | int(11) unsigned | | | 0 | | |
| max_connections | int(11) unsigned | | | 0 | | |

```
31 rows in set (0.00 sec)
mysql> SHOW COLUMNS FROM db;
```

| Field | Type | Null | Key | Default | Extra |
|---|---|---|---|---|---|
| Host | char(60) binary | | PRI | | |
| Db | char(64) binary | | PRI | | |
| User | char(16) binary | | PRI | | |
| Select_priv | enum('N','Y') | | | N | |
| Insert_priv | enum('N','Y') | | | N | |
| Update_priv | enum('N','Y') | | | N | |
| Delete_priv | enum('N','Y') | | | N | |
| Create_priv | enum('N','Y') | | | N | |
| Drop_priv | enum('N','Y') | | | N | |
| Grant_priv | enum('N','Y') | | | N | |
| References_priv | enum('N','Y') | | | N | |
| Index_priv | enum('N','Y') | | | N | |
| Alter_priv | enum('N','Y') | | | N | |

```
13 rows in set (0.01 sec)
mysql> SHOW COLUMNS FROM host;
+-----------------+-----------------+------+-----+---------+-------+
| Field           | Type            | Null | Key | Default | Extra |
+-----------------+-----------------+------+-----+---------+-------+
| Host            | char(60) binary |      | PRI |         |       |
| Db              | char(64) binary |      | PRI |         |       |
| Select_priv     | enum('N','Y')   |      |     | N       |       |
| Insert_priv     | enum('N','Y')   |      |     | N       |       |
| Update_priv     | enum('N','Y')   |      |     | N       |       |
| Delete_priv     | enum('N','Y')   |      |     | N       |       |
| Create_priv     | enum('N','Y')   |      |     | N       |       |
| Drop_priv       | enum('N','Y')   |      |     | N       |       |
| Grant_priv      | enum('N','Y')   |      |     | N       |       |
| References_priv | enum('N','Y')   |      |     | N       |       |
| Index_priv      | enum('N','Y')   |      |     | N       |       |
| Alter_priv      | enum('N','Y')   |      |     | N       |       |
+-----------------+-----------------+------+-----+---------+-------+
12 rows in set (0.01 sec)
mysql> SHOW COLUMNS FROM tables_priv;
+-------------+---------------------+------+-----+---------+-------+
| Field       | Type                | Null | Key | Default | Extra |
+-------------+---------------------+------+-----+---------+-------+
| Host        | char(60) binary     |      | PRI |         |       |
| Db          | char(64) binary     |      | PRI |         |       |
| User        | char(16) binary     |      | PRI |         |       |
| Table_name  | char(60) binary     |      | PRI |         |       |
| Grantor     | char(77)            |      | MUL |         |       |
| Timestamp   | timestamp(14)       | YES  |     | NULL    |       |
| Table_priv  |set('Select','Insert',
               'Update', 'Delete',
               'Create', 'Drop',
               'Grant', 'References',
               'Index', 'Alter')    |      |     |         |       |
| Column_priv |set('Select','Insert',
               'Update','References')|     |     |         |       |
+-------------+---------------------+------+-----+---------+-------+
8 rows in set (0.01 sec)
mysql> SHOW COLUMNS FROM columns_priv; ;
+-------------+---------------------+------+-----+---------+-------+
| Field       | Type                | Null | Key | Default | Extra |
+-------------+---------------------+------+-----+---------+-------+
| Host        | char(60) binary     |      | PRI |         |       |
| Db          | char(64) binary     |      | PRI |         |       |
| User        | char(16) binary     |      | PRI |         |       |
| Table_name  | char(64) binary     |      | PRI |         |       |
| Column_name | char(64) binary     |      | PRI |         |       |
```

```
| Timestamp   | timestamp(14)          | YES  |     | NULL     |       |
| Column_priv | set('Select','Insert',
               'Update','References') |      |     |          |       |
+-------------+------------------------+------+-----+---------+-------+
7 rows in set (0.01 sec)
mysql> SHOW COLUMNS FROM func;
+-------+----------------------------+------+-----+---------+-------+
| Field | Type                       | Null | Key | Default | Extra |
+-------+----------------------------+------+-----+---------+-------+
| name  | char(64) binary            |      | PRI |         |       |
| ret   | tinyint(1)                 |      |     | 0       |       |
| dl    | char(128)                  |      |     |         |       |
| type  | enum('function','aggregate') |    |     | function |       |
+-------+----------------------------+------+-----+---------+-------+
4 rows in set (0.01 sec)
```

Table 14.2 describes the various privileges.

**TABLE 14.2:** WHAT THE COLUMNS MEAN

| COLUMN | DESCRIPTION |
| --- | --- |
| Host | The host machine from which the user connects. |
| User | The username supplied for the connection (the -u option). |
| Password | The password the user connects as (the -p option). |
| Db | The database on which the user is trying to perform the operation. |
| Select_priv | Permission to return data from a table (a SELECT statement). SELECT results that can be calculated without needing to access a table still return a result even if the user does not have SELECT privileges. |
| Insert_priv | Permission to add new records to the table (an INSERT statement). |
| Update_priv | Permission to modify data in a table (an UPDATE statement). |
| Delete_priv | Permission to remove records from a table (a DELETE statement). |
| Create_priv | Permission to create databases and tables. |
| Drop_priv | Permission to drop databases or tables. |
| Reload_priv | Permission to reload the database (a FLUSH statement or a reload, refresh, or flush issued from mysqladmin). |
| Shutdown_priv | Permission to shut down the server. |
| Process_priv | Permission to view the current MySQL processes or kill MySQL processes (for SHOW PROCESSLIST or KILL SQL statements). |

*Continued on next page*

**TABLE 14.2:** WHAT THE COLUMNS MEAN *(continued)*

| COLUMN | DESCRIPTION |
| --- | --- |
| File_priv | Permission to read and write files on the server (for LOAD DATA INFILE or SELECT INTO OUTFILE statements). Any files that the MySQL user can read are readable. |
| Grant_priv | Permission to grant privileges available to the user to other users. |
| References_priv | Not currently used by MySQL. |
| Index_priv | Permission to create, modify, or drop indexes. |
| Alter_priv | Permission to change the structure of a table (an ALTER statement). |
| Show_db_priv | Permission to see all databases. |
| Super_priv | Permission to connect, even if the maximum number of connections is reached, and perform the CHANGE MASTER, KILL thread, mysqladmin debug, PURGE MASTER LOGS, and SET GLOBAL commands. |
| Create_tmp_table_priv | Permission to create a temporary table (CREATE TEMPORARY TABLE). |
| Lock_tables_priv | Permission to lock a table for which the user has SELECT permission. |
| Execute_priv | Permission to run stored procedures (scheduled for MySQL 5). |
| Repl_client_priv | Permission to ask about replication slaves and masters. |
| Repl_slave_priv | Permission to replicate (see Chapter 12, "Database Replication"). |
| ssl_type | Permission to connect is only granted if Secure Sockets Layer (SSL) is used. |
| ssl_cipher | Permission to connect is only granted if a specific cipher is present. |
| x509_issuer | Permission to connect is only granted if the certificate is issued by a specific issuer. |
| x509_subject | Permission to connect is only granted if the certificate contains a specific subject. |
| max_questions | Maximum number of queries the user can perform per hour. |
| max_updates | Maximum number of updates the user can perform per hour. |
| max_connections | Maximum number of times the user can connect per hour. |

## How MySQL Examines Permissions to Allow Access

When a user tries to connect, MySQL examines the user table first to confirm that the particular user, host, and password combination is listed. If not, the user is denied access. When a user is trying to connect directly to a database, the db table will also be examined if the user gets through the other checks. If the user does not have permission to connect to that database, access is denied.

When a connected user tries to perform an administrative operation (for example, `mysqladmin shutdown`), MySQL examines the column related to the operation from the user table. If permission for the required operation is granted, the operation goes ahead. If not, the operation fails.

When a connected user tries to perform a database-related operation (`SELECT`, `UPDATE`, and so on), MySQL examines the related field from the user table. If permission for the required operation (for the `SELECT`, `UPDATE`, and so on) is granted, the operation is permitted. If not, MySQL goes to the next step.

The db table is examined next. MySQL looks for the database on which the user is performing the operation. If this does not exist, permission is denied, and the operation fails. If the database does exist, and the host and user match, the field relating to the operation is examined. If permission is granted for the required operation, the operation succeeds. If permission is not granted, MySQL proceeds to the next step. If the database and user combination does exist, and the host field is blank, MySQL examines the host table to see whether the host can perform the required operation. If the host and database are found in the host table, the related field on both the host and db tables determines whether the operation succeeds. If permission is granted on both tables, the operation succeeds. If not, MySQL proceeds to the next step.

MySQL examines the tables_priv table taking into account the table(s) on which the operation is being performed. If the host, user, db, and table combination do not exist, the operation fails. If they do exist, the related field is examined. If permission is not granted, MySQL proceeds to the next step. If permission is granted, the operation succeeds.

Finally, MySQL examines the columns_priv tables, taking into account the table columns being used in the operation. If permission related to the required operation is granted here, the operation succeeds. If not, if fails.

The order of precedence for the MySQL permission tables is shown in Figure 14.1.

**FIGURE 14.1**

Precedence for MySQL permission tables

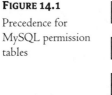
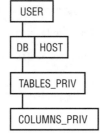

### HOW TO POPULATE THE PERMISSION TABLES

The permission tables are populated with some default values:

```
mysql> SELECT * FROM user;
+-------------------------+-----------------+-----------------+----
---------+-------------+-------------+-------------+-------------+-----
------+-------------+---------------+-------------+-----------+-------
-----+-----------------+-----------+-----------+-------------+------
------+----------------------+-----------------+--------------+------
```

```
-----------+-----------------+----------+-----------+------------+--
------------+--------------+-------------+----------------+
| Host                   | User          | Password          |
Select_priv | Insert_priv | Update_priv | Delete_priv | Create_priv |
Drop_priv | Reload_priv | Shutdown_priv | Process_priv | File_priv |
Grant_priv | References_priv | Index_priv | Alter_priv | Show_db_priv |
Super_priv | Create_tmp_table_priv | Lock_tables_priv | Execute_priv |
Repl_slave_priv | Repl_client_priv | ssl_type | ssl_cipher |
x509_issuer | x509_subject | max_questions | max_updates |
max_connections |
+-------------------------+-----------------+-----------------+----
---------+------------+-------------+------------+-------------+-----
------+------------+-------------+------------+-----------+-------
----+------------+-------------+------------+-------------+------
------+------------+-------------+------------+-------------+------
----------+-----------------+----------+-----------+------------+--
-----------+--------------+-------------+----------------+
| localhost              | root          |                   | Y
| Y          | Y          | Y          | Y         | Y         | Y
| Y          | Y          | Y         | Y         | Y
| Y          | Y         | Y         | Y         | Y
| Y                      | Y                  | Y                 | Y
|            |            |            |            |            | 0 |
0 |              0 |
| test.testhost.co.za     | root          |                   | Y
| Y          | Y          | Y          | Y         | Y         | Y
| Y          | Y          | Y         | Y         | Y
| Y          | Y         | Y         | Y         | Y
| Y                      | Y                  | Y                 | Y
|            |            |            |            |            | 0 |
0 |              0 |
| localhost              |               |                   | N
| N          | N          | N          | N         | N         | N
| N          | N          | N         | N         | N
| N          | N         | N         | N         | N
| N                      | N                  | N                 | N
|            |            |            |            |            | 0 |
0 |              0 |
| test.testhost.co.za     |               |                   | N
| N          | N          | N          | N         | N         | N
| N          | N          | N         | N         | N
| N          | N         | N         | N         | N
| N                      | N                  | N                 | N
|            |            |            |            |            | 0 |
0 |              0 |
+-------------------------+-----------------+-----------------+----
---------+------------+-------------+------------+-------------+-----
------+------------+-------------+------------+-----------+-------
```

```
-----+-----------------+------------+------------+-------------+------
------+------------------------+-----------------+-----------------+------
----------+----------------+------------+-----------+-------------+--
------------+--------------+-------------+----------------+
4 rows in set (0.05 sec)
mysql> SELECT * FROM db;
+------+---------+------+------------+-------------+-------------+----
---------+------------+----------+------------+-----------------+----
--------+------------+
| Host | Db      | User | Select_priv | Insert_priv | Update_priv |
Delete_priv | Create_priv | Drop_priv | Grant_priv | References_priv |
Index_priv | Alter_priv |

+------+---------+------+------------+-------------+-------------+----
---------+------------+----------+------------+-----------------+----
--------+------------+
| %    | test    |      | Y          | Y           | Y           | Y
| Y            | Y        | N          | Y           | Y
Y            |
| %    | test\_% |      | Y          | Y           | Y           | Y
| Y            | Y        | N          | Y           | Y
Y            |
+------+---------+------+------------+-------------+-------------+----
---------+------------+----------+------------+-----------------+----
--------+------------+
2 rows in set (0.01 sec)
mysql> SELECT * FROM host;
Empty set (0.00 sec)
mysql> SELECT * FROM tables_priv;
Empty set (0.00 sec)
mysql> SELECT * FROM columns_priv;
Empty set (0.00 sec)
```

Notice that the default settings are not secure. Anyone can connect from the local host as the root user and have total authority. An anonymous user (where no username is supplied) can connect from the local host to the default test database and to any database where the name begins with *test*.

**NOTE** *In Unix, MySQL uses the Unix login username if no username is supplied. This means that someone logged in as root can simply enter MySQL without specifying a username, and they will have full permissions.*

One of the first tasks to perform in a new installation is to set new permissions and at least a new password for the root user.

### Manipulating the Permission Tables Directly

There are two ways to set permissions—by using the MySQL GRANT and REVOKE statements or by directly changing the values in the tables. The easiest and most convenient way is with the GRANT and REVOKE statements, but it's important to understand how the tables affect permissions. For now, you're going to look at changing permissions by changing the values in the tables with the basic INSERT, UPDATE, and DELETE SQL statements. You'll see the other method later in the section titled "Using GRANT and REVOKE to Manipulate the Permission Tables." To add a password for the root user, you would write the following:

```
mysql> UPDATE user SET password=PASSWORD('g00r002b') WHERE user='root';
Query OK, 2 rows affected (0.00 sec)
Rows matched: 2  Changed: 2  Warnings: 0
```

Notice the use of the PASSWORD() function. You must use this function when updating the tables directly. It encrypts the password so that it cannot be read simply by viewing the contents of the tables. For example:

```
mysql> SELECT host,user,password FROM user;
+---------------------+------+------------------+
| host                | user | password         |
+---------------------+------+------------------+
| localhost           | root | 43b591f759a842a9 |
| test.testhost.co.za | root | 43b591f759a842a9 |
| localhost           |      |                  |
| test.testhost.co.za |      |                  |
+---------------------+------+------------------+
4 rows in set (0.00 sec)
```

**WARNING**  *Be careful when directly changing permissions. Neglecting the* WARNING *clause would mean that all passwords change, and suddenly no existing users would be able to connect.*

Changes to the permissions do not take effect immediately when made directly to the MySQL tables. MySQL needs to reread the grant tables. You can force it to do this by issuing FLUSH PRIVILEGES, mysqladmin flush-privileges, or mysqladmin reload.

```
mysql> INSERT INTO user (Host,User,Password) VALUES ('localhost',
 'administrator', PASSWORD('admin_pwd'));
Query OK, 1 row affected (0.09 sec)
```

Before the permissions are flushed, this data does not take effect. You can connect as the administrator user without any password:

```
% mysql -uadministrator;
Welcome to the MySQL monitor.  Commands end with ; or \g.
Your MySQL connection id is 6 to server version: 4.0.1-alpha-max-log

Type 'help;' or '\h' for help. Type '\c' to clear the buffer.
```

Before the database is reloaded, connecting as administrator is accepted, because, not finding the specific name, connecting is the same as for an anonymous user where no password is needed. You can see this by looking at the third and fourth records from the user table. After the flush, the administrator user can no longer connect without a password.

```
mysql> FLUSH PRIVILEGES;
Query OK, 0 rows affected (0.00 sec)
```

```
mysql> exit
Bye
 % mysql -uadministrator;
ERROR 1045: Access denied for user: 'administrator@localhost' (Using password: NO)
```

It's never good to use the root user for anything but administration. Day-to-day connections should be through users with permissions developed especially for the tasks that user performs. For this sales system, you're going to add two users—an administrator and a regular user. The administrator will have full permissions to do anything, and the regular user will have certain limitations. To add the administrator, you could simply add a record to the user table, giving a full set of permissions to the administrator. But that would mean the administrator of the sales rep system would have full access to any other database that gets developed on the system. It's almost always better to limit permissions at a user level and then activate permissions on a lower level. You're going to add a record to the user and to the database table to do this. I use an INSERT statement without specifying fields (for ease of typing) with the db table example, in case you're following these examples. Be sure that the fields match the fields in the tables from your distribution, in case they have changed:

```
mysql> INSERT INTO user (host,user,password)
VALUES('localhost','administrator',PASSWORD('13tm31n'));
Query OK, 1 row affected (0.00 sec)
mysql> INSERT INTO db
VALUES('localhost','firstdb','administrator','y','y','y','y','n','n',
'n','n','n','n');
Query OK, 1 row affected (0.01 sec)
```

The tables now contain the following:

```
mysql> SELECT * FROM user;
+---------------------------+-----------------+-----------------+----
----------+-------------+-------------+-------------+-------------+-----
------+-------------+---------------+-------------+-------------+-------
-----+-------------+---------------+-------------+-------------+-------
-----+-------------+---------------+-------------+-------------+-------
----------+-----------------+----------+-----------+-------------+--
------------+-------------+------------+-----------------+
| Host                      | User            | Password        |
Select_priv | Insert_priv | Update_priv | Delete_priv | Create_priv |
Drop_priv | Reload_priv | Shutdown_priv | Process_priv | File_priv |
Grant_priv | References_priv | Index_priv | Alter_priv | Show_db_priv |
Super_priv | Create_tmp_table_priv | Lock_tables_priv | Execute_priv |
Repl_slave_priv | Repl_client_priv | ssl_type | ssl_cipher |
x509_issuer | x509_subject | max_questions | max_updates |
max_connections |
+---------------------------+-----------------+-----------------+----
----------+-------------+-------------+-------------+-------------+-----
------+-------------+---------------+-------------+-------------+-------
-----+-------------+---------------+-------------+-------------+-------
```

```
------+-------------------------+------------------+--------------+------
----------+----------------+----------+-----------+------------+--
-----------+--------------+-----------+----------------+
| localhost               | root             |              | Y
| Y          | Y           | Y           | Y           | Y          | Y
| Y          | Y           | Y           | Y           | Y
| Y          | Y           | Y           | Y           | Y
| Y          | Y           | Y           | Y
|            |             |             |             |             | 0 |
0 |           0 |
| test.testhost.co.za     | root             |              | Y
| Y          | Y           | Y           | Y           | Y          | Y
| Y          | Y           | Y           | Y           | Y
| Y          | Y           | Y           | Y           | Y
| Y          | Y           | Y           | Y
|            |             |             |             |             | 0 |
0 |           0 |
| localhost               |                  |              | N
| N          | N           | N           | N           | N          | N
| N          | N           | N           | N           | N
| N          | N           | N           | N           | N
| N          | N           | N           | N
|            |             |             |             |             | 0 |
0 |           0 |
| test.testhost.co.za     |                  |              | N
| N          | N           | N           | N           | N          | N
| N          | N           | N           | N           | N
| N          | N           | N           | N           | N
| N          | N           | N           | N
|            |             |             |             |             | 0 |
0 |           0 |
| localhost               | administrator    | 26981a09472b4835 | N
| N          | N           | N           | N           | N          | N
| N          | N           | N           | N           | N
| N          | N           | N           | N           | N
| N          | N           | N           | N
|            |             |             |             |             | 0 |
0 |           0 |

+-------------------------+------------------+------------------+----
--------+-------------+------------+---------------+------------+----
------+-------------------+---------------+------------+----------+------
----+-------------------+-----------+-------------+-----------+------
-----+-------------------------+-------------+------------+------
----------+-------------------------+-----------+------------+--
-----------+--------------+------------+----------------+
5 rows in set (0.05 sec)
```

```
mysql> SELECT * FROM db;;
+-----------+---------+---------------+-------------+-------------+----
---------+-----------+-------------+-----------+-------------+--------
---------+-----------+------------+
| Host      | Db      | User          | Select_priv | Insert_priv |
Update_priv | Delete_priv | Create_priv | Drop_priv | Grant_priv |
References_priv | Index_priv | Alter_priv |

+-----------+---------+---------------+-------------+-------------+----
---------+-----------+-------------+-----------+-------------+--------
---------+-----------+------------+
| %         | test    |               | Y           | Y           | Y
| Y         | Y           | Y           | N         | Y
| Y         | Y       |            |
| %         | test\_% |               | Y           | Y           | Y
| Y         | Y           | Y           | N         | Y
| Y         | Y       |            |
| localhost | firstdb | administrator | Y           | Y           | Y
| Y         | N           | N           | N         | N
| N         | N       |            |
+-----------+---------+---------------+-------------+-------------+----
---------+-------------+-------------+-----------+-------------+--------
---------+-----------+------------+
```

```
3 rows in set (0.01 sec)
```

The administrator can connect to the database with the password but only perform data manipulation on the firstdb database.

Remember to flush the tables before these permissions take effect:

```
% mysqladmin reload -u root -p
Enter password:
% mysql mysql;
ERROR 1045: Access denied for user: 'root@localhost' (Using password: NO)
```

If you were not logged in as root, you'd get an error indicating that the anonymous user does not have permission:

```
% mysql mysql;
ERROR 1044: Access denied for user: '@localhost' to database 'mysql'
```

### Using GRANT and REVOKE to Manipulate the Permission Tables

Rather than updating the tables directly and having to flush the database, an easier way is to use the GRANT and REVOKE statements to manage permissions. The basic GRANT syntax is as follows:

```
GRANT privilege ON table_or_database_name TO user_name@hostname
  IDENTIFIED BY 'password'
```

To add a regular user for this sales system, you could do the following:

```
mysql> GRANT SELECT ON sales.* TO regular_user@localhost IDENTIFIED BY '13tm37n_2';
Query OK, 0 rows affected (0.00 sec)

mysql> SELECT * FROM user;
+-------------------------+------------------+-----------------+----
---------+-------------+-------------+-------------+-------------+-----
------+-------------+---------------+--------------+-----------+------
-----+----------------+-------------+-------------+-------------+------
------+----------------------+------------------+-------------+------
----------+------------------+-----------+-----------+-------------+--
------------+--------------+-------------+----------------+
| Host                    | User             | Password        |
Select_priv | Insert_priv | Update_priv | Delete_priv | Create_priv |
Drop_priv | Reload_priv | Shutdown_priv | Process_priv | File_priv |
Grant_priv | References_priv | Index_priv | Alter_priv | Show_db_priv |
Super_priv | Create_tmp_table_priv | Lock_tables_priv | Execute_priv |
Repl_slave_priv | Repl_client_priv | ssl_type | ssl_cipher |
x509_issuer | x509_subject | max_questions | max_updates |
max_connections |
+-------------------------+------------------+-----------------+----
---------+-------------+-------------+-------------+-------------+-----
------+-------------+---------------+--------------+-----------+------
-----+----------------+-------------+-------------+-------------+------
------+----------------------+------------------+-------------+------
----------+------------------+-----------+-----------+-------------+--
------------+--------------+-------------+----------------+
| localhost               | root             |                 | Y
| Y         | Y           | Y           | Y           | Y           | Y
| Y           | Y             | Y            | Y         | Y
| Y         | Y               | Y          | Y          | Y
| Y         | Y                     | Y                | Y
|           |                  |          |            |             |
0 |              0 |
| test.testhost.co.za     | root             |                 | Y
| Y         | Y           | Y           | Y           | Y           | Y
| Y           | Y             | Y            | Y         | Y
| Y         | Y               | Y          | Y          | Y
| Y         | Y                     | Y                | Y
|           |                  |          |            |             |
0 |              0 |
| localhost               |                  |                 | N
| N         | N           | N           | N           | N           | N
| N           | N             | N            | N         | N
| N         | N               | N          | N          | N
| N         | N                     | N                | N
|           |                  |          |            |             |
0 |              0 |
```

```
| test.testhost.co.za    |                |                        | N
| N          | N          | N          | N          | N          | N
| N          | N          | N          | N          | N
| N          | N          | N          | N          | N
| N          | N          | N          | N
|            |            |            |            |            | 0 |
0 |          0 |
| localhost              | administrator  | 26981a09472b4835 | N
| N          | N          | N          | N          | N          | N
| N          | N          | N          | N          | N
| N          | N          | N          | N          | N
| N          | N          | N          | N
|            |            |            |            |            | 0 |
0 |          0 |
| localhost              | regular_user   | 1bfcf83b2eb5e59  | N
| N          | N          | N          | N          | N          | N
| N          | N          | N          | N          | N
| N          | N          | N          | N          | N
| N          | N          | N          | N
|            |            |            |            |            | 0 |
0 |          0 |
+------------------------+----------------+------------------+----
---------+------------+------------+------------+------------+-----
------+----------------+------------+------------+------------+-------
----+------------+------------+------------+------------+-------
------+------------------+------------+------------+-------
----------+----------------+----------+------------+------------+--
-----------+----------------+------------+----------------+
6 rows in set (0.05 sec)
mysql> SELECT * FROM db;
+----------+--------+---------------+------------+------------+----
---------+------------+------------+------------+------------+-------
---------+------------+-----------+
| Host     | Db     | User          | Select_priv | Insert_priv |
Update_priv | Delete_priv | Create_priv | Drop_priv | Grant_priv |
References_priv | Index_priv | Alter_priv |
+----------+--------+---------------+------------+------------+----
---------+------------+------------+------------+------------+-------
---------+------------+-----------+
| %        | test   |               | Y          | Y          | Y
| Y        | Y          | Y          | N          | Y
| Y        | Y          |
| %        | test\_% |              | Y          | Y          | Y
| Y        | Y          | Y          | N          | Y
| Y        | Y          |
| localhost | firstdb | administrator | Y          | Y          | Y
| Y        | N          | N          | N          | N
| N        | N          |
```

```
| localhost | sales   | regular_user  | Y           | N            | N
| N         | N       | N             | N           | N
| N         | N       |
+-----------+---------+---------------+-------------+-------------+----
---------+-------------+-------------+------------+------------+--------
---------+------------+------------+
4 rows in set (0.01 sec)
```

The password is automatically encrypted when issued with GRANT, so there is no need to use the PASSWORD() function to encrypt it. In fact, if you do, you'll re-encrypt the password! You can change the password by reissuing the same permissions with a new password.

You can also revoke permissions in the same way as you grant them:

```
mysql> REVOKE SELECT ON sales.* FROM regular_user@localhost;
Query OK, 0 rows affected (0.01 sec)
mysql> SELECT * FROM user;
+--------------------------+------------------+------------------+----
---------+-------------+-------------+------------+------------+-----
------+-------------+---------------+-------------+------------+-------
-----+-------------------+-------------+------------+---------------+------
------+--------------------------+-------------+---------------+------
----------+------------------+----------+------------+-------------+--
------------+---------------+-------------+-----------------+
| Host                     | User             | Password         |
Select_priv | Insert_priv | Update_priv | Delete_priv | Create_priv |
Drop_priv | Reload_priv | Shutdown_priv | Process_priv | File_priv |
Grant_priv | References_priv | Index_priv | Alter_priv | Show_db_priv |
Super_priv | Create_tmp_table_priv | Lock_tables_priv | Execute_priv |
Repl_slave_priv | Repl_client_priv | ssl_type | ssl_cipher |
x509_issuer | x509_subject | max_questions | max_updates |
max_connections |
+--------------------------+------------------+------------------+----
---------+-------------+-------------+------------+------------+-----
------+-------------+---------------+-------------+------------+-------
-----+-------------------+-------------+------------+---------------+------
------+--------------------------+-------------+---------------+------
----------+------------------+----------+------------+-------------+--
------------+---------------+-------------+-----------------+
| localhost                | root             |                  | Y
| Y         | Y           | Y           | Y          | Y          | Y
| Y         | Y           | Y             | Y           | Y
| Y         | Y               | Y           | Y          | Y
| Y         | Y                     | Y                |
|           |             |          |              |              | 0 |
0 |          0 |
| test.testhost.co.za      | root             |                  | Y
| Y         | Y           | Y           | Y          | Y          | Y
| Y         | Y           | Y             | Y           | Y
```

```
| Y           | Y            | Y          | Y          | Y
| Y           |             | Y          | Y          | Y
|            |            |            |            |            | 0 |
0 |           0 |
| localhost                  |            |            | N
| N           | N            | N          | N          | N          | N
| N           | N            | N          | N          | N
| N           | N            | N          | N          | N
| N           | N            | N          | N
|            |            |            |            |            | 0 |
0 |           0 |
| test.testhost.co.za        |            |            | N
| N           | N            | N          | N          | N          | N
| N           | N            | N          | N          | N
| N           | N            | N          | N          | N
| N           | N            | N          | N
|            |            |            |            |            | 0 |
0 |           0 |
| localhost                  | administrator    | 26981a09472b4835 | N
| N           | N            | N          | N          | N          | N
| N           | N            | N          | N          | N
| N           | N            | N          | N          | N
| N           | N            | N          | N
|            |            |            |            |            | 0 |
0 |           0 |
| localhost                  | regular_user     | 1bfcf83b2eb5e59  | N
| N           | N            | N          | N          | N          | N
| N           | N            | N          | N          | N
| N           | N            | N          | N          | N
| N           | N            | N          | N
|            |            |            |            |            | 0 |
0 |           0 |
+-------------------------+-----------------+-----------------+----
---------+------------+------------+-------------+------------+-----
------+-------------+-----------------+------------+------------+-------
-----+-------------+------------+------------+------------+------
------+-------------------------+------------+-------------+------
----------+------------------------+-----------+-----------+------------+--
------------+---------------+------------+------------------+
6 rows in set (0.05 sec)
mysql> SELECT * FROM db;
+----------+---------+--------------+------------+------------+----
---------+-------------+------------+-----------+------------+-------
---------+-----------+-----------+
| Host     | Db      | User         | Select_priv | Insert_priv |
Update_priv | Delete_priv | Create_priv | Drop_priv | Grant_priv |
References_priv | Index_priv | Alter_priv |
```

```
+-----------+---------+---------------+-------------+-------------+----
---------+-------------+-------------+-----------+-------------+--------
---------+-------------+-------------+
| %         | test    |               | Y           | Y           | Y
| Y           | Y           | Y           | N           | Y
| Y           | Y           |
| %         | test\_% |               | Y           | Y           | Y
| Y           | Y           | Y           | N           | Y
| Y           | Y           |
| localhost | firstdb | administrator | Y           | Y           | Y
| Y           | N           | N           | N           | N
| N           | N           |
+-----------+---------+---------------+-------------+-------------+----
---------+-------------+-------------+-----------+-------------+--------
---------+-------------+-------------+
```

3 rows in set (0.00 sec)

Notice that all trace of the user has been removed from the db table but that the user still exists in the user table. There is no way to remove this from the table without directly deleting it. A user with no permissions (called USAGE permission) can still connect to the server and access some information, such as, for early versions of MySQL 4, viewing the existing databases! For example:

```
mysql> exit
Bye
% mysql -uregular_user -pl3tm37n_2
Welcome to the MySQL monitor.  Commands end with ; or \g.
Your MySQL connection id is 21 to server version: 4.0.1-alpha-max-log

Type 'help;' or '\h' for help. Type '\c' to clear the buffer.

mysql> SHOW DATABASES;
+----------+
| Database |
+----------+
| firstdb  |
| mysql    |
| test     |
+----------+
3 rows in set (0.00 sec)
```

To remove all traces of the user, delete them from the user table directly (while connected as root):

```
mysql> exit
Bye
% mysql mysql -uroot -pg00r002b
Welcome to the MySQL monitor.  Commands end with ; or \g.
Your MySQL connection id is 22 to server version: 4.0.1-alpha-max-log
```

Type 'help;' or '\h' for help. Type '\c' to clear the buffer.

```
mysql> DELETE FROM user WHERE user='regular_user';
Query OK, 1 row affected (0.00 sec)
mysql> SELECT * FROM user;
+------------------------+------------------+------------------+----
---------+------------+-------------+-------------+-------------+-----
------+-------------+--------------+-------------+-----------+-------
-----+-------------------+--------------+-------------+-------------+------
------+-------------------+-------------+--------------+-------------+------
----------+-----------------+----------+------------+-------------+--
------------+--------------+-------------+-----------------+

| Host                   | User             | Password         |
Select_priv | Insert_priv | Update_priv | Delete_priv | Create_priv |
Drop_priv | Reload_priv | Shutdown_priv | Process_priv | File_priv |
Grant_priv | References_priv | Index_priv | Alter_priv | Show_db_priv |
Super_priv | Create_tmp_table_priv | Lock_tables_priv | Execute_priv |
Repl_slave_priv | Repl_client_priv | ssl_type | ssl_cipher |
x509_issuer | x509_subject | max_questions | max_updates |
max_connections |
+------------------------+------------------+------------------+----
---------+------------+-------------+-------------+-------------+-----
------+-------------+--------------+-------------+-----------+-------
-----+-------------------+--------------+-------------+-------------+------
------+-------------------+-------------+--------------+-------------+------
----------+-----------------+----------+------------+-------------+--
------------+--------------+-------------+-----------------+

| localhost              | root             |                  | Y
| Y          | Y           | Y           | Y           | Y
| Y          | Y           | Y           | Y           | Y
| Y          | Y           | Y           | Y           | Y
| Y          | Y           | Y           | Y           | Y
|            |             |             |             |             | 0 |
0 |              0 |
| test.testhost.co.za    | root             |                  | Y
| Y          | Y           | Y           | Y           | Y
| Y          | Y           | Y           | Y           | Y
| Y          | Y           | Y           | Y           | Y
| Y          | Y           | Y           | Y           | Y
|            |             |             |             |             | 0 |
0 |              0 |
| localhost              |                  |                  | N
| N          | N           | N           | N           | N
| N          | N           | N           | N           | N
| N          | N           | N           | N           | N
| N          | N           | N           | N           | N
|            |             |             |             |             | 0 |
0 |              0 |
```

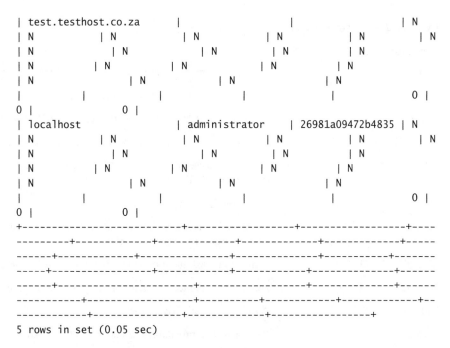

```
| test.testhost.co.za     |                 |                   | N
| N          | N          | N          | N          | N          | N
| N          | N          | N          | N          | N
| N          | N          | N          | N          | N
| N          | N          | N          | N
|          |          |          |          |          0 |
0 |          0 |
| localhost               | administrator   | 26981a09472b4835 | N
| N          | N          | N          | N          | N          | N
| N          | N          | N          | N          | N
| N          | N          | N          | N          | N
| N          | N          | N          | N
|          |          |          |          |          0 |
0 |          0 |
+---------------------------+-----------------+-------------------+-------------------+----
---------+-------------+-------------+-------------+-------------+-----
------+-------------+---------------+-------------+-------------+-------
-----+---------------+-------------+-------------+-------------+-------
------+---------------------+-------------------+-------------+-------
----------+-------------------+----------+------------+------------+--
------------+---------------+-------------+-----------------+
5 rows in set (0.05 sec)
```

Table 14.3 describes all the privileges available.

**TABLE 14.3:** PRIVILEGES

| PRIVILEGE | DESCRIPTION |
| --- | --- |
| ALL | Grants all the basic permissions. |
| ALL PRIVILEGES | Same as ALL. |
| ALTER | Permission to change the structure of a table (an ALTER statement), excluding indexes. |
| CREATE | Permission to create databases or tables, excluding indexes. |
| CREATE TEMPORARY TABLES | Permission to create a temporary table (CREATE TEMPORARY TABLE statement). |
| DELETE | Permission to remove records from a table (a DELETE statement). |
| DROP | Permission to drop databases or tables, excluding indexes. |
| EXECUTE | Permission to run stored procedures (scheduled for MySQL 5). |
| FILE | Permission to read and write files on the server (for LOAD DATA INFILE or SELECT INTO OUTFILE statements). Any files that the MySQL user can read are readable. |

*Continued on next page*

**TABLE 14.3:** PRIVILEGES *(continued)*

| PRIVILEGE | DESCRIPTION |
| --- | --- |
| GRANT | Permission to grant permissions owned by the user to another user. |
| INDEX | Permission to create, modify, or drop indexes. |
| INSERT | Permission to add new records to the table (an INSERT statement). |
| LOCK TABLES | Permission to lock a table for which the user has SELECT permission. |
| PROCESS | Permission to view the current MySQL processes or kill MySQL processes (for SHOW PROCESSLIST or KILL SQL statements). |
| REFERENCES | Not currently used by MySQL. |
| RELOAD | Permission to reload the database (a FLUSH statement or a reload, refresh, or flush issued from mysqladmin). |
| REPLICATION CLIENT | Permission to ask about the replication slaves and masters. |
| REPLICATION SLAVE | Permission to replicate from the server (slaves need this to replicate). |
| SHOW DATABASES | Permission to see all databases. |
| SELECT | Permission to return data from a table (a SELECT statement). |
| SHUTDOWN | Permission to shut down the server. |
| SUPER | Permission to connect, even if the maximum number of connections is reached, and perform the CHANGE MASTER, KILL thread, mysqladmin debug, PURGE MASTER LOGS, and SET GLOBAL commands. |
| UPDATE | Permission to modify data in a table (an UPDATE statement). |
| USAGE | Permission to connect to the server and perform statements available to all (for early versions of MySQL 4 this included SHOW DATABASES). |

The earlier example granted permissions for all tables in the sales database. You can easily manipulate this by changing the database and table names you grant on (see Table 14.4).

**TABLE 14.4:** DATABASE AND TABLE NAMES

| NAME | DESCRIPTION |
| --- | --- |
| *.* | All tables in all databases |
| * | All tables in the current database |
| databasename.* | All tables in the database *databasename* |
| databasename.tablename | The table *tablename* in the database *databasename* |

For example:

```
mysql> GRANT SELECT ON *.* TO regular_user@localhost IDENTIFIED BY '13tm37n_2';
Query OK, 0 rows affected (0.00 sec)
```

Because permission is granted on all databases, there is no need for an entry in the database table; just the user table, with the field select_priv set to Y:

```
mysql> SELECT * FROM user;
+--------------------+--------------+------------------+------------
+------------+------------+------------+------------+----------+--
----------+--------------+-------------+-----------+------------+---
-------------+------------+------------+----------+------------+------
-------+--------------+
| Host               | User         | Password         | Select_priv
| Insert_priv | Update_priv | Delete_priv | Create_priv | Drop_priv |
Reload_priv | Shutdown_priv | Process_priv | File_priv | Grant_priv |
References_priv | Index_priv | Alter_priv | ssl_type | ssl_cipher |
x509_issuer | x509_subject |
+--------------------+--------------+------------------+------------
+------------+------------+------------+------------+----------+--
----------+--------------+-------------+-----------+------------+---
-------------+------------+------------+----------+------------+------
-------+--------------+
| localhost          | root         | 43b591f759a842a9 | Y
| Y          | Y          | Y          | Y          | Y          | Y
| Y          | Y          | Y          | Y          | Y
| Y          | Y          | NONE       |            |            |
|
| test.testhost.co.za | root        | 43b591f759a842a9 | Y
| Y          | Y          | Y          | Y          | Y          | Y
| Y          | Y          | Y          | Y          | Y
| Y          | Y          | NONE       |            |            |
|
| localhost          |             |                  | N
| N          | N          | N          | N          | N          | N
| N          | N          | N          | N          | N
| N          | N          | NONE       |            |            |
|
| test.testhost.co.za |           |                  | N
| N          | N          | N          | N          | N          | N
| N          | N          | N          | N          | N
| N          | N          | NONE       |            |            |
|
| localhost          | administrator | 74126e0c6742d7e9 | N
| N          | N          | N          | N          | N          | N
| N          | N          | N          | N          | N
| N          | N          | NONE       |            |            |
|
```

```
| localhost              | regular_user  | 1bfcf83b2eb5e591 | Y
| N          | N         | N         | N          | N          | N
| N          | N         | N          | N          | N
| N          | N         | NONE      |            |            |
|
+--------------------+---------------+-------------------+------------
+------------+------------+-------------+-------------+-----------+--
-----------+-------------+------------+------------+----------+------------+---
--------------+-----------+------------+-----------+----------+-------------+------
-------+-------------+
6 rows in set (0.00 sec)
```

### Using SET to Set User Passwords

Another way to change passwords is with the SET PASSWORD statement. Any nonanonymous user can change their own password in this way. (This is another reason to assign users carefully. It's not unheard of for a user to change their password, denying others access, because they do not realize they share this username!)

You can set a password for the user you're connected as follows:

```
mysql> SET PASSWORD=PASSWORD('g00r002b2');
Query OK, 0 rows affected (0.00 sec)
```

A user with access to the user table in the mysql database can set passwords for other users too, by specifying the user:

```
mysql> SET PASSWORD FOR root=PASSWORD('g00r002b');
Query OK, 0 rows affected (0.00 sec)
```

Remember to use the PASSWORD() function to encrypt the password. If you don't, the password is stored in the user table as plain text, but because on connection the given password is automatically encrypted before being compared to the password in the user table, you will not be able to connect (if you try this, you'll need to refer to the section titled "What to Do If You Can't Connect..." afterward to continue):

```
mysql> SET PASSWORD FOR root='g00r002b';
Query OK, 0 rows affected (0.00 sec)
```

Now, after exiting you won't be able to reconnect as root:

```
% mysql -uroot -pg00r002b2
ERROR 1045: Access denied for user: 'root@localhost' (Using password: YES)
```

### Using mysqladmin to Set User Passwords

When using mysqladmin, as with the GRANT statement, you should not use the PASSWORD() function:

```
% mysqladmin -uroot -pg00r002b password g00r002b
```

### Wildcard Permissions

There's no need to enter 1,001 hosts if that's how many hosts to which you need to grant access. MySQL accepts wildcards in the host table. For example, the following allows a user to connect from a host ending with marsorbust.co.za:

```
mysql> GRANT SELECT ON sales.* TO regular_user@"%.marsorbust.co.za"
 IDENTIFIED BY '13tm37n';
Query OK, 0 rows affected (0.03 sec)
mysql> SELECT * FROM user WHERE host LIKE '%mars%';
+--------------------------+-----------------+-----------------+----
---------+------------+-------------+-------------+------------+-----
------+------------+-----------------+-------------+----------+-------
-----+-----------------+-------------+------------+---------------+------
------+------------+-------------------+-------------+------------+------
----------+-----------------+-------------+------------+------------+--
------------+---------------+-------------+----------------+
| Host                     | User            | Password        |
Select_priv | Insert_priv | Update_priv | Delete_priv | Create_priv |
Drop_priv | Reload_priv | Shutdown_priv | Process_priv | File_priv |
Grant_priv | References_priv | Index_priv | Alter_priv | Show_db_priv |
Super_priv | Create_tmp_table_priv | Lock_tables_priv | Execute_priv |
Repl_slave_priv | Repl_client_priv | ssl_type | ssl_cipher |
x509_issuer | x509_subject | max_questions | max_updates |
max_connections |
+--------------------------+-----------------+-----------------+----
---------+------------+-------------+-------------+------------+-----
------+------------+-----------------+-------------+----------+-------
-----+-----------------+-------------+------------+---------------+------
------+------------+-------------------+-------------+------------+------
----------+-----------------+-------------+------------+------------+--
------------+---------------+-------------+----------------+
| %.marsorbust.co.za       | regular_user    | 1bfcf83b2eb5e591 | N
| N            | N           | N            | N            | N
| N            | N           | N            | N            | N
| N            | N           | N            | N            | N
| N            | N           | N            | N            | N
|             |             |              |              |          0 |
0 |             0 |
+--------------------------+-----------------+-----------------+----
---------+------------+-------------+-------------+------------+-----
------+------------+-----------------+-------------+----------+-------
-----+-----------------+-------------+------------+---------------+------
------+------------+-------------------+-------------+------------+------
----------+-----------------+-------------+------------+------------+--
------------+---------------+-------------+----------------+
1 row in set (0.05 sec)
```

The quotes in the GRANT statement allow wildcards, or any special characters, to be used. You can of course also insert wildcards into the MySQL tables directly.

## What to Do If You Can't Connect or Have No Permissions

It's not impossible. Maybe you revoke yourself into oblivion, use DELETE where you shouldn't have, or even damage the files holding the permission tables, and now you can't connect at all, even as root. Fear not; there is a solution!

First, stop MySQL completely. As the root user on Unix, if you run MySQL out of /init.d, you may be able to run the following:

```
% /etc/rc.d/init.d/mysql stop
Killing mysqld with pid 5091
Wait for mysqld to exit\c
.\c
.\c
.\c
.\c
020612 01:14:41  mysqld ended

done
```

If not, still as root, you'll need to kill the specific MySQL-related processes:

```
% ps -ax |grep mysql
 5195 pts/0     S        0:00 sh /usr/local/mysql/bin/mysqld_safe --datadir=/usr/lo
 5230 pts/0     S        0:00 /usr/local/mysql-max-4.0.1-alpha-pc-linux-gnu-i686/bi
 5232 pts/0     S        0:00 /usr/local/mysql-max-4.0.1-alpha-pc-linux-gnu-i686/bi
 5233 pts/0     S        0:00 /usr/local/mysql-max-4.0.1-alpha-pc-linux-gnu-i686/bi
 5234 pts/0     S        0:00 /usr/local/mysql-max-4.0.1-alpha-pc-linux-gnu-i686/bi
 5235 pts/0     S        0:00 /usr/local/mysql-max-4.0.1-alpha-pc-linux-gnu-i686/bi
 5236 pts/0     S        0:00 /usr/local/mysql-max-4.0.1-alpha-pc-linux-gnu-i686/bi
 5237 pts/0     S        0:00 /usr/local/mysql-max-4.0.1-alpha-pc-linux-gnu-i686/bi
 5238 pts/0     S        0:00 /usr/local/mysql-max-4.0.1-alpha-pc-linux-gnu-i686/bi
 5239 pts/0     S        0:00 /usr/local/mysql-max-4.0.1-alpha-pc-linux-gnu-i686/bi
 5240 pts/0     S        0:00 /usr/local/mysql-max-4.0.1-alpha-pc-linux-gnu-i686/bi
 5241 pts/0     S        0:00 /usr/local/mysql-max-4.0.1-alpha-pc-linux-gnu-i686/bi
% kill 5195 5230 5232 5233 5234 5235 5236 5237 5238 5239 5240 5241
mysqld ended
```

In the eventuality that this doesn't work, you may have to use kill -9 (followed by the process ID) to really kill the process.

On Windows, you can simply use the task manager to close MySQL.

Then, restart MySQL without the grant tables (this ignores any permission restrictions):

```
% mysqld_safe --skip-grant-tables
```

And now you should be able to add a root password, either through directly manipulating the tables directly, with GRANT, or with mysqladmin:

```
% mysqladmin -u root password 'g00r002b'
```

Don't forget to stop the server, and restart it without `--skip-grant-tables`, to activate your root password.

### WHAT TO DO IF THE USER TABLE BECOMES CORRUPTED

Sometimes it can happen that the user table has become corrupted, so you still cannot change the password with mysqladmin. This happened to me once after a crash and could conceivably happen if someone tampers with the files directly. If you want to follow this example, you can simulate the loss of the user table by renaming it, and then flushing the tables (the original will probably still be cached otherwise):

```
% mv user.MYD user_bak.olddata
% mysql -uroot -pg00r002b;
Welcome to the MySQL monitor.  Commands end with ; or \g.
Your MySQL connection id is 6 to server version: 4.0.1-alpha-max-log

Type 'help;' or '\h' for help. Type '\c' to clear the buffer.

mysql>FLUSH TABLES;
mysql> SELECT * FROM user;
ERROR 1016: Can't open file: 'user.MYD'. (errno: 145)
```

If this is the case, you should still start MySQL without the grant tables and then try dropping the table:

```
mysql> DROP TABLE user;
Query OK, 0 rows affected (0.01 sec)

CREATE TABLE user (
  Host varchar(60) binary NOT NULL default '',
  User varchar(16) binary NOT NULL default '',
  Password varchar(16) binary NOT NULL default '',
  Select_priv enum('N','Y') NOT NULL default 'N',
  Insert_priv enum('N','Y') NOT NULL default 'N',
  Update_priv enum('N','Y') NOT NULL default 'N',
  Delete_priv enum('N','Y') NOT NULL default 'N',
  Create_priv enum('N','Y') NOT NULL default 'N',
  Drop_priv enum('N','Y') NOT NULL default 'N',
  Reload_priv enum('N','Y') NOT NULL default 'N',
  Shutdown_priv enum('N','Y') NOT NULL default 'N',
  Process_priv enum('N','Y') NOT NULL default 'N',
  File_priv enum('N','Y') NOT NULL default 'N',
  Grant_priv enum('N','Y') NOT NULL default 'N',
```

```
        References_priv enum('N','Y') NOT NULL default 'N',
        Index_priv enum('N','Y') NOT NULL default 'N',
        Alter_priv enum('N','Y') NOT NULL default 'N',
        Show_db_priv enum('N','Y') NOT NULL default 'N',
        Super_priv enum('N','Y') NOT NULL default 'N',
        Create_tmp_table_priv enum('N','Y') NOT NULL default 'N',
        Lock_tables_priv enum('N','Y') NOT NULL default 'N',
        Execute_priv enum('N','Y') NOT NULL default 'N',
        Repl_slave_priv enum('N','Y') NOT NULL default 'N',
        Repl_client_priv enum('N','Y') NOT NULL default 'N',
        ssl_type enum('','ANY','X509','SPECIFIED') NOT NULL default '',
        ssl_cipher blob NOT NULL,
        x509_issuer blob NOT NULL,
        x509_subject blob NOT NULL,
        max_questions int(11) unsigned NOT NULL default '0',
        max_updates int(11) unsigned NOT NULL default '0',
        max_connections int(11) unsigned NOT NULL default '0',
        PRIMARY KEY  (Host,User)
    ) TYPE=MyISAM COMMENT='Users and global privileges';
    Query OK, 0 rows affected (0.00 sec)
```

This probably still won't give you permission, however:

```
mysql> GRANT SELECT ON sales.* TO regular_user@localhost IDENTIFIED BY '13tm37n';
ERROR 1047: Unknown command
mysql> exit
Bye
[root@test mysql]# mysqladmin -uroot password 'g00r002b'
mysqladmin: unable to change password; error: 'You must have privileges
 to update tables in the mysql database to be able to change passwords
 for others'
```

You'll need to insert some values into the table once more. Here you add the default values. Be sure they match the columns for the user table you created, if it is different:

```
[root@test mysql]# mysql mysql
Welcome to the MySQL monitor.  Commands end with ; or \g.
Your MySQL connection id is 5 to server version: 4.0.1-alpha-max-log

Type 'help;' or '\h' for help. Type '\c' to clear the buffer.
mysql>INSERT INTO user VALUES ('localhost', 'root', '', 'Y', 'Y', 'Y',
 'Y', 'Y', 'Y', 'Y', 'Y', 'Y', 'Y', 'Y', 'Y', 'Y', 'Y', 'Y', 'Y', 'Y',
 'Y', 'Y', 'Y', 'Y', '', '', '', '', 0, 0, 0);
Query OK, 1 row affected (0.01 sec)
mysql>INSERT INTO user VALUES ('%', 'root', '', 'Y', 'Y', 'Y',
 'Y', 'Y', 'Y', 'Y', 'Y', 'Y', 'Y', 'Y', 'Y', 'Y', 'Y', 'Y', 'Y', 'Y',
 'Y', 'Y', 'Y', 'Y', '', '', '', '', 0, 0, 0);
Query OK, 1 row affected (0.00 sec)
```

```
mysql> INSERT INTO user VALUES ('localhost', '', '', 'N', 'N', 'N',
 'N', 'N', 'N', 'N', 'N', 'N', 'N', 'N', 'N', 'N', 'N', 'N', 'N', 'N',
 'N', 'N', 'N', 'N', '', '', '', '', 0, 0, 0);
Query OK, 1 row affected (0.00 sec)
mysql> INSERT INTO user VALUES ('localhost', '', '', 'N', 'N', 'N',
 'N', 'N', 'N', 'N', 'N', 'N', 'N', 'N', 'N', 'N', 'N', 'N', 'N', 'N',
 'N', 'N', 'N', 'N', '', '', '', '', 0, 0, 0);
Query OK, 1 row affected (0.00 sec)
```

You'll need to reload (or flush the privilege tables) in order to activate the permissions, and then once again you can start issuing commands:

```
mysql> exit
Bye
[root@test mysql]# mysqladmin reload
[root@test mysql]# mysql
Welcome to the MySQL monitor.  Commands end with ; or \g.
Your MySQL connection id is 7 to server version: 4.0.1-alpha-max-log

Type 'help;' or '\h' for help. Type '\c' to clear the buffer.

mysql> GRANT SELECT ON sales.* TO regular_user@localhost IDENTIFIED BY '13tm37n';
Query OK, 0 rows affected (0.00 sec)
```

### OTHER GRANT OPTIONS

By default, MySQL does not allow a user to pass their permissions onto someone else. And, being a control freak, I don't suggest you allow your users to do this. You've probably got a good reason for not granting them the permission in the first place, and you wouldn't want another user to override this. But, if you must—perhaps in a situation where there are multiple trusted users—there is a way. The WITH GRANT OPTION will allow a user to grant any permissions that they have to another user.

The following demonstrates this in action, using two databases: sales and customer. The administrator creates a regular_user2, with permission to perform SELECT queries on the sales database, and then grants the GRANT option to the first regular_user, who has permission to SELECT on the customer database, who will then in turn grant the same rights to regular_user2:

```
mysql> GRANT SELECT ON sales.* TO regular_user2@localhost IDENTIFIED BY '13tm37n';
Query OK, 0 rows affected (0.01 sec)
mysql> GRANT SELECT ON customer.* TO regular_user@localhost IDENTIFIED
 BY '13tm37n' WITH GRANT OPTION;
Query OK, 0 rows affected (0.00 sec)
mysql> exit
Bye
% mysql -u regular_user2 -p13tm37n
Welcome to the MySQL monitor.  Commands end with ; or \g.
Your MySQL connection id is 3 to server version: 4.0.1-alpha-max-log
```

```
Type 'help;' or '\h' for help. Type '\c' to clear the buffer.
mysql> GRANT SELECT ON customer.* TO regular_user@localhost IDENTIFIED
 BY 'l3tm37n' WITH GRANT OPTION;
ERROR 1044: Access denied for user: 'regular_user2@localhost' to database 'customer'
```

Regular_user2 cannot grant anything to another user:

```
mysql> exit
Bye
[root@test /root]# mysql -u regular_user -pl3tm37n
Welcome to the MySQL monitor.  Commands end with ; or \g.
Your MySQL connection id is 4 to server version: 4.0.1-alpha-max-log

Type 'help;' or '\h' for help. Type '\c' to clear the buffer.
mysql> GRANT SELECT ON customer.* TO regular_user@localhost IDENTIFIED
 BY 'l3tm37n' WITH GRANT OPTION;
Query OK, 0 rows affected (0.00 sec)
```

However, regular_user can grant permissions to regular_user2.

There are some other useful options that help avoid the possibility of one user hogging connections. These limit queries, updates, or connections to a certain number per hour. The three options are as follows:

```
MAX_QUERIES_PER_HOUR n
MAX_UPDATES_PER_HOUR n
MAX_CONNECTIONS_PER_HOUR n
```

Without these three options, the only limit on user activity is the max_user_connections variable. But this is global, and you cannot limit one kind of user from an activity.

### Where Could User Limitation Be Useful?

Limiting database-intensive queries, such as searches that involve many joins of large tables, can be useful. The application could connect as a different user with this limit. The application is still a better place to do this limiting, but an hourly limit may be useful in some situations—for example, situations where there is potential for denial of service attacks, or situations where one user could make multiple connections and cause the performance of the database server to degrade.

### Which Type of User Limitation to Use?

Connections usually have the lowest impact on the database, but there is still the possibility that max_user_connections could be taken up by one user. Setting MAX_CONNECTIONS_PER_HOUR is the most cautious option.

Sometimes you may not be worried about the number of connections, but rather about a user performing multiple queries at the same time or performing extraneous queries. You could set MAX_QUERIES_PER_HOUR to avoid users performing unnecessary queries and wasting resources or performing too many of a possible heavy query in a short space of time.

UPDATEs have a higher performance impact than SELECTs and a very marked impact where table locking is used (such as the default MyISAM table type). You may use MAX_UPDATES_PER_HOUR to limit updates for performance reasons or where users need not make many updates.

**TIP**   *It pays to be paranoid. Users can abuse the database, intentionally or not. If you cannot see a use for them to have certain permissions, do not grant them. It's always easier to add permissions than to take away permissions once they've been granted. I've encountered large systems where the security consisted only of one user and one password. When this was compromised, it proved impossible to gracefully add limitations.*

As an example of user limitations, you can limit regular_user2 to two connections per hour:

```
mysql> GRANT SELECT ON sales.* TO regular_user2@localhost IDENTIFIED BY '13tm37n'
    WITH MAX_CONNECTIONS_PER_HOUR 2;
Query OK, 0 rows affected (0.00 sec)
```

If regular_user2 exceeds the number of connections, they'll get an error such as follows:

```
ERROR 1226: User 'regular_user2' has exceeded the 'max_connections'
  resource (current value: 2)
```

Similarly, if MAX_QUERIES_PER_HOUR was assigned and exceeded, the error message would be as follows:

```
ERROR 1226: User 'regular_user2' has exceeded the 'max_questions'
  resource (current value: 4)
```

**TIP**   *Be reasonable with your limitations. If a user should only perform one query an hour, realize that they could enter an incorrect query and have to perform a second one.*

## A Strategy for Managing Users Securely

The more complex your needs, the more complex your strategy will have to be. Simple websites can often suffice with two users: an administration user who can update data and a user for the website application who can only perform SELECTs from certain tables, for example. The general principle is to grant the user only the privileges they need and no more. If they need more at a later stage, it is easy to grant them additional ones. But taking them away is another matter!

MySQL users are mostly of three kinds: There are individual people (for example, Anique or Channette), applications (for example, a salary system or the news website), and roles (for example, updating the news or updating the salaries). These may overlap to various degrees—for example, Anique may update both salaries and news, using both applications and performing both roles. The DBA needs to decide whether to issue Anique and Channette their own passwords, issue passwords to the news and salary systems, or create a user based upon whether the news or salaries are being updated.

If you opt for users as individuals and issue Anique her own password, she only has to remember one login to the database. But then she needs to be given access to update both the salary and news databases. If she, or the application she is using, makes a mistake, there is the possibility of her damaging data on which she should not even be working. For example, if the salary and news databases both have a days_data table—with the news database version growing continually until it is archived and the salary data being manually removed after it has been processed—there is the possibility of her removing the news table when she meant to remove the salary table.

If you opt for users as applications, you solve some of these problems. However, it seems a user now has to remember two passwords. Also, you cannot track which user has made which changes to the database. You have a solution, however, because where security is necessary, it's likely that the individual will have to log into the application (potentially allowing you to track the changes an individual makes to the database), and the application then logs into the database. The user could have the same username and password to both applications, but they could never destroy news data when connected as the salary application (as you'd not have given the salary user permission to update the news database).

Applications, though, often have many roles, with many levels of user. Perhaps anyone may view their own salary details, but only an administrator can update them. Giving the application permission to update data potentially allows an ordinary user to update the data. Consider also the development process: A trusted senior developer builds the salary administration component of the application, and a team of junior developers builds the salary-viewing component. Issuing the same password to the application allows the junior developers to update the data when they don't need to and probably shouldn't be allowed to update it. In this case, you could issue usernames based upon a combination of role and application (salary administration, salary viewing, news administrator, news viewing).

Some principles to keep in mind include the following:

◆ Never issue a user the root password. They should always be connecting with another username and password.

◆ Always issue the minimum permissions you can. (But be reasonable! You'll always get some sadists who take great glee in granting permission on a query-by-query basis. For example, allowing the user to read the surname column, then forcing them to come begging for more permission when they need to read the first name shortly afterward.) The global permissions assigned in the user table should always be N, though, and then access to specific databases granted in the db table.

◆ For critical data, it must be possible to trace changes made by individuals. In general, people interact with the database through an application. The burden for managing access on an individual level then usually falls on the application.

## Avoiding Granting Dangerous Privileges

Although you should always issue the minimum privileges required, there are some privileges that are particularly dangerous, where the security risk may outweigh the convenience factor. Remember that you should never grant access on a global level.

The following privileges in particular could be security risks:

**Any privileges on the mysql database**    A malicious user can still gain access even after being able to only view the encrypted passwords.

**ALTER**    A malicious user could make changes to the privilege tables, such as renaming them, which renders them ineffective.

**DROP**    If a user can DROP the mysql database, the permission limitations will no longer be in place.

**FILE**   Users with the FILE privilege can potentially access any file that is readable by all. They can also create a file that has the MySQL user privileges.

**GRANT**   This allows users to give their privileges to others who may not be as trustworthy as the original user.

**PROCESS**   Queries that are running can be viewed in plain text, which includes any that change or set passwords.

**SHUTDOWN**   It's unlikely a DBA will be fooled into granting this privilege easily, and it should go without saying that users with the SHUTDOWN privilege can shut down the server and deny access to everyone.

# SSL Connections

The connection between the client and the server is by default not encrypted. In most network architectures, this would not be a risk because the connection between the database client and server is not public. But there are instances where data needs to be moved over public lines, and an unencrypted connection potentially allows someone to view the data as it is moved.

MySQL can be configured to support SSL connections, although this does impact on performance. To do this, perform the following steps:

1. Install the openssl library, which can be found at www.openssl.org/.
2. Configure MySQL with the --with-vio --with-openssl option.

If you need to check whether an existing installation of MySQL supports SSL (or whether your installation has worked), check to see whether the variable have_openssl is YES:

```
mysql> SHOW VARIABLES LIKE '%ssl';
+---------------+-------+
| Variable_name | Value |
+---------------+-------+
| have_openssl  | YES   |
+---------------+-------+
1 row in set (0.00 sec)
```

Once SSL is supported, you can make use of it with various grant options (see Table 14.5).

**TABLE 14.5:** SSL Grant Options

| OPTION | DESCRIPTION |
| --- | --- |
| REQUIRE SSL | The client must connect with SSL encryption. |
| REQUIRE X509 | The client has to have a valid certificate to connect. |
| REQUIRE ISSUER cert_issuer | The client has to have a valid certificate issued by cert_issuer to connect. |
| REQUIRE SUBJECT cert_subject | The client has to have a valid certificate with the subject cert_subject. |
| REQUIRE CIPHER cipher | The client has to make use of the specified cipher. |

REQUIRE SSL is the least restrictive of the SSL options. SSL encryption of any kind is acceptable. This would be useful where you don't want to send plain text, but simple encryption of the connection is sufficient:

```
mysql> GRANT ALL PRIVILEGES ON securedb.* TO root@localhost IDENTIFIED
  BY "g00r002b" REQUIRE SSL;
Query OK, 0 rows affected (0.01 sec)
```

REQUIRE X509 is the same, but it is marginally more restrictive because the certificate must be a valid one:

```
mysql> GRANT ALL PRIVILEGES ON securedb.* TO root@localhost IDENTIFIED
  BY "g00r002b" REQUIRE X509;
Query OK, 0 rows affected (0.01 sec)
```

REQUIRE ISSUER and REQUIRE SUBJECT are more secure because the certificate has to come from a specific issuer or contain a specific subject:

```
mysql> GRANT ALL PRIVILEGES ON securedb.* TO root@localhost IDENTIFIED
  BY "g00r002b" REQUIRE ISSUER "C=ZA, ST=Western Cape, L=Cape Town,
  O=Mars Inc CN=Lilian Nomvete/Email=lilian@marsorbust.co.za";
Query OK, 0 rows affected (0.01 sec)
mysql> GRANT ALL PRIVILEGES ON securedb.* TO root@localhost IDENTIFIED
  BY "g00r002b" REQUIRE SUBJECT "C=ZA, ST=Western Cape, L=Cape Town,
  O=Mars Inc CN=Benedict Mhlala/Email=benedict@marsorbust.co.za";
Query OK, 0 rows affected (0.01 sec)
```

REQUIRE CIPHER allows you to ensure that weak SSL algorithms are not used, as you can specify a specific cipher:

```
mysql> GRANT ALL PRIVILEGES ON securedb.* TO root@localhost IDENTIFIED
  BY "g00r002b" REQUIRE CIPHER "EDH-RSA-DES-CBC3-SHA";
Query OK, 0 rows affected (0.01 sec)
```

You can specify any or all of the previous options at the same time (the AND is optional):

```
mysql> GRANT ALL PRIVILEGES ON securedb.* TO root@localhost IDENTIFIED
  BY "g00r002b" REQUIRE ISSUER "C=ZA, ST=Western Cape, L=Cape Town,
  O=Mars Inc CN=Lilian Nomvete/Email=lilian@marsorbust.co.za" AND
  SUBJECT "C=ZA, ST=Western Cape, L=Cape Town, O=Mars Inc CN=Benedict
  Mhlala/Email=benedict@marsorbust.co.za" AND CIPHER "EDH-RSA-DES-CBC3-SHA";
Query OK, 0 rows affected (0.01 sec)
```

## Application Security

Most security holes are caused by poor applications. There are a number of common pitfalls to avoid:

- ◆ Never trust user data. Always verify any data entered by a user.
- ◆ Inserting quotations in a website form is a common cause of breakages. For example, an application takes a username and password and runs a query such as SELECT * FROM passwords WHERE

username='$username' AND password='$password'. Poorly designed applications will allow $password to contain something like aaa';DELETE FROM passwords;. MySQL parsing the query thinks the single quote after the three *a*'s is the end of the query and then happily performs the next query. Most languages have simple functions to avoid this, escaping any quotations in the string, such as mysql_real_escape_string() in C or addslashes() in PHP.

- Check the size of the data. A complex calculation may work well with a single digit number, but a 250-digit number passed by a user may cause the application to crash.
- Remove any special characters from strings passed to MySQL.
- Use quotes around numbers as well as strings.

## System Security

By default, MySQL runs as its own user on Unix. The user and group are mysql. Never be tempted to allow anyone access to the system as the mysql user—it should only be for the database itself. MySQL also creates a separate directory where it places data files. This directory is accessible only to the mysql user. The default settings have been chosen for a reason; keep to these principles:

- Separate the data directory.
- Secure the data directory (no one else should be able to read, much less write, in the MySQL data directory).
- Run MySQL as its own user.

## Security Issues with *LOAD DATA LOCAL*

Restoring from a client machine may be convenient, but it does come with a security risk. Someone could use LOAD DATA LOCAL to read any files to which the user they are connecting as has access. They could do this by creating a table and reading from the table after they have loaded the data. If they were connecting as the same user as the web server, and have the right access to run queries, this becomes dangerous. By default, MySQL allows LOAD DATA LOCAL. To prevent this and disallow all LOAD DATA LOCAL, start the MySQL server with the --local-infile=0 option. You could also compile MySQL without the --enable-local-infile option.

## Summary

The MySQL user management mechanism is powerful, flexible, and often misused. The mysql database contains the various permission tables that allow access to be controlled based on user, host, and the action being performed. You can update the tables directly with SQL statements (in which case flushing the tables activates the changes) or through the more convenient GRANT and REVOKE statements.

The first task in a new installation should be to issue a root password. Until then, anyone can connect as root and have full access to everything. You can use mysqladmin, the SET statement, or GRANT to do this.

MySQL allows SSL connections for added security. This is not installed by default because it has performance implications.

You also learned some general principles for securing your data:

◆ Never issue a user the root password. They should always be connecting with another username.

◆ Never give anyone access to the user table, even for reading. Just viewing the encrypted password is enough to potentially allow a user full access.

◆ Always issue the minimum permissions you can. Issuing minimum permissions means that the user table contains N for all columns.

◆ For critical data, it must be possible to trace changes made by individuals. In general, people interact with the database through an application. The burden for managing access on an individual level then usually falls on the application.

◆ Ensure you cannot connect as the root user without a password from any server.

◆ Passwords should never be stored in plain text and should not be dictionary words.

◆ Check the user privileges every now and again and make sure that no one has granted anyone else inappropriate privileges.

# Chapter 15

# Installing MySQL

PERHAPS YOU'RE A BEGINNER and need to install your own copy of MySQL to have something on which to practice. Or perhaps you're lucky enough to have had systems administrators performing this task for you until now, and you're just curious. Whatever the reason, if you use MySQL extensively, you're likely to need to install MySQL yourself at some stage. And if you're approaching the task with trepidation, this chapter aims to ease you through the process and make you wonder afterward what all the fuss was about.

Featured in this chapter:

- Deciding between a source and a binary distribution
- Installing on Windows
- Installing on Unix
- Installing source and binary distributions
- Compiling MySQL optimally
- Installing multiple servers on the same machine
- Using mysqld_multi to manage multiple servers
- Upgrading from MySQL version 3.23 to version 4

## Deciding Whether to Install a Source or Binary Distribution

MySQL is an open-source development, which means the source code is available to anyone who wants it for free. Operating systems such as Linux and FreeBSD are also open source, but Windows is proprietary software, meaning the source code is owned and controlled by Microsoft. Because the MySQL source code is available, you have two ways to install MySQL:

- Installing from binary, which means you use a distribution that has already been compiled by the MySQL developers (or another party)
- Installing from source, which means you compile the MySQL source code yourself and install it

Installing a binary is usually the easiest and quickest way to install MySQL, but the choice depends on a number of factors, as well as how comfortable you are with compiling software. Windows users rarely need to do this, but FreeBSD users, for example, may find themselves doing this quite often. There are a number of reasons you may want to install from source:

◆ The system you are installing on does not have a binary distribution. Binary distributions were available for Linux, FreeBSD, Windows, Solaris, MacOS X, HP-UX, AIX, SCO, SGI Irix, Dec OSF, and BSDi at the time of writing, although not all of these had distributions for the latest version of MySQL.

◆ You think you can better optimize MySQL by using a different compiler or different compilation options.

◆ You want something that is not available in a binary distribution, such as additional character sets, a bug fix, or a different configuration.

Tables 15.1 and 15.2 provide overviews of the directories in a default binary and source installation, respectively.

**TABLE 15.1:** DIRECTORIES OF A BINARY INSTALLATION

| DIRECTORY | DESCRIPTION |
| --- | --- |
| bin | This is where the binary executables are found, including the all-important mysqld, as well as all the utilities such as mysqladmin, mysqlcheck, and mysqldump. |
| data | The actual databases, as well as log files. |
| include | The C header files. |
| lib | The compiled libraries. |
| scripts | This contains the mysql_install_db script. |
| share/mysql | A directory for each language containing files with the error messages for that specific language. |
| sql-bench | Benchmark results and utilities. |

**TABLE 15.2:** DIRECTORIES OF A SOURCE INSTALLATION

| DIRECTORY | DESCRIPTION |
| --- | --- |
| bin | This is where the binary executables for the client programs and utilities are found, such as mysqladmin, mysqlcheck, and mysqldump. |
| include | The C header files. |

*Continued on next page*

**TABLE 15.2:** DIRECTORIES OF A SOURCE INSTALLATION *(continued)*

| DIRECTORY | DESCRIPTION |
| --- | --- |
| info | Documentation files in Info format. |
| lib | The compiled libraries. |
| libexec | The mysqld server goes here, not in the bin directory, in a default source installation. |
| share/mysql | A directory for each language containing files with the error messages for that specific language. |
| sql-bench | Benchmark results and utilities. |
| var | The actual databases, as well as log files. |

# Installing MySQL on Windows

You need the following to install MySQL on a Windows machine:

- ◆ An operating system in the Windows family—in other words, currently Windows 95/98/Me or Windows NT/2000/XP.
- ◆ A copy of either the MySQL executables or the MySQL source (if you want to compile MySQL yourself).
- ◆ A program to unzip the distribution file.
- ◆ Enough space on your system for MySQL.
- ◆ Support for TCP/IP (Transmission Control Protocol/Internet Protocol). If your machine can connect to the Internet, you have this already. If not, install it (it's a network protocol).
- ◆ If you want to connect to MySQL via ODBC (Open Database Connectivity)—for example, to connect Microsoft Access to MySQL—you'll also need the MyODBC driver.

## Installing a Binary Distribution on Windows

To install onto one of Windows NT/2000/XP, you'll need to ensure that you're logged on as a user with administrator privileges. To upgrade from an earlier installation of MySQL, you'll need to stop the server. If it's running as a service, stop it with the following:

```
C:\> NET STOP MySQL
```

Or you can use mysqladmin:

```
C:\mysql\bin> mysqladmin -u root -pg00r002b shutdown
```

If you want to change the executable you're using (such as from mysqld-max-nt to mysqld-opt), on Windows NT/2000/XP you'll have to remove the service:

```
C:\mysql\bin> mysqld-max-nt --remove
```

Now perform the following steps:

1. Unzip the zipped distribution file and place it in a temporary directory.

2. Run the executable `setup.exe`, which begins the installation. By default MySQL is installed into `C:\mysql`, although many Windows users prefer to place it in a location such as `C:\Program Files\MySQL\`. If you change the location, you must specify the new location in the configuration file (usually `my.ini`):

   ```
   basedir=D:/installation-path/
   datadir=D:/data-path/
   ```

3. MySQL comes with a number of executable files. Choose the one you want depending on your needs (see Table 15.3).

**TABLE 15.3:** EXECUTABLE FILES

| FILE | DESCRIPTION |
| --- | --- |
| mysqld | A binary that supports debugging, automatic memory allocation checking, transactional tables (InnoDB and BDB), and symbolic links. |
| mysqld-opt | An optimized binary that comes with no support for transactional tables (InnoDB or BDB). |
| mysqld-nt | An optimized binary that supports named pipes (for use with NT/2000/XP). It can run on 95/98/Me, but no named pipes will be created, as these operating systems do not support it. |
| mysqld-max | An optimized binary that supports transactional tables (InnoDB and BDB) and symbolic links. |
| mysqld-max-nt | An optimized binary that supports transactional tables (InnoDB and BDB), which are named pipes when run on NT/2000/XP, and symbolic links. |

### INSTALLING MYSQL AS A SERVICE ON WINDOWS NT/2000/XP

If you're serious about running MySQL on Windows, you'll of course want to run it as a service. This allows the process to start automatically (which you'd want for a database server) when Windows starts, and shut down automatically when Windows shuts down. Services are run by Windows itself and are not affected by users logging in and out.

With NT/2000/XP, install MySQL as a service as follows:

```
C:\> c:\mysql\bin\mysqld-max-nt --install
```

If you don't want MySQL to start automatically, but still want it as a service, run the same command with the `manual` option:

```
C:\mysql\bin> mysqld-max-nt --install-manual
```

You can then start the service with the following:

```
C:\> net start mysql
The MySql service is starting.
The MySql service was started successfully.
```

And stop it with the usual `mysqladmin shutdown` or the following:

```
C:\> net stop mysql
The MySql service is stopping...........
The MySql service was stopped successfully.
```

To remove it as a service, run the following:

```
C:\> c:\mysql\bin\mysqld-max-nt -remove
```

You can also use the Services Control Panel, and click Start or Stop.

Note that Windows NT has a problem shutting down MySQL automatically because it doesn't wait long enough for MySQL to shut down before killing it (so the shutdown is not clean, increasing the chances of corruption).

To overcome this in NT, open the Registry editor `\winnt\system32\regedt32.exe` and set a new value in milliseconds for `WaitToKillServiceTimeout` at `HKEY_LOCAL_MACHINE\SYSTEM\CurrentControlSet\Control` in the Registry tree.

For more details on starting MySQL, see Chapter 10, "Basic Administration." Refer to Table 15.1 earlier in this chapter for a brief overview of the contents of the newly created directories.

# Installing MySQL on Unix

You'll need the following to install MySQL on a Unix machine:

- An operating system in the Unix family (Linux, FreeBSD, and so on)
- A copy of either the MySQL binaries or the MySQL source (if you want to compile MySQL yourself)
- gunzip (gzip or zcat) and tar to extract and decompress the distribution file (the GNU versions are recommended)
- Enough space on your system for MySQL
- make and a C++ compiler (such as gcc) if you're planning to compile from source

## Installing a Binary (tar) Distribution on Unix

To install MySQL on Unix from a binary distribution, perform the following steps:

1. Change to the root user. You'll most likely need to be root to perform the commands that follow:

   ```
   % su -
   Password:
   ```

**2.** Add the MySQL user and MySQL group, which MySQL will run as. *Never run MySQL as root!* You can give the user and group another name if you want:

```
% groupadd mysql
% useradd -g mysql mysql
```

**NOTE** *The commands may be slightly different on your version of Unix (for example,* adduser *and* addgroup*).*

**3.** Change to the directory you want to place MySQL in. By default, MySQL expects to be in /usr/local from a binary installation, but you can place this anywhere you like. If you change the location, you'll need to make some changes to the setup and to some of the utilities distributed with MySQL to point them to the new location:

```
% cd /usr/local
```

**4.** Now extract the file:

```
% gunzip -c /home/ mysql-max-4.x.x-platform-os-extra.tar.gz | tar -xf -
```

The filename you'll see will depend on the distribution you're using. I'm seeing mysql-max-4.0.2-alpha-pc-linux-gnu-i686 at present. Make sure you have the right version for your system.

**WARNING** *The Sun version of tar has been known to give problems, so use the GNU version of tar instead.*

Once this is complete, a new directory will have been created, based on the name of the distribution you're installing, as follows:

```
% ls -l my*
total 1
drwxr-xr-x  13 mysql    users          1024
  Jul  1 14:15 mysql-max-4.x.x-platform-os-extra
```

That name is a bit clunky for everyday use, and you'll most probably want to create a symlink mysql pointing to the new directory so that /usr/local/mysql/ can be the path to MySQL:

```
% ln -s mysql-max-4.x.x-platform-os-extra mysql
% ls -l my*
lrwxrwxrwx   1 root     root             40
  Jul 27 23:07 mysql -> mysql-max-4.x.x-platform-os-extra
```

The newly installed directory contains the following:

```
% cd mysql
% ls -l
total 4862
-rw-r--r--  1 mysql    users         19106 Jul  1 14:06 COPYING
-rw-r--r--  1 mysql    users         28003 Jul  1 14:06 COPYING.LIB
-rw-r--r--  1 mysql    users        122323 Jul  1 13:16 ChangeLog
-rw-r--r--  1 mysql    users          6808 Jul  1 14:06 INSTALL-BINARY
```

```
-rw-r--r--    1 mysql    users        1937 Jul  1 13:16 README
drwxr-xr-x    2 mysql    users        1024 Jul  1 14:15 bin
-rwxr-xr-x    1 mysql    users         773 Jul  1 14:15 configure
drwxr-x---    4 mysql    users        1024 Jul  1 14:15 data
drwxr-xr-x    2 mysql    users        1024 Jul  1 14:15 include
drwxr-xr-x    2 mysql    users        1024 Jul  1 14:15 lib
drwxr-xr-x    2 mysql    users        1024 Jul  1 14:15 man
-rw-r--r--    1 mysql    users     2508431 Jul  1 14:06 manual.html
-rw-r--r--    1 mysql    users     2159032 Jul  1 14:06 manual.txt
-rw-r--r--    1 mysql    users       91601 Jul  1 14:06 manual_toc.html
drwxr-xr-x    6 mysql    users        1024 Jul  1 14:15 mysql-test
drwxr-xr-x    2 mysql    users        1024 Jul  1 14:15 scripts
drwxr-xr-x    3 mysql    users        1024 Jul  1 14:15 share
drwxr-xr-x    7 mysql    users        1024 Jul  1 14:15 sql-bench
drwxr-xr-x    2 mysql    users        1024 Jul  1 14:15 support-files
drwxr-xr-x    2 mysql    users        1024 Jul  1 14:15 tests
```

MySQL is now installed. To install the permission tables (see Chapter 14, "Database Security"), run the `mysql_install_db` script:

```
% scripts/mysql_install_db
Preparing db table
Preparing host table
Preparing user table
Preparing func table
Preparing tables_priv table
Preparing columns_priv table
Installing all prepared tables
020701 23:19:07  ./bin/mysqld: Shutdown Complete
```

Now, change the ownership to ensure that MySQL and the data directory are controlled by the newly created MySQL user, if they're not already:

```
% chown -R root /usr/local/mysql
% chgrp -R mysql /usr/local/mysql
% chown -R mysql /usr/local/mysql/data
```

After this, MySQL will be ready to roll with mysqld_safe:

```
% /usr/local/mysql/bin/mysqld_safe --user=mysql &
```

**TIP** *Remember to assign a root password with* `mysqladmin` *as soon as you have finished installing; otherwise, MySQL will be wide open to anyone on the system. Also, you should immediately set about getting your configuration file right for your setup.*

See Table 15.1 earlier in this chapter for an overview of the contents of the newly created directories.

## Installing a Binary (rpm) Distribution on Unix

Red Hat Linux allows you to install MySQL from an RPM (Red Hat Package Manager) file as well. Table 15.4 shows the full list of RPMs available. (The version numbers will reflect the version you are using.)

**TABLE 15.4:** RED HAT PACKAGE MANAGER FILES

| FILE | DESCRIPTION |
| --- | --- |
| `MySQL-4.x.x-platform-os-extra.rpm` | The MySQL server software, needed unless you're merely connecting to an existing server. |
| `MySQL-client-4.x.x-platform-os-extra.rpm` | The MySQL client software, needed to connect to a MySQL server. |
| `MySQL-bench-4.x.x-platform-os-extra.rpm` | Various MySQL tests and benchmarks. The Perl and msql-mysql rpm files are required. |
| `MySQL-devel-4.x.x-platform-os-extra.rpm` | Various libraries and include files required if you want to compile other MySQL clients. |
| `MySQL-shared-4.x.x-platform-os-extra.rpm` | The MySQL client shared libraries. |
| `MySQL-embedded-4.x.x-platform-os-extra.rpm` | The MySQL embedded server. |
| `MySQL-4.x.x-platform-os-extra.src.rpm` | The source code for the previous rpm files. Not required if you're doing a binary installation. |
| `MySQL-Max-4.x.x-platform-os-extra` | MySQL Max rpm (with support for InnoDB tables etc.). |

To install the rpm files, simply run the rpm utility with each rpm you want to install listed. The client and server are typically the minimum you'll want to install:

```
% rpm -i MySQL-4.x.x-platform-os-extra.rpm MySQL-client-4.x.x-platform-os-extra.rpm
```

Installing via rpm results in a slightly different structure than that resulting from an ordinary binary installation. The data is placed in the /var/lib/mysql directory, and, by placing entries in the /etc/rc.d/ directory—as well as creating a /etc/rc.d/init.d/mysql script—MySQL is set up to begin automatically upon booting up. Be careful about installing over a previous installation in this way because you'll have to redo any changes you'd made.

After this, MySQL will be ready to roll with mysqld_safe:

```
% /usr/local/mysql/bin/mysqld_safe --user=mysql &
```

Don't forget to assign a root password and look at your configuration file.

## Installing from Source on Unix

You are unlikely to want to compile MySQL from source for production use unless you are experienced at these sorts of things. But some of you may enjoy the challenge, so this section explains the process in detail.

*TIP    It's important to look at the latest MySQL documentation because the following information can become dated quite quickly as new distributions replace older ones.*

To install from a source distribution, you'll need the following:

◆ gunzip (gzip or zcat). The GNU version is known to work.

◆ tar (the GNU tar works, but the Solaris tar has caused problems in the past).

◆ make (the GNU make is recommended, the Solaris and FreeBSD make have been known to cause problems).

◆ gcc or pgcc (or another ANSI C++ compiler). Version 2.95.2 is recommended currently, although different distributions are usually compiled with different compilers. I suggest looking at the most recent MySQL documentation to see what they compile with for your operating system and whether there are any reported problems with other compilers.

To install from source, perform the following steps:

**1.** To start with, as when installing binaries, change to be the root user and add the MySQL user and group:

```
% su -
Password:
% groupadd mysql
% useradd -g mysql mysql
```

**2.** Move to the directory where you want to place the files (for example, /usr/local/src or wherever your convention dictates).

**3.** Unpack the files:

```
% gunzip -c /tmp/ mysql-4.x.x-platform-os-extra.tar.gz | tar -xf -
```

**4.** Once complete, a new directory will have been created. Move into the new directory, which is where you're going to configure and build MySQL from:

```
% cd mysql-4.x.x-extra
```

**5.** Run the configure script, which is a useful little script supplied with the distribution that allows you to set various options for you installation. There are a large number of options available. Some of the more useful ones are described next; others are mentioned in the "Compiling MySQL Optimally" sidebar later.

**6.** By default, MySQL compiled from source will install into /usr/local, with the data and log files being stored in /usr/local/var. To change these locations, use the prefix option, for example:

```
% ./configure --prefix=/usr/local/mysql
```

This changes the prefix of the entire installation to /usr/local/mysql instead. Alternatively, you can change the location of the data directory to /usr/local/mysql/data, while leaving the rest of the installation the same with the following:

```
% ./configure --prefix=/usr/local \
        --localstatedir=/usr/local/mysql/data
```

You can do one of the following instead if you prefer:

◆ If you don't want to compile the server but just the client programs for connecting to an existing server, use the --without-server option:

```
% ./configure --without-server
```

◆ To use libmysqld.a, the embedded MySQL library, you'll need to employ the --with-embedded-server option:

```
% ./configure --with-embedded-server
```

◆ To change the location of the socket file from the default (usually /tmp), use configure as follows (the path name must be absolute):

```
% ./configure --with-unix-socket-path=/usr/local/sockets/mysql.sock
```

◆ For a full set of available options, run the following:

```
% ./configure --help
```

**7.** Once this is complete (which may take a little while depending on your setup), you'll need to build the binaries, with the make command:

```
% make
```

**8.** Next, you'll need to install the binaries:

```
% make install
```

**9.** Now, continue as you would have if you'd installed a binary, creating the permission tables and changing ownership of the files. These examples assume you decided on /usr/local/mysql as prefix:

```
% cd /usr/local/mysql
% scripts/mysql_install_db
Preparing db table
Preparing host table
Preparing user table
Preparing func table
Preparing tables_priv table
Preparing columns_priv table
Installing all prepared tables
010726 19:40:05  ./bin/mysqld: Shutdown Complete
% chown -R root /usr/local/mysql
% chgrp -R mysql /usr/local/mysql
% chown -R mysql /usr/local/mysql/data
```

**10.** After this, MySQL will be ready to roll with mysqld_safe:

```
% /usr/local/mysql/bin/mysqld_safe --user=mysql &
```

Don't forget to assign a root password and look at your configuration file.

### COMPILING MYSQL OPTIMALLY

The standard MySQL distributions are fairly close to optimal compiles, but if you're out to get every last drop of performance, you can make some improvements. It's also quite easy to do the reverse and slow things down, so be careful when using the following tips:

◆ You can define flags or the compiler name used by the compiler—for example:

```
% CFLAGS=-O3
% CXX=gcc
% CXXFLAGS=-O3
% CC=gcc
% export CC CFLAGS CXX CXXFLAGS
```

◆ Link statically, not dynamically (in other words, use the --static option). This uses more disk space but runs faster (13 percent on Linux according to MySQL measurements).

◆ MySQL binaries are mostly compiled with gcc because pgcc (Pentium gcc) has been known to cause problems on non-Intel processors. Compiling with pgcc if your processor is from the Intel Pentium family may result in some gains (1 percent according to MySQL tests, up to a reported 10-percent improvement). Similarly, on a Sun server, the SunPro C++ compiler has been about 5 percent faster than gcc in the past.

◆ Optimize to the highest possible level (-O3 with gcc).

◆ Compile without debug (the --without-debug option). This runs from between 20 and 35 percent faster than if you use the --with-debug=full option, and about 15 percent faster than if you use --with-debug.

◆ MySQL distributions come with support for all character sets. Use the --with-extra-charsets=none option if you're just using the default ISO-8859-1 (Latin1) character set. Use the --with-charset= xxx option to compile just the character set(s) you plan to use.

◆ If you're running Linux on x86 machines, compiling without frame pointers (-fomit-frame-pointer or -fomit-frame-pointer -ffixed-ebp) results in an improvement of between 1 and 4 percent.

# Installing Multiple MySQL Servers on the Same Machine

There are few reasons you would want to run multiple MySQL servers on the same machine. You will not gain any performance, and you will almost definitely not want to allow the multiple versions to access the same data. Most likely, you'll be doing this to test a new version of MySQL without removing your previous installation.

If you plan to run multiple versions of MySQL on the same machine, you'll need to ensure that they do not attempt to use the same socket file or listen on the same TCP/IP port. They will also have their own pid file. The defaults are port 3306 and /tmp/mysql.sock on most systems.

A convenient way of managing this is with the mysqld_multi utility, discussed later in this chapter. You can change the default port and TCP/IP settings in the configuration file, assuming it's a different configuration file than the other server. For example:

```
socket=/tmp/mysql2.sock
port=3307
```

Clients can connect to servers running on a different socket by using the `--socket` option:

```
% mysql --socket=/tmp/mysql2.sock -uroot -pg00r002b
```

You can also specify the server to connect to by specifying the configuration file to use for the client. For example:

```
% mysql --defaults-file=/usr/local/mysql2/etc/my.cnf -uroot -pg00r002b
```

If you're compiling MySQL, configure the second server with a new port number, socket path, and installation directory. For example:

```
% ./configure  --with-tcp-port=3307 \
               --with-unix-socket-path=/tmp/mysql2.sock \
               --prefix=/usr/local/mysql2
```

**WARNING** *Never have more than one server controlling the same data, which is a foolproof recipe for corruption! They should not need to write to the same log files either.*

MySQL distributions come with a handy utility by the name of mysqld_multi, which is a useful tool for managing multiple MySQL servers (running on different sockets and ports). To use mysqld_multi, you'll need to set up your configuration file with a mysqld_multi section, as well as sections for each MySQL server you'll be running. For example:

```
[mysqld_multi]
mysqld      = /usr/local/bin/mysqld_safe
mysqladmin = /usr/local/bin/mysqladmin
user        = root
password    = g00r002b
[mysqld1]
socket      = /tmp/mysql.sock
port        = 3306
pid-file    = /usr/local/mysql/var/hostname.pid
datadir     = /usr/local/mysql/var
language    = /usr/local/share/mysql/english
user        = hartmann
[mysqld2]
socket      = /tmp/mysql.sock2
port        = 3307
pid-file    = /usr/local/mysql/var2/hostname.pid
datadir     = /usr/local/mysql/var2
language    = /usr/local/share/mysql/french
user        = yves
```

```
[mysqld3]
socket      = /tmp/mysql.sock3
port        = 3308
pid-file    = /usr/local/mysql/var3/hostname.pid
datadir     = /usr/local/mysql/var3
language    = /usr/local/share/mysql/german
user        = cleo
[mysqld4]
socket      = /tmp/mysql.sock4
port        = 3309
pid-file    = /usr/local/mysql/var4/hostname.pid
datadir     = /usr/local/mysql/var4
language    = /usr/local/share/mysql/english
user        = caledon
```

The syntax for mysqld_multi is as follows:

```
mysqld_multi [option/s] {start|stop|report} [group_no,group_no2...]
```

Assuming a setup as in the example you've just seen of a configuration file, the following example shows mysqld_multi reporting on the status of a server and then being used to shut it down:

```
% mysqld_multi --user=root --password=g00r002b report 1
Reporting MySQL servers
MySQL server from group: mysqld1 is running
% mysqld_multi --user=root --password=g00r002b stop 1
% 020729 04:20:50  mysqld ended
% mysqld_multi --user=root --password=g00r002b report 1
Reporting MySQL servers
MySQL server from group: mysqld1 is not running
```

Table 15.5 describes the mysqld_multi options.

**TABLE 15.5:** MYSQLD_MULTI OPTIONS

| OPTION | DESCRIPTION |
| --- | --- |
| --config-file=... | Set an alternative configuration file for the groups. (It will not affect the [mysqld_multi] group.) |
| --example | Provides a sample configuration file. |
| --help | Displays help and exits. |
| --log=... | Specifies the log file, taking the full path and name of the file. If this file already exists, logs will be appended on the end of the file. |
| --mysqladmin=... | The full path and name of the mysqladmin binary, used to shut down the server. |

*Continued on next page*

**TABLE 15.5:** MYSQLD_MULTI OPTIONS *(continued)*

| OPTION | DESCRIPTION |
|---|---|
| `--mysqld=...` | The full path and name of the mysqld binary to be used, or more often the mysqld_safe binary. Options are passed to mysqld. You'll need to make changes to mysqld_safe or ensure that it's in your PATH environment variable. |
| `--no-log` | Outputs to standard output instead of a log file. The default is to write to a log file. |
| `--password=...` | The password for the user for mysqladmin. |
| `--tcp-ip` | Causes mysqld_multi to connect to the MySQL servers via TCP/IP instead of a Unix socket. By default the connection is via socket on Unix. |
| `--user=...` | The user for mysqladmin. Make sure this user has the correct privileges to do what is needed (shutdown_priv). |
| `--version` | Displays the version number and exits. |

# Avoiding Common Installation Problems

It can be extremely frustrating when things go wrong, and you haven't even managed to get started yet. For novices especially, it's difficult to know what to do when faced with an esoteric error message (if you're even lucky enough to get one). The following sections looks at some of the common problems when installing.

## Problems Starting mysqld

Problems starting mysqld usually make themselves noticed when you try to install the permission tables and have no success. There are many reasons for problems, as you'll see in the following list, and examining the error log is the best way to see what the problem could be.

♦ You may have a problem with your configuration file (`my.cnf` or `my.ini`). Check your syntax carefully, or use the standard configuration file that came with your distribution to see if you can start MySQL.

♦ Another common error is the following:

```
Can't start server: Bind on unix socket....
```

or the following:

```
Can't start server: Bind on TCP/IP port: Address already in use
```

This error occurs when trying to install a second copy of MySQL onto the same port or socket as an existing installation. Make sure you specify a different port or socket before starting.

♦ Permission problems are common, too. Make sure you've followed the steps listed in the installation section so that at least the MySQL directories are correct. If you're using sockets, you need to make sure you have permission to write the socket file as well (usually to `/tmp`).

◆ Another common problem is with libraries. For example, if you run Linux and have installed shared libraries, make sure the location of these shared libraries is listed in your /etc/ld.so.conf file. For example, if you have:

/usr/local/lib/mysql/libmysqlclient.so

Make sure /etc/ld.so.conf contains:

/usr/local/lib/mysql

Then run ldconfig.

◆ When starting MySQL where there are existing BDB tables, you may find a problem such as the following:

```
020814 19:18:02  bdb:  warning: ./bdb/news.db: No such file or directory
020824 19:18:02  Can't init databases
```

This means that BDB had a problem recovering an existing log file. You can either start MySQL with the --bdb-no-recover option, or move the log files away.

## Compile Problems

If you run into problems compiling and need to do it a second time, you'll need to make sure configure is run from a clean slate; otherwise, it uses information from its previous incarnation, stored in the file config.cache. You'll need to remove this file each time you configure. Also, old object files may still be in existence, and to ensure a clean recompile, you should remove these. Run the following:

```
% rm config.cache
% make clean
```

You can also run distclean, if you have it.

Your compiler may be out of date. Currently MySQL suggests using gcc 2.95.2, or egcs 1.0.3a, but this is likely to have changed, so check the latest documentation.

Other problems could result from an incompatible version of make. Currently, MySQL recommends GNU make, version 3.75 or higher.

If you get an error when compiling sql_yacc.cc, you may have run out of disk space. In some situations, compilation of this file uses up too many resources (even when there is seemingly lots available). The error could be one of the following:

```
Internal compiler error: program cc1plus got fatal signal 11
Out of virtual memory
Virtual memory exhausted
```

Running configure with the --low-memory option usually solves the problem:

```
% ./configure --with-low-memory
```

If you're having problems with related libraries, such as g++, libg++, or libstdc++ (perhaps they're unavailable), try setting gcc to be your C++ compiler, as follows:

```
% CXX="gcc -03" ./configure
```

Linking statically, besides being more optimal, can also solve problems with undefined references.

### Windows Problems

If you double-click `setup.exe`, and the process begins but never completes, you may have something interfering with MySQL. Try one of these procedures:

◆ Close all Windows applications, including services and ones from the system tray.

◆ Alternatively, try the install in Safe mode (by pressing F8 when booting, then choosing the option from the menu).

◆ At worst, you may have to reinstall Windows and install MySQL first, before anything else gets in the way. The problem is less likely to occur in production machines dedicated as MySQL database servers. Rather, they're likely in multipurpose computers where you're running all kinds of other applications.

## Upgrading from MySQL 3.x to MySQL 4

MySQL has made major strides in its development from version 3.23.*xx* to version 4, and there are quite a few differences to look out for when upgrading:

◆ The script `mysqld_safe` replaces `safe_mysqld`.

◆ There are a large number of new privileges in the user table (in the `mysql` database). MySQL has supplied a script to add these new permissions, while maintaining the existing permissions. Called `mysql_fix_privilege_tables`, it takes the REPLICATION SLAVE and REPLICATION CLIENT privileges from the old FILE privilege, and the SUPER and EXECUTE privileges from the old PROCESS. Without running this script, all users will have SHOW DATABASES, CREATE TEMPORARY TABLES, and LOCK TABLES privileges.

◆ The attributes of `length` and `max_length` (in the `MYSQL_FIELD` structure) are now `unsigned long` instead of `unsigned int`.

◆ The old `--safe-show-database` option is deprecated (it no longer does anything, being replaced by the SHOW DATABASES privilege in the user table).

◆ A number of variables have been renamed:

`myisam_bulk_insert_tree_size` to `bulk_insert_buffer_size`
`query_cache_startup_type` to `query_cache_type`
`record_buffer` to `read_buffer_size`
`record_rnd_buffer` to `read_rnd_buffer_size`
`sort_buffer` to `sort_buffer_size`
`warnings` to `log-warnings`

◆ A number of mysqld startup options have a new name:

`--skip-locking` to `--skip-external-locking`
`--enable-locking` to `--external-locking`

◆ The size of the startup parameters `myisam_max_extra_sort_file_size` and `myisam_max_extra_sort_file_size` are now given in bytes, not megabytes.

◆ A number of startup options have been deprecated (they will still work for now):

```
record_buffer
sort_buffer
warnings
```

◆ External locking is now turned off by default.

◆ The following SQL variables have a new name (the old names still work but are deprecated):

```
SQL_BIG_TABLES to BIG_TABLES
SQL_LOW_PRIORITY_UPDATES to LOW_PRIORITY_UPDATES
SQL_MAX_JOIN_SIZE to MAX_JOIN_SIZE
SQL_QUERY_CACHE_TYPE to QUERY_CACHE_TYPE
```

◆ SIGNED is a reserved word.

◆ Columns of type DOUBLE and FLOAT no longer ignore the UNSIGNED flag.

◆ BIGINT columns now store integers more efficiently than strings.

◆ Default behavior for the STRCMP() function is now case insensitive because it uses the current character set when doing comparisons.

◆ TRUNCATE TABLE is faster than DELETE FROM tablename because it does not return the number of rows deleted.

◆ The LOCATE() and INSTR() functions are now case sensitive if one of the arguments is a binary string.

◆ The HEX() function now, when passed a string, converts each character to two hexadecimal digits.

◆ The SHOW INDEX statement has two extra columns: Null and Index_type.

◆ You will no longer be able to run the TRUNCATE TABLE or DROP DATABASE statements when there is an active lock (whether from LOCK TABLES or a transaction). An error will be returned instead.

◆ The ORDER BY column_name DESC clause will sort NULL values first in all cases, where previously it did so inconsistently.

◆ Results of all bitwise operators (<<, >>, |, &, ~) are now unsigned, as is the result of subtraction between two integers when either of them is unsigned (the latter can be disabled by starting MySQL with the --sql-mode=NO_UNSIGNED_SUBTRACTION option).

◆ If you want to use the statement MATCH ... AGAINST (... IN BOOLEAN MODE), you'll have to rebuild your tables with ALTER TABLE table_name TYPE=MyISAM. This applies even if the tables are already MyISAM.

◆ You need to specify an IGNORE clause when using a statement of the type INSERT INTO ... SELECT, or else MySQL will stop and possibly roll back.

◆ The RAND(seed) function now returns a different random number series than before (to further differentiate RAND(seed) from RAND(seed+1)).

◆ The format of SHOW OPEN TABLES has changed.

◆ The old mysql_drop_db(), mysql_create_db(), and mysql_connect() C API functions are no longer supported. You can compile MySQL with the CFLAGS=-DUSE_OLD_FUNCTIONS option, but instead update your clients to use the version 4.0 API.

- If you're using the Perl DBD::mysql module, you'll need to use a version more recent than 1.2218, as earlier versions used the old `drop_db()` function.

- Instead of using `SET SQL_SLAVE_SKIP_COUNTER=#`, you need to use `SET GLOBAL SQL_SLAVE_SKIP_COUNTER=#`.

- Multithreaded clients should use the functions `mysql_thread_init()` and `mysql_thread_end()`.

## Summary

Installing MySQL is not difficult. If you choose a binary distribution, which is recommended in most cases, it's a matter of pointing and clicking in Windows and a few simple commands in Unix. There are valid reasons for choosing a source distribution, though—perhaps MySQL is not yet available in binary on your platform, or you need to get the most out of MySQL by compiling it more optimally. Whatever your reason, with careful tweaking of the compile options, you can get a fast yet stable installation of MySQL.

# Chapter 16

# Multiple Drives

DATABASES OFTEN GROW TO become quite large, and a huge amount of data on one drive means that the drive and drive controller become a serious bottleneck. Using multiple disks and controllers (using RAID) is one method to overcome this, and most flavors of RAID have extra redundancy features.

Symbolic links are a way of splitting databases or tables across multiple disks without using RAID. By creating a link from one drive to another, the bottleneck of one overused drive is eased.

Featured in this chapter:

◆ Using RAID
◆ Using symbolic links

## Understanding RAID

RAID stands for *redundant array of inexpensive disks*. It doesn't stand for *redundant array of independent disks*; it's amazing how quickly one wrong source gets duplicated on the Internet, though the term *independent* has some accuracy. The original term comes from a paper written in 1987 by researchers David Patterson, Garth Gibson, and Randy Katz. It improves performance and fault tolerance. The alternative is often described as single large expensive disk (SLED).

There are a number of different kinds of RAID, described in the following sections. All of them are built upon three basic concepts: *mirroring* (repeating writes on another drive), *striping* (dispersing data over multiple drives), and *parity* (examining bits to prevent and recover from errors).

### RAID 0

RAID 0 (sometimes just called *striping*, as it's not really a true type of RAID) is where data is broken into blocks and spread across multiple drives. Block sizes are the same for each drive, but different block sizes can be set initially depending on the circumstances. This allows for increased performance, as one of the major bottlenecks is moving the drive head. RAID 0 improves the chances of data requested at the same time being on different drives, meaning the read can take place at the same time without having to wait for the one to finish, reposition the head, and then read the second set of data.

In general, the more drives there are, the better the performance. Performance is even better if each drive has its own controller, though this is not critical. Just make sure the controllers can handle the load if it is responsible for multiple drives. RAID 0 allows for no fault tolerance, however. In fact, it increases the chance of a failure, as there is more than one drive that can fail, rendering the set of data unavailable.

RAID 0 should not be used in environments where data availability is critical. You need at least two drives to implement RAID 0. It is not a true type of RAID and is sometimes humorously referred to as AID because it contains no form of redundancy (the *R* in RAID).

In Figure 16.1, which shows RAID 0 implemented on three devices, the first block of data is written on device A, the second on device B, and the third on device C. The next block will then be written on the first device again, and so on. The first and third blocks of data can then be read at the same time, as they exist on different devices.

**FIGURE 16.1**
RAID 0

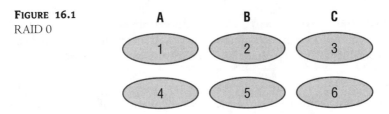

## RAID 1

RAID 1 (also called *mirroring*) is where writes to one drive are repeated on another drive. This improves fault tolerance because there is an up-to-date backup in case of one drive failing. Drive failures are the most common type of hardware failure, and RAID 1 protects against this kind of failure. Write performance is poor, as there are simultaneous writes taking place, although reads are slightly quicker, as there are multiple drives to access. You need at least two drives to implement RAID 1.

Figure 16.2 shows RAID 1 being implemented with two drives, each containing an identical copy.

**FIGURE 16.2**
RAID 1

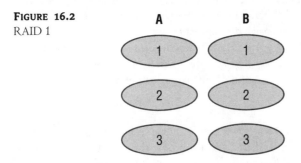

## RAID 2 and RAID 3

RAID 2 is a rarely used version that makes use of Hamming error correction codes (which uses 3 bits of a 7-bit word for error checking and correction) and is mainly useful for drives that do not do any form of error-protection (SCSI drives do).

RAID 3 is the same as RAID 0, except that it also sets aside a dedicated drive for error correction, providing some level of fault tolerance. Data is striped at a byte level across multiple drives. Another drive stores parity data. Parity is determined during a write and checked during a read. Parity information allows recovery if one drive fails. You need at least three drives to implement RAID 3. It usually requires hardware implementation to be of much use. Small writes and reads are fast, but large blocks of data usually require data to be read from all data drives, meaning that performance can be as slow as a single drive.

Figure 16.3 shows RAID 3 being used to stripe data across two drives (A and B), with a third drive (C) being used to store parity.

**FIGURE 16.3**
RAID 3

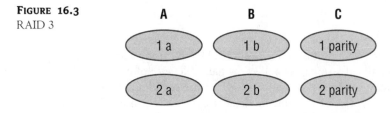

## RAID 4

RAID 4 is similar to RAID 3, except that striping is performed at block level, not byte level. Reads smaller than one block in size will be fast (generally getting faster as each new drive is added). As with RAID 3, it requires at least three drives, and the parity data allows recovery if one drive fails. The parity drive can become a bottleneck, and choosing RAID 5 can overcome this limitation.

Figure 16.4 shows RAID 4 being used to stripe data across three drives (A, B, and C), with a fourth drive (D) being used to store parity.

**FIGURE 16.4**
RAID 4

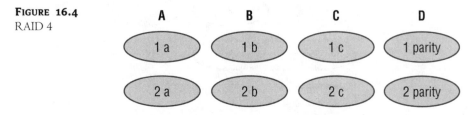

## RAID 5

RAID 5 also allows for striping, as well as stripe error correction data, improving both performance and fault tolerance. It is similar to RAID 4, except that parity data is stored on each drive. Writes are faster than RAID 4 (there is no one drive bottleneck), but reads are slower, as parity information takes up space on each drive and has to be skipped over. RAID 5 is often recommended for database servers, as it builds in redundancy and improves performance.

A minimum of three drives is required to implement RAID 5.

Figure 16.5 shows RAID 5 being used to stripe data across three drives (A, B, C), each of which contain parity data.

**FIGURE 16.5**
RAID 5

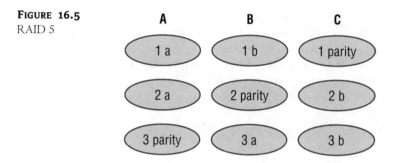

## RAID 10

RAID 10 is a combination of RAID 1 and RAID 0 (mirroring and striping). It provides all the performance benefits of striping, as well as the fault tolerance of mirroring. It's the best of both worlds, but the cost is high. It requires at least four drives to implement.

Figure 16.6 shows RAID 10 being implemented across four drives (A, B, C, and D). A and B mirror the data (blocks one to four of data appear on both drives), and drives C and D provide the performance boost with data being striped across them. RAID 10 is often suggested for database servers, as it gives the greatest level of performance boost and fault tolerance, albeit at a cost penalty (for the number of drives).

**FIGURE 16.6**
RAID 10

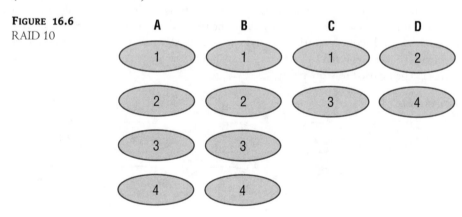

## RAID 0+1

RAID 0+1 is often confused with RAID 10. Where RAID 10 is a striped array of drives, whose segments are mirrored, RAID 0+1 is a mirrored array of drives, whose segments are striped. Generally RAID 0+1 is chosen when performance is a higher priority than reliability, and RAID 10 is chosen when reliability is a higher priority than performance. RAID 0+1 is also expensive and requires at least four drives to implement. Figure 16.7 shows RAID 0+1 being implemented across four drives (A, B, C, and D).

FIGURE 16.7
RAID 0+1

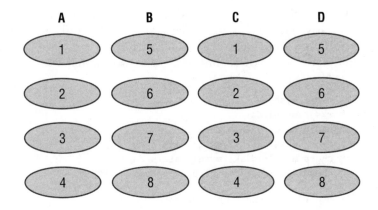

## Other Types of RAID

The previous RAID types are not all the possible types; there are others, some of little practical use.

You can implement RAID using either hardware or software (*hardware RAID* and *software RAID*), or a combination of the two. MySQL's `--with-raid-option` is a limited form of software RAID (RAID 0 currently). Its primary purpose is to overcome the limitation on file sizes. Later versions will extend its usefulness. Replication, although not strictly speaking RAID, is another MySQL software feature similar to RAID (RAID 1). Hardware RAID is usually easier to use because once it's up and running, the hardware device presents multiple drives as one drive to the software and takes care of all redundancy and striping, leaving MySQL to continue as usual. Software RAID makes use of software (for example, vinum, a tool that runs on FreeBSD and implements RAID 0, RAID 1, and RAID 5), which in consequence draws upon the central processing unit (CPU). If you have a CPU with free cycles, software RAID can be as good.

# Using Symbolic Links

You can easily utilize symbolic links (*symlinks*) to improve performance of your database and reduce disk latency. The idea is that instead of storing all your data and indexes on one disk, you create a symlink from that one disk to another disk, which actually stores the data. Currently, you can only symlink MyISAM tables and databases. Earlier versions of MySQL had fundamental problems symlinking tables (they would revert to their original location when certain operations were performed on them), but version 4 has taken care of many of the problems.

## Symbolic Linking of Databases

To create a symlink for a MyISAM database, follow these steps:

1. Create the database directory on the new location.
2. Make sure the permissions and ownership are correct (700 and mysql.mysql).
3. Create a symlink in the data directory pointing to the new location.

Let's test the creation of a new database, *s_db*, which you're going to symlink. Assuming you already have a directory, *disk2*, which is the secondary disk you want to place the database on, create the directories where you're going to store the data (*/disk2/mysql/data/s_db*) and change the permissions and ownership, first on a Unix system, as follows:

```
% cd /disk2
% mkdir mysql
% mkdir mysql/data
% mkdir mysql/data/s_db
% chown mysql /disk2/mysql/data/s_db/
% chgrp mysql /disk2/mysql/data/s_db/
% chmod 700 /disk2/mysql/data/s_db/
```

Now, back in the data directory, create the symlink:

```
% cd /usr/local/mysql/data
% ln -s /disk2/mysql/data/s_db s_db
```

Once you've done this, your database will be created (remember MyISAM databases are just subdirectories in the data directory). You can confirm this by connecting to MySQL:

```
% /usr/local/mysql/bin/mysql -uroot -pg00r002b
Welcome to the MySQL monitor.  Commands end with ; or \g.
Your MySQL connection id is 6202 to server version: 4.0.2-alpha-max-log

Type 'help;' or '\h' for help. Type '\c' to clear the buffer.
mysql> SHOW DATABASES LIKE 's_db';
+-----------------+
| Database (s_db) |
+-----------------+
| s_db            |
+-----------------+
1 row in set (0.00 sec)
```

Now, to see that data is actually placed on the second disk, create and populate a small table, as follows:

```
mysql> USE s_db
Database changed
mysql> CREATE TABLE s1( f1 INT);
Query OK, 0 rows affected (0.23 sec)
mysql> INSERT INTO s1 VALUES(1);
Query OK, 1 row affected (0.03 sec)
```

Check that the new data has been created on the secondary disk:

```
mysql> exit
Bye
% ls -l /disk2/mysql/data/s_db/
total 14
```

```
-rw-rw----  1 mysql  mysql     5 Jul  8 02:26 s1.MYD
-rw-rw----  1 mysql  mysql  1024 Jul  8 02:26 s1.MYI
-rw-rw----  1 mysql  mysql  8550 Jul  8 02:25 s1.frm
```

To create a symlink for a database on a Windows system, there are a number of differences. Permissions are simpler, and to create a symlink, instead of using ln -s, you just create a text file with the extension .sym. First, create a file called s2_db.sym in your data directory containing the following text:

```
D:\s_db
```

Because this is inside your data directory, it will appear on the same level as all your other MyISAM databases (in this case, *firstdb*, *mysql*, and *test*), and when you connect to MySQL, you'll see it as an existing database:

```
C:\mysql\bin>dir ..\data\
  ...
Directory of C:\mysql\data
09/03/2002  08:58p    <DIR>          .
09/03/2002  08:58p    <DIR>          ..
09/03/2002  08:31p    <DIR>          firstdb
09/03/2002  08:22p    <DIR>          mysql
09/03/2002  08:23p            4,342 mysql.err
09/03/2002  08:57p                7 s2_db.sym
09/03/2002  08:22p    <DIR>          test
              2 File(s)        4,349 bytes
  ...
C:\mysql\bin>mysql
Welcome to the MySQL monitor.  Commands end with ; or \g.
Your MySQL connection id is 8 to server version: 4.0.3-beta-nt

Type 'help;' or '\h' for help. Type '\c' to clear the buffer.
mysql> SHOW DATABASES;
+----------+
| Database |
+----------+
| firstdb  |
| mysql    |
| s2_db    |
| test     |
+----------+
4 rows in set (0.00 sec)
mysql> USE s2_db
Database changed
mysql> CREATE TABLE s1(f1 INT);
Query OK, 0 rows affected (0.23 sec)
mysql> INSERT INTO s1 VALUES(1);
Query OK, 1 row affected (0.03 sec)
C:\mysql\bin>dir d:\s2_db
  ...
```

```
Directory of d:\s2_db
09/03/2002  09:38p      <DIR>          .
09/03/2002  09:38p      <DIR>          ..
09/03/2002  09:38p                8,550 s1.frm
09/03/2002  09:38p                    5 s1.MYD
09/03/2002  09:38p                1,024 s1.MYI
               3 File(s)          9,579 bytes
  ...
```

**NOTE**    *If the previous code doesn't work, you may be running an earlier version of MySQL (in which case you have to add* --use-symbolic-links *to a line in your* my.ini *configuration file). It's also possible your version of MySQL was not compiled with* -DUSE_SYMDIR, *in which case symlinks will not work at all. Usually, mysql-max and mysql-max-nt servers are compiled with this option; however, you should check the latest documentation.*

## Symbolic Linking of Tables

Using symbolic tables on individual tables is not recommended because there are few features that do not work properly with symlinked tables (though check your latest documentation, as this will likely change soon).

Features that don't yet work with symlinked tables include the following:

♦ BACKUP TABLE and RESTORE TABLE (the symlinks will be lost).

♦ mysqldump does not store symlink information in the dump.

♦ ALTER TABLE (it ignores INDEX/DATA DIRECTORY="path" CREATE TABLE options).

To symlink a table when you create it, you should use the INDEX or DATA DIRECTORY PATH option. DATA DIRECTORY creates a symlink for the .MYD file, and INDEX DIRECTORY places the .MYI file. The following example places the data file of a new table in the *firstdb* database in the new directory you created earlier.

```
mysql> USE firstdb;
Database changed
mysql> CREATE TABLE s_table (a int) DATA DIRECTORY =
 '/disk2/mysql/data/s_db';
Query OK, 0 rows affected (0.20 sec)
mysql> INSERT INTO s_table VALUES(1);
Query OK, 1 row affected (0.01 sec)
```

You can see that the .frm file (containing the structure) is in the usual data directory, and the .MYD data file is in the new location:

```
% cd /usr/local/mysql/data/firstdb/
% ls -l /disk2/mysql/data/s_db/
total 16
-rw-rw----  1 mysql  mysql     5 Jul  8 02:26 s1.MYD
-rw-rw----  1 mysql  mysql  1024 Jul  8 02:26 s1.MYI
-rw-rw----  1 mysql  mysql  8550 Jul  8 02:25 s1.frm
-rw-rw----  1 mysql  mysql     5 Jul  8 05:35 s_table.MYD
```

```
% ls -l s*
lrwxrwx--x  1 mysql  mysql    34 Jul  8 05:34 s_table.MYD ->
 /disk2/mysql/data/s_db/s_table.MYD
-rw-rw----  1 mysql  mysql  1024 Jul  8 05:35 s_table.MYI
-rw-rw----  1 mysql  mysql  8548 Jul  8 05:34 s_table.frm
```

MySQL has created the symlink for the table. You could also have explicitly created this symlink yourself (taking the same care with permissions as you did with creating the database symlink).

The data and index files can be created in different locations as this example demonstrates, assuming the existence of the directory /disk3/mysql/data/indexes:

```
mysql> CREATE TABLE s2_table (a int) DATA DIRECTORY =
 '/disk2/mysql/data/s_db' INDEX DIRECTORY =
 '/disk3/mysql/data/indexes';
Query OK, 0 rows affected (0.04 sec)
```

View the files in their new locations:

```
% ls -l /disk3/mysql/data/indexes/
total 2
-rw-rw----  1 mysql  mysql  1024 Jul  8 06:01 s2_table.MYI
% ls -l /disk2/mysql/data/s_db/
...
-rw-rw----  1 mysql  mysql     0 Jul  8 06:01 s2_table.MYD
...
% ls -l /usr/local/mysql/data/firstdb/
...
lrwxrwx--x  1 mysql  mysql    35 Jul  8 06:01 s2_table.MYD ->
 /disk2/mysql/data/s_db/s2_table.MYD
lrwxrwx--x  1 mysql  mysql    38 Jul  8 06:01 s2_table.MYI ->
 /disk3/mysql/data/indexes/s2_table.MYI
-rw-rw----  1 mysql  mysql  8548 Jul  8 06:01 s2_table.frm
...
```

**NOTE**  *The* INDEX DIRECTORY *and* DATA DIRECTORY *options do not work when running MySQL on Windows (although check your latest documentation).*

# Summary

RAID is a method of using multiple disks to store data. RAID 0 (striping) spreads blocks of data across multiple disks. It speeds up performance but has no redundancy capability. RAID 1 (mirroring) slows down write speed and can speed up reads, but it is mainly used for protection from drive failure. RAID 2, 3, 4, and 5 all make use of striping and use various forms of parity for fault tolerance. RAID 10 and RAID 0+1 combine mirroring and striping (although they implement them slightly differently—RAID 10 with a greater focus on reliability, and RAID 0+1 focusing more on speed).

Symbolic links allow you to place MyISAM databases or tables in a different location from the usual data directory, usually a different drive.

# Appendixes

# Appendix A

# MySQL Syntax Reference

THIS APPENDIX CONTAINS THE SQL statements and syntax used by MySQL version 4.0. For newer versions, you should see the documentation that comes with your distribution, or visit the MySQL site (www.mysql.com).

The convention used throughout the appendixes is as follows:

- Square brackets ([]) denote something optional. For example:

```
SELECT expression [FROM table_name [WHERE where_clause]]
```

indicates that the expression is compulsory (for example SELECT 42/10) and that the WHERE clause is optional but can only exist if the optional FROM table_name clause exists. (You can have SELECT * FROM t1, but not SELECT * WHERE f1>10, because the table_name clause is then missing.)

- A vertical bar (|) separates alternatives. For example:

```
CREATE [UNIQUE | FULLTEXT] INDEX
```

indicates that UNIQUE and FULLTEXT are separate options.

- Curly brackets ({}) indicate that one of the options must be chosen. For example:

```
CREATE TABLE ... [TYPE = {BDB | HEAP | ISAM | InnoDB | MERGE |
MRG_MYISAM | MYISAM }]
```

If the optional TYPE clause is specified, one of BDB, HEAP, ISAM, InnoDB, MERGE, MRG_MYISAM or MYISAM must be specified.

- Three dots (...) indicate that the option can be repeated. For example:

```
SELECT expression,...
```

indicates that the expression can be repeated (separated by a comma), as follows: SELECT f1,f2,f3.

## *ALTER*

The ALTER syntax is as follows:

```
ALTER [IGNORE] TABLE table_name alter_specification [, alter_specification ...]
```

The alter_specification syntax can be any of the following:

```
ADD [COLUMN] create_definition [FIRST | AFTER field_name ]
ADD [COLUMN] (create_definition, create_definition,...)
ADD INDEX [index_name] (index_field_name,...)
ADD PRIMARY KEY (index_field_name,...)
ADD UNIQUE [index_name] (index_field_name,...)
ADD FULLTEXT [index_name] (index_field_name,...)
ADD [CONSTRAINT symbol] FOREIGN KEY index_name
 (index_field_name,...)[reference_definition]
ALTER [COLUMN] field_name {SET DEFAULT literal | DROP DEFAULT}
CHANGE [COLUMN] old_field_name create_definition [FIRST | AFTER field_name]
MODIFY [COLUMN] create_definition [FIRST | AFTER field_name]
DROP [COLUMN] field_name
DROP PRIMARY KEY
DROP INDEX index_name
DISABLE KEYS
ENABLE KEYS
RENAME [TO] new_table_name
ORDER BY field_name
    table_options
```

ALTER TABLE allows you to change the structure of an existing table. You can ADD columns, CHANGE column names and definitions, MODIFY (non-ANSI Oracle extension) column definitions without changing the name, DROP columns or indexes, RENAME tables, ORDER data, and DISABLE or ENABLE indexes.

A non-ANSI MySQL extension is that ALTER TABLE can contain multiple components (CHANGE, ADD, and so on) in one statement.

You need ALTER, INSERT, and CREATE permission on the table to use ALTER TABLE.

IGNORE (non-ANSI MySQL extension) causes MySQL to delete records that would result in a duplicate primary or unique key. Usually MySQL would simply abort and the ALTER would fail.

FIRST and ADD...AFTER allow you to specify where a field is to be added in the definition.

## *ANALYZE TABLE*

```
ANALYZE TABLE table_name [,table_name...]
```

For MyISAM and BDB tables, this analyzes and stores the key distribution for the specified tables. It locks the table with a read lock for the operation's duration.

## *BACKUP TABLE*

```
BACKUP TABLE table_name [,table_name...] TO 'path_name'
```

For MyISAM tables, this copies the data and data definition files to the backup directory.

## *BEGIN*

```
BEGIN
```

The BEGIN statement begins a transaction, or set of statements. The transaction remains open until the next COMMIT or ROLLBACK statement.

## *CHECK TABLE*

```
CHECK TABLE tbl_name[,tbl_name...] [option [option...]]
```

The option can be one of the following:

```
CHANGED
EXTENDED
FAST
MEDIUM
QUICK
```

This checks a MyISAM or InnoDB table for errors and, for MyISAM tables, updates the index statistics. The QUICK option doesn't scan the rows to check links. The FAST option only checks tables that weren't closed properly. The CHANGED option is the same as FAST, except that it also checks tables that have changed since the last check. The MEDIUM option verifies that deleted links are correct, and the EXTENDED option does a full index lookup for each key in each row.

## *COMMIT*

```
COMMIT
```

The COMMIT statement ends a transaction, or set of statements, and flushes the results to disk.

## *CREATE*

The CREATE syntax can be one of the following:

```
CREATE DATABASE [IF NOT EXISTS] database_name
CREATE [UNIQUE|FULLTEXT] INDEX index_name ON table_name (field_name[(length)],... )
CREATE [TEMPORARY] TABLE [IF NOT EXISTS] table_name [(create_definition,...)]
  [table_options] [select_statement]
```

The create_definition syntax can be any of the following:

```
field_name type [NOT NULL | NULL] [DEFAULT default_value]
   [AUTO_INCREMENT] [PRIMARY KEY] [reference_definition]
```

```
PRIMARY KEY (index_field_name,...)
KEY [index_name] (index_field_name,...)
INDEX [index_name] (index_field_name,...)
UNIQUE [INDEX] [index_name] (index_field_name,...)
FULLTEXT [INDEX] [index_name] (index_field_name,...)
[CONSTRAINT symbol] FOREIGN KEY [index_name] (index_field_name,...)
 [reference_definition]
CHECK (expr)
```

The type syntax can be any of the following:

```
TINYINT[(length)] [UNSIGNED] [ZEROFILL]
SMALLINT[(length)] [UNSIGNED] [ZEROFILL]
MEDIUMINT[(length)] [UNSIGNED] [ZEROFILL]
INT[(length)] [UNSIGNED] [ZEROFILL]
INTEGER[(length)] [UNSIGNED] [ZEROFILL]
BIGINT[(length)] [UNSIGNED] [ZEROFILL]
REAL[(length,decimals)] [UNSIGNED] [ZEROFILL]
DOUBLE[(length,decimals)] [UNSIGNED] [ZEROFILL]
FLOAT[(length,decimals)] [UNSIGNED] [ZEROFILL]
DECIMAL(length,decimals) [UNSIGNED] [ZEROFILL]
NUMERIC(length,decimals) [UNSIGNED] [ZEROFILL]
CHAR(length) [BINARY]
VARCHAR(length) [BINARY]
DATE
TIME
TIMESTAMP
DATETIME
TINYBLOB
BLOB
MEDIUMBLOB
LONGBLOB
TINYTEXT
TEXT
MEDIUMTEXT
LONGTEXT
ENUM(value1,value2,value3,...)
SET(value1,value2,value3,...)
```

The index_field_name syntax is as follows:

```
field_name [(length)]
```

The reference_definition syntax is as follows:

```
REFERENCES table_name [(index_field_name,...)] [MATCH FULL
   | MATCH PARTIAL] [ON DELETE reference_option] [ON UPDATE reference_option]
```

The reference_option syntax is as follows:

```
RESTRICT | CASCADE | SET NULL | NO ACTION | SET DEFAULT
```

The `table_options` syntax can be any of the following:

```
TYPE = {BDB | HEAP | ISAM | InnoDB | MERGE | MRG_MYISAM | MYISAM }
AUTO_INCREMENT = #
AVG_ROW_LENGTH = #
CHECKSUM = {0 | 1}
COMMENT = "string"
MAX_ROWS = #
MIN_ROWS = #
PACK_KEYS = {0 | 1 | DEFAULT}
PASSWORD = "string"
DELAY_KEY_WRITE = {0 | 1}
ROW_FORMAT= { default | dynamic | fixed | compressed }
RAID_TYPE= {1 | STRIPED | RAIDO } RAID_CHUNKS=#  RAID_CHUNKSIZE=#
UNION = (table_name,[table_name...])
INSERT_METHOD= {NO | FIRST | LAST }
DATA DIRECTORY="absolute_path_to_directory"
INDEX DIRECTORY="absolute_path_to_directory"
```

The `select_statement` syntax can be as follows:

```
[IGNORE | REPLACE] SELECT ...  (select statement)
```

The `CREATE` statement creates a database, table, or index.

MySQL returns an error if the database or table already exists unless the `IF NOT EXISTS` clause is used.

`TEMPORARY` tables exist only for as long as the connection is active. You need to have `CREATE TEMPORARY TABLES` permission to do this.

Fields definitions default to `NULL`. Numeric fields default to 0 (except with `AUTO_INCREMENT`), and string fields default to an empty string (except for `ENUM` fields, which default to the first option). Date and time fields by default fill the field with zeros.

`AUTO_INCREMENT` fields begin counting at 1 by default and increment by one each time a new record is added.

`KEY` and `INDEX` are synonyms in this context.

A `PRIMARY KEY` specifies that the index cannot contain duplicates, and the field (or combination of fields) must be specified as `NOT NULL`.

`UNIQUE` specifies that the index cannot contain duplicates.

The `RAID_TYPE` option helps operating systems that cannot support large files to overcome the file size limit. The `STRIPED` option is the only one currently used. For MyISAM tables, this creates sub-directories inside the database directory, each containing a portion of the data file. The first 1024 * `RAID_CHUNKSIZE` bytes go into the first portion, the next 1024 * `RAID_CHUNKSIZE` bytes go into the next portion, and so on.

The `DATA DIRECTORY="directory"` and `INDEX DIRECTORY="directory"` options specify absolute paths to where the data or index file is stored.

The `PACK_KEYS=1` option packs numeric fields in the index for MyISAM tables (as well as strings, which it does by default). This is only useful if you have indexes with many duplicate numbers.

Use AVG_ROW_LENGTH to give MySQL an idea of the average row length for the table. This is only useful where the table is large and has variable size records.

CHECKSUM can be set to 1 for MyISAM tables if you want to keep a checksum for all rows, which makes it easier to repair the table if it becomes corrupted but does slow down the table.

COMMENT is a comment of up to 60 characters for the table.

MAX_ROWS and MIN_ROWS specify the maximum and minimum rows, respectively, that you plan to store in the table.

PASSWORD encrypts the data definition file (.frm) with a password.

DELAY_KEY_WRITE causes MySQL to wait until a MyISAM table is closed before updating the index, which speeds up mass UPDATEs and INSERTs.

ROW_FORMAT specifies whether a MyISAM table should be FIXED or DYNAMIC.

## DELETE

The DELETE syntax can be any of the following:

```
DELETE [LOW_PRIORITY | QUICK] FROM table_name [WHERE
    where_clause] [ORDER BY ...] [LIMIT rows]
DELETE [LOW_PRIORITY | QUICK] table_name[.*]
    [,table_name[.*] ...] FROM table-references [WHERE where_clause]
DELETE [LOW_PRIORITY | QUICK] FROM table[.*], [table[.*]
    ...] USING table-references [WHERE where_clause]
```

The DELETE statement deletes records from the table (or tables) that adhere to the where_clause (or all records if there is no clause).

The LOW PRIORITY keyword causes the DELETE to wait until no other clients are reading the table before processing it.

The QUICK keyword causes MySQL not to merge index leaves during the DELETE, which is sometimes quicker.

LIMIT determines the maximum number of records to be deleted.

The ORDER BY clause causes MySQL to remove records in a certain order (which is useful with a LIMIT clause).

## DESC

DESC is a synonym for DESCRIBE.

## DESCRIBE

```
DESCRIBE table_name {field_name | wildcard}
```

DESCRIBE returns the definition of the specified table and fields (the same as SHOW COLUMNS FROM table_name).

The wildcard can be part of the fieldname and can be a percentage sign (%), meaning a number of characters, or an underscore (_), meaning one character.

# DO

The DO syntax is as follows:

```
DO expression, [expression, ...]
```

DO has the same effect as a SELECT, except that it does not return results (making it slightly faster).

# DROP

The DROP syntax is as follows:

```
DROP DATABASE [IF EXISTS] database_name
DROP TABLE [IF EXISTS] table_name [, table_name,...] [RESTRICT | CASCADE]
DROP INDEX index_name ON table_name
```

DROP DATABASE removes the database and all its tables.
DROP TABLE removes the specified table.
DROP INDEX removes the specified index.
MySQL returns an error if the database doesn't exist, unless the IF EXISTS clause is used.
DROP TABLE automatically commits active transactions.
RESTRICT and CASCADE are not currently implemented.

# EXPLAIN

```
EXPLAIN table_name
EXPLAIN select_query
```

The select_query is the same as specified in the SELECT description.
Using EXPLAIN with a table name is a synonym for DESCRIBE table_name. Using EXPLAIN with a query provides feedback about how the query will be executed, which is useful for optimizing the query and making the best use of the associated indexes.

# FLUSH

```
FLUSH flush_option [,flush_option] ...
```

The flush_option can be any of the following:

```
DES_KEY_FILE
HOSTS
LOGS
QUERY CACHE
PRIVILEGES
STATUS
TABLES
[TABLE | TABLES] table_name [,table_name...]
TABLES WITH READ LOCK
USER_RESOURCES
```

Flushing the DES_KEY_FILE reloads the DES keys. With the HOSTS option, the host's cache is emptied (which you use after changing IP addresses, for example). Flushing the LOGS closes and reopens log files and increments the binary log. Flushing the QUERY CACHE defragments the query cache. Flushing the PRIVILEGES reloads the permission tables from the *mysql* database. Flushing the STATUS resets the status variables. Flushing the TABLES is the same as flushing the QUERY CACHE, but it also closes all open tables. You can specify only certain tables to flush. You can place a READ LOCK on the tables, which is useful for locking a group of tables for backup purposes. Flushing the USER_RESOURCES resets user resources (used for limiting queries, connections, and updates per hour).

## GRANT

```
GRANT privilege_type [(field_list)] [, privilege_type [(field_list)]
...] ON {table_name | * | *.* | database_name.*} TO user_name
[IDENTIFIED BY [PASSWORD] 'password'] [, user_name [IDENTIFIED BY
'password'] ...] [REQUIRE NONE | [{SSL| X509}] [CIPHER cipher [AND]]
[ISSUER issuer [AND]] [SUBJECT subject]] [WITH [GRANT OPTION |
MAX_QUERIES_PER_HOUR # | MAX_UPDATES_PER_HOUR # |
MAX_CONNECTIONS_PER_HOUR #]]
```

GRANT gives a privilege of a particular kind of permission to a user. Table A.1 describes the available privileges.

**TABLE A.1:** PRIVILEGES

| PRIVILEGE | DESCRIPTION |
| --- | --- |
| ALL | Grants all the basic permissions. |
| ALL PRIVILEGES | Same as ALL. |
| ALTER | Permission to change the structure of a table (an ALTER statement), excluding indexes. |
| CREATE | Permission to create databases and tables, excluding indexes. |
| CREATE TEMPORARY TABLES | Permission to create a temporary table. |
| DELETE | Permission to remove records from a table (a DELETE statement). |
| DROP | Permission to drop databases or tables, excluding indexes. |
| EXECUTE | Permission to run stored procedures (scheduled for MySQL 5). |
| FILE | Permission to read and write files on the server (for LOAD DATA INFILE or SELECT INTO OUTFILE statements). Any files that the mysql user can read are readable. |
| INDEX | Permission to create, modify, or drop indexes. |

*Continued on next page*

**TABLE A.1:** PRIVILEGES *(continued)*

| PRIVILEGE | DESCRIPTION |
|---|---|
| INSERT | Permission to add new records to the table (an INSERT statement). |
| LOCK TABLES | Permission to lock a table for which the user has SELECT permission. |
| PROCESS | Permission to view the current MySQL processes or kill MySQL processes (for SHOW PROCESSLIST or KILL SQL statements). |
| REFERENCES | Not currently used by MySQL and provided for ANSI SQL compatibility (it applies to the use of foreign keys). |
| RELOAD | Permission to reload the database (a FLUSH statement or a reload, refresh, or flush issued from mysqladmin). |
| REPLICATION CLIENT | Permission to ask about the replication slaves and masters. |
| SHOW DATABASES | Permission to see all databases. |
| SELECT | Permission to return data from a table (a SELECT statement). |
| SHUTDOWN | Permission to shut down the server. |
| SUPER | Permission to connect even if the maximum number of connections is reached and perform the CHANGE MASTER, KILL thread, mysqladmin debug, PURGE MASTER LOGS, and SET GLOBAL commands. |
| UPDATE | Permission to modify data in a table (an UPDATE statement). |
| USAGE | Permission to connect to the server and perform statements available to all (for early versions of MySQL 4 this included SHOW DATABASES). |

# *INSERT*

The INSERT syntax can be any of the following:

```
INSERT [LOW_PRIORITY | DELAYED] [IGNORE] [INTO] table_name
    [(field_name,...)] VALUES ((expression | DEFAULT),...),(...),...
INSERT [LOW_PRIORITY | DELAYED] [IGNORE] [INTO] table_name
    [(field_name,...)] SELECT ...
INSERT [LOW_PRIORITY | DELAYED] [IGNORE] [INTO] table_name
    SET field_name=(expression | DEFAULT), ...
INSERT [LOW_PRIORITY] [IGNORE] [INTO] table_name [(field list)] SELECT ...
```

INSERT adds new rows into a table. Without the initial field list, fields are assumed to be in the same order as they were defined, and a value must exist for each field. Any columns not explicitly set are set to their default value.

The LOW PRIORITY keyword causes the INSERT to wait until no other clients are reading the table before processing it. With the DELAYED keyword, MySQL frees the client but waits to perform the INSERT.

IGNORE causes MySQL to ignore INSERTs that would causes a duplicate primary key or unique key, instead of aborting the INSERT.

INSERT...SELECT allows you to INSERT into a table from existing rows in one or more tables.

## JOIN

MySQL accepts any of the following join syntaxes:

```
table_name, table_name
table_name [CROSS] JOIN table_name
table_name INNER JOIN table_name condition
table_name STRAIGHT_JOIN table_name
table_name LEFT [OUTER] JOIN table_name condition
table_name LEFT [OUTER] JOIN table_name
table_name NATURAL [LEFT [OUTER]] JOIN table_name
table_name LEFT OUTER JOIN table_name ON conditional_expr
table_name RIGHT [OUTER] JOIN table_name condition
table_name RIGHT [OUTER] JOIN table_name
table_name NATURAL [RIGHT [OUTER]] JOIN table_name
```

The table can simply be a table_name, use an alias (with AS), or specify or ignore indexes (with USE/IGNORE index).

The condition syntax is as follows:

```
ON conditional_expr | USING (field_names)
```

The conditional_expr is the same as what can exist in a WHERE clause.

## KILL

```
KILL thread_id
```

Kills the specified thread. You can use SHOW PROCESSLIST to identify thread IDs. The SUPER privilege is required to kill processes not owned by the current connection.

## LOAD DATA INFILE

The LOAD DATA INFILE syntax is as follows:

```
LOAD DATA [LOW_PRIORITY | CONCURRENT] [LOCAL] INFILE
    'file.txt' [REPLACE | IGNORE] INTO TABLE table_name
    [FIELDS [TERMINATED BY '\t'] [[OPTIONALLY] ENCLOSED BY
    ''] [ESCAPED BY '\\' ]] [LINES TERMINATED BY '\n']
    [IGNORE number LINES] [(field_name,...)]
```

LOAD DATA reads data from a text file and adds it to a table. This is a quicker way of adding high volumes of data than using INSERT.

The LOCAL keyword indicates that the file is on the client machine; otherwise the file is assumed to be on the database server. LOCAL will not work if the server was started with the --local-infile=0 option, or the client has not been enabled to support it.

Files on the server must be readable by all or be in the database directory, and you need the FILE permission to use LOAD DATA for a file on the server.

On the server, the file is assumed to be in the database directory of the current database if no path is given. If the path is relative, it is assumed to be from the data directory. Absolute paths can also be used.

The LOW PRIORITY keyword causes the LOAD DATA to wait until no other clients are reading the table before processing it.

The CONCURRENT keyword allows other threads to access a MyISAM table at the same time as the LOAD DATA is executing (which will slow down the LOAD DATA).

The REPLACE keyword causes MySQL to delete and replace an existing record if it has the same primary or unique key as the record being added. IGNORE causes MySQL to continue with the next record.

If a FIELDS clause is specified, at least one of TERMINATED BY, [OPTIONALLY] ENCLOSED BY, and ESCAPED BY is required. If no FIELDS clause is specified, the defaults are assumed to be FIELDS TERMINATED BY '\t' ENCLOSED BY '' ESCAPED BY '\\'. These clauses specify the character at the end of a field (default tab), surrounding a field (default nothing), and the escape character (default backslash). Be careful when using Windows paths to escape the path correctly.

Without a LINES clause, the default is assumed to be LINES TERMINATED BY '\n'. This specifies the character at the end of a record (default newline).

The IGNORE number LINES option ignores a number of lines at the top of the file (which is useful when the file contains a header).

LOAD DATA INFILE is the complement of SELECT...INTO INFILE.

## *LOCK TABLES*

```
LOCK TABLES table_name [AS alias] {READ | [READ LOCAL] | [LOW_PRIORITY]
  WRITE} [,table_name {READ | [LOW_PRIORITY] WRITE} ...]
```

LOCK TABLES places a lock on the specified tables. The lock can be READ (other connections cannot write, only read), READ LOCAL (same as READ except that writes from other connections that do not conflict are allowed), or WRITE (which blocks reading or writing from other connections). If the WRITE lock is LOW PRIORITY, READ locks are placed first. Usually WRITE locks have higher priority.

## *OPTIMIZE*

```
OPTIMIZE TABLE table_name [,table_name]...
```

For MyISAM tables, this sorts the index, updates the statistics, and defragments the data file. For BDB tables, this is the same as ANALYZE TABLE.

This locks the table for the duration of the operation (which can take some time).

## RENAME

The RENAME syntax is as follows:

```
RENAME TABLE table_name TO new_table_name[, table_name2 TO new_table_name2,...]
```

RENAME allows you to give a table (or list of tables) a new name. You can also move a table to a new database by specifying database_name.table_name, as long as the database is on the same disk.

You need the ALTER and DROP permissions on the old table, and the CREATE and INSERT permissions on the new table.

## REPAIR TABLE

```
REPAIR TABLE table_name [,table_name...] [EXTENDED] [QUICK] [USE_FRM]
```

Repairs a corrupted MyISAM table. With the QUICK option, only the index tree is repaired. With EXTENDED, the index is re-created row by row. With USE_FRM, the index is repaired based upon the data definition file (for when the index is missing or totally corrupted).

## REPLACE

The REPLACE syntax can be one of the following:

```
REPLACE [LOW_PRIORITY | DELAYED] [INTO] table_name
    [(field_name,...)] VALUES (expression,...),(...),...
REPLACE [LOW_PRIORITY | DELAYED] [INTO] table_name [(field_name,...)] SELECT ...
REPLACE [LOW_PRIORITY | DELAYED] [INTO] table_name SET
    field_name=expression, field_name=expression, ...
```

REPLACE is exactly like INSERT, except that when MySQL encounters a record with a primary or unique key that already exists, it will be deleted and replaced.

## RESET

```
RESET reset_option [,reset_option] ...
```

The reset_option can be any of the following:

```
MASTER
QUERY CACHE
SLAVE
```

RESET MASTER deletes all binary logs and empties the binary log index. RESET SLAVE resets a slave's position for replicating with a master. RESET QUERY CACHE empties the query cache.

## RESTORE TABLE

```
RESTORE TABLE table_name [,table_name...] FROM 'path'
```

Restores a table backed up with BACKUP TABLE. It will not overwrite existing tables.

## *REVOKE*

```
REVOKE privilege_type [(field_list)] [,privilege_type [(field_list)]
...] ON {table_name | * | *.* | database_name.*} FROM user_name
[, user_name ...]
```

Removes previously granted privileges from the specified users. The privilege_type can be one of the privileges listed for GRANT.

## *ROLLBACK*

```
ROLLBACK
```

The ROLLBACK statement ends a transaction, or set of statements, and undoes any statements in that transaction.

## *SELECT*

The SELECT syntax is as follows:

```
SELECT [STRAIGHT_JOIN] [SQL_SMALL_RESULT] [SQL_BIG_RESULT]
    [SQL_BUFFER_RESULT] [SQL_CACHE | SQL_NO_CACHE]
    [SQL_CALC_FOUND_ROWS] [HIGH_PRIORITY] [DISTINCT |
    DISTINCTROW | ALL] expression, ... [INTO {OUTFILE |
    DUMPFILE} 'file_name' export_options]
[FROM table_names
[WHERE where_clause] [GROUP BY {unsigned_integer |
    field_name | formula} [ASC | DESC], ... [HAVING
    where_definition] [ORDER BY {unsigned_integer |
    field_name | formula} [ASC | DESC], ...] [LIMIT
    [offset,] rows] [PROCEDURE procedure_name] [FOR UPDATE | LOCK IN SHARE MODE]]
```

SELECT statements return data from tables. The expression is usually a list of fields (with a function if required), but it can also be a computation or function that has nothing to do with the table fields. For example:

```
SELECT VERSION();
```

or as follows:

```
SELECT 42/10;
```

Fields can be specified as field_name, table_name.field_name, or database_name.table_name.field_name. The longer forms are required if there's any ambiguity.

The expression can also be given an alias with the keyword AS. For example:

```
SELECT 22/7 AS about_pi
```

The expression can be used elsewhere in the statement (but not in the WHERE clause, which is usually determined first).

The table_names clause is a comma-separated list of tables used in the query. You can also use an alias for a table name. For example:

```
SELECT watts FROM wind_water_solar_power AS n;
```

You can also control MySQL's index usage if you're unhappy with MySQL's choice (which you can view by using EXPLAIN) with the USE INDEX and IGNORE INDEX clauses after the table name. The syntax is as follows:

```
table_name [[AS] alias] [USE INDEX (indexlist)] [IGNORE INDEX (indexlist)]
```

The ORDER BY clause orders the returned results in ascending (default, or using the ASC keyword) or descending (DESC) order. It does not have to use items explicitly returned in the expression. For example:

```
SELECT team_name FROM results ORDER BY points DESC
```

The WHERE clause consists of conditions (which can contain functions) that a row needs to adhere to in order to be returned:

```
SELECT team_name FROM results WHERE points > 10
```

GROUP BY groups output rows, which are useful when you use an aggregate function. Two non-ANSI MySQL extensions that you can use are ASC or DESC with GROUP BY, and you can also use fields in the expression that are not mentioned in the GROUP BY clauses. For example:

```
SELECT team_name, team_address, SUM(points) FROM teams GROUP BY team_name DESC
```

The HAVING clause is also a condition, but it is applied last so it can apply to items you group by. For example:

```
SELECT team_name, SUM(points) FROM teams GROUP BY team_name HAVING SUM(points) > 20
```

Do not use it to replace the WHERE clause, as it is will slow down queries.

DISTINCT and its synonym, DISTINCTROW, indicate that the returned row should be unique. ALL (the default) returns all rows, unique or not.

HIGH_PRIORITY (non-ANSI MySQL extension) gives the SELECT a higher priority than any updates.

SQL_BIG_RESULT and SQL_SMALL_RESULT (non-ANSI MySQL extensions) assist the MySQL optimizer by letting it know whether the results returned will be large or small before it begins processing. Both are used with GROUP BY and DISTINCT clauses and usually result in MySQL using a temporary table for greater speed.

SQL_BUFFER_RESULT (non-ANSI MySQL extension) causes MySQL to place the result in a temporary table.

LIMIT takes one or two arguments to limit the number of rows returned. If one argument, it's the maximum number of rows to return; if two, the first is the offset and the second the maximum number of rows to return. If the second argument is –1, MySQL will return all rows from the specified offset until the end. For example, to return from row 2 to the end, use this:

```
SELECT f1 FROM t1 LIMIT 1,-1
```

SQL_CALC_FOUND_ROWS causes MySQL to calculate the number of rows that would have been returned if no LIMIT clause existed. This figure can be returned with the SELECT FOUND_ROWS() function.

SQL_CACHE gets MySQL to store the result in the query cache, and SQL_NO_CACHE causes the result not to be cached. Both are non-ANSI MySQL extensions.

STRAIGHT_JOIN (non-ANSI MySQL extension) causes the optimizer to join the tables in the order in they are listed in the FROM clause, which can speed up queries if tables are joined non-optimally (use EXPLAIN to check this).

SELECT...INTO OUTFILE 'file_name' writes the results into a new file (readable by everyone) on the server. You need to FILE permission to use this. It is the complement of LOAD DATA INFILE, and it uses the same options.

Using INTO DUMPFILE causes MySQL to write one row into the file, without any column or line terminations and without any escaping.

With InnoDB and BDB tables, the FOR UPDATE clause write locks the rows.

# *SET*

```
SET [GLOBAL | SESSION] variable_name=expression, [[GLOBAL | SESSION |
LOCAL ] variable_name=expression...]
```

SET allows you to set variable values. SESSION (or LOCAL, a synonym) is the default, and it sets the value for the duration of the current connection. GLOBAL requires the SUPER privilege, and it sets the variable for all new connections until the server restarts. You still need to set it in the configuration file for an option to remain active after the server restarts. You can find the full list of variable names using SHOW VARIABLES. Table A.2 describes the variables that you set in a nonstandard way.

**TABLE A.2:** VARIABLES YOU SET IN A NONSTANDARD WAY

| SYNTAX | DESCRIPTION |
| --- | --- |
| AUTOCOMMIT= 0 \| 1 | When set (1), MySQL automatically COMMITs statements unless you wrap them in BEGIN and COMMIT statements. MySQL also automatically COMMITs all open transactions when you set AUTOCOMMIT. |
| BIG_TABLES = 0 \| 1 | When set (1), all temporary tables are stored on disk instead of in memory. This makes temporary tables slower, but it prevents the problem of running out of memory. The default is 0. |
| INSERT_ID = # | Sets the AUTO_INCREMENT value (so the next INSERT statement that uses an AUTO_INCREMENT field will use this value). |

*Continued on next page*

**TABLE A.2:** Variables You Set in a Nonstandard Way *(continued)*

| SYNTAX | DESCRIPTION |
|---|---|
| LAST_INSERT_ID = # | Sets the value returned from the next LAST_INSERT_ID() function. |
| LOW_PRIORITY_UPDATES = 0 \| 1 | When set (1), all update statements (INSERT, UPDATE, DELETE, LOCK TABLE WRITE) wait for there to be no pending reads (SELECT, LOCK TABLE READ) on the table they're accessing. |
| MAX_JOIN_SIZE = value \| DEFAULT | By setting a maximum size in rows, you can prevent MySQL from running queries that may not be making proper use of indexes or that may have the potential to slow the server down when run in bulk or at peak times. Setting this to anything but DEFAULT resets SQL_BIG_SELECTS. If SQL_BIG_SELECTS is set, then MAX_JOIN_SIZE is ignored. If the query is already cached, MySQL will ignore this limit and return the results. |
| QUERY_CACHE_TYPE = OFF \| ON \| DEMAND | Sets the query cache setting for the thread. |
| QUERY_CACHE_TYPE = 0 \| 1 \| 2 | Sets the query cache setting for the thread. |
| SQL_AUTO_IS_NULL = 0 \| 1 | If set (1, the default), then the last inserted row for an AUTO_INCREMENT can be found with WHERE auto_increment_column IS NULL. This is used by Microsoft Access and other programs connecting through ODBC. |
| SQL_BIG_SELECTS = 0 \| 1 | If set (1, the default), then MySQL allows large queries. If not set (0), then MySQL will not allow queries where it will have to examine more than max_join_size rows. This is useful to avoid running accidental or malicious queries that could bring the server down. |
| SQL_BUFFER_RESULT = 0 \| 1 | If set (1), MySQL places query results into a temporary table (in some cases speeding up performance by releasing table locks earlier). |
| SQL_LOG_OFF = 0 \| 1 | If set (1), MySQL will not log for the client (this is not the update log). The SUPER permission is required. |
| SQL_LOG_UPDATE = 0 \| 1 | If not set (0), MySQL will not use the update log for the client. This requires the SUPER permission. |
| SQL_QUOTE_SHOW_CREATE = 0 \| 1 | If set (1, the default), MySQL will quote table and column names. |
| SQL_SAFE_UPDATES = 0 \| 1 | If set (1), MySQL will not perform UPDATE or DELETE statements that don't use either an index or a LIMIT clause, which helps prevent unpleasant accidents. |
| SQL_SELECT_LIMIT = value \| DEFAULT | Sets the maximum number of records (default unlimited) that can be returned with a SELECT statement. LIMIT takes precedence over this. |
| TIMESTAMP = timestamp_value \| DEFAULT | Sets the time for the client. This can be used to get the original timestamp when using the update log to restore rows. The timestamp_value is a Unix epoch timestamp. |

The old SET OPTION syntax is now deprecated, so you should not use it anymore.

## SET TRANSACTION

```
SET [GLOBAL | SESSION] TRANSACTION ISOLATION LEVEL { READ UNCOMMITTED
  | READ COMMITTED | REPEATABLE READ | SERIALIZABLE }
```

Sets the transaction isolation level. By default it will be for the next transaction only, unless the SESSION or GLOBAL keywords are used (which set the level for all transactions on the current connection or for all transactions on all new connections, respectively).

## SHOW

The SHOW syntax can be any of the following:

```
SHOW DATABASES [LIKE expression]
SHOW [OPEN] TABLES [FROM database_name] [LIKE expression]
SHOW [FULL] COLUMNS FROM table_name [FROM database_name] [LIKE expression]
SHOW INDEX FROM table_name [FROM database_name]
SHOW TABLE STATUS [FROM database_name] [LIKE expression]
SHOW STATUS [LIKE expression]
SHOW VARIABLES [LIKE expression]
SHOW LOGS
SHOW [FULL] PROCESSLIST
SHOW GRANTS FOR user
SHOW CREATE TABLE table_name
SHOW MASTER STATUS
SHOW MASTER LOGS
SHOW SLAVE STATUS
```

SHOW lists the databases, tables, or columns, or it provides status information about the server.

The wildcard can be part of the database, table, or fieldname, and it can be a percentage sign (%), meaning a number of characters, or an underscore (_), meaning one character.

## TRUNCATE

```
TRUNCATE TABLE table_name
```

The TRUNCATE statement deletes all records from a table. It is quicker than the equivalent DELETE statement as it DROPs and CREATEs the table. It is not transaction safe (so will return an error if there are any active transactions or locks).

## UNION

```
SELECT ... UNION [ALL] SELECT ... [UNION SELECT ...]
```

Union combines many results into one.
Without the ALL keyword, rows are unique.

## *UNLOCK TABLES*

```
UNLOCK TABLES
```

Releases all locks held by the current connection.

## *UPDATE*

```
UPDATE [LOW_PRIORITY] [IGNORE] table_name SET field_name1=expression1 [, field_
    name2=expression2, ...] [WHERE where_clause] [LIMIT #]
```

The UPDATE statement updates the contents of existing rows in the database.

The SET clause specifies which fields to update and what the new values are to be.

The where_clause gives conditions the row must adhere to in order to be updated.

IGNORE causes MySQL to ignore UPDATEs that would cause a duplicate primary key or unique key, instead of aborting the UPDATE.

The LOW PRIORITY keyword causes the UPDATE to wait until no other clients are reading the table before processing it.

The expression can take the current value of a field; for example, to add 5 to all employees' commissions, you could use the following:

```
UPDATE employee SET commission=commission+5;
```

LIMIT determines the maximum number of records to be updated.

## *USE*

```
USE database_name
```

Changes the current active database to the specified database.

# MySQL Function and Operator Reference

MYSQL HAS MANY USEFUL operators and functions. The operators are one of the basics of MySQL, and you won't get far without them. There are many obscure functions that you'll probably never use, but it's worth going through the list because you may find some you will use and some you will store in the back of your mind for later.

## Logical Operators

Logical operators, or Boolean operators, check whether something is true or false. They return 0 if the expression is false and 1 if it's true. Null values are handled differently depending on the operator. Usually they return a NULL result.

### AND, &&

```
value1 AND value1
value1 && value2
```

Returns true (1) if both values are true.
For example:

```
mysql> SELECT 1 AND 0;
+---------+
| 1 AND 0 |
+---------+
|       0 |
+---------+
mysql> SELECT 1=1 && 2=2;
+------------+
| 1=1 && 2=2 |
+------------+
|          1 |
+------------+
```

## OR, ||

```
value1 OR value2
value1 || value 2
```

Returns true (1) if either `value1` or `value2` is true.
For example:

```
mysql> SELECT 1 OR 1;
+--------+
| 1 OR 1 |
+--------+
|      1 |
+--------+
mysql> SELECT 1=2 || 2=3;
+------------+
| 1=2 || 2=3 |
+------------+
|          0 |
+------------+
```

## NOT, !

```
NOT value1
! value1
```

Returns the opposite of `value1`, which is true if `value1` is false and false if `value1` is true.
For example:

```
mysql> SELECT !1;
+----+
| !1 |
+----+
|  0 |
+----+
mysql> SELECT NOT(1=2);
+----------+
| NOT(1=2) |
+----------+
|        1 |
+----------+
```

# Arithmetic Operators

Arithmetic operators perform basic mathematical calculations. If any of the values are null, the results of the entire operation are also usually null. For purposes of the calculation, strings are converted to numbers. Some strings are converted to the equivalent number (such as the strings '1' and '33'), but others are converted to 0 (such as the strings 'one' and 'abc').

**+**

```
value1 + value2
```

Adds two values together.
For example:

```
mysql> SELECT 1+3;
+-----+
| 1+3 |
+-----+
|   4 |
+-----+
mysql> SELECT 15+"9";
+--------+
| 15+"9" |
+--------+
|     24 |
+--------+
```

**−**

```
value1 - value2
```

Subtracts value2 from value1.
For example:

```
mysql> SELECT 1-9;
+-----+
| 1-9 |
+-----+
|  -8 |
+-----+
```

**\***

```
value1 * value2
```

Multiplies two values with each other.
For example:

```
mysql> SELECT 12 * 10;
+---------+
| 12 * 10 |
+---------+
|     120 |
+---------+
```

## /

```
value1 / value2
```

Divides value1 by value2.
For example:

```
mysql> SELECT 4/2;
+------+
| 4/2  |
+------+
| 2.00 |
+------+
mysql> SELECT 10005.00000/10004.00000;
+-------------------------+
| 10005.00000/10004.00000 |
+-------------------------+
|               1.0001000 |
+-------------------------+
```

## %

Returns the modulus (remainder after value1 is divided by value2).
For example:

```
mysql> SELECT 3%2;
+------+
| 3%2  |
+------+
|    1 |
+------+
```

## Comparison Operators

Comparison operators compare values and return true or false (1 or 0) depending on the results. If there's a null value, the operator will return NULL as a result in most cases. Different types can be compared (strings, numbers, dates, and so on), though if the types are different, you need to be careful. MySQL converts the types to an equivalent as well as it can.

If you're comparing strings, they are compared case insensitively, unless they are BINARY. For example, A is the same as a, but BINARY A is not the same as BINARY a. Capitals come first in this case, so BINARY A is less than BINARY a. Similarly, the string 10 is less than the string 2 because, being a string, it's compared from left to right. The first check is then whether 1 is less than 2, which it is, and the check stops there (the same way as az is before b).

## =

```
value1 = value2
```

True if both value1 and value2 are equal. If either is null, this will return NULL.

For example:

```
mysql> SELECT 1=2;
+-----+
| 1=2 |
+-----+
|   0 |
+-----+
mysql> SELECT 'A' = 'a';
+-----------+
| 'A' = 'a' |
+-----------+
|         1 |
+-----------+
mysql> SELECT BINARY 'a' = 'A';
+------------------+
| BINARY 'a' = 'A' |
+------------------+
|                0 |
+------------------+
mysql> SELECT NULL=NULL;
+-----------+
| NULL=NULL |
+-----------+
|      NULL |
+-----------+
```

## !=, <>

```
value1 <> value2
value1 != value2
```

True if value1 is not equal to value2.
For example:

```
mysql> SELECT 'a' != 'A';
+------------+
| 'a' != 'A' |
+------------+
|          0 |
+------------+
mysql> SELECT BINARY 'a' <> 'A';
+-------------------+
| BINARY 'a' <> 'A' |
+-------------------+
|                 1 |
+-------------------+
```

## >

```
value1 > value2
```

True if `value1` is greater than `value2`.
For example:

```
mysql> SELECT 1>2;
+-----+
| 1>2 |
+-----+
|   0 |
+-----+
mysql> SELECT 'b'>'a';
+---------+
| 'b'>'a' |
+---------+
|       1 |
+---------+
```

## <

```
value1 < value2
```

True if `value1` is less than `value2`.
For example:

```
mysql> SELECT 'b' < 'd';
+-----------+
| 'b' < 'd' |
+-----------+
|         1 |
+-----------+
mysql> SELECT '4' < '34';
+------------+
| '4' < '34' |
+------------+
|          0 |
+------------+
```

## >=

```
value1 >= value2
```

True if `value1` is greater than or equal to `value2`.
For example:

```
mysql> SELECT 4 >= 4;
```

```
+--------+
| 4 >= 4 |
+--------+
|      1 |
+--------+
```

## <=

    value1<= value2

True if `value1` is less than or equal to `value2`.
For example:

```
mysql> SELECT 4 <= 3;
+--------+
| 4 <= 3 |
+--------+
|      0 |
+--------+
```

## <=>

    value1 <=> value2

True if `value1` is equal to `value2`, including nulls. This allows you to pretend that NULL is actually some value, and therefore get a true or false result (rather than NULL) when using NULLs in comparison with non-NULLs; by contrast, MySQL refuses to give a definite answer to the question, "Is 4 equal to NULL?" Instead, it correctly says that the expression 4 = NULL evaluates to something undecidable (NULL).
For example:

```
mysql> SELECT NULL<=>NULL;
+------------+
| NULL<=>NULL |
+------------+
|          1 |
+------------+
mysql> SELECT 4 <=> NULL;
+------------+
| 4 <=> NULL |
+------------+
|          0 |
+------------+
```

## *IS NULL*

    value1 IS NULL

True if `value1` is null (not false).

For example:

```
mysql> SELECT NULL IS NULL;
+--------------+
| NULL IS NULL |
+--------------+
|            1 |
+--------------+
mysql> SELECT 0 IS NULL;
+-----------+
| 0 IS NULL |
+-----------+
|         0 |
+-----------+
```

## BETWEEN

```
value1 BETWEEN value2 AND value3
```

True if value1 is inclusively between value2 and value3.
For example:

```
mysql> SELECT 1 BETWEEN 0 AND 2;
+-------------------+
| 1 BETWEEN 0 AND 2 |
+-------------------+
|                 1 |
+-------------------+
mysql> SELECT 'a' BETWEEN 'A' and 'B';
+-------------------------+
| 'a' BETWEEN 'A' and 'B' |
+-------------------------+
|                       1 |
+-------------------------+
mysql> SELECT BINARY 'a' BETWEEN 'A' AND 'C';
+--------------------------------+
| BINARY 'a' BETWEEN 'A' AND 'C' |
+--------------------------------+
|                              0 |
+--------------------------------+
```

## LIKE

```
value1 LIKE value2
```

True if value1 matches value2 on an SQL pattern match. A percentage (%) refers to any number of characters, and an underscore (_) refers to one character.
For example:

```
mysql> SELECT 'abc' LIKE 'ab_';
```

```
+-----------------+
| 'abc' LIKE 'ab_' |
+-----------------+
|               1 |
+-----------------+
mysql> SELECT 'abc' LIKE '%c';
+-----------------+
| 'abc' LIKE '%c' |
+-----------------+
|               1 |
+-----------------+
```

## IN

```
value1 IN (value2 [value3,...])
```

True if `value1` is equal to any value in the comma-separated list.
For example:

```
mysql> SELECT 'a' IN('b','c','aa');
+---------------------+
| 'a' IN('b','c','aa') |
+---------------------+
|                   0 |
+---------------------+
mysql> SELECT 'a' IN('A','B');
+-----------------+
| 'a' IN('A','B') |
+-----------------+
|               1 |
+-----------------+
```

## REGEXP, RLIKE

```
value1 REGEXP value2
value1 RLIKE value2
```

True if `value1` matches `value2` with a regular expression. Table B.1 lists the regular expression characters.

**TABLE B.1:** REGULAR EXPRESSION CHARACTERS

| CHARACTER | DESCRIPTION |
| --- | --- |
| * | Matches zero or more instances of the subexpression preceding it |
| + | Matches one or more instances of the subexpression preceding it |
| ? | Matches zero or one instances of the subexpression preceding it |

*Continued on next page*

**TABLE B.1:** REGULAR EXPRESSION CHARACTERS *(continued)*

| CHARACTER | DESCRIPTION |
| --- | --- |
| . | Matches any single character |
| [xyz] | Matches any of x, y, or z (the characters within the brackets) |
| [A–Z] | Matches any uppercase letter |
| [a–z] | Matches any lowercase letter |
| [0–9] | Matches any digit |
| ^ | Anchors the match from the beginning |
| $ | Anchors the match to the end |
| \| | Separates subexpressions in the regular expression |
| {n,m} | Subexpression must occur at least n times, but no more than n |
| {n} | Subexpression must occur exactly n times |
| {n,\| | Subexpression must occur at least n times |
| () | Groups characters into subexpressions |

For example:

```
mysql> SELECT 'pqwxyz' REGEXP 'xyz';
+----------------------+
| 'pqwxyz' REGEXP 'xyz' |
+----------------------+
|                    1 |
+----------------------+
mysql> SELECT 'xyz' REGEXP '^x';
+------------------+
| 'xyz' REGEXP '^x' |
+------------------+
|                1 |
+------------------+
mysql> SELECT 'abcdef' REGEXP 'g+';
+---------------------+
| 'abcdef' REGEXP 'g+' |
+---------------------+
|                   0 |
+---------------------+
mysql> SELECT 'abcdef' REGEXP 'g*';
+---------------------+
| 'abcdef' REGEXP 'g*' |
+---------------------+
|                   1 |
+---------------------+
```

```
mysql> SELECT 'ian' REGEXP 'iai*n';
+----------------------+
| 'ian' REGEXP 'iai*n' |
+----------------------+
|                    1 |
+----------------------+
mysql> SELECT 'aaaa' REGEXP 'a{3,}';
+----------------------+
| 'aaaa' REGEXP 'a{3,}' |
+----------------------+
|                    1 |
+----------------------+
mysql> SELECT 'aaaa' REGEXP '^aaa$';
+----------------------+
| 'aaaa' REGEXP '^aaa$' |
+----------------------+
|                    0 |
+----------------------+
mysql> SELECT 'abcabcabc' REGEXP 'abc{3}';
+---------------------------+
| 'abcabcabc' REGEXP 'abc{3}' |
+---------------------------+
|                         0 |
+---------------------------+
mysql> SELECT 'abcabcabc' REGEXP '(abc){3}';
+-----------------------------+
| 'abcabcabc' REGEXP '(abc){3}' |
+-----------------------------+
|                           1 |
+-----------------------------+
mysql> SELECT 'abcbbcccc' REGEXP '[abc]{3}';
+-----------------------------+
| 'abcbbcccc' REGEXP '[abc]{3}' |
+-----------------------------+
|                           1 |
+-----------------------------+
mysql> SELECT 'abcbbcccc' REGEXP '(a|b|c){3}';
+-------------------------------+
| 'abcbbcccc' REGEXP '(a|b|c){3}' |
+-------------------------------+
|                             1 |
+-------------------------------+
```

# Bit Operators

The bit operators are not used often. They allow you to work with bit values and perform bit calculations in your queries.

## &

```
value1 & value2
```

Performs a bitwise AND. This converts the values to binary and compares the bits. Only if both of the corresponding bits are 1 is the resulting bit also 1.

For example:

```
mysql> SELECT 2&1;
+-----+
| 2&1 |
+-----+
|   0 |
+-----+
mysql> SELECT 3&1;
+-----+
| 3&1 |
+-----+
|   1 |
+-----+
```

## |

```
value1 | value2
```

Performs a bitwise OR. This converts the values to binary and compares the bits. If either of the corresponding bits are 1, the resulting bit is also 1.

For example:

```
mysql> SELECT 2|1;
+-----+
| 2|1 |
+-----+
|   3 |
+-----+
```

## <<

```
value1 << value2
```

Converts value1 to binary and shifts the bits of value1 left by the amount of value2.

For example:

```
mysql> SELECT 2<<1;
+------+
| 2<<1 |
+------+
|    4 |
+------+
```

**>>**

```
value1 >> value2
```

Converts `value1` to binary and shifts the bits of `value1` right by the amount of `value2`. For example:

```
mysql> SELECT 2>>1;
+------+
| 2>>1 |
+------+
|    1 |
+------+
```

# Date and Time Functions

You use date and time functions when working with time, such as when returning the current time in a certain format or seeing how many days until a certain date. In most cases, values of type `date` are stored as YYYY-MM-DD (for example, 2002-12-25), and values of type `time` are stored as hh:mm:ss (for example, 11:23:43). There is also the `datetime` type, stored as YYYY-MM-DD hh:mm:ss. Most functions that accept dates or times will accept the `datetime` format and ignore the part they don't need. Similarly, if you are short of values (when asked for a hh:mm:ss, you only enter the mm:ss portion), MySQL will assume the rest are zeros and perform the calculation correctly. You can use any delimiter in the date and time strings, rather than colons (:) and dashes (–) as long as you are consistent.

Certain functions make use of a specific date type (for example, `DATE_ADD()`, which needs a type interval to perform its calculation).

The following are the date and time types:

- SECOND
- MINUTE
- HOUR
- DAY
- MONTH
- YEAR
- MINUTE_SECOND: "mm:ss" (for example, "41:23")
- HOUR_MINUTE: "hh:mm" (for example, "12:23")
- DAY_HOUR: "DD hh" (for example, "11 09")
- YEAR_MONTH: "YYYY-MM" (for example, "2002-12")
- HOUR_SECOND: "hh:mm:ss" (for example, "11:24:36")
- DAY_MINUTE: "DD hh:mm" (for example, "09 11:31")
- DAY_SECOND: "DD hh:mm:ss" (for example, "09 11:31:21")

To perform date calculations, you can also use the usual operators $(+, -,$ and so on) rather than the date functions. MySQL also correctly converts between units. When, for example, you add 1 month to month 12, MySQL will increment the year and correctly calculate the months.

## ADDDATE

```
ADDDATE(date,INTERVAL expression type)
```

A synonym for DATE_ADD().

## CURDATE

```
CURDATE()
```

A synonym for the CURRENT_DATE() function.

## CURRENT_DATE

```
CURRENT_DATE()
```

Returns the current system date as either the string YYYY-MM-DD or the numeric YYYYMMDD depending on the context.

For example:

```
mysql> SELECT CURRENT_DATE();
+----------------+
| CURRENT_DATE() |
+----------------+
| 2002-09-10     |
+----------------+
mysql> SELECT CURRENT_DATE()+1;
+------------------+
| CURRENT_DATE()+1 |
+------------------+
|         20020911 |
+------------------+
```

## CURRENT_TIME

```
CURRENT_TIME()
```

Returns the current system time as either the string hh:mm:ss or the number hhmmss, depending on the context of the function.

For example:

```
mysql> SELECT CURRENT_TIME();
+----------------+
| CURRENT_TIME() |
+----------------+
| 23:53:15       |
+----------------+
```

```
mysql> SELECT CURRENT_TIME() + 1;
+--------------------+
| CURRENT_TIME() + 1 |
+--------------------+
|             235434 |
+--------------------+
```

## CURRENT_TIMESTAMP

CURRENT_TIMESTAMP()

This function is a synonym for the NOW() function.

## CURTIME

CURTIME()

A synonym for the CURRENT_TIME() function.

## DATE_ADD

DATE_ADD(date,INTERVAL expression type)

Adds a certain time period to the specified date. You can use a negative value for the expression, in which case it will be subtracted. The type must be one of those listed at the beginning of this section ("Date and Time Functions"), and the expression must match the type.

For example:

```
mysql> SELECT DATE_ADD('2002-12-25',INTERVAL 1 MONTH);
+-----------------------------------------+
| DATE_ADD('2002-12-25',INTERVAL 1 MONTH) |
+-----------------------------------------+
| 2003-01-25                              |
+-----------------------------------------+
mysql> SELECT DATE_ADD('2002-12-25 13:00:00',INTERVAL -14 HOUR);
+---------------------------------------------------+
| DATE_ADD('2002-12-25 13:00:00',INTERVAL -14 HOUR) |
+---------------------------------------------------+
| 2002-12-24 23:00:00                               |
+---------------------------------------------------+
```

## DATE_FORMAT

DATE_FORMAT(date,format_string)

Formats the specified date based upon the format string, which can consist of the specifiers shown in Table B.2.

**TABLE B.2:** DATE FORMAT SPECIFIERS

| SPECIFIER | DESCRIPTION |
| --- | --- |
| %a | Abbreviation of the day name (Sun–Sat) |
| %b | Abbreviation of the month name (Jan–Dec) |
| %c | Numeric month from 1–12 |
| %D | Numeric day of the month with English suffix (1st, 2nd, and so on) |
| %d | Numeric day of the month with two digits, from 00–31 |
| %e | Numeric day of the month with one or two digits, from 0–31 |
| %H | Hour from 00 to 23 |
| %h | Hour from 01–12 |
| %I | Minutes from 00–59 |
| %I | Hour from 01–12 |
| %j | Day of the year from 001–366 |
| %k | Hour with one or two digits, from 0–23 |
| %l | Hour with one digit, from 1–12 |
| %M | Month name from January–December |
| %m | Numeric month from 01–12 |
| %p | A.M. or P.M. |
| %r | 12-hour time, hh:mm:ss A.M. or P.M. |
| %S | Seconds from 00–59 |
| %s | Seconds from 00–59 |
| %T | 24 hour time, hh:mm:ss |
| %U | Week from 00–53, with Sunday being the first day of the week |
| %u | Week from 00–53 with Monday being the first day of the week |
| %V | Week from 01–53 with Sunday being the first day of the week |
| %v | Week from 01–53 with Monday being the first day of the week |
| %W | Name of the day in the week from Sunday–Saturday |
| %w | Day of the week from 0 for Sunday, to 6 for Saturday |
| %X | Four-digit numeric year for the week with Sunday being the first day of the week |

*Continued on next page*

**TABLE B.2:** DATE FORMAT SPECIFIERS *(continued)*

| SPECIFIER | DESCRIPTION |
|---|---|
| %x | Four-digit numeric year for the week with Monday being the first day of the week |
| %Y | Four-digit numeric year |
| %y | Two-digit numeric year |
| %% | Escaped percentage sign |

For example:

```
mysql> SELECT DATE_FORMAT('1999-03-02','%c %M');
+----------------------------------+
| DATE_FORMAT('1999-03-02','%c %M') |
+----------------------------------+
| 3 March                          |
+----------------------------------+
```

## DATE_SUB

```
DATE_SUB(date,INTERVAL expression type)
```

Subtracts a certain time period from the specified date. You can use a negative value for the expression, in which case it will be added. The type must be one of those listed at the beginning of this section ("Date and Time Functions"), and the expression must match the type.

For example:

```
mysql> SELECT DATE_SUB('2002-12-25 13:00:00',INTERVAL "14:13" MINUTE_SECOND);
+--------------------------------------------------------------+
| DATE_SUB('2002-12-25 13:00:00',INTERVAL "14:13" MINUTE_SECOND) |
+--------------------------------------------------------------+
| 2002-12-25 12:45:47                                          |
+--------------------------------------------------------------+
```

## DAYNAME

```
DAYNAME(date)
```

Returns the name of the day for the specified date.
For example:

```
mysql> SELECT DAYNAME('2000-12-25');
+----------------------+
| DAYNAME('2000-12-25') |
+----------------------+
| Monday               |
+----------------------+
```

## *DAYOFMONTH*

DAYOFMONTH(date)

Returns the day of the month for the supplied date as a number from 1 to 31.
For example:

```
mysql> SELECT DAYOFMONTH('2000-01-01');
+-------------------------+
| DAYOFMONTH('2000-01-01') |
+-------------------------+
|                       1 |
+-------------------------+
```

## *DAYOFWEEK*

DAYOFWEEK(date)

Returns the day of the week for the supplied date as a number from 1 for Sunday to 7 for Saturday, which is the Open Database Connectivity (ODBC) standard.
For example:

```
mysql> SELECT DAYOFWEEK('2000-01-01');
+------------------------+
| DAYOFWEEK('2000-01-01') |
+------------------------+
|                      7 |
+------------------------+
```

Use WEEKDAY() to return the day index from 0–6, Monday to Sunday.

## *DAYOFYEAR*

DAYOFYEAR(date)

Returns the day of the year for the supplied date as a number from 1 to 366.
For example:

```
mysql> SELECT DAYOFYEAR('2000-12-25');
+------------------------+
| DAYOFYEAR('2000-12-25') |
+------------------------+
|                    360 |
+------------------------+
```

## *EXTRACT*

EXTRACT(date_type FROM date)

Uses the specified date type to return the portion of the date. See the list of date types before the start of the date functions.

For example:

```
mysql> SELECT EXTRACT(YEAR FROM '2002-02-03');
+--------------------------------+
| EXTRACT(YEAR FROM '2002-02-03') |
+--------------------------------+
|                           2002 |
+--------------------------------+
mysql> SELECT EXTRACT(MINUTE_SECOND FROM '2002-02-03 12:32:45');
+---------------------------------------------------+
| EXTRACT(MINUTE_SECOND FROM '2002-02-03 12:32:45') |
+---------------------------------------------------+
|                                              3245 |
+---------------------------------------------------+
```

## FROM_DAYS

```
FROM_DAYS(number)
```

Converts the specified number into a date based on the number of days since Jan 1, year 0, and returns the result. Does not take the days lost in the change to the Gregorian calendar into account.

For example:

```
mysql> SELECT FROM_DAYS(731574);
+-------------------+
| FROM_DAYS(731574) |
+-------------------+
| 2002-12-25        |
+-------------------+
```

## FROM_UNIXTIME

```
FROM_UNIXTIME(unix_timestamp [, format_string])
```

Converts the specified timestamp into a date and returns the result. The returned date will be formatted if there is a format string supplied. The format string can be any of those from the DATE_FORMAT() function.

For example:

```
mysql> SELECT FROM_UNIXTIME(100);
+---------------------+
| FROM_UNIXTIME(100)  |
+---------------------+
| 1970-01-01 00:01:40 |
+---------------------+
```

```
mysql> SELECT FROM_UNIXTIME(1031621727,'%c %M');
+----------------------------------+
| FROM_UNIXTIME(1031621727,'%c %M') |
+----------------------------------+
| 9 September                      |
+----------------------------------+
```

## HOUR

HOUR(time)

Returns the hour for the specified time, from 0 to 23.
For example:

```
mysql> SELECT HOUR('06:59:03');
+------------------+
| HOUR('06:59:03') |
+------------------+
|                6 |
+------------------+
```

## MINUTE

MINUTE(time)

Returns the minutes for the specified time, from 0 to 59.
For example:

```
mysql> SELECT MINUTE('00:01:03');
+--------------------+
| MINUTE('00:01:03') |
+--------------------+
|                  1 |
+--------------------+
```

## MONTH

MONTH(date)

Returns the month for the specified date, from 1 to 12.
For example:

```
mysql> SELECT MONTH('2000-12-25');
+---------------------+
| MONTH('2000-12-25') |
+---------------------+
|                  12 |
+---------------------+
```

## *MONTHNAME*

```
MONTHNAME(date)
```

Returns the name of the month for the specified date. For example:

```
mysql> SELECT MONTHNAME('2000-12-25');
+-----------------------+
| MONTHNAME('2000-12-25') |
+-----------------------+
| December              |
+-----------------------+
```

## *NOW*

```
NOW()
```

Returns the current timestamp (date and time in the format YYYY-MM-DD hh:mm:ss), either as a string or numeric depending on the context. The function will return the same result for multiple calls on a single query.

For example:

```
mysql> SELECT NOW();
+---------------------+
| NOW()               |
+---------------------+
| 2002-09-10 00:58:06 |
+---------------------+
```

A synonym for the `CURRENT_TIMESTAMP()` and `SYSDATE()` functions.

## *PERIOD_ADD*

```
PERIOD_ADD(period,months)
```

Adds the months to the period (specified as either YYMM or YYYYMM) and returns the result as YYYYMM. For example:

```
mysql> SELECT PERIOD_ADD(200205,3);
+---------------------+
| PERIOD_ADD(200205,3) |
+---------------------+
|              200208 |
+---------------------+
mysql> SELECT PERIOD_ADD(200205,-42);
+-----------------------+
| PERIOD_ADD(200205,-42) |
+-----------------------+
|                199811 |
+-----------------------+
```

## PERIOD_DIFF

```
PERIOD_DIFF(period1,period2)
```

Returns the number of months between period and period2 (which are specified in the format YYMM or YYYYMM).

For example:

```
mysql> SELECT PERIOD_DIFF(200212,200001);
+----------------------------+
| PERIOD_DIFF(200212,200001) |
+----------------------------+
|                         35 |
+----------------------------+
mysql> SELECT PERIOD_DIFF(199903,199904);
+----------------------------+
| PERIOD_DIFF(199903,199904) |
+----------------------------+
|                         -1 |
+----------------------------+
```

## QUARTER

```
QUARTER(date)
```

Returns the quarter of the specified date, from 1 to 4.

For example:

```
mysql> SELECT QUARTER('2002-06-30');
+-----------------------+
| QUARTER('2002-06-30') |
+-----------------------+
|                     2 |
+-----------------------+
```

## SEC_TO_TIME

```
SEC_TO_TIME(seconds)
```

Converts the seconds to time, returning either a string (hh:mm:ss) or numeric (hhmmss) depending on the context.

For example:

```
mysql> SELECT SEC_TO_TIME(1000);
+-------------------+
| SEC_TO_TIME(1000) |
+-------------------+
| 00:16:40          |
+-------------------+
```

```
mysql> SELECT SEC_TO_TIME(-10000);
+---------------------+
| SEC_TO_TIME(-10000) |
+---------------------+
| -02:46:40           |
+---------------------+
```

## SECOND

```
SECOND(time)
```

Returns the seconds for the specified time, from 0 to 58.
For example:

```
mysql> SELECT SECOND('00:01:03');
+--------------------+
| SECOND('00:01:03') |
+--------------------+
|                  3 |
+--------------------+
```

## SUBDATE

```
SUBDATE(date,INTERVAL expression type)
```

A synonym for DATE_SUB().

## SYSDATE

```
SYSDATE()
```

A synonym for the NOW() function.

## TIME_FORMAT

```
TIME_FORMAT(time,format)
```

Identical to DATE_FORMAT() except that you can only use the subset of formats dealing with time (or else you'll return NULL).

## TIME_TO_SEC

```
TIME_TO_SEC(time)
```

Converts the time to seconds and returns the result. For example:

```
mysql> SELECT TIME_TO_SEC('00:01:03');
+-------------------------+
| TIME_TO_SEC('00:01:03') |
+-------------------------+
|                      63 |
+-------------------------+
```

## *TO_DAYS*

```
TO_DAYS(date)
```

Returns the number of days since Jan 1 year 0 for the specified date. Does not take the days lost in the change to the Gregorian calendar into account.

For example:

```
mysql> SELECT TO_DAYS('2000-01-01');
+----------------------+
| TO_DAYS('2000-01-01') |
+----------------------+
|               730485 |
+----------------------+
```

## *UNIX_TIMESTAMP*

```
UNIX_TIMESTAMP([date])
```

Returns an unsigned integer representing the Unix timestamp (the seconds since midnight, Jan. 1, 1970) of either the current system time (if called without a parameter) or the specified date.

For example:

```
mysql> SELECT UNIX_TIMESTAMP();
+------------------+
| UNIX_TIMESTAMP() |
+------------------+
|       1031621727 |
+------------------+
mysql> SELECT UNIX_TIMESTAMP('1970-01-01 00:01:40');
+---------------------------------------+
| UNIX_TIMESTAMP('1970-01-01 00:01:40') |
+---------------------------------------+
|                                   100 |
+---------------------------------------+
```

## *WEEK*

```
WEEK(date [,week_start])
```

Returns the week in a given year for the specified date, from 0 to 53. The week is assumed to start on Sunday, unless the optional week_start argument is set to 1, in which case the week is assumed to start on Monday. It can also explicitly set to 0 for Sunday starts. The function will return 0 for dates before the first Sunday (or Monday) of the year.

For example:

```
mysql> SELECT WEEK('2002-06-31');
```

```
+-------------------+
| WEEK('2002-06-31') |
+-------------------+
|                26 |
+-------------------+
mysql> SELECT WEEK('2002-06-31',1);
+---------------------+
| WEEK('2002-06-31',1) |
+---------------------+
|                  27 |
+---------------------+
mysql> SELECT WEEK('1998-12-31',1);
+---------------------+
| WEEK('1998-12-31',1) |
+---------------------+
|                  53 |
+---------------------+
mysql> SELECT WEEK('1998-01-01');
+-------------------+
| WEEK('1998-01-01') |
+-------------------+
|                 0 |
+-------------------+
```

Use the YEARWEEK() function to roll the week over from the previous year if the date is before the first Sunday (or Monday) of the year.

## WEEKDAY

```
WEEKDAY(date)
```

Returns the day of the week for the supplied date as a number from 0 for Monday to 6 for Sunday. For example:

```
mysql> SELECT WEEKDAY('2000-01-01');
+----------------------+
| WEEKDAY('2000-01-01') |
+----------------------+
|                    5 |
+----------------------+
```

Use DAYOFWEEK() to return the day index according to the ODBC standard (1–7, Sunday–Saturday).

## YEAR

```
YEAR(date)
```

Returns the year for the specified date, from 1000 to 9999.

For example:

```
mysql> SELECT YEAR('2002-06-30');
+--------------------+
| YEAR('2002-06-30') |
+--------------------+
|               2002 |
+--------------------+
```

### YEARWEEK

```
YEARWEEK(date [,week_start])
```

Returns a combination of year and week for the specified date. The week is assumed to start on Sunday, unless the optional week_start argument is set to 1, in which case the week is assumed to start on Monday. It can also explicitly set to 0 for Sunday starts. The year could be the previous year to the date for dates before the first Sunday (or Monday) in the year or in the following year.

For example:

```
mysql> SELECT YEARWEEK('2002-12-25');
+------------------------+
| YEARWEEK('2002-12-25') |
+------------------------+
|                 200251 |
+------------------------+
mysql> SELECT YEARWEEK('1998-12-31',1);
+--------------------------+
| YEARWEEK('1998-12-31',1) |
+--------------------------+
|                   199853 |
+--------------------------+
mysql> SELECT YEARWEEK('1998-01-01');
+------------------------+
| YEARWEEK('1998-01-01') |
+------------------------+
|                 199752 |
+------------------------+
```

Use the WEEK() function to return the week in a given year.

## String Functions

String functions mostly take string arguments and return string results. Unlike most programming languages, the first character of the string is position 1, not 0.

### ASCII

```
ASCII(string)
```

Returns the ASCII value of the first (leftmost) character of the string, 0 if the string is empty, and NULL if the string is null.

For example:

```
mysql> SELECT ASCII('a');
+-----------+
| ASCII('a') |
+-----------+
|        97 |
+-----------+
mysql> SELECT ASCII('aa');
+------------+
| ASCII('az') |
+------------+
|         97 |
+------------+
```

Use ORD() to return the ASCII value if the character is a multibyte character.

## BIN

```
BIN(number)
```

Returns the binary value (a string representation) of the specified BIGINT number, 0 if the number cannot be converted (the function will convert as far as it can from the left), and NULL if it's null.

For example:

```
mysql> SELECT BIN(15);
+---------+
| BIN(15) |
+---------+
| 1111    |
+---------+
mysql> SELECT BIN('8');
+----------+
| BIN('8') |
+----------+
| 1000     |
+----------+
mysql> SELECT BIN('2w');
+-----------+
| BIN('2w') |
+-----------+
| 10        |
+-----------+
mysql> SELECT BIN('w2');
+-----------+
| BIN('w2') |
+-----------+
| 0         |
+-----------+
```

This function is equivalent to `CONV(number,10,2)`.

## BIT_LENGTH

`BIT_LENGTH(string)`

Returns the string length in bits.
For example:

```
mysql> SELECT BIT_LENGTH('MySQL');
+---------------------+
| BIT_LENGTH('MySQL') |
+---------------------+
| 40                  |
+---------------------+
```

## CHAR

`CHAR(number1[, number2[, ...]])`

This function returns the characters that would result if each number were an integer converted from ASCII code, skipping null values. Decimals are rounded to the nearest integer value.
For example:

```
mysql> SELECT CHAR(97,101,105,111,117);
+--------------------------+
| CHAR(97,101,105,111,117) |
+--------------------------+
| aeiou                    |
+--------------------------+
mysql> SELECT CHAR(97.6,101,105,111,117);
+---------------------------+
| CHAR(0.97,101,105,111,117) |
+---------------------------+
| beiou                     |
+---------------------------+
```

## CHAR_LENGTH

Synonym for the `LENGTH()` function, except that multibyte characters are only counted once.

## CHARACTER_LENGTH

Synonym for the `LENGTH()` function, except that multibyte characters are only counted once.

## CONCAT

`CONCAT(string1[,string2[,...]])`

Concatenates the string arguments and returns the resulting string or `NULL` if any argument is null. Arguments that are not strings are converted to strings.

For example:

```
mysql> SELECT CONCAT('a','b');
+-----------------+
| CONCAT('a','b') |
+-----------------+
| ab              |
+-----------------+
mysql> SELECT CONCAT('a',12);
+----------------+
| CONCAT('a',12) |
+----------------+
| a12            |
+----------------+
mysql> SELECT CONCAT(.3,'NULL');
+-------------------+
| CONCAT(.3,'NULL') |
+-------------------+
| 0.3NULL           |
+-------------------+
mysql> SELECT CONCAT(.3,NULL);
+-----------------+
| CONCAT(.3,NULL) |
+-----------------+
| NULL            |
+-----------------+
```

## *CONCAT_WS*

```
CONCAT_WS(separator, string1[, string2[, ...]]])
```

Similar to CONCAT, except that the first argument is a separator placed between each of the concatenated strings. Will skip any null strings (except the separator, in which case the result will be NULL). The separator does not have to be a string.

For example:

```
mysql> SELECT CONCAT_WS('-','a','b');
+------------------------+
| CONCAT_WS('-','a','b') |
+------------------------+
| a-b                    |
+------------------------+
mysql> SELECT CONCAT_WS(1,.3,.4);
+--------------------+
| CONCAT_WS(1,.3,.4) |
+--------------------+
| 0.310.4            |
+--------------------+
```

```
mysql> SELECT CONCAT_WS(NULL,'a','b');
+-------------------------+
| CONCAT_WS(NULL,'a','b') |
+-------------------------+
| NULL                    |
+-------------------------+
mysql> SELECT CONCAT_WS('-','a',NULL,'c');
+-----------------------------+
| CONCAT_WS('-','a',NULL,'c') |
+-----------------------------+
| a-c                         |
+-----------------------------+
```

## CONV

```
CONV(number,from_base,to_base)
```

Converts a number from one base to another. Returns the converted number represented as string, 0 if the conversion cannot be made (the function will convert as far as it can from the left), and NULL if the number is null. The number is assumed to be an integer, but it can be passed as a string. It is assumed to be unsigned unless the to base is a negative number. The bases can be anything between 2 and 36 (with to_base possibly being negative).

For example:

```
mysql> SELECT CONV(10,2,10);
+---------------+
| CONV(10,2,10) |
+---------------+
| 2             |
+---------------+
mysql> SELECT CONV('a',16,2);
+----------------+
| CONV('a',16,2) |
+----------------+
| 1010           |
+----------------+
mysql> SELECT CONV('3f',16,10);
+------------------+
| CONV('3f',16,10) |
+------------------+
| 63               |
+------------------+

mysql> SELECT CONV('z3',16,10);
+------------------+
| CONV('z3',16,10) |
+------------------+
| 0                |
+------------------+
1 row in set (0.00 sec)
```

```
mysql> SELECT CONV('3z',16,10);
+------------------+
| CONV('3z',16,10) |
+------------------+
| 3                |
+------------------+
```

## ELT

```
ELT(number, string1 [,string2, ...])
```

Uses number as an index to decide which string to return; 1 returns the first string, 2 the second, and so on. Returns NULL if there is no matching string.

For example:

```
mysql> SELECT ELT(2,'one','two');
+--------------------+
| ELT(2,'one','two') |
+--------------------+
| two                |
+--------------------+
mysql> SELECT ELT(0,'one','two');
+--------------------+
| ELT(0,'one','two') |
+--------------------+
| NULL               |
+--------------------+
```

The FIELD() function is the complement of ELT().

## EXPORT_SET

```
EXPORT_SET(number,on,off[,separator[,number_of_bits]])
```

Examines the number in binary, and for each bit that is set, returns on, and for each that doesn't, returns off. The default separator is a comma, but you can specify something else. Sixty-four bits is used, but you can change the number_of_bits.

For example:

```
mysql> SELECT EXPORT_SET(2,1,0,' ',4);
+-------------------------+
| EXPORT_SET(2,1,0,' ',4) |
+-------------------------+
| 0 1 0 0                 |
+-------------------------+
mysql> SELECT EXPORT_SET(7,'ok','never',' : ',6);
+------------------------------------+
| EXPORT_SET(7,'ok','never',' : ',6) |
+------------------------------------+
| ok : ok : ok : never : never : never |
+------------------------------------+
```

## FIELD

```
FIELD(string, string1 [, string2 , ...])
```

Returns the index of `string` in the list following. If `string1` matches, the index will be 1. If it's `string2` then it will be 2, and so on. It will return 0 if the string is not found.

For example:

```
mysql> SELECT FIELD('b','a','b','c');
+-----------------------+
| FIELD('b','a','b','c') |
+-----------------------+
|                     2 |
+-----------------------+
mysql> SELECT FIELD('a','aa','b','c');
+------------------------+
| FIELD('a','aa','b','c') |
+------------------------+
|                      0 |
+------------------------+
```

## FIND_IN_SET

```
FIND_IN_SET(string,stringlist)
```

Similar to `FIELD()` in that it returns an index matching the string, but this function searches either a string separated by commas or the type `SET`. It will return 1 if the string matches the first substring before the comma (or the element of the set), 2 if the second substring matches, and so on. It returns 0 if there is no match. Note that it matches whole comma-separated substrings, not just any portions of the string.

For example:

```
mysql> SELECT FIND_IN_SET('b','a,b,c');
+-------------------------+
| FIND_IN_SET('b','a,b,c') |
+-------------------------+
|                       2 |
+-------------------------+
mysql> SELECT FIND_IN_SET('a','aa,bb,cc');
+----------------------------+
| FIND_IN_SET('a','aa,bb,cc') |
+----------------------------+
|                          0 |
+----------------------------+
1 row in set (0.00 sec)
```

## HEX

```
HEX(string or number)
```

Returns the hexadecimal value (a string representation) of the specified BIGINT number, 0 if the number cannot be converted (the function will convert as far as it can from the left), or NULL if it's null.

If the argument is a number, this is converted to hexadecimal (equivalent to the CONV(number,10,16) function). If it's a string, each character in the string is converted to its numerical equivalent in the ASCII table (for example, a = 97, b = 98, and so on), and each of those numbers is in turn converted to its hexadecimal equivalent.

For example:

```
mysql> SELECT HEX(13);
+---------+
| HEX(13) |
+---------+
| D       |
+---------+
```

```
mysql> SELECT ORD('a');
+----------+
| ORD('a') |
+----------+
|       97 |
+----------+
1 row in set (0.00 sec)
```

```
mysql> SELECT ORD('b');
+----------+
| ORD('b') |
+----------+
|       98 |
+----------+
1 row in set (0.00 sec)
```

```
mysql> SELECT HEX(97);
+---------+
| HEX(97) |
+---------+
| 61      |
+---------+
1 row in set (0.00 sec)
```

```
mysql> SELECT HEX(98);
+---------+
| HEX(98) |
+---------+
| 62      |
+---------+
1 row in set (0.00 sec)
```

```
mysql> SELECT HEX('ab');
+-----------+
| HEX('ab') |
+-----------+
| 6162      |
+-----------+
1 row in set (0.00 sec)
```

## INSERT

```
INSERT(string,position,length,newstring)
```

Replaces the portion of the string starting at `position` and continuing for `length` characters with `newstring`. The length of `newstring` and the length specified can differ, in which case the original string will change in length.

The function is multibyte safe.

For example:

```
mysql> SELECT INSERT('MySQL',1,0,'What is ');
+--------------------------------+
| INSERT('MySQL',1,0,'What is ') |
+--------------------------------+
| What is MySQL                  |
+--------------------------------+
mysql> SELECT INSERT('MySQL',1,1,'P');
+-------------------------+
| INSERT('MySQL',1,1,'P') |
+-------------------------+
| PySQL                   |
+-------------------------+
mysql> SELECT INSERT('MySQL',1,1,'Py');
+--------------------------+
| INSERT('MySQL',1,1,'Py') |
+--------------------------+
| PyySQL                   |
+--------------------------+
```

## INSTR

```
INSTR(string,substring)
```

Searches the `string` case insensitively (unless either string is binary) for the first occurrence of `substring` and returns the position or returns 0 if `substring` was not found. The first letter is at position 1.

For example:

```
mysql> SELECT INSTR('MySQL','My');
```

```
+-------------------+
| INSTR('MySQL','My') |
+-------------------+
|                 1 |
+-------------------+
mysql> SELECT INSTR('Cecilia','i');
+---------------------+
| INSTR('Cecilia','i') |
+---------------------+
|                   4 |
+---------------------+
```

## LCASE

```
LCASE(string)
```

Synonym for LOWER().

## LEFT

```
LEFT(string,length)
```

Returns the leftmost length characters from the string. This function is multibyte safe. For example:

```
mysql> SELECT LEFT('abc',2);
+--------------+
| LEFT('abc',2) |
+--------------+
| ab           |
+--------------+
```

## LENGTH

```
LENGTH(string)
```

Returns the length in characters of the string. Converts the argument to a string if it can. For example:

```
mysql> SELECT LENGTH('MySQL');
+-----------------+
| LENGTH('MySQL') |
+-----------------+
|               5 |
+-----------------+
mysql> SELECT LENGTH(99);
+------------+
| LENGTH(99) |
+------------+
|          2 |
+------------+
```

CHAR_LENGTH(), CHARACTER_LENGTH(), and OCTET_LENGTH() are synonyms, except that multibyte characters are only counted once with CHAR_LENGTH() and CHARACTER_LENGTH().

## LOAD_FILE

```
LOAD_FILE(file_name)
```

Reads the file and returns the file contents as a string. The file must be on the server, you must specify the full pathname to the file, and you must have the FILE privilege. The file must be readable by all and be smaller than max_allowed_packet. If the file doesn't exist or can't be read because of one of the previous reasons, the function returns NULL.

For example, if the file /home/iang/test.txt contained the text 123456, you'd return the following with LOAD_FILE():

```
mysql> SELECT LOAD_FILE('/home/iang/test.txt');
+---------------------------------+
| LOAD_FILE('/home/iang/test.txt') |
+---------------------------------+
| 123456                          |
+---------------------------------+
```

LOAD_FILE is often used with uploading BLOBs into the database.
For example:

```
mysql> INSERT INTO table_with_blob(id,image)
  VALUES(1,LOAD_FILE('/images/pic.jpg'));
```

## LOCATE

```
LOCATE(substring, string [,position])
```

Searches the string case insensitively (unless either string is binary) for the first occurrence of substring and returns the position or returns 0 if substring was not found. If the optional position argument it supplied, the search starts at that point. The first letter is at position 1.

For example:

```
mysql> SELECT LOCATE('My','MySQL');
+----------------------+
| LOCATE('My','MySQL') |
+----------------------+
|                    1 |
+----------------------+
mysql> SELECT LOCATE('C','Cecilia',2);
+-------------------------+
| LOCATE('C','Cecilia',2) |
+-------------------------+
|                       3 |
+-------------------------+
```

This is the same as the INSTR() function but with the arguments reversed.

### *LOWER*

```
LOWER(string)
```

Returns a string with all characters converted to lowercase (according to the current character set mapping). The function is multibyte safe.

For example:

```
mysql> SELECT LOWER('AbC');
+--------------+
| LOWER('AbC') |
+--------------+
| abc          |
+--------------+
```

The LCASE() function is a synonym.

### *LPAD*

```
LPAD(string,length,padding_string)
```

Left-pads the string with the `padding_string` until the result is `length` characters long. If the string is longer than the length, it will be shortened to `length` characters.

For example:

```
mysql> SELECT LPAD('short',7,'-');
+---------------------+
| LPAD('short',7,'-') |
+---------------------+
| --short             |
+---------------------+
mysql> SELECT LPAD('too_long',7,' ');
+------------------------+
| LPAD('too_long',7,' ') |
+------------------------+
| too_lon                |
+------------------------+
mysql> SELECT LPAD('a',4,'12');
+------------------+
| LPAD('a',4,'12') |
+------------------+
| 121a             |
+------------------+
```

### *LTRIM*

```
LTRIM(string)
```

Removes leading spaces from the string and returns the result.

For example:

```
mysql> SELECT LTRIM('    Yes');
+----------------+
| LTRIM('    Yes') |
+----------------+
| Yes            |
+----------------+
```

## MAKE_SET

```
MAKE_SET(number, string1 [, string2, ...])
```

Returns a set (string where the elements are comma separated) with the strings that match the number converted to binary. The first string appears if bit 0 is set, the second string if bit1 is set, and so on. If the bit argument is set to 3, then the first two strings are returned because 3 is 11 in binary.

For example:

```
mysql> SELECT MAKE_SET(3,'a','b','c');
+------------------------+
| MAKE_SET(3,'a','b','c') |
+------------------------+
| a,b                    |
+------------------------+
mysql> SELECT MAKE_SET(5,'a','b','c');
+------------------------+
| MAKE_SET(5,'a','b','c') |
+------------------------+
| a,c                    |
+------------------------+
```

## OCT

```
OCT(number)
```

Returns the octal value (a string representation) of the specified BIGINT number, 0 if the number cannot be converted (the function will convert as far as it can from the left), or NULL if it's null.

For example:

```
mysql> SELECT OCT(09);
+---------+
| OCT(09) |
+---------+
| 11      |
+---------+
mysql> SELECT OCT('a1');
+-----------+
| OCT('a1') |
+-----------+
| 0         |
+-----------+
```

```
mysql> SELECT OCT('13b');
+-----------+
| OCT('13b') |
+-----------+
| 15        |
+-----------+
```

This function is equivalent to `CONV(number,10,8)`.

## OCTET_LENGTH

Synonym for the `LENGTH()` function.

## ORD

```
ORD(string)
```

Returns the ASCII value of the first (leftmost) character of the string, 0 if the string is empty, and `NULL` if the string is null. This is the same as the ASCII function, unless the character is a multibyte character, in which case the value is calculated as a base 256 number—that is, each byte being worth 256 times more than the next byte. For example, the formula for a two-byte character would be as follows: (byte_1_ASCII code * 256) + (byte_2_ASCII_code).

For example:

```
mysql> SELECT ORD("a");
+----------+
| ORD("a") |
+----------+
|       97 |
+----------+
mysql> SELECT ORD("az");
+-----------+
| ORD("az") |
+-----------+
|        97 |
+-----------+
```

You can use the `BIN()`, `OCT()`, and `HEX()` functions to convert decimal numbers to binary, octal, and hexadecimal, respectively.

## POSITION

```
POSITION(substring IN string)
```

Searches case insensitively (unless either argument is a binary string) for the first occurrence of `substring` in `string` and returns the position (starting at 1) or returns 0 if `substring` was not found. The function is multibyte safe.

For example:

```
mysql> SELECT POSITION('i' IN 'Cecilia');
```

```
+----------------------------+
| POSITION('i' IN 'Cecilia') |
+----------------------------+
|                          4 |
+----------------------------+
```

## QUOTE

```
QUOTE(string)
```

Escapes the single quote (`'`), double quote (`"`) ASCII NULL, and Ctrl+Z characters, and surrounds the string with single quotes so it can be safely used in an SQL statement. Single quotes are not added if the argument is NULL.

For example:

```
mysql> SELECT QUOTE("What's Up?");
+--------------------+
| QUOTE("What's Up?") |
+--------------------+
| 'What\'s Up?'      |
+--------------------+
```

## REPEAT

```
REPEAT(string,count)
```

Repeats the string argument count times and returns the result, returns an empty string if count is not positive, or returns NULL if either argument in null.

For example:

```
mysql> SELECT REPEAT('a',4);
+---------------+
| REPEAT('a',4) |
+---------------+
| aaaa          |
+---------------+
mysql> SELECT REPEAT('a',-1);
+----------------+
| REPEAT('a',-1) |
+----------------+
|                |
+----------------+
mysql> SELECT REPEAT('a',NULL);
+------------------+
| REPEAT('a',NULL) |
+------------------+
| NULL             |
+------------------+
```

## *REPLACE*

```
REPLACE(string,from_string,to_string)
```

Replaces all occurrences of from_str found in the string with to_str and returns the result. The function is multibyte safe.

For example:

```
mysql> SELECT REPLACE('ftp://test.host.co.za','ftp','http');
+----------------------------------------------+
| REPLACE('ftp://test.host.co.za','ftp','http') |
+----------------------------------------------+
| http://test.host.co.za                       |
+----------------------------------------------+
```

## *REVERSE*

```
REVERSE(string)
```

Reverses the order of the characters in string and returns the result. This function is multibyte safe. For example:

```
mysql> SELECT REVERSE('abc');
+---------------+
| REVERSE('abc') |
+---------------+
| cba           |
+---------------+
```

## *RIGHT*

```
RIGHT(string,length)
```

Returns the rightmost length characters from the string. This function is multibyte safe. For example:

```
mysql> SELECT RIGHT('abc',2);
+---------------+
| RIGHT('abc',2) |
+---------------+
| bc            |
+---------------+
```

## *RPAD*

```
RPAD(string,length,padding_string)
```

Right-pads the string with the padding_string until the result is length characters long. If the string is longer than the length, it will be shortened to length characters.

For example:

```
mysql> SELECT RPAD('short',7,'-');
+--------------------+
| RPAD('short',7,'-') |
+--------------------+
| short--            |
+--------------------+
mysql> SELECT RPAD('too_long',7,' ');
+-----------------------+
| RPAD('too_long',7,' ') |
+-----------------------+
| too_lon               |
+-----------------------+
mysql> SELECT RPAD('a',4,'12');
+-----------------+
| RPAD('a',4,'12') |
+-----------------+
| a121            |
+-----------------+
```

## *RTRIM*

```
RTRIM(string)
```

Removes trailing spaces from the string and returns the result.
For example:

```
mysql> SELECT CONCAT('a',RTRIM('b          '),'c');
+-----------------------------------+
| CONCAT('a',RTRIM('b          '),'c') |
+-----------------------------------+
| abc                               |
+-----------------------------------+
```

## *SOUNDEX*

```
SOUNDEX(string)
```

Returns a soundex string, which is a phonetic string designed as a more convenient way of indexing to overcome misspellings. Strings that sound the same will have the same soundex strings. This is usually four characters long, but this function returns a string of arbitrary length. Use the SUBSTRING() function on top of SOUNDEX() to return a standard soundex string. Nonalphanumeric characters are ignored, and non-English international alphabetical characters are treated as vowels.
For example:

```
mysql> SELECT SOUNDEX('MySQL');
```

```
+-----------------+
| SOUNDEX('MySQL') |
+-----------------+
| M240            |
+-----------------+
mysql> SELECT SOUNDEX('MySequl');
+-------------------+
| SOUNDEX('MySequl') |
+-------------------+
| M240              |
+-------------------+
```

## SPACE

```
SPACE(number)
```

Returns a string consisting of number spaces.
For example:

```
mysql> SELECT "A",SPACE(10),"B";
+---+-----------+---+
| A | SPACE(10) | B |
+---+-----------+---+
| A |           | B |
+---+-----------+---+
```

## SUBSTRING

```
SUBSTRING(string, position [,length])
SUBSTRING(string FROM position [FOR length])
```

Returns a substring of the string argument starting at the position (which starts at 1) and optionally with the specified length.
For example:

```
mysql> SELECT SUBSTRING('MySQL',2);
+--------------------+
| SUBSTRING('MySQL',2) |
+--------------------+
| ySQL               |
+--------------------+
mysql> SELECT SUBSTRING('MySQL' FROM 3);
+-------------------------+
| SUBSTRING('MySQL' FROM 3) |
+-------------------------+
| SQL                     |
+-------------------------+
1 row in set (0.16 sec)
```

```
mysql> SELECT SUBSTRING('MySQL',1,2);
+------------------------+
| SUBSTRING('MySQL',1,2) |
+------------------------+
| My                     |
+------------------------+
1 row in set (0.22 sec)
```

The function is multibyte safe. The function `MID(string,position,length)` is a synonym for `SUBSTRING(string,position,length)`.

## SUBSTRING_INDEX

`SUBSTRING_INDEX(string,delimiter,count)`

Returns the substring from the string up until count (if count is positive) or beyond count (if count is negative) occurrences of delimiter.

The function is multibyte safe.

For example:

```
mysql> SELECT SUBSTRING_INDEX('a||b||c||d','||',3);
+--------------------------------------+
| SUBSTRING_INDEX('a||b||c||d','||',3) |
+--------------------------------------+
| a||b||c                              |
+--------------------------------------+
mysql> SELECT SUBSTRING_INDEX('I am what I am','a',2);
+-----------------------------------------+
| SUBSTRING_INDEX('I am what I am','a',2) |
+-----------------------------------------+
| I am wh                                 |
+-----------------------------------------+
mysql> SELECT SUBSTRING_INDEX('I am what I am','a',-2);
+------------------------------------------+
| SUBSTRING_INDEX('I am what I am','a',-2) |
+------------------------------------------+
| t I am                                   |
+------------------------------------------+
```

## TRIM

`TRIM([[BOTH | LEADING | TRAILING] [trim_string] FROM] string)`

If none of the optional parameters are specified, `TRIM()` removes leading and trailing spaces. You specify `LEADING` or `TRAILING` to only remove the one kind or specify the default `BOTH`. You can also remove something besides spaces by specifying `trim_string`. The function is multibyte safe.

For example:

```
mysql> SELECT TRIM('   What a waste of space           ') AS t;
+----------------------+
| t                    |
+----------------------+
| What a waste of space |
+----------------------+
mysql> SELECT TRIM(LEADING '0' FROM '0001');
+----------------------------+
| TRIM(LEADING '0' FROM '0001') |
+----------------------------+
| 1                          |
+----------------------------+
mysql> SELECT TRIM(LEADING FROM '           1');
+------------------------------+
| TRIM(LEADING FROM '         1') |
+------------------------------+
| 1                            |
+------------------------------+
mysql> SELECT TRIM(BOTH 'abc' FROM 'abcabcaabbccabcabc');
+-------------------------------------------+
| TRIM(BOTH 'abc' FROM 'abcabcaabbccabcabc') |
+-------------------------------------------+
| aabbcc                                    |
+-------------------------------------------+
```

## UCASE

```
UCASE(string)
```

Synonym for UPPER().

## UPPER

```
UPPER(string)
```

Returns a string with all characters converted to uppercase (according to the current character set mapping). The function is multibyte safe.

For example:

```
mysql> SELECT UPPER('aBc');
+--------------+
| UPPER('aBc') |
+--------------+
| ABC          |
+--------------+
```

The UCASE() function is a synonym.

## Numeric Functions

Numeric functions deal with numbers, mostly taking numeric arguments and returning numeric results. In the case of an error, they will return NULL. You need to take care not to go beyond the numeric range of a number—most MySQL functions work with BIGINTs ($2^{63}$ signed, or $2^{64}$ unsigned), and if you go beyond the range, MySQL will usually return NULL.

### ABS

```
ABS(number)
```

Returns the absolute value (positive value) of a number. The function is safe for use with BIGINT values.

For example:

```
mysql> SELECT ABS(24-26);
+------------+
| ABS(24-26) |
+------------+
|          2 |
+------------+
```

### ACOS

```
ACOS(number)
```

Returns the arc cosine of number (the inverse cosine). The number must be between −1 and 1 or the function returns NULL.

For example:

```
mysql> SELECT ACOS(0.9);
+-----------+
| ACOS(0.9) |
+-----------+
|  0.451027 |
+-----------+
```

### ASIN

```
ASIN(number)
```

Returns the arc sine of number (the inverse sine). The number must be between −1 and 1 or the function returns NULL.

For example:

```
mysql> SELECT ASIN(-0.4);
+------------+
| ASIN(-0.4) |
+------------+
|  -0.411517 |
+------------+
```

## ATAN

```
ATAN(number1 [, number2])
```

Returns the arc tangent of number (the inverse tangent) or of two numbers (the point number1, number2).

For example:

```
mysql> SELECT ATAN(4);
+----------+
| ATAN(4)  |
+----------+
| 1.325818 |
+----------+
mysql> SELECT ATAN(-4,-3);
+-------------+
| ATAN(-4,-3) |
+-------------+
|   -2.214297 |
+-------------+
```

## ATAN2

```
ATAN2(number1,number2)
```

A synonym for ATAN(number1,number2).

## CEILING

```
CEILING(number)
```

Rounds up the number to the nearest integer and returns it as a BIGINT.

For example:

```
mysql> SELECT CEILING(2.98);
+---------------+
| CEILING(2.98) |
+---------------+
|             3 |
+---------------+
mysql> SELECT CEILING(-2.98);
+----------------+
| CEILING(-2.98) |
+----------------+
|             -2 |
+----------------+
```

Use FLOOR() to round down, and use ROUND() to round up or down.

## COS

```
COS(number_radians)
```

Returns the cosine of `number_radians`.
For example:

```
mysql> SELECT COS(51);
+----------+
| COS(51)  |
+----------+
| 0.742154 |
+----------+
```

## COT

```
COT(number_radians)
```

Returns the cotangent of `number_radians`.
For example:

```
mysql> SELECT COT(0.45);
+------------+
| COT(0.45)  |
+------------+
| 2.07015736 |
+------------+
```

## DEGREES

```
DEGREES(number)
```

Converts the number from radians to degrees and returns the result.
For example:

```
mysql> SELECT DEGREES(2);
+-----------------+
| DEGREES(2)      |
+-----------------+
| 114.59155902616 |
+-----------------+
mysql> SELECT DEGREES(PI()/2);
+-----------------+
| DEGREES(PI()/2) |
+-----------------+
|              90 |
+-----------------+
```

## EXP

```
EXP(number)
```

Returns the number *e* (the base of natural logarithms) raised to the specified power.

For example:

```
mysql> SELECT EXP(1);
+----------+
| EXP(1)   |
+----------+
| 2.718282 |
+----------+
mysql> SELECT EXP(2.3);
+----------+
| EXP(2.3) |
+----------+
| 9.974182 |
+----------+
mysql> SELECT EXP(0.3);
+----------+
| EXP(0.3) |
+----------+
| 1.349859 |
+----------+
```

## FLOOR

```
FLOOR(number)
```

Rounds the number down to the nearest integer and returns it as a BIGINT.
For example:

```
mysql> SELECT FLOOR(2.98);
+-------------+
| FLOOR(2.98) |
+-------------+
|           2 |
+-------------+
mysql> SELECT FLOOR(-2.98);
+--------------+
| FLOOR(-2.98) |
+--------------+
|           -3 |
+--------------+
```

Use CEILING() to round up, and ROUND() to round up or down.

## FORMAT

```
FORMAT(number,decimals)
```

Formats the number to a format with each three digits separated by a comma and rounds the result to the specified number of places.

For example:

```
mysql> SELECT FORMAT(88777634.232,2);
+-----------------------+
| FORMAT(88777634.232,2) |
+-----------------------+
| 88,777,634.23         |
+-----------------------+
```

## GREATEST

```
GREATEST(argument1, argument2 [, ...])
```

Returns the largest of the arguments. The arguments will be compared in different ways depending on the context of the return value or the argument types, which can be integer, real, or strings (which are case sensitive and the default).

For example:

```
mysql> SELECT GREATEST(-3,-4,5);
+------------------+
| GREATEST(-3,-4,5) |
+------------------+
|                5 |
+------------------+
mysql> SELECT GREATEST('Pa','Ma','Ca');
+-------------------------+
| GREATEST('Pa','Ma','Ca') |
+-------------------------+
| Pa                      |
+-------------------------+
```

## LEAST

```
LEAST(argument1, argument2 [, ...])
```

Returns the smallest of the arguments. The arguments will be compared in different ways depending on the context of the return value or the argument types, which can be integer, real, or strings (which are case sensitive and the default).

For example:

```
mysql> SELECT LEAST(-3,-4,5);
+---------------+
| LEAST(-3,-4,5) |
+---------------+
|            -4 |
+---------------+
```

```
mysql> SELECT LEAST('Pa','Ma','Ca');
+----------------------+
| LEAST('Pa','Ma','Ca') |
+----------------------+
| Ca                   |
+----------------------+
```

## LN

```
LN(number)
```

Synonym for the LOG(number) function.

## LOG

```
LOG(number1 [, number2])
```

Returns the natural logarithm of number1 if there's one argument. You can also use an arbitrary base by supplying a second argument, in which case the function returns LOG(number2) / LOG(number1). For example:

```
mysql> SELECT LOG(2);
+----------+
| LOG(2)   |
+----------+
| 0.693147 |
+----------+
mysql> SELECT LOG(2,3);
+----------+
| LOG(2,3) |
+----------+
| 1.584963 |
+----------+
```

## LOG10

```
LOG10(number1)
```

Returns the base 10 logarithm of number1. This is equivalent to LOG(number1)/LOG(10). For example:

```
mysql> SELECT LOG10(100);
+------------+
| LOG10(100) |
+------------+
|   2.000000 |
+------------+
```

### LOG2

```
LOG2(number1)
```

Returns the base 2 logarithm of number1. This is equivalent to LOG(number1)/LOG(2). For example:

```
mysql> SELECT LOG2(4);
+----------+
| LOG2(4)  |
+----------+
| 2.000000 |
+----------+
```

### MOD

```
MOD(number1,number2)
```

Returns the modulus of number1 and number2 (the remainder of number1 divided by number2). This is the same as the % operator. This is safe to use with BIGINTs. For example:

```
mysql> SELECT MOD(15,4);
+-----------+
| MOD(15,4) |
+-----------+
|         3 |
+-----------+
mysql> SELECT MOD(3,-2);
+-----------+
| MOD(3,-2) |
+-----------+
|         1 |
+-----------+
```

### PI

```
PI()
```

Returns the value of pi (or at least a close representation). MySQL uses the full double precision but only returns five characters by default. For example:

```
mysql> SELECT PI();
+----------+
| PI()     |
+----------+
| 3.141593 |
+----------+
```

```
mysql> SELECT PI() + 0.0000000000000000;
+--------------------------+
| PI() + 0.0000000000000000 |
+--------------------------+
|         3.1415926535897931 |
+--------------------------+
```

## POW

POW(number1,number2)

This function is a synonym for POWER(number1,number2).

## POWER

POWER(number1,number2)

Raises number1 to the power of number2 and returns the value.
For example:

```
mysql> SELECT POWER(2,3);
+------------+
| POWER(2,3) |
+------------+
|   8.000000 |
+------------+
```

## RADIANS

RADIANS(number1)

Converts the number from degrees to radians and returns the result.
For example:

```
mysql> SELECT RADIANS(180);
+------------------+
| RADIANS(180)     |
+------------------+
| 3.1415926535898 |
+------------------+
```

## RAND

RAND([number])

Returns a random number (a float) between 0 and 1. The argument is the random number seed. It's common to use the timestamp as a seed. The function can be used to return a result set in random order.

For example:

```
mysql> SELECT RAND();
+------------------+
| RAND()           |
+------------------+
| 0.70100469486881 |
+------------------+
mysql> SELECT RAND(20021010081523);
+----------------------+
| RAND(20021010081523) |
+----------------------+
|     0.80558716673924 |
+----------------------+
mysql> SELECT * FROM t1 ORDER BY RAND() LIMIT 1;
+----+
| f1 |
+----+
| 20 |
+----+
```

## ROUND

```
ROUND(number1 [, number2])
```

Returns the argument **number1**, rounded to the nearest integer. You can supply a second argument to specify the number of decimals to round to (the default is 0, or no decimals). The rounding behavior for numbers exactly in the middle is based upon the underlying C library.

For example:

```
mysql> SELECT ROUND(2.49);
+-------------+
| ROUND(2.49) |
+-------------+
|           2 |
+-------------+
mysql> SELECT ROUND(2.51);
+-------------+
| ROUND(2.51) |
+-------------+
|           3 |
+-------------+
mysql> SELECT ROUND(-2.49,1);
+----------------+
| ROUND(-2.49,1) |
+----------------+
|           -2.5 |
+----------------+
```

## SIGN

```
SIGN(number)
```

Returns –1, 0, or 1 depending on whether the argument is negative, zero or not a number, or positive. For example:

```
mysql> SELECT SIGN(-7);
+----------+
| SIGN(-7) |
+----------+
|       -1 |
+----------+
mysql> SELECT SIGN('a');
+-----------+
| SIGN('a') |
+-----------+
|         0 |
+-----------+
```

## SIN

```
SIN(number_radians)
```

Returns the sine of number_radians.
For example:

```
mysql> SELECT SIN(45);
+----------+
| SIN(45)  |
+----------+
| 0.850904 |
+----------+
```

## SQRT

```
SQRT(number)
```

Returns the square root of the argument.
For example:

```
mysql> SELECT SQRT(81);
+----------+
| SQRT(81) |
+----------+
| 9.000000 |
+----------+
```

## TAN

```
TAN(number_radians)
```

Returns the tangent of `number_radians`.
For example:

```
mysql> SELECT TAN(66);
+----------+
| TAN(66)  |
+----------+
| 0.026561 |
+----------+
```

### *TRUNCATE*

```
TRUNCATE(number,decimals)
```

Truncates (or increases) the number to the specified number of decimal places.
For example:

```
mysql> SELECT TRUNCATE(2.234,2);
+------------------+
| TRUNCATE(2.234,2) |
+------------------+
|             2.23 |
+------------------+
mysql> SELECT TRUNCATE(2.4,5);
+----------------+
| TRUNCATE(2.4,5) |
+----------------+
|        2.40000 |
+----------------+
mysql> SELECT TRUNCATE(2.998,0);
+------------------+
| TRUNCATE(2.998,0) |
+------------------+
|                2 |
+------------------+
mysql> SELECT TRUNCATE(-12.43,1);
+-------------------+
| TRUNCATE(-12.43,1) |
+-------------------+
|             -12.4 |
+-------------------+
```

## Aggregate Functions

Aggregate functions are functions that work on a group of data (meaning they can be used in a GROUP BY clause). If there is no GROUP BY clause, they will assume the entire result set is the group and return only one result. For the following examples, assume a simple table exists, as follows:

```
mysql> SELECT * FROM table1;
+--------+
| field1 |
+--------+
|      4 |
|     12 |
|     12 |
|     20 |
+--------+
4 rows in set (0.00 sec)
```

## AVG

```
AVG(expression)
```

Returns the average value of the expressions in the group. Will return 0 if the expression is not numeric.

For example:

```
mysql> SELECT AVG(field1) FROM table1;
+-------------+
| AVG(field1) |
+-------------+
|     12.0000 |
+-------------+
```

## BIT_AND

```
BIT_AND(expression)
```

Returns the bitwise AND of all bits in the expressions from the group (performed with 64-bit precision).

```
mysql> SELECT BIT_AND(field1) FROM table1;
+-----------------+
| BIT_AND(field1) |
+-----------------+
|               4 |
+-----------------+
```

## BIT_OR

```
BIT_OR(expession)
```

Returns the bitwise OR of all bits in the expressions from the group (performed with 64-bit precision).

For example:

```
mysql> SELECT BIT_OR(field1) FROM table1;
+----------------+
| BIT_OR(field1) |
+----------------+
|             28 |
+----------------+
```

## COUNT

```
COUNT( [DISTINCT] expression1, [expression2])
```

Returns the number of non-null values in the group.

If the expression is a field, returns the number of rows that don't contain null values in this field. COUNT(*) the number of all rows, null or not. The DISTINCT option returns the number of unique non-null values (or a combination, if more than one expression is used).

```
mysql> SELECT COUNT(*) FROM table1;
+----------+
| COUNT(*) |
+----------+
|        4 |
+----------+
```

## MAX

```
MAX(expression)
```

Returns the largest value of the expressions in the group. The expression can be numeric or string. For example:

```
mysql> SELECT MAX(field1) FROM table1;
+-------------+
| MAX(field1) |
+-------------+
|          20 |
+-------------+
```

## MIN

```
MIN(expression)
```

Returns the smallest value of the expressions in the group. The expression can be numeric or string.

For example:

```
mysql> SELECT MIN(field1) FROM table1;
```

```
+------------+
| MIN(field1) |
+------------+
|          4 |
+------------+
```

## STD

```
STD(expression)
```

Returns the standard deviation of the values in the expressions from the group.
For example:

```
mysql> SELECT STD(field1) FROM table1;
+------------+
| STD(field1) |
+------------+
|     5.6569 |
+------------+
```

## STDDEV

```
STDDEV(expression)
```

A synonym for the STD() function.

## SUM

```
SUM(expression)
```

Returns the smallest value of the expressions in the group or NULL if there are no rows. The expression can be numeric or string.
For example:

```
mysql> SELECT SUM(field1) FROM table1;
+------------+
| MIN(field1) |
+------------+
|         48 |
+------------+
```

# Other Functions

The following functions include encryption functions, comparison functions, control flow functions, and other miscellaneous functions.

## AES_DECRYPT

```
AES_DECRYPT(encrypted_string,key_string)
```

Decrypts the result of an AES_ENCRYPT() function.

### AES_ENCRYPT

```
AES_ENCRYPT(string,key_string)
```

Uses the Advanced Encryption Standard algorithm (Rijndael) to encrypt the string based upon the key_string. This uses 128-bit key length by default. AES_DECRYPT() decrypts the result.

### BENCHMARK

```
BENCHMARK(count,expression)
```

Runs the expression count times. Used mainly for testing to see how fast MySQL runs an expression. Always returns 0; the time (on the client) displayed below the function is the useful part of the output.

For example:

```
mysql> SELECT BENCHMARK(10000,SHA('how long'));
+----------------------------------+
| BENCHMARK(10000,SHA('how long')) |
+----------------------------------+
|                                0 |
+----------------------------------+
1 row in set (0.95 sec)
```

### CASE

```
CASE value WHEN [compare_value1] THEN result1 [WHEN [compare_value2]
  THEN result2 ...] [ELSE result3] END
CASE WHEN [condition1] THEN result1 [WHEN [condition2]
  THEN result2 ...] [ELSE result3] END
```

There are two incantations of the CASE statement. The first returns a result depending on the value. It compares the value to the various compare_values and returns the result associated with that value (after the THEN), returns the result after the ELSE if none are found, or returns NULL if there is no result to return.

The second compares the various conditions and returns the associated result when it finds a true condition, returns the result after the ELSE if none are found, or returns NULL if there is no result to return.

For example:

```
mysql> SELECT CASE 'a' WHEN 'a' THEN 'a it is' END;
+--------------------------------------+
| CASE 'a' WHEN 'a' THEN 'a it is' END |
+--------------------------------------+
| a it is                              |
+--------------------------------------+
mysql> SELECT CASE 'b' WHEN 'a' THEN 'a it is' WHEN 'b' THEN 'b it is' END;
+-------------------------------------------------------------+
| CASE 'b' WHEN 'a' THEN 'a it is' WHEN 'b' THEN 'b it is' END |
+-------------------------------------------------------------+
| b it is                                                     |
+-------------------------------------------------------------+
```

```
mysql> SELECT CASE 9 WHEN 1 THEN 'is 1' WHEN 2 THEN 'is 2' ELSE 'not found' END;
+------------------------------------------------------------------+
| CASE 9 WHEN 1 THEN 'is 1' WHEN 2 THEN 'is 2' ELSE 'not found' END |
+------------------------------------------------------------------+
| not found                                                        |
+------------------------------------------------------------------+
mysql> SELECT CASE 9 WHEN 1 THEN 'is 1' WHEN 2 THEN 'is 2' END;
+-------------------------------------------------+
| CASE 9 WHEN 1 THEN 'is 1' WHEN 2 THEN 'is 2'  END |
+-------------------------------------------------+
| NULL                                            |
+-------------------------------------------------+
mysql> SELECT CASE WHEN 1>2 THEN '1>2' WHEN 2=2 THEN 'is 2' END;
+-------------------------------------------------+
| CASE WHEN 1>2 THEN '1>2' WHEN 2=2 THEN 'is 2'  END |
+-------------------------------------------------+
| is 2                                            |
+-------------------------------------------------+
mysql> SELECT CASE WHEN 1>2 THEN '1>2' WHEN 2<2 THEN '2<2' ELSE 'none' END;
+-----------------------------------------------------------+
| CASE WHEN 1>2 THEN '1>2' WHEN 2<2 THEN '2<2' ELSE 'none' END |
+-----------------------------------------------------------+
| none                                                      |
+-----------------------------------------------------------+
mysql> SELECT CASE WHEN BINARY 'a' = 'A' THEN 'bin' WHEN 'a'='A' THEN 'text' END;
+---------------------------------------------------------------------+
| CASE WHEN BINARY 'a' = 'A' THEN 'bin' WHEN 'a'='A' THEN 'text' END |
+---------------------------------------------------------------------+
| text                                                                |
+---------------------------------------------------------------------+
mysql> SELECT CASE WHEN BINARY 1=1 THEN '1' WHEN 2=2 THEN '2' END;
+---------------------------------------------------+
| CASE WHEN BINARY 1=1 THEN '1' WHEN 2=2 THEN '2' END |
+---------------------------------------------------+
| 1                                                 |
+---------------------------------------------------+
```

The type of the return value (INTEGER, DOUBLE, or STRING) is the same as the type of the first returned value (the expression after the first THEN).

## CAST

```
CAST(expression AS type)
```

Converts the expression to the specified type and returns the result. The types can be one of the following: BINARY, DATE, DATETIME, SIGNED, SIGNED INTEGER, TIME, UNSIGNED, and UNSIGNED INTEGER.

MySQL usually automatically converts types. For example, if you add two number strings, the result will be a numeric. Or if any part of a calculation is unsigned, the entire result will be unsigned. You can use CAST() to change this behavior.

For example:

```
mysql> SELECT "4" + "3";
+-----------+
| "4" + "3" |
+-----------+
|         7 |
+-----------+
mysql> SELECT CAST(("4"+"3") AS TIME);
+-------------------------+
| CAST(("4"+"3") AS TIME) |
+-------------------------+
| 7                       |
+-------------------------+
mysql> SELECT CAST(50-60 AS UNSIGNED INTEGER);
+---------------------------------+
| CAST(50-60 AS UNSIGNED INTEGER) |
+---------------------------------+
|            18446744073709551606 |
+---------------------------------+
mysql> SELECT CAST(50-60 AS SIGNED INTEGER);
+-------------------------------+
| CAST(50-60 AS SIGNED INTEGER) |
+-------------------------------+
|                           -10 |
+-------------------------------+
```

Use CONVERT() for a synonym that uses ODBC syntax.

## CONNECTION_ID

```
CONNECTION_ID()
```

Returns the unique thread_id of the connection.
For example:

```
mysql> SELECT CONNECTION_ID();
+-----------------+
| CONNECTION_ID() |
+-----------------+
|               7 |
+-----------------+
```

## CONVERT

```
CONVERT(expression,type)
```

This is a synonym for CAST(expression AS type), which is the ANSI SQL99 syntax.

## *DATABASE*

DATABASE()

Returns the name of the current database or returns an empty string if there is none. For example:

```
mysql> SELECT DATABASE();
+------------+
| DATABASE() |
+------------+
| test       |
+------------+
```

## *DECODE*

DECODE(encoded_string,password_string)

Decodes the encoded string using the password string and returns the result. The decoded string is usually generated by the ENCODE() function first.

For example:

```
mysql> SELECT DECODE('g','1');
+-----------------+
| DECODE('g','1') |
+-----------------+
| a               |
+-----------------+
mysql> SELECT DECODE('wer','1sz');
+---------------------+
| DECODE('wer','1sz') |
+---------------------+
| i8                  |
+---------------------+
```

## *DES_DECRYPT*

DES_DECRYPT(encrypted_string [, key_string])

Decrypts a string encrypted with DES_ENCRYPT().

## *DES_ENCRYPT*

DES_ENCRYPT(string [, (key_number | key_string) ] )

Uses the Data Encryption Standard (DES) algorithm to encrypt the string and returns a binary string. If the optional key argument is omitted, the first key from the des-key file is used. If the key argument is a number (from 0–9), the corresponding key from the des-key file is used. If the key argument is a string, that will be the key.

If the key values change in the des-key file, MySQL can read the new values when you run a FLUSH_DES_KEY_FILE statement, which requires the reload permission.

This function only works if MySQL has Secure Sockets Layer (SSL) support.

### ENCODE

```
ENCODE(string,password_string)
```

Returns an encoded binary string. You can use DECODE(), with the same password_string, to return the original string. The encoded and decoded strings will be the same length.

For example:

```
mysql> SELECT ENCODE('a','1');
+-----------------+
| ENCODE('a','1') |
+-----------------+
| g               |
+-----------------+
mysql> SELECT ENCODE('ah','2');
+------------------+
| ENCODE('ah','2') |
+------------------+
| Uÿ               |
+------------------+
```

### ENCRYPT

```
ENCRYPT(string [, salt])
```

Encrypts a string using the Unix crypt() system call and returns the result. The optional salt argument is a string used in the encryption. Its specific behavior depends on the underlying system call.

For example:

```
mysql> SELECT ENCRYPT('keepmeout');
+----------------------+
| ENCRYPT('keepmeout') |
+----------------------+
| V9tOly.dRY55k        |
+----------------------+
mysql> SELECT ENCRYPT('keepmeout','ab');
+---------------------------+
| ENCRYPT('keepmeout','ab') |
+---------------------------+
| abpr3o3DrHzJo             |
+---------------------------+
```

### FOUND_ROWS

```
FOUND_ROWS()
```

Returns the number of rows that satisfy the previous SELECT SQL_CALC_FOUND_ROWS query (or that would have been returned if it wasn't limited with a LIMIT clause).

For example:

```
mysql> SELECT SQL_CALC_FOUND_ROWS user FROM user LIMIT 1;
+------+
| user |
+------+
|      |
+------+
1 row in set (0.00 sec)

mysql> SELECT FOUND_ROWS();
+--------------+
| FOUND_ROWS() |
+--------------+
|            4 |
+--------------+
```

## GET_LOCK

```
GET_LOCK(string,timeout)
```

Attempts to obtain a lock called string, for up to timeout seconds. It will return 1 if successful, 0 if it times out, or NULL if there was some other error. The lock is released with RELEASE_LOCK(), a new GET_LOCK(), or if the thread ends. You can use IS_FREE_LOCK() to check if a lock is free.

This is used mainly as an extra locking mechanism for applications.

For example:

```
mysql> SELECT GET_LOCK('one',1);
+-------------------+
| GET_LOCK('one',1) |
+-------------------+
|                 1 |
+-------------------+
```

## IF

```
IF(expression1,expression2,expression3)
```

Returns expression2 if expression1 is true; otherwise returns expression3. This can return a numeric or string depending on the context. expression1 is evaluated as an integer, so real comparisons may not produce the results you expect.

For example:

```
mysql> SELECT IF('a'='a',1,2);
```

```
+----------------+
| IF('a'='a',1,2) |
+----------------+
|              1 |
+----------------+
mysql> SELECT IF(9<4,1,2);
+-------------+
| IF(9<4,1,2) |
+-------------+
|           2 |
+-------------+
mysql> SELECT IF(NULL,'a','b');
+------------------+
| IF(NULL,'a','b') |
+------------------+
| b                |
+------------------+
mysql> SELECT IF(16-6-10,'a',NULL);
+---------------------+
| IF(16-6-10,'a',NULL) |
+---------------------+
| NULL                |
+---------------------+
```

The next example returns `false` because the real number 0.49 is evaluated as the integer 0:

```
mysql> SELECT IF(0.49,'true','false');
+------------------------+
| IF(0.49,'true','false') |
+------------------------+
| false                  |
+------------------------+
```

## *IFNULL*

```
IFNULL(expression1,expression2)
```

Returns `expression1` if it's not null; otherwise it returns `expression2`. The result can be numeric or string depending on the context.

For example:

```
mysql> SELECT IFNULL(1,2);
+-------------+
| IFNULL(1,2) |
+-------------+
|           1 |
+-------------+
```

```
mysql> SELECT IFNULL(NULL,'nothing here');
+----------------------------+
| IFNULL(NULL,'nothing here') |
+----------------------------+
| nothing here               |
+----------------------------+
mysql> SELECT IFNULL(RELEASE_LOCK('nonexistant'),'The lock never existed');
+-------------------------------------------------------------+
| IFNULL(RELEASE_LOCK('nonexistant'),'The lock never existed') |
+-------------------------------------------------------------+
|                                        The lock never existed |
+-------------------------------------------------------------+
```

## INET_ATON

```
INET_ATON(dotted_quad_string)
```

Returns an integer 4- or 8-byte network address from the dotted quad string.
For example:

```
mysql> SELECT INET_ATON('196.26.90.168');
+--------------------------+
| INET_ATON('196.26.90.168') |
+--------------------------+
|               3290061480 |
+--------------------------+
```

## INET_NTOA

```
INET_NTOA(network_address)
```

Returns a dotted quad address from a 4- or 8-byte network address and returns a dotted quad
string representing the dotted quad address.
For example:

```
mysql> SELECT INET_NTOA(3290061480);
+----------------------+
| INET_NTOA(3290061480) |
+----------------------+
| 196.26.90.168        |
+----------------------+
```

## IS_FREE_LOCK

```
IS_FREE_LOCK(string)
```

Used to check whether a lock named string, created with GET_LOCK(), is free.
Returns 1 if the lock is free, 0 if the lock is held, or NULL on other errors.

For example:

```
mysql> SELECT GET_LOCK('one',1);
+-------------------+
| GET_LOCK('one',1) |
+-------------------+
|                 1 |
+-------------------+
mysql> SELECT IS_FREE_LOCK('one');
+---------------------+
| IS_FREE_LOCK('one') |
+---------------------+
|                   0 |
+---------------------+
mysql> SELECT GET_LOCK('two',1);
+-------------------+
| GET_LOCK('two',1) |
+-------------------+
|                 1 |
+-------------------+
mysql> SELECT IS_FREE_LOCK('one');
+---------------------+
| IS_FREE_LOCK('one') |
+---------------------+
|                   1 |
+---------------------+
```

## LAST_INSERT_ID

```
LAST_INSERT_ID([expression])
```

Returns the last value inserted into an AUTO_INCREMENT field from this connection, or 0 if there have been none.

For example:

```
mysql> SELECT LAST_INSERT_ID();
+------------------+
| last_insert_id() |
+------------------+
|                0 |
+------------------+
```

## MASTER_POS_WAIT

```
MASTER_POS_WAIT(log_name, log_position)
```

Used for replication synching. Run on the slave, this will wait until the slave has done all updates until the specified position in the master log file before continuing.

For example:

```
mysql> SELECT MASTER_POS_WAIT('g-bin.001',273);
+-------------------------------------------+
| MASTER_POS_WAIT('g-bin.001',273)          |
+-------------------------------------------+
|                                      NULL |
+-------------------------------------------+
```

## MD5

```
MD5(string)
```

Uses the Message Digest algorithm to calculate a 128-bit checksum from the string and returns the resulting 32-digit hexadecimal number.

For example:

```
mysql> SELECT MD5('how many more');
+----------------------------------+
| MD5('how many more')             |
+----------------------------------+
| 75dea0eddd9ffb8db451448a9931e764 |
+----------------------------------+
```

Use the SHA() function for a more cryptographically secure alternative.

## NULLIF

```
NULLIF(expression1,expression2)
```

Returns expression1 unless expression1 is equal to expression2, in which case it returns NULL. This will evaluate expression1 twice if it's equal to expression2.

For example:

```
mysql> SELECT NULLIF('a','b');
+-----------------+
| NULLIF('a','b') |
+-----------------+
| a               |
+-----------------+
mysql> SELECT NULLIF(1,'1');
+---------------+
| NULLIF(1,'1') |
+---------------+
|          NULL |
+---------------+
```

## PASSWORD

```
PASSWORD(string)
```

Converts the string into an encrypted password and returns the result. This function is used for encrypting passwords in the user table of the `mysql` database. It it not reversible, and it is encrypted differently than the normal Unix password.

For example:

```
mysql> SELECT PASSWORD('a');
+------------------+
| PASSWORD('a')    |
+------------------+
| 60671c896665c3fa |
+------------------+
mysql> SELECT PASSWORD(PASSWORD('a'));
+-------------------------+
| PASSWORD(PASSWORD('a')) |
+-------------------------+
| 772a81723a030f10        |
+-------------------------+
```

ENCRYPT() converts a string to a password the Unix way.

## RELEASE_LOCK

```
RELEASE_LOCK(string)
```

Releases the lock string earlier obtained with GET_LOCK(). Returns 1 if the lock is released, 0 if it can't release the lock because this connection did not create it, or NULL if the lock does not exist (never created or already released).

For example:

```
mysql> SELECT GET_LOCK('one',1);
+-------------------+
| GET_LOCK('one',1) |
+-------------------+
|                 1 |
+-------------------+
mysql> SELECT RELEASE_LOCK('one');
+---------------------+
| RELEASE_LOCK('one') |
+---------------------+
|                   1 |
+---------------------+
mysql> SELECT RELEASE_LOCK('one');
+---------------------+
| RELEASE_LOCK('one') |
+---------------------+
|                NULL |
+---------------------+
```

## SESSION_USER

```
SESSION_USER()
```

Returns the MySQL user and host that are connected with the current thread.
For example:

```
mysql> SELECT SESSION_USER();
+----------------+
| SESSION_USER() |
+----------------+
| root@localhost |
+----------------+
```

SYSTEM_USER() and USER() are synonyms.

## SHA

```
SHA(string)
```

Uses the Secure Hash algorithm to calculate a 160-bit checksum from the string and returns
the resulting 40-digit hexadecimal number. It's a more secure encryption than that achieved with the
MD5() function.
For example:

```
mysql> SELECT SHA('how many more');
+------------------------------------------+
| SHA('how many more')                     |
+------------------------------------------+
| 38ccbb8146b0673fa91abba3239829af6f3e5a6b |
+------------------------------------------+
```

## SHA1

```
SHA1(string)
```

A synonym for SHA().

## SYSTEM_USER

```
SYSTEM_USER()
```

A synonym for SESSION_USER().

## USER

```
USER()
```

A synonym for SESSION_USER().

## *VERSION*

```
VERSION()
```

Returns the MySQL server version as a string, with -log appended if logging is enabled. For example:

```
mysql> SELECT VERSION();
+----------------+
| VERSION()      |
+----------------+
| 4.0.3-beta-log |
+----------------+
```

# Appendix C

# PHP API

PHP IS ONE OF the most popular languages to use with MySQL, particularly in a web environment. This appendix lists all the PHP functions that work with MySQL—including some not yet in the release version of PHP.

## PHP Configuration Options

The PHP configuration file is called php.ini, and it has a number of options specific to MySQL. These include the following:

**mysql.allow_persistent boolean**   This is On if persistent connections to MySQL are allowed. Defaults to On. There's usually no reason to switch this off.

**mysql.max_persistent integer**   The maximum number of persistent connections for each process. Defaults to −1 (no limit).

**mysql.max_links integer**   The maximum number of MySQL connections of all types for each process. Defaults to −1 (no limit).

**mysql.default_port string**   The default TCP port number on which to connect to MySQL. PHP will use the MYSQL_TCP_PORT environment variable if no default is set. Unix can also use, in order, the mysql-tcp entry in /etc/services or the compile-time MYSQL_PORT constant. Defaults to NULL.

**mysql.default_socket string**   The default Unix socket name to use to connect to MySQL. Defaults to NULL.

**mysql.default_host string**   The default hostname to use to connect to MySQL. Safe-mode will invalidate this option. Defaults to NULL.

**mysql.default_user string**   The default username to use to connect to MySQL. This doesn't apply in Safe mode, which will invalidate this option. Defaults to NULL.

`mysql.default_password string`    The default password to use to connect to MySQL. Doesn't apply in Safe mode, which will invalidate this option. Defaults to `NULL`. Not recommended to store a password here!

`mysql.connect_timeout integer`    The connection timeout in seconds.

# PHP MySQL Functions

The PHP functions are closely related to the C API functions. The functions listed here are the native PHP functions. Also, a number of libraries add a layer of abstraction to interfacing with MySQL in PHP, the most important of which are ADODB, PEAR, Metabase, and the older PHPLib.

## mysql_affected_rows

```
int mysql_affected_rows([resource mysql_connection])
```

Returns the number of rows affected by the last statement that has made a change to the data (`INSERT`, `UPDATE`, `DELETE`, `LOAD DATA`, `REPLACE`), or −1 if the query failed. Remember that `REPLACE INTO` will affect two rows for each affected row in the original table (one `DELETE` and one `INSERT`). If the database connection is not specified, the most recent opened open connection is used.

If you're using transactions, call `mysql_affected_rows()` before calling `COMMIT`.

To return the number of rows returned by a `SELECT` statement, use `mysql_num_rows()`.

For example:

```
// open a persistent connection to the database
$connect = mysql_pconnect($hostname, $username, $password);

// update an unknown number of fields in the database table
mysql_query("UPDATE $table SET field1=2 WHERE field1=3");

// store the number of rows updated
$num_rows_updated =  mysql_affected_rows();
```

## mysql_change_user

```
boolean mysql_change_user(string username, string password
  [, string database [, resource mysql_connection]])
```

Changes the current MySQL user (the one that logged in) to another user (specifying that user's username and password). You can also change the database at the same time or specify a new connection; otherwise the current connection and database will be used. Returns true if successful and false if not, in which case the existing user and details are maintained.

For example:

```
// open a persistent connection to the database
$connect = mysql_pconnect($hostname, $username, $password);
```

```
$change_succeeded = mysql_change_user($new_user, $new_password, $database,
    $connect);
```

### mysql_client_encoding

```
int mysql_client_encoding ([resource mysql_connection])
```

Returns the default character set (for example latin1) for the specified connection or the most recently opened open connection if none is specified. For example:

```
// open a persistent connection to the database
$connect = mysql_pconnect($hostname, $username, $password);

$charset = mysql_client_encoding($connect);
print "The current character set is $charset";
```

### mysql_close

```
boolean mysql_close([resource mysql_connection])
```

Closes the specified connection or the most recent opened open connection. Does not close persistent connections. For example:

```
// open a connection to the database
$connect = mysql_connect($hostname, $username, $password);
// ... do some processing
mysql_close($connect);
```

### mysql_connect

```
mysql_connection mysql_connect([string hostname [, string username
  [, string password [, boolean new_connection [, int client_flags]]]]])
```

Establishes a connection to a MySQL server (specified by hostname, username, and password, if required) and returns a link identifier to be used by other functions. If a second, identical call is made later in the code, the same link identifier is returned, unless the new_connection parameter is set to true.

The hostname can also take a port (the port follows a colon after the host name).

The final parameter can be one or more of the following flags, which determine elements of MySQL's behavior when connected:

**mysql_client_compress**   Uses compression protocol.

**mysql_client_ignore_space**   Allows space after function names.

**mysql_client_interactive**   Waits for the value of the interactive_timeout instead of the wait_timeout mysqld variable before closing an inactive connection.

**mysql_client_ssl**   Uses the SSL protocol.

For example:

```
// set connection settings (should usually be done outside the script)
$hostname = "localhost:3306";
$username = "guru2b";
$password = "g00r002b";

// open a connection to the database
$connect = mysql_connect($hostname, $username, $password, MYSQL_CLIENT_COMPRESS);
```

### mysql_create_db

```
boolean mysql_create_db (string database [, resource mysql_connection])
```

Creates a new database on the server using the specified connection or the most recently opened open connection if none is specified. Returns true if it succeeded and false if not.

The newly created database does not become the active database. You need to use the mysql_select_db() function to do that.

This function replaces the deprecated mysql_createdb() function, which still works.

For example:

```
// open a persistent connection to the database
$connect = mysql_pconnect($hostname, $username, $password);

if (mysql_create_db("new_db", $connect)) {
  print "Database new_db successfully created";
}
else {
  print "Database new_db was not created";
}
```

### mysql_data_seek

```
boolean mysql_data_seek (resource query_result, int row)
```

Moves the internal row pointer (0 is the first row) associated with the query result to a new position. The next row that is retrieved (from mysql_fetch_row() or mysql_fetch_array(), for example) will be the specified row.

Returns true if the move succeeded and false if not (usually because the query result does not have any or as many associated rows).

For example:

```
// open a persistent connection to the database
$connect = mysql_pconnect($hostname, $username, $password);

// select the database
mysql_select_db("database1", $connect);

// set and run the query
$sql = "SELECT field1,field2 FROM table1";
```

```
$result = mysql_query($sql, $connect);

// number of rows returned
$x = mysql_num_rows($result);

// if the tenth row exists, go straight to it
if ($x >= 10) {
  mysql_data_seek($result, 9);
}

// return the data from the 10th row
$row = mysql_fetch_array($result);
print "Field1: " . $row["field1"] . "<br>\n";
print "Field2: " . $row["field2"];
```

## *mysql_db_name*

```
string mysql_db_name (resource query_result, int row[, mixed unused])
```

Returns the name of a database. The query result would have been returned from an earlier call to the mysql_list_dbs() function. The row specifies which element of the query result set (which starts at 0) to return.

The mysql_num_rows() function returns the number of database returned from mysql_list_dbs(). For example:

```
// open a persistent connection to the database
$connect = mysql_pconnect($hostname, $username, $password);

// return the list of databases on the connection
$result = mysql_list_dbs($connect);

// loop through the results, returning the database names one by one
for ($i=0; $i < mysql_num_rows($result); $i++) {
    print mysql_db_name($result, $i) . "<br>\n";
}
```

## *mysql_db_query*

```
query_result mysql_db_query ( string database, string query
[, resource mysql_connection])
```

Returns a query result resource if the query is processed successfully and false if the query fails. The query is sent to a specified database using the specified connection (or the most recently opened open connection if none is specified).

This function has been deprecated, so instead use mysql_select_db() and mysql_query().

## *mysql_drop_db*

```
boolean mysql_drop_db(string database [, resource mysql_connection])
```

Drops the specified database for the specified connection or the most recently opened open connection if none is specified. Returns true if successful and false if the database could not be dropped.

This function and the even older `mysql_dropdb()` function are deprecated. You should use the `mysql_query()` function to drop a database instead.

For example:

```
// open a persistent connection to the database
$connect = mysql_pconnect($hostname, $username, $password);

// drop the old_db database
if (mysql_drop_db("old_db", $connect)) {
  print "Database old_db is gone";
else {
  print "Database old_db could not be dropped";
}
```

### mysql_errno

```
int mysql_errno([resource connection])
```

Returns the error number of the most recently performed MySQL function or zero if there was no error. Uses the specified connection (or the most recently opened open connection if none is specified).

This function will return zero after any successful MySQL-related function has been executed, except for `mysql_error()` and `mysql_errno()`, which leave the value unchanged.

For example:

```
// open a persistent connection to the database
$connect = mysql_pconnect($hostname, $username, $password);

// attempt to use a database that you've just dropped
mysql_select_db("old_db", $connect);

// Displays the error code - 1049
if (mysql_errno()) {
  print "MySQL has thrown the following error: ".mysql_errno();
}
```

### mysql_error

```
string mysql_error([resource mysql_connection])
```

Returns the text of the error message of the most recently performed MySQL function or an empty string ("") if there was no error. Uses the specified connection (or the most recently opened open connection if none is specified).

This function will return an empty string after any successful MySQL-related function has been executed, except for `mysql_error()` and `mysql_errno()`, which leave the value unchanged.

For example:

```
// open a persistent connection to the database
$connect = mysql_pconnect($hostname, $username, $password);

// attempt to use a database that you've just dropped
mysql_select_db("old_db", $connect);

// Displays the error text - Unknown database 'old_db'
if (mysql_errno()) {
  print "MySQL has thrown the following error: ".mysql_error();
}
```

### *mysql_escape_string*

```
string mysql_escape_string (string stringname)
```

Returns a string with all characters that could break the query escaped (with a backslash placed before them). The characters that are escaped include null ($\backslash$x00), new line ($\backslash$n), carriage return ($\backslash$r), backslash ($\backslash$), single quote ('), double quote ("), and Ctrl+Z ($\backslash$x1A).

Does not escape percentage (%) and underscore (_) characters.

This makes a query safe to use. Anytime user input is used in a query, this function should be used to make the query safe. You can also use the slightly less complete addslashes() function.

For example:

```
// orginal unsafe string
$field_value = "Isn't it true that the case may be";

// escape the special characters
$field_value = mysql_escape_string($field_value);

// now it's safe and displays: Isn\'t it true that the case may be
print "$field_value";
```

### *mysql_fetch_array*

```
array mysql_fetch_array (resource query_result [, int array_type])
```

Returns an array of strings based upon a row from a query result returned from a function such as mysql_query(), and returns false if it fails or there are no more rows available. The row returned is based upon the position of the internal row pointer, which is then incremented by one. (The row pointer starts at 0 immediately after a query is run.)

The second parameter specifies how the data is to be returned. If the array type is set to MYSQL_ASSOC, data is returned as an associative array (the same if you'd used the mysql_fetch_assoc() function). If the array type is set to MYSQL_NUM, the data is returned as a numeric array (the same as if you'd used the mysql_fetch_row() function). The third option, MYSQL_BOTH, is the default used if no option is specified, and it allows you to access the data as an associative or numeric array.

The associative array takes as a key the names of the fields only (dropping any table name prefix). If there are duplicate field names, you need to use an alias; otherwise the last-mentioned value will overwrite the earlier one.

For example:

```
// open a persistent connection to the database
$connect = mysql_pconnect($hostname, $username, $password);

// select the database
mysql_select_db("database1", $connect);

// set and run the query
$sql = "SELECT field1,field2 FROM table1";
$result = mysql_query($sql, $connect);

// return the data in both associative and numeric arrays (default)
// loop through the rows, printing the data
while ($row = mysql_fetch_array($result)) {
  print "Field1: ".$row["field1"]."<br>\n";
  print "Field2: ".$row["field2"]."<br>\n";
}
```

### *mysql_fetch_assoc*

```
array mysql_fetch_assoc (resource query_result)
```

Returns an array of strings based upon a row from a query result returned from a function such as mysql_query(), and returns false if it fails or there are no more rows available. The row returned is based upon the position of the internal row pointer, which is then incremented by one. (The row pointer starts at 0 immediately after a query is run.)

The data is returned as an associative array, which takes as a key the names of the fields only (dropping any table name prefix). If there are duplicate field names, you need to use an alias; otherwise the last-mentioned value will overwrite the earlier one. This function is the same as using mysql_fetch_array() with the MYSQL_ASSOC parameter.

For example:

```
// open a persistent connection to the database
$connect = mysql_pconnect($hostname, $username, $password);

// select the database
mysql_select_db("database1", $connect);

// set and run the query
$sql = "SELECT field1,field2 FROM table1";
$result = mysql_query($sql, $connect);

// return the data in associative array format and loop through
// the result, printing the row values
while ($row = mysql_fetch_assoc($result)) {
  print "Field1: ".$row["field1"]."<br>\n";
  print "Field2: ".$row["field2"]."<br>\n";
}
```

## *mysql_fetch_field*

```
object mysql_fetch_field(resource query_result [, int offset ])
```

Returns an object containing information about a field based upon a row from a query result returned from a function such as mysql_query(). If the offset is not specified, the next unretrieved field is returned (so you can call this function multiple times to get information about all the fields); otherwise it will be the one determined by the offset (0 for the first field).

The properties of the object are as follows:

**name**   Field name

**table**   Table name to which the field belongs

**max_length**   Maximum length of the field

**not_null**   1 if the field is cannot contain nulls

**primary_key**   1 if the field is a primary key

**unique_key**   1 if the field is a unique key

**multiple_key**   1 if the field is a nonunique key

**numeric**   1 if the field is numeric

**blob**   1 if the field is a BLOB

**type**   The type of the field

**unsigned**   1 if the field is unsigned

**zerofill**   1 if the field is zero-filled

For example:

```
// open a persistent connection to the database
$connect = mysql_pconnect($hostname, $username, $password);

// return a list of all fields in database1.table1
$result = mysql_list_fields("database1", "table1");

// loop through the fields and display the field name, type
// and maximum length
while ($row = mysql_fetch_field($result)) {
  $max_length = $row->max_length;
  $name = $row->name;
  $type = $row->type;
  print "Name:$name <br>\n";
  print "Type:$type <br>\n";
  print "Maximum Length:$max_length <br><br>\n\n";
}
```

### mysql_fetch_lengths

```
array mysql_fetch_lengths(resource query_result)
```

Returns an array of the lengths of each field in the last row fetched from a query result (the length of that result, not the maximum length), and returns false if it wasn't successful. Use the `mysql_field_len()` function to return maximum length for a field.

For example:

```
// open a persistent connection to the database
$connect = mysql_pconnect($hostname, $username, $password);

// select the database
mysql_select_db("database1", $connect);

// set and run the query
$sql = "SELECT field1,field2 FROM table1";
$result = mysql_query($sql, $connect);

// return the data in associative array format and loop through
// the result, retrieving the length of the fields, and printing
// the row values and lengths
while ($row = mysql_fetch_assoc($result)) {
  $lengths = mysql_fetch_lengths($result);
  print "Field1: ".$row["field1"]."Length: ".$lengths[0]."<br>\n";
  print "Field2: ".$row["field2"]."Length: ".$lengths[1]."<br>\n";
}
```

### mysql_fetch_object

```
object mysql_fetch_object(resource query_result)
```

Returns an object with properties based upon a row from a query result returned from a function such as `mysql_query()`. The row returned is based upon the position of the internal row pointer, which is then incremented by one. (The row pointer starts at 0 immediately after a query is run.)

Each property of the object is based upon a name (or alias) of the field from the query.

For example:

```
// open a persistent connection to the database
$connect = mysql_pconnect($hostname, $username, $password);

// select the database
mysql_select_db("database1", $connect);

// set and run the query
$sql = "SELECT field1,field2 FROM table1";
$result = mysql_query($sql, $connect);

// loop through the rows returning each as an object
// and display the fields
```

```
while ($row = mysql_fetch_object($result)) {
  print "Field1: ".$row->field1."<br>\n";
  print "Field2: ".$row->field2."<br>\n";
}
```

### mysql_fetch_row

```
array mysql_fetch_row(resource query_result)
```

Returns an array of strings based upon a row from a query result returned from a function such as mysql_query(), or returns false if it fails or there are no more rows available. The row returned is based upon the position of the internal row pointer, which is then incremented by one. (The row pointer starts at 0 immediately after a query is run.)

The data is returned as a numeric array (the same as if you had used the mysql_fetch_array() function with the MYSQL_NUM parameter).

For example:

```
// open a persistent connection to the database
$connect = mysql_pconnect($hostname, $username, $password);

// select the database
mysql_select_db("database1", $connect);

// set and run the query
$sql = "SELECT field1,field2 FROM table1";
$result = mysql_query($sql, $connect);

// loop through the rows returning each as a numeric array
// and display the fields
while ($row = mysql_fetch_row($result)) {
  print "Field1: ".$row[0]."<br>\n";
  print "Field2: ".$row[1]."<br>\n";
}
```

### mysql_field_flags

```
string mysql_field_flags(resource query_result, int offset)
```

Returns a string containing flags of the specified field based upon a row from a query result returned from a function such as mysql_query(). The offset determines which field is examined (0 for the first field).

The flags include not_null, primary_key, unique_key, multiple_key, blob, unsigned, zerofill, binary, enum, auto_increment, and timestamp.

The old mysql_fieldflags() function does the same, but it's deprecated.

For example:

```
// open a persistent connection to the database
$connect = mysql_pconnect($hostname, $username, $password);
```

```
// select the database
mysql_select_db("database1", $connect);

// set and run the query
$sql = "SELECT field1,field2 FROM table1";
$result = mysql_query($sql, $connect);

// Display the properties for fields 1 and 2
print "Field1 flags: ".mysql_field_flags($result, 0)."<br>\n";
print "Field1 flags: ".mysql_field_flags($result, 1)."<br>\n";
```

## mysql_field_len

```
int mysql_field_len (resource query_result, int offset)
```

Returns the maximum length (determined by the database structure) of the specified field based upon a row from a query result returned from a function such as mysql_query(). The offset (starting at 0) determines the field.

The old mysql_fieldlen() function does the same, but it's deprecated.

Use the mysql_fetch_lengths() function to determine the specific length of a returned field. For example:

```
// open a persistent connection to the database
$connect = mysql_pconnect($hostname, $username, $password);

// select the database
mysql_select_db("database1", $connect);

// set and run the query
$sql = "SELECT field1,field2 FROM table1";
$result = mysql_query($sql, $connect);

// Display the properties for fields 1 and 2
print "Field1 maximum length: ". mysql_field_len($result, 0). "<br>\n";
print "Field1 maximum length: ". mysql_field_len($result, 1). "<br>\n";
```

## mysql_field_name

```
string mysql_field_name(resource query_result, int offset)
```

Returns the name of the specified field based upon a row from a query result returned from a function such as mysql_query(). The offset (starting at 0) determines the field.

For example:

```
// open a persistent connection to the database
$connect = mysql_pconnect($hostname, $username, $password);

// select the database
mysql_select_db("database1", $connect);
```

```
// set and run the query
$sql = "SELECT * FROM table1";
$result = mysql_query($sql, $connect);

// loop through the fields and display the name
for($i=0; $i < mysql_num_fields($result); $i++) {
  print "Field name: ".mysql_field_name($result, $i). "<br>\n";
}
```

### mysql_field_seek

```
boolean mysql_field_seek(resource query_result, int offset)
```

Moves the internal pointer to a new field of the query result, based on the offset (starting at 0 with the first field). The next call to the mysql_fetch_field() function will start at this offset. This is not that useful because you can move the pointer directly with the mysql_fetch_field() function.

For example:

```
// open a persistent connection to the database
$connect = mysql_pconnect($hostname, $username, $password);

// select the database
mysql_select_db("database1", $connect);

// set and run the query
$sql = "SELECT * FROM table1";
$result = mysql_query($sql, $connect);

// jump to the 2nd field
mysql_field_seek($result, 1);

$field = mysql_fetch_field($result);
print "The name of the 2nd field is: " . $field->name;
```

### mysql_field_table

```
string mysql_field_table(resource query_result, int offset)
```

Returns the name of the table the field in a query result determined by the offset (starting at 0) refers to, or returns false if there's an error. The deprecated mysql_fieldtable() function is identical.

For example:

```
// open a persistent connection to the database
$connect = mysql_pconnect($hostname, $username, $password);

// select the database
mysql_select_db("database1", $connect);
```

```
// set and run the query
$sql = "SELECT field1,field2 FROM table1,table2 WHERE field1=field2";
$result = mysql_query($sql, $connect);

// Get the name of the table for field1 (offset 0)
echo "field 1 belongs to the table: ".mysql_field_table($result, 0);
```

### mysql_field_type

```
string mysql_field_type(resource query_result, int offset)
```

Returns the type of a field in a query result determined by the offset (starting at 0), or returns false if there's an error. Examples of field type include int, real, string, and blob.

For example:

```
// open a persistent connection to the database
$connect = mysql_pconnect($hostname, $username, $password);

// select the database
mysql_select_db("database1", $connect);

// set and run the query
$sql = "SELECT field1,field2 FROM table1,table2 WHERE field1=field2";
$result = mysql_query($sql, $connect);

for($i=0;$i<mysql_num_fields($result);$i++) {
  echo "Field $i is of type: ".mysql_field_type($result, $i) . "<br>\n";
}
```

### mysql_free_result

```
boolean mysql_free_result(resource query_result)
```

Frees all memory used by the resource query_result, making it available for use again. Returns true on success and false on failure. Memory is automatically freed at the end of a script even without calling this function. The deprecated mysql_freeresult() function is identical.

For example:

```
// open a persistent connection to the database
$connect = mysql_pconnect($hostname, $username, $password);

// select the database
mysql_select_db("database1", $connect);

// set and run the query
$sql = "SELECT field1,field2 FROM table1";
$result = mysql_query($sql, $connect);

// loop through the rows returning each as a numeric array
// and display the fields
while ($row = mysql_fetch_row($result)) {
```

```
    print "Field1: ".$row[0]."<br>\n";
    print "Field2: ".$row[1]."<br>\n";
}

// free the resources associated with the query
mysql_free_result($result);
```

### *mysql_get_client_info*

```
string mysql_get_client_info()
```

Returns a string containing the MySQL client library version (4.0.2, for example).
For example:

```
// displays - Client library version is: 4.0.2 (for example)
print "Client library version is: ".mysql_get_client_info();
```

### *mysql_get_host_info*

```
string mysql_get_host_info([resource mysql_connection])
```

Returns a string containing the connection information (for example, "Localhost via UNIX
socket"). The information is from the specified connection (or the most recently opened open
connection if none is specified).
For example:

```
// displays - Type of connection: Localhost via UNIX socket
// (for example)
print "Type of connection: ".mysql_get_host_info();
```

### *mysql_get_proto_info*

```
int mysql_get_proto_info([resource mysql_connection])
```

Returns an integer containing the protocol version (for example, 10) used by the connection. The
information is from the specified connection (or the most recently opened open connection if none
is specified).
For example:

```
// displays - Protocol version: 10 (for example)
print "Protocol version: ".mysql_get_proto_info();
```

### *mysql_get_server_info*

```
string mysql_get_server_info([resource mysql_connection])
```

Returns a string containing the MySQL server version (for example, 4.0.3). The information is
from the specified connection (or the most recently opened open connection if none is specified).
For example:

```
// displays - Server version: 4.0.3-beta-log (for example)
print "Server version: ".mysql_get_server_info();
```

## *mysql_info*

```
string mysql_info ( [resource mysql_connection])
```

Returns a string containing detailed information about the most recent query. Detailed information includes records, rows matched, changes, and warnings. The information is from the specified connection (or the most recently opened open connection if none is specified).

For example:

```
// open a persistent connection to the database
$connect = mysql_pconnect($hostname, $username, $password);

// select the database
mysql_select_db("database1", $connect);

// set and run the query
$sql = "UPDATE table1 set field1 = 2 WHERE field2=3";
$result = mysql_query($sql, $connect);

// displays:
// Query info: String format: Rows matched: 19 Changed: 19 Warnings: 0
//(for example)
print "Query info: ".mysql_info();
```

## *mysql_insert_id*

```
int mysql_insert_id([resource mysql_connection])
```

Returns an integer containing the most recent AUTO_INCREMENT value for that connection, or returns false if it fails (there have been no AUTO_INCREMENT values set for the connection). The information is from the specified connection (or the most recently opened open connection if none is specified).

For example:

```
// open a persistent connection to the database
$connect = mysql_pconnect($hostname, $username, $password);

// select the database
mysql_select_db("database1", $connect);

// set and run the query
$sql = "INSERT INTO table1(field1, field2) VALUES(3,4)";
$result = mysql_query($sql, $connect);

// Displays: AUTO_INCREMENT value: 10 (for example)
print "AUTO_INCREMENT value: ".mysql_insert_id();
```

## *mysql_list_dbs*

```
query_result mysql_list_dbs([resource mysql_connection])
```

Returns a resource pointing to a list of databases available on the connection, or returns false on failure. The information is from the specified connection (or the most recently opened open connection if none is specified). The result can be processed by a function such as mysql_db_name() or mysql_result().

The deprecated mysql_listdbs() function is identical.

For example:

```
// open a persistent connection to the database
$connect = mysql_pconnect($hostname, $username, $password);

// return the list of databases on the connection
$result = mysql_list_dbs($connect);

// loop through the results, returning the database names one by one
for ($i=0; $i < mysql_num_rows($result); $i++) {
    print mysql_db_name($result, $i) . "<br>\n";
}
```

### mysql_list_fields

```
query_result mysql_list_fields(string database, string table
  [, resource mysql_connection])
```

Returns a resource pointing to a list of fields from a given database and table or false on failure. The information is from the specified connection (or the most recently opened open connection if none is specified).

The deprecated mysql_listfields() function is identical.

For example:

```
// open a persistent connection to the database
$connect = mysql_pconnect($hostname, $username, $password);

// return a list of all fields in database1.table1
$result = mysql_list_fields("database1", "table1");

// loop through the fields and display the field name, type
// and maximum length
while ($row = mysql_fetch_field($result)) {
  $max_length = $row->max_length;
  $name = $row->name;
  $type = $row->type;
  print "Name:$name <br>\n";
  print "Type:$type <br>\n";
  print "Maximum Length:$max_length <br><br>\n\n";
}
```

### mysql_list_processes

```
query_result mysql_list_processes ([resource mysql_connection])
```

Returns a resource containing a list of the current MySQL processes or false on failure. You can then use a function such as mysql_fetch_assoc() to return an array containing the elements: Id, Host, db, Command, and Time. The information is from the specified connection (or the most recently opened open connection if none is specified).

For example:

```
// open a persistent connection to the database
$connect = mysql_pconnect($hostname, $username, $password);

// return all the processes
$result = mysql_list_processes($connect);

// loop through the rows displaying the various process elements
while ($row = mysql_fetch_assoc($result)){
  print $row["Id"];
  print $row["Host"];
  print $row["db"];
  print $row["Command"];
  print $row["Time"];
  print "<br>\n"
}
```

### mysql_list_tables

```
query_result mysql_list_tables(string database[, resource mysql_connection])
```

Returns a resource pointing to a list of tables from a given database, or returns false on failure. The information is from the specified connection (or the most recently opened open connection if none is specified).

For example:

```
// open a persistent connection to the database
$connect = mysql_pconnect($hostname, $username, $password);

// returns the list of tables
$result = mysql_list_tables("database1");

// loops through the rows of tables, and displays the names
for($i=0; i < mysql_num_rows($result); $i++) {
  print "Table name: ".mysql_tablename($result, $i)."<br>\n";
}
```

### mysql_num_fields

```
int mysql_num_fields(resource query_result)
```

Returns an integer containing the number of fields in a query result or NULL on error.
The deprecated mysql_numfields() function is identical.
For example:

```
// open a persistent connection to the database
$connect = mysql_pconnect($hostname, $username, $password);
```

```
// return a list of all fields in database1.table1
$result = mysql_list_fields("database1", "table1");

// Displays: Num fields in database1: 6 (for example)
print "Num fields in database1: ".mysql_num_fields($result);
```

### *mysql_num_rows*

```
int mysql_num_rows(resource query_result)
```

Returns an integer containing the number of rows in a query result, or returns NULL on error. This will not work if the query result was obtained using the mysql_unbuffered_query() function. You should use mysql_affected_rows() to return the number of rows of data changed by a query (after an INSERT or UPDATE, for example).

For example:

```
// open a persistent connection to the database
$connect = mysql_pconnect($hostname, $username, $password);

// return the list of databases on the connection
$result = mysql_list_dbs($connect);

// loop through the results, returning the database names one by one
for ($i=0; $i < mysql_num_rows($result); $i++) {
    print mysql_db_name($result, $i) . "<br>\n";
}
```

### *mysql_pconnect*

```
mysql_connection mysql_pconnect([string hostname
  [, string username [, string password [, int client_flags]]]])
```

Establishes a persistent connection (one that can be reused) to a MySQL server (specified by hostname, username, and password, if required) and returns a link identifier to be used by other functions. If one already exists, it will be reused. The final parameter can be one or more of the following flags, which determine elements of MySQL's behavior when connected:

**mysql_client_compress**   Uses compression protocol

**mysql_client_ignore_space**   Allows space after function names

**mysql_client_interactive**   Waits for the value of the interactive_timeout instead of the wait_timeout mysqld variable before closing an inactive connection

**mysql_client_ssl**   Uses SSL protocol

MySQL closes persistent connections after the wait_timeout seconds (a mysqld variable) or after the process that spawned the connection closes. For example, your web server process can reuse the same connection for several scripts, but the connection will close once the web server process closes.

For example:

```
// set connection settings (should usually be done outside the script)
$hostname = "localhost:3306";
$username = "guru2b";
$password = "g00r002b";

// open a persistent connection to the database
$connect = mysql_pconnect($hostname, $username, $password);
```

## mysql_ping

```
boolean mysql_ping ([resource mysql_connection])
```

Returns true if the MySQL server is up and false if not. The ping is attempted using the specified connection (or the most recently opened open connection if none is specified). If the ping fails, the script will try to reconnect with the same parameters.

For example:

```
// open a persistent connection to the database
$connect = mysql_pconnect($hostname, $username, $password);

// time passes...

if (mysql_ping()) {
  print "Still connected";
}
else {
  print "Connection lost";
}
```

## mysql_query

```
query_result mysql_query(string query[, resource mysql_connection
  [, int result_mode]])
```

Returns a query result (if the query was one that produces a result, such as SELECT or DESCRIBE), returns true if the query did not produce a result but succeeded (such as DELETE or UPDATE) and returns false if the query failed. The query is sent to a specified database using the specified connection (or the most recently opened open connection if none is specified).

The optional result_mode parameter can be one of MYSQL_USE_RESULT, which causes the result to be unbuffered, just like with mysql_unbuffered_query() or MYSQL_STORE_RESULT (the default).

For example:

```
// open a persistent connection to the database
$connect = mysql_pconnect($hostname, $username, $password);

// select the database
mysql_select_db("database1", $connect);
```

```
// set and run the query
$sql = "SELECT field1,field2 FROM table1";
$result = mysql_query($sql, $connect);

// return the data in associative array format and loop through
// the result, printing the row values
while ($row = mysql_fetch_assoc($result)) {
  print "Field1: ".$row["field1"]."<br>\n";
  print "Field2: ".$row["field2"]."<br>\n";
}
```

## *mysql_real_escape_string*

```
string mysql_real_escape_string (string stringname [, resource mysql_connection])
```

Returns a string with all characters that could break the query escaped (a backslash placed before them. The characters that are escaped include null ($\x00$), new line ($\n$), carriage return ($\r$), backslash ($\backslash$), single quote ('), double quote ("), and Ctrl+Z ($\x1A$). It does not escape percentage (%) and underscore (_) characters.

This makes a query safe to use. Differs to `mysql_escape_string()` in that this function takes into account the current character set.

For example:

```
// orginal unsafe string
$field_value = "Isn't it true that the case may be";

// escape the special characters
$field_value = mysql_real_escape_string($field_value);

// now it's safe and displays: Isn\'t it true that the case may be
print "$field_value";
```

## *mysql_result*

```
mixed mysql_result(resource query_result, int row [, mixed field_specifier])
```

Returns the contents of a single field from a query result. The `field_specifier` can be either an offset (starting at 0) or the field's name, with or without a table specifier (in other words, `tablename.fieldname` or just `fieldname`) if this was supplied in the query. If the field specifier is not supplied, the first field will be returned.

This function is markedly slower than the functions that return the entire row, such as `mysql_fetch_row()` and `mysql_fetch_array()`, so use one of those instead. Also, don't mix this function with functions that return the entire row.

For example:

```
// open a persistent connection to the database
$connect = mysql_pconnect($hostname, $username, $password);

// select the database
mysql_select_db("database1", $connect);
```

```
// return the average of field1
$sql = "SELECT AVG(field2) FROM table1";
$result = mysql_query($sql, $connect);

// display the average value of this field
print "Field2 average: ".mysql_result($result, 0);
```

## *mysql_select_db*

```
boolean mysql_select_db(string database [, resource mysql_connection])
```

Changes the current database to the specified database. Uses the specified connection (or the most recently opened open connection if none is specified). If no connection is open, it will attempt to call mysql_connect() with no parameters to connect. Returns true if successful, and returns false if not.

The deprecated mysql_selectdb() function is identical.

For example:

```
// open a persistent connection to the database
$connect = mysql_pconnect($hostname, $username, $password);

// select the database
mysql_select_db("database1", $connect);
```

## *mysql_stat*

```
string mysql_stat ([resource mysql_connection])
```

Returns a string containing the server status. This contains uptime, threads, questions, slow queries, opens, flush tables, open tables, and queries per second average. Uses the specified connection (or the most recently opened open connection if none is specified).

For example:

```
// displays (for example):
// Uptime: 109  Threads: 2  Questions: 199  Slow queries: 1  Opens: 4
// Flush tables: 1  Open tables: 2  Queries per second avg: 1.826
print "Server Status: ".mysql_stat();
```

## *mysql_tablename*

```
string mysql_tablename(resource query_result, int row)
```

Returns the table name from a query result returned by the mysql_list_tables() function based upon the row (starting at 0), or returns false if there's an error. You can return the number of rows in the query result with mysql_num_rows(). This function is actually an alias to mysql_result(), but it's not good programming practice to use it in the same way because its name is specific to tables, and using it in another way is confusing.

For example:

```
// open a persistent connection to the database
$connect = mysql_pconnect($hostname, $username, $password);
```

```
// returns the list of tables
$result = mysql_list_tables("database1");

// loops through the rows of tables, and displays the names
for($i=0; $i < mysql_num_rows($result); $i++) {
  print "Table name: ".mysql_tablename($result, $i)."<br>\n";
}
```

### mysql_thread_id

```
int mysql_thread_id ([resource mysql_connection])
```

Returns an integer containing the current thread ID.
For example:

```
// displays - Thread id: 2394 (for example)
print "Thread id: ".mysql_thread_id();
```

### mysql_unbuffered_query

```
query_result mysql_unbuffered_query(string query
  [, resource mysql_connection [, int result_mode]])
```

Returns an unbuffered query result (if the query was one that produces a result, such as SELECT or DESCRIBE), returns true if the query did not produce a result but succeeded (such as DELETE or UPDATE), and returns false if the query failed. The query is sent using the specified connection (or the most recently opened open connection if none is specified).

The difference between this and mysql_query() is that, because the result is unbuffered, it uses less memory and you can start working with the results as soon as the first row has been retrieved. The downside is you cannot use mysql_num_rows(). It's mainly used on large, slow queries.

The optional result_mode parameter can be one of MYSQL_USE_RESULT (the default) or MYSQL_ STORE_RESULT, which causes the result to be buffered, just like with mysql_query().

For example:

```
// open a persistent connection to the database
$connect = mysql_pconnect($hostname, $username, $password);

// select the database
mysql_select_db("database1", $connect);

// set and run the query
$sql = "SELECT field1,field2 FROM table1";
$result = mysql_unbuffered_query($sql, $connect);

// return the data in both associative and numeric arrays (default)
// loop through the rows, printing the data
while ($row = mysql_fetch_array($result)) {
  print "Field1: ".$row["field1"]."<br>\n";
  print "Field2: ".$row["field2"]."<br>\n";
}
```

# Appendix D

# Perl DBI

THE RECOMMENDED WAY TO connect to a database (not only to MySQL) in Perl is with the DBI module. This is a generic interface that allows you to access different kinds of databases in the same way. Along with the DBI module, you need a DBD module. Each DBD module is for a specific database; you should use the one associated with MySQL.

NOTE    To install Perl DBI support for MySQL, you need the DBI, DBD-mysql, Data-Dumper, and File-Spec modules. You can download the latest versions from www.mysql.com/CPAN. Full installation instructions come with the software.

Throughout this appendix, you'll see the following conventions for variable names:

**$dbh**    A database handle object, returned from the connect() or connect_cached() methods

**$sth**    A statement handle object, returned from a prepare() method among others

**$drh**    A driver handle object (rarely used in applications)

**$h**    A database, statement, or driver handle

**$rc**    A Boolean return code (true for success or false for an error)

**$rv**    A return value of sorts, usually an integer

**@ary**    An array of values, usually a row of data returned from a query

**$rows**    The number of rows processed, or −1 if unknown

**$fh**    A file handle

**undef**    A NULL, or undefined, value

**\%attributes**    A reference to a hash of attribute values, used for various purposes by the methods

To use the DBI, you need to load the DBI module at the beginning of your script, as follows:

```
use DBI;
```

Then, you need to return a database handle, usually with the connect() DBI class method. The database handle then accesses methods that can run queries and return results, usually returning a statement handle.

## DBI Class Methods

The DBI class methods are those supplied from the class as a whole. The most important is the connect() method, which, upon success, will return a database handle.

### available_drivers

```
@ary = DBI->available_drivers[($quiet)];
```

Returns a list of available drivers (DBD modules). This gives a warning if there are drivers with the same name. Setting the optional $quiet to true stills the warning.

### connect

```
$dbh = DBI->connect($datasource, $username, $password [, \%attributes]);
```

Creates a connection to the database using the specified data source, username, and password and returns a database handle. The data source consists of the DBI driver (in this case, dbi:mysql), the database name, an optional hostname (localhost if unspecified), an optional port name (3306 if unspecified) and a number of modifiers, each separated by a semicolon.

```
mysql_read_default_file=filename
```

The specified file is used as an option file (MySQL configuration file, usually my.ini or my.cnf on the server).

```
mysql_read_default_group=groupname
```

When reading an option file, the default group to use is [client]. This changes the group to [groupname].

The following option causes communication between the client and server to be compressed:

```
mysql_compression=1
```

The following option specifies the path to the Unix socket used to connect to the server:

```
mysql_socket=/path/to/socket
```

The optional username and password will take the values of the DBI_USER and DBI_PASS environment variables if not specified.

If the connection fails, it will return undef and sets $DBI:err and $DBI:errstr.

You can use the \%attributes parameter to set the various attributes, such as AutoCommit (recommended), RaiseError, and PrintError.

For example:

```
my $hostname = 'localhost';
my $database = 'firstdb';
my $username = 'guru2b';
my $password = 'g00r002b';
```

```
#Connect to the database
my $dbh = DBI->connect("dbi:mysql:$database:$hostname", $username,↵
 $password, (AutoCommit => 0, RaiseError => 1, PrintError => 0))
or die $DBI::errstr;
```

### connect_cached

```
$dbh = DBI->connect_cached($data_source, $username, $password[ , \%attributes])
```

Just like connect(), except that the details of the database handle are also stored in a hash array. This same database handle is used for further identical calls to connect_cached() if it's still valid. The CachedKids attribute (accessed via $dbh->{Driver}->{CachedKids}) contains cache data.

This is still a fairly new method and is likely to change. It is not the same as an Apache::DBI persistent connection.

### data_sources

```
@ary = DBI->data_sources($driver [, \%attributes]);
```

Returns an array of all databases available to the named driver (mysql in this case).

### trace

```
trace($trace_level [, $trace_filename])
```

This method enables or disables tracing. When called as a DBI class method, it affects tracing for all database and statement handles. When called as a database or statement handle method, it affects tracing for that handle (and future children of that handle).

The trace level can be from 0 to 9, with 0 disabling tracing, 1 best for a general overview, 2 being the most commonly used, and the other methods adding more and more driver and DBI detail.

Output goes to STDERR by default or is appended to the trace file if one was specified. For example:

```
DBI->trace(2);                         # trace everything
$dth->trace(2, "/tmp/dbi_trace.out");  # trace the database handle
                                       # to /tmp/dbi_trace.out
$sth->trace(2);                        # trace the statement handle
```

You can also enable tracing by setting the DBI_TRACE environment variable to either a number (0–9) or a file, in which case tracing will be set at level 2 and output to that file.

## DBI Methods Common to All Handles

The following methods are available to database handles, statement handles, and driver handles. They are mostly used for error handling.

### err

```
$rv  = $h->err;
```

Returns the native error code from the last method (usually an integer).

### errstr

```
$error_string = $dbh->errstr;
```

Returns an error string from the failure of the previous call.
For example:

```
my $hostname = 'localhost';
my $database = 'firstdb';
my $username = 'guru2b';
my $password = 'g00r002b';

#Connect to the database
my $dbh = DBI->connect("dbi:mysql:$database:$hostname", $username,↵
 $password) or die $DBI::errstr;
```

### func

```
$h->func(@func_arguments, $func_name);
```

Used to call other nonstandard driver methods. This takes an array of arguments and the method name as arguments.

This does not trigger the usual error detection mechanisms (such as RaiseError or PrintError) or clear a previous error (such as $DBI::err or $DBI::errstr).

### set_err

```
$rv = $h->set_err($err, $errstr [, $state, $method [, $rv]]);
```

A new method mainly used by DBI drivers and subclasses. It sets the err, errstr, and state values for the handle (to enable error handling through RaiseError and so on).

$method sets a more useful method name for the error string, and $rv sets a return value (usually undef).

For example:

```
sub doodle {
  # … try to 'doodle'
  or return $sth->set_err(1234, "Nope. Sorry. Out of luck. It all↵
went wrong", undef, "doodle");
  }
```

### state

```
$rv  = $h->state;
```

Returns an error code in SQLSTATE format. Usually returns the general S1000 code when the driver does not support SQLSTATE.

### trace

```
trace($trace_level [, $trace_filename])
```

See the earlier trace method.

### trace_msg

```
$h->trace_msg($message_text [, $minimum_level]);
```

If tracing is enabled, outputs the message text to the trace file. If the minimum level is set (default 1), this only outputs the message if the trace level is at least that level.

## DBI Utility Functions

The DBI package provides the DBI utility functions as well.

### hash

```
$hash_value = DBI::hash($buffer [, $type]);
```

Returns a 32-bit integer value, which is the result of a hash algorithm specified by $type performed upon the buffer. A type of 0 (the default) performs a Perl 5.1 hash, with a negative result. If the type is 1, the Fowler/Noll/Vo algorithm is used.

### looks_like_number

```
@bool = DBI::looks_like_number(@array);
```

Returns a Boolean array, with true for each element of the original array that looks like a number, false for each element that does not, and undef for elements that are empty or not defined.

### neat

```
$neat_string = DBI::neat($value [, $maxlen]);
```

Formats and neatens the value and quotes string for display purposes, not for passing to the database server. If the maximum length is exceeded, the string will be shortened to $maxlen-4 and an ellipsis (...) will be added to the end. If $maxlen is not is not specified, then $DBI::neat_maxlen, which defaults to 400, will be used.

### neat_list

```
$neat_string = DBI::neat_list(\@listref [, $maxlen [, $field_sep]]);
```

Calls the neat() function for each element of the list and returns a string with all the elements separated by $field_sep, which defaults to a comma (,).

## Database Handle Methods

These methods are available to the database handle, so you need to open a connection before you can use any of them. Some of these methods return a statement handle, which you can then further process with the statement handle methods listed later.

### begin_work

```
$rc  = $dbh->begin_work   or die $dbh->errstr;
```

Begins a transaction and turns AutoCommit off until the transaction ends with commit() or rollback().

### column_info

```
$sth = $dbh->column_info($catalog,$schema,$table,$column);
```

An experimental method that returns an active statement handle for getting information about columns.

### commit

```
$rc  = $dbh->commit;
```

Commits the current transaction. The AutoCommit parameter needs to be off for this to have any effect.

### disconnect

```
$rc = $dbh->disconnect;
```

Uses the specified database handle to disconnect from the database. Returns true if successful or false if not.

The method does not define whether to roll back or commit currently open transactions, so make sure you specifically commit or roll them back in your applications before calling disconnect.

### do

```
$rv = $dbh->do($statement [,\%attributes [,@bind_values]]);
```

Prepares and executes an SQL statement, returning the number of rows affected. Returns 0E0 (treated as true) if no rows are affected or undef if an error occurs.

Usually used for queries that do not return results (such as INSERT and UPDATE) and that do not make use of placeholders. This method is faster than the equivalent prepare() and execute() methods.

It returns an integer.

For example:

```
my $hostname = 'localhost';
my $database = 'firstdb';
```

```
my $username = 'guru2b';
my $password = 'g00r002b';

#Connect to the database
my $dbh = DBI->connect("dbi:mysql:$database:$hostname", $username,↵
 $password) or die $DBI::errstr;

$sql = "INSERT INTO customer(id,surname) VALUES(11,'Sandman')";
$dbh->do($sql);
```

## foreign_key_info

```
$sth = $dbh->foreign_key_info($pk_catalog, $pk_schema, $pk_table↵
 [, $fk_catalog, $fk_schema, $fk_table]);
```

An experimental method that returns a statement handle for getting foreign key information. The arguments $pk_catalog, $pk_schema, and $pk_table specify the primary key table. The arguments $fk_catalog, $fk_schema, and $fk_table specify the foreign key table.

The returned result depends on which tables are supplied. If only the foreign key table is supplied (by passing undef as the primary key argument), the results contain all foreign keys in that table and the associated primary keys. If only the primary key table is supplied, the results contain the primary key from that table and all associated foreign keys. If both tables are supplied, the results contain the foreign key from the foreign key table that refers to the primary key of the primary key table.

## get_info

```
$value = $dbh->get_info( $info_type );
```

An experimental method returning implementation information.

## ping

```
$rc = $dbh->ping;
```

Checks if the database is still running and the connection is active.

## prepare

```
$sth = $dbh->prepare($statement [, \%attributes])
```

Returns a reference to a statement handle and readies an SQL statement for execution (with the execute method). You'd usually prepare statements that are to return results, such as SELECT and DESCRIBE.

## prepare_cached

```
$sth = $dbh->prepare_cached($statement [, \%attributes,[ $allow_active]]);
```

The same as prepare, except that the statement handle is stored in a hash so that future calls to identical arguments will return the same handle. The $allow_active argument has three settings. The default, 0, generates a warning and calls finish() on the statement handle before it is returned, and 1 calls finish() but suppresses the warning. If set to 2, the DBI will not call finish() before returning the statement.

### primary_key

```
@key_column_names = $dbh->primary_key($catalog, $schema, $table);
```

An experimental interface to the primary_key_info method that returns an array of fieldnames that make up the primary key, in sequence, for the specified table.

### primary_key_info

```
$sth = $dbh->primary_key_info($catalog, $schema, $table);
```

An experimental method for getting information about primary key columns.

### quote

```
$quoted_string = $dbh->quote($string [,$data_type])
```

Returns a string with any special characters escaped (such as single or double quotes) and adds outer quotation marks. If the data type is specified, Perl will use it to determine the required quoting behavior.

### quote_identifier

```
$sql = $dbh->quote_identifier( $name1[ , $name2, $name3, \%attributes ]);
```

Escapes any special characters in an identifier (such as a fieldname) for use in a query.

### rollback

```
$rc  = $dbh->rollback;
```

Rolls back the current transaction. The AutoCommit parameter needs to be off for this to have any effect.

### selectall_arrayref

```
$ary_ref  = $dbh->selectall_arrayref($statement [, \%attributes [,@bind_values]]);
```

A method that combines the prepare(), execute(), and fetchall_arrayref() methods into one for ease of use. It returns a reference to an array containing a reference to an array for each row of data returned from the query. The statement can also be a statement handle that has already been prepared, in which case the method does not do a prepare().

You can set other arguments to pass to the `selectall_arrayref()` method in `%attributes`.

### selectall_hashref

```
$hash_ref = $dbh->selectall_hashref($statement, $key_field⤦
[, \%attributes [,@bind_values]]);
```

A method that combines the `prepare()`, `execute()`, and `fetchall_hashref()` methods into one for ease of use. It returns a reference to a hash containing an entry for each row returned from the query. The key for each field is specified by `$key_field`, and the value is a reference to a hash. The statement can also be a statement handle that has already been prepared, in which case the method skips the `prepare()`.

### selectcol_arrayref

```
$ary_ref = $dbh->selectcol_arrayref($statement [, \%attributes [,@bind_values]]);
```

A method that combines the `prepare()` and `execute()` methods with fetching one or more columns from all rows returned from the query. It returns a reference to an array containing the values of the columns from each row. The statement can also be a statement handle that has already been prepared, in which case the method skips the `prepare()`.

By default it returns the first columns from each row, but it can return more with a `Columns` attribute, which is a reference to an array containing the column number to use.

For example:

```
# perform a query and return the two columns
my $array_ref = $dbh->selectcol_arrayref("SELECT first_name, surname⤦
  FROM customer", { Columns=>[1,2] });
# create the hash from key-value pairs so $hash{$first_name} => surname
my %hash = @$array_ref;
```

### selectrow_array

```
@row_ary  = $dbh->selectrow_array($statement [, \%attributes [,@bind_values]]);
```

A method that combines the `prepare()`, `execute()`, and `fetchrow_array()` methods into one for ease of use. It returns the first row of data returned from the query. The statement can also be a statement handle that has already been prepared, in which case the method does not do a `prepare()`.

### selectrow_arrayref

```
$ary_ref  = $dbh->selectrow_arrayref($statement [, \%attributes [,@bind_values]]);
```

A method that combines the `prepare()`, `execute()`, and `fetchrow_arrayref()` methods into one for ease of use. The statement can also be a statement handle that has already been prepared, in which case the method does not do a `prepare()`.

### selectrow_hashref

```
$hash_ref = $dbh->selectrow_hashref($statement [, \%attributes [,@bind_values]]);
```

A method that combines the prepare(), execute(), and fetchrow_hashref() methods into one for ease of use. It returns the first row of data returned from the query. The statement can also be a statement handle that has already been prepared, in which case the method does not do a prepare().

### table_info

```
$sth = $dbh->table_info($catalog, $schema, $table, $type [, \%attributes]);
```

An experimental method that returns an active statement handle for getting information about tables and views from the database.

### tables

```
@names = $dbh->tables($catalog, $schema, $table, $type);
```

An experimental interface to the table_info() method that returns an array of table names.

### type_info

```
@type_info = $dbh->type_info($data_type);
```

An experimental method that returns an array of hash references containing information about data type variants.

### type_info_all

```
$type_info_all = $dbh->type_info_all;
```

An experimental method that returns a reference to an array containing information about data types supported by the database and driver.

## Statement Handle Methods

These methods work on the statement handle, obtained by calling a database handle method such as prepare().

### bind_col

```
$rc = $sth->bind_col($column_number, \$column_variable);
```

Binds a field (starting at 1) in the result from a SELECT statement to a variable. See bind_columns for more information.

### bind_columns

```
$rc = $sth->bind_columns(@list_of_refs_to_vars_to_bind);
```

Calls the `bind_col()` method for each field from the SELECT statement. The number of references must match the number of fields.

For example:

```
# set RaiseError to 1 to avoid having to check each method call
$dbh->{RaiseError} = 1;
$sth = $dbh->prepare(q{SELECT first_name,surname FROM customer});
$sth->execute;
my ($first_name, $surname);
# Bind Perl variables to columns:
$rv = $sth->bind_columns(\$first_name, \$surname);
while ($sth->fetch) {
    print "$first_name $surname\n";
}
```

## bind_param

```
$rv = $sth->bind_param($bind_num, $bind_value [\%attributes | $bind_type]);
```

Used to bind a value with a placeholder, indicated with a question mark (?). A placeholder is used where you're planning to run a similar query multiple times, where only a parameter changes each time.

For example:

```
$sth = $dbh->prepare("SELECT fname, sname FROM tname WHERE sname LIKE ?");
$sth->bind_param(1, "Vusi%");  # placeholders begin from 1
$sth->execute;
```

You can't use placeholders to replace a table name or fieldname, or to replace anything but a single scalar value. For example, the following are incorrect usages of placeholders:

```
SELECT fname, ? FROM tname WHERE sname LIKE 'Vusi%'
SELECT fname, sname FROM ? WHERE sname LIKE 'Vusi%'
SELECT fname, sname FROM tname WHERE sname IN (?)
```

You can also use the optional bind type parameter to indicate what type the placeholder should have. For example:

```
$sth->bind_param(1, $bind_value, {TYPE => SQL_INTEGER});
```

or the equivalent shortcut (which requires you to import DBI with `use DBIqw(:sql_types)`:

```
$sth->bind_param(1, $bind_value, SQL_INTEGER);
```

Alternatively, you can use the `\%attributes` parameter, as follows:

```
$sth->bind_param(1, $bind_value, {TYPE => SQL_INTEGER});
```

This returns an integer.

For example:

```
my $hostname = 'localhost';
my $database = 'firstdb';
my $username = 'guru2b';
my $password = 'g00r002b';

# Connect to the database
my $dbh = DBI->connect("dbi:mysql:$database:$hostname", $username, ↵
 $password) or die $DBI::errstr;

# Create the query, with a ? to indicate the placeholder
my $query = 'SELECT first_name,surname FROM customer WHERE id=?';

# Prepare the query
my $sth = $dbh->prepare($query);

# Create an array of id's to use to replace the placeholder
my @ids = (1,4,5,6);

# Loop through the array and execute the query
for(@ids) {
  $sth->bind_param(1, $_, SQL_INTEGER);
  $sth->execute();

  my( $first_name, $surname);
  $sth->bind_columns(undef, \$first_name, \$surname);

  # Loop through the rows returned and display the results
  while( $sth->fetch()) {
    print "$first_name $surname\n";
  }
}
$sth->finish();
```

## bind_param_array

```
$rc = $sth->bind_param_array($p_num, $array_ref_or_value
  [, \%attributes | $bind_type])
```

Used to bind an array to a placeholder set in the prepared statement, ready for execution with the execute_array() method.

For example:

```
# set RaiseError to 1 to avoid having to check each method call
$dbh->{RaiseError} = 1;
$sth = $dbh->prepare("INSERT INTO customer(first_name, surname) VALUES(?, ?)");
# Each array must have the same number of elements
```

```
$sth->bind_param_array(1, [ 'Lyndon', 'Nkosi', 'Buhle' ]);
$sth->bind_param_array(2, [ 'Khumalo', 'Battersby', 'Lauria' ]);
my %tuple_status;
$sth->execute_array(\%tuple_status);
```

### bind_param_inout

```
$rv = $sth->bind_param_inout($p_num, \$bind_value,
  $max_len [, \%attributes | $bind_type])     or ...
```

The same as the bind_param() method, but you can update values (for stored procedures). MySQL does not currently support this.

### dump_results

```
$rows = $sth->dump_results($max_len, $lsep, $fsep, $fh);
```

Outputs all rows from the statement handle to $fh (default STDOUT) after calling DBI::neat_list for each row. $lsep is the row separator (with a default of \n), $fsep the field separator, with a default of comma ( , ), and the $max_len defaults to 35.

### execute

```
$rv = $sth->execute([@bind_values]);
```

Executes a prepared statement and returns the number of rows affected (for a query that doesn't return data, such as INSERT or UPDATE). Returns 0E0 (treated as true) if no rows are affected or undef if an error occurs. Use one of the fetch methods to process the data.

This returns an integer.

For example:

```
my $hostname = 'localhost'
my $database = 'firstdb';
my $username = 'guru2b';
my $password = 'g00r002b';

# Connect to the database
my $dbh = DBI->connect("dbi:mysql:$database:$hostname", $username, $password);

# Create the query, with a ? to indicate the placeholder
my $query = 'SELECT first_name,surname FROM customer WHERE id=2';

# Prepare and execute the query
my $sth = $dbh->prepare($query);
$sth->execute();

my( $first_name, $surname);
$sth->bind_columns(undef, \$first_name, \$surname);
```

```
# Loop through the rows returned and display the results
while( $sth->fetch()) {
  print "$first_name $surname\n";
}

$sth->finish();
```

### execute_array

```
$rv = $sth->execute_array(\%attributes[, @bind_values]);
```

Executes a prepared statement for each parameter set with bind_param_array() or in @bind_values and returns the total number of rows affected.

### fetch

An alias for fetchrow_arrayref().

### fetchall_arrayref

```
$table = $sth->fetchall_arrayref [[($slice[, $max_rows])];
```

Returns all rows returned from the query as a reference to an array containing one reference per row.

If no rows are returned, it returns a reference to an empty array. If an error occurs, it returns the data fetched until the error, if any.

The optional $slice can be an array reference or a hash reference. If it's an array reference, the method uses fetchall_arrayref to fetch each row as an array ref. If an index is specified, then it returns fields (starting at 0). If there are no parameters, or if $slice is undefined, the method works as if passed an empty array ref.

If $slice is a hash reference, the method uses fetchall_hashref to fetch each row as a hash reference. The fields returned will be based upon the hash keys. The hash value should always be 1.

Some examples will make this clearer. The first two examples will return references to an array of array references. First, to return just the second field of every row, use the following:

```
$tbl_ary_ref = $sth->fetchall_arrayref([1]);
```

To return the third last and last field of every row, use the following:

```
$tbl_ary_ref = $sth->fetchall_arrayref([-3,-1]);
```

The next two examples return a reference to an array of hash references. First, to fetch all fields of all rows as a hash ref, use this:

```
$tbl_ary_ref = $sth->fetchall_arrayref({});
```

To fetch only the fields called fname and sname of each row as a hash ref, with the keys named as FNAME and sname, use the following:

```
$tbl_ary_ref = $sth->fetchall_arrayref({ FNAME=>1, sname=>1 });
```

If the optional $max_rows is defined as a positive integer (it can be zero), the number of rows returned are limited to this number. You can call `fetchall_arrayref` again to return more rows. You'd use this if you don't have enough memory to return all the rows at once but still want the performance benefit of `fetchall_arrayref`.

### fetchall_hashref

```
$hash_ref = $dbh->fetchall_hashref($key_field);
```

Returns a reference to a hash that contains one entry per row at most. If the query returns no rows, the method returns a reference to an empty hash. If an error occurs, it returns the data fetched until the error, if any.

The $key_field parameter specifies the fieldname that holds the value to be used for the key for the returned hash, or it can be a number corresponding to a field (note that this starts at 1, not 0). The method returns an error if the key does not match a field, either as a name or a number.

You'd normally only use this when the key field value for each row is unique; otherwise the values for the second and subsequent rows overwrite earlier ones of the same key.

For example:

```
$dbh->{FetchHashKeyName} = 'NAME_lc';
$sth = $dbh->prepare("SELECT id, fname, sname FROM tname");
$hash_ref = $sth->fetchall_hashref('id');
print "The surname for id 8: $hash_ref->{8}->{sname}";.
```

### fetchrow_array

```
@row = $sth->fetchrow_array;
```

Returns an array of field values from the next row of data, using a previously prepared statement handle. The elements of the row can then be accessed as $row[0], $row[1], and so on. This moves the row pointer so that the next call to this method will return the following row.

### fetchrow_arrayref

```
$row_ref = $sth->fetchrow_arrayref
```

Returns a reference to an array of field values from the next row of data, using a previously prepared statement handle. The elements of the row can then be accessed as $row_ref->[0], $row_ref->[1], and so on.

This moves the row pointer so that the next call to this method will return the following row.

### fetchrow_hashref

```
$hash_ref = $sth->fetchrow_hashref[($name)];
```

Returns a reference to a hash table with the fieldname as key and field contents as value, using a previously prepared statement handle. The elements of the row can then be accessed as $hash_ref->{fieldname1}, $hash_ref->{fieldname2}, and so on.

This moves the row pointer so that the next call to this method will return the following row.

The optional `name` parameter specifies the name the attributes will be given. It defaults to `NAME`, though `NAME_uc` or `NAME_lc` (uppercase or lowercase) is suggested for portability.

The `fetchrow_arrayref` and `fetchrow_array` methods are markedly quicker.

### finish

```
$rc = $sth->finish;
```

Frees system resources associated with a statement handle, indicating that no more data will be returned from it.

Returns true if successful or false if not.

### rows

```
$rv = $sth->rows;
```

Returns the number of rows changed by the last SQL statement (after an `UPDATE` or `INSERT` statement, for example) or −1 if the number is unknown.

## DBI Attributes Common to All Handles

These attributes provide information and can apply to all handles. The most common are those used for error handling, `RaiseError` and `PrintError`. For example, `$h->{'RaiseError'}` causes errors to that handle to raise exceptions.

### Active

```
Active (boolean, read-only)
```

True if the handle object is active (connected to a database for a database handle or with more data to fetch for a statement handle).

### ActiveKids (integer, read-only)

```
ActiveKids (integer, read-only)
```

The number of current active database handles (for a driver handle) or the number of current active statement handles for a database handle. Active means connected to a database for a database handle or with more data to fetch for a statement handle.

### CachedKids (hash ref)

```
CachedKids (hash ref)
```

For a database handle this contains a reference to a hash of statement handles created by the `prepare_cached()` method. For a driver handle, it contains a hash of database handles created by `connect_cached()`.

### ChopBlanks

```
ChopBlanks (boolean, inherited)
```

Specifies whether the various fetch methods will chop leading and trailing blanks from CHAR fields. Set to true if they will and false (the default) if not.

### CompatMode (boolean, inherited)

```
CompatMode (boolean, inherited)
```

Emulation layers ensure compatible behavior in the driver.

### FetchHashKeyName

```
FetchHashKeyName (string, inherited)
```

Specifies which attribute name the fetchrow_hashref() method uses to get the fieldnames for the hash keys. It defaults to NAME, but you should instead set it to NAME_lc or NAME_uc for portability.

### HandleError

```
HandleError (code ref, inherited)
```

Allows you to create your own way to handle errors. You can set it to a reference to a subroutine, which will be called when an error is detected (when RaiseError and PrintError would be called). If the subroutine returns false, then RaiseError and PrintError are checked, as normal. The subroutine is called with three parameters, the error message string (the same as RaiseError and PrintError would use), the DBI handle, and the first value returned by the failed method.

### InactiveDestroy

```
InactiveDestroy (boolean)
```

Designed for Unix applications that fork child processes. False (the default) indicates that a handle is destroyed automatically when it passes out of scope. True indicates that the handle is not automatically destroyed.

### Kids

```
Kids (integer, read-only)
```

Contains the number of current database handles (for a driver handle) or the number of current statement handles for a database handle.

### LongReadLen

```
LongReadLen (unsigned integer, inherited)
```

Controls the maximum length of long fields (BLOB and TEXT). It should be set to slightly more than the longest field. Setting it to 0 means long data will not automatically be fetched (in other words, fetch() will return undef—rather than the field's actual value—when processing long fields). Setting it too much larger is a waste of memory.

### LongTruncOK

```
LongTruncOk (boolean, inherited)
```

False (the default) indicates that attempting to fetch long values longer than LongReadLen will cause the fetch to fail. True will return a truncated value.

### PrintError

```
PrintError (boolean, inherited)
```

When set to true (the default), errors in a method generate a warning. Usually set to false when RaiseError is set to true.

### private_*

```
private_*
```

You can store extra information of your own as a private attribute in a DBI handle by specifying a name beginning with private_. You should name it in the manner private_your_module_name_ description, and use just one attribute.

Because of the way the Perl tie mechanism works, you cannot reliably use the ||= operator directly to initialize the attribute.

To initialize, use a two-step approach like this:

```
my $descriptive_name = $dbh->{private_your_module_name_descriptive_name};
$descriptive_name ||= $dbh->{↩
  private_your_module_name_descriptive_name } = { ... };
```

You cannot use the following as you may expect:

```
my $descriptive_name = $dbh->{↩
  private_your_module_name_descriptive_name } ||= { ... };
```

### Profile

```
Profile (inherited)
```

Allows method call timing statistics to be reported. See the DBI::Profile documentation for more details.

### RaiseError

```
RaiseError (boolean, inherited)
```

False by default; when set to true this will cause errors to raise exceptions rather than just returning error codes. Usually `PrintError` is set to false when `RaiseError` is true.

### *ShowErrorStatement*

```
ShowErrorStatement (boolean, inherited)
```

When true, appends the statement text to the error messages from `RaiseError` and `PrintError`. It applies to statement handle errors and `prepare()`, `do()`, and select database handle methods.

### *Taint*

```
Taint (boolean, inherited)
```

If set to true, and Perl is running in taint mode (`-T`), all data from the database is treated as being tainted as are arguments to most DBI methods. It defaults to false. More data may be treated as tainted at a later stage, so use `Taint` carefully!

### *TraceLevel*

```
TraceLevel (integer, inherited)
```

Setting this is an alternative to using the `trace()` method to set the DBI trace level. The trace level can be from 0 to 9, with 0 disabling tracing, 1 best for a general overview, 2 being the most commonly used, and the other methods adding more and more driver and DBI detail.

### *Warn*

```
Warn (boolean, inherited)
```

True by default, enables warnings. You can use `$SIG{__WARN__}` to catch warnings.

## Database Handle Attributes

Database handle attributes are those available only to a database handle.

### *AutoCommit*

```
AutoCommit (boolean)
```

If set to true, then SQL statements are automatically committed. If false, they are part of a transaction by default and need to be committed or rolled back.

### *Driver*

```
Driver (handle)
```

Contains the handle of the parent driver.

For example:
```
$dbh->{Driver}->{Name}
```

### Name

```
Name (string)
```

The database name.

### RowCacheSize

```
RowCacheSize (integer)
```

The size the application would like the local row cache to be or `undef` if the row cache is not implemented. Setting it to a negative number specifies memory size to be used for caching, 0 has the size automatically determined, 1 disables the cache, and a larger positive number is the size of the cache in rows.

### Statement

```
Statement (string, read-only)
```

The most recent SQL statement passed to `prepare()`.

## Statement Handle Attributes

These attributes apply to statement handles that have been returned from a prepared query. Most of them are read-only and are specific to the statement handle.

### CursorName

```
CursorName (string, read-only)
```

The name of the cursor associated with the statement handle or `undef` if it cannot be obtained.

### NAME

```
NAME (array-ref, read-only)
```

A reference to an array of fieldnames. Names can be uppercase, lowercase, or mixed case. Instead, use `NAME_lc` or `NAME_uc` for portability across systems.

For example, to display the second column, use the following:

```
$sth = $dbh->prepare("select * from customer");
$sth->execute;
@row = $sth->fetchrow_array;
print "Column 2: $sth->{NAME}->[1]";
```

### NAME_hash

```
NAME_hash (hash-ref, read-only)
```

Fieldname information returned as reference to a hash. Names can be uppercase, lowercase, or mixed case. The keys of the hash are the fieldnames, and the values are the field index (from 0 for the first field). Instead, use `NAME_hash_lc` or `NAME_hash_uc` for portability across systems.

For example:

```
$sth = $dbh->prepare("select first_name, surname from customer");
$sth->execute;
@row = $sth->fetchrow_array;
print "First name: $row[$sth->{NAME_hash}{first_name}]\n";
print "Surname: $row[$sth->{NAME_hash}{surname}]\n";
```

### NAME_lc

```
NAME_lc (array-ref, read-only)
```

The same as `NAME` but only returns lowercase names.

### NAME_lc_hash

```
NAME_lc_hash (hash-ref, read-only)
```

The same as `NAME_hash` but only returns lowercase names.

### NAME_uc

```
NAME_uc (array-ref, read-only)
```

The same as `NAME` but only returns lowercase names.

### NAME_uc_hash

```
NAME_uc_hash (hash-ref, read-only)
```

The same as `NAME_hash` but only returns uppercase names.

### NULLABLE

```
NULLABLE (array-ref, read-only)
```

A reference to an array of whether the field can contain nulls. Will contain 0 for no, 1 for yes, and 2 for unknown.

For example:

```
print "Field 1 can contain a NULL" if $sth->{NULLABLE}->[0];
```

### NUM_OF_FIELDS

```
NUM_OF_FIELDS (integer, read-only)
```

The number of fields that the prepared statement will return. It will be 0 for statements that do not return fields (`INSERT`, `UPDATE`, and so on).

### NUM_OF_PARAMS

```
NUM_OF_PARAMS (integer, read-only)
```

The number of placeholders in the prepared statement.

### ParamValues

```
ParamValues (hash ref, read-only)
```

A reference to a hash containing the values bound to placeholders or `undef` if not available.

### PRECISION

```
PRECISION (array-ref, read-only)
```

This is a reference to an array of integers for each field, referring to either the maximum length of the field (nonnumeric fields) or the maximum number of significant digits (not the display size—it excludes the sign, decimal point, E character, and so on).

### RowsInCache

```
RowsInCache (integer, read-only)
```

The number of unfetched rows in the cache or `undef` if the driver does not support a local row cache.

### SCALE

```
SCALE (array-ref, read-only)
```

Returns a reference to an array of integer values for each column. `NULL` (`undef`) values indicate columns where scale is not applicable.

### Statement

```
Statement (string, read-only)
```

The last SQL query passed to the `prepare()` method.

### TYPE

```
TYPE (array-ref, read-only)
```

A reference to an array of integer values (representing the data type) for each field.

## Dynamic Attributes

These are attributes that have a short lifespan and are only available immediately after being set. They apply to the handle that's just been returned.

### *err*

```
$DBI::err
```

The same as $handle->err.

### *errstr*

```
$DBI::errstr
```

The same as $handle->errstr.

### *lasth*

```
$DBI::lasth
```

Returns the DBI handle used with the most recent DBI method call or the parent of the handle (if it exists) if the method call was a DESTROY.

### *rows*

```
$DBI::rows
```

The same as $handle->rows.

### *state*

```
$DBI::state
```

The same as $handle->state.

## A Short Perl DBI Example

Listing D.1 connects to a server, prepares a query with a placeholder, binds a number of values to this placeholder, and then loops through each row and each query to display the results.

**LISTING D.1:** *EXAMPLE.PL*

```perl
#!/usr/bin/perl -w

use strict;  # you don't have to use strict, but you should!
use DBI;     # the main module
```

```perl
# set variables with the connection details
my $hostname = 'localhost';
my $database = 'firstdb';
my $username = 'guru2b';
my $password = 'g00r002b';

#Connect to the database
my $dbh = DBI->connect("dbi:mysql:$database:$hostname", $username, $password);

# Define and prepare the query, with the ? specifying a bind variable.
my $sql = q{SELECT first_name,surname FROM customer WHERE id=?};
my $sth = $dbh->prepare($sql);

# Create an array of id's to use to replace the placeholder
my @ids = (1,4,5,6);

# Loop through the array and execute the query
for(@ids) {
  $sth->bind_param(1, $_, SQL_INTEGER);
  $sth->execute();

  my( $first_name, $surname);
  $sth->bind_columns(undef, \$first_name, \$surname);

  # Loop through the rows returned and display the results
  while( $sth->fetch()) {
    print "$first_name $surname\n";
  }
}
$sth->finish();

$dbh->disconnect;
```

# Appendix E

# Python Database API

PYTHON USES THE DATABASE-INDEPENDENT DB-API for its database connectivity. For MySQL specifically, it uses the MySQLdb module. The latest version of the API (at the time of this writing) is Python Database API Specification 2.0. It's still a fairly new API, and many features available in other APIs have not yet been implemented. However, its simplicity makes it easy to learn and use.

You can find MySQLdb and full installation instructions at `http://sourceforge.net/projects/mysql-python/`.

## Attributes

Attributes can be available to the entire module, or they can be specific to a cursor. This section describes the available attributes according to how they are available.

### Module Attributes

These attributes are available to the entire module.

#### APILEVEL

A string constant containing the supported version of the DB-API (`2.0` if you're using the version 2.0, for example).

#### CONV

Maps MySQL types to Python objects. This defaults to `MySQLdb.converters.conversions`.

#### PARAMSTYLE

A string constant containing the type of parameter marker (placeholder) formatting that the interface uses. This can be `format`, for example:

```
...WHERE fieldname=%s
```

or it can be `pyformat`, for example:

```
...WHERE fieldname=%(name)s
```

### *THREADSAFETY*

An integer constant containing the level of thread safety. It can be 0 (no thread sharing), 1 (threads can share the module only), 2 (threads can share the module and the connections), or 3 (threads can share the module, connections, and cursors). The default is 1.

## Cursor Attributes

These attributes are specific to a cursor object, returned from the `cursor()` method.

### *ARRAYSIZE*

Specifies the number of rows returned by the `fetchmany()` method, and affects the `fetchall()` method's performance. This defaults to 1, or one row at a time.

### *DESCRIPTION*

This attribute is read only and is a sequence of sequences describing the columns in the current result set, each with seven items. These are `name`, `type_code`, `display_size`, `internal_size`, `precision`, `scale`, and `null_ok`.

The `name` and `type_code` items are mandatory, and the rest are set to `None` if there are no meaningful values for them.

This is set to `None` if the query does not return any rows or has not yet been invoked.

### *ROWCOUNT*

This attribute is read only, and it indicates the number of rows the last query affected or returned, or it returns −1 if the number of rows is unknown or a query has not been invoked.

# Methods

Methods can be available to the entire module to a connection or a cursor. This section describes the various methods according to whether they are module, connection, or cursor methods.

## Module Methods

Module methods are available to the entire module. The most important is the `connect()` method:

```
dbh = MySQLdb.connect(parameters)
```

Connects to the specified hostname and database with the specified username and password, returning a connection object (or database handle). The parameters include the following:

**host**   Defaults to the localhost.

**user**   Defaults to the current user.

**passwd**   No default (empty password).

**db**   No default.

**conv**   Dictionary to map literals to the Python type. It defaults to `MySQLdb.converters.conversions`.

**cursorclass**   The class that `cursor()` uses. It defaults to `MySQLdb.cursors.Cursor`.

**compress**   Enables protocol compression.

**named_pipe**   On Windows, connects with a named pipe.

**init_command**   Specifies a statement for the database server to run as soon as the connection is created.

**read_default_file**   The MySQL configuration file to use.

**read_default_group**   The default group to read.

**unix_socket**   On Unix, connects using the specified socket. It uses TCP by default.

**port**   Defaults to 3306.

For example:

```
dbh = MySQLdb.connect(user='guru2b', passwd='g00r002b', 
    host='test.host.co.za', db='firstdb')
```

## Connection Methods

These methods are for use on a connection object, returned from the `MySQLdb.connect()` method. You'll almost always use the `cursor()` and `close()` methods. The `commit()` and `rollback()` methods are used only for transactions.

### BEGIN

```
dbh.begin()
```

Begins a transaction, turning off `AUTOCOMMIT` if it's on, until the transaction ends with a call to `commit()` or `rollback()`.

### CLOSE

```
dbh.close()
```

Closes the connection and frees the associated resources.

### COMMIT

```
dbh.commit()
```

Commits any open transactions.

### CURSOR

```
dbh.cursor([cursorClass])
```

Returns a new cursor object (which provides methods to access and manipulate data). You can specify a different class, if you want (by default it's the `cursorclass` specified in the connection, which defaults to the `Cursor` class).

### ROLLBACK

```
dbh.rollback()
```

Rolls back any open transactions. Closing the connection without explicitly calling this method will implicitly call rollback for any open transactions.

## Cursor Methods

These methods are for accessing and manipulating data; they work on a cursor object, returned from the cursor() method.

### CLOSE

```
cursor.close()
```

Immediately frees resources associated with the cursor.

### EXECUTE

```
cursor.execute(query[,parameters])
```

Prepares and executes a database query. The method also allows you to use placeholders to optimize repeat queries of a similar type by specifying various parameters. Placeholders are usually marked with a question mark (?), but MySQLdb does not currently support this. You need to use %s to indicate a placeholder (if the paramstyle attribute is set to format) because MySQLdb treats all values as strings no matter what type the fields actually are.

For example:

```
cursor.execute('INSERT INTO customer(first_name,surname) VALUES↵
 (%s, %s)',('Mike', 'Harksen'))
```

You can also use a Python mapping as the second argument if you set MySQLdb.paramstyle = 'pyformat'.

You can use lists of tuples as the second parameter, but this usage is deprecated. Use executemany instead.

### EXECUTEMANY

```
cursor.executemany(query,seq_of_parameters)
```

Prepares a database query and then runs multiple instances with placeholders to optimize repeats of similar queries.

For example:

```
cursor.executemany('INSERT INTO customer(first_name,surname) VALUES↵
 (%s, %s)',(('Mike', 'Harksen'),( 'Mndeni', 'Vidal'),( 'John', 'Vilakazi')))
```

You can also use a Python mapping as the second set of arguments if you set MySQLdb.paramstyle = 'pyformat'.

### FETCHALL

```
cursor.fetchall()
```

Fetches all rows of a query result (from the current row pointer), returning them as a sequence of sequences (list of tuples).

The `arraysize` attribute of the cursor can affect the method's performance.

This throws an exception if there's an error.

For example:

```python
cursor.execute("SELECT first_name, surname FROM customer")
for row in cursor.fetchall():
    print "Firstname: ", row[0]
    print "Surname: ", row[1]
```

### FETCHMANY

```python
cursor.fetchmany([size=cursor.arraysize]);
```

Fetches a number of rows from a query result, returning a sequence of sequences (list of tuples). You specify the number of rows with the optional size parameter or the cursor's `arraysize` if not specified. The method will not return more rows than are available.

It's best to use the `arraysize` attribute for performance reasons or to keep the size parameter the same between `fetchmany` calls.

This throws an exception if there's an error.

### FETCHONE

```python
cursor.fetchone()
```

Returns the next row from a query result set.

This throws an exception if there's an error.

For example:

```python
cursor.execute("SELECT first_name, surname FROM customer")
row = cursor.fetchone():
    print "Firstname: ", row[0]
    print "Surname: ", row[1]
```

### INSERT_ID

```python
cursor.insert_id()
```

A non-DB-API standard method that returns the previous `AUTO_INCREMENT` field value.

### NEXTSET, SETINPUTSIZES, AND SETOUPUTSIZES

```python
cursor.nextset()
```

These standard methods are not currently used for MySQL.

## A Short Python Example

Listing E.1 runs you through the basics of connecting, running queries, and processing results.

**LISTING E.1:** EXAMPLE.PY

```python
#!/usr/bin/env python

import MySQLdb
dbh = None
try:
    dbh = MySQLdb.connect(user='guru2b', passwd='g00r002b',↵
      host='test.host.co.za', db='firstdb')
except:
    print "Could not connect to MySQL server."
    exit(0)

try:
    cursor = dbh.cursor()
    cursor.execute("UPDATE customer SET surname='Arendse' WHERE↵
      surname='Burger'")
    print "Rows updated: ", cursor.rowcount
    cursor.close()
except:
    print "Could not update the table."

try:
    cursor = dbh.cursor()
    cursor.execute("SELECT first_name,surname FROM customer")
    for row in cursor.fetchall():
        print "Name: ", row[0], row[1]
    dbh.close()
except:
    print "Failed to perform query"
    dbh.close()
```

# Appendix F

# Java API

JAVA USES THE WELL-DEVELOPED JDBC API for database access. There are two main MySQL drivers: the "official" MySQL Connector/J (what was MM.MySQL), available for download from the MySQL site, and the Caucho MySQL JDBC Driver.

The basic procedure is to instantiate a connection object, a statement object, and then a result set object.

This appendix briefly describes the main methods used for database functionality in Java and provides a simple example for inserting and selecting data.

## General Methods

This section describes some sundry methods for connecting or for accessing configuration data from a file.

### getBundle

```
bundle.getBundle(filename)
```

Loads data from a properties file called `Config.properties`. Although not JDBC specific, it would be used when storing connection data in a configuration file.

For example, `Config.properties` contains the following:

```
Driver = com.mysql.jdbc.Driver
Conn = jdbc:mysql://test.host.com/firstdb?user=guru2b&password=g00r002b
```

The main program then contains the following:

```
ResourceBundle rb = ResourceBundle.getBundle("Conn");
String conn = rb.getString("Conn");
...
Class.forName(rb.getString("Driver"));
Connection = DriverManager.getConnection(conn);
```

### getConnection

```
DriverManager.getConnection(connection_details)
```

Requests a connection with the specified details, returning a connection object. Depending on the driver you use, the connection details will be specified in slightly different ways. For the Caucho driver, the format is as follows:

```
jdbc:mysql-caucho://host_name[:port]/database_name
```

For example:

```
Connection connection = DriverManager.getConnection("jdbc:mysql-caucho://↵
    test.host.co.za/firstdb", "guru2b", "g00r002b");
```

The Connector/J driver uses a slightly different format, as follows:

```
jdbc:mysql://[host_name][:port]/database_name[?property1=value1][&property=value2]
```

The properties can be any of the ones listed in Table F.1, although you'll mostly just use the password and username.

**TABLE F.1:** CONNECTION PROPERTIES

| NAME | DESCRIPTION |
| --- | --- |
| autoReconnect | Automatically attempts to connect again when the connection dies. Defaults to false. |
| characterEncoding | When Unicode is the character set, specifies the Unicode encoding to use. |
| initialTimeout | The time in seconds to wait between reconnection attempts. The default is 2. |
| maxReconnects | The maximum number of reconnection attempts. The default is 3. |
| maxRows | The maximum number of rows to return for a query or 0 (the default) for all rows. |
| password | The user's password (no default). |
| useUnicode | Specifies that Unicode be used as the character set for the connection. Defaults to false. |
| user | The user to connect as (no default). |

For example:

```
DriverManager.getConnection("jdbc:mysql://↵
    test.host.co.za/firstdb?user=guru2b&password=g00r002b");
```

### getString

```
bundle.getString(string)
```

See `getBundle` for an example of reading data from a configuration file.

# Connection Methods

The connection methods require a valid connection, returned from the `getConnection()` method.

### clearWarnings

```
connection.clearWarnings()
```

Clears all warnings for the connection, returning a void.

### close

```
connection.close()
```

Closes the database connection and frees all connection resources, returning a void.

### commit

```
connection.commit()
```

Commits open transactions.

### createStatement

```
connection.createStatement([int resultSetType, int resultSetConcurrency])
```

Returns a `Statement` object, which is a mechanism for passing queries to the database, and receives results back, through its connection object. With the optional arguments, the generated `ResultSet` objects will have the specified type and concurrency.

### getAutoCommit

```
connection.getAutoCommit()
```

Returns true if `AutoCommit` mode is set for the connection and false if it is not.

### getMetaData

```
connection.getMetaData()
```

Returns a database metadata object containing metadata about the database with which the connection has been made.

### getTransactionIsolation

```
connection.getTransactionIsolation()
```

Returns an integer containing the transaction isolation level for the connection. The transaction isolation levels can be one of the following: TRANSACTION_READ_UNCOMMITTED, TRANSACTION_READ_COMMITTED, TRANSACTION_REPEATABLE_READ, TRANSACTION_SERIALIZABLE, or TRANSACTION_NONE.

### getTypeMap

```
connection.getTypeMap
```

Returns a Map object associated with the connection.

### isClosed

```
connection.isClosed()
```

Returns true if the connection has been closed and false if it's still open.

### isReadOnly

```
connection.isReadOnly()
```

Returns true if the connection is read only and false if not.

### nativeSQL

```
connection.nativeSQL(String sql)
```

Returns a string with the supplied string converted to the system's native SQL.

### prepareStatement

```
connection.prepareStatement(String sql)
```

Prepares the statement to be sent to the database, which means you can make use of placeholders (or parameters). Use the setInt() and setString() methods to set the values of the parameters.

### rollback

```
connection.rollback()
```

Undoes all changes in the current transaction.

### setAutoCommit

```
connection.setAutoCommit(boolean mode)
```

Sets the connection's AutoCommit mode (true if set, false if not).

### setReadOnly

```
connection.setReadOnly(boolean mode)
```

Passing the method true sets the connection to read-only mode.

### setTransactionIsolation

```
connection.setTransactionIsolation(int level)
```

The level can be one of the following: `connection.TRANSACTION_READ_UNCOMMITTED`, `connection.TRANSACTION_READ_COMMITTED`, `connection.TRANSACTION_REPEATABLE_READ`, or `connection.TRANSACTION_SERIALIZABLE`.

### setTypeMap

```
connection.setTypeMap(Map map)
```

Sets the type Map object for the connection.

## Statement and Prepared Statement Methods

These methods must be invoked via a valid `Statement` or `PreparedStatement` object.

Most of these methods apply to both statements and prepared statements. Those with `preparedstatement` as an object can only be called with a prepared statement, and the methods with `statement` as an object can be called by either.

### addBatch

```
statement.addBatch(String sql)
preparedstatement.addBatch()
```

Adds the SQL statement to a current list of statements, which can then be executed with the `executeBatch()` method.

### clearBatch

```
statement.clearBatch()
```

Clears the list of statements in the batch that have been added by the `addBatch()` method.

### clearWarnings

```
statement.clearWarnings()
```

Clears all the warnings associated with the statement.

### close

```
statement.close()
```

Frees all resources associated with the statement.

### execute

```
statement.execute(String sql [,int autoGeneratedKeys | int[] columnIndexes⤦
  | String[] columnNames])
preparestatement.execute()
```

Executes a SQL statement. It returns true if the query returns a result set (such as for a `SELECT` statement), and returns false if no result set was produced (such as for an `INSERT` or `UPDATE` statement).

The options indicate that auto-generated keys should be made available for retrieval—either all of them or all in the integer or string arrays, respectively.

### executeBatch

```
statement.executeBatch()
```

Executes all statements in the batch (added by addBatch), returning an integer array of update counts, or returning false if any of the statements did not execute correctly.

### executeQuery

```
statement.executeQuery(String sql)
preparedstatement.executeQuery()
```

Executes a query that returns data (such as SELECT or SHOW) and returns a single result set.

### executeUpdate

```
statement.executeUpdate(String sql)
preparedstatement.executeUpdate()
```

Executes a query that modifies data (such as UPDATE, INSERT, or ALTER) and returns the number of rows affected.

### getConnection

```
statement.getConnection()
```

Returns the connection object that created the statement.

### getFetchSize

```
statement.getFetchSize()
```

Returns as an integer the number of the default fetch size for a ResultSet object from this statement.

### getMaxFieldSize

```
statement.getMaxFieldSize()
```

Returns as an integer the maximum number of bytes that can be returned for character and binary column values for a ResultSet object from this statement.

### getMaxRows

```
statement.getMaxRows()
```

Returns as an integer the maximum number of rows it's possible for a ResultSet object from this statement to contain.

### getMoreResults

```
statement.getMoreResults([int current])
```

Moves to the next result from the statement, returning true if there is another valid ResultSet, or returning false if not. If there's no parameter, any current ResultSet objects are closed; otherwise they are dealt with according to the value of current (which can be CLOSE_CURRENT_RESULT, KEEP_CURRENT_RESULT, or CLOSE_ALL_RESULTS).

### getQueryTimeout

```
statement.getQueryTimeout()
```

Returns the number of seconds the driver will wait for a query to execute before it times out.

### getResultSet

```
statement.getResultSet()
```

Returns a result set from the current statement.

### getResultSetType

```
statement.getResultSetType()
```

Returns the type for ResultSet objects for the current statement.

### getUpdateCount

```
statement.getUpdateCount()
```

Retrieves the current result as an update count; if the result is a ResultSet object or there are no more results, –1 is returned.

### setXXX

```
preparedstatement.setXXX(int parameter, xxx value)
```

Sets a parameter in a previously prepared statement. The parameters start at 1. The value is of the appropriate type (see Table F.2).

**TABLE F.2:** SQL Types and the Equivalent Set Methods

| SQL TYPE | JAVA METHOD |
| --- | --- |
| BIGINT | setLong() |
| BINARY | setBytes() |
| BIT | setBoolean() |

*Continued on next page*

**TABLE F.2:** SQL TYPES AND THE EQUIVALENT SET METHODS *(continued)*

| SQL TYPE | JAVA METHOD |
| --- | --- |
| BLOB | SetBlob() |
| CHAR | setString() |
| DATE | setDate() |
| DECIMAL | setBigDecimal() |
| DOUBLE | setDouble() |
| FLOAT | setDouble() |
| INTEGER | setInt() |
| LONGVARBINARY | setBytes() |
| LONGVARCHAR | setString() |
| NUMERIC | setBigDecimal() |
| OTHER | setObject() |
| REAL | setFloat() |
| SMALLINT | setShort() |
| TIME | setTime() |
| TIMESTAMP | setTimestamp() |
| TINYINT | setByte() |
| VARBINARY | setBytes() |
| VARCHAR | setString() |

For example:

```
preparedstatement = connection.prepareStatement("UPDATE customer⤸
  SET surname = ? WHERE id=?");
preparedstatement.setString(1,"Burger");
preparedstatement.setInt(2,9);
preparedstatement.executeUpdate();
```

### setCursorName

```
statement.setCursorName(String cursorname)
```

Sets the SQL cursor name to be used by later **execute()** methods.

### setEscapeProcessing

```
statement.setEscapeProcessing(boolean mode)
```

Sets escape processing (if mode is true) or disables it (if mode is false). The default is true. Escape processing has no effect with PreparedStatement objects.

### setFetchSize

```
statement.setFetchSize(int size)
```

Gives the driver an idea of how many rows should be returned from the database when more rows are needed for the statement.

### setMaxFieldSize

```
statement.setMaxFieldSize(int limit)
```

Sets the maximum number of bytes in a binary or character ResultSet column.

### setMaxRows

```
statement.setMaxRows(int limit)
```

Sets the maximum number of rows that a ResultObject can contain.

### setQueryTimeout

```
statement.setQueryTimeout(int seconds)
```

Sets the number of seconds the driver will wait for a query to execute before it times out.

## *ResultSet* Methods

These methods require a valid ResultSet object, returned from the getResultSet() method.

### absolute

```
resultset.absolute(int row)
```

Moves the cursor to the specified row from the result set (rows start at 1). You can use a negative number to move to a row starting from the end of the result set. Returns true if the cursor is on the row, false if not.

### afterLast

```
resultset.afterlast()
```

Moves the cursor to the end of the result set.

### beforeFirst

```
resultset.beforeFirst()
```

Moves the cursor to the start of the result set.

### cancelRowUpdates

```
resultset.cancelRowUpdates()
```

Cancels updates made to the current row in the result set.

### close

```
resultset.close()
```

Closes the result set and frees all associated resources.

### deleteRow

```
resultset.deleteRow()
```

Deletes the current ResultSet row from the database (and the result set).

### findColumn

```
resultset.findColumn(String field_name)
```

Maps the fieldname to the column in the result set and returns the column index as an integer.

### first

```
resultset.first()
```

Moves the cursor to the first row in the result set. Returns true if there is a valid first row, false if not.

### getXXX

```
resultset.getXXX(String fieldname | int fieldindex)
```

Returns the contents of a field of the specified type. You can identify the field by its name or its position.

Table F.3 shows the SQL types and their equivalent Java methods.

**TABLE F.3:** SQL TYPES AND EQUIVALENT GET METHODS

| SQL TYPE | JAVA METHOD |
| --- | --- |
| BIGINT | getLong() |
| BINARY | getBytes() |
| BIT | getBoolean() |
| BLOB | getBlob() |

*Continued on next page*

**TABLE F.3:** SQL TYPES AND EQUIVALENT GET METHODS *(continued)*

| SQL TYPE | JAVA METHOD |
|---|---|
| CHAR | getString() |
| DATE | getDate() |
| DECIMAL | getBigDecimal() |
| DOUBLE | getDouble() |
| FLOAT | getDouble() |
| INTEGER | getInt() |
| LONGVARBINARY | getBytes() |
| LONGVARCHAR | getString() |
| NUMERIC | getBigDecimal() |
| OTHER | getObject() |
| REAL | getFloat() |
| SMALLINT | getShort() |
| TIME | getTime() |
| TIMESTAMP | getTimestamp() |
| TINYINT | getByte() |
| VARBINARY | getBytes() |
| VARCHAR | getString() |

## getCursorName

    resultset.getCursorName()

Returns the name of the cursor used by the result set.

## getFetchSize

    resultset.getFetchSize()

Returns the fetch size for the result set object.

## getMetaData

    resultset.getMetaData()

Returns a `ResultSetMetaData` object with the number, type, and properties of the result set's columns.

### getRow

```
resultset.getRow()
```

Returns an integer containing the current row number.

### getStatement

```
resultset.getStatement()
```

Returns the statement object that created the result set.

### getType

```
resultset.getType()
```

Returns the type of the result set object.

### getWarnings

```
resultset.getWarnings()
```

Returns the first Warning triggered by a call from a ResultSet method on this result set.

### insertRow

```
resultset.insertRow()
```

Inserts the contents of the insert row into the database (and the result set).

### isAfterLast

```
resultet.isAfterLast()
```

Returns true if the cursor is after the last row in the result set, false if not.

### isBeforeFirst

```
resultset.isBeforeFirst()
```

Returns true if the cursor is before the first row in the result set, false if not.

### isFirst

```
resultset.isFirst()
```

Returns true if the cursor is at the first row in the result set, false if not.

### isLast

```
resultset.isLast()
```

Returns true if the cursor is at the last row in the result set, false if not.

### last

```
resultset.last()
```

Moves the cursor to the last row in the result set. Returns true if there is a valid last row, false if not.

### moveToCurrentRow

```
resultset.moveToCurrentRow()
```

Moves the cursor to the remembered cursor position, which is usually the current row. This has no effect if the cursor is not on the insert row. See the moveToInsertRow() method.

### moveToInsertRow

```
resultset.moveToInsertRow()
```

Moves the cursor to the insert row (a buffer where a new row can be placed with an update method). It remembers the current cursor position, which can be returned to with the moveToCurrentRow() method.

### next

```
resultset.next()
```

Moves the cursor to the next row in the result set and returns true if there is a next row, false if there is not (the end has been reached).
For example:

```
connection = DriverManager.getConnection(url, "guru2b", "g00r002b");
statement = connection.createStatement();
resultset = statement.executeQuery("SELECT first_name,surname FROM customer");
while(resultset.next()) {
  String first_name = resultset.getString("first_name");
  String surname = resultset.getString("surname");
  System.out.print("Name: " + first_name + " " + surname);
}
```

### previous

```
resultset.previous()
```

Moves the cursor to the previous row in the result set and returns true if there is a previous row, false if there is not (the start has been reached).
For example:

```
while(resultset.previous()) {
  ...
}
```

### refreshRow

```
resultset.refreshRow()
```

Refreshes the current result set row with the most recent value in the database.

### relative

```
resultset.relative(int rows)
```

Moves the cursor forward (if rows is positive) or backward (if rows is negative) by rows number of positions.

### rowDeleted

```
resultset.rowDeleted()
```

Returns true if a row has been detected as deleted in the result set, false if not.

### rowInserted

```
resultset.rowInserted()
```

Returns true if a row has been detected as inserted in the result set, false if not.

### rowUpdated

```
resultset.rowUpdated()
```

Returns true if a row has been detected as updated in the result set, false if not.

### setFetchSize

```
resultset.setFetchSize(int rows)
```

Gives the driver an idea of how many rows should be returned from the database when more rows are needed for the result set.

### updateXXX

Updates the field with a value of the specified type. Table F.4 shows the SQL types and their equivalent Java methods.

**TABLE F.4:** SQL Types and the Equivalent Update Methods

| SQL Type | Java Method |
|---|---|
| BIGINT | updateLong() |
| BINARY | updateBytes() |
| BIT | updateBoolean() |
| BLOB | updateBlob() |
| CHAR | updateString() |

*Continued on next page*

**TABLE F.4:** SQL Types and the Equivalent Update Methods *(continued)*

| SQL Type | Java Method |
|----------|-------------|
| DATE | updateDate() |
| DECIMAL | updateBigDecimal() |
| DOUBLE | updateDouble() |
| FLOAT | updateDouble() |
| INTEGER | updateInt() |
| LONGVARBINARY | updateBytes() |
| LONGVARCHAR | updateString() |
| NUMERIC | updateBigDecimal() |
| NULL | updateNull() |
| OTHER | updateObject() |
| REAL | updateFloat() |
| SMALLINT | updateShort() |
| TIME | updateTime() |
| TIMESTAMP | updateTimestamp() |
| TINYINT | updateByte() |
| VARBINARY | updateBytes() |
| VARCHAR | updateString() |

### updateRow

```
resultset.updateRow()
```

Updates the database with the contents of the current row of the result set.

### wasNull

```
resultSet.wasNull()
```

Returns true if the previous field read was a SQL NULL, false if not.

## ResultSetMetaData Methods

These methods require a valid ResultSetMetaData object, returned from the getMetaData() method. They get information about the results. Columns begin at 1 for purposes of counting and offsetting.

### getColumnCount

```
resultsetmetadata.getColumnCount()
```

Returns the number of columns in the result set.

### getColumnDisplaySize

```
resultsetmetadata.getColumnDisplaySize(int column)
```

Returns the maximum character width of the specified column.

### getColumnName

```
resultsetmetadata.getColumnName(int column)
```

Returns the fieldname of the specified column.

### getColumnType

```
resultsetmetadata.getColumnType(int column)
```

Returns the SQL type of the specified column.

### getColumnTypeName

```
resultsetmetadata.getColumnTypeName(int column)
```

Returns the database-specific type name of the specified column.

### getPrecision

```
resultsetmetadata.getPrecision(int column)
```

Returns the number of decimals in the specified column.

### getScale

```
resultsetmetadata.getScale(int column)
```

Returns the number of digits after the decimal point in the in the specified column.

### getTableName

```
resultsetmetadata.getTableName(int column)
```

Returns the table name owning the specified column.

### isAutoIncrement

```
resultsetmetadata.isAutoIncrement(int column)
```

Returns true if the specified column is an auto increment field, false if not.

### isCaseSensitive

```
resultsetmetadata.isCaseSensitive(int column)
```

Returns true if the specified column is case sensitive, false if not.

### isDefinitelyWritable

```
resultsetmetadata.isDefinitelyWritable(int column)
```

Returns true if a write on the specified column will succeed, false if it may not.

### isNullable

```
resultsetmetadata.isNullable(int column)
```

Returns the nullable status of the specified column, which can be `columnNoNulls`, `columnNullable`, or `columnNullableUnknown`.

### isReadOnly

```
resultsetmetadata.isReadOnly(int column)
```

Returns true if the specified column is read only, false if not.

### isSearchable

```
resultsetmetadata.isSearchable(int column)
```

Returns true if the specified column can be used in a `WHERE` clause, false if not.

### isSigned

```
resultsetmetadata.isSigned(int column)
```

Returns true if the specified column is a signed column, false if not.

### isWritable

```
resultsetmetadata.isWritable(int column)
```

Returns true if the specified column can be written to, false if not.

## SQLException Methods

You use these methods when a `SQLException` object has been created.

### getErrorCode

```
sqlexception.getErrorCode()
```

Returns the error code from the vendor.

### getMessage

```
sqlexception.getMessage()
```

Inherited from `Throwable`, this methods returns the message string for `Throwable`.

### getNextException

```
sqlexception.getNextException()
```

Returns the next `SQLException` or null if there is none.

### getSQLState

```
sqlexception.getSQLState()
```

Returns a `SQLState` identifier.

### printStackTrace

```
sqlexception.printStackTrace(PrintStream s)
```

Inherited from the `Throwable` class, this method prints the stack trace to the standard error stream.

### setNextException

```
setNextException(sqlexception e)
```

Adds a `SQLException`.

## *Warning* Methods

You use these methods when a `SQLWarning` object has been created.

### getNextWarning

```
sqlwarning.getNextWarning()
```

Returns the next `SQLWarning`, or null if there is none.

### setNextWarning

```
sqlwarning.setNextWarning(SQLWarning w)
```

Adds a `SQLWarning`.

## A Short Java Example

Listing F.1 takes three parameters on the command line, which it inserts into the `customer` table. Run it as follows:

```
% /usr/java/j2sdk1.4.1/bin/java InsertSelect 10 Leon Wyk
```

**LISTING F.1: INSERTSELECT.JAVA**

```java
import java.sql.*;
import java.util.*;

// The insertRecord class does the bare minimum for inserting a record
// and also performs a skeleton level of exception handling
public class InsertRecord {

  public static void main(String argv[]) {
    Connection dbh = null;
    ResultSet resultset;

    try {
      Class.forName("com.mysql.jdbc.Driver");
    }
    catch (Exception e) {
      System.err.println("Unable to load driver.");
      e.printStackTrace();
    }

    try {
      Statement sth,sth2;
      // connect to the database using the Connector/J driver
      dbh = DriverManager.getConnection("jdbc:mysql://
        localhost/firstdb?user=mysql");

      // instantiate the statement object, and run the query (an update query)
      // the three argv[] fields come from the command line
      sth = dbh.createStatement();
      sth.executeUpdate("INSERT INTO customer(id,first_name,surname)
        VALUES(" + argv[0] + ", '" + argv[1] + "', '"+argv[2]+ "')");
      sth.close();

      // instantiate the statement object, and run the SELECT query
      sth2 = dbh.createStatement();
      resultset = sth2.executeQuery("SELECT first_name,surname FROM customer");

      // loop through the result set, displaying the results
      while(resultset.next()) {
        String first_name = resultset.getString("first_name");
        String surname = resultset.getString("surname");
        System.out.println("Name: " + first_name + " " + surname);
      }
      sth2.close();
    }
```

```
        catch( SQLException e ) {
          e.printStackTrace();
        }
        finally {
          if(dbh != null) {
            try {
              dbh.close();
            }
          catch(Exception e) {}
          }
        }
      }
    }
```

# Appendix G

# C API

THE C API COMES with MySQL distributions and is included in the mysqlclient library. Many of the MySQL clients are written in C, and most of the APIs from other languages use the C API (take a look at the similarity between the C and PHP functions, for example). You can also use the C API for C++ development; for an object-oriented approach, you can use MySQL++, available from the MySQL website (www.mysql.com).

## C API Data Types

The C data types represent the data you'll be dealing with when interacting with the database server. They are of different types, some being structures and others being simple Booleans, for example. You'll need to become familiar with these types, and which functions return them or use them as arguments, to master the C API.

### my_ulonglong

A numeric type from −1 to 1.84e19, used for return values from functions such as mysql_affected_rows(), mysql_num_rows(), and mysql_insert_id().

### MYSQL

A database handle (a connection to the database server). The variable is initialized with the mysql_init() function and used by most of the API functions.

### MYSQL_FIELD

Field data, returned from the mysql_fetch_field() function, including the fieldname, type, and size. The actual field values are stored in the MYSQL_ROW structure. You can find the following members in the structure:

    **char * name**   The fieldname as a null-terminated string.

    **char * table**   The table containing the field or an empty string if there is none (such as a calculated field).

**char \* def** The field's default value as a null-terminated string. This is only available if the mysql_list_fields() function was used to return MYSQL_RES.

**enum enum_field_types type** The field type. The value here corresponds to the MySQL field type as shown in Table G.1.

**TABLE G.1:** MYSQL FIELD TYPES

| VALUE | MYSQL TYPE |
| --- | --- |
| FIELD_TYPE_TINY | TINYINT |
| FIELD_TYPE_SHORT | SMALLINT |
| FIELD_TYPE_LONG | INTEGER |
| FIELD_TYPE_INT24 | MEDIUMINT |
| FIELD_TYPE_LONGLONG | BIGINT |
| FIELD_TYPE_DECIMAL | DECIMAL or NUMERIC |
| FIELD_TYPE_FLOAT | FLOAT |
| FIELD_TYPE_DOUBLE | DOUBLE or REAL |
| FIELD_TYPE_TIMESTAMP | TIMESTAMP |
| FIELD_TYPE_DATE | DATE |
| FIELD_TYPE_TIME | TIME |
| FIELD_TYPE_DATETIME | DATETIME |
| FIELD_TYPE_YEAR | YEAR |
| FIELD_TYPE_STRING | CHAR or VARCHAR |
| FIELD_TYPE_BLOB | BLOB or TEXT |
| FIELD_TYPE_SET | SET |
| FIELD_TYPE_ENUM | ENUM |
| FIELD_TYPE_NULL | NULL-type |
| FIELD_TYPE_CHAR | Deprecated, replaced by FIELD_TYPE_TINY |

**unsigned int length** The maximum width of the field, determined by the table definition.

**unsigned int max_length** The largest width of a field in the result set. Often confused with the length member, but max_length will usually be smaller. This will contain zero if it was the mysql_use_result() function that returned MYSQL_RES.

**unsigned int flags**    Any of the flags shown in Table G.2 can be set; they provide extra information about the field.

**TABLE G.2:** FLAGS

| FLAG | DESCRIPTION |
|---|---|
| NOT_NULL_FLAG | Defined as NOT NULL |
| PRI_KEY_FLAG | Part of the primary key |
| UNIQUE_KEY_FLAG | Part of a unique key |
| MULTIPLE_KEY_FLAG | Part of a nonunique key |
| UNSIGNED_FLAG | Defined as UNSIGNED |
| ZEROFILL_FLAG | Defined with ZEROFILL |
| BINARY_FLAG | Defined as BINARY |
| AUTO_INCREMENT_FLAG | Defined as an AUTO_INCREMENT field |
| ENUM_FLAG | Defined as an ENUM (deprecated, use FIELD_TYPE_ENUM) |
| SET_FLAG | Defined as a SET (deprecated, use FIELD_TYPE_SET) |
| BLOB_FLAG | Defined as a BLOB or TEXT (deprecated, use FIELD_TYPE_BLOB) |
| TIMESTAMP_FLAG | Defined as a TIMESTAMP (deprecated, use FIELD_TYPE_TIMESTAMP) |

The following is an example of using one of these options:

```
if (field->flags & MULTIPLE_KEY_FLAG) {
 /* do something with the fact that the field is a multiple key */
}
```

The macros shown in Table G.3 ease the testing of some of the flag values.

**TABLE G.3:** MACROS

| MACRO | DESCRIPTION |
|---|---|
| IS_NOT_NULL(flags) | True if the field is defined as NOT NULL |
| IS_PRI_KEY(flags) | True if the field is, or is part of, a primary key |
| IS_BLOB(flags) | True if the field is a BLOB or TEXT (deprecated, use FIELD_TYPE_BLOB instead) |
| IS_NUM(flags) | True if the field is numeric |

**unsigned int decimals**    The number of decimal places used by a numeric.

### MYSQL_FIELD_OFFSET

Represents the position of the field pointer within a field list, beginning at 0 for the first field. It is used by the `mysql_field_seek()` function.

### MYSQL_RES

A structure containing the results of a query that returns data (such as SELECT, DESCRIBE, SHOW, or EXPLAIN).

### MYSQL_ROW

A single row of data, obtained from the `mysql_fetch_row()` function. All data is represented as an array of strings that may contain null bytes if any of the data is binary.

## C API Functions

The C API functions are for opening and closing connections to the server, performing queries, analyzing query results, debugging, and performing administrative tasks. You'll need to know them well and know how they interact with the C API data types to master the C API.

### mysql_affected_rows

```
my_ulonglong mysql_affected_rows(MYSQL *mysql)
```

Returns the number of rows affected by the last query (for example, the number of rows removed with a DELETE statement or the number of rows returned from a SELECT statement, in which case it's the same as the `mysql_num_rows` function.). It returns −1 on error.

With UPDATE statements, the row is not counted as affected if it matched the condition but no changes were made, unless the CLIENT_FOUND_ROWS flag is set when connecting with `mysql_real_connect()`.

For example:

```
/* Update the customer table, and return the number of records affected */
mysql_query(&mysql, "UPDATE customer SET first_name='Jackie' WHERE↵
  surname='Wood')";
affected_rows = mysql_affected_rows(&mysql);
```

### mysql_change_user

```
my_bool mysql_change_user(MYSQL *mysql, char
  *username, char *password, char *database)
```

Changes the current MySQL user (the one that logged in) to another user (specifying that user's username and password). You can also change database at the same time or open a new connection; otherwise, the current connection and database will be used. This returns true if successful or false if not, in which case the existing user and details are maintained.

For example:

```
if (! mysql_change_user(&mysql, 'guru2b', 'g00r002b', 'firstdb')) {
  printf("Unable to change user and or database!");
}
```

## mysql_character_set_name

```
char *mysql_character_set_name(MYSQL *mysql)
```

Returns the name of the default character set (usually ISO-8859-1, or Latin1).
For example:

```
printf("The default character set is: %s \n", mysql_character_set_name(&mysql));
```

## mysql_close

```
void mysql_close(MYSQL *mysql)
```

Closes the connection and frees the resources.
For example:

```
mysql_close(&mysql);
```

## mysql_connect

```
MYSQL *mysql_connect(MYSQL *mysql, const char *host, const char *user,
                     const char *passwd)
```

For connecting to MySQL. The function has been deprecated, so instead use `mysql_real_connect()`.

## mysql_create_db

```
int mysql_create_db(MYSQL *mysql, const char *db)
```

For creating a database. The function has been deprecated, so instead use `mysql_query()`.

## mysql_data_seek

```
void mysql_data_seek(MYSQL_RES *res, unsigned int offset)
```

Moves the internal row pointer (0 is the first row) associated with the results returned from `mysql_store_result()` to a new position. The offset is the row to move to, starting at 0.
For example:

```
mysql_data_seek(results, mysql_num_rows(results)-1);
```

## mysql_debug

```
mysql_debug(char *debug)
```

To use, the MySQL client needs to have been compiled with debugging enabled. Uses the Fred Fish debug library.
For example:

```
/* Traces application activity in the file debug.out */
mysql_debug("d:t:0,debug.out");
```

### mysql_drop_db

```
int mysql_drop_db(MYSQL *mysql, const char *db)
```

For dropping a database. The function has been deprecated, so instead use `mysql_query()`.

### mysql_dump_debug_info

```
int mysql_dump_debug_info(MYSQL *mysql)
```

Writes connection debug information into the log. The connection needs the SUPER privilege to be able to do this. This returns 0 if it succeeded; otherwise it returns a nonzero result.

For example:

```
result = mysql_dump_debug_info(&mysql);
```

### mysql_eof

```
my_bool mysql_eof(MYSQL_RES *result)
```

Checks whether the last row has been read. The function has been deprecated, so instead use `mysql_err()` or `mysql_errno()`.

### mysql_errno

```
unsigned int mysql_errno(MYSQL *mysql)
```

Returns the error code for the most recent API function or 0 if there have been no errors. You can retrieve the actual text of the error using the `mysql_error()` function.

For example:

```
error = mysql_errno(&mysql);
```

### mysql_error

```
char *mysql_error(MYSQL *mysql)
```

Returns the error message (in the current server language) for the most recent API function or an empty string if there was no error. If there have been no errors in the connection, the function returns 0.

For example:

```
printf("Error: '%s'\n", mysql_error(&mysql));
```

### mysql_escape_string

```
unsigned int mysql_escape_string(char *to, const char *from, unsigned int length)
```

Returns a string with all characters that could break the query escaped (a backslash placed before them). Instead, use `mysql_real_escape_string()` because it respects the current character set.

## mysql_fetch_field

```
MYSQL_FIELD *mysql_fetch_field(MYSQL_RES *result)
```

Returns the field data of the current field. You can call this function repeatedly to return data of the following fields in the result. This returns a null value when there are no more fields to return.

For example:

```
while((field = mysql_fetch_field(results))) {
    /* .. process results by accessing field->name, field->length etc */
}
```

## mysql_fetch_field_direct

```
MYSQL_FIELD * mysql_fetch_field_direct(MYSQL_RES * result,⤶
 unsigned int field_number)
```

Returns field data of the specified field (which starts at 0).
For example:

```
/* Return the second field */
field = mysql_fetch_field_direct(results, 1);
```

## mysql_fetch_fields

```
MYSQL_FIELD *mysql_fetch_fields(MYSQL_RES * result)
```

Returns an array of field data from each field in the result.
For example:

```
unsigned int num_fields;
unsigned int i;
MYSQL_FIELD *fields;

/* Returns the number of fields in the result */
num_fields = mysql_num_fields(result);

/* Returns an array of field data */
fields = mysql_fetch_fields(result);

/* ... Access field data as fields[0].name, fields[1].table and so on */
```

## mysql_fetch_lengths

```
unsigned long *mysql_fetch_lengths(MYSQL_RES *result)
```

Returns an array of the lengths of the fields from the current row (called with mysql_fetch_row()) in the result set, or null if there was an error.

This is the only function that correctly returns the length of binary fields (for example, BLOBs).

For example:

```
unsigned long *lengths;

/* Return the next row of data */
row = mysql_fetch_row(results);

/* Return the array of lengths */
length_array = mysql_fetch_lengths(results);

/* ... Access lengths as length_array[0], length_array[1] and so on */
```

### mysql_fetch_row

```
MYSQL_ROW mysql_fetch_row(MYSQL_RES *result)
```

Returns the next row from the result or null if there are no more rows or an error.
For example:

```
MYSQL_ROW row;

row = mysql_fetch_row(results);
/* Access the row data as row[0], row[1] and so on
```

### mysql_field_count

```
unsigned int mysql_field_count(MYSQL *mysql)
```

Returns the number of fields in the last executed query. It allows you to determine whether a NULL returned from mysql_use_result() or mysql_store_result() is because of an error or because it shouldn't return a result (a non-SELECT type query). For checking the number of fields in a successful result set, use mysql_num_fields().
For example:

```
results = mysql_store_result(&mysql);
/* test if no result set found */
if (results == NULL) {
  /* if no result, test whether  the field count was zero or not. */
  if (mysql_field_count(&mysql) > 0) {
    /* the query was a SELECT-type, so the null store_result is an error */
  }
  else {
    /* no error, as the query was an INSERT-type, which returns no fields */
  }
}
```

### mysql_field_seek

```
MYSQL_FIELD_OFFSET mysql_field_seek(MYSQL_RES *result, MYSQL_FIELD_OFFSET offset)
```

Moves the internal field pointer (which starts at 0) to the specified field. The next call to mysql_fetch_field() will the specified field. This returns the previous field position pointer.

## mysql_field_tell

```
MYSQL_FIELD_OFFSET mysql_field_tell(MYSQL_RES *result)
```

Returns the current position of the field pointer.
For example:

```
/* Record the current position */
current_pos = mysql_field_tell(results);
```

## mysql_free_result

```
void mysql_free_result(MYSQL_RES *result)
```

Frees the resources allocated to a result set.

## mysql_get_client_info

```
char *mysql_get_client_info(void)
```

Returns a string containing the client's MySQL library version.
For example:

```
/* Displays - Client library version is: 4.0.2 (for example) */
printf("Client library version is: %s\n", mysql_get_client_info());
```

## mysql_get_host_info

```
char *mysql_get_host_info(MYSQL *mysql)
```

Returns a string containing the connection information.
For example:

```
/* Displays - Type of connection: Localhost via UNIX socket (for example) */
printf("Type of connection: %s", mysql_get_host_info(&mysql));
```

## mysql_get_proto_info

```
unsigned int mysql_get_proto_info(MYSQL *mysql)
```

Returns an integer containing the protocol version (for example, 10) used by the connection.
For example:

```
/* displays - Protocol version: 10 (for example) */
printf("Protocol version: %d\n", mysql_get_proto_info(&mysql));
```

## mysql_get_server_info

```
char *mysql_get_server_info(MYSQL *mysql)
```

Returns a string containing the MySQL server version (for example, 4.0.3).
For example:

```
/* displays - Server version: 4.0.3-beta-log (for example) */
printf("Server version: %s\n", mysql_get_server_info(&mysql));
```

## mysql_info

```
char *mysql_info(MYSQL *mysql)
```

Returns a string containing detailed information about the most recent query. Detailed information includes records, rows matched, changes, and warnings.

For example:

```
/* Query info String format: Rows matched: 19 Changed: 19 Warnings: 0
(for example) */
printf("Query info: %s\n", mysql_info(&mysql));
```

## mysql_init

```
MYSQL *mysql_init(MYSQL *mysql)
```

Returns an initialized MySQL handle, ready for a mysql_real_connect().

The argument can be a null pointer, in which case a structure will be created, or a pointer to an existing MYSQL structure. The mysql_close() function frees the resources from the structure if it created it. If you passed an existing structure, you'll need to free the resources yourself after the connection is closed.

## mysql_insert_id

```
my_ulonglong mysql_insert_id(MYSQL *mysql)
```

Returns a value containing the most recently inserted AUTO_INCREMENT value or 0 if the most recent query did insert an auto incremented value.

For example:

```
last_auto_increment = mysql_insert_id(&mysql);
```

## mysql_kill

```
int mysql_kill(MYSQL *mysql, unsigned long process_id)
```

Requests that MySQL kill the thread specified by the process_id. This returns 0 if operation was successful or a nonzero value if it failed.

Requires that you have the PROCESS privilege.

For example:

```
kill = mysql_kill(&mysql, 1293);
```

## mysql_list_dbs

```
MYSQL_RES *mysql_list_dbs(MYSQL *mysql, const char *wild)
```

Returns a result set containing the names of the databases on the server that match the *wild* regular expression (equivalent to the SQL statement SHOW DATABASES LIKE 'wild') or null if there was an error. This returns all databases if passed a null pointer.

For example:

```
MYSQL_RES database_names;

/* returns a list of all databases with 'db' in the name */
database_names = mysql_list_dbs(&mysql, "%db%");

/* ... Don't forget to free the resources at a later stage
mysql_free_result(database_names);
```

## mysql_list_fields

```
MYSQL_RES *mysql_list_fields(MYSQL *mysql, const char *table, const char *wild)
```

Returns a result set containing the names of the fields in the specified table that match the *wild* regular expression (equivalent to the SQL statement SHOW COLUMNS FROM tablename LIKE 'wild') or null if there was an error. This returns all fields if passed a null pointer.

For example:

```
MYSQL_RES field_names;

/* returns a list of all fields with 'name' in the name */
field_names = mysql_list_fields(&mysql, "customer", "%name%");

/* ... Don't forget to free the resources at a later stage
mysql_free_result(field_names);
```

## mysql_list_processes

```
MYSQL_RES *mysql_list_processes(MYSQL *mysql)
```

Returns a result set containing a description of the currently running database server threads or null if there was an error. Returns the same information as returned through the SHOW PROCESSLIST statement (that is, the process ID, username, hostname, database, action, time, state, and info). You can then as usual pass the result to mysql_fetch_row() to access the results.

For example:

```
MYSQL_RES *threadlist;
MYSQL_ROW row
threadlist = mysql_list_processes(&mysql);

row = mysql_fetch_row(threadlist);
/* Access the thread data as row[0], row[1] and so on

/* ... Don't forget to free the resources at a later stage
mysql_free_result(threadlist);
```

## mysql_list_tables

```
MYSQL_RES *mysql_list_tables(MYSQL *mysql, const char *wild)
```

Returns a result set containing the names of the tables in the current database that match the *wild* regular expression (equivalent to the SQL statement SHOW TABLES LIKE 'wild') or null if there was an error. This returns all fields if passed a null pointer.

For example:

```
MYSQL_RES tablelist;

/* returns a list of all tables with 'customer' in the name */
tablelist = mysql_list_tables(&mysql, "%customer%");

/* ... Don't forget to free the resources at a later stage
mysql_free_result(tablelist);
```

## mysql_num_fields

```
unsigned int mysql_num_fields(MYSQL_RES *result)
```

Returns the number of fields in the query result. Use the mysql_field_count() function to check for errors, and use this function to check number of fields in a successful result set.

For example:

```
num_fields = mysql_num_fields(results);
```

## mysql_num_rows

```
int mysql_num_rows(MYSQL_RES *result)
```

Returns the number of rows in a query result (only the results to date if mysql_use_result() was used to get the result set).

For example:

```
num_rows = mysql_num_rows(results);
```

## mysql_options

```
int mysql_options(MYSQL *mysql, enum mysql_option option, void *value)
```

Sets extra connect options for the connection about to be made. It can be called multiple times and is called after mysql_init() and before mysql_real_connect(). This returns 0 if successful or a non-zero value if it was passed an invalid option. The options are as follows:

**MYSQL_OPT_CONNECT_TIMEOUT**   An unsigned int *, specifies the connect timeout in seconds.

**MYSQL_OPT_COMPRESS**   Uses the compressed client/server protocol.

**MYSQL_OPT_LOCAL_INFILE**   An optional pointer to uint. LOAD DATA LOCAL is enabled if the pointer points to nonzero unsigned integer or none is supplied.

**MYSQL_OPT_NAMED_PIPE**   On Windows NT, uses named pipes to connect to the server.

**MYSQL_INIT_COMMAND**   A char *, specifies a query to run as soon as the connection is established (including an automatic reconnection).

**MYSQL_READ_DEFAULT_FILE**  A char *, causes the options to be from the name file, instead of the usual configuration file (my.cnf or my.ini).

**MYSQL_READ_DEFAULT_GROUP**  A char *, causes the options to be read from the named group inside the configuration file (my.cnf or my.ini, or as set by MYSQL_READ_DEFAULT_FILE).

For example:

```
MYSQL mysql;
mysql_init(&mysql);

/* use compression, and flush the tables upon connecting */
mysql_options(&mysql, MYSQL_OPT_COMPRESS, 0 );
mysql_options(&mysql, MYSQL_INIT_COMMAND, "FLUSH TABLES" );

/* ... continue and connect */
if(!mysql_real_connect(&mysql, "localhost", "guru2b", "g00r002b",↵
  "firstdb", 0,NULL,0)) {
    printf("The following connection error occurred %s\n",
        mysql_error(&mysql));
}
```

## mysql_ping

```
int mysql_ping(MYSQL *mysql)
```

Returns 0 if the MySQL server is up or a nonzero value if not. If the ping fails, the program will try to reconnect.

## mysql_query

```
int mysql_query(MYSQL *mysql, const char *query)
```

Performs the specified query. It returns 0 if successful or a nonzero value if there was an error. To perform a query with binary data (which could contain the null character), you need to use mysql_real_query() instead. You should use this function for dropping and creating databases as well, replacing the deprecated mysql_create_db() and mysql_drop_db() functions.

You can then retrieve the result, if applicable, with the mysql_store_result() or mysql_use_result() functions.

For example:

```
query_result = mysql_query(&mysql, "CREATE DATABASE seconddb");
```

## mysql_real_connect

```
MYSQL *mysql_real_connect(MYSQL *mysql, const char *host, const char *user,↵
  const char *passwd, const char *db, uint port, const char *unix_socket,↵
  uint client_flag)
```

Establishes a connection to the MySQL server with the specified arguments, as follows:

**MYSQL *mysql**  An existing MYSQL structure, created when you called mysql_init().

**const char \*host**   The hostname or IP address of the MySQL server. It can be an empty string, same as when you connect to MySQL from a client on the same machine.

**const char \*user**   The username.

**const char \*passwd**   The password for the specified user.

**const char \*db**   The database to connect to (it can be null).

**uint port**   Specifies the port for the TCP/IP connection (if used). 0 is the default port.

**const char \*unix_socket**   Specifies the filename for the Unix socket, or name pipe, for connecting locally. This can be null to accept the default.

You can also pass any of the following optional flags:

**CLIENT_FOUND_ROWS**   Specifies that `mysql_affected_rows()` will return the number of rows that matches the query condition, not the number of rows that were actually changed.

**CLIENT_IGNORE_SPACE**   Allows you to place spaces after function names (which has the consequence of making all functions reserved words).

**CLIENT_INTERACTIVE**   Specifies that MySQL drops the connection after `interactive_timeout` seconds rather than `wait_timeout` seconds (two mysql variables). This is usually used when the client will wait a longer period of time for interactive user input before running a query.

**CLIENT_NO_SCHEMA**   Mainly used for ODBC and disallows the `database_name.tablename` `.fieldname` syntax in a query.

**CLIENT_COMPRESS**   Ensures that the connection uses compression.

**CLIENT_ODBC**   Tells MySQL that the client is an ODBC client, causing some behavioral changes.

**CLIENT_SSL**   Ensures that the connection uses Secure Sockets Layer (SSL) encryption as long as this has been compiled into the server.

For example:

```
MYSQL mysql;

mysql_init(&mysql);
mysql_options(&mysql, MYSQL_OPT_COMPRESS, 0 );
mysql_options(&mysql, MYSQL_INIT_COMMAND, "FLUSH TABLES" );
if(!mysql_real_connect(&mysql, "localhost", "guru2b", "g00r002b",↵
  "firstdb", 0, NULL,0)) {
    printf("The following connection error occurred %s\n",
         mysql_error(&mysql));
}
```

## mysql_real_escape_string

```
unsigned long mysql_real_escape_string(MYSQL *mysql, char *new_string,↵
  char *old_string, unsigned long old_string_length)
```

Escapes a string (`old_string` of length `string_length`) so that you can use it in a MySQL query, placing the result in `new_string` (which should be at least 1 byte larger than twice as large as the original string, in case every character needs escaping, as well as taking into account the null string). The characters escaped are `NUL` (ASCII 0), \n, \r, \, ', ", and Ctrl+Z. It returns the length of the new string.

For example:

```
/* the original query is 4 bytes (a,b,c and the null character) */
char *old_query = "abc\000";

/*the new length must be at least4*2+1 byted */
char new_query[9];
int new_length;
/* returns the new length */
new_query_length = mysql_real_escape_string(&mysql, new_query, old_query, 4);
```

## mysql_real_query

```
int mysql_real_query(MYSQL *mysql, const char *query, unsigned long length)
```

Executes the query (which can also use binary data), specifying the length as well (excluding a null character). You can then retrieve the result, if applicable, with the `mysql_store_result()` or `mysql_use_result()` functions.

For example:

```
query_result = mysql_real_query(&mysql, "CREATE DATABASE seconddb");
```

## mysql_reload

```
int mysql_reload(MYSQL *mysql)
```

A deprecated function that reloads the grant tables, assuming the connected user has Reload permission. Rather, use the `mysql_query()` function.

## mysql_row_seek

```
MYSQL_ROW_OFFSET mysql_row_seek(MYSQL_RES *result, MYSQL_ROW_OFFSET offset)
```

Moves the internal row pointer to the specified row, returning the original row pointer. The `MYSQL_ROW_OFFSET` should be the structure returned from either the `mysql_row_tell()` function or another `mysql_row_seek()` function, not just a row number (in which case you'd use the `mysql_data_seek()` function).

For example:

```
current_location = mysql_row_seek(result,row_offset);
```

## mysql_row_tell

```
MYSQL_ROW_OFFSET mysql_row_tell(MYSQL_RES *result)
```

Returns the current position of the row pointer. You can use this with `mysql_row_seek()` to move to the specified row. Use after `mysql_store_result()`, not `mysql_use_result()`.

For example:

```
MYSQL_ROW_OFFSET current_position = mysql_row_tell(results);

/* A little later..., move back to this position */
moved_position = mysql_row_seek(result,current_position);
```

## mysql_select_db

```
int mysql_select_db(MYSQL *mysql, const char *db)
```

Changes the current database to the specified database (assuming the user has permission to change). It returns 0 if successful or a nonzero value if there was an error.

For example:

```
mysql_select_db(&mysql, "seconddb");
```

## mysql_shutdown

```
int mysql_shutdown(MYSQL *mysql)
```

Requests that the MySQL server shut down. The user must have the SHUTDOWN privilege for this to work. Returns 0 if successful or a nonzero value if there was an error.

For example:

```
mysql_shutdown(&mysql);
```

## mysql_stat

```
char *mysql_stat(MYSQL *mysql)
```

Returns a string containing the server status. This contains uptime, threads, questions, slow queries, opens, flush tables, open tables, and queries per second average.

For example:

```
/* displays (for example):
Uptime: 109  Threads: 2  Questions: 199  Slow queries: 1  Opens: 4
Flush tables: 1  Open tables: 2  Queries per second avg: 1.826b */
printf("Server status: %s\n", mysql_stat(&mysql));
```

## mysql_store_result

```
MYSQL_RES *mysql_store_result(MYSQL *mysql)
```

For all queries that return data, you need to call either this function or mysql_use_result(). This stores the query results into the MYSQL_RES structure, or returns null in case of an error or if the query did not return data (such as after a CREATE DATABASE of an INSERT). You should use mysql_field_count() to count the number of fields expected from the query. If it's not zero (when the query was not expected to return any data), then an error has occurred.

Always free up the resources afterward.

For example:

```
MYSQL_RES results;
mysql_query(&mysql, "SELECT first_name, surname FROM customers");
results = mysql_store_result(&mysql);
/* later ... */
mysql_free_result(results);
```

## mysql_thread_id

```
unsigned long mysql_thread_id(MYSQL * mysql)
```

Returns the current thread ID of the connection, usually in order to kill it with `mysql_kill()`. For example:

```
thread_id = mysql_thread_id(&mysql);
```

## mysql_use_result

```
MYSQL_RES *mysql_use_result(MYSQL *mysql)
```

For all queries that return data, you need to call either this function or `mysql_store_result()`. This function reads the data row by row, not all at once as does `mysql_store_result()`. It is therefore faster, but it does not allow other queries to be run until all the data has been returned, making locking more of a problem than usual. It returns a null value in case of an error or if the query did not return data (such as after a `CREATE DATABASE` of an `INSERT`). You should use `mysql_field_count()` to count the number of fields expected from the query. If it's not zero (when the query was not expected to return any data), then an error has occurred.

For example:

```
MYSQL_RES results;
mysql_query(&mysql, "SELECT first_name,surname FROM customer");
results = mysql_use_result(&mysql);

/* can now use mysql_fetch_row() to access data one row at a time *

/* later ... */
mysql_free_result(results);
```

# A Short C API Example

Listing G.1 demonstrates a short sample usage of the C API with the basic components for returning data from the database. You'll need to compile and run it. Compilation instructions will differ from system to system, but could look something like this:

```
gcc -o example example.c -I/usr/local/mysql/include/mysql↩
  -L/usr/local/mysql/lib/mysql -lmysqlclient -lz
```

**LISTING G.1:** EXAMPLE.C

```c
#include <stdio.h>
#include <mysql.h>
/* the two basic includes */

/* the main function */
int main(char **args) {
  MYSQL_RES *query_result;
  MYSQL_ROW row;
/* db_handle is the connection to the database, and will be used by
 many of the functions that follow */
  MYSQL *db_handle, mysql;
  int query_error;

  /* initialize and open the connection */
  mysql_init(&mysql);
  db_handle = mysql_real_connect(&mysql,"localhost", "guru2b",↵
   "g00r002b", "firstdb", 0, 0, 0);

  /* if the connection failed, then display the error and exit. */
  if (db_handle == NULL) {
    printf(mysql_error(&mysql));
    return 1;
  }
  query_error = mysql_query(db_handle,"SELECT first_name,surname FROM customer");

  /* if the query error is not 0 (no error), display the error and exit */
  if (query_error != 0) {
    printf(mysql_error(db_handle));
    return 1;
  }

  /* Return a query result */
  query_result = mysql_store_result(db_handle);

  /* Loop through and display each row in the query result */
  while (( row = mysql_fetch_row(query_result)) != NULL ) {
    printf("Name: %s %s\n",(row[0] ? row[0] : "NULL"),↵
     (row[1] ? row[1] : "NULL"));
  }
  /* free the resources associated with the query result */
  mysql_free_result(query_result);

  /* close the connection */
  mysql_close(db_handle);
}
```

# Appendix H

# ODBC and .NET

MySQL CAN CONNECT WITH languages or environments that do not have their own developed application programming interfaces (APIs) or drivers for interacting with MySQL via Open Database Connectivity (ODBC). ODBC is a widely used API for connecting and interacting with relational databases. It is database- and language-independent. With MySQL, it's commonly used to connect to tools such as Microsoft Access or Visual Basic. To do so, you'll need to install the MyODBC driver. This is available, along with full installation instructions, from the MySQL website (`www.mysql.com/downloads/api-myodbc.html`). Installing on Windows is a matter of downloading the executable file and running it.

This appendix explains how to set up a data source on Unix and Windows, explains how to export data from Microsoft Access to MySQL, serves as a reference to the MyODBC functions for experienced programmers, and provides simple example scripts for using ODBC to connect, insert, and select records with VB .NET, C# .NET, DOA, ADO, and RDO. This appendix is not a complete description of ODBC and how to use it. For more information, examine the ODBC documentation on the Microsoft site (`www.microsoft.com/data/odbc/`), the ODBC documentation that comes with your development environment, or the information on the MySQL site (`www.mysql.com/products/myodbc/`).

## Understanding Data Sources

A *data source* can be the path to a library of files, a server, or, in this case, a MySQL database. Connection information is associated with the data source—stored, for example, in the Windows Registry. To connect to the data source, the ODBC Driver Manager looks up the connection information associated with the DSN and connects using this. To connect via ODBC, it's not always necessary to have an existing DSN. You can specify the driver directly. All of the examples except for the DAO VB example later in this appendix connect without a preset DSN.

## Setting Up a Data Source on Windows

The first step in getting a Windows application to connect to MySQL via ODBC is setting up a data source:

1. Select Start ➢ Settings ➢ Control Panel.
2. Depending on your version of Windows, you either select 32-bit ODBC or ODBC, or alternatively Administrative Tools and Data Sources (ODBC).
3. Click Add.
4. From the list that appears, select the MySQL driver you installed with MyODBC, and then click Finish.
5. The driver default configuration screen will appear. Complete the required details. The Windows DSN can be anything you want, and the host, database, username, password, and port details are the usual details required for connecting to MySQL. You can also specify a SQL command to run when you connect to the server.
6. You can click the Options button to be able to select various options to cater for the idiosyncrasies of each application (those that are not 100-percent ODBC compliant). For example, currently with Microsoft Access you should check the Return Matching Rows option. You may need to experiment to get things working smoothly, and you should look at the MySQL website as well, which will have the latest options for many common applications.
7. Click OK and the data source will be added.
8. Depending on your ODBC version, you may be able to test your connection by clicking Test Data Source. Check your connection details if the test fails.

## Setting Up a Data Source on Unix

On Unix, you can edit the ODBC.INI file directly to set up your data sources.
    For example:

```
[ODBC Data Sources]
myodbc      = MySQL ODBC 3.51 Driver DSN

[myodbc]
Driver      = /usr/local/lib/libmyodbc3.so
Description = MySQL ODBC 3.51 Driver DSN
SERVER      = localhost
PORT        =
USER        = root
Password    = g00r002b
Database    = firstdb
OPTION      = 3
SOCKET      =
```

To set the various options for non-ODBC-compliant applications on Unix, you set the OPTION value based upon Table H.1.

## Setting Connection Options

If a graphical interface is not available, you can use the option values in Table H.1 to connect. To combine options, simply add the values together (so 3 is a combination of 1 and 2).

**TABLE H.1:** CONNECTION OPTIONS

| BIT | DESCRIPTION |
| --- | --- |
| 1 | Cannot handle receiving the real width of a column. |
| 2 | Cannot handle receiving the actual number of affected rows (the number of found rows will be returned instead). |
| 4 | Makes a debug log in `C:\myodbc.log` or `/tmp/myodbc.log`. |
| 8 | Sets an unlimited packet limit for results and parameters. |
| 16 | Does not prompt for questions. |
| 32 | Toggles dynamic cursor support (enabling or disabling it). |
| 64 | Ignores the database name in a structure such as `databasename.tablename.fieldname`. |
| 128 | An experimental option that forces the use of ODBC manager cursors. |
| 256 | An experimental option that disables the use of extended fetch. |
| 512 | CHAR fields are padded to the full length of the field. |
| 1024 | The `SQLDescribeCol()` function returns fully qualified column names. |
| 2048 | Uses compressed protocol. |
| 4096 | Causes the server to ignore spaces between the function name and the open bracket and makes all function names keywords as a result. |
| 8192 | Uses named pipes to connect to a server running on NT/2000/XP. |
| 16384 | LONGLONG fields are converted to INT fields. |
| 32768 | An experimental option that returns `user` as `Table_qualifier` and `Table_owner` from the `SQLTables()` function. |
| 65536 | Reads the MySQL configuration file for the `client` and odbc group's parameters. |
| 131072 | Adds extra safety checks. |
| 262144 | Disables transactions. |
| 524288 | In debug mode, enables query logging to the `c:\myodbc.sql` *or* `/tmp/myodbc.sql` file. |

## Exporting Data from Microsoft Access to MySQL

Many novice database users start with Microsoft Access, and a common use of ODBC is to enable an upgrade to MySQL, exporting data from Access. To do so, perform the following steps (steps 1 and 2 are only required the first time you do this):

1. Install the MyODBC driver.
2. Set up a data source pointing to the MySQL server you want to export the data to, as described in the earlier section "Setting Up a Data Source on Windows."
3. Load Microsoft Access.
4. Open the Microsoft Access database window, and select the table you want to export.
5. Click File ➤ Export and choose ODBC Databases () from the Save as Type drop-down list.
6. Choose a new name if you want to change the table name, and then click OK.
7. Select the data source you defined in step 2 and click OK.
8. If the data source connection details are not correct, you'll need to change them, which you can do at this point as well. Remember that MySQL permissions have to be granted to allow access. See Chapter 14, "Database Security" for details on this.

## Using ODBC

The following examples demonstrate inserting a record into and selecting records from a MySQL database via ODBC in different programming environments. The first examples show the connection being made directly, and the DAO example shows a connection being made through a data source.

To get these examples to work, you need MyODBC installed, a preinstalled DSN (for the DAO example only—see the earlier "Setting Up a Data Source on Windows" section), and the correct environment (.NET, Visual Basic, and so on).

*WARNING*   *Be sure to keep the formatting the same or the examples may not work.*

### A Simple .NET VB Example

Listing H.1 uses VB.NET and ODBC to connect to a MySQL server, insert a record, and select and print the results. To compile the code, you'll need to specify settings appropriate for your .NET environment. The following is an example (the pause is just to make the compile options visible):

```
set path=%path%;C:\WINNT\Microsoft.NET\Framework\v1.0.3705↵
  C:\WINNT\Microsoft.NET\Framework\v1.0.3705\csc /t:exe↵
  /out:odbc_cnet.exe odbc_cnet.cs /r:"C:\Program↵
  Files\Microsoft.NET\Odbc.Net\Microsoft.Data.Odbc.dll"↵
  pause
```

**LISTING H.1:** DBNET.VB

```vbnet
Imports Microsoft.Data.Odbc
Imports System

Module mysql_vbnet
  Sub Main()
    Try

        'Set the arguments for connecting to a MySQL firstdb database↵
          with MyODBC 3.51
        Dim MySQLConnectionArgs As String = " DRIVER={MySQL ODBC 3.51 Driver};↵
          SERVER=www.testhost.co.za;DATABASE=firstdb;UID=guru2b;↵
          PASSWORD=g00r002b;OPTION=0"

        'Open the ODBC connection and ODBC command
        Dim MySQLConnection As New OdbcConnection(MySQLConnectionArgs)
        MySQLConnection.Open()
        Dim MySQLCommand As New OdbcCommand()
        MySQLCommand.Connection = MySQLConnection

        'Insert a record into the customer table
        MySQLCommand.CommandText = "INSERT INTO customer↵
          (first_name, surname) VALUES('Frank', 'Weiss')"
        MySQLCommand.ExecuteNonQuery()

        'select a record from the customer table, return the results,
        'loop through the results displaying them
        MySQLCommand.CommandText = "SELECT id,first_name,surname FROM customer"
        Dim MySQLDataReader As OdbcDataReader
        MySQLDataReader = MySQLCommand.ExecuteReader
        While MySQLDataReader.Read
          Console.WriteLine (CStr(MySQLDataReader("id")) & ":" &↵
            CStr(MySQLDataReader("first_name")) & " " & CStr(MySQLDataReader("surname")))
        End While

    'If theres an ODBC Exception, catch it
    Catch MySQLOdbcException As OdbcException
      Console.WriteLine (MySQLOdbcException.ToString)

    'If there a program exception, catch it
    Catch AnyException As Exception
      Console.WriteLine (AnyException.ToString)
    End Try
  End Sub
End Module
```

## A Simple .NET C# Example

Listing H.2 uses C# .NET and ODBC to connect to a MySQL server, insert a record, and select and print the results.

To compile the code, you'll need to specify settings appropriate for your .NET environment. The following is an example (the pause is just to make the compile options visible):

```
C:\WINNT\Microsoft.NET\Framework\v1.0.3705\csc /t:exe⤸
  /out:odbc_cnet.exe odbc_cnet.cs /r:"C:\Program⤸
  Files\Microsoft.NET\Odbc.Net\Microsoft.Data.Odbc.dll"
pause
```

**LISTING H.2:** DBNET.CS

```csharp
using Console = System.Console;
using Microsoft.Data.Odbc;

namespace MyODBC {
  class MySQLCSharp {
    static void Main(string[] args) {
      try {
        // Set the arguments for connecting to a MySQL firstdb database⤸
          with MyODBC 3.51

        string MySQLConnectionArgs = "DRIVER={MySQL ODBC 3.51 Driver};⤸
          SERVER=www.testhost.co.za;DATABASE=firstdb;UID=guru2b;⤸
          PASSWORD=g00r002b;OPTION=0";


        // Open the ODBC connection and ODBC command
        OdbcConnection MySQLConnection = new OdbcConnection(MySQLConnectionArgs);
        MySQLConnection.Open();

        // Insert a record into the customer table
        OdbcCommand MySQLCommand = new OdbcCommand("INSERT INTO⤸
          customer (first_name, surname) VALUES('Frank', 'Weiss')",⤸
          MySQLConnection);
        MySQLCommand.ExecuteNonQuery();

        // select a record from the customer table, return the results,
        // loop through the results displaying them
        MySQLCommand.CommandText = "SELECT id,
  first_name, surname FROM customer";
        OdbcDataReader MySQLDataReader;
        MySQLDataReader =  MySQLCommand.ExecuteReader();
        while (MySQLDataReader.Read()) {
          Console.WriteLine("" + MySQLDataReader.GetInt32(0) + ":" +⤸
            MySQLDataReader.GetString(1) + " " + MySQLDataReader.GetString(2));
        }
```

```
      // Close all resources
      MySQLDataReader.Close();
      MySQLConnection.Close();
    }
    // If theres an ODBC Exception, catch it
    catch (OdbcException MySQLOdbcException) {
      throw MySQLOdbcException;
    }
  }
 }
}
```

## A Simple ADO VB Example

Listing H.3 uses VB and ADO to connect to a MySQL server via ODBC, insert a record (both directly and through adding to a result set), and select and print the results.

To gain access to the ADO 2.0 objects in Visual Basic, set a reference to the ADODB type library contained in MSADO15.DLL. It appears in the References dialog box (available from the Project menu) as Microsoft ActiveX Data Objects 2.0 Library.

The code needs to appear inside a form for the Debug.Print method to work. Alternatively, you can change it to MsgBox to make the code executable.

```
Private Sub MySQLADO()
  Dim MySQLConnection As ADODB.Connection
  Dim Results As ADODB.Recordset

  Dim SQLQuery As String

  'Open a connection using ADODB and set the connection string
  'for connecting to a MySQL firstdb database with MyODBC 3.51
  Set MySQLConnection = New ADODB.Connection
  MySQLConnection.ConnectionString = "DRIVER={MySQL ODBC 3.51 Driver};↵
    SERVER=www.testhost.co.za;DATABASE=customer;UID=guru2b;↵
    PWD=g00r002b;OPTION=0"  MySQLConnection.Open

  Set Results = New ADODB.Recordset
  Results.CursorLocation = adUseServer

  'There are two common ways of inserting - the first is the direct insert
  SQLQuery = "INSERT INTO customer (first_name, surname) VALUES↵
    ('Werner', 'Christerson')"
  MySQLConnection.Execute SQLQuery

  'The second way of inserting is to add to a result set using the
  'AddNew method. First return a result set
```

```
Results.Open "SELECT * FROM customer", MySQLConnection,↵
  adOpenDynamic, adLockOptimistic
Results.AddNew
Results!first_name = "Lance"
Results!surname = "Plaaitjies"
Results.Update
Results.Close

'select a record from the customer table, return the results,
'loop through the results displaying them
Results.Open "SELECT id, first_name, surname FROM customer", MySQLConnection
While Not Results.EOF
  Debug.Print Results!id & ":" & Results!first_name & " " & Results!surname
  Results.MoveNext
Wend
Results.Close

MySQLConnection.Close
End Sub
```

## A Simple RDO VB Example

Listing H.4 uses VB and RDO to connect to a MySQL server via ODBC, insert a record, and select and print the results. Visual Basic still supports RDO, but you may want to use the newer ADO instead.

To gain access to the RDO 2.0 objects in Visual Basic, set a reference to the RDO type library contained in MSRDO20.DLL. It appears in the References dialog box (available from the Project menu) as Microsoft Remote Data Objects 2.0. The code needs to appear inside a form for the Debug.Print method to work. Alternatively, you can change it to MsgBox to make the code executable.

**LISTING H.4:** DBRDO.VB

```
Private Sub MySQLRDO()
  Dim Results As rdoResultset
  Dim MySQLConnection As New rdoConnection
  Dim SQLQuery As String

  'Open a connection using RDO and set the connection string
  'for connecting to a MySQL firstdb database with MyODBC 3.51

  MySQLConnection.Connect = "DRIVER={MySQL ODBC 3.51 Driver};↵
    SERVER=www.testhost.co.za;DATABASE=firstdb;UID=guru2b;↵
    PWD=g00r002b;OPTION=0"

  MySQLConnection.CursorDriver = rdUseOdbc
  MySQLConnection.EstablishConnection rdDriverNoPrompt
```

```
'There are two common ways of inserting - the first is the direct insert
SQLQuery = "INSERT INTO customer (first_name, surname) VALUES↵
  ('Lance', 'Plaaitjies')"
MySQLConnection.Execute SQLQuery, rdExecDirect

'The second way of inserting is to add to a result set using the
'AddNew method. First return a result set
SQLQuery = "SELECT * FROM customer"
Set Results = MySQLConnection.OpenResultset(SQLQuery, rdOpenStatic,↵
  rdConcurRowVer, rdExecDirect)
Results.AddNew
Results!first_name = "Werner"
Results!surname = "Christerson"
Results.Update
Results.Close

'select a record from the customer table, return the results,
'loop through the results displaying them
SQLQuery = "select * from customer"
Set Results = MySQLConnection.OpenResultset(SQLQuery, rdOpenStatic,↵
  rdConcurRowVer, rdExecDirect)
While Not Results.EOF
  Debug.Print Results!id & ":" & Results!first_name & " " & Results!surname
  Results.MoveNext
Wend
'Free the result set, and the connection
Results.Close
MySQLConnection.Close
End Sub
```

## A Simple DAO VB Example

Listing H.5 uses VB and DAO to connect to a DSN via ODBC, insert a record (both directly and through adding to a result set), and select and print the results. Visual Basic still supports DAO, but you may want to use the newer ADO instead.

To gain access to the DAO objects in Visual Basic, set a reference to the DAO type library contained in DAO360.DLL. It appears in the References dialog box (available from the Project menu) as Microsoft DAO 3.6 Object Library.

The code needs to appear inside a form for the Debug.Print method to work. Alternatively, you can change it to MsgBox to make the code executable.

This example requires a DSN to be set for it to work.

**LISTING H.5:** DBDAO.VB

```
Private Sub MySQLDAO()
  Dim Works As Workspace
  Dim MySQLConnection As Connection
```

```
        Dim Results As Recordset
        Dim SQLQuery As String

        'Open a workspace using DAO and set the connection string
        'for connecting to a DSN MySQL firstdb database with MyODBC 3.51
        Set Works = DBEngine.CreateWorkspace("MySQLWorkspace", "guru2b",↵
          "g00r002b", dbUseODBC)
        Set MySQLConnection = Works.OpenConnection("MySQLConn",↵
          rdDriverCompleteRequired, False, "ODBC;DSN=MyDAO")

        'There are two common ways of inserting - the first is the direct insert
        SQLQuery = "INSERT INTO customer (first_name, surname) VALUES↵
          ('Lance', 'Plaaitjies')"  MySQLConnection.Execute SQLQuery

        'The second way of inserting is to add to a result set using the
        'AddNew method. First return a result set
        Set Results = MySQLConnection.OpenRecordset("customer")
        Results.AddNew
        Results!first_name = "Werner"
        Results!surname = "Christerson"
        Results.Update
        Results.Close

        'Read customer table
        Set Results = MySQLConnection.OpenRecordset("customer", dbOpenDynamic)
        While Not Results.EOF
          Debug.Print Results!id & ":" & Results!first_name & " " & Results!surname
          Results.MoveNext
        Wend
        Results.Close

        MySQLConnection.Close
        Works.Close
    End Sub
```

## MyODBC Functions

The following sections serve as a function reference for experienced programmers. The descriptions in this appendix apply to MyODBC 3.5x.

### SQLAllocConnect

Allocates memory for a connection handle. The function is deprecated and has been replaced with SQLAllocHandle(), which is called with the SQL_HANDLE_DBC argument.

### SQLAllocEnv

Obtains an environment handle from the driver. The function is deprecated and has been replaced with SQLAllocHandle(), which is called with the SQL_HANDLE_ENV argument.

### *SQLAllocHandle*

```
SQLAllocHandle (handle_type, input_handle, output_handle_pointer);
```

Allocates a handle (either a connection, descriptor, environment, or statement handle).

The `handle_type` can be one of `SQL_HANDLE_ENV` (environment handle), `SQL_HANDLE_DBC` (connection handle), or `SQL_HANDLE_STMT` (statement handle).

The `input_handle` describes the context for allocating the new handle. This will be `SQL_NULL_HANDLE` if the `handle_type` is `SQL_HANDLE_ENV`, an environment handle if the `handle_type` is `SQL_HANDLE_DBC`, and a connection handle if it's `SQL_HANDLE_STMT`.

The `output_handle_pointer` is a pointer to a buffer to where to return the handle.

### *SQLAllocStmt*

Allocates memory for a statement handle. The function is deprecated and has been replaced with `SQLAllocHandle()`, which is called with the `SQL_HANDLE_STMT` argument.

### *SQLBindParameter*

```
SQLBindParameter(statement_handle, parameter_number, parameter_type, ⏎
    value_type, sql_type, column_size, decimal_digits, ⏎
    parameter_value_pointer, buffer_length, string_length_pointer);
```

Binds a parameter marker in a SQL statement. The `parameter_number` starts at 1. For example:

```
SQLUINTEGER id_ptr;
SQLINTEGER idl_ptr;

// Prepare SQL
SQLPrepare(sth, "INSERT INTO customer(id) VALUES(?)", SQL_NTS);

// Bind id to the parameter for the id column
SQLBindParameter(sth, 1, SQL_PARAM_INPUT, SQL_C_ULONG,
    SQL_LONG, 0, 0, &id_ptr, 0, &idl_ptr);

// ...
SQLExecute(sth);
```

### *SQLBulkOperations*

```
SQLBulkOperations(statement_handle, operation);
```

Performs bulk operations.

### *SQLCancel*

```
SQLCancel(statement_handle)
```

Cancels operations on the specified statement handle.

### *SQLCloseCursor*

```
SQLCloseCursor(statement_handle);
```

Closes any open cursors for the specified statement handle.

### *SQLColAttribute*

```
SQLColAttribute (statement_handle, record_number,↵
    field_identifier, character_attribute_pointer, buffer_length,↵
    string_length_pointer, numeric_attribute_pointer);
```

Describes attributes of a field from the result set.

The `record_number` argument is the number of the record, starting at 1.

The `field_identifier` argument specifies the field to be returned.

The `character_attribute_pointer` argument points to a buffer where the value is to be returned (if it's a string, otherwise it's not used).

The `buffer_length` argument can contain one of the following values:

- The length of the `character_attribute_pointer` (or `SQL_NTS`) if `character_attribute_pointer` points to a string.

- The result of `SQL_LEN_BINARY_ATTR(length)` if `character_attribute_pointer` points to a binary buffer.

- One of `SQL_IS_INTEGER`, `SQL_IS_UNINTEGER`, `SQL_SMALLINT`, or `SQLUSMALLINT` if `character_attribute_pointer` points to a specific data type of fixed length.

- `SQL_IS_POINTER` if `character_attribute_pointer` points to another pointer.

The `string_length-pointer` argument points to a buffer where the total number of bytes from `character_attribute_pointer` is to be returned (excluding the null byte).

For character data, if the `buffer_length` is less than the number of bytes to return, the data is truncated. For other cases, it's assumed to be 32 bits.

The `numeric_attribute_pointer` argument points to an integer buffer where to return a numeric value. It's not used if the return value is not numeric.

### *SQLColAttributes*

Describes attributes of a field from the result. The function is deprecated and has been replaced with `SQLColAttribute()`.

### *SQLColumnPrivileges*

```
SQLColumnPrivileges(statement_handle, catalog_name,
    catalog_name_length, schema_name, schema_name_length, table_name,
    table_name_length, column_name, column_name_length);
```

Returns a list of fields and privileges.

## SQLColumns

```
SQLColumns(statement_handle, catalog_name, catalog_name_length,
  schema_name, schema_name_length, table_name, table_name_length,
  column_name, column_name_length);
```

Returns a list of column names.

## SQLConnect

```
SQLConnect(connection_handle, datasource_name, datasource_name_length,
  user_name, user_name_length, password, password_length);
```

Connects to the data source with the specified username and password.

## SQLDataSources

Implemented by the Driver Manager, this function returns a list of available data sources.

## SQLDescribeCol

```
SQLDescribeCol(statement_handle, column_number, column_name,
  buffer_length, name_length_pointer, data_type_pointer,
  column_size_pointer, decimal_digits_pointer, nullable_pointer);
```

Describes a column in the result set.

The `column_number` argument is the number of the column in the result set, starting at 1.

The `column_name` argument points to a buffer where the column name is returned (read from `SQL_DESC_NAME`). Returns an empty string if the name is not available.

The `buffer_length` argument is the length in characters of the `column_name` buffer.

The `name_length_pointer` argument points to a buffer where to return the number of bytes available to return in `column_name` (excluding the null byte). If the length to be returned is greater than `buffer_length`, the column name is truncated.

The `data_type_pointer` argument points to a buffer where the SQL data type is to be returned, obtained from `SQL_DESC_CONCISE_TYPE`. It returns `SQL_UNKNOWN_TYPE` if the type is not available.

The `column_size_pointer` argument points to a buffer where the size of the column is to be returned or 0 if this is not available.

The `decimal_digits_pointer` argument points to a buffer where the number of decimals of the column is to be returned or 0 if this is not available.

The `nullable_pointer` argument points to a buffer where the nullability is to be returned (`SQL_NO_NULLS`, `SQL_NULLABLE`, or `SQL_NULLABLE_UNKOWN`).

## SQLDescribeParam

```
SQLDescribeParam(statement_handle, parameter_number, data_type_pointer,
  parameter_size_pointer, decimal_digits_pointer,
  nullable_pointer);
```

Returns a description of the parameter.

The `parameter_number` argument specifies the parameter (starting at 1).

The `data_type_pointer` points to a buffer where the SQL data type is to be returned.

The `parameter_size_pointer` argument points to a buffer where the parameter column size is to be returned.

The `decimal_digits_pointer` argument points to a buffer where the number of decimals of the column is to be returned, or 0 if this is not available.

The `nullable_pointer` argument points to a buffer where the nullability is to be returned (`SQL_NO_NULLS`, `SQL_NULLABLE`, or `SQL_NULLABLE_UNKOWN`).

### SQLDisconnect

```
SQLDisconnect(connection_handle);
```

Closes the connection specified by the connection handle.

### SQLDriverConnect

```
SQLDriverConnect (connection_handle, window_handle, in_connection,
 in_connection_length, out_connection, out_connection_length,
 buffer_length,  prompt_flag);
```

Connects to a server. Use instead of `SQLConnect` to connect without a DSN, use driver-specific connection information, or use to prompt the user for connection information.

The `window_handle` argument can be the handle of the parent window or a null pointer if either there are no dialog boxes or the window handle is not being used.

The `in_connection` argument can be a full connection, a partial connection string, or an empty string.

The `in_connection_length` argument is the length in bytes of the `in_connection` string.

The `out_connection` argument points to a buffer where the connection string is to be returned.

The `out_connection_length` argument is the length of the `out_connection` buffer.

The `buffer_length` argument points to a buffer where the number of characters available to return is to be returned. If the number of characters is greater than the `buffer_length`, the `out_connection` is truncated.

The `prompt_flag` argument specifies whether the driver must prompt for more information to connect. It can be `SQL_DRIVER_PROMPT`, `SQL_DRIVER_COMPLETE`, `SQL_DRIVER_COMPLETE_REQUIRED`, or `SQL_DRIVER_NOPROMPT`.

### SQLDrivers

Implemented by the Driver Manager, this function returns details of the installed drivers.

### SQLEndTran

```
SQLEndTran(handle_type, handle, completion_type);
```

Ends an open transaction, calling a rollback or commit.

The `handle_type` argument contains either `SQL_HANDLE_ENV` or `SQL_HANDLE_DBC` depending on the type of handle (environment or connection).

The `handle` argument specifies the actual handle.

The `completion_type` determines whether the transaction is ended with a commit or a rollback, and it can be either `SQL_COMMIT` or `SQL_ROLLBACK`.

### SQLError

This function is for returning error information and is deprecated. You can use `SQLGetDiagRec` or `SQLGetDiagField` to replace it.

### SQLExecDirect

```
SQLExecDirect(statement_handle, sql, sql_length);
```

Executes a SQL statement. Quicker than `SQLExecute` if the statement is only to be executed once, as there is no need to prepare it.

### SQLExecute

```
SQLExecute(statement_handle);
```

Executes a previously prepared statement (with `SQLPrepare`). Use `SQLExecDirect` if the statement is only to be executed once and there is no need to prepare it.

### SQLExtendedFetch

This function returns scrollable results and is deprecated. Instead use `SQLFetchScroll`.

### SQLFetch

```
SQLFetch(statement_handle);
```

Returns the next row of data.

### SQLFetchScroll

```
SQLFetchScroll(statement_handle, fetch_type, offset);
```

Returns data for the specified row.

The `fetch_type` argument can be `SQL_FETCH_NEXT` (the next row, equivalent to the `SQLFetch ()` function), `SQL_FETCH_PRIOR` (the previous row), `SQL_FETCH_FIRST` (the first row), `SQL_FETCH_LAST` (the last row), `SQL_FETCH_ABSOLUTE` (a row offset from the first row), `SQL_FETCH_RELATIVE`, or `SQL_FETCH_BOOKMARK` (a row offset from the current row).

The `offset` argument specifies the row to fetch, either from the first row or the current row, depending on the `fetch_type` argument.

### SQLFreeConnect

Frees the connection handle. The function is deprecated, so instead use `SQLFreeHandle`.

### SQLFreeEnv

Frees the environment handle. The function is deprecated, so instead use `SQLFreeHandle`.

## SQLFreeHandle

```
SQLFreeHandle(handle_type,handle);
```

Frees a handle (either connection, descriptor, environment, or statement handle).

The `handle_type` can be `SQL_HANDLE_ENV` (environment handle), `SQL_HANDLE_DBC` (connection handle), `SQL_HANDLE_STMT` (statement handle), or `SQL_HANDLE_DESC` (descriptor handle).

The `handle` argument is the specific handle to be freed.

## SQLFreeStmt

```
SQLFreeStmt(statement_handle, option);
```

Stops the processing of a statement.

The `option` argument can be `SQL_CLOSE` (closes the cursor, same as `SQLCloseCursor`, with the possibility of reopening the cursor), `SQL_DROP` (frees the statement handler and closes the cursor, although this usage has been deprecated and you should instead use `SQLFreeHandle`), `SQL_UNBIND` (frees all column buffer bound `SQLBindCol`), and `SQL_RESET_PARAMS` (frees all parameter buffers set by `SQLBindParameter`).

## SQLForeignKeys

```
SQLForeignKeys(statement_handle, primary_key_catalog_name,
  primary_key_catalog_name_length, primary_key_schema_name,
  primary_key_schema_name_length, primary_key_table_name,
  priamry_key_table_name_length, foreign_key_catalog_name,
  foreign_key_catalog_name_length, foreign_key_schema_name,
  foreign_key_schema_name_length, foreign_key_table_name,
  foregn_key_table_name_length);
```

Returns foreign keys in the specified table and foreign keys in other tables linked with the specified table.

## SQLGetConnectAttr

```
SQLRETURN SQLGetConnectAttr(connection_handle, attribute,
  value_pointer, buffer_length, string_length_pointer);
```

Returns the value of a connection attribute. The `attribute` argument can be one of the values in Table H.2.

**TABLE H.2:** ATTRIBUTE AND ASSOCIATED VALUE_POINTER CONTENTS

| ATTRIBUTE | VALUE_POINTER CONTENTS |
| --- | --- |
| SQL_ATTR_AUTOCOMMIT | Indicates whether to use auto-commit of or manual commit mode. Can be SQL_AUTOCOMMIT_OFF ( in which case transactions must be ended with SQLEndTran) or SQL_AUTOCOMMIT_ON (the default). |

*Continued on next page*

**TABLE H.2:** ATTRIBUTE AND ASSOCIATED VALUE_POINTER CONTENTS *(continued)*

| ATTRIBUTE | VALUE_POINTER CONTENTS |
|---|---|
| SQL_ATTR_CONNECTION_DEAD | Can be SQL_CD_TRUE (the connection is dead) or SQL_CD_FALSE (the connection is still alive). |
| SQL_ATTR_CONNECTION_TIMEOUT | The number of seconds to wait for a SQL statement to execute before timing out. Set to 0 (the default), it means there is no timeout. |
| SQL_ATTR_CURRENT_CATALOG | The name of the catalog. |
| SQL_ATTR_LOGIN_TIMEOUT | The number of seconds to wait while connecting before timing out. 0 indicates no timeout. |
| SQL_ATTR_ODBC_CURSORS | Indicates how the Driver Manager uses the cursor library. |
| SQL_ATTR_PACKET_SIZE | Indicates the network packet size, in bytes. |
| SQL_ATTR_QUIET_MODE | The parent window handle of the application or null if the driver does not display dialog boxes. |
| SQL_ATTR_TRACE | Can be SQL_OPT_TRACE_OFF (the default, do not perform tracing), or SQL_OPT_TRACE_ON (perform tracing). |
| SQL_ATTR_TRACEFILE | The name of the trace file. |
| SQL_ATTR_TRANSLATE_LIB | The name of the library containing the SQLDriverToDataSource and SQLDataSourceToDriver functions. |
| SQL_ATTR_TRANSLATE_OPTION | A 32-bit flag value passed to the translation DLL. |
| SQL_ATTR_TXN_ISOLATION | A 32-bit bit mask that sets the transaction isolation level. Need to end the transaction with SQLEndTran first before calling SQLSetConnectAttr with this option. |

The value_pointer argument is the pointer in which the value is to be returned. The buffer_length argument can contain one of the following values:

◆ The length of the value_pointer (or SQL_NTS) if value_pointer points to a string.

◆ The result of SQL_LEN_BINARY_ATTR(length) if value_pointer points to a binary buffer.

◆ One of SQL_IS_INTEGER, SQL_IS_UNINTEGER, SQL_SMALLINT, or SQLUSMALLINT if value_pointer points to a specific data type of fixed length.

◆ SQL_IS_POINTER if value_pointer points to another pointer.

The string_length_pointer argument points to a buffer where the number of characters available to return are to be returned (excluding null bytes). If the number of characters is greater than the buffer_length, the value in value_pointer is truncated.

## *SQLGetConnectOption*

Returns the connection option value. The function has been deprecated, so instead use SQLGetConnectAttr.

### SQLGetCursorName

```
SQLGetCursorName(statement_handle,cursor_name,cursor_name_length,
  name_length_pointer);
```

Returns the name of the cursor associated with the statement handle.

The cursor_name argument points to a buffer where the cursor name is returned.

The name_length_pointer argument points to a buffer where the number of characters available to return are to be returned. If the number of characters is greater than the name_length_pointer, the cursor_name is truncated.

### SQLGetDiagField

```
SQLGetDiagField(handle_type, handle, record_number,
  diagnostic_identifier, diagnostic_identifier_pointer, buffer_length,
  diagnostic_identifier_length_pointer);
```

Returns error, warning, and status diagnostic information.

The handle_type can be SQL_HANDLE_ENV (environment), SQL_HANDLE_DBC (connection), SQL_HANDLE_STMT (statement), or SQL_HANDLE_DESC (description).

The handle_argument contains the specific handle of type handle_type.

The record_number argument is the record (starting at 1) from which to return information, if any.

The diagnostic_identifier can be one of the values in Table H.3.

**TABLE H.3:** THE SQLDIAGFIELD DIAGNOSTIC_IDENTIFIER ARGUMENT

| DIAGNOSTIC_IDENTIFIER | DESCRIPTION |
| --- | --- |
| SQL_DIAG_CLASS_ORIGIN | Returns a string indicating the SQLSTATE class origin (for example, ISO 9075 or ODBC 3.0). |
| SQL_DIAG_COLUMN_NUMBER | Returns the column number from the result set or parameter number in a parameter set, starting at 0. If neither of these apply, it will contain SQL_NO_COLUMN_NUMBER or SQL_COLUMN_NUMBER_UNKNOWN. |
| SQL_DIAG_CONNECTION_NAME | Returns a string containing the connection name to which the diagnostics refer. |
| SQL_DIAG_CURSOR_ROW_COUNT | Returns the number of rows in the cursor. |
| SQL_DIAG_MESSAGE_TEXT | Returns a string with the diagnostic (error or warning) message. |
| SQL_DIAG_NATIVE | Returns a native error code (an integer) or 0 if there is none. |
| SQL_DIAG_NUMBER | Returns the number of status records available to the handle (currently the driver returns 1). |
| SQL_DIAG_RETURNCODE | Returns the function return code. |
| SQL_DIAG_ROW_COUNT | Returns the number of rows affected by a SQL operation that modifies data (such as INSERT or DELETE) run by SQLExecute, SQLExecDirect, SQLBulkOperations, or SQLSetPos. |

*Continued on next page*

**TABLE H.3:** THE SQLDIAGFIELD DIAGNOSTIC_IDENTIFIER ARGUMENT *(continued)*

| DIAGNOSTIC_IDENTIFIER | DESCRIPTION |
| --- | --- |
| SQL_DIAG_ROW_NUMBER | Returns the row number in a result set or parameter number in a parameter set, starting at 1. If neither of these apply, it will contain SQL_NO_ROW_NUMBER or SQL_ROW_NUMBER_UNKNOWN. |
| SQL_DIAG_SERVER_NAME | Returns a string containing the server name to which the diagnostics refer. |
| SQL_DIAG_SQLSTATE | Returns a five-character string containing the SQLSTATE code. |
| SQL_DIAG_SUBCLASS_ORIGIN | Returns a string indicating the SQLSTATE subclass origin (for example, ISO 9075 or ODBC 3.0). |

The diagnostic_id_pointer points to a buffer where the diagnostic data is to be returned. The buffer_length argument can contain one of the following values:

◆ The length of the diagnostic_identifier_pointer (or SQL_NTS) if diagnostic_identifier_pointer points to a string.

◆ The result of SQL_LEN_BINARY_ATTR(length) if diagnostic_identifier_pointer points to a binary buffer.

◆ One of SQL_IS_INTEGER, SQL_IS_UNINTEGER, SQL_SMALLINT, or SQLUSMALLINT if diagnostic_identifier_pointer points to a specific data type of fixed length.

◆ SQL_IS_POINTER if diagnostic_identifier_pointer points to another pointer.

The diagnostic_identifier_length_pointer argument points to a buffer where the number of characters available to return are to be returned (excluding null bytes). If the number of characters is greater than the buffer_length, the diagnostic_identifier_pointer is truncated.

SQLGetDiagField does not post the same diagnostics on itself. Instead it returns one of the following values: SQL_SUCCESS, SQL_SUCCESS_WITH_INFO (success but the data was truncated), SQL_INVALID_HANDLE, SQL_ERROR (if the arguments were not valid and so on), or SQL_NO_DATA.

## SQLGetDiagRec

```
SQLGetDiagRec(handle_type, handle, recorn_number, sql_state,
  native_error_pointer, message_text, message_text_length,
  text_length_pointer);
```

Returns additional diagnostic information. It is usually called when a previous call to a function has returned SQL_SUCCESS or SQL_SUCCESS_WITH_INFO.

The handle_type can be SQL_HANDLE_ENV (environment), SQL_HANDLE_DBC (connection), SQL_HANDLE_STMT (statement), or SQL_HANDLE_DESC (description).

The handle_argument contains the specific handle of type handle_type.

The record_number argument is the record (starting at 1) from which to return information, if any.

The `sql_state` argument points to a buffer where the five-character `SQLSTATE` code is to be returned.

The `native_error_pointer` argument points to a buffer where the native error code is to be returned.

The `message_text` argument points to a buffer where the diagnostic message (error or warning) is to be returned.

The `message_text_length` argument contains the length of the `message_text` buffer.

The `text_length_pointer` argument points to a buffer where the number of characters available to return are to be returned. If the number of characters is greater than the `message_text_length`, the `message_text` is truncated.

### SQLGetEnvAttr

```
SQLGetEnvAttr(environment_handle, attribute, value_pointer,
  buffer_length, string_length_pointer);
```

Returns the environment attribute value.

The `attribute` argument can be one of the supported values listed in Table H.4.

**TABLE H.4:** THE SQLGETENVATTR ATTRIBUTE ARGUMENT

| ATTRIBUTE | VALUE_POINTER CONTENTS |
| --- | --- |
| SQL_ATTR_CONNECTION_POOLING | A 32-bit value for enabling or disabling connection pooling. |
| SQL_ATTR_CP_MATCH | A 32-bit value for determining how a connection is selected from the available pool. |
| SQL_ATTR_ODBC_VERSION | A 32-bit integer for determining whether behavior is ODBC 2.x or ODBC 3.x. This can be SQL_OV_ODBC3 or SQL_OV_ODBC2. |

The `value_pointer` argument points to a buffer where the attribute value is to be returned.

The `buffer_length` argument is the length of `value_pointer` if it points to a string; otherwise it's unused.

The `string_length_pointer` points to a buffer where the number of characters available to return are to be returned. If the number of characters is greater than the `buffer_length`, the `value_pointer` is truncated.

### SQLGetFunctions

```
SQLGetFunctions(connection_handle, function_id, supported_pointer);
```

Returns the functions the driver supports.

The `function_id` argument can be an individual function ID, or it can be either `SQL_API_ODBC3_ALL_FUNCTIONS` or `SQL_API_ALL_FUNCTIONS`. The former is used by ODBC3, the latter by ODBC2.

The supported_pointer argument points to a value containing either SQL_FALSE or SQL_TRUE (if function_id was a single function, indicating whether the function is supported or not), or an array of such values (starting a 0).

## SQLGetInfo

```
SQLGetInfo(connection_handle,info_type, info_value_pointer,
  buffer_length, string_length_pointer);
```

Returns information about the driver and server.

The info_type argument contains the type of information (such as SQL_DRIVER_HDESC or SQL_DRIVER_HSTMT).

The info_value_pointer argument points to a buffer where the information is to be returned, depending on the info_type argument.

The buffer_length argument contains the length of the info_value_pointer buffer. If info_value_pointer does not point to a string, buffer_length is ignored.

The string_length_pointer points to a buffer where the total number of bytes is to be returned (excluding the null byte). If the length is greater than buffer_length, the value in info_value_pointer is truncated.

## SQLGetStmtAttr

```
SQLGetStmtAttr(statement_handle, attribute, value_pointer,
  buffer_length, string_length_pointer);
```

Returns the statement attribute value.

The attribute argument can be one of the supported options listed in Table H.5.

**TABLE H.5:** THE SQLGETSTMT ATTRIBUTE ARGUMENT

| ATTRIBUTE | VALUE_POINTER CONTENTS |
| --- | --- |
| SQL_ATTR_CURSOR_SCROLLABLE | Can be SQL_NONSCROLLABLE (scrollable cursors not required on the statement handle). If SQLFetchScroll is called with this handle, fetch_type can only contain SQL_FETCH_NEXT (the default) or SQL_SCROLLABLE (scrollable cursors required on the statement handle). If SQLFetchScroll is called with this handle, fetch_type can contain any valid handle. This attribute affects calls to SQLExecDirect and SQLExecute. |
| SQL_ATTR_CURSOR_SENSITIVITY | Can be SQL_UNSPECIFIED (the default where the cursor type is unspecified), SQL_INSENSITIVE (cursors show the result set without showing any changes made by other cursors), or SQL_SENSITIVE (cursors show all changes made to a result set by other cursors). This affects calls to SQLExecute and SQLExecDirect. |

*Continued on next page*

**TABLE H.5:** THE SQLGETSTMT ATTRIBUTE ARGUMENT *(continued)*

| ATTRIBUTE | VALUE_POINTER CONTENTS |
|---|---|
| SQL_ATTR_CURSOR_TYPE | Specifies the cursor type and can contain SQL_CURSOR_FORWARD_ ONLY, SQL_CURSOR_STATIC, SQL_CURSOR_KEYSET_DRIVEN (the driver uses the keys for the number of rows specified in the SQL_ATTR_KEYSET_SIZE statement attribute), or SQL_CURSOR_ DYNAMIC. |
| SQL_ATTR_KEYSET_SIZE | Number of rows in the keyset for a SQL_CURSOR_KEYSET_DRIVEN type cursor. |
| SQL_ATTR_MAX_LENGTH | Maximum amount of data the driver returns from character or binary columns. If the value_pointer is less than the amount of data, SQLFetch and SQLGetData data will be truncated and return SQL_SUCCESS_WITH_INFO. |
| SQL_ATTR_MAX_ROWS | Maximum number of rows the driver can return (0 is no limit). |
| SQL_ATTR_NOSCAN | Can be SQL_NOSCAN_OFF (the driver scans the SQL statement for escapes, the default), or SQL_NOSCAN_ON (the driver does not scan for escapes). |
| SQL_ATTR_PARAM_BIND_TYPE | Can be SQL_PARAM_BIND_BY_COLUMN (the default, which indicates column-wise binding), or the length of the structure or buffer for row-wise binding. |
| SQL_ATTR_PARAM_OPERATION_PTR | Points to an array containing SQL_PARAM_PROCEED or SQL_PARAM_ IGNORE that determines whether a parameter is to be ignored during execution. Can also be set to null pointer, in which case no parameter status values are returned. |
| SQL_ATTR_PARAM_STATUS_PTR | Points to an array of values (one for each row) with status information after a call to SQLExecute or SQLExecDirect containing one of the following: SQL_PARAM_SUCCESS, SQL_PARAM_SUCCESS_WITH_ INFO (successful with a warning), SQL_PARAM_ERROR, SQL_PARAM_ UNUSED (usually because SQL_PARAM_IGNORE was set), or SQL_ PARAM_DIAG_UNAVAILABLE. Can also be set to a null pointer, in which case data is not returned. |
| SQL_ATTR_PARAMS_PROCESSED_PTR | Points to a buffer where the number of processed sets of parameters, including errors, is returned. Can be a null pointer, in which case no number is returned. |
| SQL_ATTR_PARAMSET_SIZE | Number of values for each parameter. |
| SQL_ATTR_QUERY_TIMEOUT | The number of seconds to wait for a SQL statement to execute before timing out. If the value_pointer is 0 (the default), there will be no timeout. |

*Continued on next page*

**TABLE H.5:** THE SQLGETSTMT ATTRIBUTE ARGUMENT *(continued)*

| **ATTRIBUTE** | **VALUE_POINTER CONTENTS** |
| --- | --- |
| SQL_ATTR_ROW_ARRAY_SIZE | The number of rows returned by a call to SQLFetch or SQLFetchScroll. The default is 1. |
| SQL_ATTR_ROW_BIND_OFFSET_PTR | Points to an offset added to pointers to change binding of column data. |
| SQL_ATTR_ROW_BIND_TYPE | Sets the binding orientation. Can be either SQL_BIND_BY_COLUMN (indicates column-wise binding) or the length of the structure or buffer where the results are going to be bound (for row-wise binding). |
| SQL_ATTR_ROW_NUMBER | The number of the current row or 0 if this cannot be determined. |
| SQL_ATTR_ROW_OPERATION_PTR | Points to an array of elements (one for each row) containing either SQL_ROW_PROCEED or SQL_ROW_IGNORE, determining whether the row is to be included in a bulk operation (this does not include SQLBulkOperations). This can also be set to a null pointer, in which case an array will not be returned. |
| SQL_ATTR_ROW_STATUS_PTR | Points to an array of values (one for each row) containing row status values after a call to either SQLFetch or SQLFetchScroll. Can also be set to a null pointer, and the driver will not return the array. |
| SQL_ATTR_ROWS_FETCHED_PTR | Points to a buffer where the number of rows returned or affected from a SQLFetch, SQLFetchScroll, SQLSetPos, or SQLBulkOperations call is returned, including errors. |
| SQL_ATTR_SIMULATE_CURSOR | Can be SQL_SC_NON_UNIQUE (not definite that that simulated positioned UPDATE or DELETE statements will affect only one row), SQL_SC_TRY_UNIQUE (driver attempts to ensure that simulated positioned UPDATE or DELETE statements affect only one row), or SQL_SC_UNIQUE (definite that simulated positioned UPDATE or DELETE statements affect only one row.) |

The value_pointer argument points to a buffer where the value of attribute is to be returned. The buffer_length argument can contain one of the following values:

◆ The length of the value_pointer (or SQL_NTS) if value_pointer points to a string.

◆ The result of SQL_LEN_BINARY_ATTR(length) if value_pointer points to a binary buffer.

◆ One of SQL_IS_INTEGER, SQL_IS_UNINTEGER, SQL_SMALLINT, or SQLUSMALLINT if value_pointer points to a specific data type of fixed length.

◆ SQL_IS_POINTER if value_pointer points to another pointer.

The string_length_pointer points to a buffer where the total number of bytes is to be returned (excluding the null byte). If the length is greater than buffer_length, the value in value_pointer is truncated.

### SQLGetStmtOption

Returns the statement option value. The function is deprecated, so instead use SQLGetStmtAttr.

### SQLGetTypeInfo

```
SQLGetTypeInfo(statement_handle,data_type);
```

Returns a SQL result set with information about the specified data type.

Setting data_type to SQL_ALL_TYPES returns information about the data types returned by the server.

### SQLNativeSql

```
SQLNativeSql(connection_handle, sql_string, sql_string_length,
  modified_sql_string, modified_sql_string_length,
  string_length_pointer);
```

Returns a SQL string modified (not executed) by the driver.

The modified_sql_string argument points to a buffer where the modified SQL statement is to be returned.

The modified_sql_string_length argument points to a buffer where the number of bytes (excluding the null byte) is to be returned.

The string_length_pointer points to a buffer where the total number of bytes is to be returned (excluding the null byte). If the length is greater than modified_sql_string_length, the value in modified_sql_string is truncated.

### SQLNumParams

```
SQLNumParams(statement_handle, parameter_count_pointer);
```

Returns the number of parameters in a statement.

The parameter_count_pointer argument points to a buffer where the number of parameters is to be returned.

### SQLNumResultCols

```
SQLNumResultCols(statement_handle, column_count_pointer);
```

Returns the number of columns in the result set.

The column_count_pointer argument points to a buffer where the number of columns is to be returned.

### SQLParamData

Used in conjunction with SQLPutData to supply parameter data at execution time. (This is useful for long data values.)

### SQLPrepare

```
SQLPrepare(statement_handle, sql_string, sql_string_length);
```

Prepares a SQL statement for later execution.

### SQLPrimaryKeys

```
SQLPrimaryKeys(statement_handle, catalog_name, catalog_name_length,
  schema_name, schema_name_length, table_name, table_name_length);
```

Returns the primary key columns from the specified table.

### SQLPutData

```
SQLPutData(statement_handle, data_pointer, data_pointer_length);
```

For sending column or parameter data at execution time.

The `data_pointer` argument points to a buffer containing the parameter or column data (the type is that specified by the `value_type` argument of `SQLBindParameter` or the `target_type` argument of `SQLBindCol`).

The `data_pointer_length` argument specifies the length of the data sent to `SQLPutData` (`SQL_NTS`, `SQL_NULL_DATA`, or `SQL_DEFAULT_PARAM`).

### SQLRowCount

```
SQLRowCount(statement_handle, row_count_pointer);
```

Returns the number of rows affected by a SQL statement that modifies data (such as `INSERT` or `DELETE`).

The `row_count_pointer` argument points to a buffer where the row count is returned or −1 if not available.

### SQLSetConnectAttr

```
SQLSetConnectAttr(connection_handle, attribute, value_pointer, string_length);
```

Sets a connection attribute.

See `SQLGetConnectAttr` for a list and description of possible attributes.

The `value_pointer` argument points to value of the attribute, of which the type depends on the `attribute`.

The `string_length` argument can contain one of the following values:

- The length of the `value_pointer` (or `SQL_NTS`) if `value_pointer` points to a string.
- The result of `SQL_LEN_BINARY_ATTR(length)` if `value_pointer` points to a binary buffer.
- One of `SQL_IS_INTEGER`, `SQL_IS_UNINTEGER`, `SQL_SMALLINT`, or `SQLUSMALLINT` if `value_pointer` points to a specific data type of fixed length.
- `SQL_IS_POINTER` if `value_pointer` points to another pointer.

### SQLSetConnectOption

Sets a connection option. This function has been deprecated, so instead use `SQLSetConnectAttr`.

### SQLSetCursorName

```
SQLSetCursorName(statement_handle,cursor_name,cursor_name_length);
```

Specifies a cursor name.

### SQLSetEnvAttr

```
SQLSetEnvAttr(environment_handle, attribute, value_pointer, string_length_pointer);
```

Sets an environment attribute. See `SQLGetEnvAttr` for a list of possible attributes.

### SQLSetPos

```
SQLSetPos(statement_handle, row_number, operation, lock_type);
```

Moves a cursor to a position in a fetched block of data and can also refresh data in the row set or update and delete the underlying data.

The `row_number` argument selects the row in the result set the operation affects (starting at 1). Setting it to 0 applies the operation to `every` row.

The `operation` argument specifies the operation to perform and can be `SQL_POSITION`, `SQL_REFRESH`, `SQL_UPDATE`, or `SQL_DELETE`. Table H.6 describes the `operation` argument.

**TABLE H.6:** THE OPERATION ARGUMENT

| OPERATION | DESCRIPTION |
| --- | --- |
| SQL_POSITION | Driver positions the cursor on row `row_number`. |
| SQL_REFRESH | Driver positions the cursor on row `row_number` and refreshes data for that row. The row's data is not refetched, which is different from a refresh call to `SQLFetchScroll` with a `fetch_type`. |
| SQL_UPDATE | Driver positions the cursor on row `row_number` and updates the associated data with the values in the row set buffers from the `TargetValuePtr` argument in `SQLBindCol`. |
| SQL_DELETE | Driver positions the cursor on row `row_number` and deletes the associated data. |

The `lock_type` argument specifies the row locking operation after the operation is executed, and can be `SQL_LOCK_NO_CHANGE`, `SQL_LOCK_EXCLUSIVE`, or `SQL_LOCK_UNLOCK`.

### SQLSetScrollOptions

Sets options affecting cursor behavior. This function is deprecated, so instead use `SQLSetStmtAttr`.

### *SQLSetStmtAttr*

```
SQLGetStmtAttr(statement_handle, attribute, value_pointer, string_length);
```

Sets a statement attribute.

For the list of possible `attribute` values, see `SQLGetStmtAttr`.

The `value_pointer` argument points to value of the attribute, of which the type depends on the `attribute`.

The `string_length` argument can contain one of the following values:

◆ The length of the `value_pointer` (or `SQL_NTS`) if `value_pointer` points to a string.

◆ The result of `SQL_LEN_BINARY_ATTR(length)` if `value_pointer` points to a binary buffer.

◆ One of `SQL_IS_INTEGER`, `SQL_IS_UNINTEGER`, `SQL_SMALLINT`, or `SQLUSMALLINT` if `value_pointer` points to a specific data type of fixed length.

◆ `SQL_IS_POINTER` if `value_pointer` points to another pointer.

### *SQLSetStmtOption*

Sets a statement option. This function has been deprecated, so instead use `SQLSetStmtAttr`.

### *SQLSpecialColumns*

```
SQLSpecialColumns(statement_handle, identifier_type, catalog_name,
  catalog_length, schema_name, schema_length, table_name,
  table_name_length, scope, nullable);
```

Returns column information that uniquely identifies a row in the specified table or the automatically updated columns when a value in the record is updated by a transaction.

The `identifier_type` argument contains the type of column to be returned. It must be either `SQL_BEST_ROWID` or `SQL_ROWVER`. `SQL_BEST_ROWID` returns the smallest set of columns that uniquely identifies a record. (The returned columns can be designed to enable this.) `SQL_ROWVER` returns the columns that are automatically updated when a value in the record is updated by a transaction.

The `scope` argument is the minimum required scope of the row ID. It can be one of the following: `SQL_SCOPE_CURROW` (The row ID is definitely valid only while on that row), `SQL_SCOPE_TRANSACTION` (The row ID is definitely valid for the duration of the current transaction), or `SQL_SCOPE_SESSION` (The row ID is definitely valid for the entire session).

The `nullable` argument indicates whether to include columns that can contain nulls. It can be either `SQL_NO_NULLS` (excluding columns that can contain nulls) or `SQL_NULLABLE` (including columns that can contain nulls).

### *SQLStatistics*

```
SQLStatistics(statement_handle, catalog_name, catalog_name_length,
  schema_name, schema_name_length, table_name, table_name_length,
  index_type, reserved);
```

Returns table and associated index statistics.

The `index_type` argument can be either `SQL_INDEX_UNIQUE` or `SQL_INDEX_ALL`.

The reserved argument can be SQL_ENSURE (return the CARDINALITY and PAGES columns) or SQL_QUICK (return the CARDINALITY and PAGES columns only if they're readily available).

### SQLTablePrivileges

```
SQLTablePrivileges(statement_handle, catalog_name, catalog_length,
Schema_name, schema_name_length, table_name, table_name_length);
```

Returns a list of tables and associated privileges.

### SQLTables

```
SQLTables(statement_handle, catalog_name, catalog_length,
Schema_name, schema_name_length, table_name, table_name_length,
 table_type, table_type_length);
```

Returns the list of tables, catalog, or schema names and table types.

### SQLTransact

Ends a transaction. This function has been deprecated, so instead use SQLEndTran.

# Index

**Note to the reader:** Throughout this index **boldfaced** page numbers indicate primary discussions of a topic. *Italicized* page numbers indicate illustrations.

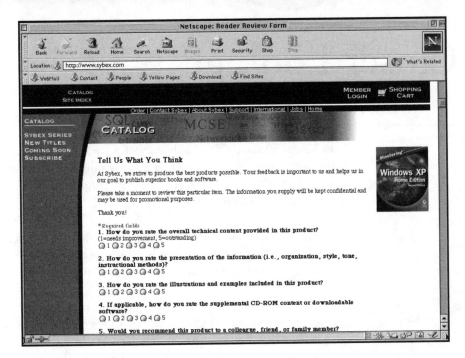

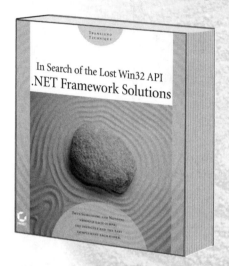

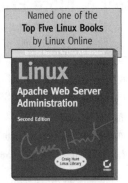